0211591

KT-486-285

The TERRORIST TRAP

AMERICA'S

EXPERIENCE

WITH TERRORISM

SECOND EDITION

——————————*Jeffrey D. Simon*

INDIANA

UNIVERSITY

PRESS

Bloomington and Indianapolis

HAROLD BRIDGES LIBRARY
ST MARTINS SERVICES LTD.
LANCASTER

0253339839

To my sister, Ellen Sandor, and in memory of our parents,
and in memory of Martha Haruko Asakura and Richard D. Schmitt

This book is a publication of

Indiana University Press
601 North Morton Street
Bloomington, IN 47404-3797 USA

http://iupress.indiana.edu

Telephone orders 800-842-6796
Fax orders 812-855-7931
Orders by e-mail iuporder@indiana.edu

© 2001 by Jeffrey D. Simon
All rights reserved. First edition 1994

No part of this book may be reproduced or utilized in any form or
by any means, electronic or mechanical, including photocopying and
recording, or by any information storage and retrieval system,
without permission in writing from the publisher. The Association
of American University Presses' Resolution on Permissions constitutes
the only exception to this prohibition.

The paper used in this publication meets the minimum requirements
of American National Standard for Information Sciences—
Permanence of Paper for Printed Library Materials, ANSI Z39.48-1984.

Manufactured in the United States of America

Library of Congress Cataloging-in-Publication Data

Simon, Jeffrey D. (Jeffrey David), date
       The terrorist trap : America's experience with terrorism / Jeffrey D.
    Simon.—2nd ed.
         p. cm.
       Includes bibliographical references and index.
       ISBN 0-253-33983-9 (cloth : alk. paper)—
    ISBN 0-253-21477-7 (paper : alk. paper)
       1. Terrorism—United States. I. Title.

HV6432 .S55 2001
363.3′2′0973—dc21
                                                                    2001039180

1 2 3 4 5 06 05 04 03 02 01

Contents

Illustrations follow pages 59 and 294

Preface to the Second Edition

As the second edition of *The Terrorist Trap* was about to go to press, America was rocked by a wave of terrorist attacks unprecedented in history. On September 11, 2001, four planes were hijacked and then used in a suicide mission that established a new threshold for terrorist violence. Two of the jetliners crashed into the World Trade Center in New York City, one into the Pentagon, and one, aborted in its mission, into a field near Pittsburgh, Pennsylvania. Preliminary estimates in the days following the catastrophe put the death toll at more than 5,000 people.

Television viewers around the world watched in horror as one plane struck the south tower of the World Trade Center after the north tower had earlier been hit. Then, when the burning jet fuel weakened the steel support columns, each of the 110-floor twin towers collapsed. All the hijacked planes were originally bound for California from eastern cities; at the beginning of their cross-country flights, they were loaded with fuel. Among those killed were hundreds of firefighters, police officers, and other rescue workers who had rushed into the buildings after the plane crashes.

Although details are still emerging as this preface is being written less than a week after the tragedy, investigators have already linked the hijackers to Saudi-exile terrorist Osama bin Ladin, who is discussed in the introduction to this book. In a clearly coordinated assault, teams of four to five hijackers, several of whom were pilots, seized the planes, armed with box cutters and small knives. All four planes crashed within a period of ninety minutes.

While this assault upon America was shocking, it should not have been surprising. As the reader will discover in the following pages, terrorism is an endless conflict. Terrorists will continue to find new and more devastating ways to perpetrate their violence. The terrorists who wreaked havoc upon America in September 2001 employed a tactic that had been used only once before (Palestinian extremists hijacked four planes on the same day in Europe and the Middle East in September 1970) and turned it into a new and more frightening one: suicide attacks from the air. I noted in the first edition of this book and again in the introduction to the second edition that one of the future trends in terrorism would indeed be suicide attacks from the air, although I suggested it was likely to be in planes packed with explosives. The terrorists in this case did not even need explosives, as the burning jet fuel from the crashes was sufficient to bring down a world landmark.

Reflecting the anger and shock of the nation, President George W. Bush called the attacks on the World Trade Center and the Pentagon "acts of war" and vowed to "do generations a favor by coming together and whipping terrorism, hunting it down, binding it, and holding them accountable."* The reader will see, however, that previous U.S. presidents issued similar statements, only to be frustrated in their efforts to defeat terrorism. In the struggle against this global threat, the advantage unfortunately lies with the terrorists since they only need to commit one spectacular act to reverse all perceptions of counterterrorist progress. What separates terrorism from all other types of conflict is the ability of a single major incident—whether a bombing, an embassy seizure, or a suicide attack—to throw an entire nation into crisis and to create repercussions far beyond the original event.

The recent attacks demonstrated another theme discussed in this book; namely, the deep psychological impact that terrorism can have upon a nation. For the surviving victims of terrorist incidents and the families of those killed by terrorists, the emotional scars will last a lifetime. The heart-

---

*Katharine Q. Seelye and Elisabeth Bumiller, "Bush Labels Aerial Terrorist Attacks 'Acts of War,'" *New York Times*, September 13, 2001, p. A16; Elisabeth Bumiller and Jane Perlez, "Bush and Top Aides Proclaim Policy of 'Ending' States That Back Terror; An Arrest Shuts New York Airports," *New York Times*, September 14, 2001, p. A1.

wrenching cellular phone calls that some of the passengers on the doomed jets made to loved ones will haunt those relatives forever. The public also feels the emotional impact of terrorism, as each new incident heightens the fear of being the next victim. It may take a long time before people feel safe again about boarding an airplane. And in this age of extensive media coverage of terrorist events, we all vicariously live through the pain and suffering of the victims and their families. It was therefore not surprising to find an overwhelming expression of public grief and sorrow over the tragedy.

Terrorism can also have a profound effect upon presidents since they bear the ultimate responsibility for determining how this country will deal with the terrorist threat. The reader will see how U.S. presidents since the early days of the republic have had to make difficult choices when faced with terrorist crises. In some cases their actions became the defining moment of their presidencies. President Bush is likely to find the same is true in his case as he shapes America's response to the worst terrorist assault in history.

The image of this country's military and financial centers being struck with such devastating force by terrorists, and the loss of so many innocent lives, will be etched in the minds of all Americans for many years to come. How much this country will be permanently changed as a result of the attacks on the World Trade Center and the Pentagon remains to be seen. Clearly, Americans have experienced the horrors of terrorism at home in ways they never could have imagined before. If, however, the result of the suicide attacks upon America is that we begin to live our lives in constant fear of terrorism and take measures that erode our basic democratic values, then the terrorists would have achieved a major victory.

Jeffrey D. Simon
Santa Monica, California
September 2001

————Introduction to the Second Edition

When *The Terrorist Trap* was first published in 1994, America was still re-covering from the shock of the World Trade Center bombing the previous year. Islamic extremists in New York City had dispelled the myth that the United States could remain safe from terrorism at home. Then, in 1995, a second major bombing within U.S. borders occurred. This time the target was the Alfred P. Murrah Federal Building in Oklahoma City. Terrorists appeared to be extending their battleground from urban centers to the heartland of the country. But when it was discovered that the perpetrators of the Oklahoma City bombing were homegrown American extremists, the public was again shocked. They were learning that terrorists can come from all types of backgrounds and have different motivations for their attacks; and that, no matter what precautions a government may take, there can never be perfect security against this age-old form of violence.

There have been many developments in the world of terrorism since the first edition of this book was published. On the international front, a wealthy Saudi exile, Osama bin Ladin, emerged as one of the most dan-gerous terrorists, coordinating and financing anti-U.S. terrorist attacks throughout the world. In Japan, a religious cult, Aum Shinrikyo, released the chemical agent Sarin inside the Tokyo subway system, raising fears everywhere about terrorists using weapons of mass destruction. On the domestic front, in addition to the Oklahoma City bombing, America experienced a diverse array of terrorist incidents, ranging from the escalating violent behavior of the "Unabomber," who sent bombs through the mail, to the activities of environmental militants who made "ecoterrorism" a growing concern in law enforcement circles.

There have also been many legal victories in the battle against terrorism, with several trials and convictions of terrorists in the United States and around the world. Among those tried and convicted for their terrorist crimes were Timothy McVeigh (who was subsequently executed) and Terry Nichols for the Oklahoma City bombing; Ramzi Ahmed Yousef for being the mastermind of the World Trade Center bombing and for plotting to blow up twelve U.S. airliners flying to the United States from Asia over a two-day period in 1995; Sheik Omar Abdel Rahman for leading a group of Islamic extremists in a conspiracy to destroy several New York City landmarks; and Mir Aimal Kansi for murdering two Central Intelligence Agency employees outside CIA headquarters. In addition, the infamous terrorist from the 1970s, Illich Ramirez Sanchez, alias "Carlos the Jackal," was apprehended, tried, and convicted for his terrorist attacks, as was the leader of the Kurdistan Workers' Party (PKK), Abdullah Ocalan.

Technology has also marched forward, with both terrorists and those who combat it taking advantage of the latest developments in weaponry, computers, and other fields. Improved surveillance and intelligence techniques have aided governments and law enforcement agencies in their efforts to thwart terrorist attacks, while the information revolution and the global village spurred by the growth of the Internet have provided terrorists with a wealth of information on potential targets, tactics, and weapons.

Yet the old adage "the more things change, the more they stay the same" is also true when assessing the terrorist phenomenon. This introduction to the second edition of *The Terrorist Trap* is therefore aimed at bringing the information contained in the first edition up to date and, at the same time, assessing how the arguments that were made about terrorism nearly a decade ago hold up in light of recent developments. Hopefully, it will confirm my own biased view that *The Terrorist Trap* is as relevant today as when it was originally published. This new introduction also gives me an opportunity to once again look toward the future and describe what I see on the horizon in the world of terrorism.

The Emergence of Domestic Terrorism

The 1990s was the decade when domestic terrorism emerged alongside the more familiar international terrorism threat as a high priority issue for the United States. Although there had been numerous domestic terrorist incidents throughout American history, the overwhelming majority of terrorist attacks aimed at the United States had occurred overseas. Beginning with the World Trade Center bombing in 1993—which is discussed in chapter 1—and continuing with the Oklahoma City bombing two years later, the United States entered a new phase in its never-ending battle against terrorism.

Whereas the World Trade Center bombing awakened the public to the reality that terrorists could indeed strike in dramatic fashion on America's shores, the Oklahoma City bombing made a deeper psychological impact upon the nation. It became the worst terrorist act ever on U.S. soil when 168 people, including a rescue worker, died from the blast that occurred shortly after 9 A.M. on the morning of April 19, 1995. The 4,800-pound bomb, made from a mixture of ammonium nitrate fertilizer and fuel oil, left the federal building looking like one of the many bombed-out buildings from war-torn Beirut in the 1980s or Sarajevo in the 1990s. Adding to the haunting images was a photo of a fireman carrying a dying baby from the wreckage. Nineteen children, including many who had been in a second-floor day-care center, were killed in the blast, as were eight federal agents who were in the building.

Speculation on who was responsible for the bombing centered on Islamic terrorists who had used a similar type of bomb in the World Trade Center attack. Although most of the perpetrators of that bombing had already been convicted and were serving long prison terms, there was still concern that additional Islamic terrorist cells were active in the United States. The public was therefore stunned to learn that a former U.S. soldier, Timothy McVeigh, was arrested for the bombing. McVeigh had parked a Ryder truck packed with the explosives in front of the federal building and then detonated the bomb. Also arrested was Terry Nichols who helped McVeigh make the bomb and place it in the truck. Nichols had served in the same army unit with McVeigh at Fort Riley, Kansas.

Both men had attended meetings of the Michigan Militia, one of several dozen anti-government, right-wing militia groups that was organized throughout the country in the early 1990s. The militia movement believed that the government intended to confiscate all citizens' weapons, thereby abrogating the Second Amendment's right to keep and bear arms. Some of the more extreme elements in the militia believed that they must prepare, through paramilitary training, for a war with the U.S. government in order to save the country from tyranny. McVeigh and Nichols were particularly upset about the 1993 government raid on the Branch Davidian headquarters in Waco, Texas. More than eighty members of that religious cult, which authorities said possessed large numbers of illegal weapons, died when their compound burst into flames during the government's final assault. The Oklahoma City bombing occurred on the second anniversary of that raid.

Not surprisingly, the Oklahoma City bombing was followed by a national focus on the terrorist threat posed by militia and right-wing extremists, just as the World Trade Center bombing had led to fears that a wave of additional Islamic terrorist attacks was on the horizon. The tendency to view the terrorist threat mainly in terms of the latest incident, however, ignored the diversity of terrorism and the potential for any number of groups or individuals to stage future attacks.

This was demonstrated shortly after the Oklahoma City bombing when an enigmatic terrorist known as the "Unabomber" single-handedly created a national crisis by threatening to place a bomb on an airliner flying out of Los Angeles International Airport. The terrorist, whose real name was Theodore Kaczynski, had credibility since he had committed sixteen attacks over a seventeen-year period—mostly through sending package bombs to his targets—killing three people and injuring twenty-two others. The FBI had given the code name "Unabom" to its investigation since Kaczynski's early targets were primarily people associated with universities and airlines ("UN" for universities, "A" for airlines). Although the airlines bomb threat turned out to be a hoax, it nevertheless increased public anxiety over terrorism, disrupted the U.S. Postal Service as a temporary ban was placed on all airmail packages sent from California weighing more than twelve ounces, forced authorities to increase security measures at California airports, which in turn led to major delays for travelers, and even caused the Secretary of Transportation, Federico Pena, to fly to Los Angeles to explain how the government intended to handle the crisis.

Kaczynski then threatened to resume sending package bombs to people unless the *New York Times* or the *Washington Post* published a 35,000-word manifesto calling for a revolution against the industrial-technological society. This was not the first time terrorists had demanded that a manifesto be published in a newspaper. Croatian extremists had made similar demands during a 1976 hijacking which is discussed in chapter 3. The *Washington Post*—with the *New York Times* sharing the printing costs—published the Unabomber's manifesto in September 1995. Kaczynski's brother, David, later discovered writings by Kaczynski that resembled the published manifesto and he contacted the police, leading to Kaczynski's arrest in a remote Montana cabin in April 1996.

It was not just Islamic extremists, right-wing militia terrorists, and self-proclaimed anarchists such as the Unabomber who were committing domestic terrorist acts in the United States during the 1990s. An anti-abortion militant, Eric Rudolph, was charged with setting off a bomb at the 1996 Summer Olympic Games in Atlanta, Georgia, that killed one person and injured a hundred others. A television cameraman also died when he suffered a heart attack while running to the site of the bombing. Rudolph was also charged in several bombings at abortion clinics and a nightclub in the late 1990s. "Ecoterrorists"—groups and individuals that commit terrorist acts related to ecological and environmental issues—made their presence felt with a variety of attacks, including setting multiple fires to eight structures at the Vail, Colorado, ski resort in October 1998 that caused $12 million in damage. The Earth Liberation Group claimed responsibility for the arson fires, stating it was done to stop the planned expansion of the resort facility that they felt would destroy a natural habitat of lynx.

The latter part of the 1990s also witnessed the most extensive effort in U.S. history to deal with a potential terrorist incident; namely, terrorists unleashing weapons of mass destruction, or "WMD," upon U.S. cities. These weapons have also been referred to by other acronyms, including "NBC" for nuclear, biological, or chemical weapons, and "CBRN" for chemical, biological, radiological, and nuclear weapons. The catalyst for the concern over terrorists using WMD was Aum Shinrikyo's release of Sarin nerve gas in the Tokyo subway system in March 1995. Twelve people were killed and more than 5,500 injured in that attack. There would have been many more casualties had Aum Shinrikyo manufactured a more potent batch of the nerve agent and had they used a more effective delivery method to release the Sarin. The cult members simply left several punctured containers of Sarin on the floor of five subway trains.

The Tokyo incident eventually led to legislation in the United States aimed at improving the readiness of the United States to respond to WMD terrorism. The Domestic Preparedness Program in the Defense of Weapons of Mass Destruction was established in 1996. Its goal was to enhance the capabilities of first-responders—emergency medical personnel, police, firefighters—in cities throughout the United States for dealing with a nuclear, biological, or chemical terrorist attack. There was also the formation of specially trained National Guard units to assist in responding to terrorist incidents involving weapons of mass destruction.

Despite this growing concern, however, the U.S. government still knew very little about the nature of the WMD terrorist threat. With the exception of the Tokyo attack, there had never been a major terrorist incident involving a chemical weapon, and none involving a nuclear or biological weapon. Policymakers therefore had no track record of incidents, groups, tactics, or targets to guide them in determining the best strategies for combating this threat. In that regard, America at the beginning of the twenty-first century was, with respect to WMD terrorism, where it was in the late 1960s with respect to "conventional" terrorism. A new international threat was emerging then—hijackings, bombings, hostage crises—yet nobody could be sure as to the direction it would take. It took many years before the diverse nature of conventional terrorism became clear and governments began designing effective countermeasures. WMD terrorism, however, will not allow the U.S. government and the international community the luxury of time to watch the threat unfold before taking action, since just one major WMD attack could have catastrophic effects in terms of the number of lives lost and the medical, political, and social crises that it would cause. Preparing for WMD terrorism, therefore, is likely to remain a top priority for the United States in the years ahead.[1]

The Continuing Threat of International Terrorism

While domestic terrorism became a growing concern for the U.S. public and government during the 1990s, there were several reminders that the international terrorist threat had not disappeared. Over the years, the United States had faced several adversaries in its battle against international terrorism. Many of them were the leaders of states that sponsored terrorism, such as Iran's Ayatollah Ruhollah Khomeini, Libya's Muammar Qaddafi, and Iraq's Saddam Hussein. Occasionally, individual terrorists achieved notoriety through audacious and highly publicized attacks, such as the elusive terrorist "Carlos," who seized the headquarters of the Organization of Petroleum Export Countries in Vienna in 1975 and took the OPEC ministers hostage; and Sabri al-Banna, who as leader of a terrorist group bearing his alias, Abu Nidal, staged several terrorist attacks in the 1980s, including the simultaneous massacres of passengers at the Rome and Vienna airports in 1985.

By the late 1990s, a new name could be added to the list of terrorists with whom the American public had become familiar. Osama bin Ladin, the wealthy son of a Saudi billionaire, was linked to several high-profile, anti-U.S. terrorist attacks overseas. These included the near-simultaneous bombings of the U.S. embassies in Kenya and Tanzania in August 1998 that killed over two hundred people and injured more than 5,000 others, and a suicide bombing of the USS Cole, a guided-missile destroyer, while it was refueling at a port in Yemen in October 2000 that killed seventeen sailors. Bin Ladin was also suspected of plotting to stage terrorist attacks in the United States and Jordan during the millennium celebrations at the end of 1999. Furthermore, there was a belief among some U.S. intelligence officials that bin Ladin had ties to the extremists who blew up the World Trade Center.[2]

What distinguished bin Ladin from other terrorists was the vast amount of funds at his disposal. In addition to his personal wealth, he raised money for his group, Al Qaeda ("The Base"), through business ventures and donations from supporters. With a seemingly unlimited amount of funds, a growing army of Islamic militants, and a fervent hatred of the United States and pro-Western Middle Eastern governments, bin Ladin embarked upon an escalating campaign of terror around the world during the 1990s. His terrorist attacks led to his being placed on the FBI's Ten Most Wanted Fugitives list in June 1999 and to the U.S. government offering a reward of up to $5 million for information leading directly to his arrest or conviction. In testimony before Congress in February 2001, CIA Director George Tenet described bin Ladin and his organization as "the most immediate and serious threat" to this nation.[3]

Bin Ladin, who helped finance, recruit, and train nationals of predominantly Muslim states who volunteered to fight with the Afghan resistance following the Soviet invasion of Afghanistan in 1979 (the United States supplied weapons, including Stinger antiaircraft missiles, to the Afghan Muslim rebels), established Al Qaeda in the late 1980s in order to launch a global *jihad,* or holy war. He viewed terrorism as a means toward achieving his organization's goal of bringing Islamic rule to Muslim countries and ridding them of what he called corrupt, Western-oriented governments. Among his objectives has been the elimination of the U.S. military presence in the Middle East. He has also made it clear, however, that his terrorism will not be limited to military or government targets. In February 1998, bin Ladin and other terrorist leaders issued a *fatwa,* or Muslim religious order, under the name "World Islamic Front for Jihad Against the Jews and Crusaders," stating that it was the religious duty of all Muslims to kill Americans and their allies, both civil and military, anywhere in the world.[4]

Meanwhile, a bombing in Saudi Arabia in June 1996 demonstrated that for U.S. military troops and personnel, terrorism could be just as dangerous, if not more so, than engagement in an actual war. A truck bomb exploded about one hundred feet of the U.S. military's Khobar Towers housing facility near Dhahran, Saudi Arabia, killing nineteen U.S. servicemen and wounding many others. A Pentagon investigative report by retired General Wayne A. Downing faulted U.S. military commanders for lax security around the complex, but a subsequent U.S. Air Force inquiry cleared the commanders of any blame for the incident. Although the Saudi government arrested and detained several people in connection with the attack, they had still not reached a conclusion in their investigation by early 2001.

That terrorist investigations can sometimes take years, even decades to resolve, was illustrated in the case of the bombing of Pan Am Flight 103 over Lockerbie, Scotland, in 1988, which killed 270 people. After years of refusing to comply with a U.N. Security Council resolution to hand over for trial two Libyan suspects in the bombing, Libya finally agreed to do so in 1999. Abdel Basset al-Megrahi and Laman Khalifa Fhimah, both of whom had been on the FBI's Ten Most Wanted Fugitives list until their surrender, were tried in the Netherlands under Scottish law with Scottish judges presiding. The trial began in April 2000 and ended nine months later with al-Megrahi, who was a senior Libyan intelligence official, being found guilty of murder and given a life sentence. Fhimah, however, was found not guilty. Following the guilty verdict, the United States called for Libya to accept responsibility for the bombing and to pay compensation to the families of the victims. Libyan leader Muammar Qaddafi's response was to give the acquitted Libyan a hero's welcome when he returned home.

The Terrorist Trap: Reevaluating the Central Themes

While only seven years have passed since publication of *The Terrorist Trap*, in the world of terrorism that could be considered an eternity. The multitude of groups active around the world and the consequences of various actions and responses can make previous assumptions about terrorism seem obsolete very quickly. How, then, have the major arguments of *The Terrorist Trap* held up with the passage of time?

One of the central themes in my book is that terrorism is an endless conflict and is destined to grow in the coming years. That is still the case today, with terrorist campaigns related to a variety of causes dotting the globe and no end in sight to this age-old form of violence. That religiously motivated attacks have become a prevalent form of terrorism at the beginning of the twenty-first century brings terrorism full circle to its origins. During the first century, the Jewish Zealots used terrorism as a means to instigate an uprising against their Roman rulers in Palestine and chose to commit suicide rather than be captured by Roman forces when surrounded at their fortress at Masada.

The "zealousness" of the religious terrorist, though, is not the only reason that terrorism is an endless phenomenon. Terrorists are driven by many different causes and issues—political, religious, ethnic-nationalist, social, economic—and the threat or use of violence has proven effective, even if only temporarily in some cases, for extremist groups and individuals throughout history. That is why elimination of one type of terrorist threat does not result in an end to terrorism. For some time, it was thought that if the Arab-Israeli and Palestinian-Israeli conflicts could be resolved peacefully, then there would be a sharp decline, if not an end to major international terrorist incidents, since those conflicts had fueled many attacks and counterattacks during the last several decades. Yet the rise of Islamic terrorism worldwide in recent years demonstrates that regardless of how one conflict might turn out, there are always other issues that can take its place as a major cause of terrorism. And since terrorism can be just one person with one bomb and one cause, it becomes clear why there can never be an end to this form of violence.

The endless nature of terrorism was again illustrated in 1998 when a new terrorist group emerged in protest to the Northern Ireland peace process. The Real IRA, consisting mostly of former Irish Republican Army (IRA) members opposed to the IRA's cease-fire, was responsible for several terrorist attacks, including a car bombing in Omagh, Northern Ireland, in August 1998 that killed twenty-nine people and injured 220 others; the firing of a rocket at the Thames-side headquarters of the British MI-6 intelligence agency in September 2000; and a March 2001 car bombing outside the television headquarters of the British Broadcasting Corporation in West London.

The formation of the Real IRA fits a pattern in the history of terrorism in which factions break away from existing groups due to divisions over strategies and tactics. For example, the Popular Front for the Liberation of Palestine–General Command (PFLP-GC) split from the Popular Front for the Liberation of Palestine (PFLP) in 1968, asserting that it wanted to focus more on fighting and less on politics. Then, in the mid-1970s, the Palestine Liberation Front (PLF) broke away from the PFLP-GC, and then later split into pro-Palestine Liberation Organization (PLO), pro-Syrian, and pro-Libyan factions. The Abu Nidal Organization split from the PLO in 1974, while the Abu Sayyaf Group, a radical Islamic separatist group operating in the southern Philippines and responsible for several bombings, assassinations, and kidnappings, split from the Moro National Liberation Front in 1991. Although divisions within an extremist group can be beneficial to law enforcement and counterterrorist officials when they lead to defections, informants, and disruption in the group's activity, it also can contribute to the endless nature of terrorism when the factions are "reborn" as new terrorist groups that continue the violence no matter what may eventually happen to the original group.

The endless nature of terrorism can also be seen in the long-time survival of some terrorist organizations. No matter what may happen in the world at large—including the end of the Cold War—and despite the efforts of law enforcement and counterterrorist forces, some terrorist groups continue to make their presence known. One such group is the Greek leftist Revolutionary Organization 17 November, also known as N-17. Formed in 1975 and named for the November 1973 student uprising against the Greek military regime, N-17 is believed to have fewer than twenty members, none of whom have ever been arrested. They have attacked U.S., British, Greek, Turkish, North American Treaty Organization, and European Union targets over the years. Demonstrating the truism that "the more things change, the more they stay the same," just as N-17 posed a threat in the 1970s, so too do they pose a threat in the first decade of the twenty-first century. One of the major concerns for security planners for the 2004 Summer Olympic Games in Athens is the prospect of terrorist attacks by N-17.

Terrorism's endless nature also becomes apparent when terrorist tactics that were thought to have been abandoned years ago by extremist groups suddenly reappear, making it seem as though we are back to the beginnings of the modern era of terrorism. When the modern era of international terrorism began in the late 1960s and early 1970s, hijackings and embassy seizures were among the tactics frequently used by a variety of terrorist organizations. Yet as security improved at airports and embassies, these types of attacks subsided. Occasionally, though, a major hijacking or embassy-type seizure occurs, reminding people that, in the world of terrorism, no type of tactic can ever be ruled out.

That was the case in the latter half of the 1990s, when in December 1996, the leftist Peruvian Tupac Amaru Revolutionary Movement (MARTA)—a group that many observers had thought was finished due to arrests, defections, and loss of support—seized the Japanese ambassador's residence in Lima during a diplomatic reception and took several hundred people hostage; and in December 1999 when Kashmiri militants hijacked an Indian Airlines jet with 190 people aboard. In both cases, the terrorists' demands were similar to demands that had always been made by terrorists who hijacked planes or seized government facilities: namely, the release of imprisoned colleagues. These incidents, however, had dramatically different outcomes. The Peruvian incident lasted more than four months and ended with Peruvian military forces storming the residence and rescuing all but one of the remaining hostages (several had been released by the terrorists during the ordeal) and killing all fourteen terrorists. The Indian Airlines incident lasted one week with the hijacked plane finally landing in Kandahar, Afghanistan, after an odyssey spanning several countries; one hostage was killed and several others released during the crisis. It ended when the Indian government agreed to free three Kashmiri militants and deliver them to the hijacked plane. The terrorists and the freed militants then drove away as the hostages were released.

Whether a hostage crisis ends with the terrorists being captured or killed as in the Peruvian case, or emerging "victorious" as in the Indian case, future terrorists will continue to be drawn to hostage-taking as one way to achieve their goals, thereby contributing to the endless nature of terrorism.

A second theme of *The Terrorist Trap* is the key role played by U.S. presidents in determining terrorism's impact on this nation. Through their actions and statements, presidents can either help fuel a crisis atmosphere over terrorism or they can help defuse it. They also have a responsibility to pursue counterterrorist policies that are in the best, long-term interests of the United States and are not immediate reactions to a highly charged emotional and political atmosphere. Since the publication of the first edition of this book, Bill Clinton served two terms as U.S. president and demonstrated once again the importance that this office plays in setting the tone for how the nation responds to terrorism.

As noted in the first edition, Clinton displayed a low-key style in dealing with terrorism during the first year of his presidency, although that style gave way to increased rhetoric on terrorism by the time he left office. He avoided any overreactions in the aftermath of the World Trade Center bombing, and did the same following the Oklahoma City bombing. Unlike many of his predecessors, Clinton did not have a major hostage crisis to deal with, so it is not known how he would have reacted had Americans been taken captive overseas.

Clinton did, however, demonstrate an ability to put events into a proper context for the public. For example, following the midair explosion of TWA Flight 800 off Long Island shortly after takeoff from New York City's Kennedy International Airport in July 1996—an incident that killed all 230 people on board and which occurred just two days before the opening of the Summer Olympic Games in Atlanta, suggesting to some observers that this was the beginning of a terrorist campaign in the United States— Clinton was asked at a press conference if he was worried about an increased threat of terrorism in the United States. "I want to caution the American people," Clinton responded, "[that] we have no evidence on this flight yet that would indicate the cause of the accident. And I want to remind you that when we had the terrible tragedy in Oklahoma City, a lot of people immediately concluded that this must have been done by some force outside our country, and it appears that that was not the case now. So let's wait until we see the evidence."[5] After two long and extensive investigations by the FBI and the National Transportation Safety Board (NTSB), no evidence was found indicating that the explosion was due to an act of terrorism, sabotage, or missile attack. The NTSB issued its final report in August 2000, ruling that the crash was the result of a short circuit in the plane's wiring that probably led to a fuel-tank explosion that tore the aircraft apart.

While Clinton's words after the TWA crash were reassuring to a public concerned about terrorism, his actions were contradictory. At the same time that he was telling the American people to withhold judgment on the cause of the crash until the investigations were over, he nevertheless established the White House Commission on Aviation Safety and Security, headed by Vice President Al Gore. Although the word "terrorism" was not in the title of the commission, its focus nevertheless was strictly on terrorism. Among its recommendations were better screening of airline passengers using computerized profiles, mandatory full baggage match between passengers and their luggage, and more teams of bomb-sniffing dogs at airports. When Clinton signed a bill that incorporated many of the commission's recommendations, the president acknowledged that it was the TWA crash that propelled him into action: "After the TWA 800 disaster last summer, I asked Vice President Gore and a commission of experts to recommend improvements in our aviation security practices to protect against terrorist or criminal attacks. The [commission] delivered its recommendations to me on September 9—forty-five days after it began its deliberations—and this bill complements and builds upon those recommendations."[6]

Thus, a midair plane explosion that was not an act of terrorism nevertheless launched two lengthy investigations and led to the creation of a highly publicized government commission to study ways to protect the nation against terrorist attacks. The TWA crash illustrated that the United States was then, as it still is today, in a pre-crisis mode of thinking about terrorism. A terrorist incident—or perceptions that a terrorist attack has taken place—can immediately raise anxiety throughout the country about terrorism and fears that additional attacks are imminent. It will continue to be the president's responsibility, as the major molder and shaper of public opinion, to put events in their proper perspective and thereby avoid any overreactions on the part of the public or others to a specific incident.

Presidents also have to be careful not to raise unrealistic expectations about what can be accomplished in the battle against terrorism. Statements such as terrorism will be "defeated" or that the United States is at "war" with terrorists only serve to frustrate the public when the next incident occurs and the "war" never ends. Although for the most part Clinton resisted rhetoric on terrorism during his presidency, there were moments when it seemed as though the country was going back in time to the "tough talk on terrorism" that was a cornerstone of the Ronald Reagan years. Just as President Reagan warned terrorists that "you can run but you can't hide," so too did President Clinton tell terrorists after the bombing of the USS Cole in Yemen that "you will not find a safe harbor. We will find you and justice will prevail."[7]

In the shadowy world of terrorism, however, terrorists can often "run and hide" or find "safe harbor," thereby making universal promises about capturing them only that much more frustrating to the American public. Although the Clinton administration enjoyed many successes in apprehending terrorists around the world—primarily through the so-called "long arm of the law" legislation that allowed the FBI to assert extraterritorial jurisdiction in cases involving acts of terrorism—all efforts to apprehend Osama bin Ladin had failed as of the spring of 2001. Despite the indictment of bin Ladin by the United States for the embassy bombings in East Africa, and despite U.S. and U.N. sanctions against the Taliban who rule most of Afghanistan where bin Ladin has his headquarters and training camps, the terrorist was not handed over to the United States or a third country to stand trial.

Clinton also fell into the trap of building up the public's expectations concerning the results of a counterterrorist military operation. While the military option is an important one to use since it demonstrates resolve and a willingness to use force in dealing with terrorists, it is advisable that presidents refrain from making grandiose statements or inferences about what can be accomplished in a particular operation. When the United States launched scores of cruise missiles against bin Ladin's training camps and facilities in Khost, Afghanistan, on August 20, 1998, in retaliation for the embassy bombings in East Africa (the United States also attacked a factory in Sudan that it believed was associated with the bin Ladin network and which was suspected to be manufacturing chemical warfare agents), Clinton announced the raids in a live televised address from the Oval Office, thereby giving the operation added prestige. "Our target was terror," he told the American people. "Our mission was clear: to strike at the network of radical groups affiliated with and funded by Osama bin Ladin, perhaps the preeminent organizer and financier of international terrorism in the world today."[8] Yet the raids did not significantly disrupt bin Ladin's terror network, as evidenced by the terrorist plots linked to Al Qaeda at the end of 1999 and the attack on the USS Cole in 2000.

Clinton's legacy in the battle against terrorism, however, will most likely lie in his efforts to prepare the United States for terrorist attacks involving weapons of mass destruction. As president, he oversaw the largest federal expenditure in history for this type of terrorism—the fiscal year 2001 budget included $1.6 billion for combating WMD terrorism (part of $11.3 billion budgeted for dealing with all types of terrorism)[9]—and made the issue one of the most important of his presidency. He signed Presidential Decision Directive (PDD) 39 in 1995, making the prevention and management of the consequences of a terrorist attack with a weapon of mass destruction "the highest priority" for the United States. He later signed PDD 62 in 1998, that established the Office of the National Coordinator for Security, Infrastructure Protection, and Counter-Terrorism. Its responsibilities included overseeing policies and programs related to counterterrorism, protection of critical infrastructure, and preparedness and consequence management for weapons of mass destruction.

This was a dramatic change from years past when analysts, government officials, or others who spoke or wrote about the possibility of terrorists using weapons of mass destruction would be accused by some people of giving new ideas to terrorists. The assumption then was that terrorists did not know much about these weapons, so the less said or written about the subject, the better. In recent years, though, there were numerous congressional hearings, government reports, and television and newspaper commentaries devoted to this issue. It would have been unimaginable during the 1970s or 1980s to witness a U.S. secretary of defense holding up a five-pound bag of sugar at a news conference, and explaining that, if instead of sugar in the bag there was anthrax, which is a biological warfare agent, half the population of Washington, D.C., could be killed. Yet that is exactly what Secretary of Defense William Cohen did in 1997. The mayor of New York City, Rudolph Giuliani, built a multimillion-dollar emergency control center that was designed to withstand a nuclear blast, and contained a ventilation system that could be closed in case there was a terrorist attack with chemical or biological weapons. And a presidential advisory panel recommended in 1998 that the United States stockpile enough vaccines and antibiotics to treat up to six million people infected by biological warfare agents.

Emergency response teams from federal, state, and local agencies and specialized military units were formed to deal with WMD terrorism. Training exercises were held throughout the country. Yet the irony of these massive government programs to deal with a terrorist attack involving a weapon of mass destruction was that the most likely victims of such an attack were left in the dark. Terrorists who use weapons of mass destruction, particularly biological warfare agents such as anthrax or botulinum toxin, will be attracted to the mass killing potential of these weapons. That means that people living in metropolitan centers will be the likely targets of an attack. During the Clinton presidency, however, there were no civil defense programs involving the public, nor were there any public information or education campaigns to alert people as to what to expect, or what to do in the aftermath of a terrorist attack with a biological agent. Policymakers were understandably concerned about unnecessarily raising public anxieties and fears for an event that has not yet happened and for which they had hoped never will. But leaving the public out of the loop in contingency planning makes little sense since the consensus in Washington had already shifted away from a belief that bioterrorism could be prevented to an acknowledgment that it was only a matter of time before a major incident occurs.[10]

The third theme of *The Terrorist Trap* is the interrelationship of technology and terrorism. This is even more true today as there have been numerous technological advances in several fields, including communications, computers, information systems, and weaponry that have been taken advantage of by both terrorists and those who combat them.

The threat of "cyberterrorism" has received the most attention in terms of terrorists using technology to wreak havoc on governments and societies. Cyberterrorism usually refers to the ability of terrorists to use the Internet and other communication and information systems that are linked by computers to cause disruptions and chaos in government, business, and society. Among the scenarios often talked about are terrorists sabotaging air traffic control systems and thereby causing plane crashes; sabotaging electric power systems and thereby causing power blackouts; penetrating government databases; or sending computer viruses around the world that cause disruption or even collapse of international financial and banking systems. Concern about cyberterrorism led President Clinton to sign PDD 63 in 1998 which stated that "the United States will take all necessary measures to swiftly eliminate any significant vulnerability to both physical and cyber attacks on our critical infrastructures, including especially our cyber systems."[11]

The growth of the Internet in the last decade has also had a profound effect on terrorist plans and operations. Terrorists can now use the Internet to gather information about targets, including obtaining diagrams and maps of airports, train stations, government and private buildings, and other types of facilities. They can find documents and reports on the Internet that describe many different types of weapons, including information on how to build homemade weapons of mass destruction. Electronic mail, or "E-mail" provides terrorists with free and instant communications with each other which can be protected against interception by government authorities through the use of encryption technology. And some terrorist groups have designed their own Web pages to attract potential recruits and spread their message and ideology around the world.

Terrorists have also used technology as a means for designing innovative ways to perpetrate their violence. For example, Pakistani authorities found two toy cars packed with explosives in Ramzi Yousef's suitcases after his arrest in Pakistan. The Japanese religious cult Aum Shinrikyo attempted to build laser guns and electromagnetic weapons, in addition to their experimentation and use of weapons of mass destruction. The leadership of the cult "systematically targeted top universities, recruiting brilliant but alienated young scientists from chemistry, physics, and engineering departments."[12] Other terrorist groups can do the same, ensuring that they will have members who are able to take advantage of our increasingly technological society.

Technology, of course, has been vital to the efforts of counterterrorist and law enforcement agencies. From designing detection equipment for explosives and other types of terrorist weapons to developing state-of-the-art surveillance and communications systems, technology has always played a key role in the battle against terrorism. One of the latest additions was the use of face-recognition technology at the 2001 Super Bowl in Tampa, Florida. Police video cameras were focused on each person among the estimated 100,000 fans and workers who walked through the turnstiles at Raymond James Stadium. Cables instantly carried the images to computers in a law enforcement control room inside the stadium. The computers spent less than a second comparing the images with thousands of digital portraits of suspected terrorists and known criminals. Although no terrorists were found and the only "hit" was reported to be a ticket scalper who then vanished into the crowd, the technology is expected to be used at future sporting events.[13]

There are limits, however, to what technology can accomplish in the battle against terrorism. Detection systems that are being designed today to deal with the threat of terrorists using biological agents, for example, can only warn *after* an agent has been released, not before. That allows terrorists in possession of biological agents to move around freely prior to an attack. And despite the use of the latest military technology in counterterrorist raids and hostage-rescue missions, there is still no guarantee that the correct targets will be hit or that all the hostages will be rescued unharmed. Combating terrorism will remain a technological race with terrorists holding the ultimate advantage since they only need to be successful once in penetrating a security system to make it appear that they are gaining the upper hand in the endless conflict.

There were a few omissions that were made in the first edition that should be corrected. In chapter 2, I discuss the kidnapping of Ion Perdicaris by the Moorish pirate Raisuli in Morocco in 1904, and point out how that incident revealed the complex web of international intrigue, suspense, and negotiations that often accompanies a hostage crisis. There was, however, another kidnapping that took place nearly three years earlier that also had international repercussions and was followed closely by the American public.[14] Ellen Stone, an American missionary in Macedonia, was kidnapped on September 3, 1901, along with a Macedonian woman, Katarina Stefanova Tsilka. The women's captors were members of the Internal Macedonian Revolutionary Organization (IMRO), who orchestrated the kidnapping in part to raise ransom money to support their activities against Turkish rule in Macedonia, and also to possibly complicate U.S. relations with Turkey—the kidnappers were in Turkish disguises when they seized their captives. The kidnappers at first demanded 25,000 Turkish lira (about $110,000), but eventually settled for $65,000, which was raised by contributions from the American public at the urgings of Stone's family in Massachusetts. After the ransom was paid, the hostages, including a baby that Tsilka had given birth to a couple of months after the kidnapping, were released unharmed on February 23, 1902. Although the IMRO failed in its objective to involve the United States in a dispute with Turkey, and a rebellion a year later that became known as the Ilinden uprising of 1903 was short-lived, the group did succeed in obtaining funds for the uprising, and also drew attention in the United States and elsewhere to the issue of Macedonian independence.

There was also no mention in my book of the 1920 Wall Street bombing, which was significant in that it could be considered the forerunner to today's car and truck bombings. On September 16 of that year, a terrorist or terrorists parked a horse and wagon in front of the J.P. Morgan and Co. building. The wagon was packed with a TNT bomb and a timer set to go off at noon. The explosion killed thirty-five people and injured hundreds more. Although anarchists or radicals were suspected of the bombing, nobody was ever officially charged for the attack.

I would also like to revise my discussion in chapter 7 of the future of media and its impact on terrorism. In discussing the potential for terrorists to exploit "integrated systems of digital networks" (ISDN) through which data, voice, and pictures are carried over networks linked to other networks, there was no mention of the Internet. At the time I wrote that chapter, which was in the early 1990s, the Internet was still evolving and was not the force that it is today in everyday life. Thus the observation that ISDN "will be the closest realization yet to [Marshall] McLuhan's 'global village'" and that "people will be linked together through computer terminals and various other devices, even in the most remote parts of the earth," has already been achieved with the incredible growth of the Internet.

Back to the Future Again

There were several future trends in terrorism that were identified in the first edition of the book, including the continual evolution of terrorist tactics with terrorists attempting to conceive of new ways to commit their violence; the rise of a new generation of terrorists, born from the ethnic-nationalist and religious conflicts that were then, and in some cases still are, raging around the world; the proliferation of high-tech weapons and their likelihood to fall into terrorists' hands; the increased risk of terrorists acquiring, and using, weapons of mass destruction; terrorists' exploitation of future communications and media technologies; and the likelihood of additional terrorist attacks within U.S. borders.

Many of these trends have become even more apparent since publication of the book. For example, we have seen terrorists introduce a new tactic—suicide boat bombings—to their repertoire of violence with the attack on the USS Cole in Yemen. Suicide bombings at sea must now be considered a threat along with the more familiar suicide car and truck bombings and individual "human bomb" attacks on land. The next innovation in suicide attacks, as noted in the first edition, may very well be attacks from the air in single-engine, low-flying planes or helicopters that are packed with explosives and can avoid radar. In terms of ethnic-nationalist and religious conflicts, there has already been a spillover of the turmoil in the former Soviet Union into the international terrorism arena, with Chechen rebels hijacking a Russian-bound ferry in the Turkish Black Sea port of Trabzon in January 1996 and a Russian airliner shortly after takeoff from Istanbul in March 2001. It is still likely that the past conflicts in Bosnia, Kosovo, and other areas will give rise to new terrorist groups that will carry on the violence.

The proliferation of high-tech weapons such as shoulder-fired Stinger antiaircraft missiles continues to be a concern of the U.S. government, and it may only be a matter of time before a terrorist group uses one in an attack on a civilian airliner or another target. In terms of weapons of mass destruction, we have seen a religious cult use one—Sarin nerve gas—inside the Tokyo subway system, and the threat of terrorists acquiring and using other weapons of mass destruction remains one of the most serious issues facing the United States and other nations. Terrorists have also been exploiting advances in media and communications in recent years, particularly with respect to the Internet. And there have been additional terrorist attacks inside U.S. borders since this book was published, including the Oklahoma City and Atlanta Summer Olympic Games bombings.

These trends, as well as others that were discussed in the first edition, such as the growing lethality of terrorist attacks, the increase in religious terrorism around the world, and the emergence of technically advanced and more creative terrorists, are likely to continue in the coming years. In addition, the future of terrorism will likely see a significant role played by the lone operator. We have already seen what lone operators such as the Unabomber can accomplish in terms of spreading fear and anxiety about terrorism throughout the country. There are likely to be additional terrorist attacks in the future by these types of terrorists. The technological society that we live in plays into the hands of lone operators, who could gather information from the Internet on tactics, targets, and weapons—including how to build homemade bombs or manufacture chemical and biological agents—without ever having to leave one's house. One of the advantages that lone operators have over a larger terrorist group or even just two individuals who plan a terrorist attack, is that by working alone they are unlikely to be discovered by law enforcement or intelligence agencies prior to an attack. There will not be any communications between members of a group to intercept, nor will there be any terrorist group members to arrest and gain further information from about planned operations.

The case of the Alphabet Bomber, which was not discussed in the first edition, demonstrates the threat posed by the lone operator, particularly with respect to weapons of mass destruction. In 1974, a mentally ill Yugoslav immigrant, Muharem Kurbegovic, who claimed to be the leader of a fictitious group called "Aliens of America," set off a bomb at Los Angeles International Airport that killed three people and injured several others. In a tape that he left with the media after the bombing, he said that the first bomb was marked with the letter "A" which stood for airport, a second bomb would be associated with the letter "L," a third with the letter "I," and so forth, "until our name has been written on the face of this nation in blood." He thus became known as the Alphabet Bomber, and in several other tapes that he sent to the media he threatened to release Sarin nerve gas over Washington, D.C., unless all immigration and naturalization and sex laws were declared unconstitutional.

Kurbegovic also claimed to have sent postcards to the nine U.S. Supreme Court justices with toxic material placed in metal disks underneath the stamps. Postal authorities intercepted the cards when they became caught in the canceling machine in a Palm Springs post office, but no toxic material was found in the metal disks. When police searched the Alphabet Bomber's apartment after his arrest, they found pipe bombs, explosive materials, books and manuals on germ and chemical warfare, gas masks, catalogues for purchasing chemicals and laboratory equipment, and maps of Washington, D.C., and London's Heathrow Airport. In subsequent searches of his apartment, police found twenty-five pounds of sodium cyanide, which is a precursor chemical for the manufacture of the nerve agent Tabun, and can also be used to generate toxic hydrogen cyanide gas.

Kurbegovic learned about chemical warfare agents by checking out books from a public library and obtaining declassified government documents. What it took him a few months of research in the 1970s to learn would probably take a person today only a few hours by searching the Internet. The Alphabet Bomber case also demonstrated that lone operators can sometimes be ahead of their time in terms of devising terrorist scenarios. Kurbegovic was one of the first terrorists to threaten to release nerve agents in populated areas, to acquire sodium cyanide, and to use the media in a systematic way to communicate his message and spread fear among the public. Lone operators have fewer constraints on the violence they perpetrate than do members of a terrorist group since there are no group decision-making processes to worry about and no constituency to be concerned with in terms of a possible negative backlash to an incident. That is why lone operators have been among the most innovative in terms of terrorist tactics throughout history, and will continue to be so in the coming years.[15]

The first edition of *The Terrorist Trap* ended with a story about the unveiling of a plaque at Syracuse University in memory of the thirty-five students who were killed in the bombing of Pan Am 103 in 1988. As I write this new introduction in the spring of 2001, it is perhaps a coincidence, or perhaps symbolic of the endless nature of terrorism, that another dedication ceremony has recently taken place for victims of a different terrorist attack. On February 19, 2001, President George W. Bush dedicated the opening of a museum in Oklahoma City at the site where the federal building had once stood before it was bombed by terrorists in 1995. The museum is devoted to the memories of the victims of that blast. "Memorials do not take away the pain," Bush told his audience. "They cannot fill the emptiness. But they can make a place in time and tell the value of what was lost. The debris is gone and the building is no more. Now, this is a place of peace and remembrance and life."[16]

Unfortunately, there are likely to be more memorial ceremonies for America's victims of terrorism in the years ahead. Whether the violence takes place overseas or at home, terrorism can leave an indelible mark upon this nation. Perhaps the best memorial to all victims of terrorism, both past and future, is to vow to continue the fight against this perpetual form of violence, all the time remembering that while we will not be able to prevent every act of terrorism from occurring, we will be able to prevent the terrorists from destroying the soul and spirit of this country.

Notes

1. Jeffrey D. Simon, "Biological Terrorism: Preparing to Meet the Threat," *The Journal of the American Medical Association*, August 6, 1997, vol. 278, no. 5, pp. 428–30.

2. Craig Pyes, Judith Miller, and Stephen Engelberg, "One Man and a Global Web of Violence," *New York Times*, January 14, 2001, p. 13.

3. *Statement by Director of Central Intelligence George J. Tenet before the Senate Select Committee on Intelligence on the "Worldwide Threat 2001: National Security in a Changing World,"* February 7, 2001, http://www.cia.gov/cia/public_affairs/speeches/UNCLASWWT_02072001.html.

4. *Patterns of Global Terrorism: 1999*, Department of State Publication 10687, Office of the Secretary of State, Office of the Coordinator for Counterterrorism, U.S. Department of State, Washington, D.C., April 2000, p. 31.

5. *Clinton Statement on TWA 800 Crash*, July 18, 1996, http://www.avweb.com/other/pres9629.html.

6. *Statement by the President*, October 9, 1996, The White House, Office of the Press Secretary.

7. *Remarks by the President During USS Cole Memorial Service, Pier 12 Norfolk, Virginia*, October 25, 2000, The White House, Office of the Press Secretary.

8. *Transcript: Clinton Oval Office Remarks on Anti-Terrorist Attacks*, United States Information Agency, August 20, 1998.

9. "Combating Terrorism: Linking Threats to Strategies and Resources," *Statement of Norman J. Rabkin, Director, National Security Preparedness Issues, National Security and International Affairs Division, United States General Accounting Office, Testimony Before the Subcommittee on National Security, Veterans Affairs, and International Relations, Committee on Government Reform, House of Representatives*, July 26, 2000, GAO/T-NSIAD-00-218.

10. For a discussion of the utility of providing gas masks to civilian populations as one measure of protection in the event of a bioterrorist attack, see Karl Lowe, Graham S. Pearson, and Victor Utgoff, "Potential Values of a Simple Biological Warfare Protective Mask," in Joshua Lederberg, ed., *Biological Weapons: Limiting the Threat*, BCSIA Studies in International Security, Cambridge, Massachusetts, The MIT Press, 1999, pp. 263–81.

11. Presidential Decision Directive 63, Critical Infrastructure Protection, May 22, 1998, The White House, Office of the Press Secretary.

12. David E. Kaplan and Andrew Marshall, *The Cult at the End of the World: The Incredible Story of Aum*, London, Arrow Books, Limited, 1996, p. 3.

13. Robert Trigaus, "Cameras Scanned Fans for Criminals," *St. Petersburg Times*, January 31, 2001, p. 1A; and Peter Slevin, "At Tampa's Turnstiles, Crowd Wasn't Faceless," *Washington Post*, February 1, 2001, p. A1.

14. I would like to thank Dennis Pluchinsky of the U.S. State Department for bringing this to my attention.

15. Jeffrey D. Simon, "The Alphabet Bomber," in Jonathan B. Tucker, ed., *Toxic Terror: Assessing Terrorist Use of Chemical and Biological Weapons*, BCSIA Studies in International Security, Cambridge, Massachusetts, The MIT Press, 2000, pp. 71–94; and Jeffrey D. Simon, "Lone Operators and Weapons of Mass Destruction," in Brad Roberts, ed., *Hype or Reality?: The "New Terrorism" and Mass Casualty Attacks*, Alexandria, Virginia, The Chemical and Biological Arms Control Institute, 2000, pp. 69–81.

16. Frank Bruni, "Bush Dedicates Museum at Site of Oklahoma City Bombing," *New York Times*, February 20, 2001, p. A12.

THE TERRORIST TRAP

Prologue

Terrorism was not on the minds of Midwood High School's honor students when they gathered in the spring of 1967 for a graduation yearbook photo. The word itself was hardly in use in those days, since it would still be another year before Palestinian guerrillas ushered in the age of international terrorism with a series of hijackings in Europe and the Middle East. Yet in that Arista picture, as the Brooklyn, New York, high school's honor society was known, was a foreshadowing of America's coming experience with this threat. One of the students would become a researcher and writer on terrorism, spending many years trying to understand this phenomenon. Another would become a hostage in the most spectacular hijacking in terrorism history. And a third would join a terrorist group, eventually sentenced to seventy-five years to life in prison for her activities.

I was in the front row of the Arista picture, and had no idea when I began writing this book in 1990 that my journey would take me back to my high school yearbook and the fates of two classmates. In the back row of Arista was Miriam Beeber, a lanky teenager with beautiful, long auburn hair and an enthusiasm for people and school. In addition to being in the honor society, she was also the leader of the school's extracurricular activities club, a member of the "boosters" that led the pep rallies before sporting events, and the cochairperson of the freshman sing committee. After graduating from Midwood, Beeber went to George Washington University in Washington, D.C. At the end of her junior year in 1970, she spent the summer in Israel working on a kibbutz and was returning home to New York when she became a pawn in the deadly game of terrorism.

It was the dawn of the age of international hijackings, and the Popular Front for the Liberation of Palestine, a faction of the Palestine Liberation Organization, made its presence felt by hijacking *four* planes on September 6, including TWA Flight 741, on which Beeber was a passenger. That plane, along with a hijacked Swissair jet, was diverted to Jordan, while a Pan American jet was forced to land in Cairo. The fourth hijacked plane was an El Al jet where Israeli security guards were able to kill one hijacker and capture the other while the plane was still airborne. After landing in London, the surviving hijacker was arrested, but the PFLP responded by hijacking yet another plane a few days later. This time it was a British airliner, which was also brought to the Jordanian desert. All of the hijacked planes were blown up on the ground after the passengers were removed.

The first prolonged hostage crisis in aviation history was under way, and Beeber was caught right in the middle. She was held captive for three weeks, being among the last group of about fifty hostages to be released from an original total of more than three hundred. Her anger and frustration led her and five other hostages to send a letter to the American embassy in Amman, calling on President Nixon and Israeli Prime Minister Golda Meir to do something to win their freedom: "We the passengers of the hijacked planes TWA 741 and Swissair 100 have as of today, September 12, become political prisoners after a week of captivity due to the negligence and political paralysis of our government. The lives of women, girls, and men are literally in jeopardy every moment. We demand that human consideration transcend all other political considerations so that we may be immediately released and returned to our homes."[1]

Beeber was finally freed after a series of deals—which nobody admitted were deals—were made to release Palestinian prisoners held in European and Israeli jails. Nixon, who was in Rome when the hostages were freed, met with them and spoke briefly to Beeber at the Rome airport before the former hostages were flown back to the United States. What Beeber found upon her arrival at Kennedy Airport would become commonplace for hostages and their families in future terrorist episodes. The media were out in full force, with television cameras, bright lights, and reporters and anchor people all crowded into a TWA terminal waiting room. Upon seeing this, Beeber quickly fled, eager to resume a life that had been unexpectedly interrupted by an act of terrorism.[2]

In the second row of Arista was Judith Clark. An attractive and bright student, Clark, like Beeber, was very active in high school. She was a member of the math team and sophomore sing committee, and was also the deputy commissioner of the codification committee, the group that set the rules and regulations for Midwood. But Clark's commitment to revolutionary causes would soon find her breaking the laws of the United States and thrust into the ranks of a terrorist group.

Clark joined the Weathermen, a violent faction of the Students for a Democratic Society (SDS), while at the University of Chicago in 1969. The Weathermen would claim responsibility for more than twenty bombings between 1970 and 1975, including attacks on the U.S. Capitol and the State Department. Clark was expelled from the university early in 1969 for participating in an illegal demonstration and was arrested in October of that year for attacking an armed forces induction center in Chicago along with a hundred other women wielding clubs and wearing crash helmets. She jumped bail in March 1970 and was arrested in December of that year when spotted by an FBI agent in New York. She served nine months in prison in Chicago, but all charges against her and other Weathermen were dismissed following a 1973 Supreme Court ruling that the U.S. government had used illegal wiretapping and other surveillance methods to convict the radicals. Clark and several other activists filed a civil suit against the government, which was settled in 1982.[3]

Meanwhile, during the 1970s, the Weathermen changed their name to the Weatherpeople and then to the Weather Underground in order to avoid any innuendoes of male chauvinism that were associated with the original name. Arrests and retirements reduced their ranks to around fifteen people from the several hundred radicals of the earlier days. Clark was still among the active members and subsequently became involved with the May 19th Communist Organization, a radical group named for the joint birthday of Malcolm X and Ho Chi Minh. In September 1981, Clark traveled to Beirut, Lebanon, to represent the May 19th group at a PLO conference.[4] She was now meeting with the very organization that had terrorized one of her classmates a decade earlier.

When Clark returned to the United States shortly after the conference, her belief in revolutionary politics took a turn that changed her life forever. On October 20, 1981, she participated in a robbery of a Brink's armored truck in Nanuet, New York. One Brink's guard was killed and two policemen were slain later at a roadblock set up in the town of Nyack to capture the gunmen. Clark was in one of the two getaway cars, and although she did not commit any of the murders, she was convicted of three counts of second-degree murder in September 1983 for being an accomplice to an armed robbery that resulted in the deaths of innocent people. She was also convicted of four counts of first-degree armed robbery. During the trial, she and her two codefendants, who acted as their own attorneys, read revolutionary statements and claimed that the Brink's robbery, which netted $1.5 million, was an "expropriation" needed to finance their revolution against the U.S. government. After their conviction they issued a statement that "we will continue to maintain our position as freedom fighters."[5] Judith Clark told the court before her sentence was read that "we believe that whatever happens to us as individuals, the forces that produce struggle remain and the movement will continue to struggle and grow."[6] After the three revolutionaries left the courtroom, the judge vented his frustration. "I harbor no illusions," said Judge David Ritter. "Everything that the defendants have said indicates that they will repeat their lawless conduct. Each defendant represents a clear and present danger to society."[7] The court reporter would later recall that of the three defendants, Judith Clark appeared to be the most angry with society. "Clark threw me," said Robert Cummings, "because she seemed like she was probably the most—I don't want to say scorned—but she seemed like she had the most hate for some reason."[8]

The experiences of Miriam Beeber and Judith Clark illustrate the opposite poles of terrorism, a conflict where anybody can become a victim—a fear that terrorists thrive upon—and where the perpetrators can come from all walks of life. Terrorists are not the faceless enemies that we have become accustomed to reading or hearing about, but rather are individuals who become so committed to a particular cause that they can justify in their own minds, and sometimes in those of their supporters, the terrorizing and killing of innocent people. The slogan that one person's terrorist is another person's freedom fighter is more than just a cliché. It goes right to the heart of a global phenomenon that will continue to plague governments and societies well into the next century.

This book is the story of America's experience with terrorism: where we have been in the past, where we are now, and where we are heading in the future. American symbols have long been a favorite target of a diverse array of terrorist groups. This will be even more so in the post–Cold War era with the United States as the world's remaining superpower. Attacking Americans or U.S. targets abroad or at home guarantees results and immediate reactions.

The reader will be taken on a journey through history and current affairs to uncover the dynamics of a conflict that impacts all our lives. The end of the Cold War and the return of American hostages from Lebanon led some to believe that terrorism was over. But terrorism evolves in cycles, and the World Trade Center bombing proved that a new wave of terrorism can approach at any time.

The 1970s was the decade of international airplane hijackings and terrorist assaults on foreign embassies. The 1980s was the decade of hostage taking, suicide truck bombings, and midair plane bombings. The 1990s still has to make its mark, but likely candidates are terrorists with chemical and biological weapons, terrorist attacks with modern, sophisticated weapons such as shoulder-fired antiaircraft missiles, and terrorist attempts to sabotage the global information and communication networks that are linking people and nations together.

Each new cycle of terrorism brings with it remnants from the past. We have not seen the last of major hijackings, bombings, or hostage taking. No other form of violence approaches the mystery and uniqueness of terrorism. For the relatively simple act of hijacking a plane, or kidnapping a person, or blowing up a building, a whole sequence of global events can unfold that can last months, years, or even decades beyond that brief moment of violence.

The most immediate impact is upon the victims who may be killed or psychologically scarred for life, and their families and loved ones who experience great suffering. There is also the effect upon the public at large, which vicariously experiences their fellow citizens' terror from media coverage of the event. There is the effect upon governments, which scurry to react and demonstrate resolve in the face of attacks against their legitimacy. And there is the impact upon issues such as regional peace efforts, which can be harmed by the acts of terrorists.

The allure of terrorism lies in its danger, the seemingly unpredictable nature and randomness of the violence. Terrorism, though, is neither senseless nor random. It is a highly purposeful act committed by deadly serious people with big payoffs in mind. A Frenchman, Emile Henry, coined a phrase in the late nineteenth century that many terrorist groups utilize today. Henry, an anarchist, had hurled a homemade bomb into a crowded café in Paris in 1894 to avenge the recent execution of a fellow anarchist. The bombing resulted in several injuries and one death. When the judges at his trial expressed bewilderment at the crime, pointing out that most of the victims were small shopkeepers, clerks, and workers— people who were innocent of any wrongdoing—Henry simply replied, "There are no innocent."[9]

Several decades of experience with terrorist tactics, incidents, and results leads to a somber conclusion: *terrorism pays off*. For all the terrorists who have been killed or captured, repented or simply burned out, there remain countless others who have seen how great powers can be brought to their knees and thrown into a state of crisis by the simple act of hijacking a plane, kidnapping a number of citizens, or threatening to initiate a terror campaign within its borders. Terrorism has become one of the most effective means by which small groups and even states can achieve results otherwise unobtainable.

Understanding why terrorism pays off is a critical part of understanding the dynamics of the terrorist threat and why it has endured over the years. It is often said that terrorists are "irrational" and that their violence is counterproductive. Many terrorist incidents are followed by official government statements calling the violence the work of "madmen" or of "sick" individuals. This helps foster the image of terrorists as lacking roots, motivations, or clear-cut strategic objectives. Yet terrorism is as much a part of international politics and the world we live in as are revolutions, coups, and other acts of violence. During a 1976 hijacking of a Trans World Airlines plane, Croatian separatists acknowledged that their act of seizing an airplane would be viewed as a terrorist act. But they pointed out that "we must remember that today's 'terrorists' are often tomorrow's policymakers, having participated in the formation of a new, independent state." And just to prove that they were open to self-criticism, they invited anybody who disagreed with them to send a critique to a post office box in Grand Central Station in New York City.[10]

Terrorism has allowed some states to acquire large sums of ransom money for hostages, as Iran did during the 1980s. Iran obtained millions of dollars from several governments, including France, West Germany, and Japan, in return for exerting their influence on pro-Iranian Islamic fundamentalists in Lebanon to free some of the foreign hostages they were holding. Terrorism also allowed Iran to acquire arms from the government it had called the Great Satan—the United States—again using hostages as bait.

Some terrorist groups have used well-timed attacks to sabotage peace initiatives in a region, or to keep the tension level high when things appear to be calming down. This has occurred frequently in the Middle East, with Palestinian terrorist groups launching raids into Israel, attacking Israeli targets in other countries, or targeting moderate Arab governments and other Palestinian factions as progress toward peace is under way. After the PLO signed a peace accord with Israel in September 1993, terrorist groups opposed to the pact increased their attacks in Israel and in the occupied territories. In February 1994, a Jewish settler opposed to the peace accord massacred at least twenty-nine Muslims as they prayed in a mosque in the occupied–West Bank city of Hebron.

Extremist groups have used terrorism to settle scores. Sometimes they even hire other groups to do their work, as was the case with the Japanese Red Army's massacre at Lod airport in Israel in 1972. Three JRA members, with no particular ideological conflict with Israel, except in the realm of trying to foment "world revolution" by attacking Western and capitalist targets, were recruited by the Popular Front for the Liberation of Palestine to launch a terrorist attack against Israel. The JRA terrorists flew to Tel Aviv, and after disembarking, hurled grenades and fired assault rifles at the passengers, killing twenty-six people and wounding seventy-six others. That most of the victims were Puerto Rican pilgrims on a visit to the Holy Land did not matter to the JRA. In terrorism, the location of an attack and the impact that it can have upon the government of that country is often more important than who the actual victims are.

Governments also hire terrorists to settle scores. Despite the U.S. indictment of two Libyan agents for the 1988 bombing of Pan Am Flight 103 over Lockerbie, Scotland, many intelligence analysts believe that it was actually Iran that first approached Ahmed Jabril, head of the Popular Front for the Liberation of Palestine–General Command, to place a bomb aboard the plane, and then turned to the Libyans after several PFLP-GC members were arrested in Germany before the bombing. The motive was retaliation for the accidental shooting down of an Iranian civilian airliner by the U.S.S. *Vincennes* in the Persian Gulf.

Terrorism has also paid off for groups who want their comrades freed from prisons around the world. The September 1970 hijackings by the PFLP, of which Miriam Beeber was one of the hostages, was aimed in part at gaining the release of fellow members in foreign prisons. When the surviving hijacker of the El Al plane was captured and imprisoned in Britain, the PFLP realized that they did not have any British hostages to gain her release. So they simply hijacked a British Overseas Airways Corporation plane and managed to win her release in exchange for the new hostages.

The hijacking of a Kuwaiti airliner in 1988 was ordered by the relative of one of several pro-Iranian Lebanese terrorists serving time in a Kuwaiti prison for blowing up the United States and French embassies in 1983. The hijackers' demand, which was not met, was the release of all the prisoners. In 1990, Hizballah, the pro-Iranian, Shiite, extremist group in Lebanon, released a French hostage, and the French government soon after reciprocated by releasing an Iranian who was in jail for his role in terrorist attacks in France.

Terrorism has also proven effective for individuals and groups intent on damaging a country's export trade. Product contamination was used by Palestinian extremists who poisoned Israeli oranges, by Sri Lankan rebels who claimed they contaminated Sri Lankan tea, and by Chilean leftist guerrillas who were suspected of placing cyanide in Chilean grapes. Terrorism has also paid off for the criminal element, giving them a political platform to hide their basic greed or homicidal tendencies.

With all the death and destruction, fear and frustration that terrorism causes around the world, it is not surprising that people and governments seek some type of a solution, or at least a diminishing of the threat. Combating terrorism, though, can be a frustrating experience for governments and law-enforcement officials. International cooperation is not always present. "Victories" over terrorists, whether in arrests, counterterrorist operations, or good physical security measures, can be quickly reversed with the next airplane bombing or hostage episode. Even though substantial progress has been made in the fight against terrorism, it is easy for people to think that we are back to square one after each major terrorist attack. In terrorism and counterterrorism, images and symbols are as important, if not more so, than the realities of the threat.

For the United States, these images have been quite stark. In 1979, the American people watched on television as their own citizens were paraded blindfolded in front of the U.S. embassy in Tehran with angry crowds shouting, "Death to America." A decade later, it was Saddam Hussein holding thousands of Americans and other foreigners as hostages and then as "human shields" in Iraq. In between these events, there were dramatic scenes of U.S. Marines being killed by a suicide truck bomber in Lebanon; a Trans World Airlines pilot in Beirut conducting a television interview while a terrorist held a gun to his head; and holiday travelers losing their lives aboard Pan Am 103, with many of the victims young college students. No matter who the perpetrators are, terrorism has left an indelible mark on the public's mind.

It has also linked permanently in history two American presidents who otherwise would have little in common. Jimmy Carter and Ronald Reagan were as different in personality, ideology, and style as any two leaders could be: Carter, the low-keyed Southern Democrat with a liberal foreign policy stance and a seemingly uncomfortable presence before the media, and Reagan, the "great communicator," whose conservative Republican credentials made him the standard-bearer for a renewal of a strong U.S. military presence around the world. Yet terrorism proved to be the Achilles' heel for both men, providing poignant portraits of two individuals who, regardless of their other accomplishments, will always be remembered for falling into the terrorist trap.

For Carter, the trap lay in allowing the Iran hostage crisis of 1979–81 to virtually paralyze his presidency, as all other issues lost importance to ending the crisis. It was not just individuals that were held hostage during this crisis; so too was the president of the United States, and by extension, the country as a whole. For Reagan, the trap involved becoming so emotionally involved with the issue of hostages in Lebanon that U.S. regional and geopolitical interests were swept aside—by his own admission—as the U.S. sought any possible way to gain freedom for eight hostages in Lebanon. The United States thus entered into an arms-for-hostages deal with Iran even though Tehran had been consistently denounced by Washington for supporting terrorism around the world.

This book explores the terrorist trap: the psychological, political, and social elements that make terrorism unlike any other type of conflict. It is the story of presidents, terrorists, media, and society, all entangled in the dramas of international violence. Firsthand accounts of terrorism's impact are provided through in-depth interviews with people who have had different experiences with the terrorist threat. These range from former secretaries of state and presidential advisers to the victims of terrorism and the terrorists themselves. There are also reflections by anchor people, reporters, and news executives on the issue of who is manipulating whom in the interrelationship between terrorists and the media. These interviews yield an oral history of America's experience with this deadly conflict.

Three central themes emerge in the following pages. The first is the endless nature of terrorism and its likely growth in the coming years. Terrorism is a conflict that is based on political, economic, and social grievances that can never be fully resolved. The attention given to terrorism in recent years makes it quite easy to assume that the terrorist threat is a product of modern times. Terrorism, however, has plagued governments and societies for many centuries. It may not always have been called "terrorism," but the tactics used, and the problems it caused, had an uncanny resemblance to today's phenomenon.

Religious fanaticism, ethnic-nationalist conflicts, political and revolutionary ideologies, and criminal greed are only some of the factors that have always propelled individuals and groups into terrorist campaigns. The roots of terrorism are also found in widespread poverty, unemployment, and alienation. Despite these realities, the myth of defeating terrorism continues to be spread by politicians and policymakers. The very first sentence of the executive summary of the President's Commission on Aviation Security and Terrorism—which was established in the aftermath of the Pan Am 103 bombing—is indicative of the tendency to view terrorism as a finite problem: "National will and the moral courage to exercise it are the ultimate means for defeating terrorism."[11] Yet terrorism can no sooner be eliminated or defeated than one can wipe out poverty, solve the drug problem, or cure all diseases. The phenomenon is too pervasive, it is linked to too many different causes, and it has too many potential targets at its disposal. Terrorism would continue even if there were no more state-sponsors, such as Libya, Syria, Iran, and Iraq, and even if every state that allowed terrorists safe passage ended their conciliatory policies. The terrorists would simply adapt to the new realities as they always have in the past, finding new hiding places and becoming more deceptive in their movements.

Living with terrorism will be an inescapable part of life in the coming years. The explosion of ethnic, nationalist, and religious conflicts that has proliferated around the globe in the early 1990s is a harbinger of a post–Cold War era in which various groups will assert themselves to fill the power vacuums left by the collapse of the old order. And terrorism will be one of the tools used to meet their various objectives. The tendency to view terrorism in black-and-white terms with identifiable enemies will become more obsolete as the range of participants increases and the lines between terrorism, political violence, and freedom fighting become further blurred.

The second theme that emerges from America's experience with terrorism is the central role played by U.S. presidents in determining terrorism's impact on this country. From the earliest days of the republic, American presidents have been key players in the terrorist dramas that have unfolded. Terrorism is a complex and frightening experience for the general public, and it becomes natural to look toward Washington for guidance and reassurance. It also becomes natural to rally around presidents in the aftermath of terrorist attacks against Americans. This high level of public support gives presidents a great amount of leverage in choosing their response options—economic, diplomatic, military—but it also places a heavy burden on them to act in accordance with the nation's long-term interests and not in reaction to high-pitched emotional fervor.

The president's role in dealing with terrorism has been made more complicated in recent years by the tremendous growth of the mass media. The media and terrorists enjoy a symbiotic relationship where the media—television, radio, and newspapers—provide a world stage for some terrorist groups, while the terrorists provide the media with great stories and human drama. The public becomes riveted to the daily, and sometimes hourly, developments in a terrorist episode, adding pressure on presidents to resolve an incident or take firm action. Yet the media cannot really be blamed for the crises that often arise after hijackings and bombings. There was terrorism before there were mass media, and some terrorist groups today act with little concern for media attention. Despite the influence of the media, it is still the job of presidents to set the tone for how the nation will respond to terrorism. If the image that comes out of Washington is one of crisis and rhetoric, then that is what the media will report. American presidents throughout history have dealt with terrorism in a wide variety of ways, and how their experiences compare with each other may provide some valuable lessons for future leaders.

The third theme of this book is terrorism's link to the irreversible march of technology. Technological advancements in all fields have one thing in common: they do not discriminate among their users. Sophisticated weapons, communications equipment, and other technology will be there for all to take advantage of, including terrorists. This will translate into more lethal and deadly incidents in the years ahead. Technology has not only provided terrorists with a continually evolving arsenal of weapons—beginning with daggers in ancient times and then guns and dynamite, and more recently plastic explosives and shoulder-fired antiaircraft weapons—but it has also provided them with an ever-increasing supply of attractive targets. Without the existence of ships, the Barbary pirates could not have taken American sailors hostage off the high seas. Without the invention of the airplane, terrorists could not have initiated campaigns of hijackings or midair bombings. And without the automobile, car bombings and suicide truck bombings would not have taken place. The global village that is evolving, with its more accessible and faster transportation and communication mechanisms, will bring people in closer touch with each other and provide new avenues for terrorist attacks.

The role of technology in terrorism also extends to efforts to contend with the terrorist threat. This becomes a never-ending technological race in which counterterrorist authorities try to stay one step ahead of the terrorists. Each new technological device that is developed to deter or prevent a terrorist attack—metal detectors, plastic explosive detectors, bomb-resistant glass, fortified buildings—serves as a challenge to terrorists to outsmart the authorities. Many terrorist groups have within their ranks or among their supporters people capable of matching counterterrorist efforts step-for-step. The trend is for terrorists to commit more spectacular and violent attacks in order to overcome existing physical security measures, as well as to ensure continual public and government shock over terrorism.

The challenges that lie ahead for the United States will be to deal with a world in which the endless political, ethnic, and religious conflicts that give rise to terrorism are joined by continued technological advancements in weaponry and tactics, producing a potentially more dangerous era of terrorism. Of particular concern will be the potential for terrorists to utilize weapons of mass destruction—biological, chemical, and nuclear. The scare that Saddam Hussein gave the world with his threat to unleash weapons of mass destruction during the 1991 Gulf War is a lesson that will not be lost on tomorrow's terrorists.

The task for American presidents will be to identify what works and what does not work in the battle against terrorism. The terrorist threat will need to be addressed in all its elements, including the importance of providing adequate physical and personal security, enhancing intelligence gathering and analysis, and using diplomatic, economic, legal, and military countermeasures against terrorists and their state-sponsors when appropriate. But there will also be a need to move away from the useless rhetoric of defeating terrorism, and instead focus on achievable goals in combating this global problem.

America's experience with terrorism is a continual saga of events that can lead to unforeseen problems for governments, unbearable suffering for victims, and widespread fears for the general public. At the dawn of the twenty-first century, it is important to step back and look at the evolution of a phenomenon that will still be with future generations. It is the aim of this book to help unravel some of the mysteries and complexities of international terrorism, and in so doing make our response options clearer and in our best interests.

1

Welcome to Reality

Siddig Ibrahim Siddig Ali, a Sudanese Muslim living in the New York area, did not know that the man he was talking to was an FBI informant. "The operation is to make them lose millions and that is what happened," Siddig Ali said. "This is a message. We want to tell them that you are not far from us, we can get you anytime."[1] He was explaining the reason for the bombing of the World Trade Center; he would later be arrested in connection with a separate plot to blow up several other targets in New York City, including the United Nations headquarters. For Siddig Ali, terrorism was a useful tool for causing disruption and spreading fear. For most Americans, terrorism seemed to be a problem that occurred elsewhere around the globe. It took the World Trade Center bombing to shatter that illusion and bring America back to reality.

It was not as though the United States had never experienced terrorism before a small band of religious extremists exploded a bomb at the World Trade Center on February 26, 1993. As we will see later in this book, Americans have been a favorite target of terrorists abroad, and there have been numerous bombings and hijackings committed within the United States. But the continual wave of spectacular terrorist attacks that plagued the people of London, Paris, Rome, and countless other cities around the world was absent from the United States.

A myth of invulnerability thus grew in America as each year passed without a series of major terrorist incidents. Since international terrorists could find an abundance of U.S. targets overseas to strike with relative ease and avoid capture, it appeared as though they would be unwilling to risk traveling to the United States to carry out their violence. And those groups and individuals already in the country who might be inclined to terrorist violence would hopefully be deterred by the good record of U.S. law enforcement in capturing those responsible for domestic terrorism.

Yet it was only a matter of time before America joined the rest of the world in encountering terrorist assaults on its soil. The end of the Cold War increased such prospects, since there were now ethnic-religious conflicts sprouting up all over the globe, and America, the lone superpower, became a tempting target for extremists not happy with U.S. policy concerning their plight. The need to bring attention to their cause with a dramatic, unprecedented act of terrorism within the United States might be a risk they deemed worth taking. This could emanate from terrorists who managed to slip past U.S. immigration officials, or from those foreign nationals already in the United States, or even from American citizens who identify with a particular foreign grievance.

So it should not have been a surprise when a truck bomb exploded in the underground parking garage of the north tower of the World Trade Center. But the fact that it was a surprise underscores the state of denial in America concerning the threat of terrorism.

The bombing was the largest one ever to take place within the United States: 1,200 pounds of nitrate explosives hidden in a rental van. It caused hundreds of millions of dollars in damage, as Siddig Ali had noted, although much of these losses to the New York economy were offset by insurance reimbursements, federal emergency assistance, and a surge of reconstruction work for local contractors. The real significance of the event, however, lay in the symbolism of the target. The terrorist message was clear: If they could launch a successful attack in one of America's most populated cities and against one of the world's most famous business and financial structures, then no city, building, or person in America could be considered safe from terrorists.

Adding to the drama were television pictures of frantic office workers trapped in the skyscraper as smoke rushed upward through the elevator shafts. More than fifty thousand people were believed to be in the 110-story, twin tower World Trade Center at the time of the explosion, and many of them had to walk down scores of flights of stairs in darkness, as the blast blew out power for the elevators and for some of the lights. The continual flow of people being led to waiting ambulances—six people were killed and more than one thousand injured, most of them by smoke inhalation—made this terrorist incident a truly unforgettable one for the country.

It was also an unforgettable experience for Ptor Gjestland, a twenty-six-year-old trader with Sumitomo Bank in New York. Gjestland was at his desk on the ninety-sixth floor of the north tower, or tower one, when the bomb exploded. The lights flickered off for a second. "We were all just kind of looking around at each other and we all came to the same conclusion: lightning hit the building," said Gjestland. "There were no alarms. We figured if there was a fire and explosion there should be alarms going off."[2]

The first inclination Gjestland had that something was wrong was when a business associate who worked in tower two of the trade center made a frantic telephone call to him. "He came screaming over my line, 'Pete, there's smoke coming out of your building,' " Gjestland said. He then ran over to the window and could see smoke pouring out from the lower floors. There were also fire trucks in the street. While some of his colleagues immediately left, Gjestland remained at his desk, thinking the situation was under control since no alarms were sounded. But when he began to smell smoke, he knew it was time to go.

By the time Gjestland left his office, smoke was already flowing from the elevators. The stairwell was packed with other workers. "People were just walking down, no one was really worried yet," said Gjestland. "But then it became a point where you weren't really moving. There were so many people trying to get in all at once. Everybody is running out [of their offices] at that point. You have a couple of people [who] start whimpering, and other people getting worried about it, and other people are [saying], 'We're never going to get out of here.' And then the hysteria just kind of builds."

Gjestland and his small group of fellow traders thought they would only have to walk down to the seventy-eighth floor, where they could then take another set of elevators that operate from the first floor to the seventy-eighth. But when they got there they found smoke once again pouring from the elevators. They now realized that they had no choice but to continue the trek by foot. Confusion and concern were growing by the minute. "You just kind of follow people down. And this is when people start getting worried because the smoke is really bad. Everyone is starting to cough. The people who are really heavy are having problems. They're having problems breathing. People start crying, and we're still in the seventies [floors]," said Gjestland.

As he continued his descent, he passed by more people who had given up hope. "People [were] sitting down [saying], 'What do we do? We're not going to get out of this,' " Gjestland said. With his eyes burning and vision impaired from the smoke, Gjestland continued the journey. At around the fiftieth floor, those who were trying to direct the evacuation told people to rest and get some fresh air through broken windows. Gjestland and his group would have no part of that. "We just said, 'Forget it, we're not waiting around.' " They took off and continued down the stairs. "We knew it was getting really weird because there was actually a mink coat lying in the stairwell," Gjestland said.

People had discarded their briefcases and heavy coats as the ordeal of the flight down the stairs took its toll. At around the fortieth floor there was complete darkness. "So all we did is we put our hands on each other's shoulders in front of you," said Gjestland. "And we just walked down, we just counted the steps. And we just kind of did like [a] double-, triple-time kind of deal. And then when we got down on the eighteenth floor we finally saw a fireman coming up. And we said, 'Is there any fire?' And [he] said, 'No,' and we knew [then] we were going to get out."

The climb down the ninety-six floors took Gjestland approximately two-and-a-half hours. Those who rested and who moved slower did not get out of the building for about four or five hours. By the time Gjestland reached the first floor, he was dead tired. He had soot all over him; his white shirt was now black. But despite the trauma of the long descent, he was not prepared for the sight that awaited him when he opened the door at the last stairwell and entered the lobby of the trade center. "When we got out [at] the first floor, it looked like a war zone," said Gjestland. "I had never seen anything like it, the haze of the smoke, the broken glass, everywhere. It was like a movie set. It was just surreal."

The magnitude of the situation now hit him. "This was the first time we realized what had happened," said Gjestland. "The fireman [had] told us there had been an explosion and now we could see where it was. We were [saying], 'Oh, my God. What could have really happened to us!' Because we didn't really know [previously] what had really happened. And then you see what the devastation was. And you're [saying], 'Oh, my God, the building could have fallen over, who knows.' "

After realizing a bomb caused the explosion, his thoughts turned to terrorism. "You always thought, well, America, no one touches us," said Gjestland. He could not understand why the terrorists would want to inflict so much death and destruction. "Why do they want to blow us up?" Gjestland asked himself. And he reflected the sentiment of the nation when he noted, "Basically, you're upset. You know, like this stuff shouldn't happen in America. It never does. What's going on?"

Terrorists had struck America, and the public was understandably anxious. But whereas most people throughout the world had long ago learned that terrorism was an unfortunate yet inevitable part of life, a threat that needed to be combated but one that they knew could never be completely defeated, Americans somehow could not accept this reality. The postmortem on the World Trade Center bombing thus became a national search for blame. *Something* had to have gone wrong for this event to have taken place. Perhaps it was lax security at major office buildings, some critics argued. Others put the blame on police and law enforcement officials for failing to prevent the attack. Still others pointed to U.S. immigration laws, since several of those arrested in connection with the bombing were Islamic extremists who had emigrated to the United States.

The level of alarm over the bombing was fueled by an endless stream of pundits who appeared on television talk shows or wrote Op-Ed articles in newspapers. The title of one of these articles best captured the growing anxiety in the country: The piece was bluntly headlined "The Terrorists among Us."[3]

Then, while the investigation into the World Trade Center bombing was continuing, the other shoe dropped. The FBI announced the arrest in June 1993 of eight more Islamic extremists for plotting to blow up four targets in New York on or near Independence Day. "The subjects were actually mixing the witches' brew," James Fox, the head of the FBI's New York office, told reporters, describing the scene as agents raided the terrorists' hide-out in Queens, New York, as they were making their bombs.[4] Their plan was to set off car bombs at the United Nations headquarters, the Lincoln and Holland tunnels that carried thousands of motorists, and the Federal building in Manhattan that houses the FBI and other government agencies.

It was a classic terrorist strategy. Follow up one attack with an even more spectacular one to ensure public and government attention and reaction. America now had *two* major terrorist episodes to worry about, with the prospect of more attacks looming. Who, then, were these "terrorists among us," and what did they really want?

The Old Man from Jersey City

Sheik Omar Abdel Rahman cut an unlikely figure for a terrorist guru. In fact, most Americans probably would have helped the Muslim cleric to cross a street had they run into him in any city in the country. Rahman was blind and diabetic, and with a gray beard and slow gait, appeared much older than his fifty-five years. Yet he had a loyal following that consisted of militant and alienated youths from the Middle East who were living in the New York area and a much larger group in Egypt.

The faithful flocked to his sermons in a mosque in Jersey City, just across the Hudson River from New York, and also to one in Brooklyn where he occasionally preached. His stature was such that Siddig Ali, the Sudanese Muslim arrested on terrorism charges, told the FBI informant, "I don't make a step unless I check with the law of our religion from Sheik Omar."[5]

How the Sheik wound up in the United States in the first place was a source of embarrassment for the U.S. government. Rahman was tried, but acquitted, in Egypt for involvement in the 1981 assassination of President Anwar Sadat. One of the people executed for the murder testified that Rahman issued a *fatwa*, or religious blessing, for the assassination, but the Egyptian government could not prove the charges. Rahman was tried in 1989 for instigating a riot that left hundreds of people dead, but he was once again acquitted.

Rahman, who remained the spiritual leader of the extremist al-Gama'a al-Islamiyya (the Islamic Group) in Egypt, was deported to Sudan in 1990. He was given a visa at the American embassy in Khartoum to enter the United States despite being on a State Department list of suspected terrorists. He was then issued a green card to remain in the United States as a religious worker. U.S. government officials claimed that the visa and green card were issued in error.

Once in the United States, Rahman lost no time in preaching against the evils of Western life. He called for a *jihad*, or holy war, and for the overthrow of the secular Egyptian government. One of his followers was El-Sayyid Nosair, who, like Rahman, worked on behalf of the Afghan rebels in their war with Soviet forces in Afghanistan in the 1980s. He was arrested in 1990 for the assassination of Rabbi Meir Kahane, an ultranationalist in Israeli politics. Although Nosair was acquitted of the murder, he was convicted on related charges. Siddig Ali visited him in prison, as did another Rahman follower, Mohammed Salameh.

The twenty-five-year-old Salameh came to the United States from Jordan in 1987 in the hopes of building a better life for himself. Instead, he gained the distinction of being the first person arrested for the World Trade Center bombing. It was Salameh who rented the yellow van that carried the explosives into the parking garage. After investigators retrieved the vehicle identification number from the wreckage, they traced the van to a New Jersey rental office of the Ryder Corporation. There, they discovered Salameh's name on the rental papers. Using his own name to rent the vehicle was not a very smart move by the young man. He then compounded his error by reporting the vehicle stolen after the bombing in an effort to get back his $400 deposit. Salameh was taken into custody when he appeared at the rental office, and the roundup of Rahman's followers soon began.

Several people arrested for the World Trade Center bombing had worshiped at Rahman's Jersey City mosque. The same was true for those apprehended for plotting to blow up the four targets in New York. But Sheik Rahman was not initially arrested for any terrorist-related activity. Instead, he was detained in July 1993 for falsifying his visa application—he lied about a prior arrest in Egypt for check forgery—and for being a polygamist, both grounds for deportation. A federal judge in August 1993 upheld the deportation order and also denied the sheik's request for political asylum, calling Rahman "a danger to the security of the United States." Then, as the legal fate of the sheik was being determined—Egypt had earlier requested his extradition while Rahman was reportedly requesting Afghanistan as his final destination—a federal grand jury indicted Rahman for being the leader of a group that conspired to engage in terrorism.

Sheik Rahman was only the latest in a long list of adversaries that has marked America's experience with terrorism. We will see in the following pages how the Khomeinis and Qaddafis of the world have continually frustrated America in its battles against terrorism. While Rahman did not have the full powers and resources of a government to call upon, he did have a fervent following that felt morally justified in its actions. Rahman and his supporters caused a great deal of havoc in the United States—although labeling him a threat to U.S. national security greatly exaggerated his capabilities. America was not going to fall from the actions of any group of terrorists. But what the World Trade Center bombing and the additional terrorist plot clearly demonstrated was that America was going to be caught up in the cycle of violence and revenge that marks current ethnic and religious conflicts throughout the world.

Four days after the World Trade Center bombing, the *New York Times* received a letter from an unknown group, the Liberation Army Fifth Battalion, claiming responsibility for the attack. Police subsequently determined that the letter was authentic, tracing it to the personal computer of Nidal Ayyad, who was among the first group of people arrested for the bombing. Ayyad was believed to have accompanied Mohammed Salameh in renting the van that carried the explosives into the garage of the World Trade Center. In the letter, the group claimed that the bombing was to protest "the American political, economical and military support to Israel, the state of terrorism, and to the rest of the dictator countries in the region." The letter also stated, "The American people are responsible for the actions of their government and they must question all of the crimes that their government is committing against other people. Or they—Americans—will be the targets of our operations that could diminish them."[6]

But Sheik Rahman's wrath was directed mainly at Egypt. In an interview published in the *Wall Street Journal* prior to the World Trade Center bombing, Rahman said that "it is the duty of all good Muslims to rebel against tyrants. The Egyptian people will not accept being whipped and raped and robbed by the corrupt [President Hosni] Mubarak regime."[7] And Siddig Ali, in an interview published in the *New York Times* after his arrest, vented his anger at secular Arab states. "Islam condemns aggression and violence," Siddig Ali said. "[But] the presidents of Egypt, Algeria, Tunisia, [and] many [other] countries are terrorists. They're killing our people. They're torturing them. They are arresting them."[8]

The United States was viewed as an appropriate target for the Islamic militants due to its support for their "enemies." If the targets they could strike in America had global significance, then all the better as far as they were concerned. The World Trade Center represented the world's financial and economic activity, while the United Nations headquarters represented the world's political body. When the FBI informant asked Siddig Ali why he and his confederates were planning to attack the United Nations—"Are you out for a particular person or do you want to demolish the whole building?"—Siddig Ali replied, "This is the world's government. Who governs the world today?"[9] Terrorism thus provided the Islamic extremists with the means for attacking several symbolic targets at once: America, Israel, Egypt, the global economy, and the world political establishment.

In March 1994, Mohammed Salameh, Nidal Ayyad, and two other men were convicted in a Federal Court in New York for the Trade Center attack; they were subsequently sentenced to 240 years each. If most Americans were unfamiliar with Islamic extremism before the World Trade Center bombing, they certainly were not afterward. There was intense focus by the media and government on the threat posed by Islamic militants in the United States. But had the bombing been the work of a different group, it would then have been those extremists and their cause that America would have been preoccupied with in 1993 and 1994. Among the many telephone calls made to the police emergency number by groups claiming responsibility for the attack was one by the Serbian Liberation Front, an unknown group. Speculation that Serbian extremists may have committed the bombing was fueled by the fact that the United States had been threatening to initiate air strikes in Bosnia against Serbian targets in order to end the fighting in the former Yugoslav republic.

The World Trade Center bombing raised fundamental questions about dealing with terrorism in an open, democratic society. The calls for new immigration controls were an overreaction to the incident: it would only punish the vast majority of law-abiding future immigrants due to the actions of a few violent ones. Since there are plenty of people born in America who can easily commit terrorist acts—and have done so in the past—changing immigration laws will not prevent terrorism from occurring in the United States.

The calls for better physical security at large office buildings and tourist facilities were more understandable. But as Stanley Brezenoff, the executive director of the Port Authority of New York and New Jersey, which operates the World Trade Center, pointed out in testimony before a congressional committee, "the World Trade Center was designed to be a crossroads, not a fortress. We, along with operators of major business and tourist complexes[,] must maintain free and open access to the facilities while providing adequate security to our tenants and patrons."[10]

His remarks touched on the dilemma that those responsible for dealing with the aftermath of a terrorist incident must face. Whether it be enhancing physical security or introducing new laws aimed at curbing terrorism, care must be taken that the response is an appropriate one. Once terrorists are allowed to change the way people live or negatively affect a country's national or international interests, they will indeed have achieved an important victory.

No matter what happens in America's future experience with terrorism, the World Trade Center bombing will have a permanent place in this country's history. One bomb transformed the nation from thinking of terrorism as a distant phenomenon to one that could strike right at home. "The world changed on February 26th," said Allen Morrison, a spokesperson for the Port Authority. "It will never be the same for us."[11] For John Yao, a Port Authority engineer who was trapped in the building, the bombing taught him a valuable lesson about terrorism. "It hits home," he said. "It could happen to anybody, anyplace."[12] And for Ptor Gjestland, the bombing was seen in a different light six months later. Gone was the shock of the ordeal on that wintry day, replaced with a more philosophical view of the whole experience. "It's [now] kind of like something to tell your kids," he said in the summer of 1993.[13] *His* story would be that of the trade center bombing. But other Americans would have different stories to tell of their own and of their ancestors' encounters with terrorism. They are stories that go back to the founding days of the republic.

2

The Endless Nature of Terrorism

A parable about two Druze in Lebanon best captures the endless nature of terrorism. One Druze is walking down the road with grenades, machine guns, and daggers weighing him down from head to foot. He passes by a fellow Druze who inquires why his friend is carrying so many weapons. The first Druze replies that he is going to the Abdullah house to kill all the people there because they killed his ancestors one hundred years ago. The second Druze looks at his friend in amazement and exclaims, "One hundred years ago?!! What's the rush?"

Time is indeed on the side of those who seek revenge. Some of today's conflicts have their roots in ancient times. The ethnic violence between Armenians and Azerbaijanis over the disputed territory of Nagorno-Karabakh dates back many centuries. Islamic fundamentalism, which has led to terrorist episodes in the Middle East, Europe, Asia, and the United States, has its origins in the split between the Shiite and Sunni sects in the seventh century. Ethnic tension between Croats and Serbs, which exploded into civil war in Yugoslavia in 1991, dates back to the fourteenth century.

Long-simmering anger and revenge characterizes several other contemporary conflicts. Many Armenians today seek revenge for the killings of more than one million of their ancestors by Turks in 1915. In Northern Ireland, "some Irishmen still bitterly dispute the future of their country in terms of the religious wars of the seventeenth century."[1] The Arab-Israeli and Indian-Pakistani conflicts go back many years. And there are those disputes yet to be born from the "new world order" that George Bush proclaimed in the fall of 1990. The proliferation of independent states and the desire of ethnic and religious groups to settle old scores and attain new power ensure that the new world order will have its share of old-world types of conflicts.

Terrorism has long been and will continue to be a part of many of these grievances. "If a single common emotion drives the individual or group to terrorism, it is vengeance," observes terrorist scholar Martha Crenshaw.[2] Terrorism's link to the endless conflicts of history ensures that it will continue unabated in the future. Recourse to violence—and to terrorism—has always been seen as legitimate by revolutionary groups worldwide. The distinction between guerrilla warfare and terrorism was never a clear one. Many guerrilla wars had aspects of terrorism perpetrated both by the guerrillas and the counterinsurgency forces. Guerrilla units sometimes use assassinations to show the ineffectiveness of the government to protect its citizens. Government troops sometimes inflict terror and violence upon villagers suspected of supporting the guerrillas. Guerrilla armies also kidnap businessmen for ransom or perpetrate a variety of other acts that could be considered outside the boundaries of accepted forms of warfare.

Terrorism is a tool that can be used in different ways under varied conditions, and it usually does not take a great effort to activate. A state-sponsor can easily recruit individuals to carry out its violence, while independent terrorist cells are formed from just a few individuals. When groups are "defeated"—in the sense that leaders are arrested or killed in counterterrorist operations, or members are co-opted into the political system—new factions often arise to continue the violent struggle. As long as there is one person left with access to some type of weapon and any type of grievance, there will always be terrorism.

Since it takes just *one* well-timed and publicized incident to put terrorism back before the public eye, terrorists can reverse all perceptions of counterterrorist progress with a single attack. No other conflict or phenomenon quite has this characteristic. For example, the 1986 U.S. raid on Libya, a state-sponsor of terrorism, quieted Muammar Qaddafi for a while, leaving the impression that terrorists had been defeated. That illusion was shattered on the night of December 21, 1988, when Pan Am 103 was blown up over Lockerbie. After that incident faded from the public agenda, the belief once again surfaced that terrorism might be on the decline. This too was shattered in the summer of 1989 when pro-Iranian Hizballah terrorists threatened to kill American hostages in Lebanon.

When that crisis subsided, it once again appeared that terrorism might be on the wane. But one year later, Saddam Hussein took thousands of foreigners hostage and threatened to unleash weapons of mass destruction during the Gulf War. Another lull in terrorism followed the end of the Gulf War, until the World Trade Center bombing in 1993 put terrorism front and center for the American people.

The lulls in terrorism are a significant part of the terrorist trap. It leads publics, governments, and the media to believe the worst is over, thereby making the next major incident that much more dramatic and difficult to accept. That is why statistics on terrorism are extremely misleading. The U.S. State Department and several research organizations produce annual reports on international terrorism that, among other things, compare the number of incidents over time, depict the geographical distribution of terrorist episodes, identify the targets of terrorists, and so forth. Some of these findings can sound an optimistic note, such as the one noted in the first paragraph of the 1990 State Department annual report: "The continuing decline in the number of international terrorist incidents during 1990 is encouraging. From a peak of 856 in 1988, the number of incidents decreased to 455 in 1990."[3]

But while statistical reports might be beneficial for business forecasts, health trends, traffic safety, and other subjects, they have less relevance for understanding terrorism. Statistics tend to mask the endless nature of terrorism by presenting it in a way that leaves the impression that terrorism is either on the rise or in decline, when in fact the *volume* of terrorist activity has little bearing upon its present and future course or its impact upon governments and societies. For example, of the 856 incidents that occurred in 1988, the one that mattered most to the American public and government was the bombing of Pan Am 103. Similarly, of the 455 incidents for 1990, the most significant one as far as the U.S. and most Western nations were concerned was Saddam Hussein's taking of thousands of hostages after his invasion of Kuwait. In 1985, it was the combination of just a few major events, including the hijacking of TWA 847, the seizure of the *Achille Lauro* cruise ship, and massacres at Rome and Vienna airports that intensified the worldwide concern about terrorism, and not the fact that there were almost 800 incidents recorded that year.

The frustration in dealing with terrorism was best expressed by one journalist following the 1972 massacre of Israeli athletes at the Munich Olympics. "Can anything be done to curb international terrorism, or must we accept that it will simply continue to grow—and if so, where can we expect it to end?" asked Colin Legum.[4] The answer is that it will not end, for terrorism has proven to be an enduring phenomenon for America and the world from its earliest days.

The Early Years

The origins of terrorism can actually be traced back to biblical times. The Jewish Zealots and Sicariis viewed assassinations and other forms of violence as a means for provoking a revolutionary uprising against Roman rule in Palestine during the first century. They committed their murders with short swords that they hid in their coats. "Consecutive atrocities kept narrowing the room for a political or mutually agreeable solution," observed terrorist scholar David Rapoport, "and this served to destroy the credibility of moderates on both sides while expanding the conflict by steadily enlisting more and more participants."[5] The revolt ended when more than nine hundred Zealots took their own lives rather than surrender to Roman forces who were about to enter their fortress at Masada in the year 73 A.D.

Between the eleventh and thirteenth centuries another terrorist group emerged that was appropriately named the Assassins. They were drawn from the ranks of the Ismailis, a revolutionary Shi'a Islamic sect. Through the use of selective murders, almost always by dagger, the fanatically loyal and secretive Assassins spread fear and terror throughout the Middle East. The Assassins were willing to die for their cause, and usually made no attempt to escape after thrusting daggers into their victims. They committed the killings in front of many witnesses, ensuring their capture and execution.

The Assassins viewed their killings as a holy mission, much like contemporary Islamic fundamentalist terrorist groups. They were convinced they would be rewarded in the afterlife, thanks to the indoctrination provided by their leader, Hassan Sabbah. The "Old Man of the Mountain," as Hassan was known, was born in the holy city of Qom, about a hundred miles south of Tehran, in the mid-eleventh century. He grew up as a Shiite in Sunni-dominated Persia, which at that time was ruled by the Turkish Seljuk Dynasty. He persuaded his loyal followers that their killings would result in entry into "paradise," and most of his troops willingly went to their deaths.[6] The legend of the Assassins spread to Europe where they caught the interest of poets who became fascinated by their devotion to their leader. "Just as the Assassins serve their master unfailingly, so I have served Love with unswerving loyalty," a Provençal troubadour tells his lover. Another says, "You have me more fully in your power [than] the Old Man has his Assassins, who go to kill his mortal enemies. . . . "[7]

But it was their terrorism that alarmed most people at that time. One rumor arose that Hassan would drug his followers while they were asleep and transport them to a beautiful pleasure garden. When they awoke, he would tell them they were in paradise. Hassan would then drug them again and transport them back to their ordinary quarters while they were asleep. When they awoke the second time, Hassan would then tell them he would return them to paradise after they completed their killings for him. However, there was no evidence to support this myth. Rather than being irrational murderers, the Assassins' strategy was clear and calculated. Their terrorism in Persia and Syria was "designed to frighten, to weaken, and ultimately to overthrow" the Sunni establishment. Although they failed in their revolutionary objective— they were eventually suppressed by the Mongols in the thirteenth century, who spread their own terror by leaving pyramids of skulls in villages to serve as a warning to would-be resisters—they nevertheless demonstrated a basic principle of contemporary terrorism: the ability of small groups to wage effective campaigns of terror against much stronger opponents.[8]

Terrorism continued after the demise of the Assassins, with the most notable group being the Thugs, who were active in India from around the eleventh century up until the nineteenth century, when they were finally destroyed by the British. Their terrorist tactic was to strangle and rob their victims, who were usually highway travelers. The Thugs claimed allegiance to the goddess Kali, and according to legend killed in order to supply her with blood for nourishment.[9]

The next significant period in the evolution of terrorism occurred in the aftermath of the French Revolution. Just as the medieval Ismailis extremists gave birth to the term "assassin," and the worshippers of the goddess Kali to the term "thug," so too did Maximilien Robespierre give birth in the eighteenth century to the very term "terror." The Committee on Public Safety that ruled France during the turbulent years following the French Revolution was the first case of state-terror imposed upon a people. It was the forerunner of twentieth-century terror governments such as Stalin's Russia, Hitler's Germany, and Pol Pot's Cambodia. Robespierre unleashed his "Reign of Terror" between 1793 and 1794 upon all strata of French society. For Robespierre, terror was viewed as the only way to save the revolution from anarchy at home and the threat of invasion from abroad by European monarchs. Even when these threats appeared to subside, he continued to use terrorism to stay in power and mold the people into a single will.[10]

More than seventeen thousand people—peasants, workers, aristocrats, moderate revolutionaries, and others—met their deaths by the guillotine. This became one of the first technological innovations in terrorist weaponry. It was designed by Dr. Joseph Guillotin, who actually viewed the sharp blade as a "humane" device that made the deaths of the victims quicker and less painful than traditional methods of decapitation. "The mechanism falls like lightning; the head flies off; the blood spurts; the man no longer exists," Dr. Guillotin told the National Assembly in 1789 when he first proposed his invention. "Gentlemen, with my machine, I'll take your head in a flash, and you won't even feel the slightest pain."[11] The guillotine, though, only served to facilitate Robespierre's efforts to eliminate all opponents to his rule. And it was not the only method used to kill people during the Reign of Terror. More than twenty-five thousand others were shot or killed by different methods throughout the country.[12]

Terrorism, though, cannot be measured only by the number of casualties. Robespierre's rule created "nervousness, apprehension, fear of secret denunciation [that] haunted thousands whom the guillotine did not touch." More than one hundred thousand political prisoners were taken and several hundred thousand others were declared suspects. As with the Assassins, Robespierre did not view terrorism as an evil or immoral act, but instead thought of it as a virtuous deed. Virtue and terror were inseparable in Robespierre's thinking. "If the basis of popular government in time of peace is virtue," Robespierre argued, "the basis of popular government in time of revolution is both virtue and terror: virtue without which terror is murderous, terror without which virtue is powerless."[13]

The terror included hauling victims onto old ships and sinking them in the Loire, sometimes killing the children of guillotined parents, and allowing thousands of prisoners to die of disease and famine. People lived in fear of the long reach of Robespierre since any seemingly innocent act could be viewed as treason. In one case, a man was sent to the guillotine for violating the Committee's laws on economic austerity since he was found with several small loaves of bread that had actually been baked for him on a doctor's orders. In another case, the teenaged daughter of a painter was executed for having in her possession thousands of candles. Sometimes the grandparents and great-grandparents of prisoners would also be thrown in jail. People accused of being against the revolution or violating various laws and principles did not always receive a trial. "No court sentence is needed," one general told the National Convention. "My saber and my pistols do their job."[14]

The French people even had to fear the way they looked in public, lest they arouse the suspicions of Robespierre's spies. The government's agents "would join the conversation of men and women in public places like street corners or cafés and attempt, in this way, to net a potential victim for the Tribunal. A facial expression could be enough to arouse suspicion. A depressed or unhappy look would attract attention and often prompt an inquiry into the identity and circumstances of anyone who had such a dissatisfied air."[15]

Robespierre himself fell victim to the guillotine in July 1794 as internal divisions within the government turned the terror machinery against the dictator and his supporters. In his last speech to the National Convention, two days before he was to be executed, Robespierre attempted to justify his actions as the will of the people:

> They call me a tyrant. . . . One arrives at a tyrant's throne by the help of scoundrels. . . . What faction do I belong to? You yourselves. What is that faction which, since the Revolution began, has crushed the factions and swept away hireling traitors? It is you, it is the people, it is the principles of the Revolution. . . . [16]

Robespierre, like the Assassins before, used highly publicized murders to spread fear to countless others whom he was trying to control. At about the same time that the French people were experiencing terrorism carried out by their own government, the United States was forced to deal with another form of terrorism that originated from abroad: hostage taking. The founding fathers were thus faced with a problem that would become all too familiar to U.S. leaders more than two centuries later.

The image many people have of pirates is a mysterious band of adventurers stalking the high seas, boarding ships, taking gold and other valuables, then vanishing into the night. And that has been a major aspect of piracy throughout the centuries. But the Barbary Coast states—Morocco, Algiers, Tunis, and Tripoli—perfected the art of piracy into a profitable and integral part of their foreign policy. They became the first state-sponsors of terrorism, utilizing pirates to target foreign vessels in the Mediterranean and Atlantic and taking hostages as a way of obtaining large sums of ransom payments from the victims' governments. Payments to the various rulers of the Barbary states, who were known as deys (Algiers), beys (Tunis), bashaws (Tripoli), and emperors (Morocco), were also made on a regular basis to prevent ships from being seized. But these extortion payments, which many governments felt were cheaper than the risk of losing their ships, still did not ensure that their ships would not be seized.

When the United States won its independence from Britain, it had to fend for itself against the activities of the Barbary states. Thomas Jefferson, sent to Paris in 1785 to negotiate treaties for the United States, became increasingly frustrated with the ability of the Barbary states to attack U.S. vessels and take American citizens as hostages. For Jefferson, the sight of a weak America being plagued by piracy was difficult to accept. In a correspondence to Nathanael Greene, Jefferson wrote of being torn between "indignation and impotence." Although he realized that continual ransom payments would only encourage further acts of terrorism and that a military response would be preferable, Jefferson had very few options. The United States was a weak military power in the late eighteenth century; not even a navy was available to respond to the Barbary attacks. The frustration of not being able to retaliate against the Barbary states, themselves not major powers, convinced Jefferson of the need to build a strong navy. Even before such a force could be built, Jefferson still hoped for a military response. He was convinced that John Paul Jones "with half a dozen frigates would totally destroy their commerce . . . by constant cruising and cutting them to pieces piecemeal."[17]

In this first U.S. debate over how to respond to terrorism, Jefferson did not have much support for his advocacy of a strong American response. John Adams argued that the United States should continue paying tribute since he believed that was a wiser economic policy than spending the much larger sums of money needed to build a navy. He also argued that the U.S. would not be able to significantly harm the Barbary states since they had no commerce upon which retaliatory strikes could be directed. The U.S. Congress was also initially against the idea of building a navy in the 1780s, and instead instructed Jefferson to continue to make payments to the Barbary states. In fact, an amount of money—not to exceed $80,000—was set aside for this very purpose. Yet over a ten-year period, the United States ended up paying more than $2 million as ships continued to be seized and American hostages taken. Between 1776 and 1816, several hundred Americans were taken captive by the terrorist states. Their treatment was usually harsh; after being captured, they were placed in chains and put into prisons infested with disease. Most of the hostages were also forced to perform hard labor.[18]

Much like the hostages in Lebanon in the 1980s, the Barbary hostages appealed to the American public and government to come to their aid. "Remember us, your unfortunate brethren, late members of the family of freedom, now doomed to perpetual confinement," wrote one hostage to U.S. ministers in 1792. "Pray, earnestly pray, that our grievous calamities may have a gracious end. . . . We ask you in the name of your Father in heaven, to have compassion on our miseries. . . . Lift up your voices like a trumpet; cry aloud in the cause of humanity. . . . "[19]

The plight of the hostages was not forgotten by the American people. The "incarceration of over four hundred and fifty citizens drawn from all parts of the Atlantic seaboard could not, and did not, fail to excite commiseration throughout the land."[20] Even when the number of hostages was only eleven, their fate was still a major concern of the government. President Washington presented a report on the hostages to Congress on December 30, 1790, and Congress referred the matter to a committee, which eventually recommended that a naval force be built as soon as public finances would permit. Congress, though, did not act immediately on this recommendation.

Jefferson was particularly affected by the sufferings of the hostages and tried all that he could to win their release. Ironically, one strategy he pursued resulted in the hostages actually accusing him of not caring about their fate. In 1787, he became convinced that the more attention the U.S. gave to the Barbary states, the more likely it would be that additional hostages would be taken and that those already in captivity would not be released. He decided that ignoring the issue might reduce the price that Algiers was demanding for the hostages' freedom. He left the false impression with the dey that the United States no longer intended to pay ransom and was not preoccupied with the hostage issue. This only resulted in the hostages blaming him for their prolonged captivity.[21]

The Barbary states were experts at playing the hostage game. They continued to up the ante for the release of American hostages, even setting prices for different types of hostages. A master required $6,000, a mate $4,000, and a sailor $1,500. Passengers on ships had a $4,000 price tag. These figures constantly changed as the Barbary leaders reneged on promises and kept the U.S. and other countries continually guessing what their next demands would be. Negotiations would be held with the different Barbary states, hopes would be raised that the hostages would be freed, only to have complications arise. The U.S. even tried using the services of a religious sect, the Mathurins, whose mission was to aid countries in negotiations with the Barbary states. The Mathurins, who were officially known as the Order of the Holy Trinity and Redemption of Captives, was founded in 1199 in Paris by the Church of St. Mathurin. For centuries its members devoted their lives to helping the victims of the Barbary pirates by raising ransom for their release and setting up missions and hospitals in the Barbary states.

Jefferson met with the general of the religious order in 1787, hoping he could resolve America's hostage crisis. Although he was eager to help, nothing came of these efforts as delays and complications, including the continual raising of ransom demands by the dey, arose before anything could be accomplished. The Mathurins were ultimately dissolved along with other religious orders during the French Revolution.[22]

The United States was also frustrated in its efforts to gain international cooperation in neutralizing the Barbary threat. Since the pirate states were themselves weak military powers, they would have been no match for any concerted effort by more powerful European nations, who also were victimized by the pirates. Yet this period in world history was characterized by escalating economic warfare among nations and "the very advantages gained by one country from the depredations on the commerce of another would have made co-operation . . . difficult." Or as a popular phrase of the time illustrated, "if there were no Algiers, it would be worth England's while to build one."[23]

The desire to resolve the Barbary problem led to the first arms-for-hostages deal in U.S. history. In 1795, the U.S. secured a peace treaty with the dey of Algiers that included a cash payment, annual tributes, and naval arms and frigates that eventually totaled almost $1 million. While this led to the release of a hundred hostages, it encouraged the other Barbary states to increase their demands upon the United States. It also did not prevent Algiers from taking more hostages in later years. The U.S. agent in Algiers, Joel Barlow, described one of the deys in terms that could easily apply to some contemporary state-sponsors of terrorism. According to Barlow, Hasan Pasha, who ruled from 1791 to 1798, was "a man of a most ungovernable temper, passionate, changeable, and unjust to such a degree that there is no calculating his policy from one moment to the next."[24]

The United States was finally able by 1816 to significantly reduce the Barbary threat through a combination of factors. These included the emergence of a U.S. Navy that was used in wars with Tripoli and Algiers, Barbary wars with other European countries, and internal problems within the Barbary states themselves. Ironically, the first U.S. military operation against a state-sponsor of terrorism took place against Tripoli—"the least considerable of the Barbary States," according to Jefferson[25]—just as the most decisive U.S. military strike against a state-sponsor in the 1980s would be the bombing of Libya's capital, Tripoli. During this war—which began during Jefferson's first year as president in 1801 when the bashaw, or ruler, cut down the flagstaff of the American consul's residence after the United States refused to pay an increased ransom for hostages—Stephen Decatur and a small raiding party burned the frigate *Philadelphia*. The ship had been seized in 1803 when it ran aground in the harbor of Tripoli and was used by the Tripolitans to increase their demands for ransom. Although the sabotage of the *Philadelphia* in 1804 was a dramatic act that received widespread approval in the United States and made a hero out of Decatur, it was not decisive in the war, which ended when the bashaw of Tripoli faced mounting domestic problems. But in terrorism and counterterrorism, the symbolic act can be as important as actual decisive events. For the United States, the war with Tripoli and the burning of the *Philadelphia* indicated that after years of capitulation to state-sponsors of terrorism, the United States would fight back.

That the terrorist threat did not end due to any specific U.S. response was among the early lessons on terrorism that the Barbary experience held for the United States. Many of the traits about terrorism that would haunt U.S. policymakers in later years were evident during this first U.S. experience with state-sponsored terrorism. These included the continual taking of hostages, the raising of false hopes for their release, the constantly increasing ransom demands, frustration in not being able to completely eliminate the threat, debates over military responses, and difficulty in acquiring international cooperation. The emotional grasp that hostages can have on presidents and the public was also evident during this period, as was the ability of terrorists to play upon human compassion and fears.

It would be another one hundred years before an American president had to face a major hostage crisis overseas. If Jefferson can be said to have faced a formidable threat with respect to the Barbary pirates, then Teddy Roosevelt helped exaggerate one with respect to a Moorish pirate named Raisuli and a hostage named Perdicaris. What became known as the "Perdicaris incident" had all the elements of a soap opera that began in the African highlands, spread to European capitals and the Mediterranean Sea, and culminated at the Republican National Convention in Chicago in 1904.

Ion Perdicaris was a wealthy, elderly man who had been living on the outskirts of Tangier, Morocco, since the 1880s. He was born in the United States, the son of a South Carolina woman with property and a Greek man who had become a naturalized American. He was well known and liked in Tangier, having contributed money and support to the Moors, a Muslim people in northwestern Africa, and having helped to build a modern sanitation system for Tangier. But on the evening of May 18, 1904, Perdicaris was abducted from his villa—a magnificent compound named the "Palace of Nightingales"—along with his stepson, who was a British citizen. The kidnappers were Raisuli and 150 of his armed men, who took their hostages on a twenty-four-hour journey into the mountain area that they controlled, thereby eliminating the possibility for a successful rescue. Along the way the two hostages were clubbed with rifles and threatened with daggers.

Raisuli—whose full name was Sherif Mulai Ahmed ibn-Muhammed er Raisuli—had no gripe with Perdicaris; he wasn't even angry with the United States. His conflict was with the bashaw of Tangier, who was his foster brother and most bitter enemy. Raisuli had a significant following among several Moorish tribes and therefore posed a threat to the bashaw. The latter had Raisuli imprisoned for several years, and during that time waged a campaign of harassment against Raisuli's people, including burning his tribes' villages, taxing them, and arresting them. When Raisuli was released from prison, he returned the favor to the bashaw by ambushing his troops and murdering emissaries when they were sent to offer peace talks. In 1903 he kidnapped a news reporter from *The Times of London*, and used that hostage to win the release of several imprisoned fellow tribesmen. More prisoners were subsequently taken by the bashaw, however, and Raisuli's followers continued to be harassed by the local government in Tangier. Raisuli wanted revenge.

The idea of taking American and British hostages seemed to be a brilliant scheme. If all went well, Raisuli could in one quick move force the United States and England to become involved in his personal squabbles. They would have to put pressure on the sultan of Morocco, who appointed the local bashaw, to address his grievances if they wanted their citizens back alive. The French would also have to take an interest in the developments since they had just concluded an agreement with England, whereby France was given free reign in Morocco for England doing as it pleased in Egypt.[26] The prospects of hostage crises and further unrest in Tangier was thus something France did not want. For Raisuli, the more foreign governments involved in this incident the better.

When word of the kidnapping reached Samuel Gummere, the U.S. consul general in Tangier, he sent a telegram to Washington stating, "Situation serious. Request man-of-war to enforce demands."[27] Gummere and the British minister in Tangier, Sir Arthur Nicolson, were convinced that further violence against foreigners in Morocco would ensue unless the hostage crisis was quickly resolved. There was actually very little, however, that a show of U.S. military force could accomplish against Raisuli. The kidnapper and his victims were entrenched in the mountains and any attempt by the U.S. Navy to bombard his position or land Marines—rumors circulated that U.S. Marines would also be landing in Tangier—would likely result in the deaths of the hostages. The request for a naval ship was really to demonstrate to the sultan of Morocco that the United States viewed the situation seriously and wanted his government to negotiate with Raisuli. The State Department instructed Gummere to "demand of the Moorish Government that it take the most sweeping measures to secure the release of Mr. Perdicaris, even, if necessary, to accede to the terms of the brigands."[28]

When President Roosevelt received Gummere's cable, he saw a golden opportunity to expand the role of the U.S. Navy in world affairs, part of the "big stick" policy he envisioned for the United States at the beginning of the twentieth century.[29] He therefore dispatched *four* warships to the region. The drama gripped the nation as the public and media regarded Raisuli as a bandit and eagerly awaited the U.S. confrontation with the terrorist—even though the real strategy was negotiations through the sultan of Morocco. When Raisuli's demands were made, they turned out to be of such magnitude that even today's terrorists would be quite impressed. Raisuli wanted no less than the removal of the bashaw of Tangier from power and the arrest of some government officials who had harmed him in the past; the payment of a $70,000 ransom that must be raised from the sale of the bashaw's property and that would constitute compensation for past wrongs; the appointment of himself as governor of two districts around Tangier; the release of his comrades from prison; and safe-conduct for all his tribesmen.[30] He later increased these demands to include a guarantee of them by the United States and England.

The Moroccan government refused Raisuli's terms, and Roosevelt and Secretary of State John Hay denounced Raisuli. But while the United States could not agree to be the enforcer of any settlement, it nevertheless still wanted the Moroccans to continue to deal with Raisuli. On May 29, Raisuli threatened to kill the hostages if his demands were not met in two days. The U.S. and British envoys in Morocco accelerated their efforts to get the sultan to acquiesce. The deadline passed with no harm done to the hostages.[31]

The negotiations and threats dragged on through June, with U.S. warships and a British ship now off the coast of Tangier. The French issued a loan to the Moroccan government and pressed it to settle with Raisuli. Meanwhile, the *New York Times* printed an editorial that suggested Perdicaris's life might not be in great danger, and revealed a basic principle of hostage taking: "For Raisuli to kill Perdicaris would be to destroy the goose that lays the golden eggs. To threaten to kill him, on the other hand, is distinctly business. He says to the sultan, Give me this, that, and the other, or I will kill this American, and you will be held responsible. Up to date the sultan has acknowledged the force of this view. But let Raisuli once kill PERDICARIS, and there is end to his blackmail." The editorial concluded that the hostage was so valuable to his captor, that "the most conservative life insurance company would regard PERDICARIS as a most eligible 'risk.' "[32]

Raisuli, meanwhile, tried to shore up his own image in Tangier and elsewhere by sending a letter to a newspaper pleading his case. He argued that he was not some type of savage beast intent on driving all foreigners from Tangier. He explained the reasons for the kidnapping—persecution of his tribe by the bashaw and his ancestors—and stated that he was being miscast as a villain. "All that has been said at Tangier about me, as well as the statement that I hate the Christian Europeans and want to drive them from Morocco, is wrong. I desire to do no wrong to any Christian." Raisuli stated that his hostages were safe and that "I hope I have made my position clear to the English and American peoples."[33]

An optimistic note was sounded by Gummere on June 19, when he cabled Washington that an agreement had been reached and the hostages would be set free on June 21. But the next day the release was postponed, as Raisuli became suspicious of the Moroccan government's true intentions. Gummere also put the blame on the "intrigue of authorities here." He sent another cable to Washington on June 21, stating that Moroccan delays in reaching an agreement were "humiliating" to the United States and requested permission to issue an ultimatum to the Moroccans, demanding compensation for every day that an agreement was delayed, and to land Marines and seize the customs house as security for the claim.[34]

While all this excitement was unfolding in Africa and was being closely followed by the American public, the Republicans gathered in Chicago in June for a rather dull nominating convention. Roosevelt was assured of being the candidate, but wanted something to stir the convention to life and send him off flying high into the presidential campaign. On June 21, as the delegates were sitting through another boring day of speeches, the chairman of the convention, Speaker of the House Joe Cannon, interrupted the proceedings to inform the delegates of a news bulletin from Washington. Secretary of State Hay had sent a telegram to Consul General Gummere, Cannon told the delegates, instructing him to deliver a message to the Moroccans. Cannon then had the secretary of the convention read the cable aloud: "We want either Perdicaris alive or Rais Uli dead."[35]

Had Cannon offered lifetime political office to all who were present, it probably would not have exceeded by much the pandemonium that broke out on the convention floor. "For fully a minute the delegates applauded, cheered, stood on their seats, and shouted, while 'Uncle Joe' Cannon beamed on them and at his judgment in picking out the psychological moment to spring the announcement from the White House," the *New York Times* wrote the next day on its front page. "Roosevelt and Hay at last had succeeded in creating artificial respiration and heart action in the convention through saline treatment."[36] One congressman exclaimed that "the people want an administration that will stand by its citizens, even if it takes the fleet to do it."[37]

What was not revealed to the delegates—or to the rest of the public— was that the cable went on to instruct Gummere *not* to take any military action. "Do not land Marines or seize customs without Department's specific instructions," Hay wrote.[38] It also was not disclosed that a settlement of the crisis had actually been reached before the telegram was received by the Moroccans. Roosevelt, though, "needed an opportunity for another demonstration."[39] But the biggest secret of all was a revelation about Perdicaris that Roosevelt and Hay kept from virtually everybody except a small circle of government officials. While seven U.S. warships were poised to do battle in Morocco—three more cruisers had been sent—and the American people were fired up over the fate of one of their countrymen, there was just one little problem: Perdicaris was not an American citizen!

The administration had learned early in June that Perdicaris went to Greece at the outbreak of the Civil War and had become a naturalized Greek citizen in 1862 to avoid either being drafted into the Confederate army or having his property in South Carolina confiscated. He returned to the United States and lived on and off in New Jersey, England, and Morocco, before finally settling in Tangier in 1884. He never attempted to regain his American citizenship.

This information came to the attention of the administration when a North Carolina man wrote to the State Department on May 30 that he had been in Athens in the 1860s when Perdicaris arrived to apply for Greek citizenship. The State Department quietly checked out the story, and to its horror found it to be true. When Hay was told about this by the head of the Citizenship Bureau at the State Department, he instructed the official to inform Roosevelt. The president chose to ignore this information and continued on with the confrontation with Morocco and Raisuli. He was reaping the benefits at home with the rally round the flag crisis, and at the same time extending American power and influence abroad. No need to tell the people that a man who had long ago given up his American citizenship was the focal point of all this concern. The information was closely guarded throughout the fall election campaign, which culminated with a Roosevelt victory.[40]

The hostage crisis ended on June 24 with the release of Perdicaris and his stepson. Raisuli got almost everything he wanted. Although the United States and England would not guarantee the agreement, Raisuli was quite satisfied. His comrades were released from prison, the bashaw was removed from power, a ransom was paid, and Raisuli was made governor of several districts around Tangier.[41] His prestige reached its "highest point" and he was "regarded by the tribesmen as a hero."[42] His captive Perdicaris had only kind words for his former captor. He told French officials in Paris a few weeks after his release that Raisuli was not a bandit but rather a "seriously sincere" man who was the best person available to deal with the problems of Tangier.[43] When addressing the annual dinner of the New York Library Club the following April, Perdicaris, who by now had become the most famous ex-hostage of his time, writing and speaking on the affairs of the world, heaped more praise upon Raisuli: "I consider my captor a true patriot who is leading his people in the fight for independence."[44] This was almost seventy years before the "Stockholm syndrome" would be proposed as an explanation for why hostages may have positive feelings about their captors—a much exaggerated theory that is discussed later in the book. But the *New York Times* got to the heart of the matter in an editorial the next day:

There is a peculiar satisfaction for us in the fact that Mr. Ion Perdicaris speaks kindly, and even admiringly, of the man who violently abducted him from his home, carried him off into the mountains to the considerable peril of his life, and released him only after the payment of a heavy ransom. While this exciting affair was in progress and everybody was calling the Rais Uli a robber chief and a ruthless blackmailer, we somehow acquired the notion that instead of being as black as he was painted, his complexion was only about as dark as was to be expected from a resident of Northern Africa, and that, while his acts would be highly reprehensible in a civilized country, in Morocco they were a fair approximation to wisdom, virtue, and patriotism. . . . [Raisuli] did what he could, and apparently about the only thing he could, to mitigate unendurable conditions, not only for himself, but for his fellow-tribesmen, who had been the victims of cruel wrongs that could not be redressed in any legal way. By abducting Mr. PERDICARIS he attracted outside attention and so was able to treat with his irresponsible over-lord on something like equal terms.[45]

One person's terrorist is another person's freedom fighter, even back in 1904.

The Perdicaris affair was another example of how governments do negotiate for the release of hostages, and the incredible web of international intrigue, politics, and conflict that can arise from the taking of just one or two hostages. With the exception of the Perdicaris kidnapping, for most of the nineteenth and early twentieth centuries, the major form of terrorism confronting the United States came from within the country rather than outside. These were primarily incidents of domestic violence associated with the anarchists and labor movements. One anarchist, Leon Czolgosz, assassinated President William McKinley in 1901, which led to Teddy Roosevelt becoming president. Czolgosz was tried, sentenced, and executed within two months of the terrorist act. Other anarchists emigrated to the United States in the hope of launching a revolution against capitalism. Jonathan Most—known as the anarchist without a country after being expelled from his native Germany and Austria, and imprisoned in Britain—arrived in the United States in 1882 and embarked on a speaking tour to rally the masses. He published a pamphlet that set forth specific instructions in the making of bombs, fuses, and poisons. He also included in his book details on how to place explosives for maximum effect in such public gathering places as churches and ballrooms.[46]

But violence for the sake of violence did not take hold in the United States, and the anarchist movement failed to achieve its goal of uprisings and revolution. The labor movement, on the other hand, waged a long and successful struggle for better working conditions and more pay.

Terrorist-related incidents were a part of labor-management conflicts and were perpetrated by both sides. Strikers were killed by company-hired guards, vigilante committees, and soldiers, while factory and mine operators and foremen were murdered by individual workers. In one case, violence in the Pennsylvania coal mines in the 1860s and 1870s led to rumors that an Irish terrorist group, the Molly Maguires, was on the rampage. The name originated in an Irish folk story about the widow Molly Maguire, who after being evicted from her farm in Ireland fought back against landlords and government officials with the aid of young Irishmen. The Molly Maguires in the Pennsylvania coal mines were believed to be connected with an Irish fraternal society, the Ancient Order of Hibernians.

Franklin Gowen, the president of the Philadelphia and Reading Railroad and its subsidiary, the Philadelphia and Reading Coal and Iron Company, decided to exploit public fears about terrorism by linking the Molly Maguires with organized labor and thus crush the emerging labor movement. Gowen hired the Pinkerton detective agency in 1873 to infiltrate the Mollies and gather evidence for their arrests. In a letter from Alan Pinkerton to one of his superintendents, he compares the Molly Maguires to the Thugs of India and calls for tough action against them:

> The M.M.'s are a species of Thugs. You have probably read of them in India. Their religion taught them to murder, to mark out their victims, and their plans by which they were to strike, and not to divulge anything even if they were brought to the stake. So it is with the M.M.'s. They are bound to stick by their oath, and to carry out their revenge. He, who they think does a wrong, is marked out, and he must die. It is impossible to believe that a jury in the mining districts would not give a verdict of guilty against the M.M.'s should they be brought to trial but I believe that some one on the jury would hang on, and get the guilty men to escape. The only way then to pursue that I can see is, to . . . get up a vigilence committee. It will not do to get many men, but let him [one of Pinkerton's men] get those who are prepared to take fearful revenge on the M.M.'s. I think it would open the eyes of all the people and then the M.M.'s would meet with their just deserts. It is awful to see men doomed to death, it is horrible. Now there is but one thing to be done, and that is, get up an organization if possible, and when ready for action pounce upon the M.M.'s when they meet and are in full blast, take the fearful responsibility and disperse.[47]

But Pinkerton did not need to use any vigilantes against the Molly Maguires. By the end of the summer of 1875, his undercover agent, James McParland, had spent two years with the Mollies in the Pennsylvania coal mines and produced enough names, dates, and places of various murders to bring several Irish miners to trial. These trials, however, were not very fair, as some defense witnesses were charged with perjury and immediately arrested and put in jail after testifying, thereby intimidating others from coming forth for the defense. Furthermore, McParland's testimony, which was the heart of the state's case, was suspect and corroborated only by disreputable individuals who received immunity from prosecution for their crimes by testifying for the state. But all of this did not matter to Gowen, who was a brilliant orator, businessman, and prosecutor and knew how to play upon public fears about violence and terrorism. He told the jury during one of the trials that if the Molly Maguires were destroyed, then "we can stand up before the whole country and say: 'Now all are safe in this country; come here, with your money; come here with your families and make this country your residence; help us to build up this people and you will be safe.' "[48]

The Mollies were convicted and sentenced to death, with ten members hanged on June 21, 1877, and nine more hanged within the next two years. To this day there is still debate among historians whether the Molly Maguires were in fact an organized group of terrorists or instead just an exaggerated threat fostered by Gowen for his own purposes. Gowen continued to use the threat of brandishing labor militants as Molly Maguires to crush any fledgling union. "It was sufficient to hang a man to declare him a Molly Maguire," Gowen once boasted.[49]

Meanwhile, terrorist-related violence continued to characterize labor-management struggles throughout the country. Among the more notable incidents was the Haymarket Square riot in Chicago on May 4, 1886, where a bomb was tossed into a column of policemen, killing seven officers. The police had been trying to break up a protest by thousands of people who were upset with the police for firing into a crowd of striking workers the day before at the McCormick harvester plant. But it was not until the early part of the twentieth century that the impact that a single terrorist bomb can have upon the American public was clearly demonstrated.

A long period of union-management disputes and strikes at the *Los Angeles Times* culminated with the dynamiting of the *Times* building on October 1, 1910. The bombing shocked the nation, as twenty-one non-union workers were killed and an estimated $500,000 in damages resulted. "Los Angeles seemed to be in a state of panic," wrote William Burns, the country's most famous detective, who would be hired by the city of Los Angeles and *Times* owner Harrison Otis to track down the bombers. "Another earthquake would not have created such fear as the citizens were experiencing. An earthquake is an act of nature, but what was going on in Los Angeles was the act of a cunning, heartless, ruthless enemy of society."[50] Two other bombs were discovered that same day:

one at the home of Otis and another at the home of the secretary of the Merchants and Manufacturers' Association. Police were able to remove the bomb at Otis's home to an open area where it exploded harmlessly, while the second bomb failed to explode due to a weak battery.

Otis vented his anger with an editorial in his newspaper that called the bombers "anarchist scum," "cowardly murderers," and "midnight assassins . . . whose hands are dripping with the innocent blood of your victims. . . . " He lamented about "the wails of poor widows and the cries of fatherless children" and was relentless in trying to pin the bombing on organized labor. When John J. McNamara, the secretary-treasurer of the International Association of Bridge and Structural Iron Workers, and his younger brother James were arrested in Indiana the following April by Burns and police detectives and brought back to Los Angeles to stand trial for the *Times* bombing, Otis could only rejoice with a headline that implied that no trial was really necessary: "The Dynamiters of the Times Building Caught. Crime Traced Directly to High Union Labor Officials."[51]

Clarence Darrow, one of the country's most famous lawyers, was retained to defend the McNamara brothers, but as evidence against them mounted, the two brothers confessed to the crime in order to escape the death penalty. James B. McNamara admitted placing a suitcase with sixteen sticks of dynamite and a timing device in the *Times* building the night before the explosion, while John J. McNamara confessed to being an accessory to that bombing as well as to one at the anti-union Llewellyn Iron Works plant in Los Angeles. James McNamara was sentenced to life imprisonment while John McNamara was sentenced to fifteen years. The McNamaras' confessions were a blow to the labor movement since union leaders and workers throughout the country had rallied to their defense and argued that the brothers were being framed by big business as a way to destroy labor.

The bombing led to a congressional inquiry as lawmakers became concerned that the United States might be facing a new wave of violence if striking workers increasingly turned to the use of dynamite in their disputes with management. Darrow was called to testify and was urged by the committee to repudiate and condemn the McNamaras' bombing. He refused, and in his testimony implied that political terrorism was a justifiable act. "There was no element [in the bombing] that goes to make up what the world calls a criminal act, which is an act coupled with a selfish criminal motive," Darrow told the lawmakers. James B. McNamara "did not do it for malice. He was a union man in a great industrial struggle running over the years. He believed in it and believed it was necessary to the welfare of his class; . . . in his mind he thought he was serving his class, and taking his life in his hands without reward. Now, if anyone can condemn him for it, they reason differently from myself. . . . I can not."[52]

Many Americans, though, did condemn the McNamaras in particular and the labor movement in general for the violence. One historian noted that the bombing and its aftermath "stopped the Los Angeles labor movement dead." But a foreign journalist traveling through the United States to cover the story observed that while many newspaper editors, reporters, and the American public were opposed to the bombing, they "seemed, nevertheless, to feel that there were deep evils in the country which were in a sense responsible [for it]."[53] An examination of the causes of violence in labor-management relations was conducted by the president-appointed United States Industrial Commission. While the commission focused initially on the McNamara case, it also studied the plight of workers in America and "played an important role in educating public opinion about the realities of the labor-capital conflict."[54]

The dynamiting of the *Times* building served the same purpose as many contemporary terrorist actions: to bring public attention to a particular cause, whether it be workers' rights, territorial demands, or ethnic and religious grievances, through a spectacular violent act. While the short-term effect is negative public reactions or official government crackdowns, the long-term benefit can be the raising of a nation's consciousness on the issue that propelled the terrorists into action in the first place.

Technological innovations in weaponry played a key role in the labor and anarchist violence of the late nineteenth and early twentieth centuries. It provided militants with dynamite, a new weapon to use against government, military, and big business. Dynamite was invented in 1867 by Swedish chemist Alfred Nobel, who intended it for peaceful purposes and was dismayed to see it used for violence. He left millions of dollars in his will to establish the annual Nobel prizes, including the Nobel Peace Prize. But dynamite was hailed by anarchists who believed that "in providing such a powerful but easily concealed weapon, science was thought to have given a decisive advantage to revolutionary forces."[55] For labor militants, the existence of dynamite meant that a new tactic could be used against management efforts to break up the unions. The International Association of Bridge and Structural Iron Workers—the McNamara brothers' union—decided in 1906 that traditional labor tactics of strikes and protests were failing to prevent U.S. Steel and other companies from imposing the open-shop at various plants. They therefore turned to dynamite, and between 1906 and 1911 was responsible for more than one hundred explosions at bridges, factories, and plants across the country.[56] Thirty-eight members of the union were ultimately convicted of these crimes, which resulted mostly in minor property damage and no casualties until the bombing of the *Times* building.

The terrorism of American·labor militants was for the most part not directed at loss of life. This was not true for other foreign terrorist groups that were active during the late nineteenth century. The Russian anarchist group Nardodnaya Volya, which was the first organization to use dynamite on a wide scale between 1878 and 1881, killed many government and business officials. Their most spectacular terrorist attack was the assassination of Tsar Alexander II in 1881. Irish terrorists also used dynamite in the 1880s in their effort to drive the British out of Ireland. While both these revolutionary movements failed at that time, they nevertheless succeeded in demonstrating how dynamite could be used by small groups in carefully planned attacks against much stronger foes for maximum effect.

Domestic violence and related terrorist incidents in the United States continued in various forms through the first half of the twentieth century. But it would not be until after World War II that a new age of terrorism truly began to emerge.

The Postwar Years

The years following the end of World War II were among the most creative and significant in American foreign policy. Decisions made at that time forged a role for the United States in world affairs that would last until the end of the Cold War more than forty years later. Emerging from the war as the strongest Western power, the United States assumed the mantle of leadership for the free world.

It was not surprising, then, that during this period of the Marshall Plan and the Truman Doctrine that Europe and the containment of the Soviet Union were the major policy concerns for the United States, and the threat of terrorism was only of passing interest. Most of the terrorism that occurred in the late 1940s did not involve U.S. targets, but instead focused on the internal conflicts in the Middle East, India, and other regions. Terrorism played an important role in the founding of the state of Israel, and many of the tactics used by Jewish militant groups against British rule in Palestine would be copied by future terrorist groups, including Palestinian extremists.

The conflicts in Palestine were many, and included the Jews against the British, the Arabs against the British, and the Jews and Arabs against each other. The British ruled Palestine under a League of Nations mandate following the end of World War I. The Balfour Declaration, calling for the establishment in Palestine of a national homeland for the Jewish people, was written into the mandate. This was naturally not well received by the Arab population, which rioted in 1920, beginning a cycle of violence that would last until today. As Jewish immigration from Europe swelled, Arab terrorism increased, being directed by the Grand Mufti, or senior judge in Jerusalem, Haz Amin el-Husseini. Arab extremists killed Jews, Arab moderates, and British soldiers and officials. There were several Arab riots between 1920 and World War II, including a full-scale rebellion in 1936 that lasted for three years until it was crushed by the British, but not before more than 1,350 Jews, Arabs, and British were killed and injured.[57]

Meanwhile, the Jews formed their own militant groups, including the Irgun Zvai Leumi, or the National Military Organization, under the command of future Israeli Prime Minister Menachem Begin, and LEHI, the Fighters for the Freedom of Israel, also know as the Stern Gang, since it was led by Abraham Stern, who was killed by British police in 1942. Both Irgun and Stern were responsible for numerous terrorist attacks, ranging from the sending of letter bombs to the assassination of British officials to the blowing up of immigration and tax offices, police stations, and other buildings. The British were seen by the militant groups as the enemy of the Jewish state since they were continuing to rule Palestine and restricting Jewish immigration to the future homeland. The goal was to drive the British out of Palestine rather than wait for the Balfour Declaration to be fulfilled.

The most spectacular attack by the Stern Gang occurred in November 1944, when a two-man assassination team traveled to Cairo and murdered Lord Moyne, the British minister of state in the Middle East. Moyne was a close personal friend of Prime Minister Winston Churchill, and the assassination led Churchill to lose his enthusiasm for the establishment of a Jewish state. "If our dream of Zionism should be dissolved in the smoke of revolvers of assassins and if our efforts for its future should provoke a new wave of banditry worthy of the Nazi Germans, many persons like myself will have to reconsider the position we have maintained so firmly for such a long time," Churchill told the House of Commons in a eulogy to Moyne.[58] Fearful that terrorism might be hurting their interests, moderate Jews as well as the main Jewish paramilitary organization, Haganah, cooperated with the British in leading them to hundreds of suspected terrorists.

But terrorism continued, and Irgun implemented its most daring terrorist operation in the summer of 1946. The King David Hotel in Jerusalem was a grand structure that served as headquarters for the British mandate in Palestine. Shortly after the noon hour on July 22, six members of Begin's Irgun group, dressed as Arabs, infiltrated the hotel through a rear kitchen entrance and placed several milk churns filled with gelignite and TNT in the unoccupied Regence Bar on the ground floor. The bombs exploded at 12:37 P.M., destroying the south wing of the hotel, which had been bristling with people. When the smoke cleared, ninety-one victims lay dead, including twenty-eight Britons, forty-one Arabs, and seventeen Jews. Forty-six other people were injured in the attack. Begin claimed Irgun had given the British sufficient time in a telephone warning to evacuate the hotel, but that the British chose to ignore the warning.

The reaction was predictable. Condemnation came from all sides, including many Jews. David Ben-Gurion, who would become the first prime minister of Israel, called Irgun "the enemy of the Jewish people." The Haganah, even though they had been in on the planning of the bombing, also denounced the attack. And a Jewish newspaper in Palestine, the *Hatsofeh*, called for a purge of Irgun and its "evil gang of fascists."[59]

But Irgun again survived and continued its terrorist campaign. In July 1947, they kidnapped two British sergeants in retaliation for the British capture of three Irgun members. In a forerunner to some of the hostage dramas of 1980s Lebanon, Irgun held the two British soldiers captive for seventeen days while their parents pleaded for their lives. When the three Irgun members were executed by the British, the fate of the sergeants was sealed. They were hanged, and their bodies were strung upside down from a tree in a eucalyptus grove, with booby traps and mines placed around the area. "We repaid our enemy in kind," Begin wrote a few years later. " . . . He forced us to answer gallows with gallows."[60]

The British finally gave up on Palestine, asking the United Nations to take responsibility for resolving the conflict. The U.N. voted in November 1947 to partition the territory into a Jewish and Arab state, making Jerusalem an international city. The British then announced that they would leave Palestine the following May. The terrorism by both Jews and Arabs increased, and by the end of 1947, Arab terrorists were murdering an average of fifty Jewish civilians a week. The Irgun retaliated with a bombing on December 29 at Jerusalem's Damascus Gate that killed fifteen Arabs. In April 1948, Irgun and Stern terrorists attacked the Arab village of Dir Yassin, killing 254 men, women, and children.[61] After the British left on May 14, the state of Israel was declared by Ben-Gurion and immediately recognized by the United States. The next day Arab armies from Egypt, Jordan, Lebanon, Syria, Iraq, and Saudi Arabia invaded the new state, the first of four wars that would be fought over the next twenty-five years between Israel and its Arab neighbors.

Many factors contributed to Britain's decision to leave Palestine. The effectiveness of moderate Zionist forces in bringing international pressure to create a Jewish state, the moral repulsion of the world following the killing of six million Jews by the Nazis during World War II, and the beginning of the end of the British empire in the aftermath of the war. But the role of terrorism in forcing Britain's hand cannot be underestimated. "Terrorism led Britain to wash her hands . . . of the Palestine problem," writes historian Paul Johnson.[62] Other observers agree, noting that the terrorist campaign by itself was not sufficient to force the British out, but that it did "accelerate an historical process,"[63] and that it "provided the often horrific spark which would stir and incite the British to the point where they were ready to leave Palestine."[64]

While terrorism in the Middle East was unfolding and laying the groundwork for decades of conflict that would affect many countries, including the United States, a new form of terrorism was emerging in Asia and North America. This was being introduced by criminals, who, in 1949, combined the technology of dynamite explosives with the growing trend toward airplane travel to produce the first wave of midair bombings in aviation history. Their motives were greed, but their tactics would later be adopted by political terrorists with even more deadly force.

The first reported midair bombing in the United States occurred near Chesterton, Indiana, on October 10, 1933, when a United Airlines transcontinental passenger plane exploded. All seven people aboard were killed, including the first stewardess to die in a plane crash. No motive or suspects were uncovered. Then, in 1949, in the Philippines, a woman and her lover hired two ex-convicts to place a bomb loaded with TNT on a Philippines Airlines plane. The plane crashed into the sea on May 7, killing thirteen people aboard. She wanted to kill her husband, who was a passenger on the plane, in order to collect his inheritance. The next midair bombing occurred only a few months later, this time in Canada when a Canadian Pacific Airlines plane exploded on September 9, near Sault Au Cochon, forty miles from Quebec. The plane, en route from Quebec to Baie Comeau, crashed after a time bomb exploded in the forward baggage compartment. All twenty-three people aboard were killed, including the wife of the person responsible for the bombing, J. Albert Guay.

Albert Guay was a dashing young man with a taste for women and money. Women were no problem but money always was. He had a twenty-eight-year-old wife, a nineteen-year-old mistress, and a forty-one-year-old former girlfriend that he remained close to. When his teen-aged lover, Marie Ange Robitaille, later nicknamed "Angel Mary" by the press for her youth and beauty, broke off her affair with Guay in the summer of 1949, the thirty-year-old Canadian jeweler believed he had to do something quickly to win her back. Killing his wife and making some money at the same time didn't seem like a bad idea to Guay.

Guay decided he would dupe his wife into traveling alone to the town of Sept Iles to retrieve suitcases of jewelry that he would tell her he had left there on a previous trip. Since Guay had worked in a munitions factory during World War II, blowing up a plane and collecting a $10,000 insurance policy on her life that he would take out a few days before the flight seemed to be the perfect plan. Guay faced a problem, though, that any criminal or terrorist faces when planning an operation for which there is little precedent: How exactly does one go about blowing up a plane in midair? While Guay probably read in the newspapers about the Philippines bombing, he still needed to learn exactly what it would take to blow up the Canadian Pacific Airlines plane he planned to put his wife on, and do so without arousing suspicion from the people he would have to consult. His prior work in the munitions factory gave him some knowledge of explosives, but not enough. He needed help.

Guay first turned to his friend and part-time employee, Genereux Ruest. The forty-seven-year-old paralyzed watchmaker could provide Guay with the technical skills necessary for making timing devices and other parts for the bomb. But he still needed specific information on explosives for blowing up planes.

Guay and Ruest began consulting experts on explosives, using the cover story that they wanted to blow up a pond in order to catch "a carload of fish." They asked a former arsenal worker how much dynamite would be necessary for such a task. The puzzled man told them that "there's no sense fishing that way; you'll only get yourselves arrested." But he nevertheless gave them information on dynamite caps, fuses, and batteries that helped them construct a time bomb. They also consulted with a mechanic and a construction worker, continuing to use the cover story of needing the explosives for a fishing trip. While all of this sounded odd to the workers, nobody became suspicious that a midair bombing was the real plan.[65]

With this information, as well as Ruest's own expertise in electronics and Guay's drawings of the type of detonator he wanted, the two men were able to construct a bomb consisting of twenty sticks of dynamite, an alarm clock, and a dry-cell battery. Guay's former girlfriend, Margueritte Pitre, who was also Ruest's sister, purchased the dynamite and delivered the bomb to the plane. She took a taxi to the airport shortly before the plane was to take off, and told a freight handler that the package contained clothing that needed to be sent to an address—which turned out to be fictitious—in Baie Comeau.[66] Since airport security in the late 1940s was virtually nonexistent, the bomb was put in the forward baggage compartment without receiving any inspection.

The plane was delayed five minutes before takeoff, spoiling Guay's plan to have it explode and crash into the St. Lawrence River and thus destroy most if not all the evidence. Instead, the plane crashed into a rocky bluff that rose several hundred feet above the north shore of the river and police were able to recover traces of the bomb from the wreckage. The prime suspect was initially Pitre, as both the freight operator and the taxi driver told investigators about the nervous woman delivering a package to the plane. The taxi driver recalled her telling him the package was fragile and to avoid bumps. When Guay learned, through news accounts, that a mysterious woman was being sought by police, he tried to convince Pitre to kill herself since she had been responsible for so many deaths and that the "police were out to trap her." The distraught woman took an overdose of sleeping pills, but survived and confessed her role in the bombing, though still claiming that she did not know the contents of the package. Guay was subsequently arrested.[67]

Among the victims of the crash, in addition to Guay's wife, were three top American executives of the U.S.-based Kennecott Copper Corporation, including its president. The son of one of the executives killed was arrested two months later by police in Massachusetts after robbing a liquor store, claiming that he wanted to finance a trip to Montreal in order to kill Guay. The interest in the Guay case riveted Canada, much like future terrorist episodes would grip the world. Air travel itself was in its relatively early period and whatever fear people had of flying was now multiplied by the knowledge that bombs could easily be put aboard by individuals or groups. The Guay incident remained incomprehensible to many people. The contempt and anger that Canadians felt for Guay was evident in one reporter's description of Guay on the day he was convicted of his crime:

> The long chain of evidence in one of the most diabolical crimes in history, today became a hangman's noose for a little man of evil who sent 23 persons to their death, one of them his wife, in the time-bombing of a Canadian Pacific airliner last Sept. 9. Albert Guay, his narrow shoulders shaking and his thin lips trembling, stood in the prisoner's dock and heard the unsteady voice of Judge Albert Sevigny sentence him to death for murder. Ladies' man Guay, the chain-smoking, dapper Guay of Lower Quebec, who snuffed out 22 other lives because he wanted to kill his wife, trembled and swayed from side to side as he watched the jury file to their seats after an absence of only 17 minutes. . . . This was the rope for the thin neck of the slight figure in the dock. This was the end of the road for the ferret-like man with the pencil moustache who coupled lust for a 19-year-old waitress with a consuming greed for money. . . . To the chalky faced Guay [the judge's sentence] . . . was the voice of his executioner. Gone was the bravado, the indifference of his demeanor maintained throughout the 15 days of trial.[68]

The judge burst into tears as he sentenced Guay, telling the doomed man, "Your crime is infamous! It has no name!"[69] Guay, Ruest, and Pitre were all hanged for their part in the bombing, with Guay's final words being, "At least I die famous." Pitre won a sort of moral victory before her conviction: she was acquitted of her attempted suicide! Although Guay did not have a political cause, the impact that seemingly random violence, whether perpetrated by a political terrorist or a clever criminal, could have upon a country was clearly evident.

A criminal was also responsible for a midair bombing in the United States in the 1950s. Not exactly a devoted son, John Gilbert Graham, a twenty-three-year-old Denver youth, put his mother on board a United Airlines DC-6B jet in Denver on November 1, 1955, along with a dynamite time bomb hidden in her suitcase. Graham then waited in an airport coffee shop along with his wife and son, who did not know about his deed, until he heard word that the plane had crashed shortly after takeoff en route to Portland. He later telephoned the airlines office to find out if his mother was indeed killed in the crash. When a sympathetic United Airlines official informed him that it was very likely that she was among the forty-four dead, Graham simply replied, "Well, that's the way it goes." His motive was greed: a $37,500 insurance policy on his mother's life that he bought from an airport vending machine shortly before she boarded the plane. What he collected, though, was the electric chair a year and a half later.

The investigation into the Graham bombing was a path-breaking effort on the part of the FBI. It set the standards for future scientific analysis of airplane bombings. Investigators on the scene of the crash knew that the plane had disintegrated in the air based on witness reports and the fact that debris was scattered for over ten miles, but they did not know the exact cause. The pressure on the FBI to solve the case was intense, since if a bomb had caused the plane to crash, the disaster would become one of the largest mass murder cases in U.S. history.

The chief FBI chemist involved in the case, Dr. J. William Magee, had no guidelines to follow for conducting a bombing investigation. "It was pretty lonely in those days," recalled Magee, "because there were no outside people to consult. Nobody had any experience with that."[70] The investigation of the Denver crash marked the first time that residues from parts of a plane were examined in a scientific manner to determine the exact cause of an explosion. Magee went back and forth from the FBI laboratory in Washington to Denver four times in a matter of a few days, looking at parts of the wreckage and sending them back to the lab for further analysis. After virtually round-the-clock study of the parts, Magee identified sodium carbonate on parts of the aircraft. This led him to conclude that the plane was brought down by a dynamite explosion.

Meanwhile, FBI agents in Denver were scanning the passenger list to determine if there was anybody on board who might be the target of a murder plot by somebody who was familiar with explosives. When they came across the name of Mrs. Graham, they checked further and discovered that her son had a prior arrest record for forgery and knew how to use explosives, having worked in construction and logging companies where dynamite was used. The insurance policy was another piece of information that led them to Graham, who confessed to placing twenty-five sticks of dynamite, a timing device, two dynamite caps, and a dry cell battery in his mother's suitcase.[71]

Graham planned to have the bomb explode when the plane was over the rugged mountains in Wyoming, where wreckage would be more difficult to recover. Bad weather would also probably delay any investigation in that area until the spring. He set the timer to its maximum ninety minutes, which did not leave him much time to place the bomb in his mother's suitcase, drive her to the airport, and then watch as the suitcase was placed aboard the plane. The flight was delayed thirty-five minutes, which caused the plane to explode only eleven minutes after takeoff over a sugar beet field near Longmont, Colorado, where recovery of the wreckage was much easier than in the mountains.[72] As had occurred in the 1949 Quebec bombing (and would occur in the 1988 bombing of Pan Am 103 over Lockerbie, Scotland) delays in the takeoff of the aircraft caused them to explode over land rather than water or rugged mountains, leaving evidence that the terrorists had not planned for.

President Dwight Eisenhower, as was true for most of the American public, was outraged at this new form of violence. Graham, meanwhile, remained stoic and unremorseful throughout his trial. He was executed under Colorado law for murder in 1957, since at that time there was no federal law to cover his offense. Ironically, even if Graham had never been caught, he would not have been able to cash the insurance policy because his mother never countersigned it. The bombing led Congress to pass a bill in 1956 that established the death penalty for anyone convicted of causing loss of life by damaging an airplane, bus, or commercial vehicle. An existing statute covered the sabotage of trains.

Following the Graham bombing, the FBI and Civil Aviation Administration conducted studies on measures that might be taken to detect explosives in luggage. However, sophisticated technology was not yet available to aid in designing effective and speedy airport security systems. "The rigmarole involved in merely running the [metal] detector over every suitcase and hat box going aboard a plane would make present baggage routine, a frequent annoyance, seem like the essence of convenience," wrote one reporter shortly after the Graham bombing. "So if the airlines continue current policy, the suitcase with the bomb inside is unlikely to be detected."[73]

The publicity surrounding the Graham case also led to the "copycat" phenomenon that is a main characteristic of terrorist behavior. U.S. airlines began receiving bomb threats on the average of one a month following the Denver bombing, whereas previously there had been few threats of this nature.[74] The American public now had to fear the destruction of planes by criminals motivated by greed, and eventually by individuals and groups motivated by political objectives.

Prior to the Graham bombing, terrorism in the United States during the early 1950s was centered mainly on the issue of Puerto Rican independence. Since 1898, when the United States acquired Puerto Rico after the Spanish American War, there were movements on the island for independence. The National Party under the leadership of Pedro Albiza Campos initially tried to work through the political system. However, after gaining only 2 percent of the vote in the 1932 elections, the movement turned to violence. In 1936, the party was accused of killing a police commander in Puerto Rico. That same year, Campos and seven other National Party members were sentenced to ten years in prison for plotting to overthrow the U.S. government. Campos was released after serving seven years and returned to Puerto Rico where he resumed his violent campaign for independence.[75]

The independence movement reached its height during a two-day uprising in the fall of 1950. Rebel bands attacked various targets throughout the island, disrupting registration that was taking place for a plebiscite on the Puerto Rican constitution. Among the rebels' targets was the governor of Puerto Rico, Luis Muñoz Marín, who escaped an attempt on his life. The rebellion was crushed, but not without leaving the extremists more determined than ever to continue their struggle. Two of them, Griselio Torresola and Oscar Collazo, who were in New York during the uprising, decided that more dramatic action was necessary. On November 1 (exactly five years before the Graham bombing and just one day after the rebellion was crushed), the two men traveled to Washington to assassinate President Truman.

In those days, security against terrorism was not seen as a high priority, and the would-be assassins had little trouble reaching the steps of Blair House, where Truman was residing while the White House was being remodeled. Torresola and Collazo were not even sure that Truman was present, but nevertheless intended to shoot their way into his quarters. Torresola was carrying a letter with him from Campos that stated that if it became necessary, Torresola was to assume the leadership of the Puerto Rican nationalist movement in the United States.

Collazo and Torresola approached Blair House from different directions along the sidewalk and tried to climb the stairs. They were spotted by security guards and a gun battle ensued. Torresola and one guard were killed, while Collazo was wounded. He was arrested, convicted, and sentenced to death, but Truman commuted the sentence to life imprisonment. Truman was inside Blair House during the incident, taking his usual afternoon nap. The gunfire woke him, and as he went to the window to see what was happening, one of the guards shouted at him to move away.[76] Truman was not hurt in the attack, which was followed by a number of bombings and bomb threats against the Puerto Rican community in New York.

Although there was public shock over the attempt on the president's life, the issue of terrorism as a threat to the United States never arose. Truman played down the incident, not wanting to give any more attention than was necessary to this act of violence. There were no major presidential statements denouncing terrorism, and Truman himself, writing to a friend about the attack, simply said, "I hope it won't happen again."[77] World events also quickly overshadowed the assassination attempt as Chinese troops entered the Korean War. Dean Rusk, at that time assistant secretary of state for Far Eastern Affairs, recalled that the attempt on Truman's life was not viewed by the administration as the beginning of a wave of anti-U.S. terrorism. It was "looked upon more or less as an isolated incident," said Rusk. "We didn't make a big deal out of it at the time in terms of the possibility of the continuation of this kind of effort by Puerto Rican nationalists."[78]

However, there would be another dramatic attack by Puerto Rican extremists in 1954. This time the target was the U.S. Congress. On March 1, four Puerto Rican nationalists, clutching a Puerto Rican flag and shouting "Viva Puerto Rico," opened fire from the gallery of the House of Representatives. Five congressmen were wounded in the attack. A note found on one of the members of the group, Lolita Lebron, pledged loyalty to nationalist leader Campos and called for the independence of Puerto Rico. After being arrested, Lebron told authorities that the attack was timed to coincide with the opening of the Inter-American Conference in Caracas, Venezuela. The group's intention was to embarrass the United States. It was also reported that the group may have been plotting to overthrow the U.S. government by assassinating President Eisenhower and other government officials.[79]

The assault on Congress, along with the 1950 attempt on Truman's life, represented the first time that terrorism was directed against U.S. targets on U.S. soil in order to affect specific U.S. foreign policies. But for the Eisenhower administration, as was true for the Truman administration, the main concern was not terrorism but rather the threat of Soviet expansionism. Thus, when Secretary of State John Foster Dulles addressed the Caracas meeting a few days after the shootings in Congress, he did not dwell upon the terrorist incidents, except to put them in the context of the Soviet threat. Dulles told the conference that while the Puerto Rican extremists "may not themselves be Communists . . . they have [nevertheless] been subjected to the inflammatory influence of communism, which avowedly uses extreme nationalism as one of its tools. What they did is precisely in the Soviet Communist pattern."[80]

The four Puerto Rican nationalists served twenty-five years in prison before being pardoned (along with Oscar Collazo) by President Carter in 1979. For many Puerto Ricans, these individuals were viewed as heroes, not terrorists, giving further credence to the "one person's terrorist is another person's freedom fighter" slogan. When they were freed, large crowds of cheering Puerto Ricans greeted them in New York, Chicago, and San Juan.[81]

Although the attack on Congress was the second major terrorist incident against U.S. officials within four years, there was again no real concern that the United States was facing a wave of terrorism associated with Puerto Rican independence. General Andrew Goodpaster, the staff secretary for President Eisenhower and his closest aide both during and after his presidency, recalled that intelligence assessments conducted by the FBI and CIA determined that the shooting in Congress was a confined and isolated attack. "There was nothing to indicate," Goodpaster said, "that this was something of substantial proportion."[82]

Eisenhower and Hostages

Before the 1950s were over, the United States faced its first major hostage episode since the Perdicaris incident. This time it would be Cuban revolutionaries who took Americans captive, and the manner in which Dwight Eisenhower handled this episode revealed a great deal about presidential leadership during hostage crises.

During the late 1950s, several incidents occurred where American military personnel were detained by Communist governments. The Communists wanted to use the servicemen as bargaining chips in the Cold War. On June 7, 1958, a U.S. Army helicopter strayed across the border into East Germany and was forced to land. After surrendering to East German police, the crew of nine Americans was turned over to Soviet army officials. Moscow, though, wanted to use the incident to force the United States to recognize the East German Communist government. They returned the servicemen to the East German authorities, claiming that the dispute was between that country and the United States. The East German government then announced that the Americans would be released only if the United States signed an agreement recognizing its regime as a legal government. Eisenhower refused, although he favored almost any other type of approach to win the soldiers' freedom. During this time there were also four Americans being held captive in Communist China.

As the Eisenhower administration came under increased pressure from Congress and others to do something about the detention of Americans abroad, it was confronted with a new hostage situation. On June 28—the same day that a U.S. Air Force plane was forced down more than one hundred miles inside the Soviet Union's border with Turkey, resulting in the detaining of nine more U.S. airmen—a bus carrying twenty-nine U.S. Navy men from Guantanamo Bay was seized by Cuban rebels. Several other American and Canadian workers in Cuba had also been taken hostage a few days earlier. The rebels, led by Fidel Castro's brother Raul, claimed that the United States was supplying arms to the government of President Fulgencio Batista, even though the Eisenhower administration had announced an end to such shipments in March 1958.[83]

For Raul Castro, the kidnappings served two main purposes. The first was the motivation that drives many groups to utilize terrorist tactics: publicity. "The outcome of the kidnappings to the Sierra fighters was much more positive than Raul could have even imagined," writes journalist and author Georgie Anne Geyer. The Cuban rebels "caught the attention of the world; the American public became more aware of the United States' role in the increasingly threatening Cuban Revolution."[84] Raul stated that the hostages were taken in order to "attract world attention" to the supplying of arms to the Batista regime. The second reason for the kidnappings, Raul claimed, was to "deter the criminal bombardments" of the Cuban government against the rebel forces[85]—a strategy of "human shields" that Saddam Hussein would use more than two decades later during the 1990 Persian Gulf crisis. And, as we will see below, this strategy was also used by rebels in the Congo in 1964.

Fidel Castro, though, did not see things the same way as his brother. In a caustic letter to Raul, Fidel warned him that "you cannot act on your own initiative, nor go beyond certain limits without any consultation." Castro complained that the kidnappings had become "an affair of major importance inside and outside of Cuba" that threatened to turn international public opinion against the rebels. "We must consider the possibility that elements of the dictatorship, exploiting this incident, are hatching a plan for physical aggression against North American citizens," Castro wrote. The Cuban revolutionary leader feared that any deaths of Americans would now be blamed on the rebels. "It is essential to declare categorically that we do not utilize the system of hostages, however justified our indignation may be against the political attitudes of any government," Castro told his brother.[86]

Fidel Castro's concern with public perceptions of the rebels' actions was not surprising. A hostage situation could be risky since it could backfire and create a wave of sympathy for the captives and animosity for the kidnappers. The editor of the Cuban rebels' newspaper, and the man in charge of public information for the revolution, Carlos Franqui, noted that "propaganda, or public information, was a decisive weapon in our struggle. We defeated Batista's army and his forces of repression with a minimum of physical destruction and a maximum of psychological penetration."[87] For this reason, a hostage situation involving foreigners was the last thing that the rebel movement wanted in its efforts to project a favorable image. But Raul had taken the hostages, and the stalemate between the United States and the Cuban rebels had begun.

The hostage crisis set off an angry session in Congress. Eisenhower came under severe attack from both parties for not taking retaliatory measures against the rebels. Representative Robert Byrd, a Democrat from West Virginia, called for "an immediate firming of policy by the Eisenhower administration." In a speech on the House floor, Byrd said that "the headlines tell a sad story of the decline of American prestige. American airmen are made prisoners in Eastern Germany—thirty American Navy men are kidnaped by Cuban rebels. What a sickening recital of insult and injury to America and Americans."[88]

Another member of Congress, Representative Victor Anfuso, a Democrat from New York, sent a telegram to Secretary of State Dulles urging him to "demand from both rebels and legal Government of Cuba the release of our citizens within 48 hours with no strings attached, or we will treat banditry for what it is and take such action as may be necessary to protect our citizens and preserve our national prestige."[89] And it was not only the Democrats who were attacking the Eisenhower administration. William Knowland, Republican Senate minority leader from California, called for the United States to send arms to the Batista government unless the rebels released the American hostages within forty-eight hours. Another Republican senator, Styles Bridges of New Hampshire, also called for a tough response.

The congressional uproar became a problem for the patient approach that Eisenhower wanted to pursue to resolve the hostage situation. The president decided that the best course would be to try to persuade the rebels that they had made a mistake in believing the United States was still supporting the Batista regime. Eisenhower did not want to force an escalating and irreversible conflict by threatening the rebels with U.S. retaliatory measures. A diplomatic effort was launched with American consuls in Cuba instructed to contact the rebels. He understandably became upset when Dulles informed him about the forty-eight-hour ultimatums being called for by some members of Congress. He told Dulles that people such as Bridges and Knowland were only making matters worse by throwing "roadblocks at those who were trying to help."[90] Andrew Goodpaster recalled that the president "would really flare up with that kind of contribution from the Hill [and see it as] just for show, just for rhetoric."[91]

Goodpaster also recalled how Eisenhower, as a military man, would always be clear as to his ultimate objectives in any crisis he faced. "We learn that from a very early time at West Point the one cardinal sin is to forget your mission—forget what it is that you are really trying to do and get captured by the tactics," Goodpaster said. "Eisenhower was a man who would think through to what outcome are we working here. He was very elusive in being pinned down. A 48-hour ultimatum, he would just question the sense of it. It's grandstanding, 'posturing' is the term he would use, and he was not going to do that. That's not the way to handle it."[92]

Telegrams arrived at the White House from angry state and local officials around the country. Many of these were from the president's own party, no doubt concerned about the effect a soft response to terrorism would have on their own election prospects in the fall. In one such telegram, a Republican precinct committeeman from Indianapolis told the president that "our tradition that being a U.S. citizen [means] something has been destroyed. [This is] the last straw [of] Castro of Cuba's actions against our citizens. It is time to show some Yankee guts. Tell them 'our citizens back alive and well or Castro dead.' We'd rather tell the world we will go down fighting for our principles than be overcome as sniveling cowards."[93]

The families of the hostages also expressed their concern about the situation. Some complained that they were not being kept informed about developments or exactly what the United States planned to do to get their loved ones back. "I have not been notified or contacted by any government agency as to my husband's condition or what is being done to secure his release," wrote the wife of one of the hostages to Eisenhower. "The families of these men deserve the courtesy of being informed. My husband is 62 years old and I am very much concerned about his health under these conditions. I would appreciate it very much if you would have someone keep me notified of current developments."[94]

With pressure growing for a tough response, Dulles held a press conference on July 1. He stated that the United States would never "pay blackmail to get people out." The hard-line Dulles also said that giving in to blackmail "would only encourage further efforts to use Americans as hostages."[95] To complicate matters, while the Cuban hostage situation was unfolding, the East German government put the nine Americans they were holding on public display at a news conference. The servicemen complained that they were being held as political hostages.

The day after Dulles's press conference, Eisenhower held one himself. Dulles sent the president a memorandum before the session with the media, suggesting how he should respond to questions concerning the hostage crisis in Cuba. The thrust of Dulles's memo was a strong condemnation of the kidnappers. He advised Eisenhower to state that "we strongly deplore the action taken by the rebel forces in an apparent attempt to involve the United States in Cuba's internal conflict. The rebel leaders should now understand that they have completely misjudged the American reaction to this act of irresponsibility and that it will be highly counterproductive for them."[96]

Eisenhower, though, favored a less confrontational approach, believing that a war of words between Washington and the rebels would only make matters worse for the hostages. He used his press conference to try to change the angry tone of Congress and the American public over the hostage crisis. The president stated that "we are trying to get live Americans back; we are not disposed to do anything reckless that would create consequences for them that would be final." Eisenhower continued:

> So, I would like to have that kind of thinking in our minds as we discuss this matter a bit. Now, the cases that come up are not similar in their circumstances. For example, the case in Russia, the case in East Germany, the one in China is entirely different from the one in Cuba. Here it is a dissident portion of the nation which, alleging that this country—and I might say inaccurately, but nevertheless alleging that this country has been giving improper support to the Government of Cuba, have taken these individuals apparently as hostages to secure some kind of accommodation or support for themselves.
>
> This is completely, as I say—it has no foundation in fact and it is unjustifiable to have innocent people seized to be held as hostages for this kind of a purpose. So that, in every way that we can do, we are trying to convince these people of the errors they have made and to release our people instantly.[97]

The hostages were gradually released in groups. The last Americans were freed shortly after U.S. Marines landed in Lebanon in response to instability in that country and in Iraq. The Cuban rebels, trying to find a way out of what clearly had become a major miscalculation on their part as U.S. and world opinion turned against their tactics, claimed that they were releasing the remaining Americans since they "did not want to interfere" with U.S. efforts in Lebanon.[98]

The pragmatic Eisenhower succeeded in preventing the hostage episode from turning into a full-blown crisis that could affect the cautious approach the United States was pursuing toward the Cuban Revolution at that time. He also did not fall into a terrorist trap of escalating rhetoric or hasty action that would increase the risk to the hostages' safety. By using such terms as "trying to convince" the rebels of their "errors," and not issuing any ultimatums, he avoided putting their backs against the wall and leaving them no room to save face.

Eisenhower also became the first president to attempt to educate the American people, Congress, and the media about the diversity of hostage situations. The detaining of Americans in Cuba, the Soviet Union, East Germany, and China were indeed separate situations that called for different responses. He used his press conference to make that point and to emphasize that each hostage situation needed to be assessed in terms of who the perpetrators were and what their motives might be. As Fred Greenstein, a scholar on the Eisenhower presidency, notes, Eisenhower pursued a "hidden hand presidency" during his years in office. Behind the scenes actions were deemed to be more critical than the public presidency. Eisenhower also favored a "no-personalities" approach to his office. He avoided rhetoric or public conflicts with those whom he might nevertheless have personally detested. "Rhetoric periodically has served the needs of presidents to vent their feelings rather than as a tool of leadership . . . [and] Eisenhower had a remarkable capacity to hold his tongue," writes Greenstein.[99] A more bellicose stance by Eisenhower during the hostage episode might have satisfied congressional and public anger about the Cuban rebels' actions, but it probably would have done little to help the situation.

Even though he was criticized by many for not exhibiting energetic leadership during his time in office, Eisenhower's low-key style was a calculated strategy that served him well. The president was "very skillful at kind of defusing and reducing the voltage on a particular issue," recalled Goodpaster. Eisenhower was also aware of the influential role of the media during a crisis. "The whole desire of the media, and I have to say, a lot of other people, is that every issue be taken into the White House," said Goodpaster. Eisenhower "was deliberately pushing them out and limiting his own engagement to those issues. Often times it cost him considerable criticism but he felt he could take the heat from the media." The media and Congress did give Eisenhower quite a bit of heat during the Cuban hostage episode, but the president was spared the round-the-clock media coverage that has become common in terrorist crises today. "We were trying to keep it out of crisis dimension," said Goodpaster. But "it was not easy and I think it would be much harder today even than in Eisenhower's time."[100]

The Cuban rebels had also hijacked at least two, and possibly three planes belonging to Cubana Airlines during the course of the revolution. One of these planes crashed during a forced landing in eastern Cuba in November 1958, killing seventeen people, including six Americans. Castro denied involvement in that hijacking, although survivors of the crash argued otherwise. The rebels did claim responsibility for two other hijackings in the fall of 1958. But despite these incidents—in one of the other hijackings an enlisted Navy man stationed at Guantanamo Bay was aboard, but he and twenty-five other hostages were eventually released, although a small child was reported to have died during the captivity[101]—the problem of hijackings never became a serious matter for the Eisenhower administration. These were brief episodes that were over before a crisis could develop.

By the time Eisenhower left office, the United States had experienced a diverse array of political and criminal terrorist events. The country had come full circle from its origins when American hostages were taken captive by the Barbary pirates. Now it was Cuban rebels demonstrating that hostage taking would likely be a continuing problem. The spate of bombings during the labor-business conflicts at the turn of the century and the blowing up of airplanes by criminals in the post–World War II period all pointed to the endless nature of terrorism.

But for most Americans, terrorism still seemed more of a sporadic occurrence than a continuing threat. Compared with the rest of the world, the United States and its citizens were relatively safe from the destruction and agony that terrorists wrought. There was no experience like that of Algeria, where a war of independence against the French was raging in the 1950s with terrorist atrocities a daily part of peoples' lives. Nor was there a terrorist history like that of Ireland, where the Irish Republican Army launched a terror campaign during the 1919–1921 rebellion that was a preview of what was to come decades later in Northern Ireland. Countless numbers of other countries endured periods of terrorism that remained etched in peoples' minds.

America's isolation from much of the terrorism around the world was about to change, however, as the forces of technology, which made air travel more common, and political events brought increasing numbers of Americans face to face with the terrorist threat. And a new group of American presidents would grapple with the issue of how best to respond to this growing form of violence.

The 1967 Midwood High School honor society with author (first photo, front row, fourth from left), Miriam Beeber (third row, ninth from left), and Judith Clark (second photo, second row, sixth from left). Within a few years, Beeber would be a hostage on a hijacked plane in the Jordanian desert, while Clark would join the Weather Underground radical group in the United States. Author's high school yearbook.

Miriam Beeber (center) along with two other former hostages in Cyprus after their release in September 1970. AP/Wide World Photos.

Judith Clark after her arrest in 1981 for involvement in a Brink's armored truck robbery in Nanuet, New York, that resulted in the death of a Brink's guard and of two policemen later at a roadblock in the town of Nyack. She was sentenced to seventy-five years to life in prison. NYT Pictures.

Jordanian army tanks and armored cars surround a TWA jet and a Swissair jet while Palestinian guerrillas hold hundreds of hostages inside the planes. Miriam Beeber is on the TWA jet. UPI/Bettmann.

Police surround a street in Nyack, New York, as Judith Clark and two others are arraigned for the Brink's armored truck robbery and murders. NYT Pictures.

The taking of American hostages by the Barbary pirate states led Thomas Jefferson to send the fledgling U.S. Navy to intervene. Stephen Decatur became a hero at home for his actions against the Barbary pirates. Library of Congress.

THE STRIKE IN THE COAL MINES—MEETING OF "MOLLY M'GUIRE" MEN.—DRAWN BY FRENZENY AND TAVERNIER.—[SEE PAGE 106.]

A meeting of the Molly Maguires in the coal mines of Pennsylvania. The "Mollies" engaged in violent confrontations with mine operators and foremen in the 1860s and 1870s and were portrayed as terrorists by coal company president Franklin Gowen. "It was sufficient to hang a man to declare him a Molly Maguire," Gowen once boasted. Library of Congress.

THE ANARCHIST RIOT IN CHICAGO—A DYNAMITE BOMB EXPLODING AMONG THE POLICE.—Drawn by T. de Thulstrup from Sketches and Photographs furnished by H. Jeaneret.—[See Page 313.]

A bomb explodes among a column of policemen during the Haymarket Square riot in Chicago on May 4, 1886. The police had been trying to break up a protest by thousands of people who were upset with the police for firing into a crowd of striking workers at the McCormick harvester plant the day before. Library of Congress.

Ion Perdicaris, a wealthy American-born businessman, was taken from his palace in Tangier by the Moorish tribal leader Sherif Mulai Ahmed ibn-Muhammed er Raisuli. Raisuli would defend himself against accusations that he was a criminal by writing that "all that has been said at Tangier about me . . . is wrong." *Illustrated London News.*

The *Los Angeles Times* building after a dynamite bomb exploded on October 1, 1910. The incident shocked the nation, as twenty-one nonunion workers were killed in the explosion. Henry E. Hunting-

James B. McNamara (right) admitted placing a suitcase with sixteen sticks of dynamite and a timing device in the *Times* building the night before the explosion. His older brother, John (left), who was the secretary-treasurer of the International Association of Bridge and Structural Iron Workers, confessed to being an accessory to the crime. Library of Congress.

Where President Viewed Gun Battle

Guard House

TORRESOLA

Blair House Entrance

Collazo Crumples At Foot of Steps

Guard House

Floyd Boring

Path of Toresola, Slain Assassin

Path of Collazo, Wounded Gunman

Birdzell

President Harry Truman was the target of an assassination attempt by two Puerto Rican nationalists on November 1, 1950. In a gun battle outside of Blair House, Truman's temporary residence, one of the gunmen, Griselio Torresola, was killed, and the other, Oscar Collazo, was injured. A White House policeman, Leslie Coffelt, was killed, and two others, Donald Birdzell and Joseph Downs, were injured. Reprinted with permission of *The Washington Post*.

Collazo (center) leaving district court in Washington, D.C., flanked by two unidentified prisoners. Copyright *The Washington Post*; reprinted by permission of D.C. Public Library.

Puerto Rican nationalists struck again on March 1, 1954, when they opened fire from the gallery of the House of Representatives, injuring five congressmen. One of the extremists, Raphael C. Miranda, is shown being led away from the Capitol. Copyright *The Washington Post*; reprinted by permission of D.C. Public Library.

The governor of Puerto Rico, Luis Muñoz Marín, meets with President Dwight Eisenhower to express the regret of the people of Puerto Rico for the shooting. Courtesy Dwight D. Eisenhower Library/National Park Service.

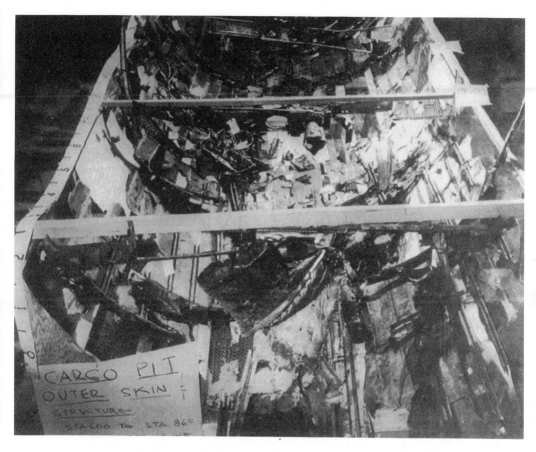

The shattered skeleton of the rear baggage compartment of a United Airlines DC-6B. The plane exploded soon after takeoff from Denver on November 1, 1955, in the first midair bombing in U.S. history in which the perpetrator was eventually caught. *Denver Post.*

John Gilbert Graham (center) appears in a Denver courtroom to face a charge of murder in connection with the bombing of the United Airlines plane. Graham put several sticks of dynamite in his mother's luggage, hoping to collect a $37,500 insurance policy on her life. Forty-four people, including Graham's mother, were killed in the bombing. *Denver Post.*

President John Kennedy at an August 1961 press conference where he implored the public to "not get overexcited" about a wave of hijackings to Cuba. Seated on the podium are (left to right) White House Press Secretary Pierre Salinger, Assistant White House Press Secretary Andrew Hatcher, and Undersecretary of State George Ball. The John F. Kennedy Library.

Roche in The Buffalo Courier-Express
"Well, whatcha goin' to do about it, Sam?"

A cartoon depicts the growing frustration in the United States over the hijackings of planes to Cuba. Although Fidel Castro did not support the air piracy, he kept one hijacked plane to press his demand for the return of several Cuban planes that had been hijacked to the United States. Buffalo and Erie County Historical Society and E. H. Butler Library, State University College at Buffalo (SUCB).

President Lyndon Johnson meets with his Cabinet to discuss the hostage crisis in the former Belgian Congo in November 1964. The United States provided transport planes for a rescue mission by Belgian paratroopers. Although two thousand hostages were saved, a number were slain while the rescue operation was under way, among them an American missionary. Courtesy Cecil Stoughton/LBJ Library Collection.

The massacre of Israeli athletes at the 1972 Olympics in Munich stunned the world and made combating terrorism a high priority for the United States. Here, a Black September terrorist wearing a mask peers out from the balcony of the Israeli Olympic squad's headquarters at the Olympic Village. UPI/Bettmann.

With U.S. diplomats being held hostage by Palestinian terrorists in the American embassy in Khartoum, President Richard Nixon said at a news conference in March 1973, "we will not pay blackmail" to gain their release. Newly arrived U.S. Ambassador Cleo Noel and departing U.S. chargé d'affaires George Moore were subsequently killed by the terrorists. Courtesy Richard Nixon Presidential Materials Project.

One of the most unusual hijackings in American history involved Croatian separatists who hijacked a TWA plane out of New York in 1976 and demanded that leaflets promoting their cause be dropped over several cities in North America and Europe. The hijackers were arrested in Paris. Zvonko Busic, the leader of the group, is on the far left, while his wife, Juliene, looks downcast. "I could never consider myself a terrorist," she would later say. AP/Wide World Photos.

3

The Threat Emerges

When John F. Kennedy took office in 1961 with the promise of a new frontier and a vigorous American foreign policy, he could not have imagined that airplane hijackings would become an issue that he would have to address before his first year was completed. There were no guidelines for dealing with the seizure of airplanes by hijackers. Even airport security was not a major concern since there had not been another midair bombing since the 1955 Denver incident. An array of other policy issues, ranging from the Cold War to the potential for instability in regions around the world, demanded the attention of the new president.

The administration, though, faced a problem with respect to maritime hijacking just two days after Kennedy was sworn in as president. On January 22, 1961, the Portuguese cruise liner *Santa Maria* was hijacked to the West Indies with 700 people aboard, including several Americans. The ship was seized by Portuguese rebels, who killed the officer of the watch and wounded other crew members. As soon as the Portuguese government learned of the hijacking, it sent naval warships in search of the vessel. The Portuguese also asked other nations for assistance in finding and detaining the hijacked ship.

The Portuguese ambassador to the United States, Pedro Theotonio Pereira, would later complain that the United States did not do all that it could have done to help the Portuguese regain control over the cruise liner. "It was first alleged that contact had been lost with the hijacked liner, a fact that appears very strange when one realizes that the Caribbean Sea is a small maritime space strongly patrolled by aircraft and ships of the American Navy. It is beyond all doubt that the latter would have intercepted the *Santa Maria* in a question of hours if they had not received orders to the contrary."[1]

Why would the United States be reluctant to help another government in its problems with hijackings at sea? For one, the United States wanted Lisbon to end its colonial rule in Africa; Kennedy eventually sent a special envoy to Portugal to make these intentions clear. Aiding a colonial power in a counterterrorist operation against rebels might therefore send the wrong signal as far as Washington was concerned. "Not even the information that there were a good number of American passengers aboard the liner was sufficient argument to outweigh the temptation to take advantage of the opportunity to publicly weaken the ties of friendship with a country of 'colonialist and medieval' concepts," said Pereira.[2]

However, Secretary of State Dean Rusk believed that the Portuguese were never quite sure what they wanted other nations to do during the hijacking. In addition, there was the practical problem of finding the ship. "We had quite a problem in locating the ship to begin with," said Rusk. "The South Atlantic is a big place. Even the use of air reconnaissance can't help too much. But our problem, from our point of view, was that we had to ask the Portuguese to be very clear as to what their own purposes were. Did they want to get the ship back? Or did they want to punish the rebels who were on board? And they finally told us that their first priority was to get the ship back."[3] The hijacking ended when the ship was spotted by a U.S. naval plane and persuaded to enter a harbor at Recife, where all the passengers and most of the crew disembarked on February 2. The leader of the hijacking, Captain Henrique Galvao, formally surrendered the next day to Brazilian authorities, and was granted political asylum along with his followers.

The *Santa Maria* episode presented a new problem for nations in dealing with maritime violence. Whereas in the days of the Barbary states the seizure of ships could be labeled as "piracy" since they were boarded from the outside, in the case of the *Santa Maria*, the ship was seized by people already on board. "We decided that we could not treat this incident as a piracy because this was a mutiny of passengers," said Rusk. ". . . And so we didn't want to proceed on the basis of piracy. We didn't want to disable the ship [and] endanger all the passengers on board. The problem of actually getting aboard this liner was quite a problem in terms of any armed resistance by the crew of the liner. So that our choices were rather meager. I think we were rather fortunate that we were able to winkle this ship into a Brazilian harbor where then processes of law can take over. But we had some trouble with the Portuguese in clarify[ing] what it was they really wanted."[4]

Since the United States was not the primary target of the *Santa Maria* hijacking, the incident did not raise serious concerns among the American public concerning the safety of cruise liners. But when a rash of airplane hijackings erupted a few months later, the reaction in Congress and around the country was quite different.

Kennedy and Hijackings

On May 1, a National Airlines twin-engine Convair en route to Key West from Marathon, Florida, was hijacked to Cuba by a passenger wielding both a pistol and a knife. Cuban President Fidel Castro returned the plane and the ten passengers and crew that same day. The hijacker, Antulio Ramirez Ortiz, a Puerto Rican extremist, claimed that his goal was to assassinate Castro. The next hijacking occurred on July 24, when an American citizen of Cuban birth, Alfredo Oquendo, entered the cockpit of an Eastern Airlines turboprop Electra bound for Tampa from Miami after a stewardess had passed through the door. Oquendo forced the pilot to fly to Cuba at gunpoint. The thirty-one passengers and crew were allowed to return to the United States the next day on another plane. Castro, however, kept the Electra plane, stating that he would surrender it to the United Nations Security Council only if the U.S. returned ten Cuban aircraft that had been hijacked to the United States. Those aircraft had been sold, or were in the process of being sold, in Florida under writs of execution related to a judgment in favor of an American company against Cuba.[5]

The wave of hijackings continued the next day when a man despondent over his marital problems attempted to seize a Mohawk Airlines plane on the ground in Binghamton, New York, with a .22 caliber pistol. He intended to commit suicide, but was persuaded by the copilot to first telephone his wife. He was then arrested by police at the airport. Another attempted hijacking occurred on August 1, when a man who was being chased by the California Highway Patrol boarded a Pacific Airlines DC-3 without a ticket and demanded that it fly to Arkansas so he could visit his estranged wife. When ordered to deplane, he shot a passenger agent and then shot the pilot when he refused to take off. He was finally disarmed by a copilot and several passengers. The pilot was blinded in the attack. The hijacker stated that he got the idea for his crime from newspaper reports about the Eastern Airlines hijacking.[6]

The hijackings to Cuba resumed on August 3, when a Continental Airlines B-707 jet en route from Phoenix to El Paso was seized by an ex-convict and his son. They ordered the plane to fly to Havana, but FBI agents, border patrol, and local police sharpshooters shot out the tires of the plane while it was on the ground in El Paso for refueling. The two hijackers were captured, and President Kennedy, clearly concerned about the epidemic of hijackings, sent telegrams of commendation to the law enforcement officers who had helped resolve the incident.[7]

The El Paso hijacking represented the fifth case of an airplane hijacking or attempted hijacking in just over three months. Although some of these were carried out by people with psychological problems or ex-convicts with no connection to any terrorist campaign orchestrated by Fidel Castro, there was nevertheless growing anger and frustration in Congress and among the American public. Senator Clair Engle, a Democrat from California, coined a phrase that would become familiar in later years, calling the hijackings "act[s] of war [that] should be dealt with accordingly." Representative Bruce Alger, a Republican from Texas, referring to the Eastern Airlines plane that Castro refused to return, said that the United States should invade Cuba if it was not returned immediately. Senator Ralph Yarborough, a Democrat from Texas, called for an embargo and blockade of Cuba if the plane was not returned, claiming that the American people "have been very, very, patient with Mr. Communist Castro, but patience ceases to be a virtue when it permits the practice of international piracy and banditry." Yarborough believed that U.S. national security interests were threatened by this new form of terrorism. "This banditry, if continued, will ultimately ground the American air fleet," Yarborough said, "because passengers will simply refuse to ride planes if Communist bandits are permitted to seize them at will."[8] And a cartoon in the *New York Times* following the Eastern Airlines hijacking illustrated the growing pressure that Kennedy was coming under to take strong measures against Castro. The cartoon showed a confident Castro, smoking a big cigar and holding the Eastern Airlines Electra plane in one hand, exclaiming, "Well, whatcha goin' to do about it, Sam?"[9]

The Kennedy administration, though, avoided rhetoric in responding to the criticism that it was not doing enough to end the hijackings. Instead, it focused on ways to strengthen aviation security. Kennedy supported a bill to make the hijacking of an airliner punishable by life imprisonment. The Federal Aviation Administration sent a telegram to all airlines serving Florida on July 27, requesting that they bolt the cockpit door and provide sidearms to crew members if they had recent training and were proficient in such weapons. Special civil air regulations were adopted that prohibited people from assaulting, threatening, intimidating, or interfering with crew members or diverting a flight. There were also regulations against carrying concealed weapons aboard aircraft. A directive was sent on August 3 to all U.S. airlines requiring that passengers boarding an aircraft be closely watched by senior station or traffic personnel and that the airlines establish liaison with local law enforcement officials. The July directive to airlines in Florida was extended to all airlines. A $10,000 reward for capturing hijackers was also offered through the Department of Justice. However, after several meetings with air carriers and airline pilots, it was determined that there was "no panacea" to airplane hijackings.[10]

Among the measures the administration considered to prevent hijackings was that the U.S. Immigration and Naturalization Service make available several hundred border patrolmen to ride airliners as guards, either in uniform or plain clothes. While that number would be "completely insufficient for guarding all flights . . . the publicity might deter potential hijackers, none of whom appear to be expert gunmen." Consideration was given to using U.S. Marines for guard duty on planes, but the Pentagon opposed that idea. The FBI also indicated that it would not be able to supply agents for anti-hijacking duty, although in subsequent years all FBI agents were required to be armed when flying aboard commercial aircraft, and in effect performed anti-hijacking duties. The FAA began working with firms to design metal devices at airport gates for detecting weapons, but it was determined that "this does not appear to be promising as a rapid solution." The FAA also consulted with the Air Defense Command to develop codes that would allow hijacked crews to signal the ground when there was trouble and if they wanted to have intercept fighters come to their aid. However, it was decided that this type of action could endanger the aircraft and make the hijackers nervous. There was also consideration by the FAA of providing stewardesses with "knockout drops" to give to hijackers if they could be persuaded to have coffee or champagne during their hijacking. A previous hijacker had in fact taken a drink after announcing the plane had been hijacked.[11]

In the midst of the rising tide of anger in both Congress and the public over the lack of a "tough" U.S. response to the hijackings, another plane was hijacked on August 9. This incident touched off an even angrier session in Congress than the one following the El Paso hijacking. In fact, for many congressmen and the public, it was the last straw, and they demanded action. The attention given to this hijacking, both in the press and in Congress, overshadowed concern over the brewing crisis in Berlin, which a few days later would see the construction of the Berlin Wall. Kennedy interrupted deliberations over the Berlin issue to address this latest hijacking.

The August 9 hijacking was perpetrated by a Frenchman, Albert Charles Cadon, who seized a Pan American World Airways DC-8 shortly after takeoff from Mexico City on a scheduled flight to Guatemala City.

Cadon ordered the plane diverted to Cuba, but not for any reasons connected with Castro or the situation in that country. Cadon told the crew, "I am not a Communist, and not a Cuban. I do not like the way Washington interfered in the Algerian situation—I am taking this means to show my protest."[12] Despite the absence of any connection to Cuba, rumors quickly circulated in Washington that Castro had orchestrated this latest hijacking.

No one was more surprised than Castro when news of the hijacking hit the wires. The Cuban dictator had grown tired of the planes that kept coming to his country and causing problems with the United States. Yet until the August 9 hijacking, these matters were basically between the United States and Cuba. This time, though, it became an international incident, for one of the passengers on board the plane was the Colombian foreign minister, Julio Cesar Turbay Ayala, along with his wife and other Colombian officials. To make matters worse for Castro, Turbay was one of his most bitter critics, and had been in Mexico City to confer with President Adolfo Lopez Mateos on concerted action against Cuba. Turbay had called for a meeting of Latin American foreign ministers to demand that Castro define his role and relations to the inter-American system.[13]

Castro was reported to be "mortified" when he learned that Turbay was on the hijacked plane coming to Havana.[14] The Colombian and Mexican governments issued protests to Cuba, still assuming Castro had ordered the hijacking. Colombia said it would consider any unjustified delay in allowing Turbay and his party to continue to their original destination an act of hostility. A telegram was sent to Kennedy from a Colombian, Enrique Ariza, urging the president to take strong action against Castro: "It is not possible that your Excellency will permit more cowardly insults and crimes by Cuba. As a Colombian, I am distressed over the fate that may be suffered by Foreign Minister Turbay and by compatriots. The whole world is with your Excellency. Cuban bullies should receive exemplary punishment. See that you are respected."[15]

Meanwhile, in Havana, Castro pulled out the red-carpet treatment for Turbay and his party. He sent his foreign minister, Raul Roa, to greet Turbay at the airport and then had dinner with him. Castro quickly arranged for all passengers to be allowed to continue on their trip and the plane was returned to the United States. Wishing to avoid yet another escalation in the hijacking situation, Cuba issued a statement that "the return of the plane is proof of the repeated statements issued recently in a note addressed to the U.S. government concerning the piracy of airplanes and about the necessity that the two governments should adopt the necessary steps to prevent the continuation of such incidents."[16]

In Washington, the mood in Congress was one of anger and frustration over the growing number of hijackings. Terrorism is a dramatic act by itself; many congressmen added to the drama with theatrical antics as word of the Pan Am hijacking reached the halls of Congress. One senator, Andrew Schoeppel, a Republican from Kansas, interrupted a Senate debate on the 1961 Foreign Assistance Act to read to his colleagues the news wire account of the unfolding hijacking. Another senator, Warren Magnuson, a Democrat from Washington, called for the suspension of Senate rules so that a week-old anti-hijacking bill—which provided for a mandatory life sentence for hijackers—could be immediately considered. Magnuson then amended the bill to allow juries to impose the death penalty. The level of excitement on the floor was such that Senator Thruston Morton, a Republican from Kansas, had to shout for calm. He complained that what was unfolding in Congress was "ticker-tape legislation." Morton told his colleagues that "this is no time to legislate on this matter. This is 'ticker-tape legislation' we are talking about. We are all excited by something that is on the ticker. Let us sit down. Let us think about this a little bit. Let us know what we are doing. Let us not sweep something through here in an emotional fit just because it happens to be politically popular at home or elsewhere."[17]

The range of calls for tough measures crossed all parts of the political spectrum. Senator Styles Bridges, a Republican from New Hampshire, stated that "the issue is far greater than a single airplane. It is, in simple terms, merely a matter of whether or not the United States, as a great sovereign nation, is going to permit its citizens to be kidnaped, its commercial carriers hijacked, and be subjected to ridicule by Castro and his Communist co-conspirators." Senator Robert Kerr, a Democrat from Oklahoma, called for a forty-eight-hour ultimatum; Senators Barry Goldwater, a Republican from Arizona, and Hubert Humphrey, a Democrat from Minnesota, called for a twenty-four-hour ultimatum; and Senator Strom Thurmond, a Democrat from South Carolina, not to be outdone, called for a twelve-hour ultimatum to Castro to return the plane or face a U.S. invasion. Typical of the sentiment in Washington was the comment by Representative James Haley, a Democrat from Florida. Haley chided the Kennedy administration for not taking strong measures against hijackings: "Maybe they will take some action after the Cubans steal one of the helicopters off the White House lawn."[18]

Senator Gale McGee, a Democrat from Wyoming, was making a speech in the Senate in support of the 1961 Foreign Assistance Act when news of the hijacking interrupted the debate. McGee warned his colleagues against hasty action: "When there is such a hijacking," McGee said on the Senate floor, "there is a strong temptation to seek a quick solution. The incident is aggravating and disturbing and makes one wish to take quick action, and the great danger is that we shall take a drastic step in an attempt to appease an emotional frustration. This action may do a great deal of harm, instead of good, which would result from a sober consideration and solution of the problem."[19]

The immediate problem for Kennedy was how to defuse the rising tide of anger and frustration over terrorism that was brewing not only in Congress, but across the nation. This hijacking occurred at the same time that the Inter-American Council for Social and Economic Cooperation was meeting in Montevideo, Uruguay, to adopt the charter of the Alliance for Progress, Kennedy's major program for development in Latin America. The Uruguay meeting represented an opportunity for Kennedy to highlight his plans for improving the plight of Latin American nations with a massive program of economic aid and political and social development. The danger was that overreactions to the wave of hijackings could divert attention away from the policies and goals that the administration wanted to pursue in Latin America.

An indication of the growing anger among the American people was illustrated in an article in the *Washington Post* that was appropriately titled "Impatient Nation Taking on Belligerent Mood." The article pointed out that the plane hijackings, following the Bay of Pigs fiasco, put an "increasing number of Americans . . . in a 'let's do something' mood and damn the consequence. . . . For many people, confronting Khrushchev militarily might seem too dangerous, but they believe that it would not be very risky to take a poke at Castro. The plane incidents seem to provide an occasion . . . [even though] so far no complicity in the hijackings by the Cuban government has been proven. The fact that the Cubans are holding one plane seems enough."[20]

Another article in the *New York Times* called for Kennedy to use his scheduled press conference of August 10—the day after the Pan Am hijacking—to make a strong statement against Castro and hijackings: "The task of reversing growing world doubts of the diplomatic resourcefulness and internal vigor of the United States confronts President Kennedy with unusual imperativeness at his news conference today. The Administration's laissez-faire policy toward the Castro regime, following its failure to give military support to the [Bay of Pigs] invasion of the anti-Castro forces it had equipped and countenanced, had begun to put this government on the defensive before the latest hijacking incident occurred. But now this policy has become a political and popular liability among the American people. . . . Today's demands on Havana require the presidential imprimatur which strong words from Mr. Kennedy alone can supply."[21] An editorial on the front page of the *Los Angeles Times* called for the United States "to destroy this pirate nest." It pointed out that "we have made war for less injury than Castro has done us and for less threat to our legitimate interests in this hemisphere. . . . The

United States ought to move now and move with all necessary military strength.""[22]

Kennedy, though, did not want to be forced into taking hasty action against Castro. "First of all, Kennedy felt that they were not Cubans who had come to the United States to hijack, so it was not a Cuban terrorist act against the United States," said Pierre Salinger, Kennedy's press secretary. "And second, he was still in that mood of heavy embarrassment about the Bay of Pigs, which he considered the most stupid thing that he ever did. Time after time he would say, 'Why did I allow this whole operation to be handed over to me by a previous administration and not bring in my own people to deal with it,' which he didn't. He didn't deal with the people that had surrounded him during the campaign and whom he had confidence in. But he dealt with CIA people, with military people that he never met before and took their word for it, whereas if he had brought it in to some of the people around him they would have said 'Hey, wait a minute, this is not going to work.' He had also been forced by this mistake to impose a boycott on Cuban products in the United States, and he didn't see any reason why there was any necessity of imposing anything else on Castro as long as Castro was willing to send the planes back and liberate the people. He did hold the hijackers but at some point later on he gave them back. So that was mostly his attitude. And then of course he was also very concerned about launching the Alliance for Progress and that was in the Latin American context of which Cuba was a member even though it was a Communist country. Mexico was quite linked to Cuba at that time. They had good relations. He thought that might interfere with what he was trying to do on the Alliance for Progress."[23]

In fact, Kennedy's reluctance to force a confrontation with Cuba was evident in his own skepticism about having to ban Cuban products in the United States. Salinger remembers an unusual request the president made one evening at five o'clock: "The president calls me into his office and said, 'I need your help.' I said, 'What do you want, Mr. President?' He said, 'I want some cigars, Cuban cigars.' He smoked the little cigar called a Petite Upmann. I said, 'How many do you want?' He said, 'A thousand.' I said, 'When do you need them?' He said, 'Tomorrow morning.' I said, 'That's a tough assignment.' I smoked Cuban cigars in those days. The next morning he calls me into his office at eight o'clock and says, 'How did you do?' I said, 'Very well. I got twelve hundred.' [He says], 'Great!' He [then] pulls out the decree and signs the ban on Cuban products."[24]

Kennedy was determined to prevent the furor over the hijackings from diverting attention away from his foreign policy goals. Even though the August 9 hijacking was already over when he held his press conference, there was still the prospect of additional hijackings. Kennedy, like Eisenhower before him, decided to use his press conference to help mold public and congressional opinion about how the United States should respond to terrorism. The president emphasized that the objectives of the Uruguay conference must take precedence over emotional reactions to hijackings:

> I hope that all of us will not get so occupied with other matters occurring in this hemisphere that we forget perhaps one of the most significant meetings in the history of the Western Hemisphere, in this century, is now taking place in Montevideo, and that if we can reach a successful conclusion we can come out of that meeting, all of these republics with a real hope that we can move ahead in improving the life of the people of this continent. And that's where the great struggle is going on. If we fail there, and if we fail here in the United States to recognize that this is the issue to which we should now be devoting our attention, then the spread of communism is—and the failure of the free society—is going to be far more assured.

Kennedy outlined the steps that the United States was taking to stem the tide of hijackings:

> We . . . have ordered today on a number of our planes a border patrolman who will ride on a number of our flights. We are going to insist that every airplane lock its door, and that the door be strong enough to prevent entrance by force, and that the possession of the key be held by those inside the cabin so that pressure cannot be put on the members of the crew outside to have the door opened.
>
> In addition, I am hopeful that governments everywhere will use their maximum influence to discourage this kind of action which endangers the lives of the crew and of the people involved, and which is an exercise in futility. And that is the view of this government and we will take every means that we can to prevent not only the hijacking of our own planes but the hijacking of other planes. I'm hopeful that all concerned will do the same. It just endangers the lives of people who should be protected.

In specific reference to the public furor over the hijackings and the faulty accusations that they were orchestrated by Castro, Kennedy issued a plea for calm over this new form of piracy:

> Because yesterday's hijacking aroused such great public excitement, and the week before, even though we now see that neither one of these hijackings was done by Cubans, does, it seems to me, make it important

for us to act with the prudence which is worthy of a great power which bears responsibilities for the defense of freedom all around the globe, and not to make determinations on policy until our information is more complete. . . . The point I want to make is that what is going on in Montevideo is so important that we should not get overexcited about matters when our information is so faulty, so incomplete.[25]

For Senator McGee, Kennedy's press conference was a major boost to those who were trying to counter the bellicose statements about terrorism and Cuba that were coming from some quarters in Congress. "I still regard it as one of his high points. I thought that at that dramatic moment, when there was such wild stuff coming from individuals because they wanted to be heard, . . . Kennedy became a rallying point. . . . He had the guts to stand."[26]

Kennedy's determination not to allow the hijackings to divert attention away from other issues was characteristic of his presidency. Dean Rusk recalled that Kennedy "was very conscious of the fact that he was the first president born in the twentieth century. And he was very active in taking a look at the underlying policies of the conventional wisdom of the day and maybe getting a fresh start on some of it. But he was a man who managed to keep his eye on the main ball. For example, in his handling of the Cuban missile crisis, he kept his eye on the business of getting the missiles out of Cuba. He didn't want to let other factors influence his decision. So that I think he looked upon these acts of terrorism as more or less unwelcome, but side shows to the main policies that he was interested in. That attitude of his doesn't surprise me at all."[27]

McGeorge Bundy, Kennedy's special assistant for national security affairs, notes that "we didn't really have a sense that the top priority was to find a way of toppling Castro, and therefore it would not have occurred to Kennedy to use something as accidental and episodic as these hijackings to stir up political pressure or to be his reason for a stronger program of direct hostility to Castro, because his mind is simply not working that way. He isn't just trying to turn off the hijackers when he shifts the spotlight towards the Alliance for Progress. He's trying to get attention to what he himself thinks is the most important thing in American policy."[28]

Kennedy succeeded in avoiding any clash with Cuba over the issue of hijackings. A dispute would likely have disrupted the Montevideo conference, which Cuba was also attending. The Inter-American Council for Economic and Social Cooperation eventually adopted the charter of the Alliance for Progress, and the Kennedy administration was able to again focus attention on the issues of Latin America and Europe. Congress and the public, who had been so upset over the hijacking episodes, soon shifted their attention to the building of the Berlin Wall and the heating up of the Cold War.

Johnson and Hostages

Hijackings remained a major concern for the international community throughout the 1960s. The first international agreement to address the hijacking problem was reached in 1963. "The Tokyo Convention on Offenses and Certain Other Acts Committed On Board Aircraft" required countries to establish jurisdiction over offenses that jeopardize the safety of aircraft or passengers that occur outside their own territory. The convention assigned the country where the aircraft was registered jurisdiction over the incident, regardless of the location of the aircraft during or after the hijacking. But it did not oblige signatories to prosecute or extradite hijackers. Stricter measures would be agreed to in the 1970s.

Better physical security measures at airports, along with Castro's willingness to return hijackers and planes to the United States, temporarily halted the wave of hijackings to Cuba. However, the Johnson administration did face a major crisis in Africa that involved the centuries-old practice of hostage taking. This time it would not be Barbary pirates or Cuban rebels that were abducting American citizens, but rather guerrillas in the Congo. The situation in that troubled country would eventually deteriorate to the point where it required the U.S. to launch its first counterterrorist military rescue operation in the postwar period.

The Congo was a perennial headache for the United States throughout the 1960s. When Belgium granted independence to its African colony on June 30, 1960, it opened up an internal power vacuum that was soon filled with tribal and political conflicts. For the next several years, there would be fighting between rebel troops and the Congolese government and United Nations forces. The United States provided military assistance to the U.N. and the Congolese troops, including airlifting U.N. forces. The United Nations, however, withdrew from the Congo on June 30, 1964, after four years of futilely attempting to maintain peace.

The situation rapidly deteriorated throughout the summer of 1964. Rebel forces made gains in many parts of the country, eventually capturing Stanleyville, the capital of Katanga province. The United States, meanwhile, had reversed its initial opposition to Moshe Tshombe, who in 1960 had led Katanga in revolt. Now he was the Congolese prime minister and faced a rebellion of his own throughout the country. Tshombe was not a popular figure in Africa, having used white mercenaries during his secessionist war in 1960. The United States nevertheless provided aid to Tshombe and the Congolese army since U.S. policy was to support the central Congolese government—no matter who the leader was—in order to prevent instability from tearing apart the country and potentially leading to Communist inroads in the region. The United States and Belgium therefore increased their security assistance to the Congo in the aftermath of the U.N. pullout, with the Johnson administration sending four C-130 transport planes with maintenance and guard personnel to provide airlift for the Congolese forces.

The guerrilla war moved into the realm of international terrorism when the rebels seized foreign hostages in August 1964. The rebels sent a message to U.N. Secretary General U Thant that they were now holding all white men, women, and children as hostages against air raids by the Congolese central government. Most of the hostages were Belgians, but there were also forty Americans, including officials from the U.S. consulate in Stanleyville. In October, the rebels announced that an American missionary, Dr. Paul Carlson, had been arrested on charges of "spying" and would be executed.[29]

The American and other foreign hostages were treated extremely poorly by the rebels. Intelligence reports reaching the White House told of swollen and bruised bodies, and that some U.S. consulate officials had been forced to eat American flags that were taken from their cars.[30] Several foreign hostages were beaten to death, while others were shot. As is true in most hostage episodes, those who controlled the fate of the captives used them to either raise or lower the tension level of the conflict. Thus, at one time during the crisis, the rebels stated that they would bury twelve Americans alive for each Congolese rebel or citizen who was killed.[31] But when the Congolese army was on the verge of attacking the rebel stronghold in Stanleyville and delivering a potentially devastating defeat to the guerrillas, they offered to negotiate with the United States concerning the fate of the hostages. Their demand was that the United States help bring about a cease-fire in the war—a tactic aimed at stalling for time while the rebels could regroup.

Intelligence assessments of the hostage situation were continually updated as new information was received. At times the assessments provided hope that the hostages' lives might be spared. For example, on October 20, a CIA report concluded that the "threat to the lives of the Americans in Stanleyville—including the five-man U.S. consular staff and some twenty to twenty-five missionaries, missionary wives, and children—apparently has abated for the time being." A rebel leader had sent a message to the King of Burundi assuring him that the "lives of foreign citizens in Stanleyville are not in danger."[32] But the rebels' future plans could not be predicted, and the situation remained tense into November.

Early that month, Congolese troops liberated the town of Kindu and rescued several European hostages. The former captives reported that the rebels were ready to kill them when they saw the central government troops advancing on their positions. This caused concern in Washington that a Congolese army assault on Stanleyville, which was imminent, would be the period of greatest danger for the hostages. Since there were no assurances that the government troops could get to the hostages before the rebels would massacre them, the sense of urgency to implement a rescue operation grew both in Washington and Brussels. Reports about cannibalism did not help matters.

Urgent messages and cables began pouring into Washington from the embassy in Leopoldville. The explosive political nature of the Congo and the likelihood of anti-U.S. sentiment throughout Africa following any unilateral U.S. military effort led the Johnson administration to seek international cooperation for an effort to save the hostages. Earlier in the crisis, McGeorge Bundy, who was now Johnson's national security adviser, sent the president a memo advising against the use of U.S. Special Forces unless other nations were also willing to participate. The possibility of using C-130 transports to evacuate Americans was kept open.[33]

Johnson, meanwhile, received personal pleas from the family of the hostage Carlson to do everything he could to save the missionary's life. While the United States and Belgium were discussing potential joint efforts to rescue the hostages, Rusk received a telephone call from the Belgian foreign minister, Paul Spaak, who had just left a cabinet meeting. Spaak needed clarification about the U.S. position on a possible rescue operation. "I said, 'Well, our position is to do whatever Belgium wants to do,' " Rusk recalled. " 'They're your paratroopers. If you decide you want to commit them, we'll make the planes available and do everything we can to make the matter a success. But if you decide that you do not wish to commit the Belgian paratroopers, we will understand.' There was a silent moment on the other end of the phone. He said, 'Do you mean that the great United States of America is leaving this decision to Belgium?' I said, 'Yes, that's the position.' He said, 'That's incredible. No decision affecting Belgium has ever been made in Belgium before!' "[34]

The Belgians decided to commit their paratroopers, and the United States provided the transport planes. The paratroopers moved first to the British Ascension Island in the South Atlantic—which was twenty-two hours from Stanleyville—after gaining approval from the British government. The Belgians then moved their force to Kamina in Katanga province, which was only four hours from Stanleyville. Bundy sent a memo to Johnson on November 16, telling him that it was best to allow the Belgians to take the lead on the rescue operation since "they know the Congolese better, and their nationals [who were taken hostage] outnumber ours by 30 to 1." Bundy also informed Johnson that the United States still hoped that a rescue operation would not be necessary "because any action of this kind will have real political cost in the Congo and may involve the death[s] of innocent Americans by panicky rebel reaction. Nevertheless, the possible cost of opposing the Belgian recommendation seems clearly greater than the cost of concurrence."[35]

A State Department Bureau of Intelligence and Research (INR) assessment pointed out one problem facing the United States—as would be true in later hostage episodes in Lebanon—was determining who actually controlled the fate of the hostages. The assessment questioned the ability of the Congolese rebel leaders to deliver upon any negotiated deal. "The real danger to the hostages derives not from the political leaders but from the "simbas" [troops] and particularly the "jeunesse" [youths], over whom the political leaders have little control. A "negotiated solution" . . . is devalued since there is no assurance that the political leaders could deliver their end of the bargain."[36]

The INR assessment also pointed to the possible negative effects of a U.S. military operation to rescue the hostages. "No amount of careful calculation probably will be able to give us a precise reading on the degree of risk to the hostages in the absence of an air rescue operation. We can only conclude that the Stanleyville air drop probably would reduce the risk to the Stanleyville hostages, while somewhat increasing the risk to non-Congolese in the outlying towns. Finally, given these many imponderables, we cannot strike anything approaching an accurate balance between gains and losses if one does or does not proceed with Dragon Rouge [the code name for the rescue operation]."[37]

The situation deteriorated rapidly in November. The U.S. mission in Geneva sent a cable to Washington on November 3, advising that the rebel military position was weakening in the wake of advances by the Congolese army. The cable warned that the "rebels may be panicking," which "makes concern for hostages even greater." Efforts for a diplomatic solution were accelerated. One faint hope centered on the possibility of African leaders convincing the rebels that they would be held "responsible in the eyes of [the] world" for the fate of the hostages. But the cable concluded that little could be expected from further diplomatic efforts, and that the rebels can "be expected to become more barbarous and unapproachable as their fortunes wane."[38]

The Congolese rebels demonstrated a high skill in using the hostages for maximum effect. On November 17, Stanleyville Radio announced the conviction and condemnation to death of Carlson for "espionage." The United States protested to the OAU Ad Hoc Commission, which was under the leadership of President Jomo Kenyatta of Kenya, urging that steps be taken to prevent the killing. The Johnson administration also sent a message to rebel leaders saying that "it holds the authorities at Stanleyville directly and personally responsible for the safety of Dr. Carlson and of all American citizens in areas under your control."[39]

Pressure mounted on the Johnson administration from some African states to convince Tshombe to agree to a cease-fire, even for a week, in order to prevent the hostages from being killed. But the situation was greatly complicated by the fact that the United States could not dictate to Tshombe what he should do in his war with the rebels, especially when he was finally gaining the upper hand. Any U.S. attempt to impose a cease-fire would make it appear that the Johnson administration was only concerned with saving "white" hostages when thousands of Africans had already lost their lives in the turmoil in the Congo. This theme was repeatedly stressed in U.S. government assessments of the crisis. Furthermore, Tshombe had a different perception of the effect of a massacre of the hostages. "The hostages do not have the same value for Tshombe as they do for the West," the INR assessment of November 18 stated. "Atrocities against the hostages, he might reason, would further discredit the rebels and end all talk in Washington and Brussels of some form of political accommodation."[40]

In one of the earliest references in the age of terrorism to the distinction between "negotiating" and "talking," the U.S. embassy in Leopoldville advised that the Johnson administration consider "talking with [rebel leaders] even at some risk to our relations with GDRC [Congo government] if these talks, as against negotiations, could lead to saving Carlson or at least buy [the] hostages time. However, we are convinced that any real negotiations with rebels at this time are against our interests if price involves slow down of military advance on Stanleyville. In view of not only Belgian and U.S. Embassies but also in view of all our knowledgeable diplomatic colleagues here, only sustained military pressure likely to save lives of hostages. If protracted negotiations start and we or GDRC do not go along with rebel demands, it quite possible that first Carlson and then other Americans and Belgians will be executed to show rebels mean business. . . ."[41]

The United States did not negotiate for the release of the hostages. Meanwhile, on November 21, the five American consular officials, along with four other American hostages and several European and Congolese hostages, were taken to the Lumumba monument in Stanleyville and exhibited before a crowd of five thousand rebel supporters. Some of the hostages were beaten in front of the angry crowd and told by the rebels that they had been sentenced to death.[42]

With the risk to the hostages' lives increasing daily, the decision was made to launch a rescue operation on November 24. With lightning action, six hundred Belgian paratroopers landed with the assistance of twenty U.S. Air Force C-130 transport planes. The Belgian paratroopers linked up with the Congolese army and secured the Stanleyville airport with minimum casualties and little resistance. Upon seeing the approaching paratroopers, the rebels fired indiscriminately into a group of hostages at the airport hotel, killing fifteen. The rebels then gathered 250 more hostages into Lumumba Square and again fired into the crowd, killing several more. The rebels were about to shoot more hostages when paratroopers rescued them while government troops gained control of the city. When the operation was complete, thirty-one hostages were dead, including two Americans. One of the dead hostages was Carlson. One other American had been killed by the rebels earlier in the year.

After completing the rescue operation in Stanleyville, the Belgian paratroopers moved on to the town of Paulis, where the rebels were holding additional hostages. The entire operation took about four days and there were 101 hostages killed. However, more than two thousand hostages of twenty different nationalities, including Congolese, were saved and evacuated by U.S. aircraft to Leopoldville.

Dean Rusk recalled that the Congo rescue operation "was very nip and go. Our own consulate general, who was among the hostages, told us after his release that he thought that if the paratroopers had arrived maybe five or ten minutes later, then a lot of them would have been killed because the simbas who were holding the prisoners were drugged and were [going] around firing tommy guns in the air and were about to turn on the people themselves."[43] In light of the problems that the United States would face in subsequent years with respect to using military operations to rescue hostages, the Congo operation was a resounding success. It had required international cooperation among three countries, with the United States, Belgium, and Great Britain all preparing together for the mission in utmost secrecy.

But it also demonstrated that the success of a counterterrorist military operation depended upon the unique aspects of each hostage situation. Cyrus Vance, who in 1980 opposed the military effort to free the hostages in Iran and would resign his post as secretary of state because of that operation, nevertheless supported the Congo rescue mission when he was deputy secretary of defense in the Johnson administration. "That was very different," Vance said. "Those [hostages] were all being held in a discreet place . . . and it was therefore possible to plan a rescue operation where you can come in and extract [them]. Therefore, you could plan how to help [the Belgians] get them out without the kind of danger to the hostages that you have in a situation such as we faced in Iran: a major urban center where we didn't even know the exact location of where they were being held. So the Congo kind of operation was a very simple kind of an operation."[44]

President Johnson strenuously avoided any personal or emotional attachment to the hostage crisis, a fate that future presidents such as Jimmy Carter and Ronald Reagan would not escape. Working in Johnson's favor was the fact that in the mid-1960s there was not the extensive media attention, particularly televised coverage, of hostage crises that is now commonplace. Also, the Congo crisis occurred right in the midst of the 1964 presidential campaign, and Johnson's attention was naturally focused on the business of getting elected. Jack Valenti, the special assistant to the president, recalled that during the campaign, the hostage crisis "was not something that the president lived and died with every day. Keep in mind that the most ineffective president I know is one who is out of office. So the first thing that you have to do is to stay in office. . . . I don't recollect [the hostage situation] as quickening his pulse and causing him sleepless nights."[45]

Johnson, who would become emotionally involved with the casualties that would result from the Vietnam War, was not any less compassionate over the fate of Americans taken hostage than recent presidents. However, he most likely viewed a hostage episode differently from a situation where peoples' lives were at risk due to his own decisions. "Hostages are different than adventures in which the president orders men into battle," said Valenti. "I think when you order troops to go to the Dominican Republic or Vietnam . . . casualties have a personal subtraction inside your gut because you forced them in there. Hostages are a different proposition. So while there is a grieving and a regret that goes deep in one's stomach and heart, I really don't think that it's the same kind of emotional wrenching where you ordered somebody into battle and they come back in a body bag. That extracts upon you a lot of pain and torment."[46]

Johnson, as was true for Eisenhower and Kennedy before him, used a press conference to set the tone for how the nation should react to terrorism. When asked by a reporter if "you plan any sort of reprisals against the rebels in the Congo to hold them responsible for killing Americans," Johnson avoided falling into a trap of escalating rhetoric and bellicose warnings. He wanted to make sure that people understood it was not just Americans who suffered from the terrorism in the Congo. He replied that the United States is "outraged by the actions that were taken not only against some of our people but against the Congolese themselves that [has] resulted in thousands losing their lives. . . . We certainly hope that the perpetrators of these outrages are brought to justice." Johnson attempted to put the Congo crisis in perspective for the public:

> I would like to stress to those of you here . . . this morning that the United States has no political goals to impose upon the Congo. We seek

no narrow interest. We have no economic gain to be served in the Congo. We seek to impose no political solution, neither our own nor that of some other outsider. We have tried only to meet our obligations to the legitimate government, and to its efforts to achieve unity and stability and reconciliation in the Congo. So we hope now that everyone who has had a part in this four-year agony of the Congo will bury past differences and try to work together in that spirit of compassion, to help reach these goals of unity and stability and reconciliation.[47]

Unfortunately, the Congo continued to experience instability throughout the 1960s. U.S. transport planes were once again needed to aid the central government in putting down a rebellion and rescuing several hostages in 1967. The most drawn-out hostage crisis for Johnson occurred during his last year in office when a U.S. naval intelligence ship, the *Pueblo,* was seized by North Korea in January 1968. The failure of the crew to take military action when challenged by the North Koreans resulted in a considerable amount of criticism in the United States. Yet this controversy did not diminish the pressure that was put on the Johnson administration to do something to get the hostages back. The North Koreans informed the United States that the hostages would be released if the United States stated that the ship had been in North Korean territorial waters, which was not true. Johnson refused to make such a statement, and the hostage drama dragged on for eleven months.

National Security Adviser Walt Rostow recalled the deliberations in Washington after the ship and crew were seized. "The options were, we can show pique and bomb somebody, or bomb the ship [and] sink it," said Rostow. "[But] all you do is leave those guys up there." Thus, unlike the Congo hostage crisis, Johnson dismissed the possibility of a military rescue operation right from the start. Rostow went on: "There were thoughtful discussions on what our interest was. The *Pueblo* crisis occurred in the middle of the Tet offensive and it was meant to divert us. We weren't about to be diverted."[48]

In addition to the concern for becoming involved in a military conflict with North Korea at a time of crisis in the Vietnam War—the 1968 Tet offensive demonstrated that the North Vietnamese had the ability to launch a major offensive throughout South Vietnam—there was also the problem of locating exactly where the hostages were. "The president was concerned about the lives of the hostages and felt there was no easy, simple way to find out where they were and to rescue them," said Cyrus Vance. "The best thing to do was to accept it as a fait accompli and figure out how you were going to work over time a way of getting them out. It was a clean, early decision on this, and [we] proceeded along that line."[49]

The *Pueblo* hostages were treated very harshly by the North Koreans.

Rostow even considered at one point in late 1968 not sending Johnson the intelligence accounts of their treatment in order to save the president the pain of having to read about their sufferings.[50] He did, of course, send it to Johnson, who, while remaining stoic, nevertheless greatly wished to see the Americans released before his term in office expired. Diplomatic efforts finally proved fruitful in December 1968, when the United States agreed to the North Korean demand that it sign a confession that the *Pueblo* had violated North Korean waters on a spy mission. However, the U.S. negotiators added the line that "we are instructed to inform you that there is not one word of truth in the above." The North Koreans accepted this quite odd confession, and the hostages were released.[51]

The two major hostage episodes of the Johnson years were both re-solved with most of the hostages safely returned. In one case, it took a military rescue operation, while in the other, patient diplomacy proved effective. What tied the two episodes in the Congo and North Korea together was the determination by the Johnson administration not to allow U.S. foreign policy interests to be negatively affected by the issue of hostages. This did not take away from the natural concern for their safety and the desire to gain their freedom. But just as the United States would not force a cease-fire on an advancing Congolese government army in order to possibly save the lives of hostages held by rebels, so too would it not become diverted from the Vietnam War by North Korea's holding of American military hostages. And in both cases, Johnson avoided any emotional attachment to the hostages.

The most active American domestic terrorist group at the end of the 1960s was the Weathermen, born from the anti–Vietnam War movement sweeping the college campuses. The Weathermen was a breakaway fac-tion of the leftist Students for a Democratic Society (SDS), whom the group felt were not violent enough to bring about a "revolution" in the United States. The split occurred at the June 1969 SDS convention in Chicago, when a number of alienated SDS members signed a statement titled "You Don't Need a Weatherman to Know Which Way the Wind Blows," a lyric taken from a Bob Dylan song "Subterranean Homesick Blues." The document called for immediate militant confrontations with the establishment.[52]

True to their word, the Weathermen staged four days of violent clashes with police in Chicago the following October, protests that the group advertised as their "Days of Rage." Two days before this began, they bombed a statue of a policeman commemorating the 1886 Haymarket Square riot, in which several policemen were killed. During the demon-strations, hundreds of Weathermen rampaged through the fashionable areas of Chicago as well as the downtown business district, smashing windows of banks, restaurants, and automobiles. At one point, a group of about one hundred women wearing helmets and carrying clubs, including Judith Clark, the former Midwood High School honor student, attempted to storm a military induction center but were stopped by the police. When several of the Weathermen who were arrested later decided to jump bail, the group essentially became an underground movement and stepped up its bombing campaign against the establishment.

Hundreds of bombings on college campuses during 1969–70 were attributed to the Weathermen. Three members of the group became victims of their own violence when they were killed in an accidental explosion at a Greenwich Village, New York, townhouse in March 1970. They were making bombs in the basement of the house, which was owned by the father of one member of the Weathermen. Several Weathermen escaped after the blast, including Kathy Boudin, who would be arrested along with Clark years later for the 1981 Brink's armed robbery and murders in Nanuet, New York.

During the early 1970s, the Weather Underground—the original name having been changed to avoid alienating women's liberation supporters—claimed responsibility for several high-profile bombings. These included attacks on New York City police headquarters in 1970, the U.S. Capitol in 1971, and the U.S. State Department in 1975. A book published by the group in 1974, titled *Prairie Fire,* set out the rationale for their violence: "We believe that carrying out armed struggle will affect the people's consciousness of the nature of the struggle against the state. . . . Action teaches the lessons of fighting and demonstrates that armed struggle is possible."[53] But Americans didn't want armed struggle, and the terrorism of the Weather Underground failed to ignite any "revolution." Even their bombings did not evoke the same fear of terrorism or government reactions that would occur when international terrorists began attacking Americans. It was almost as if terrorism by Americans within the United States seemed less frightening and more manageable than terrorism by foreign groups directed at U.S. citizens.

It would not be until the early 1970s that international terrorism became an acknowledged threat to the world community and to Americans, as the volume and intensity of terrorist attacks grew. And it fell upon the Nixon administration to venture into the uncharted waters of formulating the first official U.S. policy on combating terrorism.

Nixon and the Emergence of International Terrorism

The year 1968 is generally acknowledged as the beginning of international terrorism as we know it today. The significant breaking point was the launching of a sustained campaign of airline hijackings and sabotage by Palestinian guerrillas that was on a scale of violence and intensity never before seen by the international community. The Popular Front for the Liberation of Palestine (PFLP), under the command of a Palestinian physician named George Habash, dramatically publicized its struggle against Israel by hijacking an El Al plane in July 1968 on a flight from Rome to Tel Aviv and diverting it to Algeria. Then, in December, they attacked an El Al plane at the Athens airport, killing one passenger. The PFLP campaign of terror continued throughout 1969, with further attacks on El Al airliners. A TWA Boeing 707 was hijacked on August 29 on a flight from Rome to Tel Aviv and diverted to Damascus, where all passengers were released except for two Israelis, who were exchanged for two Syrian pilots held by Israel. One of the two hijackers threw a hand grenade and explosive devices into the cockpit, destroying the front section of the plane. The PFLP-General Command (PFLP-GC) perpetrated two midair bombings on February 21, 1970, blowing up a Swissair Transport Company plane over Switzerland, killing all forty-seven people aboard, and detonating a bomb aboard an Austrian Airlines plane near Frankfurt, where the pilot was able to land the aircraft safely with no casualties. A West German leftist terrorist group, the Baader-Meinhof Gang, also known as the Red Army Faction, attacked Western and Israeli targets in West Germany.[54]

It was not just Europe and the Middle East where international terrorism was growing. There were attacks in Latin America, including the 1969 kidnapping of the U.S. ambassador in Brazil by leftist guerrillas and the 1970 kidnapping and murder in Uruguay of an American adviser by the leftist Tupumaros. In Asia, the Japanese Red Army (JRA) made their presence felt with a 1970 hijacking of a Japanese airliner to North Korea. Two years later the JRA would massacre passengers at Lod airport in Tel Aviv.[55]

But despite the fact that international terrorism was increasing and Americans were at times the victims, for the most part the wave of international terrorist episodes of the late 1960s did not directly target U.S. symbols. This situation came to a sudden end on September 6, 1970, in a PFLP operation that has yet to be duplicated. The Palestinian extremists hijacked four planes bound for New York with more than six hundred people on board. A Pan American World Airways plane was seized by two PFLP guerrillas at gunpoint shortly after takeoff from Amsterdam. The plane was diverted to Beirut, where another PFLP member joined the hijacking team. The Pan Am jet then flew to Cairo, where, after releasing all passengers and crew, the terrorists blew up the plane. Trans World Airlines and Swissair planes were also hijacked after takeoffs from Frankfurt and Zurich, respectively, with both aircraft diverted to Dawson Field, an airstrip twenty-five miles from Amman, Jordan. Several hostages were released shortly afterward, but most were kept on the planes. The fourth plane hijacked was an El Al jet, but security guards were able to kill one hijacker and capture the other as the plane landed in London.

The capture of one of the PFLP hijackers, Leila Khaled—who had also hijacked the TWA plane in 1968—caused a problem for the PFLP. They now had one of their people in a British jail but no British hostages to use as bargaining chips to gain her release. Demonstrating the ability of terrorists to plan and implement an operation in a short period of time if necessary, the PFLP simply hijacked a British airliner three days later, demanding the release of Khaled in exchange for the new British hostages. That plane, with more than one hundred people on board, was also diverted to "Revolution Airport," as the guerrillas renamed Dawson Field, in Jordan.[56]

The world now had its first large-scale, multinational airplane hijacking episode. More than three hundred hostages from the United States, Great Britain, West Germany, Switzerland, and Israel were being held in the Jordanian desert along with the three planes as the various governments involved tried to resolve the incident. The hostages were subjected to psychological torment as they did not know why they were being held or what the demands of the terrorists were. Adding to their fears was the fact that in the middle of the night the PFLP would come on the plane with flashlights and remove some of the male passengers. Six were taken to the northern Jordanian city of Irbid, which was controlled by the guerrillas, and ten others were taken to a Palestinian refugee camp near Amman. The remaining hostages would thus awaken each morning to find some of their fellow hostages missing, not knowing what had happened to them.[57]

Thirteen-year-old Catherine Hodes and her twelve-year-old sister, Martha, were returning to New York on the TWA plane after visiting their mother in Israel. When the plane landed in Jordan, Catherine Hodes saw a frightening sight. "There was an entire Palestinian village outside our plane window," recalled Hodes. "Tents, trucks, dogs, children, all kinds of machinery and equipment [including] machine guns. There were Palestinians in full military regalia with the cloths around their heads. And it was very scary to look at. I felt like I was sitting in the middle of a war."[58] The PFLP guerrillas reminded her and the other captives that the hardships that they were temporarily experiencing were similar to what they, the Palestinians, had to endure all the time. When they allowed the passengers off the plane to wash, they used it as a lesson of life in the desert. "They had this big plastic thing of water," said Hodes. "And they were tipping it over and letting people run the water over their hands and wash their faces. And every time they would do it for someone, they would say, 'This is how we have to wash every day.' "[59]

The PFLP increased the tension level of the crisis on September 12. They removed the hostages to buses nearby and had them watch as they blew up all three planes. The buses then traveled through the desert and past a village where people lined the streets and cheered. Several hundred hostages were taken to the Intercontinental Hotel in Amman where they were released, but the hijackers kept forty others and moved them to several locations in and around Amman. There were now a total of fifty-six hostages in guerrilla hands (including the sixteen men taken earlier from the plane). The nationalities of the hostages were as follows: eight British, six Swiss, two German, two Dutch, and thirty-eight American. The two Dutch hostages were soon released.[60]

Miriam Beeber, the other former Midwood High School honor student, was among the hostages the PFLP kept. They accused her of being in the Israeli army after finding an army shirt and a picture of an Israeli soldier in her luggage, mementos from her summer working on a kibbutz in Israel. While still on the plane they took her into the cockpit and held a gun to her head. "We know you are in the Israeli army and we are going to kill you unless you tell us more information about what your role was in the army," the hijackers told Beeber. They refused to believe her when she said the soldier was just a friend. "After that interrogation they took me back to my seat and they held a gun up to my head again and they said, 'We're going to kill you.' It was scary," recalled Beeber.[61]

Beeber watched the planes being blown up, thinking to herself how childlike the hijackers who had earlier threatened her life were now behaving. "They were like school kids, they were cheering when they blew it up. They blew it up one, two, three. It was incredible," Beeber said. The buses traveled down a desert road, but then took two different directions. One went on to downtown Amman, where most of the hostages were released and put up in the Amman hotel, while the other bus—the one Beeber was on—went down another road to a refugee camp on the outskirts of Amman. The hostages there were pushed through throngs of people and placed in a structure where they were told that they were now prisoners and would not be released until the PFLP's demands were met. They were then moved to another house where the men were separated from the five remaining women hostages. There were now thirty-two Americans held captive in one building, six Americans in Irbid, and the sixteen other foreign hostages in another refugee camp at Al Wahdat.

One of the women hostages was an Egyptian Jew who lived in the United States and spoke both English and Arabic. She served as an interpreter for the hostages, who were now able to have lengthy conversations with their captors. The Palestinians told them about their own hardships, and this shed a new light on the hijacking for Beeber. "I got a real insight into their lives, so I didn't really hate them," said Beeber. "They were just trying to get us to understand what their life was like. That immediate fear [for my life] was [thus] lessened."[62] But as weeks went by and they remained captives, the hostages thought they were forgotten by the world and would probably die in Jordan. Civil war had broken out between King Hussein's forces and Palestinian guerrillas, and the hostages could hear bombs whistling every day. They would huddle together in the hallway of the house since that was the safest area. They saw houses blown up in their area and one of their guards was killed by a bomb when he walked down the street from the house.

Meanwhile, at the White House, President Nixon was holding meetings with his top aides on how to respond to the hijacking. He was receiving concerned messages from the Vatican about a possible U.S. military response. Nixon was scheduled to visit Rome and meet with the pope at the end of September, but the Vatican did not want to be associated with any possible U.S. military action to free the hostages. It requested that the secretary of defense, Melvin Laird, not accompany Nixon to Rome. The Vatican also requested that Nixon not make a scheduled visit to the Sixth Fleet immediately after meeting with the pope. This prompted White House aide Dwight Chapin to send a memo to Chief-of-Staff Bob Haldeman, stating that the Vatican was "overreacting," but that "if there is any action in Jordan on our [part], then the visit to the Vatican would be definitely off."[63]

There would be no U.S. military rescue effort during this hostage episode. The situation in Jordan was complicated by the fact that in addition to the hostage crisis, King Hussein was in the midst of a civil war. A U.S. military operation to save the hostages could make matters worse for King Hussein, who would be seen as having to enlist the U.S. military to resolve his own troubles. With regional tension very high because of the possibility of Syria and Iraq entering into the Jordan civil war, the United States was not anxious to pursue a military solution to the crisis.

There was also the problem that the United States was not prepared for military responses to hijacking episodes. The hostage rescue operation in the Congo, although complicated by the need for a joint U.S.-Belgian operation, was still a rather straightforward military operation. Attempting to rescue hostages on planes, or dispersed in different areas in Jordan, would be more difficult. The United States also did not have any specially trained troops for this kind of counterterrorist raid.

Despite these obstacles, the United States still considered military options during the first few days of the hostage crisis. Secretary of State Henry Kissinger has written how many wild ideas were circulated, including the use of poison gas against the terrorists. "[C]onsiderable time was devoted to the possible use against the hijackers of some nerve gas that paralyzed victims without their knowledge. The lack of knowledge of whether a suitable gas existed in our arsenal impeded the discussion no more than the absence of a concept of how it was to be delivered, indeed, how any military action was to be organized or sustained."[64]

The Nixon administration, though, wanted to keep the Palestinian guerrillas guessing about the intentions of the United States, and thus did not dispel the notion of a possible U.S. military strike. The Sixth Fleet aircraft carrier *Independence* was moved just off the coast of Lebanon, along with several destroyers. Kissinger and Nixon were convinced that the United States had to demonstrate military resolve, even if it was not going to pursue a military response. This was calculated to give a psychological lift to King Hussein, to prevent radical Arab regimes from intervening in Jordan, and to respond to a growing Soviet military presence in the region during the crisis. It was also aimed at preventing "the negotiations [on the hostages] from dragging on endlessly." Kissinger believed that the United States had to "begin conveying determination and start exerting pressure. An attitude of impotent scolding would only prolong our agony. American resolution was alike crucial for the fate of the hostages and for the survival of the king. Indeed, in a curious way, the future of the king and of the hostages had begun to merge. If hundreds of hostages were killed on his soil, the collapse of royal authority in Jordan would be plain for all the world to see. Each successive inconclusive crisis had weakened Hussein a little further; matters were drifting toward showdown. Either Hussein in desperation would move against the fedayeen [guerrillas] or the fedayeen would overthrow him."[65]

The multinational nature of the hijackings complicated efforts to resolve the crisis. The PFLP took advantage of the Western governments' natural concerns for the safety of their own citizens by trying to make separate deals with some of the countries, offering to exchange their citizens for Palestinian prisoners held in those countries. The hijackers also sought to put the blame for the hostages' fate on Israel for its refusal to release Palestinian guerrillas imprisoned there. There were also threats to treat all American hostages as Israelis.

The Nixon administration, however, successfully countered this strategy by putting pressure on its allies not to break ranks and make separate deals. Eventually all the hostages were released—Miriam Beeber and her group on September 26, and the six men who were held in Irbid on September 29—in exchange for Palestinian guerrillas in prisons in Switzerland, West Germany, and Great Britain. (King Hussein claimed his troops rescued the British, German, and Swiss hostages at the Al Wahdat refugee camp, but when the troops arrived on September 25, the guards had already fled.) Israel released a number of Palestinian and Libyan prisoners after the hostages were freed, but denied that this was part of any deal with the hijackers.

The end of captivity did not occur as Beeber and her fellow hostages had anticipated. They figured they would be killed by the terrorists or by the bombs falling near them, be rescued by the Jordanian army or perhaps the United States, or be released in some formal ceremony. Instead, they were simply told by their captors they were now free. "One morning they just came in and they said, 'Now pick up your things and [you're] leaving. And you will go to the Red Cross and they will take you away. Take something that is white [to use as a white flag],'" recalled Beeber. They gave the former hostages vague directions to Red Cross buses in Amman.

The good news was they were no longer hostages; the bad news was they were lost in the streets of Jordan in the midst of a civil war. There were piles of dead bodies in the street as the former captives made their way to freedom. Beeber and two other young women were barely outside the house when a group of three young guerrillas came up to them with guns and made them walk next to a wall. The hostages were able to convince the guerrillas to leave them alone. For Beeber, making her way to freedom was the scariest and most poignant part of the whole ordeal: "We walked a little bit further and some woman ran up to us from the street and she said, 'Please take my baby. Take my baby with you. My child has no hope in this country. Please take it back to your country.'"[66]

The hostages then walked further down the street where a new group of guerrillas forced them into an old arsenal building, demanding to know where they were going. Beeber and the hostages again had to convince them that they had been released and were trying to find the Red Cross. These Palestinian guerrillas then accompanied them to the Red Cross buses that drove through "no man's land"—roads that had been mined—in order to get to downtown Amman. There, the former hostages were brought to a Red Cross hospital where Palestinian nurses made sure they didn't leave Jordan without one final memory. "The nurses gave us, particularly the women, the tour of the hospital. They took us to the ward showing the children who had been maimed and harmed and arms blown off and all this during this war and they said, 'This is because of your imperialist country. This is what your country has done to our children,'" Beeber said. "So this was sort of like the grand finale."[67]

For the Nixon administration, the end of the hostage crisis was a welcome development. The president had succeeded in handling his first major terrorist episode with exceptional skill. The legacy of the hijackings for American policy was that it provided a good example of how to manage a hostage crisis. There were no actions taken or statements made that might have satisfied the public and congressional desire for tough measures. The fate of the hostages, although a concern in the White House, had to take second priority behind the issue of stability in the Middle East. Kissinger advised Nixon on September 8, two days after the hijacking began, that the United States "faced two problems, the safety of the hostages and the future of Jordan. If the fedayeen could use Jordan as their principal base and in the process destroy the authority of the king— one of the few rulers in the region distinguished by moderation and pro-Western sympathies—the entire Middle East would be revolutionized."[68] Thus, despite the understandable concern for the lives of the hostages— Nixon would later send a letter to two of them explaining how "those days were almost as long for us as they were for you, and we shared keenly in the deep concern for you and your colleagues in confinement"[69]—the real threat to U.S. interests lay in the possible overthrow of the Hussein regime and the radicalization of Jordan.

That the Nixon administration was able to keep these concerns paramount and clear was demonstrated by the decision not to have the president assume a high public profile during the hostage crisis or make bellicose and threatening statements about U.S. military retaliation against the hijackers. Nixon's low public profile during the crisis led one newspaper to describe his behavior as "aloof."[70] Senator Charles Goodel, a Republican from New York, delivered a speech at the American Zionist Federation in New York City during the first week of the hijacking, lamenting the relative absence of comment by Nixon, which he hoped "conceals the most massive effort in quiet diplomacy to free our trapped fellow Americans."[71]

Nixon, though, was very much involved in the behind-the-scenes deliberations, negotiations, and decisions during the hostage crisis. He was "close enough to the process to give impetus to the ultimate decisions; yet he (was) not . . . so involved in the details that he preclude[d] a thorough examination of alternatives."[72] Richard Tufaro, a Nixon aide who served on the Working Group on Terrorism that would be established in 1972, recalled how Nixon was a "behind-the-scenes kind of personality. More comfortable with it and probably more effective as a result of the way he operated. So I don't think he tried as much to use the drama and the media to promote positions on these issues. And his staff tended to reflect that."[73]

There was a great deal of media attention to the Jordan hijackings. Several commentators pointed to the problems facing the president in handling this first major international terrorist hijacking for the United States. James Reston, in an article titled "The Impotence of Power," wrote that "Nixon, for all his power, cannot even perform the first duty of government, which is to protect its own citizens, not because he is weak, but because his strength is so great that he dare not use it."[74] C. L. Sulzberger wrote that "the immediate issue is whether lives can be saved without yielding principles and without destroying hope of Middle East peace."[75]

Despite this reaction, the Nixon administration did not have to face the same type of media coverage, particularly by television, that would be common in later years. The technology for satellite reporting and remote location interviews with released hostages, families, and terrorists was still in its infancy. According to Cable News Network (CNN) Executive Vice President Ed Turner, the Jordan crisis occurred ten years too soon for the kind of media effect it would have today. "If that had gone on in the eighties, you would have seen damn near nonstop coverage from the desert or the capitals," said Turner. "It just fell out of the period in technology when something could have been done on a continuous basis. . . . But if that event occurred after 1980, when CNN came into existence . . . that event, those planes being blown up and all, would have been continuous presentation on CNN. And it would have forced it on the other networks to a lesser or greater degree."[76]

The Jordan hijackings were a watershed in the evolution of terrorism. Never before had so many governments been forced to deal with terrorists and their demands in order to resolve a single episode. And the cause of the Palestinians was now publicized throughout the world. The impact of terrorism was also felt by the innocent victims. Miriam Beeber had difficulty resuming her life and her friends when she returned to the United States. "It was really hard," said Beeber. "I was really scared. I was really paranoid about people and their intentions and people getting too close to me. And that there was going to be land mines on the road. That just doesn't end just because you're free." Several of Beeber's friends, who, like her, had been opposed to the Vietnam War and were part of the counterculture of the late 1960s and early 1970s, could not empathize with her three weeks of hell in Jordan, but rather made light of her experience. "They thought that what had happened to me was really 'far out,'" said Beeber. "They thought that was really 'radical,' really sort of 'been with the terrorists.'"[77]

Other hostages also suffered. Catherine and Martha Hodes were among those released after the first week of the hijacking, but had difficulty burying their experience when they returned to New York. Both girls had lost a lot of weight and had nightmares for weeks about the hijacking. More than twenty years later, Catherine Hodes still has flashbacks about her brief encounter with terrorism. "There's always a [personal] reaction when I hear about [a] hijacking," said Hodes. "When hijackings began to be more fatal [and] on a more regular basis, I would occasionally have dreams running through planes and things like that. Dreams that [were] related to the hijacking and to the fact that there were hostages now that were dying. That was disturbing to me. It's still disturbing to me."[78] Martha Hodes became sick for a week after returning home, but recalls trying to see the bright side of things. "My sense after the hijacking was that nothing was ever gonna happen to anyone in our family again because the odds were so against it. . . . That's it, nothing bad is gonna happen to anybody on an airplane because it's happened to us already and it can't happen twice."[79]

While it didn't happen again to the Hodes family, it would happen to countless others as international terrorism grew in the early 1970s. But it took one more spectacular terrorist event, this time before an entranced worldwide audience, to push terrorism into the realm of a major threat that the international community could not ignore.

The Olympic Games are supposed to be entertaining sporting contests that bring together for a few weeks some of the best athletes in the world. The 1972 games were well under way when the fun stopped and the terror began, just before dawn on September 5. Eight members of the Black September Organization—a Palestinian extremist group named after the expulsion of Palestinian guerrillas from Jordan following the September 1970 civil war—scaled the fence surrounding the Olympic Village and proceeded to the dormitory where the Israeli team was staying. After killing two Israelis, they took nine others hostage and threatened to execute them unless more than two hundred prisoners in Israeli jails and several others in West German prisons were released. The terrorists also demanded three planes to fly them out of West Germany. This was later reduced to one plane.

Israel refused to release any prisoners and urged the West Germans to do likewise. When the terrorists later demanded to be flown to Cairo with the hostages, the Germans agreed, although in fact they had decided to launch a rescue operation at the airport. On September 6, two helicopters flew the terrorists and their captors to a NATO airfield, which the terrorists were led to believe was Munich airport. When four terrorists left the helicopter to inspect the plane, German police sharpshooters opened fire, killing two terrorists. The others returned the fire, killing one policeman. A gun battle ensued for more than an hour. Finally, around midnight, as the Germans began to assault the helicopters, the terrorists shot the hostages and tossed a grenade into one of the helicopters. When the smoke cleared, all nine hostages lay dead, as well as three more terrorists. The remaining three terrorists were captured. But they would not remain in custody long, for less than two months later two Black September members hijacked a West German Lufthansa plane and demanded the release of their comrades in return for the safety of the passengers and crew. The West German government agreed and the three captured terrorists were soon in Libya, being hailed as heroes by Libyan leader Muammar Qaddafi. While still in a German prison, one of them explained the group's motives for the attack: "We wanted revenge, to stir up the world, to free Arab prisoners in Israel. We figured there would be people killed."[80]

The death toll from the Munich massacre was seventeen—eleven Israeli athletes, five terrorists, and one policeman. Black September did indeed stir up the world as millions of people watched the tragedy unfold on television. World leaders condemned the violence, with Pope Paul VI stating that the massacre "truly dishonors our time."[81] President Nixon telephoned Israeli Prime Minister Golda Meir after the first two Israelis were slain at the Olympic Village to express "my shock and horror at the news of the murderous act. . . ."[82] An editorial in the *New York Times* pointed to the escalation in terrorist violence: "That Arab fanatics could engage in indiscriminate murder, kidnapping, and aerial hijacking was proved long ago. But yesterday's murderous assault in Munich plumbed new depths of criminality. By choosing the Olympic Games as the occasion for their bloody foray, the Arab terrorists made it plain that their real target was civilized conduct among nations, not merely Israel or the Israeli athletes captured and killed yesterday. If the Olympic Games could provide a setting for release of their homicidal hatreds, then the same threat would hang over every United Nations meeting and all other international gatherings called to promote peace and friendship among nations."[83] The massacre of Israeli athletes left no doubt that terrorism was not just a sporadic phenomenon, but was a threat that was growing in both scope and intensity.

It was in the aftermath of the Munich massacre that the Nixon administration created an official organizational structure to deal with the terrorist threat. The Cabinet Committee to Combat Terrorism met on October 2, 1972, with lofty goals but a difficult task. The committee, as envisioned by Nixon in a memorandum to Secretary of State William Rogers, was to consist of all the heavy hitters in the administration. Membership included the secretaries of state, treasury, defense, and transportation; the attorney general, the director of the CIA, the national security advisor, the ambassador to the United Nations, the assistant to the president for domestic affairs, the acting director of the FBI, "and such others as the Chairman may consider necessary." The secretary of state was to chair the committee, whose mandate was to "consider the most effective means by which to prevent terrorism here and abroad." Among the committee's tasks were to "coordinate, among the government agencies, ongoing activity for the prevention of terrorism"; to be the lead group for the "collection of intelligence worldwide and the physical protection of U.S. personnel and installations abroad and foreign diplomats and diplomatic installations in the United States"; and to "devise procedures for reacting swiftly and effectively to acts of terrorism that occur."[84]

Not surprisingly, such a broad-based, high-level interdepartmental coordination on terrorism proved too bureaucratic to be effective. The committee met only once—its inaugural October 1972 meeting—during its five years in existence. The bulk of the committee's work was done by the Working Group on Terrorism, which was comprised of senior representatives of the members of the committee and headed by the secretary of state's special assistant for combatting terrorism. That post would be elevated to ambassadorial rank by the end of the 1970s. The Working Group met more than a hundred times between 1972 and 1977, with bureaucratic problems growing by leaps and bounds as more agencies and departments were added to both the cabinet committee and the working group. Complicating matters was the tendency for the different organizations not to exchange necessary information with each other.[85]

The early U.S. efforts to fight terrorism were also made difficult by the reluctance of other nations to form a united front against international terrorism. Part of the problem was the diverse nature of terrorism, where different governments faced different types of threats. Some governments also believed that they could make deals with terrorists where they would not arrest or expel terrorist groups that used their territory for a safe haven and the terrorist groups in return would not perpetrate terrorist acts on their soil. This would prove to be a naive view, as terrorists would strike virtually every country at some time. Tufaro, the Nixon aide on the Working Group on Terrorism, recalled that there was "a reasonable level of cooperation" with groups such as Interpol concerning the exchange of information, "but on broader policy issues, it was sometimes difficult."[86]

Despite these obstacles, the Nixon years accomplished an impressive record in international diplomacy with respect to terrorism. During his terms in office, there were four international agreements on terrorism concluded. These included the 1970 Hague Convention for the Suppression of Unlawful Seizure of Aircraft, which required parties to either prosecute or extradite aircraft hijackers and mandated severe punishment for those who were convicted; the 1971 Montreal Convention for the Suppression of Unlawful Acts against the Safety of Civil Aviation, which applied the same criteria to persons who committed acts of violence, including the placing of bombs, aboard aircraft; the 1973 Chicago Convention, Annex Seventeen to the International Civil Aviation Organization (ICAO) Convention on International Civil Aviation, which established standards and recommendations for airport security; and the 1973

New York (United Nations) Convention on the Prevention and Punishment of Crimes against Internationally Protected Persons, Including Diplomatic Agents, which required governments to view all violent acts against diplomats and other "internationally protected persons" and their property as criminal offenses and to extradite or prosecute any perpetrators of such acts found within their territory.

Implementing these agreements proved difficult since some governments gave only token support for firm steps against terrorism. A number of Third World nations resisted efforts to condemn terrorism at the United Nations, and instead passed a resolution in 1972 that called for a study on the causes of terrorism. Nevertheless, the international agreements and the leading role that the United States played in establishing the accords signaled that the U.S. would vigorously pursue diplomatic, legal, and other means to combat international terrorism.

Nixon faced one of his most agonizing terrorist episodes in March 1973. Black September terrorists stormed a farewell party at the Saudi Arabian embassy in Sudan for the departing U.S. chargé d'affaires, George Curtis Moore. They took Moore and four other diplomats, including the newly arrived U.S. ambassador, Cleo A. Noel, Jr., as hostages. Among their demands was the release of Sirhan Sirhan—the man who assassinated Robert Kennedy—from U.S. prison; the release of Palestinian guerrillas being held in Jordan; Arab women detained in Israel; and Baader-Meinhof Gang terrorists in West German prisons. When asked at a press conference how the U.S. would respond to the demand to free Sirhan Sirhan, Nixon took a firm stand even though the lives of the diplomats were at stake. The president told the newspeople that "as far as the United States as a government giving in to blackmail demands, we cannot do so and we will not do so. . . . We will do everything that we can to get them released, but we will not pay blackmail." He pointed out that terrorism has made "the position of ambassador, once so greatly sought after, now, in many places . . . quite dangerous . . . but it is a problem and it is a risk that an ambassador has to take."[87] He also announced that he had dispatched Deputy Undersecretary of State for Management William Macomber, Jr., to Sudan to assist in efforts to resolve the hostage drama. Macomber had no instructions on what exactly he was supposed to do once he arrived in Khartoum. But the fact that a senior State Department official was on his way to Khartoum was used by Sudanese and U.S. officials as a stalling tactic to prevent any immediate killing of the hostages. The implication conveyed to the terrorists was that Macomber was coming to negotiate with them.

But while Macomber was en route, the Palestinians killed Moore and Noel, along with the Belgian chargé d'affaires Guy Eid. They had heard through radio reports about Nixon's "we will not pay blackmail" comment.[88] They also mistakenly believed that a military rescue attempt was being planned. The tough U.S. stance against terrorism angered many Foreign Service workers who felt that the Macomber mission might have saved the lives of the hostages—or at least should have been allowed to make its attempt—if not for Nixon's hard-line stance. A study conducted by international terrorism expert Brian Jenkins for the U.S. government several months after the Khartoum killings concluded that there was little benefit in having high-level officials, including the president, making "no negotiations, no concessions" statements. These types of comments only add to the theatrics of a terrorist incident, but do little to resolve it or deter future acts. Jenkins recommended that high-level government officials remain silent during hostage episodes.[89]

Nixon's abandonment of his low-key public approach that worked so well during the Jordan hostage crisis was less a calculated decision than a spontaneous response to a reporter's question. "The guidance given to him, if asked about the affair, was to remain noncommittal," Jenkins wrote in his report.[90] The president's comments and the subsequent deaths of the diplomats in Khartoum meant that "no negotiations, no concessions" was now the public policy of the United States for dealing with terrorism. "It was a policy already sealed in blood so there was no backing away from [it]," said Jenkins.[91] The cornerstone of the U.S. approach to terrorism for decades afterward thus had its origins not in any careful consideration of alternative policies, but rather in an off-the-cuff comment by a president and unfortunate events a continent away.

Despite the tragedy of the diplomats' deaths, Nixon's handling of the Sudan crisis was still consistent with his ability to avoid allowing hostage situations to paralyze a presidency. The major positive contribution of the Nixon years to America's battles against terrorism lay not in its enunciation of a "no negotiations, no concessions" policy—which could never really be followed consistently—but rather in the establishment of a principle that terrorists would not be allowed to use the threat of violence to alter U.S. foreign policy.

Ford and the Croatian Hijackers

Gerald Ford was in the middle of a tough presidential election campaign in September 1976 when terrorists seized a plane over the skies of New York. It was the first domestic hijacking in the United States in several years, and before it was over it would span five countries and two continents and result in a temporary relaxation of the "no negotiations, no concessions" policy of the Nixon administration. It was also one of the most unusual hijacking episodes in the history of terrorism.

James Roscoe, a telephone lineman, almost missed TWA Flight 355 on September 10, 1976. He had just come home from work and rushed to La Guardia airport from his home on Long Island in order to make the Friday evening New York to Chicago flight. He planned to continue on to Tucson, Arizona, to visit his father. As the plane took off from La Guardia, he became curious about the man and woman sitting next to him. They appeared nervous and were speaking in a foreign language. When they leaned over to peer out the window, Roscoe thought they might be excited tourists. He pointed to the lights below from Shea Stadium, home of the New York Mets, and said, "Shea Stadium! Baseball, baseball!" But they didn't respond and Roscoe sat back in his seat. "A few minutes later, the two of them got up and one at a time went to the bathroom," recalled Roscoe.[92] When they emerged, the man had what appeared to be explosives and switches wrapped around his waist, and the two ran down the aisle toward the cockpit. There were joined by three other members of the hijacking team, who were carrying packages they claimed were bombs. One other man also had what he claimed were explosives attached to his body. A short time later, the pilot announced that the plane had been hijacked by Croatians and was heading for Montreal.

"Thank God it's not the Arabs," thought passenger Warren Benson, reflecting the views of most people on the plane.[93] The couple that had sat next to Roscoe turned out to be Zvonko Busic, the thirty-year-old leader of the five-person Croatian hijacking team, and his twenty-seven-year-old American-born wife, Juliene. The two had met in Vienna in 1969, where she was a nurse and he a student at the University of Vienna. Zvonko was dedicated to the cause of Croatian independence from the Serbian-dominated Yugoslav federation, and Julie, as she was known, soon joined him in the struggle. She was arrested that same year in Zagreb, the capital of Croatia, for passing out antigovernment leaflets and spent a month in prison. She was then expelled from Yugoslavia.

Throughout the early 1970s, Croatian separatists and the Yugoslav secret police were engaged in a violent conflict that saw Yugoslav diplomats and Croatian dissidents assassinated in countries throughout Western Europe. The issue of Croatian independence, which exploded into civil war in Yugoslavia in 1991 and finally independence for the republic, was unknown to most people outside of Yugoslavia at this time. In fact, most people had never even heard of Croatia. The U.S. government, by virtue of its support for the Yugoslav central government, was seen by Croatian revolutionaries as aiding the enemy. By the mid-1970s, Zvonko Busic, now living in New York City with Julie, decided that a dramatic act was necessary to bring world attention to their cause.

Zvonko began planning the hijacking early in 1976. "It just gets to the point where you figure you just cannot bear the injustice any longer and you had to do something drastic to force somebody to deal with these issues," recalled Julie Busic in the spring of 1992.[94] Although she was opposed to the hijacking plan when told about it, she decided to participate anyway. "I just didn't feel that it was an effective tool. I felt that it would alienate more people but I couldn't think of a different or a better option, either." After realizing that she could not dissuade Zvonko, she felt her place was by her husband's side no matter what the consequences. She awaited the September hijacking with trepidation, hoping something would happen in the preceding months to change their plans.

Nothing happened, and the September 10 date with terrorism was at hand. Julie Busic was quite nervous as she realized that within a few hours she would be seizing a jetliner with close to one hundred people on board. "I felt like I was going to puke every minute before [the hijacking]," said Busic. "It was horrible. It's just [like] 'I don't want to do this. I don't want to do this. What am I doing?' " But there was no turning back. "So I just tried to ignore it and just go through things mechanically. Because that's the only way I could handle what was happening. It was just so unreal and so bizarre. . . . I couldn't say, 'Well, yeah, I'm hijacking a plane.' . . . I just [had] to be completely objective about it, because that's the only way that I could get through that experience without having some kind of a breakdown."[95]

Zvonko Busic was also nervous. "I felt fear," he recalled in a telephone interview from Lewisburg Federal Penitentiary in 1993. "I felt excitement. [I felt an] adrenaline rush and worry that I would be stopped. I was sweating a lot. I was almost like a sleepwalker." The anxiety finally ended when he entered the cockpit of the plane. "Once I took over the controls, I relaxed totally," Zvonko Busic said.[96]

The plane landed in Montreal for refueling, where the hijackers notified authorities that they had placed a bomb in a locker across the street from Grand Central Station in New York, along with two long statements about Croatian independence that they wanted published in the *New York Times*, the *Washington Post*, the *Chicago Tribune*, the *Los Angeles Times*, and the *International Herald Tribune*. "We didn't have $50,000 to put a full page ad in the *New York Times*," said Julie Busic. "And people disregard those for the most part, anyway, when they see it's a paid ad."[97] The hijackers gave instructions as to which locker the bomb was in, and warned that another bomb was placed "somewhere in the United States" and would be activated if their demands were not met. Police found one bomb in a sealed pressure cooker in the locker and removed it to a police demolition area where they attempted to trigger it by remote control. When nothing happened after fifteen minutes, the bomb experts approached the device—without wearing protective gear—and the explosive unexpectedly went off, killing one officer and injuring three others. No other bomb was found.[98]

The hijacked plane flew to Gander, Newfoundland, for another refueling, with the Croatians unaware of the policeman's death. Thirty-five hostages from the original ninety-three passengers and crew on board were released in Gander in exchange for the dropping of Croatian independence leaflets by helicopter over the skies of New York, Chicago, and Montreal. The leaflets were given to the released hostages, who gave them to the authorities. The hijackers demanded that the plane take off for Europe to drop more leaflets over London and Paris. They wanted to fly to a Croatian island, where thousands of Croatians would be gathered for a religious ceremony, and drop more leaflets. The hijacked plane would then fly back to a European city where they would surrender.

Rudy Bretz, a television consultant, was a hostage on the TWA plane and felt quite certain that he and his seatmate, Alan Jaffee, would be released at Gander. Both had engaged Julie Busic in conversation before the plane landed there. In fact, she had sat down next to them and explained the reasons for the hijacking, the importance of bringing publicity to the cause of Croatian independence, and so forth. "So we were getting quite friendly," Bretz recalled. "And then she came down the plane picking people that would be kept or people who would be let off. We thought, 'Boy, we got the inside track. We're her only friends on board!' [But] she went right past us!"[99] Busic was selecting those who appeared either too fragile or anxious to make the trip to Europe, or who had a pressing family need to leave the plane. "A lot of people came up and said, 'We don't want to get off,' " said Busic. "Several of them said, 'Well, this is an adventure and I'm going to follow it to the end.' "[100]

Since the hijacked plane, a Boeing 727, was used only on domestic flights, it was not equipped with navigational instruments for a cross-Atlantic flight. It also did not have the capability to drop leaflets from the sky. A second TWA jet, a Boeing 707 with such equipment and capabilities, flew to Gander and escorted the plane to Europe. After another refueling stop in Reykjavik, Iceland, the luggage filled with leaflets was transferred to the escort plane. Both planes flew on to England, where the escort plane dropped the leaflets over central London. The same procedure was repeated in Paris before the hijacked plane finally landed at Charles de Gaulle airport. The other leaflets were dropped by helicopter over the North American cities.[101]

While the plane was flying to Europe, President Ford ordered Secretary of Transportation William Coleman back to Washington from a vacation in Vermont to attend a meeting at the White House with Federal Aviation Administrator John McLucas. The purpose of the meeting, which was held on a Saturday, was to determine how the hijackers had eluded security at La Guardia to seize the plane and smuggle their weapons on board. This was, after all, the most serious hijacking ever to originate in the United States. Most of the previous hijackings were to Cuba without loss of life. Now it seemed as though international terrorism had finally come to the United States. After the meeting, Ford instructed McLucas to investigate the breakdown in security.[102]

At one point during the hijacking, hostages Bretz and Jaffee suspected that the explosives around Zvonko Busic's waist might be fake. Jaffee had returned to his seat after stretching his legs. "He came back and sat down and said, 'You know, I just saw something funny. You know this leader that goes up and down [the aisle] with the dynamite strapped to his chest and wires and everything, and switch and so forth? I just saw him smoking a cigarette!' And I said, 'Maybe the dynamite isn't real.' And then it was just dismissed. You just forgot it. You got to believe it's real. You can't take a chance."[103]

Meanwhile, at the urging of the FBI and the FAA, the *New York Times,* the *Washington Post,* the *Chicago Tribune,* and the *Los Angeles Times* printed all or part of the hijackers' two texts. The *International Herald Tribune,* published in Paris, had already printed their edition before the hijacking began. One of the texts was titled "An Appeal to the American People" and stated that "if our goal [of publicizing the Croatian cause] is accomplished, we gladly accept all punishment and consider these ideas worthy of suffering for," while the other was a "Declaration of the Headquarters of the Croatian National Liberation Forces," which claimed that "Croatians are oppressed, humiliated, and insulted because of their pride and national dignity. In their home, as well as in their homeland, they have no rights whatsoever. . . ."[104]

Despite her nervousness before the hijacking, Julie Busic was a calming influence on the anxious passengers. One of the hostages released in Gander told reporters that Busic "acted almost like a stewardess walking up and down the aisle talking politely to people and calming them."[105] While the plane was in Europe, one of the hostages, the Right Reverend Edward O'Rourke, a Roman Catholic Bishop, tried to convince Julie Busic to tell Zvonko to end the hijacking. She told him that she would have little effect on her husband now, but that everything would turn out all right and the passengers would not be harmed. Bishop O'Rourke then went into the cockpit and asked to address the passengers over the plane's intercom. Hostage Bretz remembers what happened next: "He said, 'I don't think that we really realize the gravity of our situation.' And he went on in that vein for a while and he said, 'Those of you of the Catholic faith would probably appreciate [this],' and he said something in Latin. And a woman behind me gasped and said, 'My God! Those are the Last Rites!' "[106] Some of the passengers began to cry, others became agitated and upset, and Julie Busic immediately went through the cabin to reassure everyone that the situation had not deteriorated and not to pay any attention to what Bishop O'Rourke had said. "Oh, I was so mad at him," recalled Busic. "All these people just turned around and looked at me like, 'You betrayed us, now we are going to die.' So I had to go around and I had to tell everybody, 'I have no idea why he is doing this. Nothing has changed. Nothing is going to happen. You all are going to be home today [or] tomorrow.' "[107]

The most tense period came when the plane was on the ground in France. "We sat on the airport," said James Roscoe, "and they wouldn't let us raise the curtains in the plane to see outside. But I did raise it and I looked outside [and] I could see troops on the ground [around] the plane."[108] The French had shot out the tires so the plane could not take off and surrounded the aircraft with hundreds of police and troops. The pilot of the TWA jet, Richard Carey, became concerned that the French were going to attack the aircraft. In a conversation via radio with U.S. Ambassador Kenneth Rush, who was in the control tower at the airport, Carey let out his frustration. "All we know is that these people had a message that they wanted to put in the papers and wanted to drop leaflets on cities, and for this you are asking that this whole ship full of innocent people can be killed to prove that you can take a stand against terrorists?" Carey also asked French officials, "Tell me, please, what are we being killed for?"[109]

The Croatians were becoming anxious too when they realized that the French were not going to allow the plane to fly to Croatia. They were also concerned that their demands for publication of Croatian independence literature might not have been met. "They were coaxing the people on the plane, nobodies, virtual nobodies, to see if anyone knew a statesman or congressman, or mayor, or whatever, to get the government to do what they wanted to do," said Roscoe.[110]

Julie Busic was allowed to leave the TWA jet to telephone a contact in the United States to verify that the Croatian independence statements had been published in the newspapers and that the leaflets were dropped over the North American cities. After confirming this, she was arrested. Meanwhile, the hostages had been ordered by the remaining hijackers to gather around the bombs they claimed they had in their possession. The French issued the hijackers an ultimatum to surrender and be sent to either the United States or Yugoslavia—they could choose the country—or face execution in France if they threatened the lives of the hostages. The Croatian separatists chose to surrender and be sent back to the United States. The "bombs" turned out to be fake, some of them made from clay. They had been assembled in the airplane's bathroom, two of them from cooking pots wrapped in black tape and switching devices. Shortly before surrendering, they cut up pieces of the clay bombs and gave them to the passengers as souvenirs.[111]

Zvonko and Julie Busic were found guilty of air piracy resulting in a death and were sentenced to life in prison. Two other hijackers were found guilty of air piracy but cleared of the murder charge since it was determined they had no knowledge of the bomb in the locker. The fifth hijacker pleaded guilty to air piracy. All received lesser sentences than the Busics and were released from prison in the 1980s. Julie Busic was released on parole in March 1989, after serving twelve and one-half years, while Zvonko Busic remained in federal prison as of the spring of 1994.

The hijacking was covered extensively by the media, giving the Croatian separatists the worldwide publicity they sought. One observer noted that "for thirty hours, five unknown people had monopolized the attention of millions and had transformed the name of an obscure Balkan province into a household 'issue.' For them terror worked and worked spectacularly." But as is true for many acts of terrorism, once the drama is over, the memory fades for most of the public. ". . . [A]fter the hijackers' return to New York, interest in the story waned. Outrage and indignation are momentary emotions."[112]

For some of the participants, however, the effects can last a lifetime. One hostage refused to be interviewed for this book, stating the experience was too frightful and claiming that he had been threatened afterward by other Croatian separatists. Rudy Bretz still felt the impact almost sixteen years later. "Talking about it, I'm like this [shaking] again," said Bretz in the spring of 1992. "They took my pulse [after the hijacking] [and] your pulse is supposed to be about seventy-three. Mine was about 130." But he also felt he came out of the hijacking ordeal a much stronger person: "I am less afraid of death because I've been there and I can handle it."[113] His wife, Emily, who anxiously awaited the outcome of the hijacking from her home in California, learned a different lesson. "What you do is to hang on to [your] loved ones. You figure you might not have them forever," she said.[114]

Warren Benson received hate mail for a comment he made to a reporter after being released in France. He was asked what he thought about the Croatian hijackers. According to Benson, who was unaware of the policeman's death, he told the reporter that they should be prosecuted to the full limit of the law, but that in the Christian spirit of forgiveness, he wished them well. The quote, "I wish them well," was printed on the front page of the *New York Times* and carried by many other newspapers. "Some of the hate mail was worse than the hijacking," Benson recalled. One person wrote Benson that "I wish people like you would dismantle bombs so if they blew up there would be no loss."[115]

Julie Busic suffered in ways she never anticipated. She was ready to go to prison for her actions and even die if that was the case. But she never planned on being responsible for another human being's death. Busic had been in the helping professions her whole life; she was a nurse, a teacher, and a mental health therapist for abused teenagers. Now she was a murderer in the eyes of the law. When she found out about the policeman's death while in the control tower in Paris, she went into complete denial. "I was just praying the whole time that it was a trick, that it wasn't true. I mean the whole time that we were on the plane going back to New York, Zvonko kept saying, 'It's not true, it couldn't be true.' I mean the way he put everything together, he gave exact instructions. It was so childishly simple, it could not have exploded by accident. It was impossible."[116]

But it did explode, and Busic had to make peace with herself. A picture on the front pages of most major newspapers in the United States showed a downcast and depressed Julie Busic, chained and handcuffed to the four other hijackers. "Every day we would have to pick up the paper and see ourselves being described as maniacs and thugs and terrorists and criminals. That really broke my heart because I never did anything but good my entire life. And it was like everything was canceled. I was just a nonperson before that. That really hurt. It really hurt a lot."[117] The first few weeks in prison were the darkest period of her life. She thought that turning to God might help her emotional pain. "When I really realized that it [the policeman's death] was true, I felt that I had to do something immediately to atone for it. It wasn't enough that I was in jail and charged with murder and air piracy and did all this to my family, I had to do something more. And I felt like, no, I couldn't kill myself because then I wouldn't be suffering." So Busic decided that she would become a nun after her prison time was completed. But that idea no longer appealed to her when she was released. "I had suffered enough and I didn't have to become a nun," said Busic.[118]

Julie Busic returned to school to complete her master's degree in German language and literature, and by 1991 was working for the Office of Croatian Affairs in San Francisco. When Croatia won its independence following the civil war in Yugoslavia, many of her friends who had been political prisoners there were now heading up the new Croatian government. The former hijacker is viewed as a heroine by many people in Croatia, another example of the slogan "one person's terrorist is another person's freedom fighter." She has had poets write to her and Croatian television, newspapers, and magazines interview her. While she expresses deep sorrow for her actions—"it's just a horrible thing to realize that something that you did inadvertently caused so much tragedy"—to this day she cannot see herself as a terrorist:

> I could never consider myself a terrorist. I'm just not a terrorist. I'm not a criminal, I mean in so far as I have no criminal nature, no criminal mind. . . . When I think of a terrorist, I think of people applying indiscriminate and intentional terror upon innocent people. Not somebody who tries to reassure and avoid that at all costs. Although I know it is difficult to argue that when people are suffering fear on the plane and don't know whether they are going to be blown up. But I think the intentions are different. We didn't intend to terrorize anybody. We didn't arbitrarily cause them to suffer and to be afraid. We tried to, in fact, we assured them that the opposite was the case, that they were not going to be hurt. That was it. We didn't intend for them to be harmed or anything.[119]

Zvonko Busic shared his wife's grief over the death of the policeman. "When I learned of the policeman's death, I was shocked," he said. "I felt sorrow. I don't know how worse I could feel if they told me my whole family was killed in a car. This was the worst thing I could possibly know. My pure idealism was then gone."[120] Although he expresses sorrow for what happened, he does not feel remorse. "Remorse means you regret your actions, and I don't regret my actions," he said.[121] Since he believed that Serbian agents intended to assassinate him, the hijacking, in his view, was the only way to expose his situation and also "rekindle the spirit of Croatian people outside who were becoming hopeless." Busic believes his actions were fully justified:

> I had a moral right to hijack [that] plane. Morally, I shouldn't have taken the innocent people. But I knew that the innocent people wouldn't suffer. I didn't abuse them. Sure, it's illegal. [But] I just borrowed it illegally. It was not a hijacking. . . . [And] the bomb [that killed the policeman] wouldn't hurt anyone because we would give it to the experts to defuse.[122]

The hijacking of TWA Flight 355 touched many lives, as is true for most acts of terrorism. But because it was over within two days, it did not lead to any crisis for the Ford administration. It did, though, clearly demonstrate the problem any government has in trying to maintain a consistent counterterrorist policy. In an age when hijackers' demands usually involved freeing imprisoned colleagues, the Croatian separatists' demands caught U.S. officials off-guard. Could they possibly justify the loss of many lives by sticking with a "no negotiations, no concessions" policy, when all that appeared necessary to end the hijacking peacefully was the publication and distribution of the hijackers' propaganda? The Ford administration decided that in this case, at least, it could not. While the president refused a request by the hijackers to speak with either him or Secretary of State Henry Kissinger while the plane was on the ground in France, he did allow Ambassador Rush to talk with them even though the administration denied there were any "negotiations." As one West German diplomat observed, "In general, you should take a hard line. But don't say 'never.' You can always make room for special cases."[123]

President Ford stated that the hijacking was "renewed evidence of the urgent need for international cooperation to cope with hijacking and terrorism."[124] But he did not have to face any more hijackings, as his days in office were coming to an end. He was the target, though, of two assassination attempts earlier in his presidency by mentally ill women, one of whom had been associated with the Charles Manson group. He also faced a *Pueblo*-type incident in 1975, when a U.S. container ship, the *Mayaguez*, was seized by Cambodian forces. The administration was determined to avoid a similar yearlong ordeal for the crew as had occurred during the *Pueblo* crisis. U.S. aircraft and Marines were ordered into action quickly to rescue the crew with a land and sea assault. As the U.S. strike force was on its way to the mainland—where all the crew had been removed—U.S. intelligence intercepted a radio message that suggested the Cambodians intended to free the crew. But the strike was ordered to continue anyway, partly to demonstrate that the United States would still respond to threats against its interests in Asia despite the final withdrawal of U.S. troops from Vietnam. The rescue operation was not without its costs; eighteen Marines were killed in the military hostilities during the rescue effort, while another twenty-three Marines lost their lives in a helicopter accident in Thailand as they prepared for the rescue mission.

Brent Scowcroft, the special assistant for national security affairs during the Ford administration, believed the *Mayaguez* crisis could have been even worse had the Cambodians acted differently. "Again we were lucky," Scowcroft told the Oral History Project of the Fletcher School of Law and Diplomacy at Tufts University. "If the Cambodians had said, 'no, we are not going to release these people and every time you bomb us we are going to kill one or two of them,' we would have been in a very, very difficult position. So we were lucky."[125]

The next American president would not be so lucky. Terrorists were about to demonstrate how the leader of a great power could become caught up in the same web of emotions and reactions to terrorism that the immediate victims experienced. From the end of World War II until the late 1970s, successive U.S. presidents had managed to avoid paralyzing crises over terrorism. An unstated principle of U.S. counterterrorist policy seemed to be that terrorists' actions would not be allowed to harm U.S. foreign policy or vital national interests. Yet when Americans were taken captive in their own embassy in Iran in November 1979, it marked more than the beginning of a yearlong period of agony and frustration for the United States. It also marked the first time since the days of Jefferson and the Barbary pirates that the United States would fall into the terrorist trap.

4

The Setting of the Terrorist Trap

No American president was more wounded by a terrorism crisis than Jimmy Carter. While Ronald Reagan was able to recover from the Iran-Contra fiasco and leave office with his popularity ratings still high, President Carter would not enjoy such a turnaround. While many factors led to his overwhelming defeat by Reagan in the 1980 presidential election—including the economy with its double-digit inflation and high unemployment and interest rates, and foreign policy issues ranging from the Soviet invasion of Afghanistan to the growing image of a militarily weak America—it was the hostage crisis in Iran that in the end destroyed his presidency.

It is a difficult experience for any incumbent president to endure the two-and-one-half months between an election defeat and the inauguration of a new president. The "lame duck" label hangs over every decision and statement that is made. For Carter, though, the experience was exacerbated by the captivity of fifty-two Americans in Iran. The hostages would be a constant reminder to Carter of how the United States was manipulated and humiliated by a foreign government that knew how to play the hostage game. In fact, as a final insult to the president who desperately wanted to see the hostages brought home before his term expired, the Iranian government refused to allow the plane with the freed hostages aboard to take off until a few moments after Reagan was sworn in as the new president.[1]

The legacy of the 1979–81 Iran hostage crisis is a lesson in the power of terrorism. Without causing a single casualty to any American—although there would be the tragic loss of eight U.S. servicemen during the failed effort to rescue the hostages and one death early in the takeover of the embassy—the Iranian government, militants, and others in postrevolutionary Iran were able to carry out the longest and most agonizing crisis for the United States in the post–World War II era. The 1962 Cuban missile crisis may have brought the world to the brink of nuclear war, but it was over in less than two weeks. The hostage episode in Iran, in contrast, continuously gnawed at the American people and government, touching a nerve that even the militants who climbed the embassy wall on November 4, 1979, could not have imagined.

Once the crisis began, the Iranians continuously frustrated all efforts by the United States and other parties to gain the release of the hostages. The United States could not control the actions of those who took its citizens captive; it could, though, control the direction and scope of its own responses. It was in this realm that the Carter administration fell victim to the terrorist trap almost immediately after the embassy was seized. To understand why this occurred, it becomes necessary to examine the personality and style of the president himself.

When Carter defeated Gerald Ford in the 1976 election, it was, in many respects, a statement by the American people that the Watergate era was finally to be put to rest. Ford had done a credible job in guiding the country in the difficult months following the resignation of President Nixon. He tried to get the American public thinking about things other than the scandals associated with the cover-up of the 1972 break-in of Democratic headquarters in Washington, D.C. But he could not extricate himself from Watergate even though he was not involved in the events himself. His decision to pardon Nixon, his retention of most of the high-level officials from the Nixon administration, and the short time period between his becoming president and the 1976 election prevented Ford from forging his own identity as president. Carter was thus able to exploit the "outsider" theme of a Southern politician coming to clean up Washington and begin a new era of morality both at home and abroad. One journalist described Carter as the best "one-on-one" presidential candidate in recent times, while another observer noted how he "created a public persona of morality rather than one of power."[2]

The human rights campaign for reform in the Third World was the foreign policy manifestation of Carter's deep inner convictions. But as National Security Adviser Zbigniew Brzezinski writes, "his personal qualities—honesty, integrity, religious conviction, compassion—were not translated in the public mind into statesmanship with a historical sweep."[3] In fact, it would be these highly positive personal traits that would not serve him well in dealing with the tough and often seemingly immoral world of terrorism. A hostage incident early in his presidency offers a glimpse as to how the new president would respond to future cases of hostage taking.

On March 7, 1977, a twenty-five-year-old former Marine, Corey Moore, entered the city hall complex in Warrensville Heights, Ohio, and took two people hostage after firing shots from a handgun. Moore, who was black, seized the two white hostages, a forty-eight-year-old diabetic police captain and an eighteen-year-old high school girl, to protest the treatment of blacks in the United States. His demands ranged from the ludicrous—that all white people evacuate the earth in seven days—to the improbable, that he be allowed to talk with President Carter. Moore wanted the president to apologize for the misdeeds of whites against blacks since the year 1619. About eleven hours after the siege began, Moore released the high school student in exchange for a television set. He told reporters that he would release the police officer, Capt. Leo Keglovic, and surrender if Carter would talk with him by telephone. The president agreed to do so if Moore surrendered first.

During a press conference that was held while the hostage drama was unfolding, Carter was asked by a reporter if he was "concerned that this might be regarded as a precedent" for dealing with terrorists. The president stated that he was indeed worried "[but] that I weighed that factor before I made my own decision." Carter told the newspeople that "I understand that Mr. Moore has promised to release the police officer after this news conference, regardless of any comment that I might make on it and I hope that the police officer will be released. But if he should be released I will talk to Mr. Moore."[4] After viewing Carter's press conference on television, Moore emptied his handguns and gave them to Keglovic, who led him outside to surrender to police. Moore then spoke with Carter over the telephone, telling reporters that the president "wished me luck." The White House acknowledged the extraordinary call by issuing a one-sentence press release stating that "The president spoke briefly with Corey Moore at 4:13 P.M. EST."

Less than two months into his presidency, Carter had completely abandoned any pretext of following the Nixon-Kissinger doctrine of "no negotiations, no concessions." Although the Moore case was not an act of terrorism on the international stage, it was political terrorism perpetrated within the United States. Why, then, would a president of the United States become directly involved in a hostage situation to the point of personally communicating with the hostage taker? For Carter, the primacy of saving lives over any rules or procedures for dealing with terrorists was his motivation. The racial overtones of the incident made it even more potentially explosive for Carter to become directly involved.

It was a decision that was widely criticized, even by prominent black leaders. Richard Hatcher, the black mayor of Gary, Indiana, said that Carter's communication with Moore was "very courageous. It showed compassion. But I still think he was wrong to do it. It sets a bad precedent."[5]

Soon after the hostage episode in Ohio ended, another one began in the nation's capital. On March 9, a small band of Hanafi Muslims—a breakaway faction of the larger Black Muslims—seized three buildings in Washington, D.C.: the B'nai B'rith headquarters, the Islamic Center and Mosque, and city hall. One reporter was killed and several people injured as the Hanafis took more than a hundred people hostage. The leader of the group, Hamaas Abdul Khaalis, made several demands, including the cancellation of the premiere of a movie, *Muhammad, Messenger of God,* which he believed was sacrilegious since it portrayed the life of Muhammad on film. He also demanded that the men convicted of killing several Hanafi Muslims in 1973—four of his children were among the victims, and his wife and daughter were seriously injured—be brought to him along with those convicted of assassinating Malcolm X. Khaalis also wanted the return of a $750 fine he paid in 1973 for contempt of court when he disrupted the Hanafi murder trial by shouting at one of the defendants.

The money was returned and the movie premiere canceled. But the convicted killers of his family and of Malcolm X were not delivered to Khaalis. During the course of the hostage drama, Khaalis held several telephone interviews with reporters. When one reporter informed Khaalis that everybody was worried about the fate of the hostages, the Hanafi Muslim leader replied that nobody showed any concern when his family was killed several years earlier. He told the reporter to "get on the phone and call President Carter and some of those senators that never even sent a call, a condolence message. Do you realize when my family was wiped out, [no] one said one word? Not one. Not even a preacher. Not even a minister. Not even a spiritual adviser. Not even a City Council member. So, I'm very glad you're worried now. When they wiped out my family, I didn't hear about your sympathy and emotions. I got a letter the other day from my brother telling me how the brother was swaggering around in jail, the killer of Malcolm, walking around with guards protecting him. Well, tell him it's over. Tell him it's payday."[6]

This was retaliatory terrorism at its height. Khaalis also stated a common theme among terrorists when the reporter pointed out that the hostages had nothing to do with his personal grievances: "Stop all this piety," Khaalis said. ". . . How many civilians do have anything to do with it when war comes? Don't they pay the higher price? Come on now, we're at war."[7] The incident was finally resolved with the assistance of three Muslim diplomats—the ambassadors of Pakistan, Iran, and Egypt—who met with Khaalis and other Hanafi leaders for more than three hours and read to them from the Koran, appealing to their consciences. The hostages, including a number of Egyptians, were released, and the Hanafi Muslims surrendered. The chief of police for Washington, D.C., Maurice Cullinane, stated that "if any one thing turned this around it was the face-to-face negotiations" between the ambassadors and Khaalis.[8] Also joining in the negotiations were United States Attorney for the District of Columbia Earl Silbert, and Deputy Attorney General-Designee Peter Flaherty.

These two hostage episodes in the early days of the Carter presidency illustrated the direction that the United States would take with respect to domestic terrorism. A patient, nonforceful approach would be pursued with direct presidential involvement utilized if necessary. During the Hanafi incident, both the director of the FBI, Clarence Kelley, and the attorney general, Griffin Bell, went to the command post at the scene of the confrontation. They reported to the White House that "enough agencies were already involved and that additional assistance from the chief executive was not needed at that time."[9] Following Khaalis's surrender and arrest, Bell authorized the temporary release of the Hanafi Muslim leader on his own recognizance despite criticism of this action by many congressional leaders. Bell believed that "given the release of the hostages . . . it was not a drastic thing to do."[10] An editorial in the *New York Times* agreed, stating that even if the temporary release of Khaalis was part of a deal made to free the hostages, it was well worth it. "The Washington authorities appear at this juncture to have acted wisely and well. Their first concern was 134 real lives, not some abstract, contradictory, speculative argument over precedent. Fortunately, they found themselves in a position where negotiation was possible. . . ."[11]

Concern for the fate of hostages dictated the administration's approach to the Moore and Hanafi incidents. But what worked at home would not necessarily work abroad.

The Long Crisis

When militants seized the U.S. embassy in Tehran, Iran, on November 4, 1979, it was not the first time that year that the embassy had been overrun by an angry mob. On February 14, a group of Marxist Fedayeen urban guerrillas attacked the embassy compound, forcing U.S. Ambassador William Sullivan and his staff to take refuge in secure rooms. Sullivan telephoned the revolutionary committee of the Ayatollah Ruhollah Khomeini for help. Khomeini, who had recently returned in triumph from exile in France to assume leadership of the Islamic revolution, had not yet embarked on his Great Satan campaign against the United States. Pro-Khomeini forces, led by Deputy Prime Minister Ibrahim Yazdi, arrived and forced the guerrillas out of the embassy, freeing the Americans.

At the same time that the embassy siege in Iran was unfolding, another hostage crisis was taking place in Afghanistan, where Muslim extremists abducted U.S. Ambassador Adolph Dubs. Despite pleas by the United States to the Afghan government not to attack the hotel where Dubs was being held, government troops assaulted the hotel anyway, leading the rebels to kill Dubs. Both crisis situations were being monitored in the same operations center room in the State Department. In one corner were a group of senior officials trying to coordinate efforts to win Dubs's release, while in another part of the room there was a second group in communication with Sullivan as he was trapped inside the besieged embassy in Tehran. The two crises threatened to force postponement of a scheduled trip to Mexico the next morning by President Carter. Although the visit was viewed as an important step in improving U.S.-Mexican relations, administration officials were ready to cancel it if the embassy in Iran was still under siege and Dubs's life was still in danger. After both situations were resolved—although tragically in the case of Dubs—Secretary of State Cyrus Vance recommended that the trip to Mexico proceed.[12]

Following the February 14 attack on the embassy, there was some speculation that the United States might completely phase out its presence in Iran until a sense of calm was restored to the country. However, it was decided to maintain at least a minimum official presence in a nation that was still of vital importance to the United States. The embassy staff was thus reduced from more than 1,400 to approximately sixty. Steps were also taken to improve physical security at the embassy compound, including the installation of bullet-proof glass, steel doors, and other measures aimed at creating a safe haven in case of an attack. The objective was to provide a few hours of protection against an angry crowd—a time frame that was deemed to be sufficient to allow for government forces to arrive at the scene and disperse the mob.[13]

The United States was planning for a scenario whereby the Iranian authorities would once again come to their aid. This seemed reasonable given their previous response to trouble at the embassy and the fact that there had not been a hostage situation in recent times in which the host government supported the captivity of foreigners by its citizens. Adding to this sense of guarded optimism were assurances given by Iranian officials to the United States in the fall of 1979 that Americans would be protected. This assurance was sought by U.S. chargé d'affaires Bruce

Laingen in a meeting with Prime Minister Mehdi Bazargan and newly appointed Foreign Minister Ibrahim Yazdi on October 21. Since the United States was about to allow the deposed shah to enter the country for medical treatment, the Carter administration was concerned about the reaction in Iran. Although the Iranian officials warned Laingen of potential anti-U.S. demonstrations, they nevertheless sent extra police to guard the embassy. And when the Iranian government kept the bulk of a massive demonstration several miles away from the embassy on November 1, the Carter administration felt the government would continue to provide protection if necessary.[14]

However, the scenario the United States had planned for fell through when thousands of militant students attacked the American embassy on November 4. In a revolutionary situation, assurances given one day can easily be broken the next as events take on a life of their own. The moderate secular Iranian government did not want to be seen as opposing the desires or policies of the Ayatollah Khomeini. Thus, when Khomeini threw his support behind the students, who had taken sixty-three Americans hostage, the government had little choice but to fall in line. Laingen and two other U.S. officials had just left the foreign ministry building when the attack was under way. When they returned to seek assistance, they soon realized that the government had little power to control the situation. In fact, the Bazargan government would collapse two days later. Meanwhile, the Americans in the embassy retreated to secure rooms while waiting for the expected help from the government. When it became apparent that no such help would be forthcoming, they surrendered, and the hostage crisis was under way.

Despite the absence of a strong central government in Iran, the United States still expected that the crisis would be resolved shortly through negotiations. The Carter administration sent former Attorney General Ramsey Clark and an ex-foreign service officer who spoke Farsi, William Miller, to Tehran to meet with Khomeini. However, despite the good relations that Clark had previously established with the Ayatollah, the Iranian spiritual leader refused to allow the two Americans into the country.[15]

Even as the hostage episode continued through November, nobody really anticipated the fourteen-month ordeal that would subsequently ensue. "In the first month or so," recalled Secretary of State Cyrus Vance, "we had a feeling that perhaps we could get them freed in a reasonably short period of time—a month or two. However, as we went into the second month, it then became clear to me that we were probably in for a long and difficult haul. That didn't mean we shouldn't continue to try the various efforts which we undertook, but it was clearer and clearer that we were in for a long haul."[16]

The hostages realized this when the first few days of their captivity failed to bring any quick solution. "We didn't have any idea how long we'd be held," said Robert Ode, a retired Foreign Service officer who had the misfortune of accepting a temporary State Department assignment to Iran in October 1979.[17] His consulting agreement called for a forty-five-day stint in Tehran, where he would work in consular affairs. The State Department assured Ode that it was safe to work at the embassy since everything was returning to normal in Iran, or so they thought. He was on the job for one month and was making his travel arrangements to return home when the embassy was seized.

At sixty-five he was the oldest hostage, but that did not result in any special treatment by the militants. They took all the hostages' personal belongings, including Ode's gold wedding ring. The protests of a Marine guard—"Leave him alone, he's an old man"—didn't stop the Iranians. Like the other hostages, Ode was blindfolded with his hands tied to a chair and forced to sleep on the floor at night. The hostages were not allowed to talk with one another during the first few weeks of their captivity.[18]

Preparations for a possible military rescue operation were begun almost immediately. The decision on actual implementation, though, would be delayed until a feasible plan could be designed and rehearsed, since this was a unique situation with the host government supporting the hostage takers. The diplomatic approach was deemed to be the best means for attaining the safe release of the hostages. At times, Vance would express dismay with other foreign ministers for not joining with the United States to put pressure upon Iran to release the hostages. "I had some rather sharp words," Vance recalls, "because I felt that they were not being sufficiently helpful in working with us to try and put economic sanctions and political sanctions on the Iranians."[19]

The first dilemma brought on by the hostage crisis was whether Carter should proceed with a scheduled trip to Canada on November 8. The state visit was to be the first by a U.S. president in more than a decade to a nation that was facing its own difficulties with respect to Quebec separatism. Reassuring Ottawa of the importance that the United States placed on its "special relationship" with Canada was a key objective of the trip. However, White House Chief of Staff Hamilton Jordan was convinced that under no circumstances should the president go to Canada. "Here we were in the middle of an international crisis," Jordan writes, "with the lives of numerous American diplomats at stake, and the President was leaving the country."[20]

Carter initially opposed Jordan's recommendation, pointing out that he could readily stay in touch with the White House Situation Room while in Ottawa, would have all his top foreign policy advisers along with him, and that a cancellation could set back U.S.-Canadian relations. Jordan persisted and sent Carter a memorandum outlining his reasons why the trip should be canceled. He then met with Vance, who also opposed canceling the trip, but who told Jordan that if the president felt strongly enough about not going to Canada, then it could be arranged. Carter eventually decided to cancel the trip. "I walked back to my office," writes Jordan, "satisfied that the president had done the right thing, and more than a little proud of myself for changing his mind."[21]

But this strategy backfired, as Carter felt compelled to remain in Washington for several more months as the crisis worsened. He became a virtual prisoner in the White House, afraid to leave any impression that he was not on top of the situation. "That [decision to cancel the Canada trip] took the president completely out of remaining involved in his campaign for re-election," said Vance, "and sort of consigned him to the Rose Garden as it was described and that did set a pattern that in the long run was the wrong pattern."[22]

In fact, even when Carter was ready to abandon his self-imposed exile and begin campaigning after the ill-fated hostage rescue effort in April 1980, he could not find the proper forum to make the announcement. The president expected that a question would be raised at his first regularly scheduled news conference after the raid concerning the possible end of the Rose Garden strategy. But that question was not asked by the press corps. "We had gotten tired of asking him because he always gave the same answer," said ABC White House correspondent Sam Donaldson. Carter had continually stated that he could not leave his post while the hostages were in Iran. "So the next day, since we hadn't asked him, they had to stage a little ceremony in the White House in which they got Charles Manatt, the national [Democratic] chairman, to stand up and ask the question and he said, 'Yes, as a matter of fact he thought he could now go out.' "[23]

Jordan himself would later regret his part in forging the "stay-at-home" strategy to deal with the crisis. "Months later, when we were bogged down in what the press labeled our 'Rose Garden strategy,' unable to bring the hostages home and committed not to campaign until the crisis was resolved, I kept remembering that incident [the cancellation of the Canada trip]. It was the first time we had placed Iran above everything else in Carter's Presidency, and I felt largely responsible for the public trap we later found ourselves in."[24]

The canceling of the Canada trip was the first mistake the Carter administration made in the early days of the hostage crisis. The second was the belief that a full-scale public relations campaign would be necessary to rally the American public behind the president. But the public normally rallies around a president in times of crisis—for instance, President

Kennedy's highest ratings followed his worst foreign policy fiasco, the Bay of Pigs invasion. But when a concerted effort is made by a president's staff to portray the president as being on top of developments, the short-term benefits can be outweighed by the long-term costs if the crisis drags on. The president then becomes the personification of the nation's frustration in not "resolving" the situation, just as he was the personification for their rallying and patriotic expressions at the early point of the crisis.

Memorandums circulated among Carter aides during the first few days after the hostages were taken illustrate how some of the president's own people inadvertently helped set the terrorist trap. On November 8, White House Staff Director Al McDonald sent a memo to Jordan, titled "Timely Public Responses to the Iranian Situation." McDonald suggested that Carter issue a public statement on the hostage situation that would state that "this is an unprecedented event and is demanding the constant attention of the senior officials of our country, including myself." McDonald urged that the president be portrayed as handling this crisis virtually by himself:

> This brief announcement should be made before the television cameras, ideally after the departure of the Irish Prime Minister [who was visiting Carter that day] rather than in connection with that departure statement. The President should clearly be seen alone as the American leader in charge of handling of this problem. Each statement by the Secretary of State should indicate that he has been "authorized by the President to make the following statement." . . . Jody [White House Press Secretary Jody Powell] would make the following points: . . . Indicate the President is devoting a great deal of personal attention to the effort [to free the hostages] and has called the NSC into multi-sessions daily to stay abreast of the situation. Mention that the President is in regular conversation with the Secretary of State several times each day. Comment that the President has instructed that his and the Vice President's schedules be reviewed to assure that one of them will be in the While House in direct charge of the situation at all times until it is resolved.[25]

The "president in control" strategy was augmented by a large-scale media campaign to encourage editors and news directors around the country to rally behind Carter. Press Secretary Powell sent a letter to eight thousand people on the White House media liaison list and a mailgram to 1,500 people in broadcasting suggesting two ways that the American people could show their concern for the fate of the hostages. The first suggestion, set forth by Bruce Laingen, the American chargé d'affaires in Iran who was being held as a hostage in the Iranian foreign ministry building (and allowed to remain in contact with Washington), was that "church bells be rung each noon until the hostages are re-leased." The recommendation of Attorney General Benjamin Civiletti and several members of Congress that "Americans write the Iranian Mission at the United Nations to demand the release of the hostages" was also mentioned. The implication of this appeal to the media was that those in television, radio, and print news could do their part for the country and the president by giving wide publicity to the plight of the hostages. "Your support for these two suggestions will help prevent any miscalculation [by Iranian authorities] of where Americans stand in this time of crisis."[26]

Many people in the media did respond to this personal appeal from the White House. The general manager of a radio station in Dubuque, Iowa, wrote to Carter to inform him that his station had drafted a letter to be sent to Khomeini demanding the release of the hostages, and that more than four thousand listeners had added their names to the letter. "We know that this, in itself, is not enough to free the American hostages," wrote Philip Kelly, president and general manager of WDBQ radio, "but it does show that the people of Dubuque, Iowa, a great American city, and the people of the surrounding area do care. You have our support!" The text of the letter to Khomeini was symbolic of the mood and temperament of the country: ". . . We American people are outraged by the reprehensible and totally unjustified taking of innocent American hostages at our embassy in Tehran. We join our government in demanding their immediate release. We support our government in its efforts to secure that release. . . . We address you as a free people, free to address you in any way we see fit, a people who need no guidance from our government in what to say, or how to say it, for we speak with one calm but clear and unmistakable collective voice. You can hear it in our church bells. LET OUR PEOPLE GO. NOW."[27]

It was not just in the heartland of America that the president's call for unity and expressions of concern for the hostages were enthusiastically received. The governor of Alaska, Jay Hammond, issued a press release that "called on Alaskans to join a national movement to set aside a time each day to pray for the safe release of the hostages. The governor said he supports the President's efforts to achieve the safe return of the hostages and the call by members of Congress for daily prayers by Americans until the hostages are freed. . . . Hammond asked churches, organizations and individual Alaskans to unite to pray, each in his or her own way, for the quick and safe return of all the American hostages in Iran." Powell thanked Hammond's press secretary for the governor's actions, stating that "these are crucial days for our nation, it is clear. But it also is clear that there is a wonderful sense of unity and all demonstrations of that unity will be helpful in the long run to our hostages."[28]

The "wonderful" sense of unity, though, would soon evaporate as the hostage crisis lingered into 1980. The ringing of church bells, the national days of prayer, and the tying of yellow ribbons around the homes of hostages' families would all be constant reminders to the American people that the United States in general, and President Carter in particular, were seemingly helpless. The image of America that was projected both at home and abroad was that of a great power reduced to calling for prayers and sympathy. When Carter aides Anne Wexler and Bob Maddox sent the president a memorandum in mid-November 1979 suggesting that Carter call for a special prayer for the hostages on Thanksgiving Day—a suggestion that Carter approved—they claimed that "such a call would further rivet the nation's attention on the problem and could lead us to an even deeper sense of unity in the midst of these crises."[29] But the last thing Carter and the country needed was any further attachment to the hostage crisis. The more attention that was focused on the plight of the hostages, the worse it would become for Carter as the hostages remained in captivity. What was needed in the early months of the seizure of the embassy was a clear message from the White House that while all efforts to attain the release of the hostages would be pursued, the situation would not be allowed to paralyze the government or to dictate the course and direction of American foreign policy. That message never came.

Carter made his first public address on the hostage issue in a speech before the AFL-CIO in Washington on November 15. A few days earlier, the White House released a statement by Carter that called for restraint on the part of the American people in responding to the crisis. Powell said that "the President expects every American to refrain from any action that might increase the danger to the American hostages in Tehran." The statement said that Carter shares with the American people their feelings of "outrage," "frustration," and "deep anger" over the taking of the hostages, but that his effort to resolve the crisis "require[s] the calmest possible atmosphere."[30] However, in his address to the AFL-CIO members, Carter denounced Iran in what would be the toughest speech he would ever make on the hostage crisis. He also inadvertently helped fuel the "day count" of how long the hostages remained in captivity:

> I have reflected for several weeks about what I would say to you this afternoon about our mutual goals, our legislative successes together, our National Accord, and our solid working relationship. With great pride I had intended to point out our accomplishments during the last 34 months. . . . But I must leave these subjects. . . . [T]oday we have other important matters to consider. . . . This is the 12th day that more than 100 innocent human beings, some 60 of whom are members of the

United States' diplomatic mission, have been held hostage in our Embassy in Iran. For a rare time in human history, a host government has condoned and even encouraged this kind of illegal action against the sovereign territory and official diplomatic relations of another nation. *This is an act of terrorism—totally outside the bounds of international law and diplomatic tradition.*[31]

After repeating his call for restraint—"This crisis calls for firmness and it calls for restraint. I am proud that this situation has brought forth calm leadership by officials and private citizens throughout the country"— Carter then issued the following warning to Iran:

The actions of Iranian leaders and the radicals who invaded our Embassy were completely unjustified. They and all others must know that the United States of America will not yield to international terrorism or to blackmail.[32]

The speech drew enthusiastic cheering and whistling from the delegates, but also criticism from Republican presidential hopeful John Connally, who accused the president of pursuing a double standard on the hostage issue. Connally said that on the one hand, Carter had appealed for calm on the part of the American people, "yet he chooses the opportunity to appear before the A.F.L.-C.I.O. convention to go down and make a ringing speech, talking about the terrorists in Iran, and using the inflammatory language himself."[33] Carter, who was trying to project a tough image at times in order to deflect criticism of his patient approach to the crisis, sometimes gave mixed signals about his intentions concerning Iran. Following a presidential breakfast meeting with congressional leaders on November 27, Senator Bennett Johnston, a Democrat from Louisiana, told reporters that "the President made it clear simply by releasing the hostages, the slate [with Iran] is not wiped clean. He did not say, did not suggest, what further action might be taken, but I think all of us feel, including the President, that he will do something else after the hostages are released."[34]

While much of the country rallied behind Carter in the immediate aftermath of the embassy seizure, there were some visible cracks in the "unity" drive as early as November 1979. The daily tabulation of mailgrams, telegrams, and telephone calls to the White House on November 21, for example, found that out of 1,153 mailgrams and telegrams sent that day, 750 urged military intervention, while the others pleaded with the administration to "do something." Telephone callers urged further action such as military intervention or a cutoff of food shipments to Iran.[35]

The public relations campaign at times found the Carter administration in a sparring role with those in the media who saw the situation differently from the president. The White House occasionally became testy when negative feedback came in concerning how Carter was handling the crisis. A few days after the hostages were taken, the publisher of the *Sacramento Union*, John McGoff, wrote an editorial in his newspaper calling for the resignation of Carter. "This nation can no longer afford the luxury of even fourteen more months of this moralistic mountebank," wrote McGoff. "We are in the fix we are because of Carter. . . . Now we have been forced to stand before the world as a helpless sap while a tinhorn fanatic humiliates us. . . . We call—with all solemnity and seriousness—for James Earl Carter to step down and turn over the presidency to a vice president whose politics may be equally as abhorrent to us, but who at least has some notion of what government and leadership is all about. While there is still time." Robert Henley, the president and general manager of radio station KGNR in Sacramento, sent a copy of the editorial to Powell, informing him that his station conducted a "people poll" to determine how much support there was for McGoff's recommendation. "In a 24-hour period, the station received 4,100 calls," Henley informed Powell. "Of these, 2,220, 54% disagreed and 1,890, 46% agreed with McGoff's views. . . . Just thought you might like to know." Powell shot back a letter to Henley: "It may be indigenous to your area of California, or it may be that people who are angry are more likely to call. But the mail and telephone calls coming into the White House are running consistently 89% to 90% in support of the President. *Thought you might like to know.*"[36]

The unity drive was also directed at Congress, as the administration tried to gain bipartisan support. In presidential aide Wexler's November 7 memorandum to Jordan and Powell, she stated that "there is too much at stake here to play politics on this issue." However, the White House itself was not above playing politics when Senator Edward Kennedy, who was mounting a strong challenge for the 1980 Democratic presidential nomination, made a blunder by denouncing the shah and stating that the deposed Iranian dictator should never have been allowed into the United States. Tehran Radio exploited Kennedy's statement, claiming it represented a significant change in American public opinion on the hostage crisis. "Regardless of the real goals behind Kennedy's recent statements," Tehran Radio said on December 4, "we realize that they reveal to us, as well as to the entire world, the real stand of the American people, who are beginning to understand the various dimensions of the crisis. The American people are now blaming those who agreed to accommodate the deposed Shah, the Pharoah of the 20th Century." When Carter read the transcript of the radio broadcast, he sent a copy to Powell with a brief but clear message: "Jody—Use as appropriate."[37]

Some people in the administration were not hesitant to point out that public expressions of sympathy for the hostages by Carter could help his political fortunes. On the day before Thanksgiving, one aide wrote to Powell that "we might . . . consider having JC ask everyone to observe 1-2-5 minutes of silence tomorrow for hostages and/or dead marine. This is something JC could do that would involve everyone, corny as it might seem to sophisticates like those (in press) covering JC, it might play well in the country."[38]

Carter enjoyed a tremendous rise in public support in the aftermath of the seizure of the embassy. The Gallup poll's traditional question, "Do you approve or disapprove of the way Carter is handling his job as president?" garnered only a twenty-nine percent positive response in October 1979. On the day the hostages were taken, his approval rating was still at a low of thirty-two percent. But it then began to climb to thirty-eight percent by mid-November, and to sixty-one percent by December. This marked one of the most substantial gains ever for a president in such a short period of time. An NBC/Associated Press poll asked whether the respondent approved or disapproved of the way Carter was handling the hostage situation; it found a seventy-five percent approval rating in November and almost eighty percent in December. But Carter's popularity then began to decline steadily as the hostage drama extended into 1980. In January, the president's approval rating on the hostage crisis fell to sixty percent, by April it was below fifty percent, and by May it had fallen to forty percent. It remained around that level through Carter's defeat in the 1980 presidential election.[39]

The support from the American people during the first few months of the hostage episode reinforced the administration's belief that it was responding to the crisis in the right way. The Carter administration had taken some significant steps against Iran once the hostages were seized. These included the freezing of Iranian assets and property in the United States, suspending purchases and shipments of Iranian oil to the United States, reviewing the visas of fifty thousand Iranian students in this country, and discouraging the granting of permits for demonstrations either against or in favor of the Iranian government on federal property.

Carter felt particularly strong about the need to prevent domestic demonstrations concerning the situation in Iran. "I . . . forbade any Iranian demonstrations on federal property, and became quite irritated when my legal advisers and some staff leaders came back repeatedly to argue that this order might infringe on the constitutional right of free speech," writes Carter in his memoirs. "I was certain I was right. American citizens—including the president—were in no mood to watch Iranian 'students' denouncing our country in front of the White House. I was convinced that the demonstrators might precipitate a riot, in which they would be killed or cause the deaths of others. Such an event would have been bad enough in itself, but violence of this kind would very likely have been highly publicized in Iran, and might have caused Americans to be killed or injured in retaliation."[40]

Thus, when Attorney General Civiletti sent a memorandum to Carter on November 15, stating that "it is my firm opinion that we cannot legally deny the right to persons, Iranian or American, who do not have some provable record of violence themselves, to demonstrate on federal properties in Washington in support of or in opposition to United States policy in Iran," Carter responded with a handwritten note on the original memo: "I strongly prefer that we do our best to prevent permits being issued for Pro- or Anti-Iranians until hostages are free. Take our case to court if necessary." To ensure that the president did not misunderstand his own personal distaste for pro-Khomeini sympathizers, Civiletti wrote back to Carter: "I share deeply revulsion at the views of students or anyone here supporting the vicious acts of terrorism against our people in Tehran. I pray for your strength and their freedom."[41]

The permits were denied, but the issue continued throughout the hostage ordeal. During the summer of 1980, the park police in Washington, D.C. granted a few permits for Iranian demonstrations that subsequently took place in Lafayette Park, near the White House. Carter became upset and informed his legal counsel, Lloyd Cutler, that he wanted to be "personally . . . involved in any *approval* of an Iranian demonstration in the vicinity of the White House."[42] In the early days of the crisis, Carter told Jordan that "I'm not going to risk a fight in front of the White House that gets shown in Iran and brings harm to the hostages. I may have to sit here and bite my lip and show restraint and look impotent, but I am not going to have those bastards humiliating our country in front of the White House! And let me tell you something else, Ham, if I wasn't President, I'd be out on the streets myself and would probably take a swing at any Khomeini demonstrator I could get my hands on."[43]

It was more compassion for the hostages, though, than anger toward Iran that drove Carter and much of his administration throughout the 444 days that Americans remained in captivity. An emotional bond developed between the president and many of his top aides with the hostages and their families. When the relative of one of the hostages wrote to Carter to express her anxiety over her sister's situation—"I feel very frustrated and depressed at this time. I wish there were more that I could do personally"—Carter added a handwritten note to the White House response, saying, "P.S. I work on this *every* day, and *never* forget the hostages—J."[44] After meeting with the families of the hostages at the State Department a few days after the embassy was seized, Carter was moved deeply by the experience. "Although the building was only a few hundred yards from the White House, the trip seemed long to me," Carter writes. "There was no way for me to know how the families would react, but when we finally met, it was obvious that they and I shared the same feelings of grief and alarm. Secretary Vance and I briefed them on what had occurred, and explained some of the steps we were taking to insure the safety of their loved ones in Iran. The conversation was emotional for all of us, and afterward I was pleased when the families issued a statement of support for me and called on the nation to remain calm. This meeting was the beginning of a close relationship between us, which never faltered during the succeeding months."[45]

Carter's sentiments were shared by many in the administration, who were also touched and troubled by the capture of Americans. Many of the hostages were diplomats whom they knew personally. Gary Sick, the Middle East analyst on the National Security Council, writes that "I remember discussing the crisis with my family shortly after the hostages were seized and telling them that until the hostages were freed, their welfare would take priority over everything else in my life. It was almost like taking religious vows, and that sense of personal dedication remained vivid and strong until the Algerian plane carried the hostages safely out of Iranian airspace many months later."[46] Secretary of State Vance felt the daily strain of concern for the hostages. "All of us in senior positions didn't think about the hostages [without asking] ourselves the question, 'Is there anything that we ought to [do] that we are not doing?' "[47]

At one point early in the crisis, Carter left the impression with congressional leaders that the fate of the hostages would not be the paramount issue for the United States in dealing with the situation. Senator Johnston, in his talk with reporters following the November 27 congressional leaders' breakfast meeting with Carter, claimed that "the President said that his first concern was the honor of this country. He didn't say that in a way that'd show less concern for the hostages, but a real resolve on his part which I think everyone supported that we not do anything to sully the honor of this country by negotiating for hostages, negotiating away the honor of the country." Johnston said that Carter "emphasized that the honor of the country comes first, before the lives of the hostages."[48]

But the hostages would always come first for Carter, and the honor of the country would, unfortunately, suffer. Jack Valenti, the former special assistant to President Johnson, puts it more bluntly: "The worst thing a president can do is to go on television and talk about hostages or kidnapped people. . . . Carter publicly anguished and that was just like feeding raw, red meat to those kidnappers. They loved it. Here they had the most powerful leader in the free world humbling himself on his goddamn' knees and they kicked his ass all over the place."[49]

The taking of the hostages complicated U.S. foreign policy during Carter's last year in office. Under normal conditions, formulating and implementing American foreign policy is a difficult enough task. In times of crisis, though, the task becomes more difficult since all the energy and attention of the president and his senior policymakers are focused on the particular crisis. Yet prior to the Iran hostage episode, most U.S. foreign policy crises were rather brief affairs. Once the high point of a crisis subsides, life gets back to normal. In the case of the Iran hostage crisis, life never really got back to normal for the Carter administration, as the hostage issue never went away.

Cyrus Vance was determined not to allow the hostage drama to detract from his efforts to complete the foreign policy agenda of the first term of the Carter administration. "It didn't change my focus as secretary of state," said Vance. "It meant that there was another excruciatingly difficult problem to deal with along with all the others, but in no way in which I can let it interfere with carrying out the many other things which we were involved in."[50] That included solidifying the peace treaty between Israel and Egypt, working toward attaining some degree of stability in the always turbulent Middle East, winning ratification in Congress for the SALT II treaty (which would become derailed following the Soviet invasion of Afghanistan in December 1979), maintaining the normalization of relations with China, and a host of other issues.

But most of all, the hostage crisis remained at the top of the U.S. foreign policy agenda for the last fourteen months of the Carter administration. It drained away the energy and vision that was needed to direct the entire course and content of America's foreign relations. Even when other events arose that had a potentially more significant impact upon U.S. security and geopolitical interests than the seizure of the embassy, the hostage crisis was never far from the president's thoughts. When the Soviets invaded Afghanistan—an engagement that would become their "Vietnam War" and lead to the formulation of the Carter Doctrine, which pronounced the Persian Gulf as vital to U.S. interests—the hostage crisis continued to take center stage. "Throughout the crisis over Afghanistan," Carter writes, "the meetings between me and my advisers about the hostages had continued without slackening. In spite of my other responsibilities, the hostages were always in my mind."[51] For Vance, the hostage crisis demanded a great amount of his attention. "Obviously, it took people's time away [from] concentrating on other things," Vance said, "important problems that we were dealing with. But I think that we all recognized that we have to be careful that we did not let the hostage crisis divert us from what we had to do in those other areas. And it's very difficult to do because it did take a lot of the President's time and it took a considerable amount of my time, but I had these other things to do, and I just had to go ahead and do it."[52]

The Iranians would do their best to prevent the United States from getting on with the business of being a great power. For the militants and for Khomeini, paralyzing the United States and dominating its foreign policy agenda was not its main purpose or strategy. This was just an added and unexpected benefit to the seizure of the embassy. The initial purpose of the November 4 attack—to protest the entry of the hated shah into the United States and to demand his extradition—soon gave way to a much more important objective for the militants. The hostages could now become the focal point for solidifying and consolidating the Islamic revolution, which was still less than a year old. Khomeini sent his son to the embassy the day after it was seized to demonstrate his support for the militants.

By January 1980, it had become clear that the militants had gained the upper hand in the struggle to prevent any moderate government from assuming control over events in Iran. Gary Sick sent a memo to Jody Powell on January 8, emphasizing the advantages that the militants had gained from the hostage crisis. Titled "The Militants vs. the Government—Who Leads Whom?" Sick pointed out that "the kidnappers have . . . succeeded in moving Iranian policy—and Khomeini himself—into more extreme and militant positions than would have been likely in the absence of the hostage situation. By keeping Iranian public attention inflamed with their militance, they have served Khomeini's purposes by deflecting criticism of the failures of the present regime and popular concern about the implications of the new constitution. But the price of that service has been that Khomeini has lent his own great authority to the militants and their purposes." Sick then summed up the situation in Iran as the Carter administration entered the third month of the crisis:

> If it is fair to assume that the objective of the militants is to destroy relations between the United States and Iran, to move the revolution into a more militant path, and to identify and bring down any political leadership within the country which has doubts about the wisdom of such a policy; if those are their objectives, they have succeeded to a very considerable extent over the past ten weeks. By crushing or diverting any obstacles which have appeared along the way, they have demonstrated very effectively who is leading whom.[53]

In this way, the hostages became rallying points for *both* Khomeini and Carter. While the White House asked the American people to ring church bells, say prayers, and write letters to the Iranian mission, so too did

Khomeini fuse religion, politics, and hostages to rally *his* masses in the struggle against the forces of evil, of which the United States was the Great Satan. The hostages were referred to by Khomeini and the militants as "spies," and they provided a ready-made platform to vent anger at all those opposed to the Islamic revolution, both at home and abroad. In fact, had a Gallup poll been conducted in Iran both prior to and after the hostages were seized, it would likely have shown Khomeini's approval rating to have soared just as Carter's did with the American people in the aftermath of the embassy takeover.

But while Khomeini could continuously tap the revolutionary fervor of the Iranian people and had that most precious of all commodities—time—on his side, Carter was not as fortunate. The patience and support of the American people was eroding at the beginning of 1980, as not only the television newscasts kept reminding the country of how many days the Americans had been held in captivity—day sixty, day sixty-one, and so forth—but so too was the White House with its continual focus on the plight of the hostages. The first few months of 1980 were characterized by tireless efforts to attain a solution to the crisis, but as was the case in November and December of 1979, the militants would not relinquish their prized assets. One obstacle to a possible end to the crisis was removed when the shah departed for Panama on December 15. His presence in the United States for treatment of cancer not only angered the Iranians and was the catalyst for the embassy takeover, it also angered some of the relatives of the hostages. "For God's sake, Mr. President," wrote the son of Moorehead Kennedy, one of the hostages, to Carter, "must my father sit bound and blind-folded daily while the recuperating Shah relaxes, and contemplates which country club he will live in? . . . I plead to you as President of this nation to ask the Shah to promptly leave this country in order that some light may be shed on this seemingly never ending crisis."[54]

But the removal of the shah from the United States did not change the situation for the Carter administration. His presence in this country and the U.S. refusal to extradite him to Iran was initially used by the militants to inflame the Iranian people and continue to build support for the Islamic revolution. But the shah soon ceased to be the central factor in resolving the crisis. "The Ayatollah had made up his mind," said Vance, "that he was going to use the holding of the hostages as a lever to bring about the establishment of the Majlis [parliament] and the establishment of a parliament that was consistent with his views of what the politics of Iran should be. And so until the Majlis was established, I think that it was really impossible that we would get them back."[55]

International efforts to gain the release of the hostages included a January visit to Iran by U.N. Secretary General Kurt Waldheim; a U.N. Security Council measure to impose sanctions against Iran, which was vetoed by the Soviet Union on January 13; and continued pressure on U.S. allies to isolate Iran and force the government to release the hostages. All these efforts failed as there was no strong central government that could impose its desires on the militants who were holding the hostages. Even the election of moderate Abolhassan Bani-Sadr as president of Iran on January 25, along with the presence of other moderates in the government such as Foreign Minister Sadegh Ghotbzadeh, could not help the United States extract itself from the quagmire of the hostage crisis. This all proved very frustrating for American officials. "From time to time we thought that we might [get the hostages back] because we had the President of Iran [and] the foreign minister siding with the view that they ought to be returned, that they had served whatever purpose they may have served," recalled Vance. "But the Ayatollah was the all-powerful. His decision was that he would use them [until a revolutionary parliament was established]."[56]

Nevertheless, secret negotiations were conducted in Europe during the first three months of 1980 between Hamilton Jordan and two intermediaries for the Iranian government, Christian Bourguet, a French lawyer, and Hector Villalon, an Argentine businessman-lawyer. Both Bourguet and Villalon were friends of Ghotbzadeh and Bani-Sadr and offered to work behind the scenes in order to help resolve the crisis.

The intricate process of secret meetings and information exchanges between the United States and Iran actually began in late November, after thirteen women and black hostages were released. Pierre Salinger, the former press secretary to President Kennedy and at the time of the hostage crisis working for ABC News, received a telephone call from another French lawyer, François Cheron, who said that he had an urgent matter to discuss with Salinger. "I was alone in my house," Salinger recalls, "and the phone rings. [It was] a French lawyer saying, 'I've got to see you. I used to be the lawyer for Ghotbzadeh and for Bani-Sadr, and for the Ayatollah Khomeini, and I've got to talk to you about the hostage problem.' Well, I mean I said come right over! So he comes over and he says, 'Look, here's what happened. The United States government has sent out word all over the place trying to find people who might serve as intermediaries, and a friend of mine . . . a lawyer in Italy [who in turn was a friend of former Italian Prime Minister Giulio Andreotti] called me knowing that I had these contacts in Iran, and said would you be willing to do it. I said yes, and we called Bani-Sadr in Tehran and said would he be willing to talk through us. And Bani-Sadr said yes.' And then [Cheron] went back to [the Italian contacts] and they said the American government has decided not to do it. 'And I'm very upset about it [Cheron told Salinger] because now I've got Bani-Sadr standing on the thing ready to talk, and we can't do anything. Would you do something about this?' "

Salinger told Cheron that although he was now a journalist and no longer in the government, he also wanted to get the hostages released and would see what he could do. He immediately telephoned the U.S. ambassador to France, Arthur Hartman, and related the conversation he had with Cheron. Shortly afterward, Salinger received a call from the political counselor at the American embassy in France, Warren Zimmerman, who asked him how he could get in touch with Cheron. The French lawyer later called Salinger to thank him for his efforts, telling him, "We'll keep you briefed on what's going on if you promise me that you will not report anything that we are doing until after the hostages are free." Salinger agreed. "I followed that thing for a year. We never reported a single thing, not once."[57]

Meanwhile, when Hamilton Jordan asked CIA Director Stansfield Turner for background checks on the two men he would be dealing with—Bourguet and Villalon—he discovered that Bourguet was a French leftist who had been representing the new Iranian government on various legal matters, while Villalon was more of an international entrepreneur who had been arrested in 1977 by French police for alleged involvement in the kidnapping of Luchino Revelli-Beaumont, a top executive of Fiat. As it turned out, Villalon was innocent of the kidnapping. He had been asked by the wife of Revelli-Beaumont to help track down the kidnappers and get her husband back. Neither Bourguet nor Villalon received any money for their efforts to help end the Iran hostage crisis. Bourguet was convinced that a prolonged crisis between the United States and Iran could actually lead to a world war and that the situation must be resolved as soon as possible. He was also a lawyer who had defended individual rights and liberties and was opposed to the holding of hostages by the Iranian militants.[58]

A detailed scenario was designed by Jordan and the two intermediaries involving a series of reciprocal steps by the United States and Iran aimed at ending the crisis. This included the formation of a U.N. Commission of Inquiry that would hear Iranian grievances and travel to Iran to visit the hostages. The hostages would be transferred to the control of the government and then set free. But on February 23, the day the commission arrived in Tehran, Khomeini issued a statement that the fate of the hostages would be decided by the Majlis, which had not yet even been elected. Then, in March, Khomeini demanded that the U.N. commission first make a public statement of its "findings" concerning the crimes of the shah before being allowed to see the hostages. There was no indication from the ayatollah that the hostages would then be transferred to the control of the government. The commission felt compromised and left Iran on March 11 without getting to visit the hostages.

In the meantime, Ghotbzadeh had made plans to transfer the hostages to the foreign ministry building on March 8 and had military helicopters ready to carry the hostages out of the embassy. He had even gone on Iranian television to say that he had Khomeini's approval for this action. But the scenario fell apart when Khomeini's office issued a statement that the ayatollah "prefers to remain silent on this" matter.[59]

A second scenario was then drawn up by Jordan, Bourguet, and Villalon that included the return of the U.N. commission to Iran and the eventual release of the hostages. Bani-Sadr secretly promised Jordan and Carter (in letters written to them after the collapse of the U.N. effort) that the hostages would still be turned over to the Iranian government in a matter of a few weeks. Public announcements were later made to that effect, leading Carter to postpone a planned statement on April 1 imposing new sanctions on Iran. But on April 7, Khomeini announced that the hostages would remain under the control of the militants. Although the Revolutionary Council voted in favor of a transfer of hostages to the government, Bani-Sadr left the matter for Khomeini to decide since the vote was not unanimous. The ayatollah vetoed the Revolutionary Council's measure, convincing Carter that Bani-Sadr had no real power to help end the crisis. "It was obvious to me," Carter writes, "that the Revolutionary Council would never act and that in spite of all our work and the efforts of the elected leaders of Iran, the hostages were not going to be released."[60]

On the same day that Khomeini killed any prospect for the transfer of the hostages, Carter announced that the United States was breaking diplomatic relations with Iran. Carter also stated that the United States was putting into effect additional sanctions prohibiting exports from the United States to Iran, except for food and medicine. All visas issued to Iranians for future entry into the United States were declared invalid, and no new visas would be reissued. It was in his closing remarks, though, that the president once again revealed the grip that the hostages had taken on him and reminded the American people of how long the hostages were in captivity: "I am committed to resolving this crisis. I am committed to the safe return of the American hostages, and to the preservation of our national honor. The hostages and their families, indeed, all of us in America, have lived with the reality and anguish of their captivity for five months. The steps I have ordered today are those that are necessary now. Other actions may become necessary if these steps do not produce the prompt release of the hostages."[61]

Meanwhile, the hostages were languishing in the embassy, subjected to mental torture and at times physical beatings. The more fortunate ones were the three diplomats who were held in the Iranian foreign ministry building during most of the crisis. They were treated much better than the majority of the hostages. After their release, the hostages told of mock executions in the middle of the night. In one instance, on February 5, a group of militants wearing white masks, fatigues, combat boots, and carrying automatic rifles, awoke twenty-one of the hostages at 1:00 a.m. and forced them to stand against a wall. The chambers of the rifles were loaded, orders were given to the "firing squad," and a round hit the floor. Colonel Charles Scott, the chief of the Military Assistance and Advisory Group, was one of the hostages brought to the wall to be "executed." He recalled his thoughts as he heard the rounds put into the chambers and the safety catches released: "My knees were knocking," said Scott. "I thought things had deteriorated so badly that they were just going to get rid of us."[62]

Robert Ode also thought it was over for him on what he calls the night of the Gestapo raid. "We didn't know whether they were going to blow our heads off or what they were going to do," recalled Ode. Later that night, when things had quieted down and the hostages were returned to their rooms, Ode suffered a delayed reaction. After about one hour of sleep, he awoke to his heart pounding extremely hard. "I thought [for] sure I was going to have a heart attack," he said.[63] But the effect of the mock execution backfired for the Iranians, for while it created intense fear the first time, it also reinforced the hostages' wills to survive. "You can just get so scared," said Scott. "[Then] you get angry and once you get angry it sustains you through many sorts of stress. I refused to think about death after that."[64]

The anger was not just directed at the Iranians, but also at Carter, since the hostages were told by their captors that the president didn't care about their fate. The hostages themselves could only wonder why they were in captivity for so long without any progress toward freedom. One of the hostages even refused to meet with Carter after they were freed in January 1981, when the former president traveled to Wiesbaden, West Germany, to greet them.[65] Sometimes the hostages would become quite despondent over what they thought was a lack of interest in their plight by the American public. Ode once wrote a letter to his wife, Rita—who was serving on the Iran Working Group at the State Department—saying that he feared that the hostages were just not an important news item in the United States. Since Rita knew from working with the State Department that all the letters sent and received to the embassy were being read by the Iranian militants, she could not come right out and say that the hostage crisis was indeed a major news story—the Iranians would have intercepted that letter. She therefore decided to send a coded message.

Since both she and her husband were avid television news junkies, she wrote to him that all his personal friends, such as "Walter" and "John"—and she used the first names of many other major newscasters at that time—talk about him *all the time*.[66]

Ode incurred the wrath of the guards when he wrote to his wife that she should not worry about him because he had made up his mind that he was going to outlive the "SOBs" who had taken him captive. He was then awakened in the middle of the night by two guards, holding the letter in front of him and demanding to know what the term "SOBs" meant. "And I said [to them], 'You know what it means. You've been to the U.S.' [They replied], 'No, we do not know, what is meaning 'SOBs.' So I said it means sons of bitches, that's precisely what it means. They were so angry they took my letter and just tore it into shreds and said you'll never, ever receive another piece of mail while you're here," Ode recalled. The guards punished Ode by withholding mail from him for over a month.[67]

There was dissension among the hostages concerning how some of them conducted themselves during their captivity; some of the hostages cooperated with the Iranians and were used as propaganda tools to denounce the United States. Sometimes, though, the hostages did not get along with each other for the same reasons people normally don't get along; they simply didn't like each other. "I absolutely couldn't stand him," hostage Bill Belk, a communications officer, said about another hostage who was brought into his cell to be his roommate. "And after forty-eight hours I was in a frame of mind where I would find fault with everything he did. I would pass my time by sitting in the corner of the cell and making up 300 reasons to hate him. I'd say to myself, 'I hate him because he's cross-eyed. I hate him because of the sucking noises he makes when he smokes his pipe.' . . . On and on. I just kept making up reasons to hate him." Belk finally decided the only way to get rid of his undesired roommate was to make the militant guards believe that he would kill him unless they removed him from his cell. One day while being escorted to the bathroom, Belk told his guard that he was going to strangle his roommate and showed the guard how he would do so with his bare hands. The guard believed him, and Belk got a new roommate that same day.[68]

The break in diplomatic relations with Iran on April 7 signaled a new phase in the hostage drama. The endless diplomatic maneuvering, which included publicized appeals to allies and Third World countries to apply pressure to Iran to release the hostages, and the secret negotiations with Bourguet and Villalon, not to mention those with Ghotbzadeh and Bani-Sadr, had left the United States exactly where it was when the militants scaled the embassy walls on November 4. American hostages were still being held, and the kidnappers and those who controlled the kidnappers were still calling the shots. They were playing to audiences both in Iran and the United States and were assured of getting attention and reaction as long as they had American hostages.

But the United States was actually in much worse shape with respect to the hostage crisis in April than it was in November. Gone was the almost euphoric feeling in the country that the president must be supported and that America would prevail against these Middle Eastern fanatics who dared to insult the United States by violating its embassy and taking its citizens captive. Gone too was the international shock over the incident, for, as is the case in many bad situations that linger on for a long time, the sense of urgency to resolve it gave way to complacency on the part of other states. The decision by the White House to portray the president as in control of the situation and the main person to handle it had clearly backfired. The president was now trapped in his self-imposed exile of not leaving his "command post" in Washington. And he was increasingly being perceived by the American people and by other governments as ineffective in dealing with Khomeini and the militants.

Carter was moving closer to the one option he wanted most to avoid: the use of military force. But with increased calls from many different quarters—Congress, the public, and many of his close advisers—for military action, he finally decided on April 11 to order a military rescue mission for the hostages. It was implemented thirteen days later.

"Hostages," "Khomeini," and "Carter" were the three words that the American public had heard almost daily since the takeover of the embassy. These words, like the main protagonists in the drama, had become interwoven and fused as the crisis dragged on into the spring of 1980. Soon, though, there would be new terms that would enter the vocabulary of the hostage crisis: "Desert One," "malfunctioning helicopters," "eight casualties."

The Rescue Attempt

"When we started," said Delta Force commander Colonel Charles Beckwith about the early plans in November for a rescue effort, "I didn't think the president had the real guts to approve an operation like that. I didn't think Carter would do that. And then I realized as time went on and I'm watching the administration and they were running out of what things to do. And so I knew that the force option would be the very last option that he would use. And he got down to that was the last one."[69]

Operation Eagle Claw, the code name for the military rescue operation in Iran, caught many people, including the Iranians, by surprise. There had been continual speculation that a rescue effort may be launched since the day the hostages were taken. But few people really expected Jimmy Carter to order American military forces into action. The president who had placed so much emphasis on the lives of hostages would surely be unwilling to risk even a single hostage death in a military venture. Carter himself repeatedly stressed that all other measures—diplomatic, economic, political—would be pursued vigorously and that he did not favor military action. Even the breakdown in the secret negotiations and the imposition of tougher economic measures against Iran on April 7 did not seem to indicate that military countermeasures were imminent.

It thus came as startling news to the American people, U.S. allies who were not consulted prior to the rescue operation, and to other governments, when the White House released the following statement at 1:00 A.M. on April 25:

> The President has ordered the cancellation of an operation in Iran which was underway to prepare for a rescue of our hostages. The mission was terminated because of equipment failure. During the subsequent withdrawal of American personnel there was a collision between our aircraft on the ground at a remote desert location in Iran. There were no military hostilities, but the President deeply regrets that eight American crew members of the two aircraft were killed and others were injured in the accident. Americans involved in the operation have now been airlifted from Iran, and those who were injured are being given medical treatment and are expected to recover.
>
> This mission was not motivated by hostility toward Iran or the Iranian people, and there were no Iranian casualties.
>
> Preparations for this rescue mission were ordered for humanitarian reasons, to protect the national interests of this country, and to alleviate international tensions. The President accepts full responsibility for the decision to attempt the rescue.
>
> The nation is deeply grateful to the brave men who were preparing to rescue the hostages.
>
> The United States continues to hold the Government of Iran responsible for the safety of the American hostages.
>
> The United States remains determined to obtain their safe release at the earliest possible date.[70]

This brief statement was followed at 7:00 A.M. by a televised address to the nation in which Carter said that the rescue mission "had an excellent chance of success" and that he ordered the operation "in order to safeguard lives, to protect America's national interest and to reduce the tensions in the world that have been caused among many nations as the crisis has continued."[71]

All these reasons, though, were questioned both in discussions among Carter administration officials prior to the raid and in public debates afterward. There was no indication that American lives were in any more danger in the weeks prior to the decision to approve the raid than in the previous five months. The risk to the hostages' lives would actually have been higher during a military rescue mission than in the absence of one, since there are usually hostage deaths when counterterrorist forces storm a barricaded building, airplane, or other structure where armed terrorists are holding the hostages. In fact, a CIA estimate in March put the "loss rate" for the planned, but not yet approved, rescue mission at sixty percent, thus casting doubt on the "safeguarding lives" justification for the raid.[72]

It was also questionable whether a raid to free the hostages was dictated by our national interests. On the one hand, the high priority that the Carter administration gave to the hostage situation and its continual frustration in resolving the problem made the United States appear weak and impotent at the hands of the Iranians. A bold military strike to rescue the hostages could be viewed as in our national interest and necessary to restore America's image. However, the holding of hostages in Iran, no matter how tragic a situation, was not a real threat to U.S national interests. Hostages can be taken at any time, in any place around the world, as events prior to and since the 1979–81 hostage crisis have indicated. To view such incidents as against our national interest meant that a terrorist can automatically perpetrate a crisis by simply taking an American hostage.

Moreover, potential repercussions of a military venture into the streets of Tehran were numerous. "In the process of carrying out that rescue operation," said Secretary of State Vance, "we would have to spray a number of bombs, and thus greatly damage an area and this could cause a lot of things which would be against our interests. Namely, that it might spark an Islamic-Western conflict because the whole peninsula at that point, the whole area, was a tinderbox and it might well explode."[73]

Vance resigned his post after failing to persuade Carter and the National Security Council (NSC) to reverse their decision to proceed with a rescue operation—a decision that was made while Vance was on a brief vacation. He did not make his resignation public until after the mission was completed in order to preserve the secrecy of the operation. Others have written about his firm devotion to the primacy of human life. "No one who was acquainted with Cyrus Vance could question the depth of his commitment to peace and nonviolence," writes NSC analyst Gary Sick. "His reverence for human life shone through every decision he made. Throughout his distinguished service as Secretary of State he was absolutely consistent in counseling against the employment of military instruments—even for purposes of political symbolism. He was prepared to accept temporary political defeats and humiliations rather than set in motion a chain of events that might at some point result in even limited loss of life."[74]

But when it came to the hostage rescue mission, Vance was prepared to go further than accept a temporary political defeat. He was prepared to make the ultimate political sacrifice. On April 21, three days before the rescue operation was launched, Vance gave Carter a handwritten letter of resignation. "I know how deeply you have pondered your decision on Iran," Vance wrote. "I wish I could support you in it. But for the reasons we have discussed, I cannot. You would not be well served in the coming weeks and months by a secretary of state who could not offer you the public backing you need on an issue and decision of such extraordinary importance—no matter how firm I remain in my support on other issues, as I do, or how loyal I am to you as our leader. Such a situation would be untenable and our relationship, which I value so highly, would constantly suffer."[75]

Seasoned White House correspondents such as Sam Donaldson could not help but marvel at Vance's integrity. "[It was an act of] political courage . . . for him to resign before the raid," said Donaldson. "It would have been an act of principle to some extent to resign afterward, [saying] 'I can't support what happened, therefore [I resign].' But to do it before" was impressive in Donaldson's view.[76] White House Chief of Staff Hamilton Jordan writes that he was convinced that the rescue operation would be successful and that Vance would later regret his opposition to the plans. "Cy was going to feel like a damn fool when the helicopters landed on the South Lawn and our hostages climbed out."[77]

Vance, though, was firm in his belief that the rescue mission would be a disaster for the United States:

> I felt that if we did this, we were going to get killed all of the hostages, because I was convinced that they had people with machine guns guarding them wherever they were located. And we really didn't know where they were located. But that if we came and tried to take them, they would all be killed. And in my conversations with the hostages afterwards, I believe that that was a correct assessment. So that was a critically important matter to explore as far as I was concerned because I was also of the belief that it was not too far distant before that they would be released because the Majlis would be established and they would have served their purpose and we would then be able to get them back.
>
> In addition to that, we had some other problems. One, we would have to do this without consulting with our allies. And for us to do this without consulting with them would be completely contrary to the pres-

sure that we had been putting on them to keep them involved so that we could put political and economic pressure. We were moving in that direction and this would set that back. In addition to that, I felt that it would tend to drive the Iranians towards the Soviets. Again, I did not see that would be in our interests.

So all I saw was a whole series of very serious negatives which I thought were against our national interests and I could see no good reason for attempting what was going to be probably a failed operation.[78]

But by April 1980, the hostage drama had taken too great a toll on the Carter administration. The prospect of ending the national nightmare with a bold and daring rescue operation was too good for Carter to resist. As he indicated in his April 25 statement, plans for a potential rescue mission had actually begun shortly after the hostages were seized. The problem, though, was how to design a plan for an event that had no precedent.

The Iranian government's decision to support the militant students after they seized the American embassy meant that the United States faced a unique counterterrorist problem. The United States was prepared for operations in a "permissive" environment where the military units are allowed by the host government to enter the country and set up operations for a final assault on the target. This had occurred in Mogadishu, Somalia, in October 1977, when West German commandos stormed a hijacked Lufthansa 737 plane on the tarmac and rescued all eighty-six passengers, killing three terrorists and capturing a fourth. The counterterrorist operation was greatly enhanced by the cooperation of the Somali government, which allowed the mission to take place on its soil. That eliminated the need for secrecy in transporting the commandos to Mogadishu, or possibly confronting Somali military forces during the operation. The Somalis also actively participated in the raid by setting a diversionary fire near the front of the plane in order to distract the attention of the hijackers while the German GSG-9 commandos quietly moved into position for an assault from the rear. While the hijackers were in the cockpit observing the fire, two British Strategic Air Services commandos who took part in the raid launched stun grenades toward the cockpit window. The Germans also benefited from prior training for rescue missions on different types of aircraft, including the Lufthansa 737, and therefore knew the best means for gaining entry to the plane and avoiding areas that would cause loud vibrations or noise.[79]

But the Iran hostage situation meant that U.S. forces would have to enter Iran undetected and then proceed to an urban center to rescue large numbers of hostages who might be scattered throughout the American embassy compound. The situation was further complicated by the fact that whatever force or equipment that would be necessary for the rescue mission would have to be flown a long distance into Iran, since the United States did not have access to military bases close by. Turkey was not considered as a possible launching point for political and security reasons. The longer the geographical distance that a counterterrorist strike force needs to travel obviously increases the risk that some kind of problem—either technological or human—will arise.[80]

Delta Force, the special unit for U.S. counterterrorist operations, was created following the Mogadishu raid. Carter sent a note over to the Joint Chiefs of Staff inquiring whether the United States had the same capability as the Germans. Since we did not, it was suggested that U.S. military personnel take a close look at the German model. "When we formed Delta, we formed it based on fact," said Beckwith. "We felt that any way we operated, that we would never have to worry about our backside. We'd never have to go into a country like Iran. . . . We always felt when we went in that the local constabulary or something would keep everything down, that we would just be a surgical force that would handle that problem." The taking of the American hostages in Iran and the Iranian government's support of the hostage takers made the German model irrelevant for the United States.[81]

When Carter decided in 1977 to create a special counterterrorist force, the task was given to Beckwith. As an Army colonel and battle-proven warrior in Korea and Vietnam, he had earned the nickname of "Chargin' Charlie." Creating Delta meant that Beckwith had to recruit, mold, and train a cohesive unit to fight a new type of conflict. He was convinced that forming such a unit would take two years, but the Pentagon was anxious for quick results. "Somebody in the Office of the Secretary of Defense called me and said, 'We don't understand why it is going to take so long,'" Beckwith said. " 'Why don't you just go out there and get some "good ole boys" and take about nine weeks and form this thing.' And I just said, 'Well, that's a way to do it, but it's the wrong way.' And I said that you have to have the right people, the right skills and a lot of things that we don't know. We are going to have to plow new ground. And so I was given two years to do it."[82]

Beckwith welcomed the challenge of creating America's first counterterrorist unit. He had been urging the establishment of such a force for many years. But it would not be an easy task, since counterterrorism and special operations were not high-priority objectives for the U.S. military in the 1970s. The military's main emphasis and interest had long been in the strategic and conventional conflict arenas, including deterring and planning for nuclear or conventional war with the Soviet Union in Europe. Unconventional warfare, including counterinsurgency and counterterrorism, were viewed by many in the armed services as extra-curricular activities not to be taken very seriously. It was certainly not the path to take for career advancement. "[When] I was assigned that task," said Beckwith, "I knew this would be my last job. The probabilities of me getting anything else [were low]. The Army was awfully good to me. . . . I stayed inside the Special Ops for over twenty-three years. And so they told me it would ruin my career. I said, 'Fine, I'm enjoying it.' But so when it came up for me to do this job, there were people standing there wanting to see me fail. I can tell you that right now. That was not an easy job."[83]

After less than one year of recruiting and training his unit, Beckwith was informed that the Army wanted to "evaluate" his force. This involved demonstrating skills through a training exercise and responding to terrorist-type incidents—such as a hijacked plane and a barricaded building with hostages—before a panel of Army evaluators. Beckwith's unit passed this test, but the Delta Force commander still felt he needed the full two years that he had originally been given to make Delta ready for an actual incident. Another exercise was held before a panel of U.S. military and government officials a year later, including representatives from the State Department, CIA, and FBI, as well as counterterrorist specialists from Great Britain, West Germany, and France. When it was over, Delta had again passed and was "validated" as America's special operations unit to combat terrorism. And in one of those ironies of history, the validation exercise was completed on November 3, 1979, barely twenty-four hours before the hostages were taken at the U.S. embassy in Tehran.[84]

Beckwith immediately sent two of his men to Washington at the request of the Army after the embassy was seized. The Pentagon did not have any contingency plans for this type of hostage situation, in which the host government was supporting the terrorists. During that first week of the crisis, Beckwith received a phone call from one of his men, who was upset with the plans that were being discussed in Washington. "Boss, you need to get up here," he said. "They are coming up with some real wild ideas." Some of these "wild" ideas were not too popular with Beckwith, including parachuting into Tehran and launching an assault on the embassy. "And so I got there," said Beckwith, "and I heard all these wild things: 'Let's take Beckwith's people and we'll parachute them in over here, and do this.' And that's crazy. I said right then and there that this is not a parachute operation. On a parachute operation, you are always going to have seven percent [military] casualties. So they started talking to me about it and I said as far as I am concerned parachute is an option, but it's the poorest option that there is."[85]

But for Beckwith, the first priority before advising on a workable rescue plan was to obtain and evaluate the intelligence on the situation at the embassy. "I said what we need to do is find out what the situation is on the inside, so why don't we frame a message and take it over to Langley [Virginia, CIA headquarters] and have them send it to somebody from CIA that's on the ground over there. A fellow took me by the arm and said, 'Can I talk to you out in the hall?' And he politely said, 'We don't have anybody in there.' "[86]

Compounding the problem of not having any human intelligence assets in Iran—U.S. agents would subsequently be infiltrated into the country to help plan the rescue operation—was the decision by the U.S. military to keep the rescue mission a secret. It was kept secret not only from other agencies in the U.S. government, but also from many of the participants in the operation themselves. This emphasis on secrecy made even routine tasks very difficult. For example, Delta Force needed pictures of the hostages and the terrorists so they could study them and know whom to shoot and whom to save when they broke down the embassy doors. The easiest way to obtain these pictures would have been to contact the State Department; it was, after all, their diplomats who were in captivity. But the military did not want the State Department to know anything about the rescue mission. This meant that creative ways had to be utilized to get the most basic information.

That task fell to Howard Bane, the CIA official in charge of the rescue operation. "They didn't want anybody to know it," said Bane about the military's plans for the rescue. "It was a well-kept secret. And from the very first day they never trusted the State Department. . . . I had to work up excuses to get these pictures from State Department." In order to ensure that Delta had as many visual images of the hostages and terrorists as possible, Bane supplemented the State Department photos that he was able to obtain with pictures gathered from television newscasts. "What I started doing, is every night I had a special office set up [with] nothing but TV screens," recalled Bane. "And all day long and all night long we copied every news broadcast that we could pick up in the world where hostages and terrorists were on the news. And we made stills from these and they stuck these up on their barracks. So when they started shooting they would know who to shoot. And they started that from Day two almost. . . . As soon as I'd give them a picture, it would go up in their shooting room or in their barracks."[87]

The emphasis on secrecy during the planning of the rescue mission would later be criticized by the Holloway Commission, which was established to evaluate the problems associated with the rescue operation. The six-man panel, which was headed by Admiral James Holloway III, a retired officer and former chief of naval operations, found that several military personnel who were given important functions in preparing for the rescue effort were not fully informed of the mission's objectives. The Holloway Commission concluded that the rescue operation could have succeeded had there been more helicopters, less secrecy, and better planning for dealing with bad weather.[88] Others have argued that the rescue mission would not have worked, that too many things could have gone wrong at any of the multiple stages of the plan. But what most everybody agrees on, including those who participated in the rescue mission, was the intricacy of the operation. "It was a very complex plan," said Beckwith, "probably the most complex plan that the military has ever taken up in its history."[89]

The first stage involved a rendezvous in the Iranian desert of eight RH-53D helicopters—which would be flown in from the aircraft carrier *Nimitz*, sixty miles south of the coast of Iran in the Sea of Oman—with six C-130 aircraft, including three MC-130s that would carry the ninety-three-member Delta team, as well as several other military personnel, and three EC-130s that carried fuel, all of which would fly in from Egypt. The helicopters and C-130s would meet at "Desert One," a small airstrip that was prepared near the town of Tabas, approximately one hundred miles southeast of Tehran. The rendezvous would be necessary since the helicopters could not get close to Tehran without refueling. The distance from the *Nimitz* to Desert One itself was six hundred miles over the desert. After refueling, the helicopters would take off with the Delta Force team and other military personnel aboard and fly to "Desert Two," a mountain hide-out outside of Tehran. There, the commandos would hide during the day and launch the assault that night. The plan called for them to travel to the embassy in trucks that would be brought to their mountain hide-out by U.S. agents who had slipped into Tehran for this mission. At the same time that Delta was rescuing the hostages at the embassy, a thirteen-man special assault team would penetrate the foreign ministry building and free the three American hostages being held there. All the hostages would then be brought to a soccer stadium where helicopters would take them and the Delta team to an abandoned airfield near Tehran. Waiting there would be C-141 transport planes that would have arrived from Egypt to carry everyone out of the country.

The rescue mission never got past the first phase. Beckwith and his men arrived at Desert One and prepared for the arrival of the helicopters. While waiting, Delta Force encountered a civilian bus along a narrow road at the rendezvous site. The passengers, mainly elderly people and young children, were searched and detained in order not to compromise the mission. There were plans to fly them to Egypt in one of the C-130s, and return them to Iran after the rescue operation was completed. Another potential risk to the secrecy of the mission occurred when a gasoline tanker truck drove along the road. One of the soldiers fired a light antitank weapon at the fuel truck, causing it to burst into flames. The driver ran out and was picked up by a smaller truck that had been following behind it. The second truck made a sharp turn and was able to escape in the darkness of the desert. Beckwith believed the two men were probably gasoline smugglers and thus unlikely to report the incident to the authorities. Furthermore, Beckwith did not think they had seen the C-130s and probably thought that it was the Iranian police that had fired at them.[90]

Meanwhile, the helicopters were late and Beckwith began to worry that he would not have enough hours of darkness left to reach the mountain hide-out. "The choppers were going to be a problem all along," recalled Beckwith. "The first time I saw one fly I said . . . this is really going to be a tough go."[91] The helicopters finally began to arrive, but not at the same time. The first one arrived almost one hour behind schedule and the sixth helicopter was almost ninety minutes late. The helicopters had to break formation due to bad weather, which also increased their travel time. Beckwith was still determined to continue with the mission even though they would be arriving at Desert Two during daybreak, thereby increasing the chances for detection. Beckwith received more bad news when he learned that the last two helicopters would not make it to Desert One. One of them was forced down when it developed mechanical problems with its rotor blade. The crew was picked up by one of the other helicopters. A second helicopter had to abort its mission and return to the *Nimitz* when it encountered a severe sandstorm that damaged its navigational instruments. That helicopter was less than one hundred miles from Desert One when it turned back. The remaining helicopters made it through the bad weather.

At that point, the mission was still on, although now there would be no back-up helicopters in case something else went wrong with the remaining helicopters. The plan called for a minimum of six helicopters to carry out the rescue operation. The crushing blow to the mission occurred when it was discovered that yet another helicopter had experienced a partial hydraulic failure en route to Desert One. The crew believed they could repair it at the refueling site. However, upon landing, it was discovered that a fluid leak had caused a hydraulic pump to fail and there was no replacement pump available. Even if there had been one, there would not have been enough time to change the pump and fix the leak.

Since there were now only five flyable helicopters, Beckwith advised Colonel Jim Kyle, the commander at Desert One, that the mission should be canceled. Kyle and Beckwith communicated this information by radio to General James Vaught, who was in charge of the overall rescue operation and was monitoring the situation from Egypt. Vaught was in communication with General David Jones, the chairman of the Joint Chiefs of Staff, and Secretary of Defense Harold Brown in Washington. He advised Jones and Brown of the recommendation to abort. They in turn informed President Carter, who agreed to cancel the long-planned rescue effort.

The inability to get past the first stage of the operation was a great disappointment for both Beckwith and the Delta Force, who had trained so hard and wanted so much to bring the hostages home. CIA Director Stansfield Turner has written that he wanted to ask Beckwith when he saw him at a luncheon soon after the failure at Desert One what his thoughts were when he decided to abort the mission. "I wanted to ask him what had gone through his mind," Turner writes. "There he was, close to the fulfillment of an ambition, having campaigned for over a decade and a half for the creation of Delta, spent two years nursing it into being, and then brought it over the past six months into fighting form for what lay just a few hours ahead. How could he have resisted not taking a chance and going on when he had assured the President he was ready to do whatever was needed to get the hostages out? It must have been the most wrenching decision of his life. I couldn't find a way to put my question directly to Charlie without the risk of sounding critical. . . ."[92]

So Turner never asked his question. But when Beckwith was asked this question in the spring of 1990, he replied that the decision to abort was based on pure military realities. He did not have any second thoughts about his decision. "It [was] real simple," recalled Beckwith. "I picked up the radio and I called back to General Vaught in Egypt and I said there ain't no way we can proceed forward. We don't have five flyable helicopters here. I said we are not going to make it like this. This is the poorest situation that we have discussed. It wasn't a difficult decision to make. And I sat there in the third day of January [and said] if we don't have these helicopters, I'm going to abort; it's an abort situation. And I want that put in the plan. They put it in the plan. It certainly wasn't a pleasant thing to do, but I'm not going to sit there and see a bunch of kids getting murdered. That's stupid."[93]

Unfortunately, eight servicemen did die at Desert One. After the decision was made to abort and Delta Force was preparing to leave, one of the helicopters crashed into a C-130 during refueling, setting off a blaze that trapped the military people on the aircraft. The surviving members then took off on the remaining C-130s, with little choice but to leave the dead soldiers and the helicopters behind. America's attempt to end the hostage crisis by military means had come to a tragic end.

The postmortem on the rescue effort included commentaries in leading newspapers with titles such as "A Puzzle of Timing," a column in which Tom Wicker criticized Carter for ordering a military strike just when U.S.

allies had agreed to impose economic and diplomatic sanctions against Iran, and "A Second Rescue Mission," in which James Reston pointed to the difficult task Carter now faced in rescuing his own presidency after the humiliating failure at Desert One. "President Carter is now engaged in a second Rescue Mission," wrote Reston. "He is trying to rescue himself, and it won't be easy. For the moment, even his political opponents are saying publicly that his military raid in Iran was a sensible operation wrecked by bad luck, but in private, even many of his best friends are saying it was a senseless operation, wrecked by bad judgment." Reston concluded his commentary by stating that "everybody is being very polite about this, but the leaders of Congress, the allies, and even members of the President's own Cabinet are deeply disturbed, not only about the tragedy of the raid into Iran, but about the way this policy was decided, and about the blunders of the Pentagon in the way it was carried out."[94]

Columnist William Pfaff wrote in the *Los Angeles Times* that the rescue mission illustrated "American military incompetence and the failure of military technology." A cartoon in the same newspaper depicted a burned-out helicopter lodged face down on the White House lawn with the inscription "Reelect Carter" on its side.[95] The Holloway Commission, as noted above, found fault with the overly secret nature of the planning process for the raid that, among other things, precluded a full-scale dress rehearsal. The commission also criticized the failure to include three additional helicopters that would have allowed the mission to continue and would not have required additional fuel at Desert One. (Additional fuel would have meant additional C-130s and would have increased the risk of detection.) The commission concluded that three more helicopters could have been hidden on the deck of the *Nimitz*, contradicting the concern that additional helicopters on the *Nimitz* would have alerted the Iranians to the existence of the mission. The commission also criticized the failure to utilize a C-130 Pathfinder weather electronics plane that could have helped the helicopters find Desert One in case of navigational problems. Finally, the Holloway Commission implied that Delta Force may not have been the best choice for the rescue mission. Criticizing the "ad hoc nature" of the planning process, the commission stated that an existing military command should have been used so that the Joint Chiefs of Staff would not have had to start from scratch "to find a commander, create an organization, provide a staff, develop a plan, select the units and train the forces."[96]

Stansfield Turner believed the Pentagon did not give Delta Force sufficient assets for the mission. He writes: "We lacked helicopters that could fly the required distance or that could be refueled in flight and go almost any distance; we did not have enough satellite communications sets to give more than one to a flight of eight helos. It was not because these requirements could not have been met. The long-distance helos, the aerial refueling capability, and the radio sets all could have been found, but they had not been given sufficient priority. Had any one of them been available to the rescue operation, the probability of success might have changed markedly."[97]

The lessons of Operation Eagle Claw went beyond specific matters related to the failure at Desert One. They also raised broader questions concerning the problems associated with hostage rescue operations in general. Unlike retaliatory air strikes against terrorist training camps or against state-sponsors of terrorism, hostage rescue missions involve greater military risks than simply dropping bombs on a target. The chances for failure, even in "permissive" environments where the host government supports the rescue operation, are high since the terrorists can kill all the hostages once the rescue effort is under way. In "non-permissive" environments, the rescue unit faces the additional problem of meeting resistance from the government and its military or police forces.

The difficulties associated with a hostage rescue operation led National Security Adviser Zbigniew Brzezinski to recommend that a retaliatory air strike be combined with the rescue operation at the embassy. "My view was that casualties in the rescue mission would be unavoidable and we had to face the fact that the attempt might even fail," writes Brzezinski. "Accordingly, it would be better if the United States were to engage in a generalized retaliatory strike, which could be publicly described as a punitive action and which would be accompanied by the rescue attempt. If the rescue succeeded, that would be all to the good; if it failed, the U.S. government could announce that it had executed a punitive mission against Iran, because of its unwillingness to release our people, and that unfortunately in the course of that mission an attempt to rescue the hostages had not succeeded."[98]

Although the landing of the C-130s and helicopters at Desert One caught the Iranians by surprise, it was possible that they may have learned of the rescue effort at the last minute and would have been waiting to ambush the U.S. commandos once they entered Tehran. "I understand from talking to some of the people that they got a little touchy about where those trucks were being held [in a warehouse] and at the last minute they had to move those things," recalled Beckwith. "So that may have been compromised and yet we didn't know it."[99]

While the risks were acknowledged by most of the participants, there was nevertheless an understandable desire in the tense days leading up to the April 24 operation to interpret any positive developments as a sign that the rescue mission was destined to succeed. On April 23, while Beckwith and his men were in Egypt preparing for the flight to Desert

One, U.S. intelligence came upon an incredible finding. A CIA agent had been on a flight out of Tehran and was sitting next to a Pakistani man who turned out to be one of the cooks at the American embassy. The cook had just been allowed to leave Iran by the militants. After engaging the Pakistani in conversation, the CIA agent convinced him to get off the plane at the next stop and be debriefed by the CIA. The cook then reported that all the hostages were being held in just one building, the chancellery. He also informed U.S. agents where the guards were stationed. While there was no time left to verify the reliability of the information, and while many people associated with Operation Eagle Claw were suspicious of the coincidence of a CIA agent and an embassy cook sitting together on the same plane, the information was nevertheless used to modify Delta Force's assault plans. Instead of searching all fourteen buildings at the compound to find the hostages, Beckwith now planned to focus mainly on the chancellery building, which would still be difficult with its ninety rooms. For Howard Bane, the CIA chief intelligence officer for the rescue mission, this information received on the eve of the mission was nothing less than a sign from above that somebody was finally watching out for the United States. "When I got the cable giving us the intelligence on that," said Bane, "I *knew* the operation was going to succeed. Because at that point I said, 'God's on our side.' I mean this just doesn't happen in real life. To have a CIA case officer sit next to a Pakistani cook for the American Embassy in Tehran [who] came out yesterday!"[100]

But fortune did not shine upon the United States on April 24, and "real life" meant that everyone associated with the failed mission had to begin picking up the pieces of their lives. For people such as Beckwith and Bane, who had lived with the mission day and night for several months, the sense of disappointment was extreme. "It was a difficult period," said Beckwith, who would meet personally with Carter to express his deepest regrets over the failure at Desert One. "It was difficult for everybody who was involved."[101] Bane recalled that "a lot of us were crying," when the mission collapsed and eight servicemen lay dead in the Iranian desert.[102]

But the heaviest burden fell on the most public figure throughout the entire hostage crisis, Jimmy Carter. After having to face the nation in a televised address on the morning after the aborted raid, Carter retreated from the public eye for several days. This so concerned his chief of staff, Hamilton Jordan, that he sent Carter a handwritten note urging him to break out of his self-imposed isolation. "Mr. President," Jordan wrote, "not to beat a dead horse, but the American people need to see you and hear from you. Since Friday morning's telecast, we have had the inevitable second guessing on the wisdom of the initial decision, the question raised of 'why now' on the operation, the sickening display of our bodies in the compound and Cy's resignation. In such turbulent and emotion laden times, the American people need to *see you and hear you*. The sooner the better. I recommend Tuesday night press conference. . . . — H. J."[103]

But as mentioned above, nobody asked Carter the question that he and his aides had been hoping for—whether the president would now finally cast aside his Rose Garden strategy and hit the campaign trails—and it was left for the White House to stage a ceremony the next day so the question could be asked and Carter answer in the affirmative. His exile in the White House was now over, but his problems remained. After almost half a year of tireless efforts on behalf of the hostages, efforts that had seen his popularity ratings soar for one month but then plummet in the winter and spring of 1980, Americans were still in captivity in Iran. And a spectacular effort to free them had ended in a humiliating defeat for the United States.

Final Agreement

"I am still haunted by memories of that day," Jimmy Carter would write a few years later in describing his feelings about the failed rescue attempt.[104] He now had to face the reality that the hostages were not going to be coming home soon and that he would most likely have to run for reelection with the situation unresolved. The prospects of trying another rescue operation were virtually eliminated as the Iranians dispersed the hostages to different locations in Tehran and outlying areas. The pursuit of economic and diplomatic sanctions against Iran continued, but these were unlikely to lead to freedom for the hostages. Their fate was tied to the internal political situation in Iran, which was still uncertain, as the clerics and the secular moderates fought for power in the turbulent post-revolutionary period. U.S. allies agreed to sanctions against Tehran, but Great Britain—the country that would become the most fervent supporter of U.S. counterterrorism policy during the Reagan years—dissented from an EEC decision to cancel all contracts that were signed with Iran after the hostages were taken on November 4, 1979. The British agreed only to adhere to a May 22, 1980, cutoff, which weakened the sanctions and highlighted the divisions that existed among U.S. allies in responding to the hostage crisis.[105]

The main hope left for Carter was to return to the secret negotiations that had been ongoing prior to the raid. Contacts were reestablished with the two intermediaries, Christian Bourguet and Hector Villalon, almost immediately after the rescue attempt. Messages were passed through them to the Iranians assuring Tehran that the rescue mission was not a hostile military act against Iran, but rather something that the United States felt it had to try since all other efforts had failed. Foreign Minister Sadegh Ghotbzadeh telephoned Bourguet to let him know that Iran would not take any revenge on the hostages. "They have been punished enough," Pierre Salinger quotes Ghotbzadeh as saying. "It's an act of God. Let's start again."[106]

The secret negotiations continued during the months following the aborted raid. Meetings were held in Europe between Bourguet, Villalon, Assistant Secretary of State for Near Eastern and South Asian Affairs Harold Saunders, and Henry Precht, head of the State Department's Iran Working Group during the crisis. But with Iranian internal politics still in turmoil, nothing came out of these meetings. Next, Islamic fundamentalists won control of the newly formed Majlis in parliamentary elections in May, a major blow to Ghotbzadeh and President Bani-Sadr's hope of establishing secular leadership over the government. Since the Ayatollah Khomeini had previously stated that the fate of the hostages would be decided by the Majlis, the victory by the hard-line Islamic clerics was not a good sign. Neither was a report in a Tehran newspaper in June that the Majlis would probably not discuss the hostage issue until September. Even the death of the shah in July did little to change the situation. His fate had long ceased to be a central issue in the hostage drama.[107]

A positive sign for the hostages occurred in September, when an Iranian official, Sadegh Tabatabai, who was related to Khomeini by marriage, contacted the West German government to indicate that he would like to meet with somebody representing the U.S. government to discuss the crisis. This marked the first time that Khomeini had authorized an Iranian official—Tabatabai was a state secretary—to meet with an American official. Khomeini also delivered a speech in which he listed four conditions for resolving the hostage crisis—conditions that Tabatabai had already told the Germans that Khomeini would endorse and that therefore enhanced Tabatabai's credibility. These were the return of the shah's assets, cancellation of all U.S. claims against Iran, a guarantee of no U.S. political or military intervention in Iranian affairs, and the freeing of all Iranian assets. Carter sent Deputy Secretary of State Warren Christopher to Bonn to meet secretly with Tabatabai in order to further discuss the Iranian proposal. The meeting went well, and Tabatabai indicated he would be returning to Tehran to make a favorable report to Khomeini and others in his government.[108]

The optimism in the White House following Christopher's return from Bonn on September 18 reached the point where discussions were even held between Carter and Jordan on how to handle the return of the hostages. Carter was concerned that it not appear that the administration was using the event to gain political points in the midst of a presidential campaign. Jordan suggested that Republican presidential candidate Ronald Reagan be invited to join Carter in welcoming home the hostages.[109] They never got to deliver that invitation to Reagan, though, as the Iran-Iraq War broke out on the very day—September 22—that Tabatabai was scheduled to return to Tehran. With the Iraqis bombing Tehran's airport, Tabatabai could not return until a week later. Meanwhile, dealing with the Iraqi invasion took precedence in Iran over the hostage issue, and the United States was once again frustrated in its efforts to end the crisis.

On November 2, the Majlis finally passed a resolution on the hostage situation, basically endorsing the same four conditions that Khomeini had listed in September. It was too late for any deal to be finalized in time for the U.S. presidential election, which was being held two days later. Further negotiations would be needed, and the Majlis specified that Algeria serve as mediator. Carter's hopes for an election eve celebration of returning hostages were dashed, and he went down to an overwhelming defeat by Ronald Reagan exactly one year to the day that the hostages were seized.

Meanwhile, the business of getting the hostages out of Iran still remained for the lame duck president. What had been in his own words an "obsession" now took on new proportions. Carter was determined to prove to the nation, and to himself, that his patient approach was the correct one. The only way left to do this would be to have the hostages freed while he was still president. Yet by January 1981, the hostages were still in Iran and Carter was running out of time. "The release of the American hostages had almost become an obsession with me," Carter writes in his memoirs. "Of course, their lives, safety, and freedom were the paramount considerations, but there was more to it. I wanted to have my decisions vindicated. It was very likely that I had been defeated and would soon leave office as President because I had kept these hostages and their fate at the forefront of the world's attention, and had clung to a cautious and prudent policy in order to protect their lives during the preceding fourteen months. Before God and my fellow citizens, I wanted to exert every ounce of my strength and ability during these last few days to achieve their liberation. I knew that if we failed, it might take many months to reweave the fabric of complex agreements that had been so laboriously created."[110]

The last few days of the hostage crisis, though, resembled more a frantic week of trading on Wall Street than the end to one of the worst foreign policy nightmares for the United States. The final sequence of the hostage crisis—a crisis that had seen a national appeal by a president for unity and sympathy for the hostages, the imposition of sanctions against Iran, a military rescue effort that cost eight servicemen their lives, and the resignation of a secretary of state—had now become a matter of moving money and beating the clock. "Can sec[urities] be sold over [the] weekend so funds can move?"; "coming up short at 7.6"; "move gold and sell sec[urities]"; "clean up trust fund for movement" were some of the rough draft notes written on White House stationery as U.S. officials scurried about to move billions of dollars to the Iranians.[111] They had thrown a snag into the negotiations in late December by demanding that the United States return $24 billion, including $14 billion in frozen assets and $10 billion that they claimed represented the shah's assets. These figures were much higher than what the United States had been prepared to offer. Carter rejected it, stating that "we will not pay any ransom," and President-elect Reagan called the Iranians "nothing better than criminals and kidnappers."[112] A few days later, the Iranians dropped their demand to $9.5 billion, an indication that they were as anxious to end the crisis as was the United States. The final figure that both sides agreed to was $7.97 billion, and the Declaration of Algiers, which officially brought the crisis to an end, was signed in Algeria by Deputy Secretary of State Christopher on January 19, 1981.

Unfortunately, it was too late for Carter, though, as the Iranians would not allow the hostages to take off from Tehran's airport until thirty minutes after Ronald Reagan had become president at noon on January 20. The hostages would finally clear Iranian air space while Carter was flying home to Plains, Georgia. The compassionate president who had seen his political fortunes rise as the hostages were taken and then fade as they remained in captivity for 444 days, would nevertheless be able to say on the tenth anniversary of the embassy seizure that "in spite of the fact that I turned over the reigns of a great nation, as President, to my successor, it [the hostages' release] was one of the happiest moments, one of the happiest days of my life."[113]

But the hostage episode in Iran was clearly an extremely painful experience for both the president and the nation. The key question is, could it have been avoided? In terms of the seizure of the embassy and the holding of American captives for fourteen months, the answer is no. In terms of the building up of a crisis atmosphere in the country and the paralysis of presidential leadership, the answer is yes.

There was very little that the United States could have done in 1979 to prevent its embassy from falling into the hands of an angry anti-U.S. mob. American support for the shah during the 1970s had alienated those who were orchestrating the Iranian revolution, and it would be natural that in a revolutionary environment, anti-U.S. demonstrations would take place. As noted above, Iran was too important to the United States, both geopolitically and strategically, to write the country off by eliminating our diplomatic presence there. Thus, the decision was made following the February 1979 takeover of the embassy to keep a U.S. diplomatic mission there, although one that was greatly reduced in personnel. The rescuing of the Americans by Khomeini's forces and their crushing of the Marxist extremists who had attacked the embassy reassured the United States that even if such an event should happen again, we could count on the Iranian authorities to come to our aid.

When they did not do so in November 1979, the fate of the Americans was sealed. Better embassy security may have prevented the takeover for a few more hours, but the mob would have eventually penetrated the building and seized the hostages. And while the decision to allow the shah into the United States for medical treatment was the catalyst for the takeover, it is likely that the Iranian militants would have seized on another issue to attack the embassy. Anti-U.S. demonstrations and sentiment were a critical part of the strategy of the Islamic fundamentalists as they tried to convert the anti-shah revolution into a clerical state that would, in Khomeini's words, pursue policies that were "neither East nor West." Any number of potential U.S. actions or foreign policy decisions—support for Israel, arms sales to a moderate Arab regime, etc.— could very well have been used by the clerics to foment anti-U.S. demonstrations in order to keep the revolution moving in the direction they wanted.

The militants may not even have needed a specific event related to the United States as an excuse to attack the U.S. embassy. Pakistani mobs assaulted the U.S. embassy in Islamabad in November 1979, burning the building to protest the seizure of the Great Mosque in Mecca by Muslim dissidents, even though the United States was not involved in that incident. The Islamic fundamentalists in Iran could have used that event to rally the masses to attack the U.S. embassy. As historian Bernard Lewis notes, the Iranian revolution, and Islamic fundamentalism, represented "a clash of civilizations." "The instinct of the masses is not false in locating the ultimate source of these cataclysmic changes in the West and in attributing the disruption of their old way of life to the impact of Western domination, Western influence, or Western precept and example," writes Lewis. "And since the United States is the legitimate heir of European civilization and the recognized and unchallenged leader of the West, the United States has inherited the resulting grievances and become the focus of the pent-up hate and anger."[114]

Just as the takeover of the embassy was unavoidable, so too was the duration of the period of captivity for the American hostages. A military rescue operation was unfeasible during the early weeks and months of the crisis because of the lack of intelligence on hostages' locations and the capabilities and strengths of the militants who were holding them.

We also did not have any contingency plans for a situation in which the host government supports the hostage takers. Even at the time of the rescue mission in April 1980, the chances were likely that many hostages would have been killed during the assault on the embassy.

As long as the American hostages were perceived by Khomeini and the clerics to be important pawns for the revolution, they were not going to be released. It was only after the Majlis was held in firm control by the clerics and the hostages had ceased to be of further value to the Islamic fundamentalists that Khomeini seriously began to consider making a deal for their release. Even then, it would still take several months before a final agreement would be reached.

If the taking of the hostages and their long captivity was unavoidable, the same cannot be said for the crisis atmosphere that prevailed in the United States as a result of the embassy seizure. The cancellation of Carter's visit to Canada, the numerous White House staff memos that urged the president to be the focal point for "handling" the problem, the appeal to the public to ring church bells and to say prayers, all served to magnify the hostage episode into a crisis of the highest proportion. Carter's continual statements about the hostages and his personal agony over their fate kept that issue at the top of the U.S. public policy agenda. It led the public to expect that the president would soon be able to bring the hostages home. "In hindsight, I think one of the major mistakes that we made," reflected Cyrus Vance, "was spending as much time talking to the media about the problem and the need to get a prompt solution to the problem. That helped to foster the continuation of the pattern used by the press of every day and every night coming on and saying that this is the 330th, or 331st, or the 332nd day. And that played into the hostage takers' hands, rather than helping to resolve the situation."[115]

An acknowledgment by the Carter administration that events might indeed be beyond the control of the United States was never made. Since the hostages were caught up in the internal politics of the Iranian revolution and were unlikely to be freed no matter what the United States said or did, the excessive focus by the administration on their plight only served to highlight U.S. impotence in the situation. The American people would not have thought a president any less compassionate if he clearly stated that while all was being done to try to gain the release of the hostages, the United States could not allow those who take hostages to bring the U.S. government to a standstill, to negatively affect its foreign policy, or to create a crisis atmosphere within the country.

Yet the hostage episode did paralyze the Carter administration and was a major factor in the president's defeat. The inauguration of Ronald Reagan as president on January 20, 1981, the departure of Jimmy Carter from Washington, and the freeing of the hostages on that same day were symbolic of a metamorphosis that was about to occur in U.S. policy toward terrorism. The patient approach of Carter would be replaced with the tough rhetoric of Reagan. The mood of the country, and of the new president, was best captured by one of the returning hostages who, when asked by a reporter whether he would like some day to go back to Iran, replied, "Yeah, in a B-52."[116] America was about to enter the period when terrorism would be defined by the United States as a "war," and one where it was expected to prevail. Yet when it came time for Reagan to deal with *his* hostage problem in Lebanon, he too would become emotionally involved with their fate, to the detriment of U.S. interests. But before he embarked on the arms-for-hostages deal with Iran, there would be a period of celebration for the returning hostages from the American embassy in Tehran and the formulation of a new approach to terrorism by a new administration.

5

Tough Talk on Terrorism

"International terrorism will take the place of human rights in our concern because it is the ultimate abuse of human rights," said Secretary of State Alexander Haig at his first news conference on January 28, 1981. "And it's time that it be addressed with better clarity and greater effectiveness by Western nations and the United States as well." One day earlier, President Reagan greeted the returning hostages from Iran with a ceremony at the White House and a ringing speech that set the tone for how his administration would deal with the problem of terrorism. "Let terrorists be aware," the president said, "that when the rules of international behavior are violated, our policy will be one of swift and effective retribution."[1] The break with the patient approach of the Carter administration was complete. Combating terrorism would now be a top priority for the United States.

For Ronald Reagan, that meant confronting the Soviet Union. Despite the fact that America had just emerged from an agonizing experience with terrorism that was not directed by the Soviets, but rather by an "independent" actor, Reagan's fervent anti-Communist and anti-Soviet philosophy made it inevitable that terrorism would be seen in black-and-white terms. The "evil empire," as Reagan liked to refer to Moscow, was a player in the terrorist game by virtue of its history of training various Palestinian and other extremist groups. It was not, though, the center of international terrorism. But the attractiveness of the Soviets as a terrorism foe for Reagan lay in their being a known quantity and the main antagonist of the Cold War.

Terrorism would thus be seen from a U.S.-Soviet conflict perspective during the early years of Reagan's presidency. "As the foundation of my foreign policy," Reagan writes in his memoirs, "I decided we had to send as powerful a message as we could to the Russians that we weren't going to stand by anymore while they armed and financed terrorists and subverted democratic governments. In my speeches and press conferences, I deliberately set out to say some frank things about the Russians, to let them know there were some new fellows in Washington who had a realistic view of what they were up to and weren't going to let them keep it up."[2]

One of those new fellows was Haig, the military man who served as Richard Nixon's chief of staff in the waning months of his presidency, and of whom Reagan would later write, "It's amazing how sound he can be on complex international matters but how utterly paranoid with regard to the people he must work with."[3] Haig made his remarks about terrorism replacing human rights when he was asked by a reporter what U.S. policy would be toward the Soviet Union. Haig told the press corps that the Soviets "are involved in conscious policy, in programs, if you will, which foster, support, and expand this activity which is hemorrhaging in many respects throughout the world today."[4] Haig knew firsthand about international terrorism. While serving his final week as supreme allied commander of NATO in 1979, he was the target of an assassination attempt suspected to be the work of the West German leftist terrorist group Red Army Faction. The RAF set off a remote controlled bomb on a road in Belgium as Haig was traveling to work at NATO headquarters. The bomb exploded near his limousine, causing the vehicle to lift into the air and leaving a deep crater in the road. A second car following behind carrying Haig's security people was demolished, but the occupants were able to escape, although one was seriously injured. Although Haig and the other people in his car were not hurt, the bombing nevertheless left a lasting impression upon him. In his farewell address a few days later, he told his audience that although he did not have any evidence linking any Communist country to the attempt on his life, their support for international terrorism made them culprits in such attacks. "Regardless of the cause that these [terrorist] organizations espouse," Haig said, "the totalitarian regimes of the East bear a large measure of responsibility for this international disease that we are all plagued with because they espouse a doctrine which justifies extra-legal measures to achieve political or social change."[5]

European leftist terrorist groups such as the RAF and the Italian Red

Brigades were indeed very active at the time the Reagan administration took power. The assumption that they were tied in some way to Moscow was easy to make. After all, they professed to Marxist-Leninist ideology, were dedicated to the overthrow of democratic governments, and were poised to attack Western targets everywhere. The Red Brigades conducted a "kneecapping" (shooting their victims in the knees) campaign and other violent attacks against Western business executives and government officials throughout the 1970s. Their most spectacular operation was the kidnapping and murder of former Italian Prime Minister Aldo Moro in 1978. The Red Brigades also abducted U.S. Army Brigadier General James Dozier in Italy in 1981. Elsewhere in Europe, the German RAF initiated a terrorist campaign against NATO and the U.S. military in the early 1980s. Their stated objective was to protest the placement of intermediate-range nuclear missiles in Europe. A popular book of the time, Claire Sterling's *The Terror Network,* provided the intellectual foundation for the Reagan administration's focus on the Soviet Union as the standard-bearer of international terrorism. In a second printing of the book in 1982, Sterling approved of Haig's comments at his press conference, stating that it "reflect[ed] a decided change in U.S. attitudes" toward Soviet behavior in international terrorism.[6]

Sterling's main thesis was that the multitude of terrorist groups that were active in the late 1960s and that grew throughout the 1970s received training, equipment, funding, and other support services from the Soviet Union and its proxies. There were three major components of the terror network. First, there was Cuba, which provided training camps for terrorists in the 1960s and sent their instructors to Palestinian fedayeen camps in the early 1970s. Then there were the Palestinians, who in turn would train others in the art of terrorism. "The third pole closing the triangle," Sterling writes, "was Soviet Russia itself, arming and training Palestinians on its own territory and turning out other professional terrorists by the thousands—European, South and North American, African, Asian—inside Russia or in the Communist states of Czechoslovakia, Hungary, Bulgaria, North Korea, South Yemen."[7]

Sterling argued that "the Kremlin took an avuncular interest in terrorist 'adventurers' of every alarming shade." Terrorists and guerrilla groups served an important function for Moscow: "Their value to the Soviet Union has been their capacity to disrupt the West in whatever way they might see fit, always stopping short at the outermost borders of the Soviet empire."[8]

It was the pinning of a Soviet label on this complex web of international terrorism that made Sterling's thesis so appealing. Terrorism is a difficult phenomenon to comprehend due to the multitude of groups that are active and the various causes that they pursue. If one source could be pointed to as the main benefactor, founder, and organizer of international terrorism, then terrorism itself would not seem so bewildering and confusing. There was also an implied "solution," or at least hope for substantial progress against terrorism, in Sterling's argument; namely, apply pressure to force the Soviets and their proxies to end their role in international terrorism.

However, there was no real terrorist "network" or center that Western governments could target. Those countries that seriously wanted to confront international terrorism would be hard pressed to find a central focus for their policies. While there were several state-sponsors of terrorism, including Syria, Iraq, Iran, and Libya, toward whom diplomatic and economic pressure could be applied, the diversity in international terrorism precluded targeting any single network for counterterrorist action.

Eliminating the Soviet connection with international terrorism would not have a great impact on reducing the overall terrorist threat. There were also limitations as to what the United States could actually do, even if it was determined that the Soviets were behind certain anti-U.S. or anti-Western terrorist attacks. It is one thing to go after states such as Libya, which would be no match for U.S. military retaliatory strikes, but quite another to target the Soviet Union. The risks of creating a much greater crisis or even a war mitigated the options available to the United States vis-à-vis the Soviets.

Despite the lack of evidence of a terror network or of a direct Soviet hand in international terrorism, the Reagan administration was determined to prove otherwise. The first Cabinet meeting of the new administration was devoted to the subject of terrorism. Haig took the lead in trying to persuade the high-ranking officials that the Soviet Union was the major state-sponsor of international terrorism. Most of the group did not need persuading, including CIA Director William Casey. However, Haig did not produce any evidence to substantiate his claims, so the CIA was asked to produce a National Intelligence Estimate on the Soviet role in international terrorism.

Casey was not satisfied when he saw the first draft of the report, which failed to accuse the Soviets of fostering international terrorism. Casey also felt that some of his analysts simply wanted to prove Haig wrong and that affected their assessment. Casey therefore asked the Defense Intelligence Agency, the Pentagon's intelligence arm, which he knew would take a harder position against the Soviets, to produce a second estimate of the Soviet link with international terrorist groups. However, the DIA estimate was so extreme in its condemnation of Moscow that it lacked credibility, even in Casey's view. The CIA director finally decided to get a third opinion from an independent review group headed by Lincoln Gordon, a former ambassador to Brazil during the Kennedy and

Johnson years and the former president of Johns Hopkins University. The Gordon draft, which ultimately became the CIA's final report, stated the well-documented fact that Moscow supported revolutionary violence that "frequently entails acts of international terrorism" and that they maintain close relationships with state-sponsors of terrorism such as Libya and with Palestinian groups that engage in terrorism. However, the CIA report did not accuse the Soviet Union of currently training or supporting terrorists.[9]

It was not until the end of 1981 that the Reagan administration experienced its first major international terrorist incident. This occurred on December 17, 1981, when the Red Brigades kidnapped General James Dozier from his home in Verona, Italy. They held him captive for more than a month, prompting a massive search effort by Italian and U.S. authorities. The Italians were certainly not new to the game of searching for kidnapped dignitaries, having a few years earlier experienced an agonizing and fruitless search for former Prime Minister Aldo Moro. The Red Brigades taunted the Italian authorities during that long kidnapping episode and finally killed Moro before the police could move in.

The search for Dozier, though, had a more positive outcome when a special Italian hostage rescue force, NOCS (Nucleo Operativeo Centrale di Sicurezza), rescued the American general. The elite group was formed after the Moro killing and was known as "leatherheads" for the leather helmets they wore. Italian authorities had learned where Dozier was being held from the driver of the truck that carried the American hostage from his home in Verona to a Red Brigades hide-out in the city of Padua. On January 28, 1982, NOCS stormed the apartment, using the noise of a bulldozer in the street to catch the terrorists by surprise. Dozier was rescued and all five Red Brigades kidnappers apprehended without a shot being fired.[10]

The successful ending of the Dozier case was a boost for Reagan, even though it was an Italian counterterrorist force, and not an American one, that rescued the general. Just one year into his presidency, Reagan had a highly publicized victory over terrorists to boast about. Compared with the long, drawn-out hostage crisis in Iran, the Dozier case demonstrated that Americans could indeed be rescued from terrorists and that prolonged terrorist crises could be averted. But victories over terrorism can be short-lived as the terrorists rebound and strike again and as other groups emerge and initiate new attacks. The Red Brigades and its various factions would stage several more high-profile attacks in the 1980s, including the murder of Leamon Hunt, the U.S. chief of the Sinai Multinational Force and Observer Group in Rome in 1984. That assassination was believed to have been coordinated with the Lebanese Armed Revolutionary Faction.

It would be in the Middle East, though, that the United States would face its toughest battles against terrorism. These conflicts took place in many countries in the region, but one in particular stood out: Lebanon. Lebanon had actually long ceased to function as a nation and by the early 1980s was instead a perpetual battleground for religious factions, foreign troops, and international terrorists. The year 1982 was a pivotal one in its history as the Israeli invasion and subsequent withdrawal set in motion a sequence of events that plagued the United States for the duration of the decade. Hostage taking, car and truck bombings, and airplane hijackings directed against the United States would all follow and lead to multiple terrorist crises for the Reagan administration.

Lebanon and Terrorism

Lebanon was to terrorism in the 1980s what Berlin was to the Cold War in the 1960s. It was a central location for the conflicts, threats, incidents, and other dramas that unfolded around this "new" form of violence. Beirut, which had once been regarded as the Paris of the Middle East for its beauty and charm, by the early 1980s had been reduced to virtual rubble. Burned-out buildings, mortar fire and rocket attacks across the Green Line that divided Christian East Beirut from Muslim West Beirut, and an endless series of car bombings in crowded civilian areas had all become trademarks of the capital. It was, in the words of *New York Times* correspondent Thomas Friedman, "a city without 'officials,' [having been] carved up into a checkerboard of fiefdoms and private armies" after civil war erupted in 1975.[11] The Palestine Liberation Organization, which shifted its command center from Jordan to Lebanon in 1970 after being ousted by King Hussein, continually interfered in Lebanese internal affairs, leading to conflicts with Christian factions and other groups. The civil war began when Palestinian guerrillas opened fire on a Christian militia in September 1975, killing two members. The Christians retaliated by firing on a bus of Palestinians, killing twenty-seven people. Fighting soon erupted throughout Beirut, eventually leading to intervention by Syrian troops in June 1976. The Syrians, although not a natural ally of the Christians, nevertheless acted in order to prevent a victory by the Palestinian forces and a likely partitioning of the country. Syrian troops remained in Lebanon and became observers, participants, and sometimes targets of the numerous battles and violence that seemed to continue endlessly.[12]

For Israel, the Palestinian presence in Lebanon was a source of anxiety that increased with each terrorist attack across the border. The PLO and its various factions used bases in Lebanon to stage guerrilla raids and mortar attacks into northern Israel. The Israelis would invariably retaliate with aerial bombardments of Palestinian camps. In 1982, Ariel Sharon, the tough-minded Israeli defense minister, decided that the time had finally come for Israel to end the Palestinian threat. His plan was to invade Lebanon and drive out the PLO. Sharon also believed that a successful Israeli invasion would neutralize the growing Syrian influence in Lebanon. Thus, after the Israeli ambassador to Great Britain was seriously wounded in an assassination attempt in London on June 3, Israel bombed PLO targets in West Beirut, knowing that would lead to a retaliatory Palestinian strike on settlements in northern Israel. When the Palestinians so responded, Israel used that as its reason for invading Lebanon on June 6.[13]

Israeli troops and tanks quickly advanced through southern Lebanon and within three days reached the outskirts of Beirut. The invasion did not go smoothly in the area around the capital as Israeli forces became engaged in battles with Syrian troops. Israeli forces chose not to enter West Beirut in what likely would have been a successful but bloody battle against the retreating and weakened Palestinians. They instead used heavy artillery fire and air strikes to force the PLO into a negotiated settlement. The agreement included a cease-fire and insisted on the expulsion of the PLO guerrillas from Lebanon. It also called for the formation of a Multinational Force (MNF) that would oversee the evacuation of the more than six thousand Palestinian guerrillas.[14] It would be the formation of this international peacekeeping force, and U.S. participation in it, that would lead one year later to the worst terrorist incident in the history of the U.S. military.

The PLO evacuated Lebanon in August 1982 in a highly publicized event. PLO leader Yasir Arafat and his troops streamed down the streets of West Beirut on their way to ships that would disperse them to other Arab countries, firing their weapons into the air and appearing more like victorious warriors than a vanquished foe. Perhaps they knew that it would not be too long before many of them would slip back into Lebanon and once again become participants in the conflicts of that troubled country.

The removal of the PLO left a vacuum to be filled by yet another terrorist group that attempted to inflame the passions of certain parts of the Lebanese population. This time, rather than Arab nationalism, the cause was Islamic fundamentalism, and the pro-Iranian Islamic extremist group Hizballah found enthusiastic followers from the ranks of the downtrodden and traditionally oppressed Shiite minority in Lebanon. Led by pro-Iranian Lebanese Shiite clergymen who had been educated in Iran and who had received substantial military and financial support from the Khomeini regime, Hizballah moved into the Bekaa Valley and organized a powerful movement that would influence Lebanese internal affairs for the remainder of the decade.[15] They would also become known throughout the world as they soon introduced new forms of terrorism into the region, such as suicide truck bombings, and became masters of an older form of terrorism—kidnappings.

At the same time that the PLO was withdrawing from Lebanon, Bashir Gemayel was elected president by the Lebanese parliament on August 23. Less than one month later he was assassinated in East Beirut. Israeli troops then moved into the capital while Christian Phalangist militiamen, who were once led by Gemayel, raided two Palestinian refugee camps that were major bases of PLO support. The Phalangists massacred hundreds of Palestinians, including women and children, at the Sabra and Shatila camps. The violence was carried out not only in retaliation for the killing of Gemayel, but also to settle scores for past killings of Phalangists by Palestinian extremists.[16] Israeli troops did not order the Phalangists to stop their activities until three days after the massacre began. Brigadier General Amos Yaron, who was the commander of the Israeli forces that remained on the periphery while the Phalangists committed their atrocities, was relieved of his field command by Israel's Kahan Commission, which investigated the incident.[17]

The situation in Lebanon continued to deteriorate during the summer of 1982, and the Lebanese government issued a call for the return of the MNF, which had departed following the PLO evacuation. The new president of Lebanon, Amin Gemayel, brother of the slain president, went to the United States in October to appeal for U.S. aid. Support had already come with the return of U.S. troops to Lebanon on September 29 as part of a second MNF. But whereas the mission of the first MNF was clearly defined—oversee the withdrawal of the PLO—the objective of the second MNF was more ambiguous. This greatly troubled Secretary of Defense Caspar Weinberger, who opposed U.S. participation in the return of the MNF to Lebanon. "The Joint Chiefs were also strongly opposed to reentry of a multinational force," writes Weinberger in his memoirs, "because without a clearly defined objective, determining the proper size and armament and rules of engagement for such a force is difficult at best."[18] The undefined mission of the second MNF was eventually clarified to be that of serving as a buffer for Syrian and Israeli troops as they withdrew from the country. The problem, however, was that there was no secured agreement for such a withdrawal, and the MNF thus existed in Lebanon without any real purpose.

To make matters worse, the MNF was seen by many warring factions as just a puppet of an unpopular Lebanese central government. The MNF was lightly armed and undermanned since it was never intended to be a fighting force. "It was not only lightly armed," Weinberger writes, "but was quite insufficient in numbers or configuration to deal militarily with either the Israelis or the Syrians, and certainly not with all the factional militias of Christians and Moslems who fought each other with great ferocity and had been doing so for many years. Indeed the second MNF was not designed or intended to deal militarily with any other forces. The militias saw that, and began their season of rising threats with the April 1983 bombing of our Embassy."[19]

The embassy bombing on April 18 was the first suicide attack against the United States in Lebanon. It was also the most devastating terrorist assault ever on a U.S. diplomatic post. A man drove a truck laden with two thousand pounds of explosives through the front gate of the American embassy in Beirut and then detonated the bomb, causing part of the building to collapse. Sixty-three people were killed, including seventeen Americans. Among the victims was the CIA station chief, Kenneth Haas, and the agency's top Middle East analyst, Robert Ames. The United States had thus suffered a serious loss in its intelligence assets in Lebanon. Furthermore, the bombing came only one month after a grenade had been hurled at a Marine patrol in West Beirut, wounding five soldiers. It was now clear that the violence that was a daily part of life in Lebanon would also be directed at any symbols of the U.S. presence in that country.[20]

The main perpetrator of the anti-U.S. terrorist assaults in Lebanon was Hizballah. Immad al-Haj Mugniyeh, chief of security for the pro-Iranian Shiite extremist group, was one of the masterminds of the embassy bombing and subsequent terrorist events, including the kidnappings of Americans.[21] Yet, as is the case with many terrorist incidents, there were several different actors involved, ranging from those who supplied the weapons to those who aided in logistics and planning. Both Iran and Syria played significant roles in many anti-U.S. terrorist attacks in the 1980s. But tracing the web of conspirators and operatives was difficult since those who take part in terrorist operations, particularly state-sponsors, are careful to cover their tracks and destroy any incriminating evidence.

The Reagan administration was beginning to realize the trap it had laid for itself by promising "swift and effective retribution" against terrorists. Reagan had made those comments in the wake of a hostage drama in Iran in which the perpetrators of the act were clearly identified. But what was he to do now with the prospects of bombings and other terrorist attacks in which the perpetrators may be more difficult to discover? And even when the individual terrorists are identified, locating their whereabouts and retaliating were likely to prove extremely difficult. There is no guarantee that even when a terrorist safe-house is identified, there will be anyone left against which a counterterrorist operation could be launched. There is also the risk of civilian casualties through the bombing of urban areas. In the case of Lebanon, any U.S. military action could easily have repercussions far beyond the original incident.

The United States decided against retaliating for the April 1983 embassy bombing. It also decided against withdrawing from Lebanon despite the mounting evidence of anti-U.S. sentiment in the country. Efforts to improve physical security for American military and government personnel were accelerated and the number of embassy personnel was reduced. But the U.S. Marines remained in the country and became a vulnerable target for the militants. Beirut International Airport was an open area that was easily within range of hostile fire from the surrounding mountains and hills. Two U.S. Marines were killed in the summer of 1983 during a mortar attack at the airport.

The risk to the Marines' safety increased substantially following the decision to actively support the Lebanese Armed Forces (LAF) in its war against the various militias. The Israeli withdrawal in September from the strategic Shouf Mountains opened up a vacuum for the warring factions to move into. The LAF soon became engaged in combat with Druze units that were backed by Syrian and Palestinian forces for control of the mountain village of Souk el-Gharb, which overlooked Beirut airport. On September 19, American guided-missile cruisers and a destroyer fired more than three hundred shells at the Druze, Palestinian, and Syrian positions.[22] Any remaining doubts among the Lebanese factions and people concerning U.S. neutrality were shattered. "The image of the USMNF, in the eyes of the factional militias, had become pro-Israel, pro-Phalange, and anti-Muslim," concluded the Long Commission, the Defense Department inquiry that was established after the October 1983 bombing of the Marines barracks. "After the USMNF engaged in direct fire support of the LAF, a significant portion of the Lebanese populace no longer considered the USMNF a neutral force."[23]

The most visible symbol of the U.S. presence in Lebanon became legitimate targets for retaliation in the minds of the Shiite extremists and their state supporters in Iran and Syria. Snipers from the surrounding hills were a continual threat. The several hundred Marines stationed in Beirut were concentrated in just one building at the Battalion Landing Team (BLT) headquarters at the airport. To make matters worse, the sentries at several posts around the building carried unloaded weapons. Their commanders did not want a guard to accidentally fire on a crowd or initiate an unauthorized attack. It was thus only a matter of time before terrorists would find this situation too tempting to resist.

On the morning of October 23, while the Marines were asleep in their barracks, a suicide truck bomber drove through a barbed wire fence and passed through two guard posts where the sentries did not have enough time to load their weapons. The terrorist continued through an open gate, maneuvered around iron pipe obstacles, and then crashed into the lobby of the headquarters building. The bomb detonated with the equivalent of more than twelve thousand pounds of TNT, killing 241 U.S. servicemen, mostly Marines. That same morning, another suicide bomber attacked the barracks of the French contingent of the MNF, killing forty-seven French troops.

There was never any conclusive evidence as to who exactly perpetrated the bombing. But as news correspondents David Martin and John Walcott noted, while "there was no smoking gun" to link Iran or any other party to the bombing, "the Reagan administration knew to a moral, if not a legal, certainty who was responsible for the massacre of the Marines. The plot had been conceived in Tehran, born in Baalbek, and wet-nursed at the Iranian Embassy in Damascus."[24] But as was the case with the bombing of the American embassy, there were no clear targets to retaliate against. "Our intelligence experts found it difficult to establish conclusively who were responsible for the attack on the barracks," Reagan writes. "Although several air strikes were planned against possible culprits, I canceled them because our experts said they were not absolutely sure they were the right targets. I didn't want to kill innocent people."[25]

The United States did respond militarily when Syrian forces fired surface-to-air missiles at U.S. reconnaissance planes in Lebanon in December. U.S. bombers attacked several Syrian missile-launching and anti-aircraft sites and a radar complex. One U.S. airman was killed and another was captured. When Syria again fired on an American reconnaissance plane on December 14, the United States retaliated as the battleship *New Jersey* fired its sixteen-inch guns on Syrian positions. Anti-U.S. terrorist incidents continued in Lebanon and elsewhere, including the bombing of the U.S. embassy in Kuwait that December and the bombing of the U.S. embassy annex in Beirut in September 1984.

The United States finally withdrew militarily from Lebanon in February 1984. U.S. Marines were moved from Beirut airport to ships offshore as the first step in bringing them back home. French, British, and Italian forces in the MNF pulled out of Lebanon shortly afterward. The Marine barracks bombing left the Reagan administration with little choice but to withdraw. The decision to put U.S. troops into this tinderbox was never a popular one at home and had led to a policy dispute—one of many—between Secretary of Defense Weinberger, who opposed the mission, and Secretary of State George Shultz—who had replaced Haig in June 1982—who supported it. The October bombing sealed the fate of U.S. policy in Lebanon. The future of that country would now be left to the warring factions.

The lesson that the Shiite terrorists and their patrons in Iran and Syria gained from the Marine barracks bombing was the wide-ranging impact that a well-timed and well-executed terrorist attack could have. By perpetrating a single, major terrorist event, extremists in Lebanon were able to affect other nations' foreign policies. The lesson for Reagan and Weinberger was more personal. They, along with other members of the administration, were deeply scarred by the deaths of the Marines. Reagan writes that "the sending of the marines to Beirut was the source of my greatest regret and my greatest sorrow as president. Every day since the death of those boys, I have prayed for them and their loved ones."[26] Weinberger echoed those sentiments, recalling that "Lebanon will, in my mind, always stand as a major reproach to me because I was not more persuasive, in all the meetings we held, to prevent the worst loss of military lives to occur during the time I was at the Pentagon."[27]

The aforementioned Long Commission that investigated the bombing chastised the Marine commanders in Beirut for concentrating hundreds of troops in one building and for not implementing adequate physical security measures. The commission also criticized the lack of a clear objective for U.S. military forces in Lebanon and the fact that the U.S. military role expanded while the political and military situation in the country greatly deteriorated, thereby increasing the risk to the safety of the USMNF.

But it was its advocacy of a strong U.S. military response to terrorism that gave the Long Commission its lasting legacy. They reinforced and gave new life to the growing belief within the administration that terrorism had to be viewed as a "war," and that the United States must garner all available resources to meet this violent conflict:

> The Commission believes that the most important message it can bring to the Secretary of Defense is that the 23 October 1983 attack on the Marine Battalion Landing Team Headquarters in Beirut was tantamount to an act of war using the medium of terrorism. Terrorist warfare, sponsored by sovereign states or organized political entities to achieve political objectives, is a threat to the United States that is increasing at an alarming rate. The 23 October catastrophe underscores the fact that terrorist warfare can have significant political impact and demonstrates that the United States, and specifically the Department of Defense, is inadequately prepared to deal with this threat. Much needs to be done, on an urgent basis, to prepare U.S. military forces to defend against and counter terrorist warfare.[28]

However, while there was an urgent need to improve physical security at U.S. government and military installations worldwide—bomb-shattering safety windows, concrete barriers, heightened personnel awareness, and other measures—there was not the same urgency for the U.S. military to "counter terrorist warfare." Such calls for U.S. military resolve in the face of terrorism sounded fine, but could have far-reaching effects that were not always in the best interest of the U.S. military or U.S. national security. Defining terrorism as a "war" placed undue pressure on the military to produce results against an "enemy" that one day could be Shiite terrorists in Lebanon, the next day could be leftist terrorist groups in Europe, and still another day could be revolutionary organizations in Latin America.

Instead of acknowledging the unique characteristics of terrorism and informing the public, Congress, and the president that it might not be amenable to military solutions, the Long Commission made recommendations that were in accordance with how the military approaches most threat situations: "The Commission recommends that the Secretary of Defense direct the development of *doctrine, planning, organization, force structure, education and training* necessary to defend against and counter terrorism."[29] Fighting terrorism, though, was not the same as planning for warfare against an invading army. "Doctrines" and "force structure" did not have much relevance in the world of terrorism. The Reagan administration discovered this when it tried to adopt the "irrefutable evidence" criteria for the occasions when the U.S. would use military force in the aftermath of a terrorist incident. That doctrine reduced U.S. flexibility since it placed an unnecessary burden upon the United States to provide "evidence" of who was responsible for a terrorist incident before military force would be used. Sometimes there might not be "irrefutable" evidence, but enough indications as to who was involved. The United States also placed itself in the position of risking the disclosure of intelligence capabilities in order to satisfy a self-imposed doctrine.

The irrefutable evidence doctrine also led the United States at times to overlook Syrian or Iranian involvement in anti-U.S. terrorism. While those countries were denounced by the Reagan administration for giving support to terrorist groups and were on the official State Department list of state-sponsors of terrorism, the administration never announced that there was "irrefutable evidence" pointing to those countries' involvement in anti-U.S. attacks. A military strike against either of those countries would have had adverse effects on U.S. foreign policy objectives in the Middle East.

The Long Commission's focus on the issue of military responses to terrorism eventually led to the signing by President Reagan of National Security Decision Directive (NSDD) 138 on April 3, 1984. This still-classified document, which has been described in numerous books and news articles, officially established the principle for the use of military force against terrorists. The introduction to NSDD 138, as reported by

Martin and Walcott, states that "the U.S. government considers the practice of terrorism by any person or group in any cause a threat to our national security." NSDD 138 reflected the adoption of the general principle of using force against terrorism. Administration officials told the press that NSDD 138 "is an effort to switch from defensive to offensive action, partly by increasing United States operatives' ability to gather intelligence in order to stop terrorists before they can act." They also said that "the general idea [of NSDD 138] is that we don't allow terrorism to go unpunished."[30]

NSDD 138 was the result of several months of reflection and discussion by key administration officials, including National Security Adviser Robert McFarlane and his deputy, John Poindexter, both of whom would soon become principal actors in the arms-for-hostages deal with Iran. While the White House never officially referred to NSDD 138 by name, it did acknowledge in an official statement on April 17 that there had been "a detailed review" of the subject of terrorism and that this resulted in "some conclusions on what we must do to protect ourselves." The White House also said that "the states that practice terrorism or actively support it cannot be allowed to do so without consequence." It said that it was "the right of every legitimate government [to combat terrorism with] all legal means available." And on April 4, one day after Reagan signed NSDD 138, Shultz delivered a speech that echoed the main thrust of the directive, stating that the United States might have to take "preventive or preemptive action" against those who perpetrate terrorist acts.[31]

Shultz was the administration's most outspoken hawk on terrorism. He wanted the United States and other democratic governments to utilize all practical means at their disposal to battle this hideous form of violence. Getting people and governments to realize there was a problem was the first step. "I think you have to proceed in series," recalled Shultz. "You have to first have a situation to work with where people see there is a problem. And unfortunately, the terrorists provide that education for you by the things they do that get on peoples' minds." Once people and governments were made aware of the threat of terrorism, efforts could then be launched to gain international cooperation in such matters as intelligence-sharing and physical security measures at embassies and airports that could help reduce the likelihood of a terrorist attack. But that was only part of the picture as far as Shultz was concerned. "It seemed to me—and this was a hard point to put across—[that you] can't simply be defensive, sitting there waiting for the terrorists to hit you. You have to let them know that you are willing to hit them. And that they can pay a price. Now, you just can't go conducting military type operations everywhere. You have to have the intelligence to be able to pinpoint things and so on. But, nevertheless, the idea . . . that they can be taken out is something that unnerves them. So you work along those policy paths. I suppose a general way to put it, is you try to lower the value of whatever the terrorists do, and you try to raise the cost to them."[32]

Shultz embarked on a public campaign during the summer and fall of 1984 to promote the idea of the "tough" U.S. response to international terrorism. Testifying before the House Foreign Affairs Committee on June 13, Shultz stated that "we are now faced with a problem which is of major and growing significance. The problem . . . is . . . represented . . . by the threat that terrorism represents to civilized life. The main target of terrorists is not just individuals but the basic interests and values of the democracies. It is a form of low-level warfare directed primarily at Western nations and institutions and their friends and allies. We are the targets because our belief in the rights of the individual is an obstacle to those who wish to impose their will on others." Eleven days later, he addressed the Jonathan Institute, an educational foundation established in memory of Lieutenant Colonel Jonathan Netanyahu, who was killed while leading the Israeli raid on Entebbe in 1976. Shultz told the group that "a purely passive defense does not provide enough of a deterrent to terrorism and the states that sponsor it. It is time to think long, hard, and seriously about more active means of defense—about defense through appropriate preventive or preemptive actions against terrorist groups before they strike."[33]

But it was in a speech at the Park Avenue Synagogue in New York City on October 25 that Shultz delivered his most aggressive message yet on terrorism. After beginning his talk with the hope that "someday terrorism will no longer be a timely subject for a speech, but that day has not yet arrived," Shultz outlined the reasons why the United States must adopt a military solution to the problem. "We now recognize," Shultz said, "that terrorism is being used by our adversaries as a modern tool of warfare. It is no aberration. We can expect more terrorism directed at our strategic interests around the world in the years ahead. To combat it, we must be willing to use military force." Shultz appealed for public support for U.S. military action against terrorists:

> What will be required, however, is public understanding *before the fact* of the risks involved in combating terrorism with overt power. The public must understand *before the fact* that there is potential for loss of life of some of our fighting men and the loss of life of some innocent people.
> . . . Our military has the capability and the techniques to use power to fight the war against terrorism. This capability will be used judiciously. To be successful over the long term, it will require solid support from the American people.

> . . . We will need the capability to act on a moment's notice. There will not be time for a renewed national debate after every terrorist attack. We may never have the kind of evidence that can stand up in an American court of law. But we cannot allow ourselves to become the Hamlet of nations, worrying endlessly over whether and how to respond. A great nation with global responsibilities cannot afford to be hamstrung by confusion and indecisiveness. Fighting terrorism will not be a clean or pleasant contest, but we have no choice but to play it.
>
> . . . If terrorism is truly a threat to Western moral values, our morality must not paralyze us; it must give us the courage to face up to the threat.[34]

The speech set off alarm bells in Washington. Administration officials were caught off-guard by the secretary's strongly worded address. Using military force against terrorists regardless of the risk to innocent lives, not allowing issues of "morality" to hamper U.S. counterterrorist efforts, and retaliating against terrorists "on a moment's notice," were pretty strong words for even the highly rhetorical Reagan team. Reporters wanted to know whether Shultz's comments reflected official U.S. policy. Only a few days earlier, Reagan himself stated in a debate with Democratic presidential candidate Walter Mondale that the United States would not strike back at terrorist targets unless it was assured that it was retaliating against the actual perpetrators of an incident. "We are not going to hit people to say, 'Oh, look—we got even,'" Reagan said. An administration official who remained anonymous played down Shultz's comments, telling a reporter that the Defense Department, the Joint Chiefs of Staff, and the CIA were all much more cautious than the secretary of state on the issue of using military force against terrorists. Vice-President Bush echoed these sentiments, stating that he did not agree with the view that the United States should be willing to risk innocent lives in retaliating against terrorists. And the president himself said that he did not think that Shultz's speech "was a statement of policy." But White House spokesman Larry Speakes claimed that "Shultz's speech was Administration policy from top to bottom."[35]

The uncertainty concerning what U.S. policy toward terrorism really was led Mondale to believe he might have an issue to seize upon in the waning weeks of the 1984 presidential campaign. "This past day," Mondale said on October 27, "we have the U.S. Government all over the map—the Secretary saying we will attack terrorists even if innocents are killed; then the Vice President saying, 'Oh, no, only if they can be attacked without touching innocents'; then the President backing up and taking a different position, underscoring the fact that there is no one in charge. All that theoretical talk yesterday, and the inconsistency only emboldens terrorists to think that this Government does not know what it is doing."[36]

George Shultz felt he knew what he was doing and that he was being consistent with Ronald Reagan's true feelings about dealing with international terrorism. "I felt I was saying what the president believed, and after he went over carefully everything, he agreed with me," recalled Shultz. "He endorsed what I [had] said. There were many people who I had a great struggle on this with—[such as] the Secretary of Defense—because when you talk about military action, you are talking about his assets. And he was basically very reluctant to have military forces engage in actions. So we had a lot of tension about that."[37]

It was indeed an anomaly that George Shultz, the pragmatic secretary of state in a highly ideological administration, would be the most hawkish U.S. government official when it came to terrorism. Shultz took a moderate view on most of the major issues of his time. For example, he did not share his president's view of the Soviet Union as an "evil empire," but rather saw it as a formidable adversary for whom negotiation, arms control, and cooperation was a wiser strategy to pursue than confrontation. Shultz argued in favor of abiding by the SALT II treaty even though it had not been ratified by the Senate following the Soviet invasion of Afghanistan in 1979. He supported SALT despite evidence of Soviet violations of the treaty, including the building of an antimissile defense system at the Krasnoyarsk radar site. Shultz was also opposed to the covert operations that CIA Director Casey had initiated in Central America in order to counter the growing Soviet-Cuban influence in the region. He felt that Casey was taking unnecessary risks and was conducting his own foreign policy without consulting the State Department. Reagan had to convince Shultz not to resign over that matter.[38]

How, then, could the man who had avoided rhetoric in his dealings with the Soviets, who had pressed for democratic reform in Third World countries, and who had once lamented that the "gradual movement [toward democracy in Latin America] does not receive the [same amount of] attention of the media as much as the sporadic guerrilla offensive,"[39] be so extreme in his approach to international terrorism? "It was something that I lived with throughout my time in office," said Shultz. The embassy bombings in 1983 and 1984, the Marine barracks bombing, the hostage episodes, and all the other terrorism episodes of the 1980s helped solidify his thinking on the issue. So did the long reach of terrorists. "Personally, I had threats on my life three times," said Shultz. "So I would say [it was] a fact of life."[40] But one that Shultz earnestly believed could be changed with firm resolve by the United States.

One reason why Shultz was so hawkish on terrorism stems in part from his ongoing feuds with Defense Secretary Weinberger. It almost seemed at times that whatever position one of them took on an issue—arms control, relations with the Soviets, policy in Lebanon, and so forth—the other took the opposite view. "[They] never got along especially well together," Reagan writes. "There was always a little chill—a tension—between them."[41] Weinberger strongly opposed Shultz's advocacy of a military approach to combating terrorism. "A number of people, particularly in the State Department, supported what is called an 'unfocused' response," Weinberger writes, "that is, an immediate retaliatory action, such as bombing a Syrian or Iranian city if we believed the terrorist act originated there. I always argued against that simple 'revenge' approach, as did the President."[42] These differences with Weinberger very likely reinforced Shultz's tough stance on terrorism.

According to Weinberger, Shultz became upset after the Long Commission published its findings on the Marine barracks bombing. Shultz believed that the commission had exceeded its original mandate by criticizing U.S. policy in Lebanon and had become a tool for Weinberger—who created the commission—to air his policy disputes with Shultz. Weinberger writes that Shultz reacted with anger following the publication of the Long Commission's report.[43] Shultz, who supported U.S. participation in the multinational peacekeeping force in Lebanon, while Weinberger opposed it, continued to press the case for a U.S. presence in the country even after the withdrawal of U.S. troops. "I think the appropriate punctuation to put after the word 'Lebanon' right now is not a period—perhaps a comma, but certainly no more than a semicolon," Shultz told the American Society of Newspaper Editors in May 1984. "We're very much engaged there."[44]

Weinberger, though, issued a speech before the National Press Club in November 1984, in which he outlined the conditions under which the United States should be willing to commit its troops to combat overseas. These included only those situations when U.S. national interests or those of our allies are at stake, when there is likely to be support for such action by the American public and Congress, when there are clear political and military objectives for such action, when we have the intention of winning, and when it is the last resort.[45] "I think in those days the Defense Department was focused on winning World War III from the Soviet Union," said Shultz. "And I was advocating the view that there were lots of conflicts around the world. They were gray area conflicts. And terrorist activities was one representation of it. And that we had to be prepared to engage with these types of conflicts. There were a lot of people in the Pentagon who agreed completely with what I said."[46]

Furthermore, although it was the military that suffered the most casualties at the hands of terrorists in Lebanon, Shultz viewed the bombing of the Marine barracks and the subsequent U.S. withdrawal from that country as a victory for terrorists at the expense of U.S. foreign policy goals. This helped harden his position with respect to U.S. responses to terrorism. He writes in his memoirs about his frustrating attempt in early 1984 to prevent the withdrawal:

> By the time I got back to Washington [from a trip to Latin America] on February 8, I found a virtual stampede just to "get out" of Lebanon. "The Defense Department," I said, "will try to get the marines out without putting new elements in. It's a rout. We haven't figured out how to cope with terrorism. The vice president said that there is nothing more important than getting those marines out. We need some thinking about our interests worldwide and what the stakes are, what it means to have staying power in difficult and ambiguous situations."[47]

It was in the year after the Marine bombing that Shultz intensified his public campaign to make military responses a part of U.S. strategy for fighting terrorism. The irony of having the State Department, the one agency of the U.S. government expected to adopt the diplomatic approach to most problems, instead taking the lead on the use of military force to deal with terrorists, while the Defense Department took the more cautious approach, is not as surprising as it may seem. The military is often asked to apply quick fixes to problems that may not be that easy to fix. And if things go wrong, it is the military that gets blamed. The State Department, on the other hand, was the official government agency responsible for U.S. counterterrorist efforts worldwide, and even had a special "Office for Counterterrorism" headed by individuals with ambassadorial rank. For the State Department, the struggle against terrorism was a high-profile task that required all the available means at the disposal of the United States.

By the end of Reagan's first term in office, then, the issue of international terrorism had risen to the top of the U.S. foreign policy agenda. Part of this was due to the high-profile incidents that terrorists had perpetrated in Lebanon, Kuwait, Europe, and elsewhere. Part of it was also due to the coverage that terrorism was given in the media. But a major reason was the expectations by the Reagan administration that the terrorist threat could be met head-on. In the aftermath of Shultz's tough speech on terrorism in New York, a State Department official supporting Shultz's views said, "We are going to move against the terrorists. There will be a war on terrorists. You just watch and see."[48]

The top U.S. counterterrorist official during the last few years of Reagan's second term, Ambassador L. Paul Bremer, did not approve of the rhetoric on terrorism that was the trademark of Reagan's first term. "The previous administration, particularly in its early years, used far too much rhetoric in describing the battle against terrorists," said Bremer. "I think there is a tendency in our politics in general to overuse rhetoric, and the problem is that the American people . . . respond to that rhetoric. It is a more general problem in that Americans, politicians, and sometimes even diplomats tend to describe situations as problems. And when you use the word *problem* you automatically imply a solution. There isn't a Middle East problem, there is a Middle East situation, and there isn't therefore going to be a solution to terrorist problems, there are only going to be ways to alleviate them."[49]

Reagan, though, would continue the rhetoric on terrorism until the end, tempering it somewhat after the arms-for-hostages deal with Iran became public in the fall of 1986. But as 1984 was drawing to a close, the president was riding high. He had just won a landslide victory in the November elections and was preparing to escalate the battle against terrorists both in words and in action. But the terrorists were also preparing for a second term of violence against the United States. Reagan would be spared another high-fatality terrorist attack, such as the Marine barracks bombing, until he was about to leave office in December 1988 and Pan Am Flight 103 was blown up over Lockerbie, Scotland. The impact of terrorism, though, lies not just in a body count, but also in the symbolic effect of high-profile attacks. In 1985, terrorists would perpetrate two attacks that would leave a lasting impression on both the American public and the American government.

Terrorism in the Air and at Sea

The year 1985 was a particularly gruesome one in international terrorism. Several countries suffered through incidents with high numbers of casualties. In June, an Air India jet exploded off the coast of Ireland, killing 329 people. Sikh extremists were suspected of placing the bomb aboard the plane before it took off from Canada. In November, leftist guerrillas belonging to the Colombian M-19 group seized the Palace of Justice in Bogota, taking several judges and civilians captive. Colombian police and the military assaulted the building in a rescue attempt, but more than one hundred people were killed, including several Supreme Court judges. That same month in Malta, Egyptian commandos stormed a hijacked Egyptair plane, but more than fifty people were killed during that rescue effort. And during the Christmas season, Abu Nidal terrorists staged simultaneous massacres at airports in Rome and Vienna, killing several people, including five Americans.

The United States did not suffer large numbers of casualties at the hands of terrorists in 1985. American deaths accounted for only three percent of the 854 casualties worldwide. Eighteen U.S. servicemen were killed in the bombing of a Madrid café in April, while two Americans lost their lives in a car bombing at Rhein-Main air base near Frankfurt in August. In that incident, the Red Army Faction killed a U.S. serviceman outside a discotheque and used his identity papers to gain access to the base.

In terrorism, though, the symbolic effect of an incident can be just as effective as killing large numbers of people. The hijacking of Trans World Airline Flight 847 in June and the seizure of the *Achille Lauro* cruise ship four months later led to only two American casualties. But the long, drawn-out dramas of both incidents, the wide degree of media exposure they attracted, and the symbolism of a terrorist event in the skies followed by one at sea greatly increased public fears about terrorism. It also increased the pressure upon the Reagan administration to "do something" to stem the growing tide of international terrorism.

On June 14, TWA Flight 847, carrying 153 passengers and crew, including 135 Americans, was hijacked shortly after take-off from Athens en route to Rome. Two Shiite extremists belonging to Hizballah and armed with handguns and grenades ordered the pilot, Capt. John Testrake, to fly to Algiers. When Testrake told them that he did not have enough fuel to reach the Algerian capital, the hijackers instead chose Beirut as their first stop. After landing and refueling there, they released several women and children. The plane then flew to Algiers, where the hijackers demanded the release of more than seven hundred Shiite prisoners in Israel. They also demanded that the plane be refueled and flown back to Beirut. The driver of the fuel truck, however, was not impressed that it was a hijacked plane that he was servicing. He refused to pump the fuel until either the terrorists or the hostages produced a credit card to pay for it. The Shiite terrorists had prepared for their hijacking with guns and grenades, but it failed to occur to them that they might need a credit card somewhere down the road. It was thus left to one of the crew members, Uli Derickson, to pay for the fuel with her personal Shell Oil credit card.[50]

The refueled plane took off for Beirut after twenty-one additional hostages, mostly women and children, were released in Algiers. In Beirut, the hijackers shot and killed U.S. Navy diver Robert Stethem, whom they had viciously beaten during the hijacking. His body was thrown onto the tarmac. Several more terrorists with additional weapons joined the original hijackers in Beirut. The plane returned to Algiers, where the hijackers released several Greek hostages in exchange for one of their comrades who had been arrested in Athens for participating in the planning of the hijacking. He joined the other terrorists on the plane, which then returned to Beirut after several more hostages were released in Algiers. There were more than thirty male hostages and three crew left on

TWA 847 as it landed in Beirut on the fourth day of the hijacking. The plane and the hostages would remain in Beirut for the duration of the episode.[51]

Although the Beirut-Algiers shuttle odyssey of TWA 847 had ended, the drama on the ground was just beginning. After the final return to Beirut, most of the hostages were released to the custody of Amal militia chief Nabih Berri. The hostages were moved to guarded places in south Beirut while three crew members and a few of the original hijackers remained on the plane. Thomas Murry, an aerospace engineer, recalled the terror of being put in a van with the other hostages and shuttled across Beirut. When the back door of the van was opened, Murry found himself in a stark building with a bare light bulb hanging from two wires on the ceiling. He could see a large wall with two young Arabs standing on each side with AK-47 automatic rifles slung over their shoulders. When the hostages were told to move out of the van, Murry thought it was all over. "I look[ed] back [at the wall] and the thing that came across my mind immediately was the [St.] Valentine's Day massacre. . . . The majority of us had the impression that this would be an execution."[52]

But Amal, which was a more secular and less extreme group of Shiites than Hizballah, had no intention of killing the hostages. They moved them across the street to an apartment building where they would be kept in small groups in different apartments. Murry was placed with seven other hostages in a one-bedroom apartment with a sitting room. The next morning one of the Amal guards came into the apartment and told the captives that they were safe and essentially in "protective custody." "They were more worried about somebody getting to us than they were about us escaping," said Murry.[53] Amal was concerned that rival factions would try to kill the Americans in order to embarrass Amal. After several days in the small apartment, Murry and the other hostages were moved to a larger place in a different area in Beirut, where they remained until the crisis was over.

Meanwhile, Berri demanded that the Shiite prisoners in Israel be released in exchange for the hostages. The Israelis, who were planning to release the prisoners anyway, did not want to appear to be yielding to the demands of terrorists. At the same time, though, they were getting nervous about alienating the U.S. government and the American public by appearing intransigent while American lives were in danger.

The Reagan administration also did not want to appear to be negotiating with terrorists, but hoped that Israel would bend just a little bit and make life easier for Washington. When the Israelis refused to release the prisoners unless they were asked explicitly to do so by the United States, Reagan became upset. "His [Berri] price is release of the 760 Shiites held by Israel," Reagan writes. "Israel is publicly saying they will, but the U.S.

at the highest level of govt. must ask them to do it. This of course means that me—not they, would be violating our policy of not negotiating with terrorists. To do so, of course, negotiate with terrorists, is to encourage more terrorism." When Algeria offered to approach Berri and suggest to him that the hostages be removed from Lebanon to Algeria in return for a promise from Israel that the Shiite prisoners would be released, Israeli Foreign Minister Yitzhak Rabin "loused things up," according to Reagan, "by going public with a statement that the U.S. should ask them to release the Shiites." This was unacceptable to Reagan since it would be "establishing a linkage we insist does not exist."[54]

While the behind-the-scenes negotiations were continuing, the terrorists were publicizing their cause with press conferences. Terrorists in the 1980s had perfected the art of utilizing the media to publicize their grievances. One news interview was held at the side of the hijacked plane, with a Hizballah guard brandishing a gun at both Testrake and the reporters. The image of a terrorist holding a gun to the head of a hostage was quite striking. Reagan saw the interview and was very impressed with Testrake. "That captain is quite a guy," Reagan wrote in his diary on June 19, "absolutely unruffled."[55] What Reagan and most people did not know, though, was that by this point in the hijacking—after several days of interactions with the hijackers—Testrake had developed a rapport with his captors that diminished the immediate threat to his life. The terrorists relied upon him to fix things that broke down in the cabin as the plane remained on the ground, including the air conditioning and the radio. There was also a great deal of give and take and friendly joking between the crew and the hijackers. In fact, when one of the hijackers opened the news conference by leaning out the window and brandishing his gun at the reporters, Testrake thought the hijacker was just showing off and enjoying the publicity a little too much. "He didn't seem to want to relinquish the stage," Testrake writes, so the TWA pilot had to yell at him, "Okay, that's enough! Come on back in here." The hijacker obeyed the hostage and Testrake began talking with the reporters. One of the points he made was that he was against any attempted rescue effort since "we would all be dead men . . . because we're continually surrounded by many, many guards."[56]

A counterterrorist raid had been planned in the early stages of the hijacking. The Pentagon did not want to activate Delta Force immediately after the plane was hijacked since it did not know where it would eventually land. But after the terrorists killed Stethem and the plane was on the ground in Beirut with all the hostages aboard, Delta was dispatched from Fort Bragg, North Carolina. The plan was to send Delta to a British military base on Cyprus, which was only one hundred miles from Beirut. But while the counterterrorist team was en route to Cyprus, the hijacked plane returned to Algiers. Delta's destination was then changed to a NATO base in Sigonella, Sicily. A force of more than two hundred commandos, mechanics, other military personnel, and helicopters landed there and waited for a call that never came. Once the hijacked plane returned to Beirut and the hostages were taken off the plane, the rescue plans were canceled. The risks to the hostages and to U.S. military personnel were deemed too high in the fortified environment of Beirut. Heavily armed Amal militia were guarding most of the hostages, which would have made any rescue attempt extremely bloody.[57] Thomas Murry was glad no rescue was tried. "We didn't want any attempt like that because we knew that it wouldn't be successful and we were going to lose at least half the people. Somebody [might] be a hero because they save eight people, but ten people over there die?"[58]

Meanwhile, the terrorists continued to play up to the media. After the cockpit-window interview, the Amal terrorists holding the majority of hostages called a press conference themselves. Five hostages were brought to the airport terminal to answer questions from reporters. But the news conference quickly turned into bedlam when reporters and photographers initiated a pushing, shoving, and shouting match in order to get closer to the hostages. This was mainly the work of a few local newspeople, but it gave the image of an out-of-control world media. "It was all of the local crazies who came in without discipline who made the whole press look like a bunch of animals, which indeed they were and which properly I think appalled the world," said Larry Grossman, who was president of NBC News during the TWA hijacking.[59] CNN Executive Vice President Ed Turner agreed, claiming that "the conduct by the journalists there was immature. I think you had less experienced hands on site. There weren't very many of them that caused that brief uproar. It was kind of a black eye, I thought."[60] Nevertheless, interviews with hostages and terrorists would continue throughout the duration of the hijacking.

The episode was finally resolved with the help of Syria. Countering terrorism can make for strange bedfellows, and the United States in its desire to end the hijacking elicited the aid of Syrian President Hafez al-Assad, even though Syria was on the State Department's list of state-sponsors of terrorism. Assad convinced Berri to release the hostages to Syrian custody. The pro-Iranian Hizballah, however, refused to free four hostages that it was holding because it objected to Reagan's public remarks calling the group "thugs and murderers and barbarians."[61] Hizballah demanded a statement from the United States that it would not retaliate against them for the hijacking, but instead settled for a statement that the U.S. would respect the sovereignty of Lebanon. The four hostages were then released with the likely approval of Iran. National

Security Adviser Bud McFarlane believed that the real reason that Hizballah had refused to release the four hostages was that they thought that rival Shiite Amal militia leader Berri would look too good in bringing about an end to the hostage drama.[62] After being escorted to Damascus in a Red Cross motorcade, all the hostages were flown to Wiesbaden, West Germany, on June 30. They returned to the United States two days later and the Israelis eventually freed their Shiite prisoners.

The hostage episode was over after seventeen days of high drama and anxiety. The impact of the ordeal upon hostage Murry was profound. While he suffered through the fears one would normally expect in a hostage situation, he also gained some new insights into the problems of Lebanon. The two-week course, provided by his captors, included a tour of some of the burned-out sections of Beirut. Amal showed the hostages the buildings and other structures destroyed by the heavy bombardment from the U.S.S. battleship *New Jersey*. One day one of their guards, whose name was Akal, was talking with the hostages about the reasons for the hijacking and told them about Hizballah's demands. But he also wanted his captives to understand why somebody might become a terrorist. "He said, 'Think about a young man in southern Lebanon, a Shiite, who [is a] poor farmer [or shepherd],' " recalled Murry. " 'And he's out in the fields working. And some of these Palestinians come in town and launch a rocket attack at the Israelis. The Israelis shoot back and [the] Palestinians are gone. And he gets home to find his family dead. And here is shell casings stuffed with American markings on it. And he's standing there looking at that, and a radical comes up and pats him on the shoulder and says, 'I'll show you how to get even.' And you've got [yourself a] terrorist."[63]

Murry's most lasting impression of Lebanon, however, was when he peered out the window one day from the apartment where he was being held and saw two little Lebanese girls playing on a nearby patio. One girl was about seven years old and the other around four. The older girl appeared to be teaching her sister how to pound mulberry leaves with a rock:

> And I'm standing there thinking about my granddaughter and my grandson—who I've never seen at this time. Then two explosions went off from shells. Kind of freezes your chest. I mean it's that close. It's not the one that you hear off as a distant boom. This is where you hear the sharp, high pitched sounds of the explosions. And working around the explosives enough to, I knew those were damn close. But I was watching these two children and *they didn't move. They didn't pay any attention to that.* And I'm sitting there thinking those two kids didn't pay any more attention to that than my kids would playing in the backyard if

somebody honked the horn. That's what they're growing up with. What must their parents feel when they see they're raising their children in that kind of environment?[64]

Most Americans back home were not exposed to these types of images about Lebanon despite extensive media coverage of the hijacking. The three major television networks devoted an average of fourteen minutes each night to the episode from their regular twenty-two minute evening newscasts. Video images of hostages, families, terrorists, and others were continually broadcast to the American public. But minimal time was spent depicting or discussing the internal problems of Lebanon.[65]

The image of a crisis over the TWA hijacking was also perpetuated at the highest levels of the U.S. government. The normally calm approach to terrorism that Weinberger had demonstrated during the first Reagan term was shattered with his statement during the hijacking that "it is a war and it is the beginning of war."[66] President Reagan added to the crisis atmosphere by returning from Camp David ahead of schedule in order to be at the White House during the episode, much like Jimmy Carter refused to leave his post while there were hostages in Iran.[67]

But it was not until the former hostages were airborne for West Germany that the extent to which terrorism had become one of the most significant issues for the United States was dramatically illustrated by Reagan. There have been few, if any, times since the invention of television that a president of the United States unexpectedly interrupted regularly scheduled programs to address the American people with news about a particular event. Yet Reagan considered the release of the hostages to be of such historic importance that he took to the airwaves at 6:00 P.M. on Sunday, June 30:

> The 39 Americans held hostage for 17 days by terrorists in Lebanon are free, safe, and at this moment, on their way to Frankfurt, Germany. They'll be home again soon. This is a moment of joy for them, for their loved ones, and for our nation. And America opens its heart in a prayer of thanks to Almighty God.

Reagan then stated that no deals were made—even though deals were actually made linking the release of the hostages to the release of the Shiite prisoners in Israel—and he renewed the call for a "war" on terrorism:

> The United States gives terrorists no rewards and no guarantees. We make no concessions; we make no deals. Nations that harbor terrorists undermine their own stability and endanger their own people. Ter-

rorists, be on notice, we will fight back against you, in Lebanon and elsewhere. We will fight back against your cowardly attacks on American citizens and property.[68]

Terrorists worldwide could not have hoped for a better script. The message to them was clear: Hijack the right plane at the right moment, or perpetrate some other dramatic attack, and you can bring the president of the most powerful nation in the world to address you and take notice of you. You could also greatly complicate U.S. foreign policy. The hostages were coming home, U.S.-Israeli relations were strained, and that paragon of U.S. trust, Hafez al-Assad of Syria, was now given worldwide prominence for helping to win the release of the hostages. Meanwhile, hostage Murry's thoughts were with the people of Lebanon as he flew to freedom. "Flying out over from Damascus directly out over the coast, we were back over Lebanon. And my thinking again [was] of those two little girls down there, hoping that they can get peace in that country. And my seatmate talking about wanting to drop a bomb and wiping it all out."[69]

The American public had barely recovered from the traumas of the TWA hijacking when news came of another spectacular terrorist attack. The seizure of the *Achille Lauro* cruise ship off the coast of Egypt on October 7 by the Palestine Liberation Front caught virtually everybody by surprise, even the terrorists themselves. Abu Abbas, leader of the PLF, had planned that four of his men would attack the Israeli port of Ashdod, one of the stops on the cruise. But when a waiter discovered the terrorists cleaning their guns in their cabin, they seized the ship instead. A dramatic hijacking at sea was indeed a unique event for the 1980s. While terrorism at sea was commonplace during the days of the Barbary pirates, modern day terrorists preferred land targets for several reasons. There was a wider variety of targets on land than at sea and planning and executing an operation at sea was much more difficult in terms of logistics, equipment, and escape routes.[70]

When the PLF gunmen seized the *Achille Lauro*, there were ninety-seven passengers on board along with a crew of 344. Most of the original 750 passengers had already disembarked earlier for a day-long tour of Egypt. The terrorists demanded the release of fifty Palestinian prisoners in Israel in exchange for the safety of the hostages. The ship sailed to the Syrian port of Tartus, but Syrian authorities refused to allow it to enter. While the ship was off the coast of Syria, the terrorists killed Leon Klinghoffer, a wheelchair-bound, elderly Jewish American citizen, and threw his body overboard. The gunmen then ordered the ship to return to fifteen miles off the coast of Port Said, Egypt. Egyptian and PLO officials persuaded the hijackers to surrender in return for safe passage out of the country. Egyptian authorities later claimed that they did not know that Klinghoffer had been killed.[71]

The hijacking was over after only two days. But the brutal killing of an invalid American, the attack on a cruise ship—something the public was not accustomed to associating with terrorism—and the wide media coverage of the episode all contributed to a heightened level of fear about terrorism. For the Reagan administration, there was no way they could sit by and allow the PLF hijackers to be flown out of Egypt after all the promises that were made to the American people about swift and effective retribution against terrorists. Thus, on October 10, U.S. Navy F-14 fighter planes intercepted the Egyptian airliner carrying Abu Abbas, one of his aides, and the four hijackers, forcing it to land at the U.S.-Italian NATO base in Sicily. The plane was then immediately surrounded by American commandos who had been aboard two C-141 transport planes following the airliner. The Joint Special Operations Command (JSOC) team, comprised of Delta Force and Navy SEALS, was prepared to capture the hijackers and bring them back to the United States to stand trial for the murder of Klinghoffer. However, Italian troops surrounded the JSOC team and refused to allow them to transfer the hijackers to U.S. custody. The Italians arrested the four hijackers themselves, but allowed Abbas and his aide to remain on the plane. The Italians likely did not want to arrest Abbas—who had close ties with PLO leader Yasir Arafat—for fear of retaliatory PLO terrorist attacks on Italian soil. Abbas and his aide were later transferred to a military base outside of Rome, then on to Rome's international airport where, disguised as Egyptian officers, they boarded a Yugoslav plane for Belgrade. Yugoslavia had diplomatic relations with the PLO, and since Abbas was a member of its executive council, he and his aide were granted diplomatic immunity at the PLO embassy in Belgrade.[72]

The four hijackers, who remained in Italian custody, along with several accomplices who were also arrested, were eventually tried and convicted by Italian courts. The most severe sentence was handed to Yussef Magid Molqi, who initially confessed to murdering Klinghoffer, but later recanted his confession. He was given thirty years in jail. The other hijackers were given lesser sentences. Abu Abbas, the mastermind of the operation, was given a life sentence in absentia.[73]

"It was a damn good operation," recalled George Shultz.[74] In part, the campaign that he had led the year before to make military responses an integral part of U.S. counterterrorist policy was paying off. With many government officials and the public thinking that military responses were justified, there was little trouble in getting President Reagan to approve the mission, even though he was in Chicago at the time.

The interception of the Egyptian airliner and the subsequent events in Italy strained U.S. relations with these countries and also caused the temporary collapse of the government of Italian Prime Minister Bettino Craxi. President Reagan, though, finally had a "victory" over terrorism to boast about. And boast he did. In a question-and-answer session with reporters on the day after the capture of the hijackers, Reagan upped the rhetoric on terrorism. Referring to the military troops and intelligence officials who captured the hijackers, Reagan said, "these young Americans sent a message to terrorists everywhere. The message: *You can run but you can't hide.*"[75]

Reagan's statement would haunt him for the remainder of his presidency. The bulk of anti-U.S. terrorist attacks take place overseas where terrorists can indeed run and hide. But for one moment, at least, Reagan had something to smile about in the frustrating war against terrorism. And he was also spared an embarrassing and potentially politically damaging situation when a Reagan gaffe was eclipsed by news of the *Achille Lauro* hijackers' capture. ABC News correspondent Sam Donaldson recalls the event well:

> The luck of the Irish, or maybe it's not luck, but one of the days that stands out in my mind is the day he went to Chicago, during the *Achille Lauro* episode. And he got off the plane and he made one of those Reaganesque booboos that again would have done in, in some major way, a normal person. He got off and he was asked whether he agreed [with what] Yasir Arafat had just said, that they [the PLO] would find and punish the perpetrators of the *Achille Lauro*. Would that be OK with Reagan? And Reagan said, "Yes, if they could find them and try them." And I said, "But we don't recognize the PLO as a sovereign nation. How can you elevate them here? You've just turned 40 years of U.S. foreign policy on its [ear]!" [Reagan said] "Well, no I think—" [National Security Adviser Bud] McFarlane, listening to all this, was just having a fit. We ran over to him and asked, "Bud, is that U.S. policy?" [McFarlane said] "Of course it isn't U.S. policy! I'll talk to him about it!" So we thought, you know, "We've got him now. *We've got him now!*" I mean, here, Ronald Reagan, five years into his term, still doesn't know what our policy is towards the PLO! [He] still doesn't understand the litany of what's to be said about it.[76]

But instead of wide news coverage and a potential controversy concerning Reagan's remarks about the PLO, the news the next day was dominated by the interception of the Egyptian airliner. "The headline the next morning," said Donaldson, "was not, *REAGAN ENDORSES PLO*, [but instead] the headline was, *ACHILLE LAURO KIDNAPPERS CAPTURED*. Because later that day, Oliver North and John Poindexter brought to him these kidnappers captured in midair. What a celebration. What a celebration!"[77] There would not be any celebration, though, for the operators of the Egyptair plane that U.S. fighters had intercepted. In what has to be a record of bad luck for one plane, less than two months later it was hijacked by pro-Libyan supporters of the Abu Nidal organization—a major opponent of Yasir Arafat and the PLO—and became the scene of one of the bloodiest rescue efforts ever launched. It was this plane that Egyptian commandos stormed in Malta with fifty-eight people, mostly hostages, killed during the operation.[78]

The Abu Nidal organization, also known as the Fatah Revolutionary Council and headed by Sabri Khalil al-Banna, a.k.a. Abu Nidal, was not yet finished with their work for 1985. They staged dramatic massacres at airports in Rome and Vienna during the Christmas holidays. On December 27, two teams of three terrorists each opened fire with automatic weapons and tossed grenades at the Israeli El Al Airlines check-in gates at Leonardo da Vinci Airport in Rome and Schwechat Airport in Vienna. A total of nineteen people, including five Americans, as well as two terrorists in Rome and one in Vienna, were killed in the attacks.

The terrorists did not fire indiscriminately in their assaults. They wanted to make sure that children were included among the victims. They succeeded in killing an eleven-year-old girl, and the lone surviving terrorist in the Rome massacre carried a note explaining why: "As you have violated our land and our honor, we will violate everything, even your children, to make known the sadness of our children. For every drop of blood shed, whether for the Tunis raid or for other things, rivers of blood will be shed in exchange."[79] The endless cycle of violence that terrorism brings was thus made clear. Abu Nidal had retaliated for the Israeli raid on PLO headquarters the previous October, which in turn was a retaliatory raid for the murder of Israeli tourists in Cyprus by Palestinian terrorists.

America's "victory" over terrorism with the capture of the *Achille Lauro* hijackers began to fade from the public memory as international terrorism continued to grow. The first few months of 1986 were fueled with speculation that the United States would finally launch a military strike against Libya. Muammar Qaddafi, the Libyan dictator, was not the only state-sponsor of terrorism in the world. He was not even the most deadly, as others such as Saddam Hussein of Iraq, Hafez Assad of Syria, and the Ayatollah Khomeini of Iran were all involved in aiding various terrorist groups. But Qaddafi—"one of the strangest heads of state in the world," as Defense Secretary Weinberger put it, and "a madman," according to Reagan, who is "not only a barbarian, [but] he's flaky"[80]—was the most visible in his anti-U.S. rhetoric and in his praise for terrorists. He was also the most vulnerable to a U.S. retaliatory strike. The United

States could bomb Libya, a weak military power, with little risk. This was not true for an attack on Syria, Iran, or Iraq. There were also fewer political risks involved in an attack on Tripoli than on other Arab states since Libya was isolated in the Arab world.

The Reagan administration's rhetoric on terrorism continued unabated throughout the winter and spring of 1986. Shortly after the United States cut all economic ties with Libya in January, Secretary of State Shultz warned that military action might still be necessary to stem the tide of international terrorism. "My opinion is that we need to raise the cost to those who perpetrate terrorist acts," Shultz said in a televised interview, "by making them pay a price, not just an economic price, so they will have to think more carefully about it."[81] President Reagan called Libya "a threat to the national security and foreign policy of the United States." Confrontations with Libya escalated in March, when Qaddafi attempted to close off international waters in the Gulf of Sidra. He had tried to do the same thing in 1981, but the United States ignored those threats and conducted naval exercises in the international waters of the gulf. When Libyan fighter planes challenged two Navy F-14s—one of the Libyan jets fired upon the U.S. aircraft and the other locked its radar on the planes— the U.S. fighters shot down the two Libyan planes. This time Qaddafi proclaimed a "Zone of Death" in the Gulf of Sidra and stated he would destroy all U.S. aircraft and ships that crossed the line. When U.S. aircraft again ignored these threats, Libya fired Soviet-made SA-5 missiles at the U.S. planes on March 24. The missiles missed their targets. The United States retaliated later that day by destroying a Libyan radar site, sinking a patrol boat, and damaging another boat that was approaching U.S. ships in the gulf.[82]

But the United States was still waiting for the "irrefutable evidence" that would link Libya to an anti-U.S. terrorist incident before it would order a military retaliatory strike. In the world of terrorism, it was a pretty good bet that Libya would soon be involved in some mischievous behavior. But the administration did not anticipate that the burden of linking Libya to a terrorist attack would also mean that important U.S. intelligence-gathering techniques and operations might also have to be revealed.

This became apparent in the aftermath of the bombing of the La Belle discotheque, a popular West Berlin nightclub that was frequented by American troops. One U.S. soldier and one Turkish woman were killed in the April 5 bombing. The blast also injured 230 others, including fifty U.S. servicemen. Weinberger, upon learning of the disco bombing, asked one of his aides whether this is "finally our smoking gun." It was, as U.S. intelligence had intercepted conversations between Libyan diplomats in the people's bureau—the name the Libyans gave to their embassies around the world—in East Berlin and Qaddafi's headquarters in Tripoli. Those conversations discussed the bombing both before and after it took place. However, since there were many discotheques in West Berlin that American servicemen frequented, it had not been possible to search each one in time to prevent the bombing. Three Abu Nidal terrorists who were arrested in connection with the incident eventually told police that it was the Syrian embassy in East Berlin that provided them with the explosives for the bombing while the Libyan people's bureau provided the operational intelligence. "The evidence was irrefutable," said Reagan. "Intelligence data provided positive proof that Libya was responsible for the bombing."[83]

As rumors circulated in Washington that the United States would now finally retaliate against Qaddafi, U.S. allies and others who were opposed to a military strike wanted to see the "irrefutable evidence" that linked Libya to the disco bombing. But revealing to the world, and particularly to the Libyans, that the United States had the intelligence capabilities to intercept communications between embassies did not go over big with the National Security Agency. The super-secret government agency, which is often referred to as "Never Say Anything," breaks codes and routinely monitors and intercepts communications around the world that could have a bearing on U.S. national security interests. NSA vigorously opposed Reagan's decision to publicly release the decoded Libyan diplomatic cables. This would not only cause the Libyans to change their codes or rely on other means of communications, such as couriers, but it would also alert other U.S. adversaries to U.S. intelligence methods. However, an unidentified White House official told a reporter that the cables had to be released in order to win public and media support for the bombing of Libya.[84]

The April 14 bombing itself was a rather straightforward military operation that almost seemed anticlimactic after all the months and years of promises of a military strike against terrorists. Combating terrorism sometimes requires unconventional military tactics, but the raid on Libya was a demonstration of how U.S. air power can be used at times to bring both physical and psychological damage to certain state-sponsors of terrorism.

The United States utilized a mix of fighter-bombers, electronic warfare aircraft, refueling tanker planes, and attack jets to strike Libya. On the evening of the raid, twenty-four F-111 fighter-bombers, twenty-eight KC and KC-135 refueling planes, and five EF-111 electronic jamming planes took off from American bases in Britain to begin a 2,800-mile journey to Tripoli. The U.S. planes were forced to fly an extra 1,200 miles over the Atlantic Ocean and the Strait of Gibraltar due to France's refusal to allow the aircraft to fly over French territory. After the first refueling, six F-111s and one EF-111, which were spare planes, returned to the British bases as planned. After three more refuelings, the fighter bombers attacked the military side of the Tripoli airport, a Libyan commando training center at Sidi Bilal port, and the el-Azzizya military barracks, where Qaddafi and his family were sleeping. In addition to the Tripoli strikes, fifteen Navy A-6 and A-7 attack jets based on aircraft carriers in the Mediterranean struck two Libyan bases near Benghazi.[85]

The raid was a military success, although problems arose with some of the aircraft. Four F-111s and two Navy A-6s were forced to abort their mission due to technological and mechanical failures. One laser-guided "smart bomb" was released early and hit an apartment building near the French embassy. One plane also crashed before reaching its target. Scores of civilians were reported to have been killed in the bombing. Qaddafi immediately struck back with a flurry of terrorist attacks, including an attempted bombing of a U.S. Air Force officers' club in Turkey, the shooting of an American who worked at the U.S. embassy in Sudan, and the execution of an American hostage in Lebanon, Peter Kilburn. Qaddafi reportedly paid a large ransom to those in Lebanon who were holding Kilburn, as well as three British hostages whom he also killed in retaliation for the use of British bases by American planes during the raid.[86]

The U.S. bombing, though, clearly left an impression upon Qaddafi. After his initial retaliatory attacks, little was heard or seen from the Libyan dictator for several months. He retreated into virtual isolation in the desert, slept in different quarters every night, and constantly moved around in case there was another U.S. raid. Although Qaddafi continued to support various terrorist groups, built a chemical weapons facility, and again challenged U.S. fighter planes in international waters in January 1989, which led to the shooting down of two Libyan MiG-24s, his public boasting about terrorism was over.[87] He got the message Reagan wanted him to get. "As we proved last week," Reagan said on April 23, "no one can kill Americans and brag about it. No one. We bear the people of Libya no ill will, but if their Government continues its campaign of terror against Americans, we will act again."[88]

The raid on Libya was a watershed for U.S. efforts to combat terrorism. One night of aerial bombings had put to rest all criticism that the United States lacked the resolve to use military force against terrorists. Public support for the raid was indeed overwhelming. A *New York Times*/CBS News poll found that seventy-seven percent of the American public approved of the bombing, while only fourteen percent opposed it.[89] The bombing was not only a success in its effect on Qaddafi, but also on the effect it had on other governments' efforts to oppose terrorism. In the wake of the raid, several countries began taking stronger measures against terrorists and cooperated more with the United States to prevent additional U.S. military strikes against Libya. (The raid was not popular in Europe; only twenty-nine percent of the British public supported the bombing while sixty-six percent were opposed.)[90] "It caused the Europeans to close down or reduce drastically the Libyan people's bureaus—their embassies—almost throughout Europe," said George Shultz. "And that reduced his [Qaddafi's] capability to operate by a lot. He was [also] shown to be isolated in the Arab world. No Arab country came to his defense in any major way at all. They all told us privately 'too bad you didn't get him in the process.' So I think it undoubtedly set his efforts back. On the other hand, it didn't stop him."[91]

If the indictments that the United States handed down in November 1991 against two Libyans for blowing up Pan Am 103 in 1988 are any indication, then the raid on Libya certainly didn't stop Qaddafi. Although there is evidence—discussed in the following chapter—suggesting that both Syria and Iran were involved in the bombing, the U.S. focus on Libya as the main perpetrator of the bombing casts a shadow on the Libyan raid. For if Libya was indeed the sole sponsor or a major player in the Pan Am bombing, then the price the United States paid for the raid may have been the subsequent loss of 270 lives, including 187 Americans, as Qaddafi sought his revenge.

But since Qaddafi was such a vocal and conspicuous proponent of terrorist attacks against the United States, there was no way that the Reagan administration could sit back and allow him to continue to flaunt his terrorism in front of the American people. "A person like that is a continuing problem," said Shultz. "Nobody suggested that the raid ended the problem. But it put a punctuation mark in our attitude and it did set him back."[92]

The raid also led to heightened security worldwide in anticipation of Libyan-sponsored retaliatory attacks. This tightened security helped avert many potential incidents, including a Syrian-sponsored plot to blow up an Israeli El Al plane at Heathrow Airport on April 17. Britain broke diplomatic relations with Syria after a November trial documented the role played by Syrian intelligence. The United States, while condemning Damascus for the attempted bombing, did not follow the British lead in severing diplomatic ties. "From a terrorism point of view, the argument was clear that we should break diplomatic relations," said L. Paul Bremer. "But [counterterrorism] is not the only objective in American foreign policy." The United States, at least with respect to this incident, put foreign policy interests in the Middle East ahead of the desire to take strong action against state-sponsors of terrorism. "It was rather curious," said Bremer, "because I was arguing against breaking diplomatic relations, not from a terrorism point of view, but because I thought there was a broader American policy interest to keep the lines open."[93]

There wasn't the same need, or interest, to keep the lines open with Libya. The less the world heard of the Libyan dictator, the better off it was as far as the Reagan administration was concerned. International terrorism, though, did not begin and end with Qaddafi. The multitude of states and groups that played this deadly game ensured that U.S. targets would continue to be hit in different ways. One type of terrorist tactic in particular frustrated Reagan. While a terrorist bombing or airplane hijacking are relatively short-term incidents that may allow for retaliatory responses at a later date, prolonged hostage episodes are a different matter. As Jimmy Carter learned during the hostage crisis in Iran, and as Reagan learned with the captivity of Americans in Lebanon, the longer it is that Americans are held against their will, the greater the pressure for the government to do something to win their release. Carter chose to wait it out, aside from one disastrous rescue attempt. Reagan eschewed the rescue option, but also decided against the wait 'em out approach. By trading arms for hostages with one state-sponsor of terrorism at the very moment that he was preparing to bomb another state-sponsor, Reagan brought to the forefront the contradictions and ambiguities in U.S. counterterrorism policy. His actions also dramatically demonstrated once again the emotional grip that hostages can have on U.S. presidents and those who serve them.

Reagan's Hostages

"My whole time, my whole three years, was in some ways determined by those first couple of weeks on the job," said Bremer, who became the special ambassador for counterterrorism in the fall of 1986, just as news of the Iran-Contra scandal was becoming public. "The effect of the arms-for-hostages [deal] was to completely undermine the basic premise of American counterterrorism policy," said Bremer. "I therefore spent a lot of time and energy in my three years at the job basically trying to re-establish the credibility of the policy. And indeed, that wound up being my main objective."[94]

Part of that policy was not to make concessions to terrorists and those governments that sponsor them. No policy on terrorism, though, could account for the human toll that having one's citizens taken captive has had on U.S. presidents. It was almost as if a president felt personally responsible for the safety of all his citizens when they were abroad and felt a sense of personal failure if he could not gain their speedy release once they became hostages. For Ronald Reagan, the need to end his personal agony over the fate of American hostages in Lebanon justified in his mind any action that he might take to win their release. "... I felt a heavy weight on my shoulders to get the hostages home," Reagan would write later. "We were coming up to another Christmas season with American citizens held captive far from home, separated from parents, wives, and children, deprived of basic freedoms, and subjected to almost unspeakable living conditions. What American trapped in such circumstances wouldn't have wanted me to do everything I possibly could to set them free? ... It was the president's duty to get them home. I didn't want to rest or stop exploring any possible avenue until they were home safe with their families."[95] Reagan, however, admitted in a May 1987 address to the nation that "I let my personal concern for the hostages spill over into the geopolitical strategy of reaching out to Iran. I asked so many questions about the hostages' welfare that I didn't ask enough about the specifics of the total Iran plan." The President's Special Review Board—also known as the Tower Commission—which investigated the arms-for-hostages deal, stated in its final report that Reagan's "intense compassion" for the hostages in Lebanon led him to support the secret arms sales to Iran. Reagan also reportedly brought up the hostage issue at ninety percent of his briefings.[96]

One of the traps that Reagan fell into, just like his predecessor Jimmy Carter, was to meet with the families of the hostages. This only served to accentuate the emotional side of presidential decision making and caused both presidents to become more involved in the personal sufferings of the families. It also added more value to the prized possessions that the terrorists were holding. "I think it is better for the president not to meet with families because it does tend to raise the profile of the issue," reflected George Shultz in 1991. "It's hard for people to accept the fact that if the value of holding the hostages is reduced, the chances of getting the hostages out is better. . . . That's the basic equation you're working with. And the more hype you give to the hostage question [and] the more the president keeps involved [in it], the more you raise the value."[97]

This was the advice Shultz gave to executives from the *Wall Street Journal* when they came to him in early 1987, asking for his help in gaining the release of one of their reporters, Gerald Seib, who had been detained by the Iranian government. Seib was one of fifty journalists visiting Iran at the request of the government, but was nevertheless seized outside his hotel room on January 31. The Iranian government later accused him of spying for Israel. Seib was most likely the victim of the endless factional fighting in Iran between the moderate forces led by Speaker of the Parliament Ali Akhbar Hashemi Rafsanjani, who had invited the journalists to Tehran in the first place, and the more extreme forces led by the Ayatollah Hussein Ali Montazeri, who saw an opportunity to embarrass Rafsanjani by seizing an American reporter.[98] But regardless of the motives behind the detaining of Seib, the Reagan administration was faced with the makings of another hostage crisis. Shultz decided that a low-key public approach—and one that did not involve the president—would be the best hope for getting Seib out quickly. Shultz recalls his meeting with Warren H. Phillips, chairman of the board of Dow Jones and Co., which publishes the *Journal;* Norman Pearlstine, the managing editor; and Karen Elliot House, the foreign editor, on February 2:

> Some of the key people at the *Journal* came to see me about it before it became a big issue. And they said, "We would like to work with you on this." And I said, "All right, I'll work with you. But if you'll take my advice . . . [which is] to play this down. Don't make a big thing out of it publicly. But let us send some messages around quietly in news organizations that this is going to cost Iran because newspeople won't go there and they're going to get very bad write-ups out of this. So they're going to pay a heavy penalty. At the same time, don't increase the value of the hostage by making a lot of publicity about how important it is that he get out." And I explained my thoughts about the strategy, and they said, "All right, we'll buy it." And we worked together. And we got him out very promptly.[99]

"I think that was good advice," Seib would later say. Seib had no idea how long he would be held by the Iranians, but thought to himself while sitting in an Iranian prison that he was at least more fortunate than the hostages in Beirut. "I was in the hands of the [Iranian] government and there can always be pressure brought on a government. . . . And from the first hour I found some solace in that. People knew who had me. If I was a real hostage as opposed to being a prisoner, I think I would have felt twice as hopeless, because not only was it unclear what leverage would work, [but] nobody was ever clear who had these people [the Beirut hostages]."[100]

Seib was released within a week, as the Shultz strategy, along with private diplomacy by the *Journal*, proved effective in averting yet another long hostage crisis for the United States. "There was never a story about what happened to me on the front page of the *Wall Street Journal* until after I got out," Seib said. "The paper did enough externally to make it clear that I was a legitimate journalist [and not a spy]. There were stories they ran that sort of explained my background. There was enough said and written by the *Journal* to make it clear that I was their representative [and] they were standing behind me, and that they were going to make sure I got out to establish my credibility. But a lot of what the paper did was done quietly." Among its behind-the-scenes actions was to have foreign editor Karen House pointedly tell the Iranian ambassador to the United Nations that his government had made a big mistake in holding Seib on espionage charges, that he was a legitimate journalist, and that the *Journal* would vouch for him. The *Journal* also enlisted the assistance of the Turkish government. The newspaper had long been supportive of Turkey in its editorials, pointing out the importance of Turkey for Western and U.S. strategic interests in the Middle East and Europe. The Turkish government therefore felt very positive about the *Journal*. The newspaper "got to [Turkish Prime Minister Turgut] Ozal directly and said, 'Would you on our behalf vouch for this guy and tell the Iranians that this is a real journalist and not a spy,' " Seib said. "And the Turks apparently did that."[101]

The Reagan administration—and the *Wall Street Journal*—had a clear target to direct their efforts upon to gain the release of Seib, namely, the Iranian government. When it came to the mysterious, shadowy terrorist groups in Lebanon that abducted Americans throughout the 1980s, the picture would not be as clear. Instead of freed hostages, the American people saw their president sink deeper and deeper into the emotional aspects of hostage taking.

The emotional grip that hostages can have on presidents is not defined by the number of hostages. Jefferson was deeply moved by the captivity of several hundred Americans in the Barbary states. Carter was greatly affected by the holding of fifty-two Americans in Iran. And Reagan was obsessed with less than ten hostages in Lebanon. The hostages during Jefferson's time were all seamen and sailors snatched from the high seas by the Barbary states. The hostages during Carter's period were mostly diplomats and those associated with the American embassy in Tehran. But Reagan's hostages, outside of having a common bond in being in the wrong country at the wrong time, were a diverse lot. They included a journalist, a priest, a university professor, a high-ranking CIA analyst, a military officer, a hospital administrator, and so forth. One had a Muslim wife and some were opposed to U.S. policy in the Middle East. The hospital administrator worked in a facility that primarily treated sick and wounded Shiites. The priest worked with schools and orphanages in Shiite areas. All of this did not matter to Hizballah and other Islamic extremist groups who abducted the Americans. For the kidnappers, any American taken hostage was a prize to be used as they saw fit.

The abduction of Americans in Lebanon was not a complicated process for the terrorists. Sometimes they simply snatched their victims off the street; other times they stormed their offices. Father Lawrence Martin Jenco, an American priest with the Catholic Relief Services in Beirut, was seized while being driven to work one morning. Several gunmen rushed to the car with their automatic weapons blasting in the air. They forced Jenco out of his vehicle and made him lie down on the floor of their car as it sped away. David Jacobsen, the director of the American University of Beirut's Medical Center, was seized after parking his car in a garage and walking the short distance to his hospital. Three men in a blue van forced him at gunpoint into their car while a Lebanese soldier and two policemen nearby simply watched. Frank Reed, the director of the International School in Beirut, was abducted as he was leaving his home to play golf in Muslim West Beirut; apparently, the numerous bombings and mortar and rocket fire had left a golf course intact somewhere in the war-torn city.

Once they had their hostages, Hizballah played a waiting game with the United States and the other countries whose citizens they had abducted. Since they did not play by any rules or feel bound by the same values that Western democracies have, they exploited the public's compassion for human life.

The total number of American hostages taken in Lebanon in the 1980s was seventeen, but their ranks were continually changing due to the release of some and the tragic killing of others. The core group that became the focus of the arms-for-hostages deal with Iran was only seven. The first kidnapping of an American in Lebanon occurred in 1982 when Hizballah abducted David Dodge, the acting president of the American University in Beirut. Although they released him the following year, Hizballah discovered that abducting Americans could be valuable because it gained them instant attention and elicited reactions from foreign governments. One of those reactions became the biggest fiasco of the Reagan presidency.

The arms-for-hostages deal with Iran was a murky mix of politics, profit, and intrigue. It started out with a vision in the summer of 1985 by some U.S. intelligence analysts that the time was ripe to open communications with Iran. The motivation was to counter potential Soviet inroads in the region and to prepare for the period following the death of Khomeini. But while a normalization of relations with Iran made perfect strategic and geopolitical sense, the manner in which it was attempted went against everything the United States had preached to its allies both about terrorism and the war between Iran and Iraq. In one swoop, the selling of arms to Iran for hostages violated U.S. pledges of not dealing with state-sponsors of terrorism and of not selling arms to either of the warring parties.

Between March 1984 and June 1985, seven Americans were kidnapped in seven separate incidents in Beirut.[102] One of these kidnappings involved William Buckley, the CIA station chief in Beirut, who was abducted on March 16, 1984, as he left his apartment on his way to work. Islamic Jihad, the loose organization of terrorist groups in Lebanon of which Hizballah was the most active, announced in October 1985 that Buckley had been executed in retaliation for the Israeli raid on PLO headquarters in Tunis. But U.S. intelligence analysts knew that Buckley had died months earlier—most likely after being tortured and forced to give a four-hundred-page confession that listed the names of U.S. agents in the Middle East—and that the terrorists were using the announcement of his death for propaganda purposes.[103] The Reverend Benjamin Weir, who had been abducted outside his home in Beirut in May 1984 and was released in September 1985, was able to tell U.S. authorities that Buckley died the previous June.[104]

None of the hostages saw Buckley beaten or tortured, but they heard his anguished cries as he lay dying the evening of June 3. David Jacobsen was in the next cubicle from Buckley, and Father Jenco was locked up in a hallway closet nearby. "I heard him say, 'I don't know what's happened to my body. It was so strong thirty days ago and now it's so very, very weak,' " recalled Jacobsen.[105] He was coughing violently and became delirious. Father Jenco heard Buckley say, "My God, I could do so much, why this?" a few hours before his death.[106] Buckley died around 10:00 that night. "I heard a [loud thud] like someone came in and whacked him one to make certain that he wasn't asleep or faking it," said Jacobsen.[107]

The Buckley case was one reason that CIA Director Casey was in favor of the arms-for-hostages deal in the summer of 1985. There was no confirmation at that point that Buckley was dead. For Casey, selling arms to Iran represented the last hope for gaining the release of Buckley if he was still alive, and if not, of at least getting a copy of the confession to assess what damage to U.S. intelligence assets in the region may have been done. Casey also felt personally responsible for the safety of Buckley. It was Casey who had asked a reluctant Buckley to take the post of CIA station chief in Beirut following the April 1983 bombing of the U.S. embassy, which killed the CIA's chief Middle East analyst, Robert Ames, as well as several other key agency personnel. Casey pulled out all the stops in an effort to rescue his man. The National Security Agency took satellite photographs of neighborhoods in Beirut in order to locate possible hiding places. Lebanese agents employed by the CIA were sent into Shiite areas in Beirut. Casey even requested that the FBI send in a team of agents to help with the search.[108] But all the technological assets of the U.S. government and all the dedicated efforts of those who looked for Buckley ultimately failed. In a kidnapping situation in a country like Lebanon, the advantage was clearly with the terrorists, who could find countless hiding places and easily move from one location to another.

Legitimate national security concerns dictated the need to free a hostage such as Buckley, and human compassion drove the desire to liberate all Americans held against their will in Lebanon. But the Iran-Contra affair—profits from the sale of arms to Iran were diverted to the Contra rebels in Nicaragua—revealed that when governments become so desperate in their efforts to free their citizens, they become tools of the kidnappers. During the numerous interactions between U.S. officials and various intermediaries and Iranian officials, the United States was continually led to believe that with the next shipment of arms, all the hostages in Lebanon would be released. But the Iranians and their Hizballah kidnappers would only release the hostages piecemeal, which greatly frustrated and angered Bud McFarlane, Oliver North, John Poindexter, and the others involved in the secret negotiations.

The Iran-Contra experience also clearly illustrated how the pool of potential hostages is a bottomless well. Whenever their "assets" get too low, the terrorists can simply dip into the well and take another. The first hostage to be released as a result of shipments of TOW antitank missiles to Iran was Weir. He was freed on September 15, 1985, after Israel transferred one hundred TOWs to Iran on August 30, and then more than another four thousand on September 14.[109] There were also direct sales of TOWs and HAWK antiaircraft missiles to Iran by the United States between 1985 and 1986. These transactions resulted in freedom for two more hostages: Jenco on July 26, 1986, and Jacobsen on November 2, 1986. But in September 1986, while the dealings with Iran were still going on, two more Americans were abducted in Beirut. A third American was then seized the following month. And in January 1987, three more Americans were kidnapped. Thus, after all the maneuvers, all the secret deals, and all the public revelations and anguish over the trading of arms for hostages, the final tally was three Americans freed and six more taken captive.

The foreign hostages in Lebanon suffered greatly. In addition to Buckley, several others died while in captivity, including Peter Kilburn and the three British hostages, as noted above, who were executed following the U.S. bombing of Libya. U.S. Marine Lieutenant Colonel William Higgins was executed most likely in the summer of 1988. Other dead hostages included a Frenchman and a Soviet diplomat.[110]

The American hostages were held in different places at first, with some imprisoned in the Bekaa Valley and others in a building near Beirut airport. By the spring of 1985, most of the Americans were brought together in the structure near the airport. They were moved a couple more times during 1985 and several more times in the ensuing years.

The hostages were chained to walls and other objects and forced to wear blindfolds in the presence of their guards. Their captors were young Shiite militants who took orders from higher-ups in Hizballah. The hostages were beaten at various times; Father Jenco lost twenty percent of his hearing due to blows to his head and face. "I was chained to a radiator and you eat off the floor and you feel like a dog," recalled Jenco. He kept his sanity by continually telling himself, "I am not an animal. I am a person of worth. And loved." One day one of the guards stood on his forehead and began to squash him. Jenco yelled, "Listen, I am not an insect!" Jenco, like the other hostages, would get depressed at times. "I can see how you can get so down that you just give up. You're so dehumanized. You cease to even be a human," Jenco said.[111]

David Jacobsen was severely beaten and placed for a short time in solitary confinement after Hizballah mistakenly thought he had sent a coded message to U.S. authorities in a videotape he made in July 1986 and which Father Jenco carried with him after his release. Jacobsen pleaded for the release of the Shiite prisoners in Kuwait in return for his and the other hostages' freedom and also criticized the U.S. government for not doing enough to win their own release. At one point in the tape Jacobsen expressed his condolences to the widow and daughters of William Buckley; however, Buckley had been a bachelor. When this was pointed out by the American news media with suggestions that Jacobsen was perhaps trying to send a coded message, Hizballah took their anger out on the hostage.[112]

There were always at least four guards present in the buildings in which the hostages were held. Some of them were less vicious than others; one in particular, who went by the name of Sayid, was the most humane, according to Jacobsen. Since he spoke English well, he talked with the hostages at length and they eventually came to learn details about his life. He had been a barber in Beirut, but the economic situation in the country left few people able to afford to pay for haircuts. So he tried to earn extra money by working for Hizballah. He was paid the equivalent of $25 a month to guard the hostages. Sayid himself suffered personal grief during the hostage episode. In the summer of 1985, his pregnant wife was mortally wounded by fragments of an artillery shell, leaving him to raise three small children. Then, in September 1986, Sayid was himself injured by an artillery shell while working on his car. He was treated—as was his late wife—in the very hospital that Jacobsen had directed before he was kidnapped.[113]

All of the terrorists were fascinated with guns and violence. They liked to watch *Rambo*-type movies and took special pleasure in pointing out to their captives where some of their own modern weapons had come from. "They used to mock me sometimes," recalled Father Jenco. "They would have brand new weapons sometimes and they would say, 'Look where they are made! They are made in Israel and the USA!'"[114]

The hostages used many coping mechanisms to deal with their plight. One was the technique of continually telling themselves they were worthwhile human beings who would one day be freed. Another was to envision being back home and driving through familiar streets. A third was to gather together in prayer—including ones such as "Dear Lord, bring Delta Force through the door."[115] The hostages would also talk with each other about their future plans. Sometimes it became a game to pass the time and keep their minds active. In a scene reminiscent of old World War II movies in which soldiers in a foxhole talk about buying that ranch in Texas or opening that candy store in Brooklyn once the war is over, the hostages traded stories about potential business investments. Terry Anderson, a correspondent with the Associated Press who was kidnapped in Beirut in March 1985, talked about having a farm in upstate New York for troubled kids from the inner cities. "He was always after Tom [Sutherland, a fellow hostage who was a professor of agriculture and animal sciences at the American University in Beirut], 'Well, [Tom], ten kids, how many cows can I have, how many pigs and chickens? How much do I feed them?' He was putting it all together [and] we had to suffer throughout that," recalled Jacobsen.[116]

Jacobsen himself kept busy by thinking about two different business plans. One was to set up a mental health facility at AUB; the other was to open a Danish fast-food restaurant in southern California. "I worked out in my mind where would be the best place to have this little fast-food [restaurant]," recalled Jacobsen, whose parents were Danish. "So I did my business projections [and] found the ideal place as far as foot traffic, automobile traffic, year-round traffic, hour-of-day traffic, [and] customers [was] Laguna Canyon Road and PCH [Pacific Coast Highway]." Jacobsen then went through a detailed analysis in his mind of the menu for the restaurant, deciding how many pieces of Danish apple cake and how many open-face sandwiches he would have to sell to make a profit, how many people he would have to hire, to whom he would submit his business plan, and so forth. "[I also] got into the design of this little shop. It kept me going. So you have to become task oriented," said Jacobsen.[117]

The hostages could also get on each other's nerves. After his release in 1991, Thomas Sutherland complained that Terry Waite, the Anglican Church envoy who tried to win the hostages' release but was himself kidnapped in 1987 and was kept with Sutherland for a while, was an egotist who had done things just for publicity. "We all irritated each other at times," Waite told Barbara Walters during an interview on ABC News "20/20." He suggested that Sutherland was only saying that he, Waite, could be "an irritating man." "He's right. I'm no saint, absolutely right," said Waite.[118]

Other hostages also fought among each other, as would be expected from a small group of men held together for an indefinite time in a confined space. "Anderson and I couldn't stand one another," recalled Jacobsen. "I couldn't tolerate him and he couldn't tolerate me. Both of us with good cause. We were both opinionated, argumentative, and you can't have two stallions in one corral."[119] They fought for dominance of their group—after Weir was released, Jacobsen, Jenco, Anderson, and Sutherland were kept together in the same room. Not surprisingly, given their occupations, Sutherland was the most academic of the group while Jenco was the most spiritual. Neither was inclined to try to take control. That left Jacobsen and Anderson to fight it out, with Sutherland usually aligning himself with his AUB colleague and Jenco siding with Anderson.

Father Jenco and David Jacobsen, who have remained good friends since their release, could also irritate each other. "David was the most difficult of all," recalled Jenco, "because he's [a] fundamentalist Christian, John Birch Society Republican, ultra-conservative, and everything's packaged in his life."[120] Jacobsen saw Jenco as a packaged liberal. "Jenco is still a bleeding-heart liberal Democrat Catholic who is deeply concerned for the poor," said Jacobsen.[121] Jenco and Terry Anderson would also fight at times. "Sometimes he'd get me angry by always insisting that he wanted a radio and a newspaper," recalled Jenco. "[And] he'd pound on the door . . . [and yell] 'I want the radio.' " Jenco would try to point out to Anderson that the guards would only get angry and not give them a radio for a long time if he carried on. "Can't you just one day not worry about a radio?" Jenco pleaded with Anderson. "Nope," was Anderson's typical reply.[122]

But the combative relationships among the hostages were good for their psyches as it kept their intellectual skills sharp. "Well, by God, I'm not going to lose this debate," was often the thought they had as they argued over various things.[123] The constant bickering that went on also masked a deep conviction they shared that whenever one of them was freed, they would work hard to win the release of their comrades left behind. "The day before I got released, Terry Anderson said to me, 'I think you are going to be the next one freed. Make sure I'm not forgotten,' " Jenco recalled.[124] So Jenco, like Jacobsen and Weir, continually publicized the hostage issue. "I would speak at any kind of an organization," said Jenco. "It would be a tea for women, and I'd go and speak. You had to keep it on the front page, on the front burner."[125]

When news of the Iran-Contra scandal became public in November 1986, that task became more difficult. The focus was now on the folly of trading arms for hostages and diverting funds to the Contras, not on the plight of the remaining hostages in Beirut. Government officials were reluctant to talk about the hostages since it was now a controversial subject. So the families of those still in Beirut leaned heavily on the released hostages to keep the issue of their loved ones alive in the media. Father Jenco received hate mail as the hostages were viewed by some as the cause of the growing scandal involving President Reagan, the thinking being that if they weren't in Lebanon in the first place they wouldn't have been taken hostage and caused problems for the president. But the official U.S. warning for all Americans to leave Beirut was not issued until January 30, 1987—a few days after three more American hostages were seized.

Prior to disclosure of the arms-for-hostages deal, the freed hostages thought that nothing had been done on their behalf by the U.S. government while they were in captivity. Father Jenco recalls being on the plane flying to Washington a few days after his release to meet with Reagan. "I was saying to my family, 'It's kind of stupid for me to be meeting with this man—to thank him for what? He said he never negotiates for my release. Why am I going there to thank him for *what*? . . . This is crazy' "[126] Reagan was also apprehensive about meeting with Jenco. The videotape that he carried with him showing Jacobsen criticizing Reagan for doing nothing for the hostages had already been broadcast. "I don't know what I expected when Father Jenco visited the Oval Office . . ." writes Reagan.[127] The former hostage had just been to Rome, delivering a letter to the pope that he had written at the request of his captors asking the pope to help the economic and social situation of the Lebanese Shiites. He gave Reagan a copy of that letter, as well as another letter he wrote to the president. ". . . [T]here were times I did not have kind and charitable thoughts about my government, my Servite order, my church, and the C.R.S. [Catholic Relief Services]. I have asked God's forgiveness for these sinful [thoughts] and ask your forgiveness, too. . . . In the future, I might still get angry—bear with me."[128]

Jenco spent most of his time at the meeting talking with Nancy Reagan. He found that soothing. "It was good for me because it was like a sister talking to a brother," he recalled. Also present was Secretary of State Shultz, who had strongly opposed the arms-for-hostages deal— along with Secretary of Defense Weinberger—when it was first discussed in a White House meeting on August 5, 1985. Shultz did not know that Jenco was released as part of the arms deal—he had been told by administration officials throughout the year that the secret dealings with Iran had ended. But the possibility that it might still be on was probably on his mind as he watched the Reagans talk with the Catholic priest. Shultz remained silent throughout the proceedings, and when it came time for him to say a few words to Jenco he could only utter, "I guess prayer works."[129]

David Jacobsen also met with President Reagan after he was released in November, but by then news of the arms-for-hostages deal had broken. A story about it had been published in a Lebanese newspaper the day after Jacobsen was freed. While Reagan and Jacobsen posed for pictures in the Rose Garden, reporters shouted questions at the president. Sam Donaldson asked a question about the arms-for-hostages deal that particularly irked Jacobsen. Before Reagan could answer, Jacobsen, still angry over media speculation that he had sent a coded message when he made a videotape, nudged the president aside and addressed the reporters: ". . . Unreasonable speculation on your part can endanger [the hostages'] lives. . . . In the name of God, will you please just be responsible and back off?"[130]

The president was thrilled with the former hostage doing battle with the hard-nosed Donaldson. "That was wonderful, wonderful," Reagan told Jacobsen as they retreated back into the Oval Office. "How do we handle the press," Nancy Reagan chimed in. "They're awful."[131] One of Reagan's assistants later remarked that when Larry Speakes, the White House press secretary, leaves his job, they should hire Jacobsen to take his place.

Jacobsen did not believe that the selling of arms to Iran was wrong. He did not see it as a deal to win his freedom, but rather as a justified way for the United States to counter Soviet influence in the region and reestablish ties with moderates in Iran. Jenco, on the other hand, was angered that his freedom was related to arms proliferation. He learned about it while at a news conference in Washington sponsored by the No Greater Love society, a support group for hostages' families and those who have lost loved ones in war or by terrorist acts. When the media asked Jenco his reaction, he told them he could not agree with what the U.S. government had done on his behalf. "That's madness," he said.[132]

The number of government officials who fell due to the Iran-Contra affair was high. Several careers were ruined, including those of National Security Adviser John Poindexter and his gung-ho subordinate, Lieutenant Colonel Oliver North. Both men were convicted of felonies, including obstruction of Congress. Their convictions were overturned when appeals courts ruled that the special prosecutor investigating Iran-Contra, Lawrence Walsh, had improperly used testimony against them that they had given to Congress under grants of immunity. Other officials tarnished by the scandal were Assistant Secretary of State for Latin American Affairs Elliott Abrams and the head of the CIA's Central American Task Force, Alan Fiers, both of whom pleaded guilty to misdemeanor charges related to aid to the Contras. The CIA's head of covert operations, Clair George, was indicted on several charges, including perjury and obstructing congressional and federal investigations. A federal jury convicted him in December 1992 on two felony counts of lying to Congress.[133]

The highest-ranking Reagan official to be indicted in the scandal was Caspar Weinberger. The distinguished secretary of defense, who had argued vehemently against the arms sale to Iran when he first learned about it in 1985, was indicted by a federal grand jury in June 1992 on five felony counts. These included perjury before congressional committees and obstruction of Congress. Weinberger was also accused by the special prosecutor's office of concealing the existence of more than 1,700 pages of notes on the arms sales to Iran that he kept in a personal diary—notes that Weinberger himself donated to the Library of Congress in 1988.[134] That charge was dismissed by a federal judge in September. There was speculation at the time of the indictments that Walsh hoped to use Weinberger in order to bring charges, in Walsh's words, against "officials at the highest level of government." There were only three officials ranked above Weinberger in the Reagan administration: Vice-President Bush, Secretary of State Shultz, and President Reagan. Weinberger was offered a plea bargain, which he refused, to one misdemeanor count in exchange for his full cooperation with investigators in gathering evidence against others.[135] Then, in December 1992, one month before he was to leave office, President Bush pardoned Weinberger, along with several other former government officials, including Abrams, Fiers, and George.

The arms-for-hostages deal cost much in personal prestige for George Shultz. Here was the highly respected secretary of state, the man who more than anybody else in the Reagan administration embodied the principles of standing firm against terrorists and their state-sponsors, forced to watch his own government make secret deals involving weapons for hostages. Why did he not resign from office as soon as he learned about the secret dealings, much like Cyrus Vance did in 1980 when he could not agree with his president's decision to attempt a military rescue of the American hostages in Iran? For one thing, Shultz was not always informed about what was really going on with the arms-for-hostages deal. When he did learn about various developments, he stayed to be a voice, along with Weinberger, against the wild schemes of others on the Reagan team:

> I was against it in 1985, [but it] went through a cycle, at the end of which I was assured . . . it was stopped. . . . Then it started again in January, the following January and I opposed it then. There was no [presidential] finding that I knew about. Later it developed that there was a finding. [But] there were many subsequent things, including a direct statement from Poindexter and Casey that the whole thing had

been, as Poindexter said, "stood down." So I thought that it was over but it wasn't. So for much of the time that the effort was going on, particularly through the whole latter half of 1986, I didn't know it was going on, so I didn't have anything to resign about. . . . I did resign in the middle of 1986, but it was a result of my feeling that I was just sort of at odds with much of the administration, and the president would be better off getting somebody who was more sympathetic to other colleagues. But he didn't wish to have me resign. So we postponed it. And then the whole crisis hit.[136]

The crisis was "an embarrassing episode"[137] for Shultz and others in the government. But newspaper reporter and author Lou Cannon, echoing the findings of the Tower Commission, writes that both Shultz and Weinberger chose not to be informed of all matters concerning the arms-for-hostages deal, thereby distancing themselves from the brewing scandal. "The real failure of Shultz and Weinberger on the Iran initiative," writes Cannon, "was their unwillingness to take concerted action to stop a proposal that both of them thought likely to prove ruinous to their country and their president and was certain to become public."[138] Cannon concludes that "neither Weinberger nor Shultz was willing to put the president to the test" by resigning from office and thereby perhaps forcing Reagan to reconsider his approval of the arms-for-hostages deal. But even Cannon admits that a dual resignation by the two highly respected members of the Reagan cabinet might still not have changed the course of events, since the president believed strongly in the righteousness and correctness of the policy.[139]

The effect of the Iran-Contra scandal was more damaging to U.S. foreign policy interests and U.S. counterterrorist policy than to Ronald Reagan himself. Reagan the man and Reagan the president survived the ordeal after a temporarily rough period. After the story of secret dealings with Iran was first reported, Reagan denied in a televised address that there was any trading of arms for hostages. Even after the Tower report was published—detailing the arrangements and meetings between U.S. government officials and Iranian officials—Reagan still denied that there was ever any quid-pro-quo arrangement involving arms for hostages. While most Americans were convinced that we did trade arms for hostages, Reagan could nevertheless tell the American people that *he* never thought it was an arms-for-hostages deal. In many respects, his genial personality and his detached, hands-off style of running his presidency helped him through this ordeal. "Those first months after the Iran-Contra affair hit the front pages were frustrating for me," Reagan writes. "For the first time in my life, people didn't believe me. I had told the truth, but they still didn't believe me."[140] White House Chief of Staff Donald Regan notes that Reagan "was baffled by his loss of credibility. He flushed and pursed his lips when he talked about it, a sure sign of dismay. He thought that he was telling the truth in his television address. Why didn't the people believe him?"[141]

But disbelieving Reagan and blaming him for the problems of Iran-Contra were two different matters. The American people did not become overly upset with the president, even when he waffled in his speeches and maintained that there was no trading of arms for hostages. The people liked Reagan, and although his approval ratings as president would decline during the episode, there was no movement to have him removed from office. "I don't know anyone else who could have survived the Iran-Contra scandal," said Sam Donaldson. "I think a normal person would have impeachment proceedings begun against him. Reagan had a low point for about two or three months. He went into a blue funk. [But] he came out of it. And left [office], as you saw, still bouncy with his popularity ratings back up. I just thought that was amazing."[142]

Reagan would indeed leave office under much better circumstances than his predecessor. Unlike inauguration day 1981, there would be no waiting for a planeload of hostages to come home after a year and a half of humiliation to the nation and to the president. In fact, many of Reagan's hostages would not come home at all during his tenure. Terry Anderson was held captive for almost the entire period of Reagan's second term, having been abducted in 1985. He and others would remain prisoners in Lebanon as a new president took power.

The American public's mood with the issue of hostages, though, was beginning to change. They still cared about the fate of Americans abroad, but they were beginning to realize the difficulties involved in battling terrorism in general and rescuing hostages in particular. They were also exhausted by the emotional roller coaster that characterizes hostage episodes. Events had finally overtaken rhetoric, which had been the major shortcoming of the Reagan team's approach to international terrorism. The one positive aspect of the arms-for-hostages episode was that it demonstrated painfully to the American people, Congress, and the president himself that an obsession with the issue of hostages could be harmful to the nation's welfare. Since hostages could be taken at any time and at any place, it was an important lesson to learn.

Reagan could look back on his two terms in office and point to some noticeable gains in the fight against terrorism. He became the first president since Jefferson to use military force against a foreign power that engaged in terrorist attacks against Americans. Reagan also pressed U.S. allies and others to cooperate more earnestly in counterterrorist efforts. Several economic summits of the industrialized democracies were held and devoted to the issue of international terrorism. Physical security was enhanced at U.S. installations worldwide and legal measures, both national and international, were pursued to bring terrorists to justice.

The United States even succeeded in finally capturing and bringing to trial in the United States an "international terrorist." True, Fawaz Younis was not among the top ten, or even the top one hundred, of the who's who in terrorism. It took an elaborate sting operation (with the FBI luring him to a boat off the coast of Cyprus under the pretense of a drug deal) to catch the Lebanese terrorist. Younis's crime was that, along with several accomplices, he hijacked a Royal Jordanian airliner in 1985. The terrorists then blew up the plane on the ground in Beirut after releasing the passengers. The objective of the hijacking was not to seize Americans, but rather to bring about the withdrawal of Palestinian militias from Lebanon. But because there were two Americans on board the plane, Younis was liable for punishment in the United States under a 1984 terrorism law that made it a federal crime to commit a hijacking if Americans were victims. Compared with the magnitude of the Marine barracks bombing in Lebanon, the anti-U.S. nature of Younis's act was minimal. But since we could not capture and bring to trial the Abu Nidals and Abu Abbases of the world, the United States had to settle for Younis. He was eventually convicted and sentenced to thirty years in prison.

By the end of 1988, the world of terrorism seemed relatively quiet. There were still terrorist incidents: a car bombing in one country, an assassination in another. But most of the attacks did not involve U.S. targets.[143] The lull in major anti-U.S. terrorist attacks led one writer to entitle an article on terrorism, "Terrorism in Decline?"[144] But in the dynamic world of international terrorism, "progress" is always relative. While Western nations could point to an impressive number of incidents that were prevented by good intelligence and dedicated police work, and could cite a greater number of terrorists being apprehended and some groups even eliminated, the terrorists had the final word. Their most powerful weapon remained their ability to reverse all perceptions of counterterrorist progress with one well-placed bomb. The Irish Republican Army best summed up the dilemma that governments face in trying to reduce the terrorist threat when, following a failed attempt to assassinate Prime Minister Margaret Thatcher at the Conservative party convention in Britain in 1984, they issued the following statement: "Today we were unlucky, but remember, we only have to be lucky once. You will have to be lucky always."

Governments cannot always be lucky, and this was painfully demonstrated on December 21, 1988. The midair bombing of Pan Am Flight 103 over Lockerbie, Scotland, shattered any illusions people had that terrorism was on the decline. Although it took place while Reagan was still president, it would fall to his successor to determine what, if anything, the United States could do to retaliate for the killing of Americans. George Bush would also be faced with his own hostage crises as terrorism continued. And there would be a "new" terrorist nemesis who would take center stage. Just as Carter had his Khomeini to deal with and Reagan had his Qaddafi, Bush would be linked in history in a duel with one of the most brutal of them all, Saddam Hussein.

6

The Mother of All Hostage Takers

It is the beauty of American politics that a candidate for a party's presidential nomination could denounce a rival's economic plans as "voodoo economics" and then become that man's running mate on the national ticket. For George Bush, accepting the second slot behind Ronald Reagan in 1980 was not what he hoped for when he set out on his quest years earlier. He wasn't even Reagan's first choice for the number two slot; a deal with former President Gerald Ford fell through at the last minute. All things considered, though, it wasn't that bad. Bush, who had not held any official position since his brief tenure as CIA director in 1976, needed some vehicle to stay in the national limelight until he could make another run at the presidency.

The vice presidency is one of the most unusual jobs in the U.S. government. It is both a "heartbeat away from the presidency" and, at the same time, eons away from the power and prestige of that office. Vice presidents attend funerals of other heads of states, perform ceremonial duties, make speeches, and are at the beck and call of the president. If a president wants his vice president to remain in obscurity, then that will be his fate.

Yet there was a reward at the end for those who endured the doldrums of the office and the endless jokes. Most of the recent vice presidents eventually got their chance at the big prize. Richard Nixon would win it outright; Lyndon Johnson and Gerald Ford would inherit it unexpectedly (with LBJ eventually succeeding and Ford failing when they went before the electorate); Hubert Humphrey and Walter Mondale would also get their chance at being elected president, but each would lose. Only Spiro Agnew and Nelson Rockefeller—the former having to resign from office in disgrace for tax evasion, bribery, and extortion and the latter well past his prime as a politician—would break the chain of vice presidents running for the top post.

George Bush therefore had good reason to expect that by putting in his time and being the loyal servant to the president he would ultimately be rewarded. It was tricky business at first for this arch-critic of Reagan during the campaign. Conservatives didn't trust him, but he gradually won their support by enthusiastically endorsing the president's programs. And Reagan gave Bush several high-profile responsibilities. He named him the chairman of a special crisis management group within the National Security Council, authorized him to lead task forces on the problems of drugs and terrorism, and generally allowed the vice president to be an active participant in the administration. "I didn't want George," Reagan writes, "in the words of Nelson Rockefeller, simply to be 'standby equipment.' "[1]

When it came to the issue of terrorism, Bush definitely did not stand by. No vice president was more prepared to deal with the problems of international terrorism. His one year at the helm of the CIA introduced him to the operational and analytical world of counterterrorism. But it was in his role as head of the Vice President's Task Force on Combatting Terrorism that Bush gained prominence on an issue that was being given the highest priority by the Reagan administration. The report that the task force issued also offered insight into how the future president would view the problems of international terrorism.

Shortly after the 1985 TWA hijacking episode in Beirut, Bush formed a committee to examine U.S. policy on terrorism. He named Admiral James Holloway—the same man who headed the investigation into the failure to rescue the American hostages in Iran in 1980—to be its executive director. Bush utilized the expertise of officials from the CIA, FBI, State and Defense departments, and also held meetings with airline executives, media officials, members of Congress, and former diplomats and Cabinet officials. As Bush put it, he wanted to ensure "that the U.S. was using every means at its disposal to combat this modern scourge."[2]

The report of the task force was released with great fanfare in February 1986, a time when the public's concern with terrorism was at its peak. The United States had just endured one of its worst terrorist years ever with the TWA and *Achille Lauro* hijackings and the airport massacres in Rome and Vienna. Not surprisingly, the report delivered the tough message on terrorism that everyone expected. Bush wrote in the introduction that "the U.S. policy and program to combat terrorism is tough and resolute. We firmly oppose terrorism in all forms and wherever it takes place. We are prepared to act in concert with other nations or alone to prevent or respond to terrorist acts. We will make no concessions to terrorists. At the same time, we will use every available resource to gain the safe return of American citizens who are held hostage."[3]

What the American people did not know at the time was that one of those resources was arms for Iran. The Tower Commission noted that Bush was present during a January 17, 1986, briefing by National Security Adviser John Poindexter on developments in the arms-for-hostages deal. This was a month before the task force report was released to the public. Bush was also briefed on Israel's role in transferring arms to Iran in exchange for the release of American hostages when he met with Amiram Nir, a counterterrorist adviser to Prime Minister Shimon Peres, in Jerusalem in July 1986.[4] Furthermore, Bush was present at a top-level meeting on August 6, 1985, with Reagan, Secretary of State Shultz, Secretary of Defense Weinberger, National Security Adviser Bud McFarlane, and White House Chief of Staff Donald Regan when the issue of arms for hostages was first being discussed. "As a result of the voluminous material [on Iran-Contra] now available, we know that Bush could not have failed to know a great deal about the problems and pitfalls [of Iran-Contra], because he was usually present, as Poindexter testified at the latter's morning briefings of President Reagan," writes historian Theodore Draper. "In the end, there was little difference between Bush's support of 'arms for hostages' and Reagan's."[5] But as long as all this was still secret, a tough policy stance against terrorism could be announced without exposing the hypocrisy and contradictions contained in the report.

The task force praised the efforts of the U.S. government in its fight against terrorism. They pointed out how "more than 150 specific activities to combat terrorism are carried out by various federal departments and agencies. . . . The total number of people—calculated in terms of man-years—assigned to these various programs in 1985 was approximately 18,000." They also noted that $2 billion was spent on fighting terrorism during that tumultuous year.[6] Many topics were covered, including brief sections—less than two pages each—on the role of Congress in opposing terrorism, the interrelationship between the media and terrorists, and public attitudes toward terrorism. The task force urged Congress to enact further legislation aimed at punishing terrorists, including the death penalty if someone was killed during a hostage situation; they called for cooperation between the media and the government during a terrorist incident and for the media to serve as its own watchdog in avoiding coverage that could be advantageous to terrorists; and they appealed to government officials to do a better job in informing and communicating with the media and the public as to U.S. policy on terrorism.[7]

The report also stated that "international cooperation offers the best hope for long-term success" in dealing with terrorism and recommended that "a full-time NSC position with support staff" be created in order to "strengthen coordination of our national [counterterrorism] program." That position would be responsible for "participating in all interagency groups; maintaining the national programming document; assisting in coordinating research and development; facilitating development of response options; overseeing implementation of the Task Force recommendations."[8] Yet at the very same time that the task force was urging a more prominent role in counterterrorism for the NSC, that agency, under the direction of Poindexter and Lt. Col. Oliver North, was operating by their own rules without regard for the law. Profits from the arms-for-hostages deal with Iran were secretly diverted to supply the Contra rebels in Nicaragua in violation of a congressional ban on such aid. In fact, during the same month that the terrorism task force report was released, North was given several encrypting devices from the NSC in order to create a private communications network to aid his secret dealings with the Contras. These devices were used, according to the Tower Commission, "to communicate, outside of the purview of other government agencies, with members of the private Contras support effort."[9] And the Tower Commission issued a scathing rebuke of the NSC for "mistakes of omission, commission, judgment, and perspective."[10] This was hardly a ringing endorsement for the agency that the Bush commission wanted at the center of formulating and implementing U.S. counterterrorism policy.

The major shortcoming of the task force, though, lay in its emphasis on the need for a clear and consistent "policy" to fight terrorism. "Terrorism deeply troubles the American people," the commission wrote. "They feel angry, victimized, vulnerable and helpless. At the same time, they clearly want the United States Government to have a strong and consistent national antiterrorist policy. While such a policy exists, the Task Force believes that better communication is necessary to educate the public to our policy. . . . "[11] However, the assumption that there is such a thing as a "national policy" for terrorism, or that a government can always be "consistent" in responding to terrorism, was not a realistic notion. What may work against one type of terrorist threat, group, or state-sponsor will not necessarily work against another one. Furthermore, as situations change around the world, it becomes increasingly difficult to remain consistent in counterterrorist policy.

The task force acknowledged at one point in its report that being consistent in the struggle against terrorism is difficult, but still proceeded to set forth "criteria" for U.S. responses, particularly those regarding military force:

> . . . The Interdepartmental Group on Terrorism should prepare, and submit to the NSC for approval, policy criteria for deciding when, if and how to use force to preempt, react and retaliate. This framework will offer decisionmaking bodies a workable set of standards by which to judge each terrorist threat or incident. The use of this framework also would reassure the American people that government response is formulated consistently. Criteria for developing response options might include the following: Potential for injury to innocent victims; Adequacy and reliability of intelligence; Status of forces for preemption, reaction or retaliation; Ability to identify the target; Host country and international cooperation or opposition; Risk and probability of success analysis; U.S. public attitude and media reaction; Conformance with national policy and objectives.[12]

The task force also reinforced the theme prevalent in the mid-1980s that terrorism, in any form and context, was a threat to our vital interests. "The U.S. Government considers the practice of terrorism by any person or group a potential threat to its national security and will resist the use of terrorism by all legal means available."[13] Yet this view only served to greatly exaggerate the capabilities of terrorists who may only be able to hijack a commercial airliner or set off a pipe bomb in the countryside.

Following the public revelations of the arms-for-hostages deal, the task force issued a follow-up report in May/June 1987—with much less fanfare that their original report—that tried to control the damage done to U.S. counterterrorist policy by the Iran-Contra scandal. Bush wrote in the cover letter that although there were "mistakes" made in dealing with Iran that caused a "temporary reduction in credibility" of U.S. counterterrorist programs, progress in combating terrorism had nevertheless been "excellent." Bush pointed to renewed international cooperation and noted that there was a decline in the number of Americans killed by terrorists overseas in 1986 (twelve) as compared with 1985 (thirty-eight), as though that were a meaningful measure of "progress" against terrorists. In an effort to finally put to rest any notion that the United States would again deal with terrorists, Bush proclaimed in 1988, "I won't bargain with terrorists, and I won't bargain with drug dealers either, whether they're on U.S. or foreign soil."[14]

The revelations of the arms-for-hostages deal led to a rethinking about the whole issue of hostages. "One of the consequences of the disaster of the Iran hostage situation," said L. Paul Bremer, the ambassador-at-large for counterterrorism from 1986 to 1989, "was that we really had to look very much more closely at how we were dealing with the issue of hostages. We basically concluded that we had to get it off the front burner. We were playing into the hands of the hostage holders. . . . "[15]

The Vice President's Task Force on Combatting Terrorism was thus a reflection of its time. It came at the height of the American public's and government's concern about the threat of international terrorism. And it automatically propelled George Bush into an important role in the Reagan administration's efforts to meet this threat. It also landed him in hot water with critics of administration policy, including some of the families of the American hostages in Lebanon. During the 1985 TWA hijacking in Beirut, Bush stated that the United States would not rule out retaliation against the hijackers once the hostages were released. This so infuriated Peggy Say (the sister of hostage Terry Anderson, who had been abducted prior to the TWA hijacking and who she feared might be killed if the United States retaliated) that she implied that Bush himself was a "terrorist." "We bandy about the word 'terrorist,' " Say said in a televised interview, "and the true meaning is 'One who inspires terror in the hearts of others.' Well, George Bush certainly did just that to seven families when he refused to rule out retaliation."[16]

But it would not be until he was elected president in 1988 that Bush would be tested with his first terrorist crisis. And this would occur just a month before he officially took office. While the president-elect was busy with his transition team during the Christmas holidays and while Reagan was winding down his affairs, terrorists struck dramatically in the skies over Scotland, sending reverberations around the world.

Pan Am 103

Terrorists have the unfortunate ability to make certain airlines and particular flight numbers a permanent part of history. Air India Flight 182 will forever be known as the plane that Sikh terrorists are suspected to have blown up over the Atlantic, killing all 329 people on board. TWA Flight 847 will always be equated with a long, drawn-out hijacking in Beirut that was televised around the world. And Pan Am Flight 103 will be indelibly linked with a midair bombing over Lockerbie, Scotland, in which 270 people perished, including all 259 people on board and eleven others on the ground. Pan Am 103 will also be remembered as prompting one of the most exhaustive, yet never fully resolved, investigations in aviation history.

The first news reports that a Pan Am Boeing 747 had crashed en route to New York from London after mysteriously disappearing from radar screens led many people to assume that this could be the work of terrorists. Although there had not been a major terrorist incident involving

Americans for some time, the public was nevertheless conditioned to fear the worst when it came to airplane crashes. The FBI, the Federal Aviation Administration, and Scotland Yard sent their top explosives experts to Lockerbie as soon as word of the crash was confirmed. The extent of the wreckage indicated that the plane had disintegrated in midair, as there were debris and bodies scattered throughout the countryside. The search teams, which were comprised of police, military personnel, and volunteers, had to cover 845 square miles. But neither the U.S. nor British governments would make any official statements about a possible terrorist connection until it could be proven that a bomb had indeed brought the jetliner down. Some aviation experts argued that the destruction of the plane might have been caused by mechanical or structural flaws.[17]

In Washington, Randy Beers, the director of counterterrorism on the National Security Council (the position previously held by Oliver North), was hoping desperately that this was not an act of terrorism. "My first reaction on the day that it occurred was it can't be a bomb. It's gotta be [bad] weather," recalled Beers. During the late fall of 1988, the United States was involved once again in trying to free the hostages from Beirut, and a major international terrorist act could greatly complicate matters. "At that particular point in time we were pursuing one of our various little will o' the wisps in terms of trying to see if we couldn't get some hostages released," said Beers, "and didn't want to have another confrontation in terms of this process. There was some suggestion that the Palestinians might intervene on our behalf to get the hostages released. And the last thing that we needed was terrorism front and center as a disrupter to what we all believed was necessary, which was calm, quiet, no attention to the problem. I mean you know this doesn't last very long. This lasts until you start getting those clear indications that the initial signs were correct, there was nothing on the air, there was no indication that there had been anything that could have caused the crash other than explosives."[18]

Two people who immediately believed it was a bombing were Rosemary Wolfe and her husband, Jim, the stepmother and father of twenty-year-old Miriam Wolfe. Miriam, a student at Syracuse University, was returning home on the doomed aircraft, along with thirty-four other students from the university's overseas study program. Rosemary and Jim watched in horror as newscasts reported the crash and showed film of the wreckage. Jim Wolfe was familiar with aviation as a hobby and knew this could not be any ordinary crash. "He said that was a bomb," recalled Rosemary Wolfe. "He said that the way it was described [on newscasts], the way it broke apart, and the initial explosion" indicated it was a bomb. When a television crew came by the next morning to interview the

Wolfes, he pulled no punches. "He went on television and said this was murder," Rosemary Wolfe said. She called for a congressional investigation. "We knew something had to be wrong."[19]

The task of determining whether a bomb exploded on board the jetliner, named the *Maid of the Seas,* was left to John Boyd, the chief constable for the district in which Lockerbie was located. Assisting him was his chief investigating officer, John Orr. Boyd's team had every piece of luggage and debris examined by an x-ray machine in order to check for explosives or explosives residue.[20] The science of analyzing airplane wreckage for proof of explosives had progressed significantly since the days of J. William Magee, the pioneering FBI scientist who had discovered that a dynamite bomb was the cause of the midair explosion of a plane near Denver in 1955. There had been enough acts of sabotage involving airplanes since the 1955 bombing—eighty-six planes were blown up completely or in part between 1955 and December 1988—to create a mini-industry of expertise for these types of aviation disasters.[21]

A baggage container retrieved from the airplane wreckage caught the attention of Boyd and the explosives experts. The metal from the container was shattered in a way that suggested the impact of a bomb. Utilizing a variety of chemical and metallurgical forensic techniques, experts at the British government's top crime laboratory at Fort Halstead, Kent, discovered traces of explosive residue on the container. The Air Accidents Investigation Branch of the British Department of Transport released a statement on December 18, asserting that there was now "conclusive evidence of a detonating high explosive. The explosive's residues recovered from the debris have been positively identified and are consistent with the use of a high-performance plastic explosive."[22]

There would be additional scientific findings in the weeks and months ahead. The investigators were eventually able to pinpoint exactly where the bomb was placed on the aircraft: in forward baggage carrier 14 L, on the left side of the plane and in front of the wing. They were also able to determine in which suitcase the bomb was situated—a Samsonite suitcase not matched to any of the passengers on board—and even where in the suitcase the bomb was hidden (in the battery pack and wiring of a radio-cassette player). They pinpointed exactly what type of explosives brought the plane down—a Czechoslovakian-made Semtex plastic explosive that can be molded into any shape. It was the most remarkable reconstruction ever conducted of an airplane after it was completely demolished in midair.

The impressive findings generated by the scientific part of the Pan Am 103 investigation were not matched by the official investigation into who was responsible for the bombing. There were no laws of politics like the laws of science and technology that could reconstruct without a shadow of doubt the planners and perpetrators of the terrorist act.

The terrorists who perpetrated the Pan Am 103 bombing, though, left plenty of traces. The prime suspect for several years following the bombing was the Popular Front for the Liberation of Palestine–General Command. A few months prior to the bombing, West German police raided residences in Frankfurt and other cities where members of the PFLP-GC were meeting. The PFLP-GC, headed by Ahmed Jabril, a former captain in the Syrian army, split from the PFLP in 1968, claiming that Palestinian groups needed to focus more on fighting than on politics. Several members of Jabril's group were arrested in the West German raid. The police also seized a Toshiba radio-cassette player that was rigged with plastic explosives, similar to the one that brought down Pan Am 103.[23]

The Pan Am bombing was among the most carefully planned in terrorism history. The radio-cassette bomb was placed on two flights prior to being put on Pan Am 103. Investigators working in many countries eventually concluded that the suitcase carrying the bomb was first placed aboard an Air Malta flight in Malta as unaccompanied baggage,[24] and then transferred first to Pan Am's connecting flight from Frankfurt to London and then to the Boeing 747 jet at Heathrow airport in London. There was no checking of interline baggage by Pan Am at either Frankfurt or Heathrow to determine if each piece was matched to a boarding passenger.

If things had worked out according to the terrorists' plans, Pan Am 103 would have exploded while it was over the Atlantic. However, a twenty-five minute delay at Heathrow foiled the terrorists' plot to leave no traces of their crime. The timer on the detonating switch expired before the plane reached the Atlantic. "If this tragedy had occurred some 10 or 15 minutes later," said Peter Frader, the Lord Advocate for Scotland, "what remained of the aircraft would have been somewhere over the Atlantic Ocean, and we would have secured virtually nothing."[25] This same twist of fate fouled up the plans of two of the earliest midair bombers in aviation history. Both Albert Guay and John Graham failed to anticipate delays in the departure of the planes they blew up, leaving evidence of their crimes.

On the day after British authorities announced that a bomb had destroyed Pan Am 103, there was a predictable response from President Reagan. "Now that we know definitely it was a bomb," the president said, "we're going to make every effort we can to find out who was guilty of this savage and tragic thing." Reagan added that whoever was responsible for the bombing "would be charged with 270 murders."[26] Two days later, on December 31, during his weekly radio address, the vintage Reagan rhetoric on terrorism came shining through for the last time while he was president. Reagan hinted at military retaliation by pointing out that Bush's task force report on terrorism, which had recommended military response as one option to consider in countering terror-' ism, "ought to be giving some people sleepless nights." Reagan further stated, "If, as seems likely, our terrorists have crawled out of their hole to threaten American lives, we can promise them this: The pledge we make to seek out the truth and punish the guilty is a sacred one, which George Bush shares."[27]

But Bush did not completely share Reagan's enthusiasm for raising the expectation level of the public on the issue of terrorism. The president-elect knew a trap when he saw one, and purposely avoided making any promises about what the United States would do in response to the Pan Am bombing. Although Bush revealed a touch of the Reagan rhetoric in answer to reporters' questions, he nevertheless added a strong dose of reality. He promised that the United States would "seek hard and punish firmly, decisively, those who did this *if you could ever find them*."[28] But the president-elect also could not resist the temptation to point out to the press that he was a key player in U.S. counterterrorist policy under Reagan, and that he would continue the battles as president. "We have a fine antiterrorist policy," Bush told reporters on December 29. "I take great pride in having coordinated and to some degree written the antiterrorist report and I think it's setting high standards around the world."[29]

In at least one corner of the world, there was concern that the United States might overreact to the Pan Am bombing and launch military retaliatory strikes once the perpetrators were known. The warning against such action came from a most surprising source, British Prime Minister Margaret Thatcher. The "Iron Lady," whose credentials for a tough policy against terrorists were beyond reproach, and who had been the United States' most loyal and vocal supporter on counterterrorist policy, said on January 1, 1989, "I do not think an eye for an eye or a tooth for a tooth is ever valid. I can understand the anger. We feel the anger very deeply. The most important thing to do is to try to get the cooperation of all nations to track down these people so that they are brought to justice."[30]

Thatcher, though, did not have to worry about any rash American response. Reagan, the ideological president, might have been tempted to at least say something about possible military action, but even he had come to recognize somewhat late in his presidency the pitfalls of promising and then following through with tough responses to terrorism. Bush was even more pragmatic than his predecessor, and more hesitant to pull the trigger when it came to terrorism.

There was also the problem of who exactly the United States would attack for the bombing of Pan Am 103. If indeed the perpetrators were the PFLP-GC, retaliation would be complicated. In addition to the ease with which terrorists can move from one safe-house to another, there is also the risk of death to innocent civilians in a counterterrorist operation. In terms of trying to apprehend the terrorists, there was no guarantee that the host government would agree to extradite them to the United States. The most concrete target then becomes the states that sponsor the terrorist activity. In the case of the PFLP-GC, there were plenty to go around.

First there was Syria, which supported, both militarily and financially, Jabril and his terrorists. The PFLP-GC leader had operated freely in Damascus and planned and commanded many of his terrorist attacks from Syrian soil. Striking back at Syria, though, was never really an option for the United States. The risks to U.S. interests in the Middle East, including the effects it would have on U.S. efforts to attain a peace accord between the Arab states and Israel and the possibility that it could initiate a Middle East war, all precluded any military action against Syria. Syrian President Hafez al-Assad had also proven very adept at turning the tables on U.S. counterterrorist policy, particularly the self-imposed criteria of "irrefutable evidence." Assad continually replied to charges that he was harboring terrorists by claiming that there was no hard evidence linking the PFLP-GC to the Pan Am bombing.

U.S. military responses against Iran, another suspected key player in the Pan Am bombing, were also precluded due to the potentially explosive repercussions on U.S. interests in the Middle East. According to one theory, Jabril reportedly went to Tehran in the summer of 1988 and negotiated an agreement with Iran's interior minister, Ali Akbar Mohtashami, to blow up an American airliner in exchange for $10 million.[31] Iran's motive was revenge for the shooting down of an Iranian civilian airliner by the U.S.S. *Vincennes* in the Persian Gulf on July 3. The *Vincennes* fired two missiles at the plane, mistaking it for a fighter jet. All 290 people on board were killed.

A third state suspected at that time of involvement in the destruction of Pan Am 103 was Libya. Qaddafi's regime had either provided the PFLP-GC with detonator switches and plastic explosives for the radio-cassette player bomb, or had used their own agents to blow up the plane. This would be in revenge for the 1986 raid on Libya. Yet for all the promises that were made by both Reagan and Bush concerning bringing to justice those responsible for the Pan Am bombing, nothing would be done against the states involved in the terrorist act. "You got three countries involved in it," said Pierre Salinger, former ABC News chief foreign correspondent, who launched a major independent investigation into the Pan Am bombing. "Libya, who provided the Semtex; Syria, which controlled the Jabril movement; and Iran, which paid for it. Now, with the hostages, they don't want to bother Syria or Iran, [and] they have already bombed Libya."[32]

The hostages in Lebanon continued to play a significant role in U.S. policy in the Middle East. There were no arms-for-hostages deals under Bush, nor were there the seemingly endless public reminders about their fate as had been the practice of the Reagan administration. There was, though, a desire by Bush to avoid any retaliatory measures against Iran, Syria, or Libya for fear of potential harm to the unfortunate captives.

Although there would be no retribution for the Lockerbie killings, there would be the typical blue-ribbon panel formed to investigate the bombing. Surprisingly, the panel reached some hard-hitting conclusions that the Bush administration did not expect.

The President's Commission on Aviation Security and Terrorism was created by Executive Order 12686 on August 4, 1989. The families of the victims of Pan Am 103 had lobbied for an independent investigation into the incident. The executive order called for "a comprehensive study and appraisal of practices and policy options with respect to preventing terrorist acts involving aviation." The major focus of the investigation, the commission noted in its report, "was not to determine who planted the bomb on Flight 103 but to ascertain how the device could have made its way onto the plane." The seven-member commission, which was appointed by Bush, included two senators, two congressmen, a former secretary of the Navy, a retired general, and a former secretary of labor, Anne McLaughlin, who served as the chairperson. The commission began its work in November 1989 and held several public hearings with representatives from the FAA, Pan Am, and other airlines. They also met with aviation security experts, administration officials, and families of the victims of the bombing. There were more than 250 interviews conducted, including many with government officials abroad. The final report was released to the public on May 15, 1990.[33]

The commission fulfilled its official task by providing a thorough examination of airline and airport security practices. It was an impressive report that detailed the flaws in the antiterrorist measures utilized by the aviation industry. The commission came down particularly hard on both Pan Am and the FAA: "The Commission found the Federal Aviation Administration to be a reactive agency—preoccupied with responses to events to the exclusion of adequate contingency planning in anticipation of future threats." They also stated that "Pan Am's apparent security lapses and FAA's failure to enforce its own regulations followed a pattern that existed for months prior to Flight 103, during the day of the tragedy, and—notably—for nine months thereafter."[34]

Among these lapses was a failure by Pan Am to follow FAA regulations concerning the matching of all interline baggage with passengers boarding the flight. The commission found that there was extremely poor training of security personnel at Frankfurt by Pan Am. They also found fault with the FAA and Pan Am concerning the lack of follow-up action after information was received that West German police had found a radio-cassette bomb in the possession of members of the PFLP-GC.

The commission also criticized the FAA and Pan Am for not releasing to the public information concerning an explicit threat to blow up Pan Am planes over the Christmas holidays. A few weeks before the Pan Am bombing, a man telephoned the U.S. embassy in Helsinki, warning that a Pan Am plane from Frankfurt to the United States would be blown up during the holidays. However, investigators determined that this was a hoax; the man making the call had made numerous other terrorist threats throughout the year. Nevertheless, even though the threat was probably an eerie coincidence, the information should have been made available to potential travelers on Pan Am. The posting of this information on a bulletin board in the U.S. embassy in Moscow led some State Department employees to change their holiday travel plans.

Pan Am anticipated the criticisms contained in the presidential commission report. The company took out a full-page advertisement in the *New York Times* the day after the report was released to the public. The advertisement, titled "Airline Security: It Is Now Time To Deal With The Issue From A Realistic Perspective," claimed that commercial airlines simply do not have the manpower, resources, or technological capabilities to provide perfect security against terrorism. What is needed, Pan Am claimed, is a more active role by the United States government and other governments in helping airlines thwart the terrorist threat to aviation. *"Is it appropriate,"* the ad asks, "that U.S. commercial airline companies, acting on their own and relying on their own means, be required to provide extraordinary, quasi-military security in face of ever-increasing terrorist determination and resources? *Should* airlines, who are victims, not targets of terrorist attacks, be held responsible for developing and maintaining such extraordinary security measures and equipment? *Should not* the one-half of U.S. citizens traveling on foreign flag airlines *know* that foreign airlines are not required to provide, and do not provide, the same level of security as U.S. flag carriers? *Should not* the governments of this world be working more aggressively in concert toward a global solution?"[35]

Pan Am—which saw its first quarter losses for 1989 soar to $151.1 million, nearly double those of a year before[36]—was not alone in appealing for tougher counterterrorist measures from governments of the world. The biggest bombshell in the report was its scathing attack on

U.S. counterterrorist policy in general, and the reluctance by the United States to utilize military measures in particular. "A swift response could be directed against the terrorist group responsible and/or its state sponsor. In this context, the Commission recommends planning, training and equipping for direct preemptive or retaliatory military actions against known terrorist hideouts in countries that sanction them. Where such direct strikes are unwise or inappropriate, the Commission recommends use of middle-level options, including covert operations to preempt, disrupt, or respond to terrorist actions. The Commission recognizes the many reasons, historical and otherwise, why the United States Government must proceed with caution in the use of covert operations. Certainly such tactics must not be used to circumvent basic democratic values. Terrorists, however, have relied upon the adherence by others to these values to permit them to attack thousands of innocent victims with impunity." The commission further stated that "state sponsors should be made to pay a price for their actions."[37]

To ensure that their message about getting tough with terrorists would not be buried deep in their 182-page report, they repeated it on the very first page of their executive summary. The first paragraph left no doubts about where they stood:

> . . . The President's Commission on Aviation Security and Terrorism recommends a more vigorous U.S. policy that not only pursues and punishes terrorists but also makes state sponsors of terrorism pay a price for their actions.
>
> . . . Rhetoric is no substitute for strong, effective action.[38]

This rebuke of administration policy was the very last thing that George Bush expected when he created the commission. Like most people, the president figured that the panel would focus solely on the issue of aviation security and not delve into the broader policy issues of combating terrorism.

The irony of the commission's criticisms of the Bush administration's counterterrorism policy could not have been lost upon the president. Here was Bush, who was so proud of the task force report on terrorism he wrote as vice-president, now having to weather criticism by a new task force on how *he* was handling the terrorist problem. Bush did not respond to the commission's report, but White House Press Secretary Marlin Fitzwater stated, "We certainly agree that we need to be aggressive as necessary to fight terrorism."[39] Nothing more was heard from the blue-ribbon panel that, as stipulated in the executive order that created it, disbanded within thirty days after submitting their report to the president.

The families of those killed on board Pan Am 103, however, did not disappear. They banded together to form a group called Victims of Pan Am Flight 103. Their aim was to ensure that all unanswered questions about the bombing would be addressed and that the criminal investigation would continue. It was also formed to give the families a source for mutual comfort. They issued newsletters and created political action committees and a press office. A similar organization was established in London for the families of the British victims.[40]

Sometimes, it took very little to reach a sympathetic ear. Tom Brokaw, the NBC News anchorman, delivered a commencement address at Boston College. The father of one of the victims of the Pan Am bombing was in the audience. He had lost his daughter, who was returning to the United States after a year abroad. Her twin sister was not on the plane. The father wrote a poignant letter to Brokaw describing his anguish. "It really just crushed him," said Brokaw. "The utter rage and frustration of this man, and the total innocence of his daughter who had no stake in this thing. It would be easier for him if there had been a malfunction on the plane. But to have his daughter killed in a deliberate act for which there probably should have been some forewarning. My heart goes out to him." And in an indication of how the plight of victims of terrorism can affect one's overall views on the terrorist threat, Brokaw said, "I think about him when I think about pushing [the issue of] terrorism on the back burner."[41]

The worldwide criminal investigation into the Pan Am bombing continued for several more years. In mid-1990, investigators believed they had finally found their smoking gun. An investigator going through some of the debris from the crash discovered a tiny piece of plastic lodged in a shirt that was in the same suitcase where the bomb had been placed. Further analysis showed that fragment to be from the circuitry of a digital electric timer that was different from the ones used by the PFLP-GC.[42] Investigators then discovered that a similar timer had been confiscated by the government of Senegal from Libyan agents and that another one had been sold by Libya to the government of Togo—all before the Pan Am bombing. Investigators then traced the timers to a Swiss company that sold twenty similar ones to Libya in the mid-1980s.[43]

In November 1991, the United States and Britain indicted two Libyan intelligence agents for the Pan Am bombing. U.S. officials also stated at the time that there was no evidence pointing to Syrian or Iranian involvement. President Bush accentuated that point by claiming that Syria had gotten "a bum rap" on Pan Am 103. That the indictment and the statements came at a time when the United States was convening a Mideast peace conference with Syrian participation and progress toward release of all remaining American hostages in Lebanon was proceeding, made many people suspicious of the administration's motives in absolving two well-known state-sponsors of terrorism such as Syria and Iran. *New York Times* columnist A. M. Rosenthal wrote shortly after the indictments that Bush had been irresponsible in stating that Syria got a bum rap. "The President committed a statement for which any civil servant would have been fired. He delivered a not-guilty verdict while the investigation of mass murder, and all its legal, moral and political connections and ramifications, was still going on. That's the rap."[44]

Former Ambassador Bremer also wrote in the *New York Times* that Syria and Iran could not be forgiven for their roles in Pan Am 103:

> . . . Libya's guilt does not necessarily prove Iran or Syria's innocence. Our Government has clear information that the Iranians contracted with the Popular Front for the Liberation of Palestine–General Command, headquartered in Damascus and headed by a former Syrian air force officer, to blow up U.S. airlines in retaliation for the accidental downing of an Iranian civilian plane by the U.S.S. Vincennes in July 1988. The Popular Front's extensive plans for attacks had to be known to the Syrians. The plans were preempted by the arrest of a large cell in Germany in October 1988. Iranian complicity in, and Syrian knowledge of the plan, cannot be overlooked.[45]

Despite the indictments, it seemed probable that Syria and Iran, along with Libya, played a part in the bombing of Pan Am 103.

As tragic as the Pan Am bombing was, it was already fading from the public agenda before Bush's first year in office was up in 1989. The half-life for public outrage over any particular terrorist event is not very long. Other issues compete for attention, and new terrorist incidents arise that push aside old ones. This is what occurred during the summer of 1989 as a chain of events set off by a daring Israeli kidnapping in Lebanon quickly propelled Bush into his first hostage crisis as president.

Higgins, Hizballah, and Hostages

Israel can always be counted on to do the unexpected. Their bold rescue operation at Entebbe in 1976 fascinated the world and is still marveled about in counterterrorist circles. Their surprise 1982 invasion of Lebanon is less warmly remembered, having led to further chaos in that already troubled country. While it succeeded in temporarily driving out the PLO, it also laid the roots for another extremist element that would plague the Israelis and the West for a long time.

Ever since the fall of the shah in 1979, the Ayatollah Khomeini had been waiting patiently for an opportunity to expand his Islamic revolution beyond the borders of Iran. He found it in the aftermath of the Israeli invasion of Lebanon. At almost the same time that Yasir Arafat and his guerrillas were being dispersed, Iranian Shiite fundamentalists moved into the Bekaa Valley. Khomeini sent more than one thousand Revolutionary Guards into the area to recruit among the poor and alienated Lebanese Shiites. The task was not too difficult, given the long-standing resentment that the Shiites harbored toward the Sunnis, who had dominated and discriminated against them for centuries. Appealing to both new-found Shiite pride in the Islamic revolution in Iran and new anger directed at both Israel and the United States for intervention in Lebanon, the ranks of the Shiite extremists swelled.[46]

Hizballah and other Islamic extremist factions quickly filled the vacuum left by the departure of the PLO. They perpetrated a wide variety of terrorist incidents, including the bombing of the Marine barracks and U.S. embassy in Beirut; the kidnapping of dozens of foreign citizens, including Marine Lieutenant Colonel William Higgins; and the killing of Israeli soldiers in southern Lebanon. And the Palestinian terrorist threat was not eliminated by the Israeli invasion of Lebanon. Syrian-backed Palestinian factions, such as the PFLP-GC, staged numerous attacks into Israel, including a daring motorized hang-glider assault by two terrorists in November 1987. One terrorist killed six Israeli soldiers before being killed himself by the soldiers, while the other terrorist died when his hang glider crashed. Both men became instant martyrs for many Palestinians.

For Israel, combating terrorism has always been a matter of national pride and national security. Surrounded by Arab states with whom they have gone to war several times and where state-sponsorship of terrorism has been rampant, it is not surprising that the Israelis' trademark is to hit back hard and fast whenever terrorists strike. Whereas other nations, including the United States, are much more cautious in the use of military force to retaliate against a terrorist incident—sometimes becoming engaged in long, drawn-out public debates on the issue—the Israelis suffer from no such doubts. Although their use of military force to fight terrorism can sometimes lead to an escalating cycle of violence, the Israelis nevertheless believe that it is better to send a "tough" message to terrorists and suffer the short-term consequences than to endure the long-term risks of terrorist attacks that go unanswered.

The Israelis also have had no qualms about using assassination as a counterterrorist tactic. Whereas in the United States there exists an executive order that bans such action, in Israel there is reported to be a "hit" list that is continually updated. "It has been the policy of every Israeli government since that headed by Golda Meir," write terrorist experts Neil Livingstone and David Halevy, "to give no quarter to those who plan and conduct terrorist operations against Israel. When the opportunity has presented itself, Israel has struck back with fury at its antagonists. Accordingly, the Israeli security services have maintained a list of those marked for death."[47]

One of these men was Khalil Ibrahim Machmud al-Wazir, also known as Abu Jihad. As the number-two man in the PLO, Abu Jihad had planned many operations against Israel and had "personally briefed, and often bade farewell to, every terrorist team sent against Israel or an Israeli target." Thus, in April 1988, a team of Israeli commandos slipped into Tunis where Abu Jihad lived, and together with intelligence agents from Mossad, killed the PLO official. It was a clear signal from Jerusalem that its policy of "an eye for an eye" would continue.[48]

The most intriguing aspect of Israel's counterterrorist policy, however, lies in that area that has proved most troublesome to governments throughout the world: that is, hostages. No matter how many raids they launched on Palestinian or Shiite terrorist camps in Lebanon or how many assassinations of terrorists they carried out over the years, Israel, like all other countries, was powerless to prevent its citizens or troops from being taken hostage. And despite its reputation for being "tough" on terrorists and never "dealing" with terrorists, Israel was never ashamed of the top priority it placed on every single Israeli life. Israel would do virtually anything, including making deals with terrorists, in order to get their people back. "We do not forsake the soldier in the battlefield," Prime Minister Yitzhak Shamir told a meeting of the United Jewish Appeal in 1989, "nor do we relent in our efforts to obtain the release of a soldier or civilian who may be abducted under any circumstances by enemies or terrorists."[49]

During the 1982 invasion of Lebanon, Ahmed Jabril's PFLP-GC captured three Israeli reservists and held them hostage for several years while Israel tried desperately to get them back. At one point the Israelis kidnapped a nephew of Jabril and offered to trade him for their people. Jabril refused, but in 1985 offered a deal to which the Israelis agreed. In the most lopsided prisoner/hostage exchange in history, Israel released more than 1,100 Palestinian and Shiite prisoners—including 400 who were serving life sentences for killing Israelis—in exchange for just the three Israeli hostages. Among the released prisoners were 300 PFLP-GC members, as well as Kozo Okamoto, the lone surviving member of the Japanese Red Army terrorist team that committed the Lod Airport massacre in 1972.[50]

The pool of hostages can always be replenished, though, and by the summer of 1989 three more Israelis were in the hands of terrorists in Lebanon. This time the captors were not the PFLP-GC, but rather Islamic Shiite extremists. The Israelis were not alone in seeing their people held captive by Hizballah and other factions; several other countries, including the United States, Great Britain, France, West Germany, Switzerland, and Ireland, all had some of their citizens held by the terrorists. By mid-1989, there were three Israelis and fourteen Western hostages in Lebanon.[51]

Israel at first tried to get their people back through secret deals. As one Israeli official later stated, "We had tried everything else. We had tried secret contacts, we had tried to negotiate, we had tried so-called peaceful methods to try to reach the Shiite Muslims who are holding a number of hostages. None of that worked."[52] So the Israelis resorted to what they do better than anyone else. They launched a surprise raid on the residence of a regional head of Hizballah, Sheik Abdel Karim Obeid. In the early morning hours of July 28, Israeli commandos landed on the outskirts of a village in southern Lebanon where the sheik lived. With Israeli jets flying overhead to mask the sound of the helicopters and make the residents believe it was an air raid and not a special commando operation, the Israelis seized Sheik Obeid and two associates at his home and flew them back to Israel.[53]

The reverberations of the kidnapping were felt in Washington. President Bush indirectly condemned it, stating, "I don't think kidnapping and violence helps the cause of peace."[54] The Israelis, though, were hoping that they could swap their new prisoners for not only the three Israelis in Hizballah's hands, but also for all of the foreign hostages in Lebanon. At a time when Israel was still under worldwide criticism for its handling of the Palestinian uprisings in the West Bank and Gaza Strip, gaining the release of all hostages in Lebanon might generate some positive publicity and perhaps some good will from other countries.

Rather than goodwill, though, the Israelis faced the prospects of a dead American hostage. Hizballah, which knew how to play the terrorist game better than most groups, struck back not at Israel, but at the United States with one of their most powerful weapons: an American hostage. They threatened to kill Higgins, the Marine lieutenant whom they had abducted in February 1988, unless Sheik Obeid was released. They set a deadline of a couple of days.

Nobody budged, and when the deadline passed, Hizballah produced a videotape that showed the limp body of Higgins hanging from a post. U.S. intelligence later became convinced that Higgins was executed much earlier, probably in the summer of 1988 following the shooting-down of the Iranian civilian airliner in the Persian Gulf by the U.S.S. *Vincennes*. Hizballah was waiting for an opportune time to "threaten" his life and then show the videotape, and decided that the time had come during the kidnapping of Sheik Obeid.

The reaction to the videotape was strong. Senator Robert Dole, the

Republican minority leader, severely criticized Israel on the Senate floor: ". . . I hope the Israelis would take another look at some of their actions, which they must know in advance will endanger American lives." Others in Congress rushed to Israel's defense, claiming it was unfair to place the burden for Higgins's death on such a close U.S. ally that had been facing a serious terrorist threat on its borders for decades. Bush, though, was still clearly upset with the Israelis and the initial reports that their kidnapping had led to Higgins's execution. "On Friday I said that the taking of any hostage was not helpful to the Middle East peace process," Bush said following reports of Higgins's death. "The brutal and tragic events of today have underscored the validity of that statement."[55]

Having "killed" an already dead hostage, Hizballah now turned its attention to a live one. They threatened to murder Joseph Cicippio, an American whom they had seized in Beirut in September 1986, unless Sheik Obeid was released. Bush now faced a rapidly deteriorating hostage situation in the Middle East as Hizballah attempted to draw a wedge between Israel and the United States. The key question was how he would handle his first test as president with the emotional issue of hostages. Would he repeat the mistakes of Jimmy Carter and Ronald Reagan and become a captive himself of a hostage episode, or would he chart new ground and handle the hostage problem in a different manner than his predecessors?

The answer came in a speech Bush made to the National Governors' Association meeting in Chicago on the day that the news of Higgins's "execution" was released. "There are unconfirmed reports that Colonel Higgins has, indeed, been executed," the president told his audience. "And I had planned to go on out to Nevada for another appearance today and then to go to Oklahoma tonight. But this matter is of such concern to me and to all of you and to the American people that I think it's appropriate that I go back to Washington. . . . We have not been able to confirm this horrible report, but I will go back to Washington and convene our top national security people and first establish to the best of our ability if the report is true and then figure out what might conceivably be done."[56]

The president could, of course, do all these things while still away from the White House. Conference calls on secure lines with his top aides and government officials, contacts with foreign leaders, intelligence reports, and so forth were always at the disposal of a president in this modern age of communications. But Bush felt compelled to rush back to the White House and portray the image of a president "in charge" as American hostages were being killed and threatened to be killed overseas. The terrorists could not have asked for anything more as they once again elicited a crisis reaction from the White House. "I think they have a victory here," said Pat Buchanan, the conservative Republican communications director for Ronald Reagan when he was president, in a televised interview. "They've gotten Bush's attention, brought him back to Washington, got the attention of the media. The Marines say you don't lose a platoon for a single man. We have eight people who are POWs. We cannot permit their fate to dictate American policy in a war against terror in the Middle East."[57]

But this hostage crisis did not last long. The United States dispatched the *Coral Sea* to within striking distance of Lebanon. This was more for show than for action, since bombing various sites in Lebanon where Hizballah was concentrated would very likely result in either retaliatory killings of all the hostages or in their deaths during the bombing. Bush nevertheless wanted to keep both the terrorists and the states that sponsor or had influence over them guessing about U.S. intentions. Neither Syria nor Iran wanted to see a U.S. military strike in Lebanon, since the consequences of such an action would be difficult to predict.

In addition to the show of military force, there were also contacts with Iran aided by intermediaries such as Algeria, which had proved helpful in negotiating an end to the 1979–81 hostage crisis in Iran. And in one of the first tangible signs that the Cold War was over, the United States asked for, and received, help from the Soviet Union in resolving the crisis. The Soviets assisted in diplomatic overtures to both Syria and Iran.

The deadline for Cicippio's execution passed without incident. Ali Akhbar Hashemi Rafsanjani, now president of Iran, reportedly intervened to have the death sentence lifted. There was no clear ending to this hostage episode, as Sheik Obeid remained in Israeli custody and the American hostages remained in captivity in Lebanon. The hostages and their families had gone through another emotional grind. "It was hell for the Cicippios," said Peggy Say, "and not much better for the rest of us." But Say saw a positive sign in the otherwise traumatic events. ". . . It did bring public attention back to the hostages. . . . With the Sheik Obeid kidnapping, at least everyone who should have been involved was talking. All I had ever wanted was for all the people who had anything to do with either abducting, holding, releasing, or taking responsibility for the hostages to be in touch with one another. . . . The Reagan and Bush Administrations' policy of never negotiating with terrorists had made talks impossible, but now finally it seemed it was going to get done."[58]

Say would be disappointed as Terry Anderson and the other foreign hostages spent yet another Christmas in captivity. By the spring of 1990, however, there were signals from Lebanon that one or more of the foreign hostages would soon be released. U.S. contacts with Syria on an official level and Iran on an unofficial level were beginning to bear results. Rafsanjani was also favoring a less militant role for Iran in the impending post-Khomeini era. The *Teheran Times*, which reflected Rafsanjani's views, had repeatedly called for the release of the hostages.[59]

But the Islamic extremist groups holding the hostages preferred to prolong the moments of anxiety for the West. In April, the Islamic Holy War for the Liberation of Palestine demanded that Bush send John Kelly, the assistant secretary of state for Near Eastern affairs, to Damascus to finalize the release of the yet-to-be-named American hostage. It was the terrorists' way of saying that while they might bend to pressure from Syria and Iran, they still wanted to humiliate the United States by dictating to the president the exact terms for a hostage release.

It was an offer that Bush could, and did, refuse. "The United States does not knuckle under to demands," Bush told reporters on April 19. While there was the risk that denying the terrorists their demand might lead to cancellation of the release, it was a risk the president deemed worth taking. The administration stated that the U.S. ambassador to Syria, Edward Djerejian, would be the person handling the pending release of the hostage. "We have a perfectly capable, accredited diplomat on the scene in Syria to work toward the release if it comes to that," Bush said.[60]

It was a seemingly small, but ultimately pivotal, step in the evolution of U.S. responses to terrorism. For the first time since American hostages were taken in Iran in 1979, a U.S. president was sending a clear message to terrorists that the possible freedom for an American hostage would not turn a president on his ear. The U.S. refusal to send Kelly to Syria surprised and angered the Shiite extremists. They called the administration's decision "arrogant, cowboy behavior."[61] Nevertheless, they released the hostage, Robert Polhill, after delaying his freedom for a few days. Soon afterward they released another hostage, Frank Reed.

Bush's firm stand against the Shiites and his refusal to make any promises to Iran and Syria concerning possible U.S. rewards if more hostages were released won the approval of the American people. It was almost as if the country needed to finally see a president not become obsessed with the hostage issue. One newspaper columnist wrote that "Bush, to his credit, has played it just right—a restrained 'thanks' to Iran and Syria for their role in securing the release of Polhill and Reed, coupled with a firm 'no deal.'"[62] Another noted how the president demonstrated that he had learned some important lessons from the past. "Mr. Bush said he thinks about the hostages every day," wrote *New York Times* reporter Robert Pear, "but the contrast between him and his two predecessors could not be more stark. Jimmy Carter became a prisoner of the White House for several months after revolutionary militants invaded the American embassy in Teheran in November 1979. Ronald Reagan was so touched by the pathos of individual cases that he sold arms to

Iran and pursued a will-o'-the-wisp into the maze of the Iran-Contra scandal. . . . President Reagan's experience with secret negotiations showed the futility of trying to sort out and satisfy the conflicting demands of rival factions in Iran and the back alleys of Beirut. . . . The lesson that Mr. Bush seems to have learned is to find a spot and dig in his heels. He seems determined to avoid any fixation on or obsession with the hostages."[63]

Bush also won praise from a diverse array of high-level officials from previous administrations. Dean Rusk, secretary of state under Presidents Kennedy and Johnson, was a firm believer in the virtues of negotiations during terrorist episodes. He nevertheless approved of Bush's handling of the Polhill and Reed episode:

> I can understand the theory that if you negotiate with the terrorists abroad, that tends to lead to more terrorism and to greater demands on their part. I understand that, but I'm rather sorrowed to see us lose the flexibility that may be required in a particular situation and that we shouldn't have iron clad rules that tie our hands in particular situations. Now I didn't object to our refusing to send Assistant Secretary of State [Kelly] over to receive the release of our hostage in Syria because it was such a superfluous kind of thing. The American ambassador in Syria after all is the alter ego of the president of the United States. I mean, when he is at his post, he is senior to the secretary of state and you could not have a more senior of individual to handle that kind of problem than the alter ego of the president. So I didn't object to their refusal to send Kelly over there.[64]

By the summer of 1990, then, George Bush was receiving quite high marks for his handling of the hostage issue. There were still Americans being held against their will in Lebanon, but Bush had sent signals to both the American people and to Hizballah and other Shiite extremists that the era of Reagan's obsession with hostages might finally be over. However, Bush had shown signs of being susceptible to the terrorist trap during the Higgins crisis when he rushed back to Washington to become captive of yet another hostage episode. How, then, would Bush react to the next terrorist crisis, as there always is a next one? The answer came before the summer was over as Saddam Hussein threw the entire world into anxiety and crisis in the early morning hours of August 2.

The Mother of All Hostage Takers

There is nothing unique about one country invading another. It has happened enough times in history to give credence to General Karl von

Clausewitz's dictum about war being the continuation of politics by other means. Some invasions, though, tend to become more famous than others. The world remembers well the German invasion of Czechoslovakia in 1939 that marked the beginning of World War II, the North Korean invasion of South Korea in 1951 that led to the Korean War, and the Soviet invasions of Czechoslovakia in 1968 and of Afghanistan in 1979 that heightened tensions between Washington and Moscow. Less famous—although certainly remembered by the participants and the victims—were those invasions that did not have global implications, such as Vietnam's invasion of Cambodia and Tanzania's invasion of Uganda in 1978.

When Saddam Hussein sent his forces streaming across the Kuwaiti border at 2:00 A.M. on August 2, he automatically added one more to the ranks of the historic invasions. With lightning speed, Iraqi troops, tanks, and supplies swept through the basically undefended country. There was some resistance mounted by the Kuwaiti Air Force, but they were no match for the much more powerful Iraqi military. The significance of the invasion lay not in the fact that another regional power had gobbled up a much weaker neighbor. Rather, the alarm throughout the world lay in the stakes that were involved in Iraq's aggression and the fears for the future of the Middle East.

The stakes involved oil, "the prize," as Daniel Yergin has so aptly described it in his book on the age-old quest for that precious resource.[65] Iraq's occupation of Kuwait placed Baghdad in a position to control Arab oil policy and prices and place a stranglehold on the flow of oil to the rest of the world. They were also in a position to threaten Saudi Arabian oil fields and potentially invade that country. As *New York Times* reporter Judith Miller and Harvard scholar Laurie Mylroie wrote, ". . . had Kuwait been, for example, a country in sub-Saharan Africa and without oil, not a single American soldier would have been deployed to protect it."[66] But Kuwait was not in Africa, but rather right in the middle of the region that has been the source of conflicts and wars for centuries.

If the potential threat to the world's supply of oil was not enough to cause great alarm, there was also the prospect of an out-of-control, unchecked, and unrestrained Saddam Hussein marching across the Middle East in the new post–Cold War era. With both U.S. and Soviet influence in the region greatly diminished from previous years and with his arsenal of chemical and biological weapons, Saddam Hussein would become the new power broker in the region.

Iraq's invasion of Kuwait thus could not be filed away among the forgotten cases of aggression in the twentieth century. It was all the more significant due to the period in which it occurred. The summer of 1990 was a time of great optimism in the United States and elsewhere concerning the future of the world community. Prospects for global peace abounded given the remarkable changes that had taken place around the world in the previous year. Communist regimes had come tumbling down throughout Eastern Europe as people's power revolutions toppled the once-monolithic Soviet bloc. In the Soviet Union itself, there was a remarkable transformation occurring in economic and political affairs and a growing movement for independence in the Baltic states. There had been pro-democracy demonstrations in China, with hundreds of thousands of students filling Tiananmen Square until the Communist authorities sent in the army to brutally suppress the movement. And guerrilla wars in Afghanistan, Angola, Nicaragua, and elsewhere were ending as "peace breaking out all over" seemed to best describe the world during the first half of 1990. There was even a debate evolving in the United States on how best to spend the "peace dividend," the billions of dollars in savings that would flow from a reduction in defense spending as there was no longer a Soviet threat to worry about.

The Iraqi invasion was a wake-up call that there was still a violent world out there. Hussein, though, had misread U.S. intentions, thinking that the Bush administration would not thwart his drive into Kuwait. Washington helped fuel this impression by sending ambiguous signals to the Iraqi dictator. In one instance, a little more than a week before the invasion, Hussein summoned the American ambassador, April Glaspie, to his office to explain his anger at Kuwait. He told Glaspie that Kuwait was waging economic warfare against Iraq by virtue of its high oil production, which kept prices low and cost Iraq billions of dollars in much-needed foreign exchange. Furthermore, Kuwait was producing oil from wells in a disputed border region with Iraq. He hinted at a possible Iraqi invasion, and did not receive a clear warning against such action from Glaspie. Instead, the American ambassador told Hussein that the Bush administration desired good relations with Iraq. She also told him that "we have no opinion on Arab-Arab conflicts, like your border disagreement with Kuwait." On July 28, Bush sent a message to Hussein in which he stated that the United States would support its friends in the region if Iraq used force to resolve its differences with its neighbors, but at the same time Bush stressed the importance that the United States placed on improving relations with Iraq. And on July 31, Assistant Secretary of State John Kelly testified before Congress that there were no treaty obligations or commitments that would require U.S. military force to thwart a potential Iraqi invasion of Kuwait. Kelly's statements were broadcast on the BBC World Service and were heard around the world, including in Baghdad.[67]

The Iraqi invasion elicited a strong response from the United States, its allies, and a new coalition of Arab countries. Many Arab states were slow at first to criticize Iraq's aggression for fear of alienating their own people. An invasion of Israel would probably have been the most popular move for Hussein to make among the Arab masses in the Middle East. But attacking Kuwait was not a bad second. Kuwait was among the richest countries in the world and not one that the downtrodden in the region could easily identify with. And Hussein played on Arab nationalism by equating Kuwait with Western interests. But this strategy ultimately failed as Egypt, Syria, Saudi Arabia, and other countries in the region—after failing in their own efforts to find an Arab solution to the invasion—supported the United States in its biggest airlift of troops, tanks, aircraft, and supplies since the Vietnam War. In announcing the decision to send troops to Saudi Arabia, on August 8, President Bush said that "a line has been drawn in the sand."[68]

The Arab states had many different reasons for joining the U.S. effort. For Saudi Arabia, there was the fear that Iraqi troops might come across their border as the next step in Hussein's plan for domination of the region. For Egypt, a powerful and influential Iraqi presence throughout the Middle East meant trouble for Cairo's hopes to become reintegrated into the Arab world following its many years of isolation since the Camp David peace accords with Israel. And for Syria, there was the intense personal animosity between President Hafez Assad and Saddam Hussein. Both dictators led rival factions of the Arab Ba'th party and had ambitions that extended beyond their borders; they were competing for supremacy in the Arab world. Syria had already gained de facto control over Lebanon by virtue of the thousands of Syrian troops that were situated in that war-torn country. Hussein's thrust into Kuwait, coming on the heels of its victory over Iran in an eight-year war, was a clear signal to Assad that Hussein would continue to flex his muscles in the region unless he was stopped.

The irony of Hussein's aggression into Kuwait was that it resulted in a tremendous gain in international prestige for his archenemy, Assad. In the ensuing months, Assad would play host to Secretary of State James Baker, who came to Damascus to persuade Syria to remain firm in the Arab coalition against Iraq. At one point Assad traveled to Geneva to meet with Bush. Whereas the Ayatollah Khomeini died just a little too early—his death came in June 1990—to see *his* hated enemy, Hussein, be confronted with the might and power of his other enemy, the United States, Assad could sit back and enjoy the developments.

Bush was convinced that the need to keep the Arab coalition together against Hussein justified his meeting with the leader of a country that was on the U.S. government's official list of state-sponsors of terrorism. "As long as I have one American troop—one man, one woman—out there [in the gulf], I will work closely with all those who stand up against this aggression," the president said shortly before his meeting with Assad in Geneva on November 23, 1990. Bush also said that "Mr. Assad is lined up with us with a commitment to force. They are on the front line, or will be, standing up against aggression."[69]

One segment of the American people that did not take kindly to the Bush administration's courting of the Syrians was the families of the Pan Am 103 victims. Pictures of the president of the United States meeting and smiling with the leader of the country that supported the terrorist group that was still considered the leading suspect in the destruction of Pan Am 103 was too much for some of them to take. Susan and Daniel Cohen, who lost their twenty-year-old daughter, Theodora, in the terrorist bombing, wrote the president a letter expressing their outrage. Bush responded by writing to the Cohens that, "If I knew for sure who had done this, action would already have been taken against the criminals. . . . As to the meeting with Assad, I had a very frank discussion with him about international terror. Having said that, it is important that we have the broadest possible support to stand against Saddam Hussein. . . . "[70] *New York Times* columnist A. M. Rosenthal, who published details about the letter and the president's response in his column, castigated Bush for meeting with Assad and for expressing ignorance about the involvement of Syria and the PFLP-GC in the Pan Am bombing. Writing on the second anniversary of the bombing, Rosenthal said:

> At this anniversary time, when the relatives meet in memorial vigil, it must be said that the President's decision to meet Mr. Assad, increasing his power in the Middle East, is not only morally depressing but also could compromise the case and block punishment of the criminals.
>
> Mr. Bush is ultimately responsible for the American investigation and prosecution of the case—prosecution by courtroom if possible, by political or military reprisal if necessary.
>
> The central terrorist organization involved calls itself the Popular Front for the Liberation of Palestine, General Command. It is based in Syria, trained by Syria, armed by Syria, sheltered to this day by Syria. Its chief, Ahmed Jebril, lives in Damascus, was a Syrian Army officer and is part of the Syrian military and terrorist apparatus.[71]

But if the Bush administration was reluctant to take any action against Syria for its possible role in the Pan Am 103 bombing prior to the Persian Gulf crisis, they certainly were not going to do anything now. The priorities of an impending war took precedence over any potential counter-terrorist responses for Pan Am 103. The focus shifted to Saddam Hussein.

The Iraqi dictator was no novice when it came to terrorism and unconventional warfare. Hussein's brutality included the use of chemical weapons in the war with Iran and against Kurdish guerrillas and civilians in his own country. He also sponsored several terrorist groups, including the Abu Nidal organization and the Arab Liberation Front. Hussein expelled Abu Nidal in 1983, but the group reportedly was allowed back into the country in 1990. Another terrorist group that received support from Hussein was the Palestine Liberation Front, led by Abu Abbas, the mastermind of the *Achille Lauro* hijacking in 1985 and an attempted seaborne attack on Israeli beaches in May 1990. Iraq also allowed the leader of the defunct 15 May terrorist group, Abu Ibrahim, to operate from Baghdad.[72]

Hussein utilized a mixture of threats, rumors, and specific steps to let the fear of terrorism take hold during the gulf crisis and eventual war. Even before the invasion of Kuwait, Hussein strongly hinted at potential terrorist activity on U.S. soil. "We know that you can harm us," Hussein told Ambassador Glaspie during their July 25 meeting, "although we do not threaten you. But we too could harm you. Everyone can cause damage according to his ability and size. We cannot come all the way to you in the United States, but individual Arabs may reach you."[73] Hussein wanted to leave the impression that he could initiate a terrorist campaign within the United States.

A few days after he invaded Kuwait, Hussein dropped the other shoe. He announced that thousands of foreigners in Kuwait and Iraq would not be allowed to leave those countries. Hussein had thus escalated the art of hostage taking to a new level. Never before had so many people from so many different nations—the United States, Great Britain, Germany, Japan, the Soviet Union, and Austria, among others—been held against their will. Many of the "guests," as Hussein referred to them, who were seized in Kuwait were eventually sent to Iraq. Some of the foreigners, including many Americans, were then distributed to strategic sites throughout the country to become "human shields." Hussein was hoping to use them to prevent a potential U.S. air strike or ground attack. The use of hostages for this purpose was not unique. As we saw earlier, Cuban rebels led by Raul Castro, Fidel's brother, took American hostages during the Cuban Revolution, partly to prevent bombardments of rebel strongholds by the Batista regime. And in 1964, rebels in the Congo did the same with several American and European hostages.

Hussein's use of the word "guests" to describe the foreigners he was holding was an unintentional favor for the Bush administration. Nobody in Washington wanted to use the "H" word, since hostages automatically conjured up images of Lebanon, the U.S. embassy under siege in Iran, presidents in crisis, and so forth. As long as the Americans and other foreigners were called "guests" or "detainees," perhaps the pressure on the Bush administration to "do something" about the problem could be kept to a minimum, since there was very little that could be done to rescue the trapped Americans without endangering their lives.

The Bush administration's sensitivity to transforming the detainee problem into a full-fledged hostage crisis was evident during the days immediately following Hussein's seizure of the foreigners. In order to make clear to both Hussein and the American public that he was not going to fall into the terrorist trap, Bush went on a scheduled twenty-five-day vacation to Kennebunkport, Maine, in August. He did not repeat the mistakes made during the Higgins crisis when he rushed back to Washington in order to maintain control over a situation that he easily could have managed wherever he might be. He also wanted to make the contrast between his administration's handling of this hostage issue and the way Carter handled the hostage crisis in Iran. "You know," Bush told reporters on August 10, "what you don't want to do is appear to be held hostage in the White House to events. And I'm not going to do that. That's why we have all this sophisticated intelligence. So I feel all right about it."[74]

But when Hussein announced on August 20 that several of the foreign "guests" were now "human shields," Bush responded angrily. In a speech before the Veterans of Foreign Wars in Baltimore, the president said there was no doubt now that the foreign citizens being held in Iraq and Kuwait were indeed hostages. "We've been reluctant to use the term hostage," Bush told the convention. "But when Saddam Hussein specifically offers to trade the freedom of those citizens of many nations he holds against their will [in return] for concessions, there can be little doubt that whatever these innocent people are called, they are, in fact, hostages. And I want there to be no misunderstanding. I will hold the government of Iraq responsible for the safety and well-being of American citizens held against their will."[75]

Bush now had a bona fide hostage crisis along with the prospects of a possible war with Iraq. Complicating the problem was that the administration never clearly or consistently explained to the American public why hundreds of thousands of its troops were being sent to the Saudi desert. Sometimes the reasons given were the need to thwart Iraqi aggression, liberate Kuwait, and ensure a "new world order" in the post–Cold War era. At other times the Bush administration pointed to the brutality of Hussein and hinted that U.S. resolve might lead to his being toppled from power. But none of these arguments sounded quite right. It was difficult for the public to identify with Kuwait, a country most people had not even heard of before Hussein invaded it. And while it was true that Hussein was a brutal dictator, so, too, were many other world leaders that the United States had supported with military and economic aid. We had helped the likes of Noriega, Marcos, the shah, and others at one time or another; we had even supplied Hussein with military weapons both prior to and during his war with Iran.

The true justification for the U.S. military response to the invasion was the need to protect one of our vital interests—oil. But even when the Bush administration raised this issue with the public, it only served to remind them that almost twenty years had passed since the first Arab oil embargo, yet the United States was still dependent on foreign oil. The country could still be threatened and pushed into drastic action when that flow was disrupted. The antiwar protesters' cries of "no blood for oil" hit home with many people.

Although the Bush administration still had the support of the majority of the American public, they felt frustrated in not finding a single "winning" argument to justify the military build-up in the gulf. They therefore fell back on what they thought would be a sure winner: hostages. As mentioned above, Bush had tried initially to de-escalate the hostage issue by remaining on vacation after Hussein seized the foreigners. He had also sent a strong signal to Hussein that the fate of the hostages was not going to dictate American foreign policy or the potential use of military force against Iraq. "Of course, our hearts go out to the hostages and their families," Bush told a joint session of Congress on September 11. "But our policy cannot change, and it will not change. America and the world will not be blackmailed by this ruthless policy."[76] Nevertheless, there was a reversal of this stance in late October, just a few days before the 1990 congressional elections.

The main advocate for placing the hostage issue at the top of the public policy agenda was once again an American secretary of state. Just as Secretary of State George Shultz took the lead in raising the terrorism issue to high priority during the Reagan administration, now it was Secretary of State James Baker who prevailed over the Bush team to make "hostages" the reason for America's largest military build-up since the Vietnam War. In late October, Baker told National Security Adviser Brent Scowcroft that the arguments the administration had thus far used to try to build public support for the gulf policy—thwart aggression in the Middle East, protect oil, and so forth—were not working. A drastic change in focus was thus needed, and the hostages provided that vehicle. Although Scowcroft was reluctant to raise the hostage issue at this point, almost three months after the gulf crisis had begun, he nevertheless went along with Baker's plan. The secretary of state delivered a strong speech on the hostage problem to the Los Angeles World Affairs Council on October 29. He stated that the Americans who were being used as human shields "are kept in the dark during the day and moved only at night. They have had their meals cut to two a day. And many are becoming sick as they endure a terrible ordeal. The very idea of Americans being used as human shields is simply unconscionable."[77]

Bush pursued the hostage line the next day both in a meeting with congressional leaders as well as in comments to reporters. He told the congressional leaders that the situation was deteriorating with respect to the plight of the hostages and that they were increasingly being maltreated. Several of those present, including Senator William Cohen, who was vice-chairman of the Senate Intelligence Committee, doubted that there really was any new "evidence" about the hostages since both CIA and DIA officials had recently testified before the Intelligence Committee that there was no new evidence of maltreatment of hostages. Some of the congressional leaders told Bush and Baker, who was also present, that the hostage issue did not justify the United States getting involved in a potential war with Iraq.[78]

Bush nevertheless kept up the rhetoric on the hostages, telling reporters on October 31 that he had "had it" with Hussein's treatment of the American hostages, as well as with the treatment of U.S. diplomats at the American embassy in Kuwait. Iraq had cut off electricity for the few remaining diplomats in the embassy. "Do you think I'm concerned about it?" Bush said. "You're darn right I am. And what I'm going to do about it? Let's just wait and see. Because I have had it with the kind of treatment of Americans, and I know others feel that way."[79]

Bush tried to temper his remarks the next day as concern in Washington and elsewhere grew that the United States might soon go to war over the issue of hostages. "I'm not trying to sound the tocsin of war," Bush said at a November 1 news conference. "I think some are saying, hey, there's a shift here, there's a dramatic shift in how we approach hostage-holding. And I don't think so. I'll tell you what is different, though. It's the sense of urgency I feel given the reports coming out of Iraq and given the status of the embassy." Bush also said, "I don't think I'm overstating it [the status of the embassy personnel in Kuwait]. I know I'm not overstating the feelings I have about it."[80]

But the situation for the hostages was not any different in October than it had been during their first few months of captivity. In many respects, the worst was over. They had already experienced the terror of being rounded up and taken to different locations. Now, with the whole world watching Hussein, and a stream of foreign dignitaries traveling to Baghdad to try to negotiate their freedom, it became a matter of waiting out the storm and hoping that they would be out of Iraq before a war began.

Hussein played the hostage card for all he could. Because of the unprecedented number of foreigners under his control and the fact that they came from so many different countries, Hussein could play all sorts of pressure games with the United States and other nations. When he wanted to raise the tension level in the crisis, he would make various threats about their safety. When he wanted to send a conciliatory note, he used the hostages by promising they would soon be released. He rewarded those foreign dignitaries who came courting him by releasing some of the hostages. Following a visit by Austrian president Kurt Waldheim, Hussein released ninety-six Austrian hostages. Muhammad Ali traveled to Iraq in December and won the release of fifteen American "human shields." After Jesse Jackson visited Baghdad, Hussein allowed American women and children to leave.

But playing the hostage game could backfire at times, as Hussein painfully learned. On August 23, Hussein met with several British hostages at an undisclosed location. The meeting, which was televised in Iraq and abroad, was intended to show a sympathetic Iraqi leader concerned for the welfare of his captives. Here was Hussein, dressed in a tailored business suit rather than his military uniform, smiling before the cameras as he assumed a paternalistic role with a seven-year-old British hostage, Stuart Lockwood. "Are you getting your milk, Stuart?" Hussein asked the frightened boy. "And with corn flakes, too. I don't think all Iraqi kids can get corn flakes [in] school?" The sight of the fragile young boy, along with the other British hostages who remained tense during the forty-minute meeting with Hussein, angered not only the British public, but also the millions of other viewers around the world who watched it on CNN. Hussein dispensed with televised meetings of hostages after the broadcast.[81]

By November, Hussein began to loosen his grip on the hostages, realizing that their value to him was diminishing. His holding them did not prevent the imposition of economic sanctions by the United Nations, nor did it seem that it would prevent an impending vote by the Security Council authorizing the use of force against Iraq if it did not withdraw from Kuwait by January 15. In a final effort to prevent such a vote, Hussein freed almost two hundred German hostages after former West German Chancellor Willie Brandt traveled to Baghdad. He also pledged—for a second time—to allow a thousand Soviet workers to leave the country. Hussein subsequently released the remaining German hostages and promised to release all the foreign hostages over a three-month period.[82]

But all these efforts failed, as the Security Council approved the resolution on the use of force on November 29. President Bush then surprised everyone by proposing that Secretary of State Baker travel to Baghdad to meet with Hussein and that Iraqi Foreign Minister Tariq Aziz come to Washington to meet with Bush in a final effort to avoid war. Hussein responded to this new overture by announcing on December 6 that all foreign hostages were now free to leave Iraq. It was a last-ditch effort by

Hussein to turn the tables on Bush and apply pressure for a peaceful solution to the crisis. Events, however, were rapidly moving toward war. After several delays in setting up the U.S.-Iraq meetings, there was only one, a fruitless one that took place in Geneva on January 9, 1991, between Baker and Aziz. The war plans of both sides were readied as the January 15 U.N. deadline approached.[83]

When the war began on January 16—"the mother of all battles" as Hussein referred to it—the Iraqi leader no longer had a hostage card to play against the West. But he still had the overall threat of terrorism, and he did not even have to do much to put that strategy into motion. One of the more powerful weapons that terrorists have at their disposal is the element of fear. And this can be self-generating as rumors take on lives of their own. Isolated terrorist incidents are seen as part of a worldwide orchestrated campaign of terror. Hussein wanted everyone to believe he had his finger on a worldwide terrorist button that could be activated during a war with the United States. But when the war came, he was too busy running for cover in the face of the U.S. aerial bombardment of Baghdad to try to issue orders to terrorists around the world to strike back.

However, people understandably feared the worst. Several international terrorist incidents occurred during the war that added to this concern. Two days after the war began, an Iraqi man was killed and another man was wounded in the Philippines when a bomb they were trying to plant at U.S. offices in Manila exploded prematurely. In Saudi Arabia, two U.S. soldiers were slightly injured in a sniper attack on a shuttle bus in the Red Sea port of Jidda on February 3. In Turkey, a retired U.S. serviceman was assassinated on February 7 and the leftist extremist group Dev Sol claimed credit for the attack. There were several bombings in Lebanon, including one at the Bank of Egypt to protest Cairo's role in the multinational coalition force fighting Iraq. In Jordan, a firebomb was hurled at a U.S. military attaché's car. And in Germany, the leftist terrorist group Red Army Faction fired shots at the U.S. embassy in Bonn on February 13, with police reportedly finding a letter stating that the attack was launched to protest the war.

These and other terrorist attacks, though, were not part of the opening of a "second front" by Hussein. Terrorist groups sometimes take advantage of any situation they can to perpetrate their violence. A war in the Middle East in which the United States was involved provided enough excuses for a whole range of terrorist groups, from Arab extremists to Islamic fundamentalists to European leftists, to commit violent incidents for their own objectives. Several members of the Japanese Red Army, whose goals include a worldwide revolution, reportedly visited Baghdad during the prewar period and pledged their support to Hussein. Philippine intelligence issued an alert for eight JRA members they believed were planning to enter the country.[84]

Other terrorist groups continue their campaigns of violence regardless of what else is happening in the world at large. Thus, terrorist attacks that took place during the war could leave the impression of being linked to the war, when in fact they were completely separate from developments in the Persian Gulf. On February 7, the Irish Republican Army launched one of their most daring attacks yet in their violent campaign to force the British out of Northern Ireland. Three mortar rounds were fired at the office and residence of British Prime Minister John Major at 10 Downing Street. The shells, which were fired from a van across the street, barely missed a room where Major was holding a War Cabinet meeting. The fact that Britain was in a war and the entire British Cabinet was almost wiped out led to a rare public denouncement of terrorism by Queen Elizabeth II, who normally does not comment on political developments. She pledged that terrorists would never "undermine Britain's democratic system." And former Prime Minister Margaret Thatcher stated that "their calculated, cold-blooded attack failed totally and will [be] met with even greater resolution to defeat the terrorists." The IRA, though, wanted to make it clear that their attack had nothing to do with British participation in the Gulf War, nor was it a personal vendetta against the new prime minister. "The operation had been planned over a number of months," the IRA said in a statement. "Its inception predates both John Major's coming to power and the beginning of British involvement in the gulf war."[85] Eleven days later the IRA struck again, setting off a bomb at Victoria Station in London, killing one person and injuring forty-three others.

In the United States, the fear of terrorism hit a peak during the war. America had long been fortunate, until the 1993 World Trade Center bombing, in terms of terrorism within its borders. While American targets overseas were a perennial favorite for all sorts of terrorists, averaging approximately one-third of all international incidents, domestically the United States was basically terrorist-free. There had been incidents associated with neo-Nazi groups such as the Aryan Nations, Puerto Rican nationalist groups such as the FALN, and various other causes ranging from anti-abortion groups to animal rights advocates, but the United States was spared the terrorism experience of most other countries. There was no wave of bombings of cafeterias and post offices in the United States as occurred in Paris during two weeks of terror in September 1986. There was no bombing of a crowded department store as took place in London during the 1984 Christmas holidays, or of a shopping center as occurred in Barcelona in 1988. And there wasn't the almost daily violence that countries from India to Northern Ireland have come to expect.

As noted earlier, one of the reasons that the United States was spared the terrorism that other countries experienced was that terrorists have enough American targets overseas to strike without having to risk penetrating U.S. borders. American diplomats, military personnel, business people, travelers, and others provided the "soft" targets for terrorists to hit. There were also plenty of "hard" targets available, such as embassies, airliners, and other facilities that terrorists were still willing to strike even though there might be physical security measures in place. It was much easier to coordinate a terrorist attack in Europe or the Middle East—and escape afterward—than would be the case in the United States. Furthermore, local, state, and federal authorities had done an excellent job in tracking down leads of potential terrorist activity within the United States.

The absence of terrorism in the United States, however, led to exaggerated fears about what might happen *should* international terrorists ever come to this country. Governments and societies around the world survive the periodic waves of terrorist campaigns that unfold in their countries. The American people, though, had no experience in this regard. Before the Gulf War erupted, America could best be described as being in a perpetual pre-crisis mode of thinking about terrorism within its borders. The right incident at the right time would likely set off alarm bells throughout the country and play right into the terrorists' hands.

This became evident during the war. Domestic air travel dropped significantly, as did overseas flights from the United States, as the fear of terrorism took hold. Local and state police departments in many parts of the country were flooded with telephone calls from concerned citizens. These included reports of potential bombs and terrorists. In one case, newspapers and television stations in Los Angeles reported that an Iraqi who might be a terrorist was on the loose in the area. David Azawi, also known as Duraid Jafar-Azawi, had failed to appear in court on earlier charges of having a pipe bomb in his car, and had now been reported to have driven his car near the gates of two military bases in southern California. He was subsequently arrested in San Francisco after a statewide manhunt. But the FBI said that it had no information linking him to terrorist activity, and that they did not believe he had ever driven his car near the military installations.[86]

There was also concern that terrorists might strike at the Super Bowl, which was scheduled for Tampa, Florida, on January 27. Cancellation of the game, though, would have played into the terrorists' hands. There was actually less of a risk of a terrorist incident occurring at the Super

Bowl than at another event where there would not be the same heightened level of security. The risk of terrorism is diminished when security can be concentrated in large numbers for a short period of time at a specific site. The element of surprise is taken away from the terrorists. The first time that there was a terrorist incident at a major sporting event was the Black September attack at the 1972 Olympic Games in Munich. This attack caught everybody off-guard. Since then, the Olympics have been free of terrorism.

The Super Bowl was held on January 27 without incident. But the fears of terrorism in the United States continued to grow. In February, several pipe bombs were discovered in chemical tanks in Norfolk, Virginia, the home for the Navy's Atlantic Fleet. This led to immediate speculation that an Iraqi terror network might now be operating within the country. The bombs, however, were part of a plot by three men to blow up the tanks and collect insurance on a chemical that was kept in the tanks. The bombs were safely defused.

The most symbolic indication of terrorism's grip on the American people was the purchase of gas masks by many citizens. Americans who were tens of thousands of miles away from the conflict certainly did not need gas masks. Not only was there no risk of Iraqi-fired Scud missiles with chemical warheads reaching the United States, there was also little risk of an Iraqi-sponsored chemical terrorist attack occurring within the country since security was at its highest level in decades. None of this, though, mattered to many people. After seeing others in the Middle East prepare for chemical warfare, they too felt they needed to be ready. Saddam Hussein was thus able to generate a level of fear and anxiety over terrorism that had been unmatched in the history of this nation.

For the troops in the Persian Gulf, the fear of terrorism was constant. While most of them felt confident that the United States would win any war with Iraq, they could not feel that secure about surviving terrorist attacks in the region. For six months they were sitting ducks as they waited in the desert for the war to begin. This was on the mind of Major Rhonda Cornum, an Army flight surgeon who was sent with her unit, the 2-229th Attack Helicopter Battalion (attached to the 101st Airborne Division [Air Assault]), to Saudi Arabia in August. Headquarters was at the King Fahd Airport near Dhahran. The only security around the facility at first was a guard at the gate. "We have 19,000 soldiers in a confined area and the memories of the Beirut bombings [was evident]. Our biggest fear was somebody driving a truck in and blowing something up or just lobbing in some kind of [bomb]," Cornum recalled.[87]

When the war began, Cornum's unit was moved closer to the front. On February 27, she was on a search-and-rescue mission inside Iraq—a U.S.

Air Force pilot had been shot down—when the UH-60 Black Hawk helicopter she was in with seven other soldiers was itself shot down by Iraqi antiaircraft fire. Five soldiers on board were killed instantly, but Cornum and two others survived, Cornum with two broken arms and an injured knee. They were captured by the Iraqis and remained in Iraq for a week. Cornum was transferred from one bunker to another that first night and finally to a small prison. During the thirty-minute truck ride to the prison, an Iraqi guard sexually molested her.[88] Cornum nevertheless felt more secure that she was a POW in Iraq rather than a hostage in Lebanon. "At least I didn't feel like a hostage. I knew I was always under the control of the military and that really makes you feel better," Cornum reflected.[89]

But her major concern was for the safety of her teenage daughter in the United States. She did not want the Iraqis to know she had a daughter for fear they might try to use her as a way of getting information from Cornum. "I denied having children because the biggest fear that I had was that if I told them I had a kid that they would target her for a terrorist act in America," Cornum said.[90]

The war ended in March, only six weeks after it began. A virtual round-the-clock aerial bombardment of Iraq by U.S. fighter-bombers and a large-scale and violent ground assault that choked off the Iraqi forces, including the elite Republican Guards, resulted in an overwhelming victory for the allied forces. The victory was tarnished by Hussein's brutal suppression of Kurdish uprisings in the northern part of Iraq and Shiite rebellions in the south after the war was over. A mass exodus of hundreds of thousands of Kurds to border areas with Turkey and Iran resulted in many thousands of deaths. And while Kuwait was liberated and the Iraqi military defeated, Saddam Hussein still remained in power.

America, though, had won the war overseas and survived the scare of terrorism at home and abroad. There are several reasons why the anticipated terrorist assault by groups aligned with Iraq did not materialize. Hussein made several threats about terrorism, but did not have an organized central command of terror networks to put into action once the war began. His ability to launch terror campaigns was also limited by the extraordinary worldwide security and intelligence alert that was in effect for much of the period leading up to and during the war. "There were more than three operations that we knew of that we aborted," said Randy Beers, the National Security Council's counterterrorism director during the war. "The general strategy that was undertaken was that we, the coalition allies, and host governments would identify [Iraqi] operatives. Whereas in a classic intelligence sense you would simply watch [them] and try to ascertain what they were about, and if you really felt there was an operation brewing, then you would probably do something about it. In this environment [prewar and war period] it was completely preempted. If you knew that somebody [an Iraqi operative] was there, then you went to the host government and sought to get them expelled. Run them out of the country. Yes, it exposed perhaps your ability to determine who was, and wasn't an agent, but at that particular point in time, nobody wanted to take a chance."[91]

The victory over Iraq gave George Bush one of the highest popularity ratings ever enjoyed by a U.S. president. His approval by the public soared to eighty-eight percent in March. Such a high rating could not be sustained, however; the euphoria of the war victory eventually faded as other problems, particularly the economic recession in the United States, took center stage.[92] Furthermore, the sufferings of the Kurds and the ability of Hussein to remain in power added to the erosion of Bush's postwar popularity.

Bush's handling of the hostage episode during the gulf crisis was, with one exception, in sharp contrast to the policies of his two immediate predecessors. His refusal to cancel a scheduled vacation in Maine, even though Americans were being held captive in Iraq and Kuwait, and his determination not to raise the hostage issue continually during the crisis were important breaks with the hostage policies of Carter and Reagan. Working to Bush's advantage were some of Hussein's actions. His release of all foreign hostages in December spared Bush the agony of the fourteen-month hostage crisis that Carter had to endure. His taking of such a large number of hostages, and from so many different countries, meant that Bush would not become personally and emotionally involved with a handful of hostages as Reagan did. And the fact that the plight of the hostages was overshadowed by the larger issue of America possibly going to war made it less likely that Bush or the American people would become obsessed with a hostage crisis. Still, the president got accolades from one who should know the traumas of managing hostage crises: George Shultz. The former secretary of state in the Reagan administration marveled at the skill with which Bush responded to Saddam Hussein's terrorism. "I think President Bush, in handling the hostages taken by Iraq, did it extremely well," Shultz observed in November 1991. "He said, 'we care about the hostages, but where you're holding them, where you're putting them in harm's way, is not going to have one iota of impact on our policy. So you get no benefit out of it. And you're going to pay a price.' So he removed the value, so to speak, even while still expressing his concern. So he did it well. And that worked and we got those people out. I thought it was handled beautifully."[93]

The one exception to making a clean break with the past was the administration's decision in late October to use the hostages as a possible rallying point for U.S. policy in the gulf. The Baker proposal to focus on the hostages as the reason for America's impending conflict with Iraq, which was endorsed by the president, resulted in a few days of rhetoric on the hostage issue by both Bush and Baker. Had the administration continued that course, it would likely have vindicated in Hussein's mind the worth of the hostages. The Iraqi leader would have been able to control events and reactions in Washington by manipulating the fate of the hostages. The administration wisely retreated from that course in November.

Of all the terrorism lessons from the war, though, the one that stood out was how Saddam Hussein, more so than any other individual terrorist or state-sponsor in recent history, demonstrated how unprepared the United States was for terrorism within its borders. The irony of the terrorist threat was that while the United States was prepared to deal with it in terms of good physical security and excellent intelligence assets, it was not psychologically prepared to deal with terrorist attacks on U.S. soil. Had there been any number of spectacular terrorist attacks here—or, given the heightened tension level, even minor ones—the effect would likely have been one of overreaction and panic. Learning how to tone down that reaction may be one of the most important lessons from the Gulf War.

George Bush continued to reap benefits after the victory over Iraq. While there was criticism in some quarters that U.S. troops should have been allowed to go all the way to Baghdad to depose Hussein and that the United States never should have abandoned the Kurds who rose up in rebellion after the war, the Bush administration nevertheless rode a wave of popularity in the postwar period. The United States was now clearly the dominant player in the Middle East, with a new coalition of former adversaries, including Syria, on its side. The collapse of communism in the Soviet Union—finalized by the failed August 1991 coup—removed Moscow from any influence in the region. Both Syria and Iran were maneuvering for better relations with the United States and some much-needed Western investment. There remained, though, one obstacle to improved ties: the hostages. Syria was now in control of Lebanon and could exert pressure on Hizballah and the other Islamic factions to free the hostages. So, too, could Tehran, which had long been the patron of many of the Shiite extremists in Lebanon. Adding to the momentum for a resolution of the hostage issue was the convening of a Mideast peace conference in the fall of 1991.

Thus, almost as quickly as they had been scooped up from the streets of Beirut and other places, the foreign hostages were let go. First came a British hostage, soon followed by an American hostage in the summer of

1991. Then a stream of other foreign hostages, including several Americans, were released in the fall. Israel was also releasing Shiite prisoners that it was holding. And then, finally, on December 4, 1991, the most famous hostage of them all, Terry Anderson, was freed by his Islamic captors. His fame came from the fact that he was the longest-held American hostage and from the media campaign that his sister, Peggy Say, conducted to keep his name, and those of the other hostages, alive during their years of captivity. With Anderson's freedom, America's long ordeal with hostages in Lebanon was finally over.

Bush got a lot of well-deserved praise for the resolution of the hostage problem. "The kidnappers, their Iranian and Syrian protectors, realized that this administration would not pay a high price for those hostages, that the value had gone down with the change of administrations. All of that had an effect on those isolated mercenary hostage takers in Beirut," stated newspaper columnist Jim Hoagland on ABC's "Nightline" the day Anderson was freed.[94] But just like America's first experience with hostages during the days of the Barbary pirates, it was a combination of factors, including the changing relationships among key players in the region and internal problems in some of these states—along with U.S. policy—that helped end the hostage ordeal. Hostage taking, though, is a cheap and easy form of terrorism. It does not require a great deal of planning or resources to carry out a successful operation. And terrorists can always play on the compassion that democratic governments show to their citizens who are taken captive. It is doubtful that America has witnessed the end of hostage episodes with the 1991 homecoming of the former captives from Lebanon.

For many of the Beirut hostages, life after captivity turned out to be anything but joyous. "Careers have been destroyed," said David Jacobsen, who had trouble finding work in his field of hospital administration when he returned to the United States in 1986. Potential employers told him that he was too big a celebrity and would probably be bored on any normal job—they were also afraid that any time there were developments regarding the remaining hostages in Lebanon, the media would descend on the hospital to interview Jacobsen, causing disruptions in the workplace. Some employers told him that the field of hospital administration had changed drastically during his absence and he would never be able to catch up. Others were afraid that since he was a former hostage, he *must* be suffering flashbacks and would probably react irrationally whenever he heard a loud noise. He finally got a job with a hospital in Colorado, but decided after a while to return to his home in southern California. Reflecting on his prospects for future employment, Jacobsen was not optimistic. "I'm 61," he said in the summer of 1992, "[and] there's age discrimination."[95]

Several other former hostages faced hardships in trying to resume their lives. Robert Polhill came out of Beirut in 1989 and had to have his larynx removed due to throat cancer—a definite hardship for anyone, but particularly for somebody whose career was in teaching. Thomas Sutherland, who was held hostage for more than six years in Beirut, could not find a teaching position in agricultural sciences upon his release in 1991, according to Jacobsen. Both his age, 61, and the length of his isolation from the outside world undoubtedly scared potential employers. Joseph Cicippio, the comptroller at American University of Beirut who was held hostage from 1986 until 1991, had a hard time finding work. The same was true for Frank Reed, the former director of the International School in Beirut, who was kidnapped in 1986 and released in 1990. "[He] has nothing," said Jacobsen. "He lost everything. Everything he had was in Lebanon."[96]

The more fortunate among the former hostages were the two men of God, Father Lawrence Martin Jenco and the Reverend Ben Weir. Neither could be fired and both had guaranteed employment. But even in the case of Jenco, life was not the same after he was freed. The priest, who had devoted his life to working with the poor, whether it be migrant farm workers in California, refugees in Thailand, or the victims of the civil war in Lebanon, wanted desperately to return to helping the downtrodden of the world after he was freed in 1986. But his superiors were afraid that lightning might strike twice and he would be taken hostage if he were sent back overseas. So they sent him to New York City to serve the spiritual needs of stockbrokers. "The first thing he got when he got back . . . [was] a church on Wall Street to say mass once a day, Monday through Friday," said Jacobsen. Father Jenco did not see this as his calling, and after a while he was sent to other places in the United States, including the University of Southern California, where he was employed as a campus minister. Jacobsen sees this as a pitiful waste of talent. "Marty doesn't need to pray all day long. He needs to go take care of refugees."[97]

None of the Beirut hostages have been able to escape their past in the eyes of the public. "We all have a big 'H' on our foreheads," said Jacobsen. "Some of that is our own fault because we cared about the guys who were [still] there [after we came out] and we politicized that."[98] Being a former hostage seemed to cancel out everything else these men had done prior to their captivity. "They don't say I'm a priest, they don't say I'm a servite, they don't say anything," said Father Jenco, " '[except Martin Jenco] comma, former hostage.' That's my whole life! I got to put that on my tombstone, 'former hostage.' "[99]

Both the hostage crises and the Persian Gulf War demonstrated the growing impact of mass media on public perceptions of events. The media was partly responsible, along with the government, for making the hostages household names and instant heroes. But when they were freed, they were no longer news nor of interest to the government and were essentially left on their own to reenter a world that had passed many of them by. The Gulf War was also a made-for-television event. Never before had millions of people around the world been able to see live coverage of bombs falling and events unfold *by the hour*. The last decade of the twentieth century had truly become the global village that futurists such as Marshall McLuhan had prophesied years earlier.

7

Media Players

Television news today has the ability to broadcast live virtually any major development in the world, and the tendency to then discuss the situation to death. It would thus be easy to forget that there was once a time in the early history of the medium when it was actually criticized for not covering and discussing *enough* news. "The public, which once had on radio a regular and sustained exposure to a variety of opinions on national and international affairs, now lives, so far as broadcasting is concerned, in a *trouble-free cathode cage*," wrote television critic Jack Gould in 1955. "Night after night, a viewer can watch TV and never be reminded that something has happened in the world which then and there should be analyzed, discussed and thought about."[1]

The era of the "trouble-free cathode cage" is long gone. It has been replaced with satellite technology that brings round-the-clock coverage of revolutions, hijackings, and other fast-breaking events. Television has come full circle from its infancy—the "golden age of television," as the 1950s are now remembered—when there was a plethora of live dramatic and comedy shows, but a scarcity of news programs and interviews. One of the last remnants of "live" television programming today is the news, which adds to its importance for viewers. Live news coverage of events gives the viewer a sense of "being there," with the added interest of not quite knowing the ultimate outcome. Television news today also provides for global hook-ups of the "talking heads," the so-called experts and commentators who can be routinely rounded up to offer instant analyses on whatever issue may arise.[2]

And it is not just television news that provides extensive coverage of events and continual commentary about them. Journalists have skillfully used the technological breakthroughs that have brought into existence personal and laptop computers, portable telephones, and fax machines to file a report from virtually anywhere and then have it printed in the next newspaper edition. Op-Ed pages abound in most newspapers, with the same "experts" who appear on television writing about the events they usually talk about. Radio, including the short-wave stations that can transmit programs from one country to several others throughout the world, and the numerous current-events magazines and newsletters are additional aspects of this global news village.

While most forms of mass media have the capability to follow a terrorist episode from beginning to end, captivating the public's interest, it is television in particular that allows for a vicarious experience. Viewers can watch the dramatic moments of a hijacking or hostage episode without ever having to leave their living rooms. When television stations used the title "America Held Hostage" to present their reports on the 1979–81 Iran hostage crisis, they could just as well have been referring to the millions of Americans who were riveted to their television sets as the crisis unfolded.

The first time Americans were captivated by continual television coverage of a tragic event was the assassination of President John Kennedy. For four long days and nights in November 1963, the public experienced nonstop television reports in the aftermath of Kennedy's murder in Dallas. It began with the first bulletins on the networks that Kennedy had been shot, continued with the swearing-in of Lyndon Johnson as president aboard Air Force One and the return to Washington of Kennedy's body, and grew in emotion with Johnson's speech upon deplaning at Dulles International Airport in which he asked the nation for its prayers. The tension and shock increased with the murder of Kennedy's assassin, Lee Harvey Oswald, before live television cameras and culminated with the funeral procession and burial of the slain president. It was truly the most remarkable and anguished event ever broadcast live by the still relatively young television industry.

But unlike the terrorist events that would unfold on television in later years and cause great anxiety and fear among the public, the television coverage of the Kennedy assassination actually had a *calming* effect on the nation. Marshall McLuhan described television in the mid-1960s as the "cool" medium: a place where people can become involved and participate in an event, yet at the same time not become too excited or agitated by what they see:

The Kennedy assassination gave people an immediate sense of the television power to create depth involvement on the one hand, and a
numbing effect as deep as grief, itself, on the other hand. Most people
were amazed at the depth of meaning which the event communicated to
them. Many more were surprised by the coolness and calm of the mass
reaction. The same event, handled by press or radio (in the absence of
television), would have provided a totally different experience. The national "lid" would have been "blown off." Excitement would have been
enormously greater and depth participation in a common awareness
very much less.[3]

The most vivid example of the "lid" being blown off by a "news"
event on radio was Orson Welles and his Mercury Theater of the Air
dramatization of H. G. Wells's "The War of the Worlds." Nothing since
then, either on radio or television, has matched the public hysteria
caused by the 1939 broadcast, which "reported" Martians landing in
New Jersey and killing people with poison gas. The broadcast came at a
time of heightened tension and concern in the United States about Nazi
Germany and war in Europe. Many people believed the "invasion" to be
real since there were "live" updates and bulletins read during the show
and several "interviews" conducted with people on the scene. Police stations throughout the country were flooded with frantic telephone calls
from worried Americans, and many people actually fled their homes.[4]

For McLuhan, panic was an anathema to the "cool" medium of TV.
"The Kennedy funeral, in short, manifested the power of TV to involve
an entire population in a ritual process," McLuhan wrote. ". . . Most of
all, the Kennedy event provides an opportunity for noting a paradoxical
feature of the 'cool' TV medium. It involves us in moving depth, but it
does not excite, agitate or arouse. Presumably, this is a feature of all
depth experience."[5]

Television today, though, involves both depth experience *and* excitabil-
ity. Its "cool" days are over. Terrorists have seen to that, bursting upon
the scene, skilled in using the medium to project images of fear and
panic. McLuhan, who in his classic book *Understanding Media* claimed
that the cool medium of TV "rejects hot figures and hot issues,"[6] did not
anticipate the phenomenon of terrorism. But in a later work written, in
part, shortly before his death in 1980, McLuhan and a colleague observed
that the era of global satellites will greatly benefit terrorists in their campaigns of violence. "The satellite will distribute terrorist paranoia around
the world in living color to match each acceleratingly disruptive event,"
McLuhan and Bruce Powers wrote.[7]

The first disruptive terrorist event shown on live television was the
massacre of Israeli athletes at the 1972 Olympic Games in Munich. Black
September timed their attack to coincide with the worldwide media cov-

erage guaranteed for the Olympics. Had their hostage seizure and killings occurred anywhere else in the world, it is doubtful that the news media would have been able to provide the coverage that it did. Terrorism was ahead of television technology at this time. It was the days before news teams could be put in place to cover a hot spot virtually anywhere, like a rapid deployment military force.

But during the Olympics, everything for a complete media perspective was already in place. ABC, which televised the games, had spent many years planning for the sporting event. The latest television equipment and cameras were already on the scene, as were hundreds of reporters from all over the world. All the terrorists had to do was crash the party. "Here is worldwide television covering all the games," said Pierre Salinger, formerly ABC's chief foreign correspondent. "And then all of a sudden they have to go off the games and focus on the Israelis getting killed."[8] The global sporting event was instantaneously transformed into a global terrorist event. Terrorism and the media would never be the same again.

It took several more years for media technology to catch up with the terrorists. By the late 1970s, with satellite newscasts becoming more common and able to produce better quality pictures, major events anywhere in the world could be covered extensively and dramatically. The Iranian revolution became the first "peoples' power" revolution to be shown on live television. There were vivid portraits of hundreds of thousands of Iranians marching in the streets, first demanding and then celebrating the downfall of the shah. But it was not until the militant students seized the U.S. embassy in Tehran and held Americans hostage for 444 days that the true power of television to cover a hostage crisis was demonstrated.

The storming of the embassy and the taking of the hostages, followed by angry crowds chanting "Death to America," was the perfect match between terrorism and media technology. The dramas could be played out nightly on television screens across America and the rest of the world, with correspondents filing reports and conducting interviews right in front of the embassy. Often, anti-U.S. demonstrations were staged by the militants for the television cameras. The image portrayed was thus one of an entire population worked up in a frenzy against the United States, even though just a few blocks from the embassy life went on as usual, with people calmly going about their business.[9] ". . . I know that I was relieved on occasion when the Ayatollah would exclude the western media from the streets of Iran," Jimmy Carter told Ted Koppel of "Nightline" on the tenth anniversary of the hostage crisis, "because then the threats against the hostages would die down, the public demonstrations would die down. Absent television cameras, Iran became much more moderate in its attitude toward the crisis itself."[10] The popular

"Nightline" television interview show was itself a creation from the intense interest that the American public expressed in the Iran hostage crisis.

It would turn out to be good practice for the media for what was to come. The early 1980s were filled with major terrorist episodes that made instant headlines and top television news stories, including the bombings of the U.S. embassy, annex building, and the Marine barracks in Beirut. The media were there at each turn, providing extensive coverage. A pattern to news coverage of terrorism was beginning to emerge. There would first be news of the terrorist attack, usually with a vivid description of what happened, how many people were killed or taken hostage, and speculation as to which group or state-sponsor of terrorism might be responsible. This would then be followed, both on television and in the newspapers, with statements and interviews by administration officials, commentators, and various experts regarding U.S. response options. Additional interviews would be held with the families of the victims. If any Americans were killed in the terrorist attack, there would be the solemn pictures of bodies being brought back home, memorial services conducted in towns and cities throughout the country, and finally the burials.

But as tragic as a bombing is with its potential loss of life, the real drama of the event is over too quickly for sustained media coverage. There may be the fear of additional bombings, but the terrorist act itself basically ends in those few seconds that the bomb explodes. This is not the case for hijackings or hostage episodes or threats where the terror is prolonged and can be effectively played out in the public eye. When the next major hijacking-hostage episode involving Americans occurred—in June 1985—the media demonstrated how far they had come since the days of the PFLP hijackings in Jordan in September 1970. Compared with that multi-plane seizure and blowing up of aircraft on the ground, the hijacking of TWA Flight 847 was far less dramatic. But now, finally, television technology was *ahead* of the terrorists and able to take a rather ordinary hijacking and transform it into one of the major media spectacles of the decade.

The media got help from President Reagan, who treated the event as a crisis of the highest order. His interruption of network broadcasting to announce that the hostages were finally freed only added drama and stature to the terrorist act. The terrorists demonstrated how adept they were in playing up to the cameras by staging a plane-side interview while a terrorist held a gun to the head of the pilot. Their holding of press conferences during the two-week episode further illustrated their media awareness. The hijacking was the top story on all the U.S. networks and in most newspapers, both in the United States and abroad.

There were continual bulletins and banner headlines on daily develop-ments. The scuffle that broke out among the press during the terrorists' news conference added to the controversy brewing over the media's role in terrorist events.

A congressional hearing was held shortly after the hijacking ended, with several legislators calling for the media to institute voluntary guide-lines for reporting on terrorism. There was a conference held by the Radio-Television News Directors Association during which network news anchors defended their actions during the TWA hijacking. Dan Rather, CBS News anchor, told the gathering that press conferences by terrorists are newsworthy events and should be covered by the media. "If you are covering a hijacking and you aren't going to cover the activi-ties of the hijackers—even if they're staged—then aren't you in the wrong business?" Rather admitted, though, that there were too many special reports on the hijacking. ABC News anchor Peter Jennings told the same group that although the media tended to focus too much atten-tion on the hostages' families and therefore underplayed other important news stories that were occurring—due to the fear of losing out to com-petitors—they had still done a good job. It was "a major improvement on our coverage of Iran," Jennings told the convention. "Generally, it had more substance and less sheer emotion."[11]

Emotion, however, is an essential characteristic of both the media and terrorism. Any topic that the media choose to cover has the potential to evoke strong emotions among the public, due either to the subject matter itself or to dramatic embellishments by the media. And any terrorist act that is perpetrated can evoke strong emotions among the victims, their families, or the nation as a whole. Since the media are influential actors in government and public affairs, their role in terrorist episodes cannot be ignored. But much of the controversy over media reporting on terror-ism stems from several misperceptions about the terrorist-media relationship.

Myths about Terrorism and the Media

"The terrorists are manipulating the media and getting great kicks," said Daniel Schorr, former CBS and CNN News correspondent and currently senior news analyst for National Public Radio. "And it's this mindless competition [among news organizations] which causes them to do it. There really ought to be a kind of voluntary code in which they say, 'We report the news, we don't dramatize it more than it is already demand-ing. [And] we don't do live interviews.' "[12] Schorr's views reflect a widely shared perception among the public, government officials, and some newspeople themselves that the media have played into the hands of terrorists by providing excess coverage of terrorist episodes and over-dramatizing certain events. Yet the media have tended to be unfairly blamed for encouraging or perpetuating terrorism. This is due to several prevailing myths about terrorist-media interaction.

The first myth is that *most terrorists try to use the media to their advantage.* This implies that terrorist groups worldwide take the media into account when they plan their operations, that they time their attacks to gain max-imum media exposure, and that they strive for as much publicity as possible for their various causes. This leads to the logical assumption that if media coverage of terrorism would be reduced significantly, then so, too, might be the terrorist threat.

This is a myth because only *some* terrorist groups utilize the media. The vast majority do not. For every press conference and interview session that has been conducted by a terrorist, and for every message or threat that a terrorist has issued through the media, there are hundreds of other terrorists who couldn't care less about media attention. When various car bombs were set off in crowded marketplaces in Beirut by warring Christian and Muslim factions in the 1980s, they were not done for media exposure. They were aimed instead at the civilian populations of each side as part of a campaign to demoralize them as well as to retaliate for previous attacks. The people in Beirut and in the Lebanese government would hear about these bombings regardless of the amount of coverage in the press or on television. It would be difficult for any-body living in the city not to know about the carnage. The same was true for other terrorist bombings in populated cities, including attacks by Tamil extremists in Colombo, the capital of Sri Lanka, or by Shining Path guerrillas in Lima, Peru.

State-sponsored and state-directed terrorists also tend to avoid media scrutiny or publicity for their actions. They "do not need publicity to generate recruits or sympathy," observes Patrick Clawson, a terrorism analyst.[13] When Bulgarian agents killed a leading Bulgarian defector, Georgi Markov, in London in 1978 with a poison-tipped umbrella con-taining ricin, the last thing they wanted was publicity. They wanted to quietly silence the defector and leave no traces of their crime. But Mar-kov lived long enough to tell his doctors that a stranger bumped into him on Westminster Bridge and apologized for prodding him with his umbrella. The remains of the poison pellet were found in Markov's thigh.[14]

Media exposure for terrorists can carry risks of identification, potential capture, and possible interference or distraction with future operations. In the aftermath of the assassination of Indian Prime Minister Rajiv Gan-dhi, a newspaper published a photograph of the alleged assassin—a female member of a Tamil Tiger suicide squad who detonated a bomb that was tied around her waist as she bowed to greet Gandhi at a campaign rally. The photograph aided investigators in their search for those involved in the killing.

Extensive press and television coverage of a particular terrorist act can also lead to increased pressure on a government to crack down on the suspected terrorist group. While some groups, such as the anarchist Japanese Red Army and German Red Army Faction, may seek such a reaction in the belief that it would lead to a repressive state and further their goals of "world revolution," most terrorist groups avoid that strategy. There have also been cases in which media attention to a particular terrorist incident forced the terrorist group to issue an "apology." The Irish Republican Army and the Basque separatist group ETA claimed they were sorry for two separate bombings in Northern Ireland and Spain that killed innocent people and led to widespread antiterrorism demonstrations in both countries.

There are, of course, terrorist groups that thrive on generating media attention. Their actions have led to the perception that all terrorism is media-related. The first group to effectively use the media was the PLO and its various factions. The wave of hijackings that began in 1968 were, in the words of columnist Charles Krauthammer, the origins of "media terrorism." "The terrorist acts of the PLO were not intended to demoralize the Israelis—the PLO has never really been at war with Israel—but to publicize political grievances," Krauthammer told a terrorism conference in 1983. "And the intended audience was not the immediate victims—the airline passengers—or even the Israelis, but the entire world. For such actions, coverage by the mass media becomes absolutely essential. This is where terrorists' utter dependence on the media begins."[15]

The Croatian separatists who hijacked a TWA plane in 1976 and demanded that an ideological statement be printed in several newspapers were certainly geared to using the media. Juliene Busic, who was part of the hijacking team, believes that had there been sufficient media attention to Croatian grievances before the hijacking, the terrorist act would not have taken place. "The media failed to play the role that they should [have] play[ed] prior to the hijacking," said Busic. "They are not aware that a lot of times their attention to certain issues will create conditions where people will not commit the desperate actions [they do] because they feel that they have a voice. . . . If they had done that before the hijacking, the hijacking probably wouldn't have happened."[16] "Z"—a pseudonym for a convicted Armenian terrorist who plotted to blow up the Turkish consulate office in Philadelphia in 1982—agreed: "Armenians have generally felt that there has been a wall of silence around their cause. . . . I know definitely . . . one of the reasons [for the bomb plot was] the media issue. . . . To target a building of some sort just to cause some financial damage and to get some coverage, media coverage."[17]

The various pro-Iranian Shiite extremists in Lebanon who seized foreign hostages throughout the 1980s were also aiming to create media attention. The terrorists were dependent on the global media to convey various messages and threats to governments about the fate of their citizens if certain demands were not met. They also knew that kidnapping Americans would get tremendous play in the U.S. press and television.

But many terrorists go about their violent business without considering media exposure. Terrorism existed before there was a mass media to cover such events, and would continue even if all reporting about terrorism ceased. The issue of terrorists manipulating the media is limited to particular terrorist groups and to particular terrorist incidents such as hijackings and hostage taking.

The second myth about terrorism and the media is that *the media foster images of "crisis" over terrorism*. This perception stems from the fact that it is on the television screens, in the newspapers, and on the radio that the general public experiences the dramas of a terrorist event. News bulletins, banner headlines, and round-the-clock coverage all lead to this view. But this tends to mask the influential role that presidents and their top aides play in creating a crisis atmosphere during terrorist incidents. When the public sees presidents become captive of the White House while a hostage episode is unfolding, or sees them declare a "war" on terrorism, it becomes quite easy to assume that a crisis is at hand.

While the media will seek statements from government officials and the president during terrorist episodes, they will also be the recipients of unsolicited information that the administration believes might be useful in resolving the incident. This could include issuing warnings through the press to terrorists or their state-sponsors about U.S. options if the hostages are not released, or simply acting in such a manner that the media will convey to the American people that their government is on top of the situation. All this adds to the sense of crisis over the event. "The press, especially the Washington press, is almost entirely dependent upon official sources," said *New York Times* correspondent Michael Wines. "Informed outside observers that do not have the stamp of government authenticity simply don't count. So when you get a tip from the inside that something is important, that makes it important to your editors. After that, it is up to the publisher and then the public."[18]

Administration officials are well aware of the influential role that they can play with the media during terrorist incidents. The Carter administration was the first to see this backfire when it tried to utilize the media during the first few months of the Iran hostage crisis to rally public support around the president. By continually talking to the press about the plight of the hostages, the administration was able to keep national and international attention focused on their fate, but also on the inability of the president to free them. "How to deal with the media is a very tricky kind of thing to do," recalled Cyrus Vance, secretary of state during the Carter administration.[19] George Shultz, secretary of state in the Reagan administration, agreed. "We live in the information age," said Shultz. "That's a fact of life. So there's no point in saying we should turn the clock back, or something like that. That's the way life is. *Achille Lauro*, we handled a lot more quickly and better because the ship was isolated . . . and there was no media. In the case of the TWA plane [TWA Flight 847], it was wild because the terrorists in effect were putting their message out over the television."[20] L. Paul Bremer, the chief U.S. counterterrorist official during the Reagan years, had his headaches in dealing with the press during terrorist episodes. "In the actual coverage of the incidents themselves, the press is a very tricky element," said Bremer. "I mean, I can tell you [that] in chairing our task forces during terrorist incidents, the question about how you deal with the press is—if not the first question—it is certainly the second question."[21]

There is no doubt that in the course of competing with each other for scoops or for the most extensive coverage of a terrorist incident, the media can make life difficult for a president. "Almost every television station in every major city in the nation now has some sort of reporter in Washington," said journalist Wines. "Newspapers that ten years ago would never have thought of covering the White House on a daily basis now pack themselves into the press room. It's a different kind of atmosphere. There is a lot more pack journalism and there is a lot more competition not just to be first with the news, but to make it as spectacular and awe-inspiring as possible. It is a temptation reporters have to resist all the time."[22]

But despite the media's pursuit to uncover the latest information—no matter how insignificant—about a terrorist episode, it is still those "high-level government officials" that can set the tone for how the story eventually plays out in the media. "If it [the government] wants to contain the impact of a news story, they don't have to get up every day and feed us stories to keep the story going," said Leslie Gelb, the foreign affairs columnist for the *New York Times*. "If they wanted to, if they want the handling of the crisis to take place more quietly, they have some influence on that process by how they treat us in the daily briefings and in the background."[23]

The third myth concerning media behavior during terrorism incidents is that *the media can limit a president's options in responding to terrorism*. This myth arises, in part, from the tendency by the media to focus on the "personal" elements of a terrorist story. Many terrorist episodes are characterized by numerous television, radio, and newspaper interviews with the families and friends of hostages or other terrorism victims. There are also profiles of the hostages. Some media critics argue that this complicates a president's ability to downplay a hostage incident or to order a military rescue or retaliatory operation, since it might lead to the deaths of the hostages.

This is a myth, however, because it has been the presidents themselves, particularly Carter and Reagan, who made the hostage issue a "personal" drama for themselves and for the country. And while presidents will surely be concerned with potential public and media reaction to a counterterrorist operation, their decisions will also be based on a variety of other factors, including the probability of success of the operation and its likely geopolitical repercussions.

Another argument that is sometimes raised against the media is that they can negatively affect U.S. counterterrorist plans by disclosing information that could be helpful to terrorists or their state-sponsors. This includes the risk of tipping them off to U.S. intentions by publishing or broadcasting reports on possible responses, or discussing in detail specific plans. This argument is part of the broader debate on the responsibilities of the media in reporting national security affairs.

While there is no consensus as to what constitutes a report that could be deemed harmful to U.S. national security—mainly because there is no consensus on what exactly is "national security"—the media have often adhered to government requests not to publish certain information.[24] The *New York Times* withheld publication in 1961 of a story on the secretly planned Bay of Pigs invasion at the request of President Kennedy. In the aftermath of his worst foreign policy fiasco, Kennedy reportedly joked that he wished the media *had* published the story so that he might have been forced to reverse his decision. When the Reagan administration asked the media not to disclose the fact that one of the hostages on board TWA 847 was a member of the National Security Agency—which possibly would have put his life in danger—they obliged. And although the news media reported that Delta Force had been deployed for a possible rescue operation during the TWA hijacking, they did not disclose that the special U.S. counterterrorist team had been sent to Cyprus.

The media came under heavy criticism for publicizing the deployment of Delta Force, even though that information was leaked to them by the Reagan administration for tactical reasons. "We did not say where it [Delta Force] was being deployed to," said former NBC News President Larry Grossman. "We decided to do it [announce the deployment] because it was leaked to us so that we would broadcast it. . . . I mean nobody told us that, but that was clear. But people who didn't know it was leaked yelled at the media as an example of their insensitivity and their failure to abide by security to say [that] Delta Force [had been deployed]. . . . But the government wanted the hijackers to know that we were not without our resources. And if we had said they were going to Cyprus and there were 3,200 guys and they had three tanks and twelve bazookas, that's a different kettle of fish. But we have guidelines."[25]

The decision on whether to broadcast or print information that might have an impact on national security is one that is left to the editors and news executives. Their natural inclination, not surprisingly, is to keep the public informed. "I will err on the side of telling more than less," said Ed Turner, CNN's executive vice-president. "There are considerations of national security sometimes—not often—but sometimes. And we damned sure pay attention to those. But those really are not frequent major factors. A politician will say it is. And what he means is the security of this administration or this policy. But that's not truly national security. It's *their* security. And you have to be sophisticated enough to divine the difference. But we will inevitably come down on the side of more reporting, and not less, at CNN."[26]

The fourth myth about the media and terrorism is that *the media help prolong terrorist episodes by giving the terrorists continuing and widespread publicity.* This myth has arisen due to the numerous times that the public has watched on television as cameras and reporters converge on the scene of a hijacking or other hostage-type event, and then see the episode continue for days, weeks, or months.

This is a myth, though, because the amount of publicity that the media give to any particular terrorist event has little effect on its duration. Terrorists may prolong or end a terrorist episode for a variety of reasons, including their perceptions of the degree of success or failure in having their demands met, pressure from third parties or state-sponsors to take certain actions, fatigue with the hijacking or hostage ordeal, or other factors related to the politics of the country or region where the episode is taking place. The TWA 847 hijacking, for example, lasted two weeks due to the intricate politics of the Middle East. This included the jockeying for power among various Lebanese factions that wanted to exploit the hijacking crisis for their own advantage, and the difficulty in arranging a "deal" with the hijackers, Amal leader Nabih Berri, Syria, and Israel, whereby the Israelis would release hundreds of Shiite prisoners in return for freedom for the hostages. Although media coverage of the TWA hijacking turned into a circus at times, their presence was not the reason the crisis lasted seventeen days.

This was also true for the Iran hostage crisis. The militants in Iran took advantage of the media presence there to stage various demonstrations for the cameras, and the crisis became the number-one media event in the United States. But the ultimate outcome of the hostage crisis had more to do with the internal politics of Iran than with the role of the media. "I doubt, however, that even if the media had not been playing up as much as it had, that we would have gotten the hostages back earlier than we did," said Cyrus Vance.[27] The Ayatollah Khomeini, as noted earlier, was using the hostages for his own purposes, which included maintaining a revolutionary fervor in Iran and creating a parliament, the Majlis, that would reflect his vision of an Islamic state. There was little hope of winning the release of the hostages until that stage was completed. The media attention played into the hands of the militants at times, but was not the decisive factor in prolonging the crisis.

The fifth myth about the media and terrorism is that *the media are not interested in providing context and causal explanations for a terrorist incident.* This myth has arisen because there *is* a disproportionate amount of air time on television and print space in newspapers devoted to the "shock" elements of a terrorist episode—the killings, the threats, the bombs, the deadlines—at the expense of a more balanced and comprehensive treatment of the issues involved. This is a problem, though, that many in the news media are concerned with, and they are continually reassessing their performances after each terrorist episode. "I wish we had done a better job early on," said CNN's Ed Turner, "at explaining the religious philosophy of the Shiites in 1980, which would have made at least careful and consistent viewers far better informed as to the why and how did we come to such a dreadful past."[28]

Another television newsman who wished his network would have covered a terrorist-related story differently is NBC News anchor Tom Brokaw. In 1986, NBC's "Nightly News" aired an interview with Abu Abbas, the Palestinian terrorist responsible for the *Achille Lauro* hijacking and murder of Leon Klinghoffer. NBC agreed not to disclose Abbas's location in exchange for the interview. This led to heavy criticism of the network by the State Department and some other media organizations. Robert Oakley, the State Department's chief counterterrorist official at the time, called the interview "reprehensible," implying that NBC had given comfort to the enemy. "When a media outlet makes deals with a terrorist not to divulge his whereabouts, the news organization is saying, in effect, 'we've become his accomplices in order to give him publicity,'" Oakley asserted. CBS correspondent Charles Osgood added that the news media "should not let [Abu] Abbas and his kind call the shots." Officials from the *New York Times* and *Los Angeles Times* also criticized the NBC deal with Abbas. But one news organization came to NBC's defense. "If NBC can find him and get his views, that's part of news gathering," said CNN's Ed Turner. "I wish we had him."[29]

The criticisms concerning NBC's refusal to disclose Abu Abbas's hideout did not bother Brokaw. "I don't have any problem with the whereabouts business," said Brokaw. "I just don't think we go around doing that [disclosing locations]. . . . There would not be that argument if we were in the jungles of Botswana with [African National Congress] commandos who were going to go across the border. No one would say, 'Well, you should have told us where they are.' No one would say that. So it is a kind of an ideological [thing] that comes into play here."[30]

What did bother Brokaw about the interview was his failure to put the situation into a better context for the public. "I do think what we didn't do enough of in that piece was to say, 'Here's who he is, this is the context of the interview, this is why it is important that you understand the import of it, and therefore you will as well, and the construct of it as we leave in your own mind,' " said Brokaw. "And people just see a guy up there who has been accused of some really outrageous crimes, appearing in their homes, and wondering what the hell is NBC doing talking to him about. . . . What you got was kind of a thug. We probably should have reinforced that in some way. And we probably should have had somebody evaluating what he had to say as well, so it had context."[31]

Newspaper reporters have also acknowledged the need for their profession to put terrorist events in their proper context so that the public is better informed about why certain things are occurring. "We are addicted to guns in the head, or the bomb under the car or in the airplane. And we do almost nothing to actually explain to people why these acts are undertaken . . . ," said *New York Times* correspondent Wines.[32] The concern for less sensational reporting on terrorism reflects the media's awareness of their potential role as educators for the public. Since the public receives the bulk of their information on current affairs from television, radio, and newspapers, the way that information is presented greatly affects public attitudes and knowledge. There are several barriers, however, to providing more balanced and measured news accounts of terrorist episodes. These lie in the competitive nature of the news business in general, and the special problems of terrorism reporting in particular.

The competition among the networks and newspapers for obtaining the latest scoop and holding viewer and reader interest puts a premium on emphasizing the fast-breaking developments of any crisis, no matter how insignificant the latest piece of information might be. Real life becomes more dramatic than fiction, putting a primacy on reporting the glitz rather than the reasons why the situation has arisen. "Crisis reporting offers opportunities for what is known in the trade as a 'continuing story,' " write media analysts Dan Nimmo and James Combs, "one that runs night after night, *simplifies complex details around a few easily grasped symbols,* and becomes almost a mini-series. When continuing stories strike a responsive chord among viewers, the possibilities for successful delivery of the audience to advertisers are increased."[33]

This is particularly true in terrorism crises, where people tend to become transfixed by the daily and hourly turn of events. The news station that focused on the historical or causal explanations for the terrorist act could risk losing its audience to its competitors. Since terrorism evokes strong emotions among the public—it is usually thought of in a "good guy–bad guy" syndrome—there is also the danger that discussions about why terrorists are committing their violent acts might seem too sympathetic and forgiving. For example, if a hijacking was under way with Americans on board and their lives threatened and a television station or newspaper devoted a significant amount of time or space to the possible underlying causes of the act—such as poverty and alienation among a particular ethnic or religious group, revenge for perceived injustices committed by various governments, and so forth—they could run the risk of being accused of being the dupes of the terrorists.

Nobody, though, would object to explanations for why a particular conflict between nations may have arisen, or why a health crisis may have erupted. In fact, it would be expected that the media and government would provide as much information as possible on the causes of the crisis to help the public better understand the event. But a different mode of thinking seems to set in when it comes to terrorism. Understanding the "whys" about a terrorist event does not forgive or excuse it; it only makes us better prepared to deal with the violence and less likely to panic over the terrorists' threats and actions. It also takes away the "faceless" nature of terrorism by placing it in the context of international conflict and affairs.

The media are clearly influential players in terrorist dramas. They can play both an educating role for the public and an alarming one. While the media have tended to be unfairly blamed for being partners for the terrorists, there is no question that they have at times overstepped the boundaries of proper behavior. The melee at the Beirut press conference during the TWA 847 hijacking was one example. Another was the media hounding of hostage families back in the United States during that same incident. Jeanne Murry, the wife of hostage Thomas Murry, was living in Newbury Park, California, about forty miles west of Los Angeles, when the hijacking began. The press would not leave her alone and virtually camped outside her home. "We were immediately inundated with media as soon as they found us," she recalled. ". . . They kept wanting an interview. And I kept saying no. Because I'll cry. And one thing I hate is crying in the driveway. And I wasn't going to perform for them."[34]

Jeanne Murry asked her daughter, Marianne, to fly out from Oklahoma and be the one to handle the media. When a reporter was particularly persistent and difficult, Marianne simply told him that unless he stopped she would tell her father when he got back from Beirut and make sure that he didn't give that reporter any interviews. "We had what they wanted," said Jeanne Murry, "and so they had to play by our rules. . . . After we got a handle on the situation, we all got along real well."[35]

Andy Ross, the owner of Cody's Bookstore in Berkeley, California, also had to deal with overzealous media during his experience with terrorism. His store was carrying Salman Rushdie's controversial novel *The Satanic Verses*, which the Ayatollah Khomeini denounced as blasphemous for its depiction of the life of the Prophet Muhammad. Iran condemned Rushdie to death in 1989—he went into hiding in Britain—and offered a $1-million bounty for his assassination. (The bounty was increased to $3 million several years later.) Riots erupted in Pakistan and other countries over publication of the book and there were a number of bombings of bookstores in Europe. Several chain stores in the United States withdrew the book for fear of terrorist attacks, but Cody's, an independent store, did not. As a precaution, though, Ross removed it from a window display. Nevertheless, his store was firebombed on the evening of February 28, 1989. Another bomb was found rolling around the floor, and the police detonated it after placing sandbags around it. Ross then held a meeting with his staff to determine if they wanted Cody's to continue to sell the book. "I believe in freedom of the press," said Ross, "but I also don't believe in exposing my employees to slaughter."[36] They voted unanimously in favor of continuing to carry the book.

Ross hoped the incident would quietly fade away. On the advice of a security consultant he turned down all requests for media interviews. "My main objective was to stay out of the media because I didn't want to call any more attention to myself than I already did," said Ross. ". . . My main struggle was not with terrorists because I really didn't know who they were and there wasn't much that I could do . . . [but rather] with the media to see that they would not exacerbate the situation."[37] But exacerbate it they did, with stories that made Ross out to be the tough hero doing battle against the evil terrorists:

> I just wanted to be out of the news entirely. But the press kept doing stories . . . and the spin that they were putting on stories was completely out of control. . . . They were trying to make me look like sort of this kind of Clint Eastwood kind of guy. You know, 'BOOKSELLER TELLS AYATOLLAH: READ MY LIPS.' That kind of story. And I definitely did not want that story in the newspaper. So in spite of the fact

that they were trying to make me look like this lone hero, it was a real dangerous situation.[38]

It was even suggested that Ross should put the book back into the window display to demonstrate resolve against terrorism!

The excesses of some of the media during terrorist episodes have led to calls for the imposition of voluntary—or even involuntary—guidelines in terrorism reporting. This, however, raises fundamental questions concerning freedom of the press and the role of the media in a democratic society.

The Guideline Debate

The question of imposing guidelines for media coverage of terrorism first surfaced following the 1977 Hanafi Muslim barricade-hostage incident that was discussed earlier. When the small sect of Hanafi Muslims seized three buildings in Washington, D.C., and took more than one hundred people hostage, reporters and television cameras maintained a vigil outside the buildings and some newspeople conducted live telephone interviews with the leader of the sect, Hamaas Abdul Khaalis. One Associated Press reporter telephoned Khaalis and asked him if he had set any deadlines. Since Khaalis had not mentioned anything about deadlines prior to the reporter's questions, there was now a new danger introduced to the hostages' safety. When Khaalis told the reporter that there were no deadlines, the reporter nevertheless continued to prod him: "Well, then, what are you waiting for?" the reporter asked. Khaalis shot back at him: "Don't you worry about it. I know what I'm doing." As the interview continued, Khaalis became more agitated with the reporter. "I'll beat the hell out of somebody over here. You'll cause somebody to get a head beating. You're not listening."[39]

Khaalis was also monitoring developments through television and radio reports, and became angry whenever the media reported something that he did not like. One television report stated that police were moving boxes of ammunition near the buildings, leading to speculation that a counterterrorist assault was imminent. Another television report showed a basket of food being lifted to a floor where several people were hiding from the terrorists. Khaalis had not been aware of these potential additional hostages until the report was telecast. Police were able to rescue the trapped people before the Hanafis could get to them.[40]

The media coverage of the Hanafi Muslim incident led many prominent figures to criticize the news media. Ronald Reagan called for an end to all live coverage of terrorist events in order to cut "off the source of inspiration for an untold number of loose nuts who harbor similar crazy ideas." Andrew Young, then the U.S. ambassador to the United Nations, said that "the First Amendment has got to be clarified by the Supreme Court in the light of the power of the mass media."[41]

CBS News announced in April of that year that it was instituting guidelines for covering terrorist incidents. These included avoiding "providing an excessive platform for the terrorist/kidnapper" by allowing them to issue demands directly into the camera. It was suggested that reporters instead paraphrase any demands. The guidelines further stated that "except in the most compelling circumstances, and then only with the approval of the President of CBS News, or in his absence, the Senior Vice President of News, there should be no live coverage of the terrorist/kidnapper since we may fall into the trap of providing an unedited platform for him." It was also recommended that newspeople not interfere with telephone communication between the authorities and the terrorists, and that experts on hostage negotiation be contacted to determine whether certain questions or phraseology might make the situation worse. Finally, the CBS guidelines called for an overall balance to the length of coverage of the terrorist event so that other important news would not be excluded from that day's newscast.[42]

Problems with some of these guidelines, though, became evident when Iranian militants took Americans hostage in Tehran in 1979. CBS, as was true for all the other networks, gave quite extensive coverage to the hostage crisis. All other news was quickly put aside. Competition for viewer interest dictated that the hostage crisis would get maximum air time. Interviews with militants and their supporters in the Iranian government were shown on all the networks, and there were televised pictures of the anti-U.S. demonstrations in front of the embassy. Even the dean of television news anchors, Walter Cronkite, became caught up in the crisis, ending each of his newscasts with a reminder to viewers of exactly how many days Americans had been held hostage.

While the Iran hostage crisis led to renewed debates about guidelines for media coverage of terrorism, it was not until the 1985 TWA 847 hijacking that the issue of guidelines and even censorship of the media during terrorism was raised in earnest. This was due to the media frenzy during the crisis, which included, as noted above, press conferences with the terrorists, plane-side interviews, and extensive coverage that scuttled all other news stories. The most blatant case occurred when the host of ABC's "Good Morning, America," David Hartman, ended a live interview with Amal Shiite leader Nabih Berri—who at the time was holding the hostages after their removal from the TWA plane—by asking him, "Any final words to President Reagan this morning?"[43] A media personality was offering a terrorist the opportunity to directly negotiate with the president of the United States during a hostage episode.

Following the TWA hijacking, television news departments grappled again with the guideline issue. NBC News President Larry Grossman sent an internal memorandum to his staff listing several questions that had been raised concerning network coverage of the episode and suggested answers for how to proceed in future terrorist incidents. These included "should NBC News give extensive coverage to hostage stories?" with the answer that it should since "we are in the business of covering news of interest and importance." Grossman suggested that reporters cover only what is happening in a situation and make no effort to change or dramatize the story. The memo concluded by stating that "professionalism and common sense provide the best guidelines to avoid undue risks, dangers and the exploitation of news reporting. There must be a delicate balance of our obligation to keep the public informed, our obligation to avoid being used, and our obligation not to exacerbate or sensationalize the situation."[44]

NBC's guidelines reflect the difficulty that the media face each time a terrorist incident occurs. "It's something out of the ordinary that has shock value," said ABC News correspondent Sam Donaldson. "From the standpoint of engaging the news media's attention, automatically, it's something you want to look at."[45] Any effort to reduce news coverage of a terrorist event due to concern for the media's impact on the event could open a floodgate for censoring other stories in which similar concerns are raised. "[We] want to continue to report that story right through to the very end," said Donaldson. "Giving it as much coverage as—again, reasonable editors can differ—but as much coverage as would normally be given a story. And I don't think you scrimp on it [coverage]. I don't think you say, well, this is a terrorist attack. The terrorists want to engage the news media, therefore we won't give them what their objective is. That seems to me to fly in the face of everything we stand for. It is not up to me to decide what is good for my audience. It is up to me to report the news. It is up to the audience, the individuals, to decide how to think about it, what to do with it. . . . We get on awfully dangerous ground when we decide to play censor because we think it is not in the best interest of American people or any other people to have a particular cause publicized."[46]

The potential for media interference in the course of a terrorist episode has troubled policymakers and law enforcement officials. Former Ambassador Bremer has proposed that the media adopt a "do no harm" credo when covering terrorism. "The basic rule is that first they should do no harm. They have to understand that they are not just observers, they are actors, they are part of the incident. They are a major reason for the incident . . . so they don't have the luxury of folding their arms and saying, 'Well, we're just reporters here.' That's nonsense. They can't get away with that. They are in fact actors. . . . [Their] first job ought to be in effect the Hippocratic oath, first—do no harm. Some of the journalists understand that, some of them don't."[47] Robert McGuire, who as police commissioner in New York City in the late 1970s and early 1980s had to deal with the media on a continuing basis, had similar experiences. "Where you do have a problem is where they're [media] vying with each other for a story that has partially broken. Then you can have trouble," recalled McGuire. But McGuire found that most of the media acted responsibly in their coverage of domestic terrorist incidents. "You would talk to them privately off the record about it and they would cooperate with you pretty much."[48]

Defining a proper role for media reporting on terrorism is complicated by several factors. One is the diverse nature of terrorist acts, which preclude any guidelines from being consistently followed. A guideline that advises the media to avoid granting interviews to terrorists might make sense in a hijacking case in which the hijackers have nothing new to say and will just use the media as platforms for world attention; it would not make sense in a kidnapping case in which hostages had been held for months or even years without any word on their condition, and an interview with the kidnappers might shed new information on that matter.

The introduction of third parties into terrorist incidents can also make media guidelines difficult to adhere to. When pro-Iranian Shiite extremists in Lebanon released British hostage John McCarthy in August 1991, they instructed him to deliver an undisclosed letter to U.N. Secretary General Perez de Cuellar. The most intriguing aspect of this was that it ensured that Islamic Jihad's letter to de Cuellar would be published by the world's press once the United Nations released its contents. Any existing media guidelines against publishing terrorist propaganda could thus be by-passed, since the media could argue it was only printing what was given to them by the United Nations. And the United Nations even provided a translation service, releasing the original Arabic letter in English. Many newspapers, including the New York Times, printed lengthy excerpts. The statement demanded that Israel release hundreds of Shiite prisoners—and that all Shiite prisoners in Europe also be released—in return for the release of the remaining foreign hostages in Lebanon. But the letter was mostly an ideological attack against the West and all who opposed Islam. The terrorists appealed to de Cuellar, "in your capacity as Secretary General of the United Nations, and to the world as a whole, to adopt Islam as an ideology, a code of law and a system and to follow the teachings of the Great Imam Khomeini. . . ." They also asserted that "the question of detainees and prisoners in the world today is one of the consequences of the confrontation between us and the forces of international arrogance led by America, the mother of iniquity throughout the world, and its offspring Israel."[49] Islamic Jihad was thus able to use the services of the United Nations to generate worldwide publicity for their ideology and demands.

Another factor that makes uniform media guidelines difficult to implement is the speed with which terrorist developments can unfold. There may be little time for reporters or news anchors at the scene of a terrorist incident to check with their superiors about whether something they are about to say or write fits within their news organization's existing guidelines. The experiences of one reporter during a hijacking episode illustrate this dilemma.

On April 5, 1988, pro-Iranian Shiite terrorists hijacked a Kuwaiti Airways jet en route to Kuwait from Bangkok. Among the more than one hundred hostages were three adult children of Sheik Khalid al-Jabir al-Sabah of Kuwait. The plane was forced to land in Iran, where additional weapons and explosives were brought on board. The terrorists demanded that seventeen comrades be freed from Kuwaiti prisons where they were serving various terms for blowing up the United States and French embassies in 1983. It would later be revealed that the hijacking was organized by the relative of one of the Shiite prisoners in Kuwait. The Kuwaiti government refused to release the prisoners, and the hijacked plane remained in northern Iran for three days. Although several hostages were released, there were still approximately fifty people on board when the plane took off for Beirut.

The last thing the authorities in Beirut wanted—the word "authorities" was stretching it for war-torn and chaotic Lebanon—was another hijacking on their soil. The Beirut airport control tower refused to grant the Kuwaiti plane permission to land. The pilot was told that the jet would be fired upon if it attempted a landing. "A gun is pointed at my head," pleaded the pilot. "I request landing permission to load to refuel." The air traffic controller replied curtly, "We have been for 14 years under gunfire." One of the hijackers took the radio and told the Beirut air traffic controller, "I shall punish control tower officials if they don't allow us to land. The passengers are all in panic now and many of them are vomiting. Among the passengers is a member of the Kuwaiti royal family with a heart condition." The air traffic controller was not impressed with this piece of information. "With all due respect to all families, permit me to say that all the Lebanese suffer heart ailments. Do not try to talk to me sentimentally." A passenger then tried to talk to the tower. "I plead with you to allow us to land in Beirut," the hostage said. "The hijackers insist on landing in Beirut and emphatically refuse to go to any other airport. There is no fuel left to take us to another airport." The pilot added that "there is no other option for us." The tower responded by again refusing permission. "There is no chance of landing," the controller said. "You will have to shoulder the responsibility of your action." The pilot then tried one last time to convince the tower of impending disaster. "If you fail to clear the runways within a few minutes, we will land in the sea," the frantic pilot said. The reply by the tower was go ahead and crash. "Do whatever you want," the tower told the pilot. "Crash on the tarmac or in the sea. . . . We shall not let you land here."[50]

The dramatic exchange between the hijacked plane and the control tower was broadcast live on Lebanese radio after local radio stations picked up the transmissions. The Lebanese people became riveted to their radios as they heard the pleas from those who were aboard the plane. The pilot decided to attempt a landing, and descended to two thousand feet above the airport. The control tower, however, dimmed all lights on the runway. Not being able to land in Beirut, the hijacked plane flew to Cyprus, where it was given permission to land. The pilot was quite happy to end his ordeal, even if it would prove to be only a temporary respite. "I'll never forget this, thank you," he told Cypriot authorities after getting clearance to land.[51]

For several days the plane remained in Cyprus, where the terrorists reiterated their demand that Kuwait release the Shiite extremists. The situation deteriorated as the Kuwaiti authorities stood fast on their refusal to give in to the terrorists' demand. On April 9, the hijackers beat and killed one passenger, dumping his body on the runway at Larnaca Airport, and a few days later killed another hostage, also dumping his body on the ground. Both were members of the Kuwaiti armed forces. They threatened to massacre all the passengers if their demand was not met. After releasing several passengers, the plane took off for Algeria on April 12 with approximately thirty hostages on board.

It was at this point that *New York Times* correspondent Youssef Ibrahim entered the picture. The Paris-based reporter began covering the hijacking in Algiers. On April 15, with the hijacking in its twelfth day, the terrorists decided that they wanted to talk with the media. "We want to hold a news conference in one hour," one of the hijackers said in a radio message to the tower.[52] He told Algerian authorities that one Algerian journalist and two other foreign journalists should come to the plane. The hijacker also stated that one of the reporters should speak Arabic, one French, and one English. Since they had already killed two hostages and were threatening to kill more, refusal or delays in granting the media interviews could result in further deaths. The interview would be the terrorists' first contact with the media since they seized the plane and might prove helpful in resolving the crisis. Three reporters were chosen by the hundreds of other press members gathered in Algiers to act as a "pool," thereby sharing information with everyone else. Ibrahim, who spoke Arabic, was one of the three reporters chosen to interview the terrorists.

Ibrahim had to decide whether to go ahead with the interview within an hour. The option of checking with his superiors at the *New York Times* was preempted by time constraints. "Clearly, you don't have the time," said Ibrahim. "I mean [if] they said at 3 o'clock, 'come on,' it's yes or no. My judgment was, 'yes.' My position was that in the end of the day this should be left to the reporter. If you assume that you have reporters who are experienced and who have covered the region or the subject for a long time, [then] it is up to them to make the decision (A) concerning their own safety (B) concerning the safety of other people involved, and (C) concerning whether it is worthwhile or not. And I saw the answer to all of these was 'yes.' "[53]

Ibrahim and the other two reporters—one was a correspondent for the Algerian press agency and the other was a reporter for Agence France-Presse—were brought to the plane amid very tight security. One of the hijackers motioned to the reporters to come up the ramp, one at a time. "They searched everybody," Ibrahim said. "We were not allowed inside the plane, but sat just outside the door [after] having climbed the stairs. And we each asked our . . . questions and the spokesman for the terrorists answered. But in fact, he wasn't really answering the questions. They wanted to make a number of statements, and they knew exactly what they wanted to say and what they didn't want to say. So in many ways, again, it became irrelevant what kind of question you were asking."[54]

The interview lasted fourteen minutes, and despite the terrorists' request for a multilingual group of journalists, the entire interview, including the terrorists' statement, was conducted in Arabic. The leader of the group was hidden from view, but whispered instructions to the hijacker who was conducting the interview. A third terrorist was standing a little way off. The terrorists repeated their demand for the release of the Shiite prisoners in Kuwait, and requested that Algerian officials refuel the plane so they could "liquidate our account with Kuwait elsewhere." They told the reporters that they "don't want to have the massacre in a friendly country."[55] The threat to kill all the passengers never materialized, however, as Algeria allowed the hijackers safe passage out of the country on April 19 after they released all remaining hostages. The United States strongly condemned the Algerians for letting the hijackers go, presumably to Lebanon or Iran.

Although the interview with the terrorists did not generate any earth-shattering information, Ibrahim believed it was still worthwhile. "I don't think we got a lot of explosively new revealing information from them,"

Ibrahim said. ". . . [But] it [did] give the readers, indeed the proper authorities, whatever they are, a much closer look, at least, [at] what's the configuration of that hijacking group, or those we saw, anyhow. . . . The other thing, the very simplest thing, is that since I speak Arabic, I could tell what accents that the terrorists had. And it was clearly Lebanese as opposed to, say, Iranian. So, [the] bottom line [is], I still think it was worthwhile, and if the situation happens again, I'll probably still do the same thing."[56]

If Ibrahim thought that his superiors would be happy that he got the interview—which although "pooled" would still give him a scoop over other reporters since he could describe in detail the characteristics of the terrorists, their behavior during the interview, his assessment of the situation, and so forth—he was wrong. His foreign editor was upset that Ibrahim had gone to the plane without first getting his approval. "I was surprised by the New York Times' reaction," said Ibrahim. "My foreign editor at the time . . . was quite angry that I accepted the initiative. And the cable that came in was, 'Never ever again accept [this], do not say yes in a situation like this, before consulting with New York.' Eventually, when things cooled down, we had a long conversation about it. And the idea was, well, were we being manipulated by these people? Are we giving them a platform to say whatever they want?"[57]

Ibrahim did not believe he had been manipulated by the terrorists. After all, he did learn some new facts about their composition and characteristics, which itself was a newsworthy event. His published report in the New York Times described the interview session in detail, pointing out that the demeanor of the terrorist who conducted the interview was "tense," that he played a subordinate role in taking commands from the leader who was hidden from view, that his apparent age was in the mid-twenties, and that his accent "suggested he was from one of the Arab nations in the eastern Mediterranean." The interview also gave Ibrahim insight into who were the likely sponsors of the hijacking. "The statement [by the hijackers] clearly echoed the rhetoric of militant religious leaders in Iran and Shiites of Lebanon," Ibrahim wrote in the Times. "He spoke of the Islamic nation as a 'nation torn apart because it has abandoned its Islamic values.' Throughout the statement, the hijacker attributed only Islamic characteristics to the Mideast region, speaking of the 'Moslem nation,' and 'Moslem lands,' never once using the word Arab to characterize the region. This closely follows the Iranian view, which opposes Arab nationalism as divisive and stresses the Islamic bond between the nations of the Middle East."[58] The public was thus better informed about the dynamics of the hijacking situation and its link to Middle East politics after the interview than they were before.

Following the interview, discussions ensued at the New York Times concerning guidelines for terrorism reporting. "The *Times'* attitude since then has become more focused," said Ibrahim. "It basically is [that] we are not going to just cover an event like this if we are serving as a platform for propaganda. I think it is a position that is not as clear among the television people. . . . [And] we just don't take [or give] anything [from the terrorists in exchange for a scoop], period. Beyond that, we don't have a clear-cut position. I think when the next time the situation arises, it will be judged on experience." Ibrahim reflected the prevailing view among journalists concerning terrorism reporting when he stated that "the bottom line, however, [is that] it's inconceivable not to report the event. And it is equally inconceivable not to present whatever demands or requests that the hijackers are making."[59]

Findings of a study conducted by Timothy Gallimore sought to determine the consistency between what the news organizations claimed to have as guidelines for terrorism coverage, and what they actually did once the terrorists went into action. Gallimore asked several news organizations what their guidelines were for terrorism reporting. He then compiled a list of ten typical types of guidelines—and intended ways of behaving—from the responses he received. These included not relying on terrorists or authorities as sole sources for information; balancing the volume of news on a particular incident so that other news is not excluded; providing a context and background to the event; not disclosing counterterrorist operations or plans; not using inflammatory words or rumors; withholding the identity of hostages whose disclosure would result in harm; not providing a platform for the terrorists; involving top management of the news organization in tough decisions about coverage; not participating in incidents or serving as a negotiator; and respecting the privacy of hostages and their families.[60]

Gallimore then analyzed media behavior by news magazines and television networks during two terrorist incidents. One was the 1986 hijacking of a Pan Am jet by Palestinian terrorists, while it was still on the runway at the airport in Karachi, Pakistan. That hijacking ended when the lights went out on the plane and the terrorists panicked, thinking that a rescue operation was under way. The hijackers began shooting passengers and tossing grenades, killing fifteen people and wounding almost one hundred others. Two terrorists were killed and two captured when Pakistani troops stormed the plane. The other incident was a hostage episode and bomb threat at the Washington Monument in Washington, D.C., in 1982. An antinuclear protester, Norman Mayer, held eight people hostage and threatened to blow up the monument with explosives that were in his van. That incident ended when Mayer, after releasing his hostages, was killed by the police as he attempted to drive away.

Gallimore found that the media did not always practice what they preached concerning guidelines. "Examples of violations of the voluntary codes and measures of responsible reporting abound," wrote Gallimore. He found, for example, that the media were responsible for publicizing Mayer's demands and that one reporter even served as a negotiator to get Mayer to release his hostages. In the Pakistan hijacking, Gallimore found that the media served as platforms for any group that called in to claim responsibility for the incident. He also found that the media did not provide much context and background to either terrorist incident and instead focused on the dramatic elements of the episodes.[61]

The issue of guidelines will be debated each time there is a major terrorist incident. Rather than rigid guidelines that would reduce the flexibility of the reporter at the scene or the news anchor at the station, the Bremer principle of "do no harm" makes the most sense. This is broad enough to cover a range of potentially dangerous and counterproductive actions, such as interfering with counterterrorists' plans and actions, unduly alarming the public with inflammatory reports, or risking the lives of hostages or the reporters themselves, while still flexible enough to maintain the freedoms of the press that are essential in a democratic society. Despite the excesses of some of the media during terrorism coverage, any significant encroachments on their freedom to report and cover world events would be against the public's and the nation's interests.

The CNN Phenomenon

Of all the media players in terrorist episodes, Cable News Network has catapulted to the top in an astonishingly short period of time. The all-news network, which is on the air twenty-four hours a day, seven days a week, and is seen in two hundred countries, has become *the* network to watch during times of crisis. Its popularity is enhanced by its live programming, nonstop coverage of any major event, and its ability to take a viewer around the world for any breaking story. What ABC's "Nightline" brought to America with its nightly half-hour news show of interviews with dignitaries around the globe, CNN developed further with its round-the-clock coverage of virtually all breaking developments. When it was first launched on June 1, 1980, CNN had a skeleton crew working in an old, leaky-roofed, white house in Atlanta—a house that a new employee insisted must have been the one that "Sherman forgot to burn"— yet by the end of the decade would be the station that the president of the United States would be watching in *his* White House during a hostage crisis in Lebanon. President Bush has "been in his study a lot watching CNN," said a Bush aide during the Higgins episode in August 1989.[62]

It was truly a remarkable metamorphosis for the network. During the period leading up to its inaugural broadcast, there was concern among the staff that CNN might miss the biggest terrorist story in decades. The United States was in the midst of the Iran hostage crisis, a made-for-television type of event. There were those Iranian crowds chanting anti-American slogans before the television cameras, the pathos of worried hostage families in towns throughout America, and an endless stream of U.S. government officials and foreign dignitaries commenting on the developments. Americans were already riveted to their television sets, and an all-news network would be a natural to fill the seemingly insatiable public desire for information about the crisis. Some of the CNN staff thus urged their bosses to move up the June start date, just in case something big happened in the crisis before then, such as release of the hostages or a rescue mission.[63]

CNN didn't make it on the air for the ill-fated rescue effort at Desert One in April 1980. But it was able to cover the jubilant celebration of the release of the hostages in January 1981. However, since CNN only started up while the hostage crisis was already at its midpoint in duration, it did not become a major media player in that drama. The network was still working out all the various kinks that would be expected in its first year of broadcasting. Its small staff and limited resources were not yet on par with the more established networks.

It would not be until the 1985 TWA hijacking that CNN demonstrated what an all-news, all-the-time, live television network could do in a terrorism episode. The bombing of the Marine barracks in Beirut in 1983, as noted above, was a relatively short-term media event. There was just not that much of sustained drama to portray on the television screen despite the tragic loss of lives. But the TWA hijacking gave CNN the opportunity to give viewers uninterrupted, live coverage of a hijacked plane in Beirut and American hostages for more than two weeks. Several media analysts took note of CNN's impact on its audience. One analyst wrote that "there was no way to be fully and immediately informed about any of this [crisis] without CNN. . . ." Another newspaper noted that the crisis gave CNN "its greatest coup since its birth just five years ago."[64]

For the rest of the decade, CNN was there for every major terrorist and counterterrorist episode, including the U.S. bombing of Libya and the various hostage crises and hostage releases. But most important of all for CNN was the fact that it became the station that people *expected* to be there during times of crises. A subculture had formed throughout the government and military in which various agencies and departments had CNN turned on all day—without the sound—ready to turn up the volume if the pictures showed a crisis brewing somewhere in the world.

The accolades for CNN began to pile up, beginning with Oliver

North's oft-quoted compliment that "CNN runs ten minutes ahead of NSA"; continuing with Bill Moyers's observation that "CNN is the network of the future, because even George Bush watched the invasion of Panama on CNN"; and Marlin Fitzwater, President Bush's press secretary, stating that CNN is often "the first communication we have." Furthermore, with CNN being seen in two hundred countries by 1993, it became a favorite station for world leaders and foreign government officials everywhere.[65] "Everyone is operating on real-time now in any crisis because it's on CNN and everybody is seeing the same imagery all over the world," noted George Shultz. "And so it's changed the way we conduct diplomacy."[66]

With all this attention and growing foreign audience, CNN was in a special position when it reported the news. Since the people who were making the news, whether they be terrorists in the Middle East or foreign leaders in Asia, could very well be tuned in to CNN's broadcasts, what the network said or did on the air could affect the course of events. Didn't this role as a potential newsmaker make CNN more careful than the other networks about what it said or did during its broadcasts? "No," said Ed Turner, reflecting on CNN's global influence as the network approached its tenth anniversary in the spring of 1990. "When I'm asked that question, I know that you expect us to say, 'Yes, we feel the burden.' But really, no more so today than when we began ten years ago. We had the same standards. They're more refined in the sense that we have more tools and better equipment. But . . . when we had a staff of only a few hundred and that many viewers, we still acted and conducted ourselves the same way then as now. It just hasn't changed that much. You don't sit down and think, 'Oh my God, they'll be watching us in Kuwait. Should we say that?' You report it because you believe it's a part of the story. It belongs there without thought of who is watching. It's what we should be doing. And I think most journalists are that way."[67]

The ten years of experience for CNN in covering the world, though, would turn out to be just a tune-up for the network's biggest moment. When U.S. aircraft bombed Baghdad on the evening of January 16, 1991, it signaled not only the beginning of the Gulf War, but also a new plateau for television reporting in general and CNN in particular. And the irony would be that the global television network would make its most important impact ever with *still* pictures and some good, old-fashioned, *radio-type* war broadcasting.

CNN had covered all the breaking events in the gulf since Saddam Hussein ordered his troops across the Kuwaiti border. From August 1990 until January 1991, the prewar coverage on CNN included the taking of thousands of foreign hostages by Hussein, the continual deployment of American troops to Saudi Arabia, Hussein's meeting with British hostages, and the various diplomatic efforts undertaken to avert war. As the January 15 U.N. deadline authorizing the use of force approached, CNN anchor Bernard Shaw and two colleagues, Peter Arnett and John Holliman, went to Baghdad to interview Saddam Hussein. Shaw was told by Iraqi officials that he would be granted the interview one or two days after the U.N. deadline passed. He was told to wait in the Rashid Hotel in Baghdad for word of when the interview would take place.

Instead of the interview, though, Shaw, Arnett, and Holliman would find themselves at the right place at the right time as far as journalists were concerned. With the aid of a telephone hookup, the CNN trio provided the most dramatic coverage of an air raid since the days of Edward R. Murrow's "This Is London" broadcasts during the London blitz in World War II. The modern-day "This Is Baghdad" found the three reporters huddled inside a room at the Rashid Hotel as the bombing raids began:

> Shaw: There is, uh, . . . something is happening outside. The skies over Baghdad have been illuminated. We're seeing bright flashes going off all over the sky. . . .[68]

The war was now under way and so was CNN. Much like a baseball game in which a pitcher is throwing a no-hitter and news quickly spreads through word-of-mouth and phone calls to friends and neighbors to tune in to the game, the audience for CNN grew astronomically that first night of the war. From its normal audience of 560,000 viewers during prime time, the audience soared to more than eleven million. And that did not include the millions of viewers watching in countries all over the world, as well as many independent U.S. local stations and network affiliates that chose to show the CNN broadcast.[69] This made CNN the major network for covering both the war and the threat of terrorism associated with it.

The drama was spellbinding. There were pictures at first of bursts of light over Baghdad as bombs exploded and antiaircraft guns were fired. But soon the video footage was eliminated as one of the bombs took out the transmission facilities for CNN. This occurred in the midst of a report by Holliman. With the video pictures from Baghdad eliminated, the drama intensified for the millions of viewers who could now only imagine, but not see, what was going on in Baghdad. Marshall McLuhan would have probably been quite interested to see his "cool" medium of television suddenly turn into a very hot medium filled with audio descriptions of a war. There were still pictures of a map of Baghdad and the Rashid hotel shown on the television screen, with a still picture of each reporter as he spoke, along with the caption "CNN Live." The reporters' voices were filled with emotion as the bombs dropped outside their hotel:

> Holliman: "Now we can hear explosions off in the distance to the west of central Baghdad, and we don't know how far to the west. But I can put the microphone out the window and maybe you'll get to hear some of the sounds of these explosions just for a moment, or at least the antiaircraft fire that is going with them."

At one point in the war, CNN reporter Charles Jaco stood on a platform in Saudi Arabia, nervously looking toward the skies and then all around him as he hurriedly told viewers:

> There's sounds of planes overhead. We don't know whose planes they are. But air raid sirens are going off incessantly. There's military convoys on both sides of me. We're being told to get off this platform and get inside into the air raid shelter immediately. But right now everyone has been training for this. And it looks like we may have to . . .

Suddenly the picture went static, and then blank, as CNN anchor David French in Atlanta tried to reassure viewers that everything *may* be okay with Jaco:

> All right, Charles Jaco. That doesn't mean that he is in any imminent danger. Of course we can't know that. He does have a place of shelter to which to go, and that's where we believe he is going. He is well equipped and cared for. We're going back to Baghdad and our reporters at the Rashid Hotel.

It was as if Orson Welles and his Mercury Theatre of the Air were back on the radio again. Only this time instead of a dramatized Martian invasion with "live" interviews with people at the scene that would suddenly go silent, this was real-time, prime-time war. CNN remained at the center of the war reporting, helped by its huge ratings coup that first night and then later by Hussein's decision to expel all U.S. media from Iraq except for Peter Arnett. Hussein was undoubtedly aware of CNN's global reach and hoped to use the network to show Iraqi citizens suffering from the war, and possibly turn international opinion against the United States.[70]

The strategy did not work, as Hussein's brutality in Kuwait was irreversible in the eyes of most of the world. CNN and Arnett came under heavy criticism from many in the U.S. government, Congress, and public for continuing to broadcast from the heart of the enemy camp. Arnett was not free to move around Baghdad and was often taken to places and people that the Iraqis wanted him to see, such as bombed-out buildings and suffering civilians. CNN informed its viewers during each Arnett report that the report had to first be cleared by Iraqi censors. This did not silence some of his critics, including a senator who called Arnett an Iraqi "sympathizer" and a media analyst who claimed that Arnett was "the equivalent . . . of Tokyo Rose in World War II."[71]

The terrorist aspects of the Gulf War were covered extensively by CNN, as they were by all the other networks and print media. There were two basic parts to this story. The first was the anticipation of a worldwide Iraqi-sponsored terror campaign, including hijackings and bombings. The second was the fear that a new form of terrorism—chemical and biological agents—would be introduced. While the public knew how to respond to the first threat, it did not know what it was supposed to do to protect itself from the second. The images portrayed by the media added to the public's anxiety.

Americans and others around the world had long experienced the terrorist threat with respect to hijackings and airplane bombings. The public's reaction was thus predictable once the Gulf War began. There were large-scale cancellations of trips abroad and numerous phone calls placed to police concerning suspicious people and packages. Many corporations prohibited their employees from traveling out of the country during the war, thereby contributing to one of the worst slumps the airline industry had ever suffered. The continual reports on CNN and the other networks concerning the prospects for Iraqi-sponsored terrorism added to the public's fears. But there would still have been an overreaction by the public even without the media attention. The public had been conditioned for so long to fear the worst concerning terrorism that any rational assessment of the risk of being a victim of a hijacking or a bombing was precluded. The irony of the Gulf War, as noted earlier, was that it was probably the safest time to travel abroad, since security at all airports and airlines was at its highest point in history.

The media played a more significant role with respect to the public's concerns that terrorists might unleash weapons of mass destruction. This role was more a byproduct of the media's live war coverage, rather than any attempt to overdramatize the threat for the public. Once people saw on television U.S. troops and Israeli citizens wearing those strange-looking gas masks, they knew that new types of death and destruction could unfold. The images portrayed on television were quite powerful. If a picture can be said to be worth a thousand words, then a live picture on television, and one during wartime, is probably worth ten times that.

CNN's war and terrorism coverage—and that of the other networks—demonstrated the impact that "pictures" can have in describing a story. "Pictures are the point of television reporting," writes Reuven Frank, former president of NBC News and one of the early pioneers in television news. "Television enables the audience to see things happen, and that is what newspapers and magazines and radio cannot duplicate, while all use basically the same words."[72] But at some point in a crisis, whether it be a war or a terrorist incident, the pictures can become repetitive. They begin to lose their fascination and grip on the viewing public, who eventually wants to know why certain events are occurring.

"The pictures just last so far," said Ed Turner. "And then it's expert opinion, analysis, and commentary. And those are words. 'Talking heads' we call them. And there's nothing wrong with a talking head as long as it has something to say. And the interviewer is smart enough to bring it out." Talking heads have been used extensively by CNN to flesh out the details of any crisis, including that of terrorism:

> I'll tell you something [that] I think that is particularly important now as insofar as the role of CNN can play in a terrorist story. And that is taking the drama, as a magnet of the event, and presenting the high drama. But as you're doing that, and there will be peeks through that story where something will occur that is pictorially fascinating. But around all of that you have these experts to explain and fill out the historical reasons why we are where we are. . . . By taking the experts, the opinion, and shaping it, and putting it around the live coverage, you can inform and educate tens of millions of people that would *never* sit through it on PBS or an hour on a Wednesday night. And that is unique to CNN and what I think we have brought to the eighties. The only similar [thing] I can recall is when Cronkite used to sit for hours live at Cape Canaveral on a space shot. And when you came away from watching Walter at a space shot, by God you knew something about that space program. But other than a few moments like that, it awaited the time of an all-news operation to serve the purpose. I don't mean it to say how good we are. No. It's just that we have the time, the natural drama is there. And the two mesh really very well.[73]

The Gulf War provided more than its share of talking heads, and it wasn't just on the American side. The British also brought out its flow of experts, many of them former military officers, to provide commentary as the events unfolded. Instant television celebrities were born on both sides of the Atlantic.[74] The problem with talking heads, however, is that they can often be wrong with their analysis on terrorism or any other subject, thereby misinforming the public. A true talking head, though, would never acknowledge that, but would instead smoothly move on to the next plateau and explain why certain things had occurred or did not occur for which they were originally dead wrong to begin with.

Talking heads can also cause undue alarm with dire or overly pessimistic assessments. This is particularly true during unfolding terrorism episodes when people are at an already heightened state of anxiety. Even though an expert may preface his remarks by noting that what is being said is only speculation, their lofty titles and affiliations with prestigious institutions can give their guesswork an air of legitimacy. Thus, when a terrorism expert tells a viewing audience that a wave of anti-U.S. terrorism attacks is imminent, it tends to be interpreted as fact rather than sheer speculation.

There is also a tendency for most of the experts that appear on television—and in newspaper quotes—to be from the same elitist institutions or hold the same type of current or former high-level government jobs. This can deprive the public of hearing new and different perspectives on the issues of the day, including terrorism. The technology is there for the networks and the press to obtain the views and commentary of qualified people wherever they may be located and with whomever they may be affiliated. "After all," observes Stephen Hess of the Brookings Institution, "the press people have WATS lines, the networks have uplinks. What's wrong with an expert in the Midwest?"[75]

Talking heads will continue to fill television airwaves in the 1990s; they have already become mainstays on popular news shows such as ABC's "Nightline" and PBS's "MacNeil/Lehrer Newshour." The future of network news, though, is more in doubt. The 1980s found the news departments at ABC, CBS, and NBC making deep budget and staff cuts and closing overseas bureaus, leading one media analyst to write that "the networks no longer qualified as a worldwide news service, if they ever did."[76] As the global village evolves due to space-age advances in computers, telephone systems, televisions, and data bases, new media players are likely to make their impact felt. But no matter how the future unfolds, CNN has already ensured itself a place in the history of both television news and world politics through its pioneering role in reporting on crises throughout the world.

Media coverage of terrorism will continue to be a hotly debated issue. The best safeguards today against inflammatory reports or excess publicity for terrorists will remain the common sense and professionalism that characterizes most journalists, correspondents, and news executives. "I think there is a certain self-censoring that begins to take hold," said former Secretary of State George Shultz, who saw the media get out of control during the 1985 TWA hijacking in Beirut. "And when the media start seeing that they're being used, they start to draw back. So I think that the problem is quite handable."[77] The excesses exhibited by some during terrorism reporting does not justify the costs to basic freedoms of the press that government-imposed restrictions would bring.

The issue of safeguards for *future* media reporting on terrorism, though, is more thorny. The shape and content of the evolving communications revolution has yet to be determined. The speed with which things have transpired in all spheres of life has been quite dazzling. It is almost as if everything that took place up until the late 1980s was just a tease for what was to come. From the proliferation of personal computers, fax machines, portable telephones, and global news reports, to the collapse of communism and the demise of the Soviet Union, the world has indeed changed rapidly. Although the communications revolution and the political revolutions have altered many aspects of our lives, for many terrorists their own private worlds have changed little. The adage "the more things change the more they stay the same" will ring true in the coming years. New groups and state-sponsors will emerge to take center stage from old ones. Different tactics will be introduced to make the terrorists' actions more effective. But some familiar causes will lie at the heart of their violence.

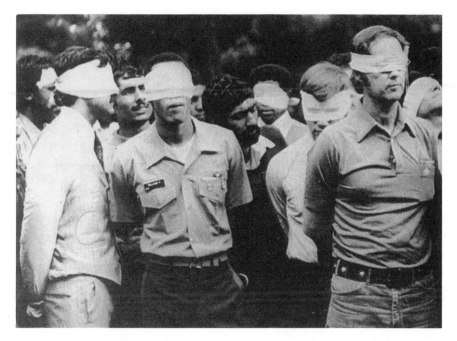

The Iranian hostage crisis began with the takeover of the U.S. embassy in Tehran on November 4, 1979. Americans were shocked at the sight of their fellow
citizens being paraded blindfolded in front of the U.S. embassy. The fate of the
American hostages would consume the presidency of Jimmy Carter for more
than a year. UPI/Bettmann.

Carter and Secretary of State Cyrus Vance talk with some of the families of the
hostages at the State Department. "All of us in senior positions didn't think
about the hostages [without] ask[ing] ourselves the question, 'Is there anything
that we ought to [do] that we are not doing?'" Vance would reflect years later.
Courtesy Jimmy Carter Library.

March 25, 1980

To Vivian Homeyer

Thank you for your letter. I understand
your feelings of frustration while your
sister remains a hostage in Iran. The
safe return of the American captives is
our paramount objective as we continue to
explore avenues to solve this crisis.

I am glad to know you have the spiritual
reserves to help you through these difficult
times. All Americans share your anticipation
of the day when we can welcome the hostages
home.

With best wishes,

Sincerely,

Jimmy Carter

*ps. I work on
this every day,
& never forget the
hostages ..*

A letter from the president to a relative of one of the hostages. In a handwritten
note, Carter added, "I work on this every day, and *never* forget the hostages."
Courtesy Jimmy Carter Library.

An attempt to free the hostages ended in tragedy in the Iranian desert. "I am still haunted by memories of that day," Carter would later write. Eight U.S. servicemen died when a helicopter collided with a C-130 transport plane during refueling after the rescue mission had been aborted. UPI/Bettmann.

RESCUE MISSION

A cartoon depicts the anticipated effect of the failed rescue mission on Carter's reelection hopes. Copyright 1980, *Los Angeles Times* Syndicate. Reprinted with permission.

Strain shows on the faces of Carter and his top aides as they await word on the hostage release on inauguration day, 1981. Iran would not allow the hostages to leave Iranian airspace until after Ronald Reagan had taken the oath of office. Courtesy Jimmy Carter Library.

A quite different mood prevailed on the White House lawn as President Reagan promises "swift and effective retribution" against terrorists as he welcomes home the former hostages from Iran in January 1981. Reagan would later learn that striking back at terrorists proved to be a most difficult task. Courtesy Ronald Reagan Library.

President Reagan and First Lady Nancy Reagan review a line of caskets for the victims of a suicide truck bombing at the U.S. embassy in Beirut in April 1983. The blast killed sixty-three people, including seventeen Americans. Courtesy Ronald Reagan Library.

A hijacker with rifle in hand appears at an open door of TWA Flight 847 in Beirut. The 1985 hijacking was covered extensively by the media and the terrorists even held a news conference during the episode. AFP photo.

The hijackers of the Italian cruise ship *Achille Lauro* wave from the deck of a tugboat in October 1985 after surrendering to Egyptian authorities. The terrorists killed an American hostage, Leon Klinghoffer, during the hijacking. AFP photo.

Libyan leader Muammar Qaddafi flaunted his support for anti-Western and anti-U.S. terrorism during the 1980s. AFP photo.

Secretary of State George Shultz was the most vocal advocate in the Reagan administration of using military means to combat terrorism. Here, he delivers a hard-line speech on terrorism at the Park Avenue Synagogue in New York in October 1984. AP/Wide World Photos.

President Reagan listens as General Charles Gabriel, chief of staff to the Air Force, delivers a briefing in the White House situation room on the damage caused by the Libyan raid in April 1986. The raid on Libya demonstrated that the United States had the resolve to use military force in the battle against terrorism. Courtesy Ronald Reagan Library.

Father Martin Lawrence Jenco waves to well-wishers and media upon his arrival at Rhein-Main Air Force Base in West Germany in July 1986. Jenco was held hostage by pro-Iranian extremists in Beirut for more than one and a half years and was released as part of the secret arms-for-hostages deal with Iran. Official U.S. Air Force photo.

Investigators examine the cockpit of Pan Am Flight 103 as it lies in a field in Lockerbie, Scotland. The December 1988 midair bombing killed all 259 people on board and eleven others on the ground. AP/Wide World Photos.

President George Bush and U.N. Secretary-General Javier Perez de Cuellar greet the last Beirut hostages, released in 1991. Standing left to right: Joseph Cicippio, Terry Anderson, Donald Sutherland, Alan Steen, Jesse Turner. Courtesy George Bush Presidential Materials Project.

Saddam Hussein took thousands of hostages during the Persian Gulf crisis in 1990, which began after Iraq's invasion of Kuwait. Here, he talks with the press after releasing some of the hostages. AFP photo.

Hussein also introduced a new fear of terrorism and warfare: attacks with chemical and biological weapons. U.S. troops in Saudi Arabia trained with gas masks. Official U.S. Air Force photo.

The World Trade Center bombing sent shock waves across America in February 1993. An investigator examines the large crater left by the explosion in the underground parking garage of the skyscraper. AFP photo.

Sheik Omar Abdel Rahman, a Muslim cleric from Egypt, was indicted by a federal grand jury in 1993 for being the leader of a group that conspired to engage in terrorism in the United States. AFP photo.

President Bill Clinton prepares for a live television address to the nation in June 1993 concerning the U.S. air strike on Iraq's intelligence command center. The raid was in retaliation for an Iraqi plot to assassinate George Bush during a 1993 visit to Kuwait. Courtesy of the White House.

8

Roots

"There's no idea worth killing for at the end of the twentieth century," proclaimed Milan Panic as he was sworn in as Yugoslavia's prime minister on July 14, 1992.[1] He could be excused for expressing such wishful thinking since he was taking over the helm of a country ravaged by ethnic-nationalist fighting that had already claimed tens of thousands of lives. As he spoke, war was still raging in Bosnia-Herzegovina among Muslims, Croats, and Serbs. That his statement was made on Bastille Day—the official beginning of the French Revolution—was just a historical coincidence. But it highlighted the fact that people have always found ideas worth killing and dying for.

This will not change as we approach the next century. In addition to revolutions and civil wars, terrorism will contribute to the death tolls in countries around the world. The roots of terrorism are as diverse as the groups that perpetrate it. They can be found in the religious, ethnic-nationalist, political, economic, and social differences that have prevented people from living together in peace.[2]

Religious Conflicts

Religious conflicts are among the oldest and bloodiest forms of violence. Before there were wars fought over political ideologies or nationalism, there was religious violence. Often, terrorism had a central role in these wars. As noted earlier, centuries before the Assassins appeared there were the Jewish Zealots and Sicariis, who believed that violence was the only way to oppose Roman rule in Palestine. And one of the most effective terrorist groups in recent times has been Hizballah, or the "Party of God," which along with its various factions has been a thorn in the side of the United States and other nations.

Religious terrorism has several characteristics that make it a particularly potent form of violence. One is the moral justification for committing the seemingly immoral acts of kidnapping and killing people. Believing that God is on one's side is a powerful incentive to action. Secular terrorists tend to justify their acts on pragmatic grounds—the means justifying the ends—whether those ends are sabotage of peace talks, revenge, territory, or other factors. Religious terrorists, though, are driven by a higher order. "The sacred terrorists believed that their ends and means were sanctioned by divine authority, which humans had no right to alter," writes one terrorism scholar. "Whereas their modern secular counterparts are concerned with the future, the sacred terrorists' eyes are on the past—on the particular precedents established in the religion's most holy era, the founding period when deity and community were on the most intimate terms and when the basic rules of the religion were established."[3] Another observer notes that the various Islamic organizations that have waged campaigns of terror in the Middle East and elsewhere "would be insulted if described as political organizations seeking political goals. They recruit their members in the name of Islam and are led by religious officials. Their long-term objective is the conversion—'by force if necessary'—of all mankind to the faith of Muhammad."[4] This trait is shared by other religious extremists in countries around the world.

A second feature of religious terrorism is the concept of "martyrdom." The belief that one will be rewarded in the afterlife has motivated some followers to perpetrate spectacular suicide terrorist incidents. These acts, in turn, provide the sect's leaders with a continual source of martyrs to assist in enticing other people into the ranks. The suicide terrorists of Hizballah and other Islamic factions, some of whom were reportedly drugged or duped, but others who willingly went to their deaths, were used by the Islamic extremists to galvanize anti-Western sentiment and gain new followers. In one case, a seventeen-year-old girl drove a car filled with TNT into an Israeli convoy in southern Lebanon in 1985, killing two Israelis and wounding two others. The "martyr," San'ah Muheidli, was part of a team of teenage girls who were known as the "Brides of Blood." Muheidli had grown up in a war-torn Lebanese Shiite village in southern Lebanon. She made a videotape before her mission, telling her mother not to mourn her impending death, but rather to celebrate it and "be merry, to let your joy explode as if it were my wedding day."[5] Thousands of Iranian teenagers volunteered to go to their death during the war with Iraq by running over mine fields to clear the way for the advancing ground troops. These suicide troops wore white headbands to symbolize their acceptance of death and shouted "Shaheed, shaheed," which translates into "Martyr, martyr," as they were blown up.[6]

The earlier religious terrorists were also ready to die for their cause, as we saw in the case of the medieval Assassins. The appeal of martyrdom has led some contemporary religious terrorists to follow in the tradition of the Assassins and commit killings for which there would be no escape. In 1981, terrorists belonging to the Islamic Group of Egypt (Al-Jihad), a Sunni fundamentalist sect, assassinated president Anwar Sadat before a horrified Egyptian public watching a military parade on television. The terrorists emerged from the parade and approached Sadat in the reviewing stand, who mistakenly thought they were going to salute him. As he rose from his chair to return the anticipated greeting, he became the victim of a barrage of gunfire and grenades. All the assassins were captured, including one who was a military officer in the parade. Seven people were killed and twenty-eight were wounded in the attack. The terrorists were prepared for martyrdom, as one of them wrote to his wife asking her to pay all his debts since "paradise has been forbidden for those who are indebted." He also told her not to cry for him when he is buried "because I consider myself a martyr and these things should not be done for martyrs."[7]

Religious terrorists are not the only ones who have committed virtual suicide by not trying to escape during their attacks. As noted earlier, the Tamil Tigers in Sri Lanka have a suicide squad that was responsible for the assassination of Indian Prime Minister Rajiv Gandhi. Members of that squad, as well as several other Tamil Tigers, follow the practice of swallowing cyanide capsules when faced with imminent capture. Some terrorists take their own lives after they are captured. Several members of the Red Army Faction, including its founders, Andreas Baader and Ulrike Meinhof, committed suicide in prison in the 1970s. The IRA created martyrs when eleven of its members fasted to death in a Belfast prison in 1981.[8] Secular terrorists, however, are more likely to believe that taking their own lives is a final act. Religious terrorists tend to more enthusiastically embrace death with their vision of the afterlife.

Fundamentalist religious terrorism—of which Islamic terrorism is the predominant mode today—may be the most difficult to alleviate or significantly reduce. The attraction of religion is that it provides hope to those whose lives are beset with poverty, oppression, and misery. The majority who embrace Islam do not become terrorists or engage in violence. Rather, they see the religion as "a homegrown answer to disorder, corruption, and inequality."[9] It has also "brought comfort and peace of mind to countless millions of men and women."[10]

Religious terrorism cannot be resolved by political agreements. There is likely to be no compromise possible in the minds of religious fundamentalists since compromise would be seen as defeat. A terrorist who is driven by the desire for a homeland or a separate state might feel satisfied if that homeland or state is granted. But terrorists who are motivated by religion can always find "infidels" somewhere in the world to justify a continual campaign of violence. This can include those within their country or elsewhere, such as novelist Salman Rushdie. "At times this hatred goes beyond hostility to specific interests or actions or policies or even countries and becomes a rejection of Western civilization as such, not only what it does but what it is, and the principles and values that it practices and professes," writes historian Bernard Lewis. "These are indeed seen as innately evil, and those who promote or accept them as the enemies of God."[11]

When Rushdie, after several years of hiding in Britain, tried to have his death sentence lifted by renouncing *The Satanic Verses* and claiming he had now converted to Islam, it had little effect on the Islamic extremists. One Iranian cleric stated that if Rushdie was indeed now a Muslim, then he should prepare to die like a good Muslim. For religious terrorists, "killing the infidel has God's blessing and is not considered to be either unethical or immoral, let alone criminal," observes one Islamic scholar.[12] Of all forms of terrorism, religious terrorism appears destined to never be resolved.

Religious terrorism is likely to grow in scope and volume. The United States and European nations have long been conditioned to think about Islamic terror primarily from the Iran-Lebanon connection. "Shadowy groups," as the pro-Iranian Islamic extremists in Lebanon have been described, have dominated Islamic terrorist activity during the 1980s. However, Islamic fundamentalist movements in Africa and Asia, including the former Soviet republics in central and southern Asia, all have the potential to give rise to militant activity in the 1990s. The victory by the Islamic Salvation Front in the first round of parliamentary elections in Algeria in December 1991 indicated that Islamic fundamentalists may gain control of governments through democratic processes. But once in power, they are likely to end all democratic rights and attempt to export their religious beliefs beyond their borders as Iran did in the early 1980s. New religious state-sponsors of terrorism may be on the horizon in the coming years. As one Muslim fundamentalist elected to parliament in the Algerian elections stated, the election "was the victory of Islam and the defeat of democracy, which is pure atheism."[13]

The fear of an Islamic state in Algeria led President Chadli Bendjedid to resign in January 1992 and a new civilian-military government to cancel the second round of voting, in which the fundamentalists were expected to win control of parliament. On June 29, the civilian head of the new government, Mohammad Boudiaf, was assassinated. Earlier that month in Egypt, a writer who was critical of Islamic fundamentalism, Faraq Foda, was assassinated by Islamic Jihad. One of the assassins was reported to have said after being captured, "We had to kill him, because he attacked our beliefs."[14] The attraction of Islamic fundamentalism to millions of people throughout the world will be one of the biggest challenges facing governments as we approach the end of the twentieth century. "We are facing a mood and a movement far transcending the level of issues and policies and the governments that pursue them," writes historian Lewis. "This is no less than a clash of civilizations—the perhaps irrational but surely historic reaction of an ancient rival against our Judeo-Christian heritage, our secular present, and the worldwide expansion of both."[15]

Ethnic-Nationalist Conflicts

Terrorism is also rooted in the centuries-old conflicts that exist among different ethnic groups and nationalities. For every case of "melting pots" or peaceful heterogeneous societies, there is an equal number of warring tribes, massacres between neighboring villagers, and lasting hatreds that are handed down from generation to generation. The violence can be temporarily suppressed under autocratic or dictatorial rule, but once that control erodes, the tinderbox explodes.

Ethnic and nationalist conflicts are sometimes limited to violent incidents in remote villages where the killings have little effect on the rest of the population or government. Other times, though, the terrorism is part of a sustained, well-organized strategy to gain a homeland, win various political rights or other freedoms, or simply to settle old scores. Ethnic-nationalist terrorism can also extend beyond the boundaries of a particular country, making the world the battleground. Armenian extremists have targeted Turkish diplomats worldwide, and Palestinian terrorists have attacked Israeli citizens and symbols in many different countries.

Unlike religious fundamentalist terrorism, ethnic and nationalist terrorism is not perceived by its perpetrators as being blessed by God. Rather, it is seen as a necessary means for achieving various political and social objectives. Since many ethnic-nationalist conflicts can also be divided along religious lines, this form of conflict has often been described as "ethnic-religious" violence. The Tamil separatist movement in Sri

Lanka pits the minority Hindu Tamils against the ruling Buddhist Sinhalese majority, the Palestinian-Israeli conflict finds Muslims on one side and Jews on the other, the violence in Northern Ireland has Catholics against Protestants. However, the religious aspects of these conflicts are secondary in significance to the secular objectives of the combatants. The zealousness of the religious fanatic is replaced by the brutal and calculating violence of the political pragmatist. The IRA's goal is to drive the British out of Northern Ireland and create a united Ireland. Sikh terrorists in the Punjab, who have been responsible for some of the most vicious crimes in recent years, including massacres on buses and trains filled with Hindu civilians, are striving for a separate state in their region. And the Palestinians' goal is a homeland, not a religious state.

While not all ethnic and nationalist groups seek autonomy or independence, those that do can attract world attention through terrorist campaigns. As noted earlier, Palestinian extremists turned to international terrorism in the aftermath of the Arab countries' defeat by Israel in the 1967 Six Day War. This was seen by the militants as the only way left to continue their war for a Palestinian homeland. Similarly, the Croatian separatists who hijacked a TWA plane in 1976 wanted to bring immediate worldwide attention to their cause. They succeeded as propaganda leaflets were dropped over several cities and a Croatian manifesto was published in leading U.S. newspapers.

When terrorism is rooted in ethnic-nationalist causes, the terrorists often find a popular base of support within their own community. While most of the ethnic population does not endorse the violence, there can still be a significant degree of passive support. While ethnic-nationalist terrorists do not go to their graves with the promise of paradise looming, they can at least die assured that they will receive heroic burials in their community. The sense of a constituency makes the terrorist groups sensitive to miscalculations in strategy that might alienate their supporters. Both the IRA and the Basque separatist ETA issued apologies, as noted above, after their bombs killed many civilians and led to widespread protests against terrorism in both Northern Ireland and Spain.

A terrorist campaign by an ethnic or nationalist group can originate in response to the refusal of government authorities to meet demands for political or social rights. Tamil separatists turned to terrorism in Sri Lanka after the government responded harshly to their demands for local autonomy and after anti-Tamil riots erupted in 1983. The terrorism continued after India sent troops to the island in 1987. The IRA began its terrorism in Northern Ireland in 1969 following anti-Catholic discrimination in the Protestant-dominated province. The terrorist campaign escalated after Britain sent troops to Northern Ireland that same year.[16]

A distinguishing trait of ethnic-nationalist and religious terrorism is its lasting power over the centuries. The divisions in society that give rise to terrorist activity never quite die out. They only await new sparks to start things going again. With each new round of fighting, fuel is added for future generations to carry the torch of revenge. The 1990s civil war in Yugoslavia is a case in point.

Yugoslavia was created as a nation by the Treaty of Versailles after the end of World War I. It was an uneasy confederation of south Slavic nations. It was hoped that granting equal federal rights to each republic would prevent potential conflicts. The plan was originally opposed by Serbian nationalists, who argued instead for the territorial expansion of their country and the creation of a "Greater Serbia."[17] The fear of Serbian expansionism had been prominent throughout the history of Croatia and the other Yugoslav republics. Meanwhile, the Serbs would later have reason to fear an independent Croatia; during World War II, the Nazis created a puppet independent state in Croatia that committed atrocities against the Serbs.

The divisions among the different nationalities in Yugoslavia was kept in check in the post–World War II era by Marshal Tito. After his death in 1980, a collective presidency took over with representatives from each of the republics taking turns at being the head of state. But this agreement broke down in 1991 after the Croatian representative, who had been arguing for his republic's independence, was denied the presidency. Croatia and Slovenia responded by declaring their independence and the country quickly slipped into civil war.

The latest emotional wounds for the Croats, Serbs, Slovenes, Bosnians, and other nationalities will last for a long time. "We do not think about what will happen tomorrow," said one young Croat during the conflict. "We do not think about what will happen when this war is over. Only one thing is certain; relations between Croats and Serbs will never be the same again. The hatred is very deep." Another put it more bluntly. "Next time, I will wipe out every Serb living in those villages. I want revenge," said a thirty-five-year-old engineer who had been wounded in the stomach when his National Guard unit was ambushed by Serbian guerrillas.[18] The feeling was mutual among the Serbs. When the Yugoslav army bombed Croatia's presidential palace in Zagreb in the fall of 1991, one Serb summed up his people's sentiments about the conflict. "It's pay time," said the Serb. "Now the Croats are being made to pay for what they did to Serbs during World War II."[19]

When another former Yugoslav republic, Bosnia-Herzegovina, declared its independence, fighting broke out between Croats and Muslims on one side, and the Serbs on the other. The Bosnian city of Sarajevo was encircled and bombarded by Serbian forces and there were reports of Serbian-run concentration camps. Eventually, the Bosnian Muslims also fought against Croatian troops. Meanwhile, Serbia forced the exile of Muslims from towns throughout Bosnia in what they called "ethnic cleansing." "I want revenge, and I am surprised at that," said a Bosnian Muslim after his home was shelled by Serbian militias. "I always considered myself a peaceful person incapable of such emotions."[20] Major General Lewis MacKenzie, the former commander of the U.N. Peace Force in Yugoslavia, was asked by CNN's Larry King to compare the Yugoslav conflict with others he had seen during his life. "Take all the others, multiply by 10, add a few points, and that's the level of hate," said Mac-Kenzie. "We are talking about people that cannot stand each other at this particular stage."[21] And most likely in future stages as well.

The makings of an ethnic-nationalist terrorist can be seen in the experiences of "Z," the young Armenian who plotted to bomb the Turkish consulate office in Philadelphia in 1982. Z grew up in Lebanon in the 1970s and left just as civil war was breaking out in 1976. The fifteen-year-old was able to see firsthand the effects of war and quickly became familiar with the use of weapons. Along with other Armenians in West Beirut, he stood guard over Armenian schools, churches, and other institutions to protect them from possible attack by local militias such as the Palestinians or Sunni Muslims. Violence was a part of life. "If you grow up in the Middle East . . . you tend to view violent means as not necessarily an impossible way of doing [things]," said Z. "[There is] the relative acceptance of violent means as a way of addressing your rights, your claims."[22]

He never saw his grandparents as a child, and when he asked what happened to them he was told that they were killed, along with one and a half million other Armenians, by the Turks in 1915. He heard graphic descriptions of how his great-uncle "was axed in front of his family, one of whom was my great-aunt who saw it and lived to describe it to me." These personal experiences intensified Z's anger when people questioned if the genocide ever took place. "You resent it very much. And if you're a certain type of personality, I guess, you try to do something about it."[23]

That feeling put Z on a collision course with terrorism when he moved to the United States. While living in Los Angeles in the early 1980s, he met regularly with other Armenians who felt as he did: that drastic action was needed to bring attention to their demands that the Turkish government apologize for the genocide, issue reparations, and grant the Armenians their territorial claims in eastern Turkey. "There was this urge to do something that was beyond just talk," said Z. Terrorism was seen as sending a message that their grievances were not something to bury in the past. "What terrorism did was say to the world community, 'Wait a minute, this [genocide] may be an issue that's seventy years old, but now what we're choosing to do is making it into a current issue. Go on and deal with it,' " said Z.[24]

Armenian terrorist groups were active in the United States and Europe during this period, some assassinating Turkish diplomats. But Z and his conspirators acted independently of any group and decided to target a Turkish consulate building without causing any loss of life. They planned the bombing for a Friday night at 8:00 P.M. when the consulate office would presumably be empty. The problem was to find one that had not already been bombed by other groups. "[The] selection process . . . was not an involved one. The consulate here in L.A., we knew that it was bombed . . . before . . . so we assumed there was going to be heavy security. The Washington embassy was out of the question [because of security]. The consulate or something of that nature in Boston was bombed. So we said, '. . . Where can we go where there will be less security?' And we went to one of those publications that has the different offices, the consulate offices, and there it came, the Philadelphia office. So we said, 'O.K., that's the one we'll go to.' "[25]

Z and the four other Armenians were arrested in October 1982 after five sticks of dynamite and a timing device were found in a search of one of the men's luggage at Boston's Logan International Airport—he had planned to eventually travel to Philadelphia. That man was later arrested with the luggage at a Boston hotel while Z and the others were arrested in the Los Angeles area. The FBI had received court authorization in September to wiretap Z's telephone, which alerted them to the details of the plot. After the arrests, an assistant U.S. attorney described Z as "the instigator and organizer" of the plan and as "the most culpable of these five defendants."[26]

The Armenian community in Los Angeles and throughout the United States raised several hundred thousand dollars for their defense, which was an insanity defense. This allowed them to argue in court that the 1915 genocide had left them psychologically scarred and was the main motivation for the terrorist act. "We had no intentions of plea bargaining," said Z, "because we sincerely thought that what we had done was morally justifiable." They were convicted in 1984 of conspiracy, transportation of explosive materials in interstate commerce, and possession of an unregistered destructive device. Z served more than four years in federal prison before being released on parole. As he looked back on his actions in the spring of 1992, Z regretted the pain he brought to his family and to the Armenian community. "The community suffered . . . in terms of Armenians being perceived as terrorists. . . . So it probably got to a point where non-Armenians were looking at Armenians as a source of unrest and as a source of terrorism."[27]

Z acknowledged that he was a terrorist, but he also viewed himself as a freedom fighter:

> Yes, this was an act of terrorism. I have no problems [with that]. I mean the prosecutor turned around as if he was trying to insult us [and] called us terrorists. I have no problems with that. I'm not one of those who would sit down and discuss the semantics between terrorists and freedom fighter. Terrorism for me is a tactic, and if you use that tactic, you can very well be called a terrorist. As long as they don't label you exclusively as that. I mean freedom fighting is more of a strategy. You can be a freedom fighter and then go ahead and implement terrorism as a form of freedom fighting. So in those terms I tried not to fall in that trap of, "Are you a terrorist, are you a freedom fighter?" I am a freedom fighter, or was. I would like to believe that I still am. And at that point I chose to use terrorism.[28]

Another ethnic-nationalist extremist who chose terrorism as a course of action was Juliene Busic. Her path to terrorism was quite different from Z's. An American blonde from Oregon would be the last person one would expect to commit a terrorist act on behalf of Croatian separatists. "I fell in love with a Croatian. I never knew what one was before," she said.[29] Through her husband, Zvonko, she learned about Croatian history and became dedicated to his quest for an independent state. As noted earlier, they met while in Vienna in the late 1960s, and she became increasingly involved in the free Croatian movement. "I knew that was foremost in his life, and I agreed with it. And I thought it was just a noble cause," Juliene Busic said. The hijacking was aimed at gaining publicity and "putting us at the most risk for doing more prison time [which] showed that we were willing to sacrifice even more," said Busic. But her decision to engage in terrorism was not an easy one:

> We were reacting against state-sponsored terrorism [by Yugoslav agents] against us and the entire Croatian nation which was being unopposed. And the point comes where . . . sometimes you have to ask yourself what is more valid for you, man-made law or some higher law. And God forbid that anybody should ever have to make that choice because it's the most excruciating choice that you'll ever have to make. Because I made the decision that I had to follow a higher, a different law. And I had to pay the price. And that's the choice that I made and I don't regret making that choice. I regret that people suffered, of course, I would never want anybody to suffer. But I had such an idealistic notion that if people knew, if they read the leaflet, and they knew we wouldn't harm them, they would be in solidarity with us and they'd say, "I'm willing to sacrifice these few hours of my life to get this truth out." I mean that's how naive and idealistic we were.[30]

Z also viewed his actions as less than practical. "You tend to be more idealistic," said Z. "You don't necessarily look at cost-benefit or what is this going to accomplish."[31] Although their individual terrorist acts accomplished little for their movements, both Z and Juliene Busic were nevertheless able to come out of prison and watch as an independent Croatia and Armenia came into existence. The history of many independent nations is filled with an assortment of terrorist attacks—some relevant to the future course of events, others not—committed in its name by a diverse range of groups and individuals.

As is the case with religious terrorism, ethnic-nationalist terrorism is destined to proliferate in the coming years. The catchwords for the 1990s are self-determination, independence, tribalism. No matter how small a state is, or how difficult the road might be once they are independent, ethnic and nationalist groups around the world are rushing to stake their claims for total freedom. The demise of the Soviet Union and the collapse of Yugoslavia portend a potential era of ethnic-nationalist violence for the remainder of this decade. Terrorism will be a byproduct of many of these conflicts since it takes only a small extremist faction to initiate a campaign of bombings, assassinations, or hijackings in order to provoke responses from other groups or governments, retaliate for any number of previous incidents, or simply gain publicity for the movement. The terrorist aspects of these conflicts will have some familiar rings to them, such as the hijacking of a Soviet Areoflot plane to Turkey by Chechen-Ingish separatists from the Soviet Union in November 1991.[32] But it may also have some new and more frightening characteristics. During that same conflict, the leader of the Chechen militants threatened to initiate terrorist attacks against nuclear facilities around Moscow if Russian federation President Boris Yeltsin continued to send troops to put down the uprising.[33]

Political-Ideological Beliefs

The roots of terrorism are also found in the ideological beliefs that can drive individuals from all parts of the political spectrum to commit violent acts. The political and social terrorists do not fight for any religion, or for territory, or for an ethnic or nationalist group, but rather for the "cause." This has included European leftist urban revolutionaries, global anarchists, right-wing fascist and neo-Nazi groups, and militants protesting specific issues.

The European leftist terrorists were among the most prominent terrorists of the 1970s and early 1980s. Groups such as the Red Brigades and the Red Army Faction were born from the ashes of the student revolts that shook many European countries in 1968. Most of its members were drawn from the middle class, with the goal being a mix of Marxist-Maoist revolution. Their main targets were capitalists and other symbols of industrialized states. Andreas Baader, who along with Ulrike Meinhof formed the RAF, stated the group's objective after it committed its first terrorist incident in 1968. By setting a fire at a department store in Frankfurt, the RAF intended to set a "torch against the capitalistic terror of consumerism," claimed Baader.[34] Meinhof further argued that the group's aim was "to hit the Establishment in the face, to mobilize the masses, and to maintain international solidarity."[35]

The RAF demonstrated a remarkable ability to adapt to changing circumstances and survive over time. When intermediate-range nuclear missiles were placed in Europe in the early 1980s, the RAF saw a golden opportunity to rally the masses to their cause. The presence of the missiles on European soil was highly unpopular among the public, and it led to large-scale, nonviolent protests in many countries. The RAF sought to capitalize on this sentiment by targeting NATO and U.S. military personnel and facilities for terrorist attack. They set off bombs at the NATO Air Force headquarters in Ramstein in 1981 and at the Rhein-Main Air Force Base in Frankfurt in 1985. The RAF also assassinated U.S. servicemen as part of their terrorist campaign.

However, the anticipated rallying to their ranks by the masses never materialized. When the nuclear missiles were finally removed as the Cold War began to wind down, the RAF had to find another issue to seize upon. They thus went back to their roots and began focusing once again on the capitalist symbols of the state. In 1989 they assassinated Alfred Herrhausen, the chairman of Deutsche Bank, and in 1991 they murdered Detlev Rohwedder, who was responsible for the economic transition of eastern Germany after the reunification of the country. The reforms, aimed at privatizing German industries, were highly unpopular since they led to the loss of thousands of jobs. The killing of Rohwedder was significant since it demonstrated that despite the reunification of Germany, the dismantling of Stasi (the secret East German police force that had given refuge and aid to the RAF), and the arrests of several RAF leaders, the group would still be able to initiate terrorist attacks. They were not going to disappear in the post–Cold War environment. "The myth of the RAF is still alive in underground circles. While Stasi fades, the nightmare of the Red Army Faction still hangs over Germany," reported Radio Deutsche Welle in a May 25, 1991, broadcast.

The RAF is also likely to find a new pool of recruits from the ranks of the former East German intelligence operatives. Ex-Stasi members will be able to bring to the RAF expert knowledge on explosives, counterterrorist and intelligence information, and special tactics in violence and psychological warfare. They will also bring money. "Such Stasi people disappeared [after the Berlin Wall came down] with millions in cash and with weapons—and with international contacts," observed a German counterterrorist official.[36] And as is true for many terrorist groups, the RAF can be propelled into a new wave of violence due to government actions. Following a police ambush in 1993 in which an RAF member was allegedly shot in cold blood, the terrorist group promised revenge.

Another leftist European terrorist group, the Red Brigades, has not demonstrated the survival skills of the RAF, although factions of the group have remained active. But in their heyday in Italy in the 1970s, few terrorist groups could match their notoriety. Their uniqueness lay in the sheer volume of their activity. At times they perpetrated more than two thousand incidents each year. But unlike terrorist groups that blew up planes or committed massacres, the Red Brigades usually kept casualties to a minimum. The favored technique, as noted earlier, was "knee-capping," or selective assassinations. Their targets were capitalists, government officials, military personnel, and journalists who opposed their movement. Their objective was to bring about a Marxist-Leninist revolution in Italy. As was true for many European leftist terrorist groups, most of the Red Brigades members were drawn from the middle class. Terrorism was seen as a way to expose the weakness of the state and lead to repressive government responses, which in turn would rally the masses to the revolution. But as it turned out, the Red Brigades' most spectacular terrorist incident ultimately led to its downfall.

On March 16, 1978, the Red Brigades kidnapped former Italian prime minister Aldo Moro, killing his five bodyguards during the abduction. At the time of the kidnapping, Moro was involved in efforts to bring the Italian Communist Party into cooperation with the ruling Christian Democrats. The trial of Red Brigades leader Renato Curcio and forty-seven other members had also begun one week earlier. But the Moro kidnapping was more than just a retaliatory act against the state or an effort to sabotage national reconciliation among the Communists and the government. It was a statement by the Red Brigades that they could take terrorism to new heights. The world had seen a wide diversity of terrorist tactics by the late 1970s, but now the terrorists had a former head of state as their captive. The vulnerability of a government to terrorists was now clearly illustrated. People in other countries could not help but imagine what it would be like had it been one of their current or former leaders who had been seized by terrorists. The pressure for the Italian government to find the kidnappers and save Moro's life was intense. And the drama unfolded while the media from many countries converged on Italy to cover the biggest terrorist story in years.

The Red Brigades toyed with the government during the nearly two months that they held Moro. On March 25, they stated that he would be tried by a "people's court." They also released a demeaning picture of him in captivity, which was printed in most Italian newspapers and carried by other newspapers and magazines abroad. On April 7, the pope appealed to the Red Brigades to save Moro's life. But the terrorists announced on April 15 that he had been condemned to death. On May 10, police found his body in the back of a car in Rome.[37]

The Italian authorities were both angered and embarrassed by the Moro affair. After all, it was not as if terrorists in one corner of the world had perpetrated an anti-Italian act and then disappeared into some remote area of a foreign land. This was done right under their noses. They later discovered that Moro was held in a Rome apartment the whole time. But the initial publicity the Red Brigades gained with the kidnapping was negated by the brutal murder and negative public reaction. The subsequent crackdown on the Red Brigades by the Italian police and security forces was not seen as repressive by the public, but as a welcome response. The Red Brigades had committed the one sin that terrorist groups try to avoid: stepping over the boundaries of "acceptable" violence and alienating the constituency they are trying to appeal to. Moro was among the most respected of all Italian politicians, and the dehumanizing way they played with his life angered many Italians.

It also angered some members of the Red Brigades, and defections in their ranks began to occur. In the aftermath of the Moro killing, several Red Brigades members were arrested, including one of the masterminds of the operation, Corrado Alunni.[38] The futility of the security forces to locate Moro also led to reforms that made Italian counterterrorist forces more effective in subsequent years. The Italian authorities ingeniously introduced the concept of "repentance" to Red Brigades members. What in other countries would be given cold, clinical names like "plea bargaining," in Italy was given the romantic-religious euphemism of "repentance." "Repent for your sins of political violence, and give us the names and whereabouts of your cohorts, and we will reduce your sentences," was the type of message that the Italian government sent out to those Red Brigades they captured and others still at large. Although the proposal was not passed by parliament until January 1982, it was unofficially used for those Red Brigadists who cooperated after the repentance law was first proposed in May 1980.

Many Red Brigadists turned in their terrorist "badges" and also turned on their former colleagues, giving Italian police further leads to pursue. The defections continued after the 1981 kidnapping of U.S. General James Dozier, which ended with Dozier's rescue and the capture of the terrorists holding him. But terrorist groups can continue operations with small numbers of militants. Although the Red Brigades never matched the volume of activity in the 1980s that they were known for during the previous decade, factions of the group perpetrated a few high-profile assassinations. These included the 1984 murder in Rome of Leamon Hunt, the U.S. chief of the Sinai Multinational Force and Observer Group, which was most likely carried out with the participation of the Lebanese Armed Revolutionary Faction, and the 1987 killing of Italian Air Force General Licio Giorgieri. The Giorgieri assassination demonstrated the simplicity of some terrorist operations. Two terrorists on a motorcycle simply drove up to Giorgieri's car on a Rome street and fired through the rear window, killing him.

Other European leftist revolutionary terrorist groups have also managed to stay active with a minimum number of members. Among these are the two major Greek terrorist organizations, the Revolutionary Organization 17 November (N–17) and the Revolutionary People's Struggle (ELA). N–17 and ELA never had the thousands of members—estimated at two thousand in the late 1970s—that the Red Brigades once had. These groups are believed to number less than twenty active members. But that simply means they are not susceptible to the mass defections, factional disputes, and arrests and plea bargaining that decimated the ranks of the Red Brigades. N–17 was formed in 1975 and took its name from the November 1973 student uprising against the Greek military junta. ELA was formed in 1971, also in opposition to the junta. Both groups have targeted U.S. military personnel, Western businessmen, and Greek and Turkish officials. N–17 was responsible for remote-control car bombings that killed a U.S. defense attaché in 1988 and a U.S. Air Force sergeant in 1991. They have also initiated attacks against U.S. military vehicles.[39]

Urban revolutionary groups can sometimes operate in the same country as ethnic-nationalist terrorist groups. In Turkey, the leftist Dev Sol group commits terrorist attacks aimed at toppling the government and bringing about a Marxist revolution, while the Kurdish Worker's Party (PKK) commits its terrorist attacks in pursuit of a separate Kurdish state in southeastern Turkey. Similarly, in Spain, the October 1st Antifascist Resistance Group (GRAPO) does not fight for a separate homeland as does the Basque separatist ETA terrorist group, but rather aims to create a Maoist revolutionary government.[40] The divergence of goals among leftist revolutionary terrorist groups on the one hand, and ethnic-nationalist terrorist groups on the other, prevents any meaningful collaboration or joint participation in terrorist attacks in the same country. While there has been some cooperation and sharing of information among the European leftist terrorist groups—in the mid-1980s, the RAF and the French Direct Action announced a formal alliance—even the

"Euroterrorists" found more differences than similarities among themselves, since they are primarily creatures of the particular country and culture in which they operate.

Leftist revolutionary terrorists are found in many regions, including the Middle Core Faction (Chukaku-Ha), which is active in Japan, and several groups in Latin America. Some terrorist organizations, such as Sendero Luminoso (Shining Path) in Peru, combine rural guerrilla insurgency campaigns with urban terrorism. But whether they are based in the countryside or urban centers, revolutionary terrorists have a more difficult task in generating public support than do their ethnic-nationalist or religious counterparts. There is no ready-made constituency based on similar religious beliefs or ethnic affiliation. It is not surprising, then, that studies of public attitudes toward terrorist groups have found that ethnic terrorists have more positive images than the revolutionary terrorists.[41]

Ideological terrorism also includes global revolutionary groups, the modern-day equivalent of the nineteenth-century anarchists. The most notable of these is the Japanese Red Army Faction (JRA). Whereas Euroterrorists aimed for revolution within their individual countries, the JRA seeks a worldwide global uprising. They are the hired guns of international terrorism. They were responsible for the Lod Airport massacre in Israel in 1972, which was committed on behalf of the PFLP. Since their goal is worldwide revolution, any terrorist act in any setting may be seen as furthering their objectives. This makes the JRA one of the more dangerous groups around. They have no constituency to worry about, and thus have fewer constraints on the threshold of their violence. Kozo Okamoto, the lone terrorist survivor of the Lod Airport massacre in which twenty-five people were killed and seventy-six injured, many of them Puerto Rican pilgrims, showed no remorse at his trial. "We believe slaughtering of human bodies is inevitable. We know it will become more severe than battles between nations," Okamoto said.[42] Patricia Steinhoff, who interviewed Okamoto in jail in the mid-1970s, paints a picture of Okamoto and by implication the JRA, in which virtually anybody in the world could be seen as the enemy:

> One of the ambiguities of Okamoto's revolutionary conception is that the enemy is not clearly defined. . . . He regards [people] as faceless, inevitable casualties of the revolution. Because he foresees total overthrow of the existing arrangements of society, he does not feel bound in any way by the moral values of the present world. . . . [But] he is not really certain of what society will be like after the revolution has occurred. This uncertainty about what will come after the all-important revolution requires that he suspend judgment about revolutionary

methods. Since his revolution is not being fought in the name of any specific values, there are no constraints on how it may be fought. It is not simply a question of ends justifying means, but a more fundamental vagueness about what are ends and what are means.[43]

This type of thinking explains the propensity for the JRA to be involved in daring plots that only world revolutionaries would think could further their cause. The adventures of JRA operative Yu Kikumura illustrate this. Kikumura entered the United States in March 1988 with a stolen Japanese passport and a visa obtained from the U.S. embassy in Paris. He found an apartment in New York City and began an eleven-state odyssey to purchase materials for three bombs that he planned to build and set off in April at several buildings in New York. The attack was likely to coincide with a suspected JRA bombing of a USO club in Naples on April 14—the second anniversary of the U.S. raid on Libya— that killed five people and injured eighteen. In order to avoid detection, Kikumura bought different elements for his bombs—wires, tape, gas cans, aluminum powder, switches—from department stores, art supply shops, and sporting goods stores.[44] Kikumura was well on his way to finalizing his plans when he was spotted on April 12 by an alert New Jersey state trooper. The officer, Robert Cieplensky, became suspicious when he noticed Kikumura acting nervously at a rest stop on the New Jersey turnpike. As Cieplensky approached Kikumura, the frightened JRA terrorist ran to his car and drove off. When Cieplensky caught up with him and searched his car, he found fire extinguishers that were loaded with gunpowder and lead shot, switches, triggers, wires, flash bulbs, nine-volt batteries, wire cutters, and a hacksaw. He also found a map of New York with three pinholes showing potential targets. These were the U.S. Naval recruiting station in the Veteran's Administration building in lower Manhattan, the United Nations building, and the garment district in Manhattan. Police also suspected that Kikumura intended to attack several New York City college campuses. Kikumura was convicted of illegal possession and interstate transportation of explosives and was sentenced to thirty years in prison.

Right-wing extremist groups provide another source of terrorism based on ideological beliefs. Like their leftist revolutionary counterparts, the right-wing terrorists are not motivated by a desire for a homeland or territory; the right-wing extremists see terrorism as a tool to bring about a repressive government response. But whereas the leftist revolutionaries view the repressive responses by the state as just the first step in a series of events that will ultimately lead to a popular uprising and the emergence of a revolutionary regime, the rightist terrorists see the repressive measures as an end in themselves. The establishment of authoritarian regimes and suppression of minorities and foreign influences are their key objectives.

In Italy, right-wing terrorism was more indiscriminate and violent than that perpetrated by the Red Brigades. While the leftists used selective assassination and high-profile kidnappings, the rightist terrorist groups committed mass casualty attacks, including the 1980 bombing of a Bologna train station, which killed eighty-five people and wounded 181. By killing large numbers of people, right-wing groups such as the New Order and National Vanguard attempted to show that violence and disorder were reigning throughout Italy and that only an authoritarian government could put an end to it. This failed, though, as the Italian government by the early 1980s had broken the back of the Red Brigades and terrorism was on the decline. Although there was a resurgence in bombings during the 1993 political corruption scandals, which authorities believed was committed by right-wing extremists in alliance with the Mafia, right-wing terrorism in Italy never reached the volume of activity that the left had perpetrated.

In one country where it did, the result was chaos and collapse of all authority and order. Turkey in the late 1970s rivaled Beirut for its daily terrorist battles. Right-wing terrorists, known as the "Grey Wolves"; leftist extremist groups such as Dev Yol, Dev Sol, and the Marxist-Leninist Armed Propaganda Union (MLAPU); and Kurdish separatists were all involved in the violence. In 1979 alone, there were 3,831 terrorist incidents. During just a nine-month period in 1980, there were more than eleven thousand terrorist incidents. This degree of violence finally led to a military coup in September of that year. As terrorist scholar Sabri Sayari notes, both the rightists and leftists miscalculated in their strategy. "By provoking an authoritarian response, Turkey's terrorists achieved one of their goals, namely, the dismantling of democracy and the creation of [a] militarized environment," writes Sayari. "However, their expectations that military rule would lead to mass resistance and revolutionary changes, or that it would result in a fascist-type political regime . . . turned out to be costly fantasies. . . . The military takeover led to a harsh crackdown on terrorism. Thousands of suspected terrorists belonging to leftist, rightist, and Kurdish separatist organizations were rounded up during the first months following the coup. By mid-1981, about 20,000 suspected terrorists were in jail awaiting trial."[45]

Right-wing terrorism has been characterized by the notorious death squads that roamed villages and towns in several Latin American countries in the 1980s and by neo-Nazi groups in the United States and Germany. There has also been right-wing terrorism associated with Cuban exiles opposed to the dictatorship of Fidel Castro.

Terrorism based on fervent ideological beliefs is also found among militants in various groups dedicated to specific ecological or environmental issues. The Animal Liberation Front, for example, has waged terrorist campaigns, including firebombing London fur shops, to protest the killing of animals. Animal rights activists were also arrested in Britain in 1991 for plotting to contaminate a popular health drink. The company that makes the drink, SmithKline Beecham, uses animals in its pharmaceutical research.[46] Anti-abortion militants firebombed abortion clinics in the United States in the 1980s, assassinated an abortion clinic doctor in 1993, and attempted to assassinate another doctor that same year. Ecological terrorist groups, such as Earth First, have engaged in violence related to the cutting of trees.

Whether ideological terrorists are motivated by single issues or by the desire for sweeping political and social change, there may be little that can be done to address their grievances. When the demand is the overthrow of democratic regimes or the preservation of authoritarian rule, there can be little room for compromise. But even in the case of animal rights, anti-abortion, and pro-ecology groups, the use of violence by these movements further polarizes the debate and makes each side more intransigent.

State-Sponsored Terrorism

Another cause of terrorism is the pursuit of power and self-interest by some governments. They use terrorist groups to facilitate various foreign-policy objectives. This is known as state-sponsored terrorism, since the governments provide direct or indirect support to the terrorist groups. A derivative of this activity is state-terrorism, in which governments use their own agents to perpetrate the terrorist attacks both at home and abroad. Libyan hit-squads have killed exiled opponents of Muammar Qaddafi in Europe, the Middle East, and the United States; Bulgarian agents, as noted earlier, used umbrellas with poison-tipped pellets to kill one defector in London and almost kill another in Paris in 1978; North Korean intelligence agents planted a bomb aboard a South Korean airliner in 1987 that exploded in flight, killing 115 people; an Iranian government official is suspected of the assassination of former Iranian Prime Minister Shahpur Bakhtiar in Paris in 1991; and two Libyan intelligence agents are wanted in the United States for the blowing up of Pan Am 103.

When terrorist groups are given assistance by a government, they enjoy benefits that their more independent counterparts have to work hard to obtain. These include financial, technical, and logistical support for various operations. State-sponsored groups gain instant access to money, sophisticated weapons, training, false passports, safe passage, and protection both before and after their attacks. They also have a basis, if necessary, to convince themselves or others that what they are doing is not "terrorism," since their actions are being sanctioned by a government.

States that provide assistance to terrorists never admit to it. Unlike some terrorist groups that claim responsibility after a bombing or assassination, state-sponsors "do not need to leave their signature on the crime." As terrorism expert Paul Wilkinson observes, "they do not resort to international terrorism to become known to the world. Their generalized public threats are enough. The real purposes of state-sponsored international terrorism are somewhat different: the hunting-down of exiled opponents and dissidents, the waging of surrogate war against an adversary state, and the export of revolution by means of supporting client terrorist groups abroad."[47]

In the murky world of international terrorism, state-sponsors ironically provide a welcomed target for governments dedicated to combating the terrorist threat. If terrorism only consisted of independent groups that struck at will and then disappeared, there would be little that governments could do to combat it. Independent terrorist groups consisting of less than twenty people are hardly affected by the policies of superpowers or international organizations. But when a foreign government is linked to a terrorist incident or to terrorist groups, then a full repertoire of responses—diplomatic, economic, legal, and military—can be initiated.

That is why the major efforts to combat international terrorism are directed at state-sponsors, even though in 1990, for example, they accounted for less than 12 percent of all international terrorist activity.[48] The United States maintains an official list of state-sponsors, as mandated by the Export Administration Act of 1979. That law and subsequent statutes "impose trade and other restrictions on countries determined by the Secretary of State to have repeatedly provided support for acts of international terrorism."[49] The list is continually updated and sent to Congress, with countries added or deleted as seems warranted. Sudan was added to the list in the summer of 1993 for its support of Islamic and Palestinian terrorist groups.

But the absence or presence of various countries on the list has proven embarrassing at times to the United States. When Iraq took thousands of Americans and other foreigners hostage in both Kuwait and Iraq in the summer of 1990, thereby committing the largest hostage-taking incident ever in history, Saddam Hussein's government was not on the list. It had been taken off years earlier after apparently ceasing its support for the Abu Nidal group. Yet even before the invasion of Kuwait, several international terrorist groups, including the Arab Liberation Front and the Palestine Liberation Front headed by Abu Abbas, were being supported by Baghdad. And the Abu Nidal organization had reestablished a base in Iraq, as did Abu Ibrahim, leader of the terrorist group 15 May. Iraq was quickly put back on the official list in September 1990.[50]

The United States has also found itself utilizing the services of Syria and Iran, two countries designated as state-sponsors of terrorism, to help resolve hostage crises. The Reagan administration enlisted the help of Syria to gain the release of the TWA hostages in Beirut in 1985 and of Iran during the ill-fated arms-for-hostages deal. The Bush administration sought both Syrian and Iranian assistance during the 1989 hostage crisis in Lebanon following the Israeli kidnapping of Sheikh Abdel Karim Obeid, and during the successful effort to win the release of all remaining American hostages in Lebanon at the end of 1991. The pivotal role of Syria and Iran in the geopolitics of the region—and particularly of Syria regarding a Middle East peace settlement—ensures that the United States will not hesitate to interact with state sponsors of terrorism when necessary. "There is no automatic [rule] that says once you are on the list we cannot have contact with you," said L. Paul Bremer, the U.S. ambassador-at-large for counterterrorism during the Reagan administration.[51] "I am a person who believes that we should have diplomatic relations with everybody," adds former Secretary of State George Shultz.[52]

Governments can provide support for terrorist groups in several different ways. At the lowest level is the passive acceptance of international terrorist groups within one's borders. Higher up the ladder of state involvement in terrorism is the active and willing provision of a home base for various terrorist groups. In addition to Iraq, both Syria and Libya have allowed Palestinian terrorist groups to set up headquarters on their territory. Several Palestinian extremist organizations, including the Popular Front for the Liberation of Palestine–General Command (PFLP-GC), have headquarters in Damascus. President Hafez Assad of Syria also gives sanctuary to non-Palestinian terrorist groups such as the JRA, the Armenian Secret Army for the Liberation of Armenia (ASALA), and the Kurdish Worker's Party (PKK). Some of these groups have bases in Syrian-controlled areas of Lebanon. Libya is the home base of operations for the Abu Nidal organization and elements of the Palestine Liberation Front (PLF), while Iran provides sanctuary to Islamic extremist groups from Lebanon.[53]

State support for terrorism also includes supplying terrorist groups with weapons, financial and logistical support, and training. In the past, the Soviet Union trained Palestinians and Third World revolutionary groups in terrorist tactics, while Cuba sponsored urban terrorist groups throughout Latin America in the late 1960s and 1970s. Syria, Iran, Iraq, and Libya continue today to provide training and support to various groups that utilize terrorist tactics. Muammar Qaddafi's regime has given training to both Palestinian and non-Palestinian groups, including the PFLP-GC, the JRA, the leftist Chilean group Manuel Rodriguez Patriotic Front (FPMR), and ASALA. The larger terrorist organizations also provide assistance themselves to other groups. In the 1960s and 1970s, Yasir Arafat's Al-Fatah group trained terrorist organizations from Europe, Asia, Africa, and the Middle East.[54]

The highest level of state-sponsorship of terrorism occurs when governments help plan the terrorists' operations. Libya has been directly involved in many terrorist operations, including the 1986 bombing of a West Berlin discotheque and the 1989 midair bombing of a French UTA plane over Niger that killed all 171 people on board. Qaddafi's government also helped plan the 1990 failed seaborne attack on Israel, in which four terrorists were killed and twelve captured.[55]

But while the Libyans have been the most visible of the state-sponsors, other governments have carried out terrorist operations more quietly than Qaddafi. Although never indicted, the Iranians are believed responsible for the bombing of the U.S. embassy and Marine barracks in Lebanon by pro-Iranian Islamic extremists. Tehran also had extensive links with the various groups that took foreign hostages in Lebanon in the 1980s. Syrian intelligence officials were involved in the failed attempt to blow up an Israeli El Al plane in Britain in 1986, and both Syria and Iran, along with Libya, are strongly believed to have been involved in the Pan Am 103 bombing. Iraqi intelligence planned the attempted assassination of George Bush in Kuwait in 1993.

When governments are directly involved in planning terrorist operations, they elevate terrorism into a new form of conflict among nation states. "Terrorists offer a possible alternative to open, interstate armed conflict," writes international terrorism expert Brian Jenkins. "Modern conventional war is increasingly impractical—it is destructive, it is expensive, and it is dangerous. World, and sometimes domestic, opinion imposes constraints. Some nations that are unable to mount a conventional military challenge see terrorism as the only alternative: an 'equalizer.'"[56] Governments have frequently accused other states of supporting terrorist operations against them. The continual violence in the northern Indian provinces of Punjab and Kashmir, which have seen thousands of deaths in recent years, led Prime Minister P. V. Narasimha Rao to accuse Pakistan in 1992 of "waging a proxy war" in both provinces and of "sponsored terrorism being carried on from across the border."[57]

The irony of state-sponsored terrorism, however, is that while it can be a most powerful form of terrorism—given the resources and expertise that governments have at their disposal—it can also be the most vulnerable to shifts in the international political arena. Whereas many terrorist groups can survive developments in world affairs, the states that sponsor terrorist groups are more affected by the world around them. Governments cease to sponsor terrorism when it no longer serves their interests, or when the risks of being caught outweigh any potential benefits. There are likely to be further additions and deletions to the State Department's list of state-sponsors of terrorism in the years ahead.

Drug-related Terrorism

By the early 1980s, a new term was introduced into the lexicon of terrorism: "narcoterrorism." This referred to the mixing of terrorist tactics and drug trafficking in Latin America, Asia, and the Middle East—the main regions where illicit drugs such as cocaine and heroin are cultivated and transported. A natural alliance evolved among terrorists and drug barons in these regions. Each had something the other wanted. "The combination of the terrorists and the drug-traffickers is a very tough thing, because the drug-traffickers have such immense sums of money and the terrorists provide them with the muscle. It's quite a combination," said George Shultz.[58] The terrorists indeed had the skills in intimidation, killing, and provoking fear in government and judicial officials trying to end the drug trade, while the drug lords had that precious commodity—money.

Drug barons can also use their own people to commit terrorist attacks. Their virtually unlimited financial resources allow them to purchase on the black market sophisticated weapons and technical apparatus, thereby forming their own private militias. Narcoterrorism is thus a special brand of terrorism, since although the tactics are similar to traditional terrorism—threats, assassinations, bombings, kidnappings—the motivations and resources are different. There are no ideological or nationalist goals, nor are there ethnic-religious or separatist causes for the violence. Rather, it is the pursuit of money and power that drives the drug lords to attack all who try to stop them. Since they do not have any political constituency to worry about, they see no limits to their violence.

One of the most spectacular terrorist incidents in Colombia's history was perpetrated by M-19 guerrillas working on behalf of drug traffickers. In November 1985, the leftist insurgents seized the Palace of Justice in Bogota, taking scores of hostages, including twelve Supreme Court justices. The operation was intended to intimidate the Colombian judiciary against extraditing drug traffickers to the United States. As government troops launched a rescue effort, M-19 killed all the justices. More than one hundred people died during the counterterrorist attack. It has been estimated that between 1982 and 1990, the Colombian drug cartels killed over one thousand public officials.[59] Their wave of terror worked and there were no extraditions of drug lords to the United States.[60]

But narcoterrorists can sometimes miscalculate the effects of their violence. The assassination in August 1989 of a leading Colombian presidential candidate, who advocated a tough stand against the drug lords, was intended to intimidate the government. Instead, it led the public to support government efforts to fight the Medellin drug cartel. It also resulted in a $65 million U.S. military aid package to Bogota for its counternarcotics policies.

However, each time drug lords are captured, extradited, or killed, new or rival ones can come along to take their place. This is likely to occur in Colombia following the December 1993 killing of Medellin drug kingpin Pablo Escobar by Colombian police. For example, during the year following the crackdown on the Medellin drug lords in mid-1989, the rival Cali cartel's share of the drug market rose from 30 percent to 75 percent.[61] Policies that are aimed at eradicating coca crops in the Andean countries—Colombia, Peru, and Bolivia—usually fail since new crops are planted as fast as the old ones are wiped out. Furthermore, since the economies of these countries are intertwined with the drug trade—it creates thousands of jobs and profits for the peasants who grow the illicit crops—there is a reluctance by the governments to completely end the illegal activity. "A swift and effective blow to the coca economy would have a devastating economic and political impact," observed one group of experts on the Andean drug trade. "The livelihoods of hundreds of thousands of citizens would be threatened, triggering massive social unrest."[62] The police and military in these countries are also "no match for narco-trafficking organizations operating transnationally and backed by private armies, advanced weaponry, and highly sophisticated intelligence systems. Security forces in the region are further hamstrung by operational inefficiency and ineffectiveness."[63]

The huge profits that can be made from narcotics trafficking has led some terrorist groups to enter into the illegal practice themselves. Lebanon is a processing center and distribution point for heroin and marijuana that is grown in Asia, leading several Middle Eastern terrorist groups, including the PLO and Hizballah, to find instant profits by selling and transporting the drugs. The Bekaa Valley in Lebanon also contains many acres of land devoted to growing hashish.[64] The incentive for various terrorist groups, either working alone or in conjunction with the drug lords, to engage in drug trafficking, and the motivation for the drug cartels to stay in business, will remain high as long as there is a huge demand for drugs and large profits to be made in countries such as the United States. George Shultz, who helped lead the war on terrorism in the Reagan administration, has more doubts about the effectiveness of the war on drugs. "As long as we create a market in the United States— it's a large market and an extremely profitable one—it will draw suppliers. And what can't be supplied from within the United States will get supplied somehow from outside the United States. And it moves from one place to another. It's very hard to contest it. So the problem is here. To start with anyway. I don't mean that we shouldn't be fighting the good fight. But I don't think you can expect to win the war on drugs by making it impossible for drugs to get into the United States from abroad. We just haven't been able to do it. Look at the record."[65]

The record shows that as of 1988 the narcotics trade, including heroin, was yielding more than $100 billion a year in the United States, $35 billion in Italy, and an additional $300 billion around the world.[66] The Drug Enforcement Administration estimated that cocaine production in Latin America rose from approximately 397 tons in 1988 to 990 tons in 1990.[67] A 1992 United Nations report stated that Colombian drug trafficking was continuing unabated, while DEA officials noted that the Colombian drug lords were expanding into heroin shipments. One kilogram of heroin is estimated to sell for as much as $200,000 in New York, where half of the estimated 750,000 American heroin addicts are believed to live. In 1991, the DEA seized 1,085 kilograms of heroin in the United States, while the previous year 637 kilos were seized.[68] But without progress in drug education and treatment for addicts, there is little likelihood that interdicting drugs at the border, launching wars on drug traffickers around the world, or trying to eradicate the crops that become the illicit drugs will have much impact upon the demand for drugs and the profit and terrorism associated with drug trafficking.

Criminal Terrorism

The quest for money, revenge, and adventure can also drive individual criminals to perpetrate terrorist attacks. When there are no political motives or organizations behind a bombing, extortion plot, kidnapping, or other violent act, it tends to be dismissed as a "non-terrorist" event.[69] There seems to be something comforting in knowing that an act of violence may only be the work of common criminals. This means that the public and government are not under attack by organized terrorists. Yet throughout history, criminals have been among the most innovative in terrorist tactics, introducing new forms of violence, with the more established political terrorists eventually following suit. Criminal terrorists can also at times evoke public and government reactions that match, and even exceed, those elicited by political terrorists.

As noted earlier, the first midair bombings of aircraft were the work of criminals. These early incidents still shocked the publics and governments of their respective countries. The fact that relatively new technology, such as the airplane, was being used by criminals to kill large numbers of innocent people—people who were not the intended target—was quite unsettling. Modern-day terrorists would perfect the art of generating fear in audiences far beyond their specific targets; the early criminal terrorists unintentionally achieved that effect.

The same was true for the first wave of hijackings in the United States. Some of the hijackers who demanded that the planes be flown to Cuba in 1961 were individual political dissidents, but others were either mentally unstable or, in one case, an ex-convict. None of the hijackers were part of any organized political group. This would come several years later when the Palestinians used hijackings to publicize their cause to the world. But the early hijackings had the same effect on the American public and politicians that later hijackings would have. They generated anger, fear, and demands that something be done to end the air piracy.

Criminals—and mentally unstable people—have also been active in product contamination. The most famous case for the United States was the Tylenol poisoning in 1982. Several people died after taking Tylenol capsules laced with cyanide. Although nobody was ever caught and no demands ever made, police suspected that it was the work of a mentally ill person. The publicity surrounding the incident led to copycat episodes throughout the country, with extortionists trying to blackmail a variety of companies with similar types of threats. Pharmaceutical firms had to introduce new forms of packaging for their products to alert consumers to potential tampering. In Japan, a group known as "The Man With 21 Faces" demanded large sums of money from private Japanese companies after placing cyanide-laced candy and food in several stores.[70]

Although the majority of product contamination incidents have been the work of criminal terrorists seeking monetary gain, political and ethnic-nationalist terrorists have also used this tactic for their own purposes. Tamil guerrillas in 1986 notified several Western embassies that they had put potassium cyanide in exported Sri Lankan tea. After extensive testing by the U.S. Food and Drug Administration, no poison was reportedly found. But in 1989, minute traces of cyanide were discovered in Chilean grapes by U.S. inspectors after a threat was received by the U.S. embassy in Santiago. All Chilean fruit in the United States was subsequently quarantined and recalled, severely damaging the Chilean economy. Leftist terrorists were suspected of this incident. And Palestinian terrorists have used the tactic of placing mercury in Israeli oranges in an effort to damage the Israeli economy.[71]

The line between the criminal terrorist and the political terrorist is often a fine one. This is due to the tendency for "criminals and psychopaths [to] sometimes clothe themselves in political slogans of justification, and by the well-known propensity of terrorist movements to recruit assistance from, and to collaborate with, the criminal underworld."[72] The case of "Commander Nemo" and a multi-million-dollar extortion plot in Cyprus illustrates how a criminal terrorist tried to fool authorities into believing he was a political terrorist. In March 1987, a thirteen-page letter was sent to the president of Cyprus, Spiros Kiprianou, signed by a man calling himself "Commander Nemo of Force Majerus." He threatened to disperse dioxin, a toxic chemical, over the Troodos mountains south of Nicosia unless he was paid $15 million. Commander Nemo claimed that the dioxin would be released by radio-controlled devices that were already in place and would be carried by wind over populated areas. Since the letter was in fluent English, Cypriot officials suspected it originated in London. (Cyprus gained independence from Britain in 1960.) The Cyprus chief of police, Frixos Yangou, went to London to collaborate with Scotland Yard. Due to the potential for panic among the Cypriot public, the entire matter was kept secret until British police arrested four people in London in May.[73]

The first task for the Cypriot and British authorities was to determine if the threat was credible. The blackmail letter was extremely detailed, including scientific data on the ingredients Commander Nemo claimed he used to make the dioxin. In order to convince the authorities that the dioxin would be carried by wind from the mountains to populated areas, he invited them to try an experiment. He told them to burn a large number of tires and watch as the black smoke drifted across populated areas. He warned them that a dioxin attack would be a thousand times worse. He cited the disaster at Seveso, Italy, where an explosion at a chemical factory in 1976 caused dioxin to escape. Several people near the plant suffered burns and sores on their skin, and large numbers of people complained of nervousness, fatigue, and loss of appetite. Many animals were killed, and Italian authorities were forced to slaughter more than eighty thousand domestic animals as a protective measure.[74] Commander Nemo also mentioned the explosion at a chemical factory in Bhopal, India, and the nuclear reactor disaster at Chernobyl in the former Soviet Union, and warned that his attack would be much worse since Cyprus is a small island.

The extortionist played on the history and economy of Cyprus to make his threat seem credible. The northern part of the island was invaded by Turkish troops in 1974 following a Greek right-wing coup, and the island has remained divided since that time. Commander Nemo claimed that each Greek Cypriot would have gladly paid some money to prevent the Turkish invasion, and since what he was planning to do was much worse, the government should simply pay him the $15 million. He also pointed out that the economy of Cyprus is dependent on agriculture and therefore could not afford the damage that would be caused by the release of the dioxin. He further argued that Cyprus would not have the medical facilities and resources to deal with the human casualties of a dioxin attack.

British scientists analyzed the blackmail letter and concluded that Commander Nemo could not make dioxin from the ingredients he listed. However, the letter was couched in enough scientific jargon that the scientists had to spend some time analyzing its contents before dismissing the threat. Commander Nemo continued to contact the Cyprus government and was finally apprehended by Scotland Yard detectives when he went to the Cyprus High Commission office in London, posing as the "scientific adviser" to Commander Nemo, to collect a passport and some money.[75]

The extortionist turned out to be a thirty-six-year-old British citizen of Cypriot origin, Panos Koupparis. Also arrested in London were his wife, who worked for the British High Commission, and two brothers, one of whom was a chemistry student at London's Polytechnic Institute. Koupparis's sister-in-law was arrested in Cyprus, but ordered released by a judge for lack of evidence. Police stated that they found documents and weapons in Koupparis's Cyprus apartment—he had an offshore company in Cyprus—which indicated he had planned a series of bombings on the island to convince the government that his dioxin threat was real.[76]

After the arrests, Scotland Yard issued a statement that although the dioxin plot was not the most practical method for causing widespread harm, it was still a viable threat. They pointed out though, that the extortionists did not have the means to carry out their threat.[77]

The aftermath of the Commander Nemo affair had Cyprus reeling. The public reaction was one of "fear, concern, and disbelief." One independent newspaper worried that the four people arrested were just part of a "criminal general staff of men of science." The government was criticized by some opposition parties for keeping the whole affair secret when lives were potentially at stake, while others criticized them for taking the hoax too seriously. One opposition newspaper called the episode a "fiasco," claiming the government was exploiting the situation for its own purposes and that the threat was "devoid of any seriousness." The ruling Democratic party newspaper defended the government's handling of the case, claiming that the extortionists had "planned the crime of the century." The Cyprus government spokesman said that "the content of the threat and the nature of the blackmail were such that it would be [an] act of lack of responsibility for the Government and the police to underestimate the affair, the more so that first assessments by British experts spoke of a realisable threat if the blackmailers had the necessary means." The government and police also stated that steps had been taken to protect lives in case the threat were real.[78]

The Commander Nemo incident was a very clever scheme by an individual criminal with psychological problems. Koupparis was under the care of two psychiatrists.[79] But he was clever enough to hatch a plan that caused two governments to consult in secrecy, brought in top-level scientists to assess the threat, and led to a mini-crisis for the Cyprus government in explaining their handling of the affair. Had the scientific data been more credible, and the terrorist's intentions more believable, the crisis would have been much worse for the government. Public revelations by Commander Nemo before he was caught, either through communications with newspapers or television stations, might well have caused great alarm and panic in Cyprus.

The history of criminal terrorism points to some very innovative tactics—midair bombings, product contamination, extortion threats—by individuals with limited resources. For the criminal terrorist, unlike the political, religious, or ethnic-nationalist terrorist, there are no group decision-making mechanisms to deal with, no theories or ideologies to worry about, and no constituency to be concerned with in terms of possible negative backlash to an incident. All that is needed is a "good" idea and the willingness to follow through.

But while some criminal terrorists are psychologically disturbed, others are not. They are just cold-blooded murderers or extortionists driven by the lure of money. What, though, can be said about the psychological makeup of political terrorists? Is there something in the personality of certain individuals that drives them to join terrorist groups and commit violent acts?

Psychological Explanations for Terrorism

One of the most enduring myths about terrorism is that it is perpetrated by irrational and psychopathic individuals. This is a logical conclusion for people to reach when they see on television or read about planes blown up in midair, suicide attacks on buildings, and a host of other seemingly senseless violent acts. Some public officials, as noted earlier, foster this myth with statements about terrorism being the work of barbarians, madmen, and sick individuals. But the terrorist who kills for his cause sees himself as no different than the soldier who kills for his country or the guerrilla or "freedom fighter" who kills for his group. All believe they are on the just and moral side of a conflict.

Among the more extreme psychological theories on terrorism is that terrorists "suffer from faulty vestibular functions in the middle ear or from inconsistent mothering resulting in dysphoria."[80] Another view is that while "terrorists do not fit into a specific psychiatric diagnostic category . . . individuals with particular personality dispositions are drawn to the path of terrorism."[81] According to Jerrold Post, a psychiatrist who worked for the U.S. government and has written extensively on the psychology of terrorism, terrorists rely on "externalization" and "splitting," which are "psychological mechanisms found in individuals with narcissistic and borderline personality disturbances." The individual "idealizes his grandiose self and *splits out* and *projects* onto others all the hated and devalued weakness within." Post points out that not all terrorists suffer from these personality disorders, but that "it is my distinct impression, however, that these mechanisms are found with extremely high frequency in the population of terrorists, and contribute significantly to the uniformity of terrorists' rhetorical style and their special psycho-logic."[82]

The main problem, though, with psychological explanations for terrorist behavior is that they obscure the ethnic-nationalist, political-ideological, religious, and other reasons that motivate the vast majority of terrorists into action. Whether or not a terrorist group has a few or even a large number of members with personality disorders is irrelevant to the course of terrorism. There will always be enough "normal" individuals in a terrorist group to carry out various attacks even if all the psychologically troubled members were weeded out or never joined in the first place. And it is not clear whether those terrorists who have abnormal personality characteristics would be any different in terms of their desire to join a terrorist group even if they were "cured." Their commitment to a particular cause could very well attract them to a life of violence anyway.

The difficulty in gaining access to individual terrorists for clinical research purposes has made the field of terrorism and psychology extremely speculative. The studies that have been conducted point more toward normality than to psychological problems. "What limited data we have on individual terrorists suggest that the outstanding common characteristic is normality," writes terrorism analyst Martha Crenshaw.[83] A psychiatrist who examined four German Red Army Faction members before their trial found that they showed "no particular personality type" and did not suffer from any psychosis or neurosis.[84] Franco Ferracuti, an Italian psychiatrist who worked for his government in combating terrorism, conducted several studies of left-wing terrorists in Italy and found that they "rarely suffer from serious personality abnormalities."[85] Furthermore, terrorist groups tend to reject potential recruits who seem more interested in danger and adventure than in a commitment to the "cause." Such members could easily place the entire group in jeopardy through their reckless behavior.[86]

Even if a terrorist personality could be identified, it would likely vary among countries and causes. The terrorist in a religious movement in the Middle East would likely have a different personality makeup than the terrorist in a leftist urban movement in Latin America, and still different personality than an ethnic-nationalist terrorist in Africa. "The paths to a life of terrorism appear to be quite different in different societies and different types of groups," notes psychiatrist Walter Reich.[87] There may very well be similar types of "mindsets" among different terrorist groups, in which perceptions of morality, violence, and so forth are similar, but that is more a belief in the ends justifying the means than in a particular psychological disposition.

Where psychology is most helpful in understanding terrorist behavior is in group dynamics. Terrorists live a life in the underground, dependent on each other and sympathizers for support and nurturing. The "us-them" dichotomy becomes paramount in the thinking of terrorists. As psychiatrist Post notes, "terrorists have a tendency to submerge their own identities into the group, so that a kind of 'group mind' emerges. The group cohesion that emerges is magnified by the external danger, which tends to reduce internal divisiveness in unity against the outside enemy."[88] Former German terrorist Michael Baumann writes in his autobiography that "the greater the pressure from the outside, the more you stick together. . . ."[89] An individual terrorist may also use the group to avoid any personal sense of guilt or responsibility for various murderous activities. If the killings are the result of a collective group decision, then the terrorist feels no shame. Once the group identity is removed, though, the terrorist is faced with his own individuality and the crimes he committed.[90] This may explain, in part, why some terrorists never leave a group and why some groups continue to exist even as the world around them goes through dramatic changes.

The psychological dynamics of a terrorist group can also be effective in pressuring reluctant members to participate in various operations. Former German RAF terrorist Peter-Jurgen Boock describes the psychological pressure that was put on fellow member Susan Albrecht to take part in an RAF plan to kidnap Dresdner Bank chairman Jurgen Ponto in 1977. The RAF wanted to exploit Albrecht's personal relationship with the Ponto family—Jurgen Ponto was her godfather—to gain access to the Ponto house. The kidnapping was to be used to demand the release of RAF members in prison. Albrecht initially refused because of her emotional involvement with Ponto. "Exactly because she based her refusal on emotional grounds, the group accused her of having no political identity and of not seriously wanting the liberation of the comrades in Stammheim [prison]," said Boock. "They put enormous pressure on her." When a reporter asked Boock why Albrecht could not have said "that for such a [emotional] price she would not do it," Boock emphasized the psychological hold that a terrorist group has on its members:

> It's easy for an outsider to say that. In the situation of group pressure it's quite a different matter. All sorts of fears play a role in that. After all, it was a small group, isolated and without outside contacts, there was no longer any normal human context. It takes more than courage to stand up against that. The pressure was applied over several days. Sometimes it seemed like brainwashing. People took turns challenging one person who was emotionally totally overwrought. In the end, her giving in was actually a breakdown.[91]

Albrecht took part in the kidnapping with two other RAF members. The plan went awry at the Ponto house when one RAF terrorist killed Ponto. In the aftermath of the murder, a distraught Albrecht finally broke down. ". . . [A]fter the horrible result of the operation, she was incapable of doing anything," said Boock. "For days on end, she was shaken by incessant crying spells. She had no strength left. . . . She had broken down completely and should, under normal circumstances, have been hospitalized."[92] Since Albrecht felt she could no longer participate in terrorist operations after the Ponto murder, the RAF arranged for her transfer to East Germany. She assumed a new name, Ingrid Jaeger, and married an East German physicist and had a child. They lived for two years in the Soviet Union but maintained a residence in East Berlin. Albrecht was finally arrested in East Berlin in June 1990, following the collapse of the Communist government.[93]

In addition to using psychological pressure on their own members, terrorist groups also employ psychological warfare on publics and governments when they threaten or carry out terrorist attacks. Each terrorist incident leaves the impression that anybody could be the next victim. A plane is blown up in midair and an entire airplane industry feels the effect as the public becomes afraid to fly. A fellow citizen is kidnapped and the terrorists play on human emotions by keeping their captive for weeks, months, or years on end, sometimes mixing promises of freedom with threats of death. A product contamination threat is received and the product is taken off shelves nationwide. Terrorists are quite skilled at using psychological techniques, often conveyed through the mass media, to compensate for their disadvantaged position against much larger and stronger adversaries.

One of the most prevalent psychological theories concerning victims of terrorism is the so-called "Stockholm syndrome." Its premise is that some hostages tend to identify with their captors, form positive emotional bonds with them, and view their own government or the police in hostile ways. This is supposedly a coping mechanism to deal with the trauma of the ordeal and the fact that they are now totally dependent on their captors for their survival.

The theory derives from a bank robbery in Stockholm, Sweden, in September 1973. An escaped convict seized several hostages after police responded to a silent alarm while the robbery was in progress. The robber demanded more than $700,000, the release of a fellow prisoner, and a getaway car. The police complied with all these demands and the released prisoner soon joined his comrade at the bank. But when the two insisted that they be allowed to take some of the hostages with them to ensure their escape, the police refused. The gunmen retreated into the bank vault with three female hostages and one male hostage as the drama was covered live by Swedish television. At one point in the six-day siege, the bank robber and one of the hostages spoke by telephone with Swedish Prime Minister Olof Palme, who also refused the criminals' demands.[94]

Various countermeasures were attempted by the police, including withholding food to force their surrender, seeking opportunities to shoot the gunmen, drilling holes in the bank vault ceiling and threatening to pump tear gas into the vault, and trying to trick the gunmen into drinking beer that was spiked with sleep-inducing chemicals. The hostages came to view their captors as their protectors, fearing that a police rescue attempt might result in their deaths. Throughout the siege, the hostages expressed anger with the police for not acquiescing to the criminals' demands. Even though they were subjected to threats on their own lives by the gunmen, including having wire nooses placed around their necks and explosives at their feet, the hostages formed positive feelings about their captors. The two gunmen "often consoled their captives when they were distraught, comforted them when they were physically miserable, and personalized themselves by empathetic self-disclosures of their own human longings and feelings."[95]

The episode ended when the gunmen surrendered after police finally decided to pump the tear gas into the vault, forcing the gunmen to open the vault door. But when the authorities ordered the hostages to come out first, the captives refused, shouting to police that they feared the lawmen would simply shoot the criminals once they were gone. They all came out together, with the hostages essentially providing a shield for the gunmen before they were arrested. The hostages and the criminals embraced each other, and it was later revealed that one of the female hostages had held hands during the siege with the prison friend of the bank robber. "Perhaps it sounds a little like a cliché, but [he] gave me tenderness," she said. "Yes, we held hands, but there was no sex. It made me feel enormously secure. It was what I needed."[96] Police, however, found traces of semen on the bank vault carpet and the twenty-one-year-old hostage admitted to allowing the criminal to caress her body.[97] She later married him while he was in prison.[98] Meanwhile, the male hostage said that he had gained a better understanding of the hardships of prison life through conversations he had with his captors. He stated that he had little interest in any type of social issue before the bank siege, but was now thinking about the condition of prisoners in general.[99]

Since the Swedish bank incident, any time political hostages fail to criticize their captors or express an understanding of their cause, they are accused of falling prey to the "Stockholm syndrome." President Reagan thought this is what happened to Beirut hostage Father Jenco. ". . . I was surprised at his reluctance to condemn his captors," writes Reagan. "I almost sensed he felt sympathy for the Muslims who had held him captive for nineteen months. He didn't seem to want to criticize them and had no apparent bitterness, making me wonder if it was an example of the 'Stockholm syndrome.' . . ."[100] Following the 1976 TWA hijacking by Croatian separatists, a newspaper columnist criticized those passengers who had positive things to say about the hijackers. In an article in the *Los Angeles Times* titled "Terrorists Are 'Nice Guys,' Their Victims Say—Why?" Georgie Anne Geyer wrote, "It seems that impressionable people, feeling utterly helpless, look to the people who now hold the power over their lives . . . for salvation. After the initial terror, they turn out to be great folks just because they didn't kill you."[101]

But the Stockholm syndrome has been greatly exaggerated. It implies a weakness in the personality and character of some former hostages simply because they do not come out of their experience seeking revenge against the terrorists. After surviving a terrorist episode, it should not seem unusual that some people would not have any animosity toward their captors, since their lives had been spared and they might have seen a human side to the criminals. Terrorists sometimes explain to the hostages the reasons for their actions and reveal personal aspects of their own lives. For some victims this may very well be the first time they learn about the various issues that motivate the terrorists. For others it may be the first time they have ever seen firsthand the risks that ethnic-nationalist, religious, or political extremists are willing to take for their cause. Therefore, even though they are the victims, they may have no inclination to condemn their captors once it is over.

Father Jenco expressed anger toward his guards at various times during his ordeal. He would scream at them and argue with them. "You don't forget any of this. What you have to do is heal the wounds," he said.[102] But his spiritual calling led him to try to see good sides of his captors. He believed they were products of the war-torn environment of Lebanon and offered to help them once he was freed. "These kids gave up their formal education at the age of ten to . . . arms," said Jenco. "That's all they know is violence. I used to say to them, 'The only gift I can give you is to send you back to school. Come and live with me, I'll send you back to school.' "[103] Another former Beirut hostage, David Jacobsen, feels otherwise. "I'm not going to kiss them on both cheeks and say you're forgiven. . . . I do have anger towards some of them . . . and I want to see those people executed. I'm going to be there when they pull the trap on them," Jacobsen said.[104] But even Jacobsen writes kindly about one of his guards. "Of all of them, only Sayid seemed to have genuine interest in our welfare. Were he suddenly to appear in the United States and ask my help, I might be favorably inclined."[105]

There can also be a tendency for some terrorists to identify or have sympathy for their victims. The guards holding Father Jenco and David Jacobsen asked for their forgiveness when they were released. During the 1976 TWA hijacking, Juliene Busic felt an emotional attachment to her hostages. "I felt like I was experiencing sort of a reverse Stockholm syndrome," recalled Busic. "It was like I identified with the passengers too to the extent that I believed that we were all on the same side."[106] After she was arrested and was in the airport control tower, she realized she had in her possession her husband Zvonko's address book. She did not want the authorities to discover this, but did not know how to get rid of it. She then saw the released passengers and crew walk by her in the tower:

> And so I go up to the steward—I'm arrested now and he's free—and I said, "Listen, you've got to hide this for me! Because this is Zvonko's address book!" And he looked at me like I was crazy. And I was so upset. Because you know we had gone through all this and we were all one big happy family. And now he wouldn't do that.[107]

Several former TWA hostages visited Julie Busic during her years in federal prison. One passenger even circulated a "Mile Hijack Club Newsletter" to all his fellow hostages calling for an annual reunion at his home where "there will be Croatian folk dancing."[108] The tendency to view terrorism as a grand struggle between good and evil makes it easy to expect that hostages should denounce their former captors. But each hijacking or kidnapping has its own unique characteristics, and the hostages' behavior is not always a product of the psychological dynamics of the captor-hostage relationship. The "Stockholm syndrome" label can become an extra burden placed on people who have already suffered.

The basic causes of terrorism will remain unchanged in the coming years. The pursuit of territory, power, ideology, religion, revenge, and personal greed will continue to motivate individuals, groups, and governments to commit terrorist acts. Some terrorist groups will also seek to exploit conditions of poverty, socioeconomic frustration, and political alienation in various countries in order to win sympathy among the masses.

The dramatic changes in the world, including the demise of the Soviet Union, will not be translated into a reduced threat of international terrorism. If anything, it will likely increase the diversity of terrorism as new terrorist groups emerge in the post–Cold War environment. While Moscow and the former Communist bloc governments provided assistance and training at times to terrorist organizations, the bulk of terrorist activity in the 1980s unfolded outside of an East-West dimension. The terrorism of the Islamic fundamentalists and Palestinian extremists in the Middle East and Europe, the campaign of violence by the IRA in Northern Ireland, and the bombings and assassinations by the drug cartels in Colombia were among the most frequent and violent terrorist incidents in recent years. None of these were directly related to East-West struggles and rivalries.

Even the world revolutionary terrorist groups such as the JRA, which perpetrated their attacks with vague notions about the type of revolutionary world they wanted to create, will not disappear because of the end of the Cold War. Their targets will remain the Western and industrialized nations that they view as the forces of imperialism and aggression. The same will be true for many European leftist revolutionary groups. They began with an anticapitalist platform in the late 1960s, moved to an anti-NATO stance in the early 1980s when public sentiment against nuclear missiles in Europe was strong, and now in the post–Cold War environment have gone back to attacking the symbols of capitalism. They have also not ceased their attacks against military targets. Their worlds still consist of the idealistic goals of overthrowing the capitalist, militaristic establishment. Their mission may take on a heightened sense of importance as some of these groups see themselves now as the last hope for revolution. And since the amount of resources and personnel necessary for some terrorist operations is not large, they should be able to continue to make their presence known.

The history of terrorism has been characterized by escalating cycles of violence. These have combined the prevailing technologies of the time—which influence the weapons that the terrorists use, the tactics that they employ, and the targets that they hit—with the political and social conflicts that may be brewing in any given area of the world. The daggers of the ancient Zealots and the medieval Assassins were small but effective weapons that could be hidden in their clothing as they gained close proximity and surprised their victims. The dagger also meant that their terrorism was limited to selective assassinations. The dynamite of the anarchists and labor militants of the nineteenth and early twentieth centuries escalated terrorism to larger numbers of casualties and facilitated the blowing up of buildings and other structures. And the plastic explosives and sophisticated timing devices of contemporary terrorist groups have allowed the killing of even larger numbers of people through powerful car bombs and midair plane explosions.

Since technology will continue to march forward along with the various conflicts of the world, we can expect another cycle of terrorism in the years ahead. Several trends point to a future terrorist environment that will be unlike any we have yet experienced.

9

Future Trends

Imagine that a book on terrorism was being written thirty years ago. After first discussing the recent terrorist environment—which would have included airplane hijackings to Cuba, midair plane bombings by criminals with dynamite that killed between twenty and forty people, hostage crises in the Congo and Cuba, and political assassinations and bombings in many countries—the author turned her attention to the future. Pointing out that there were several unresolved ethnic-nationalist conflicts around the world—including the Arab-Israeli and the British-Irish disputes—and new conflicts arising from decolonization in the Third World, she argued that terrorism was likely to continue for many years. Then, identifying emerging trends in technology, including the building of bigger and faster airplanes that made air travel more popular, and the manufacture of more powerful and lethal explosives, the author made the following dire forecast: Terrorists were likely to escalate their violence to include international hijackings with hundreds of hostages, midair plane bombings with plastic explosives and sophisticated timing devices that could kill more than three hundred people, suicide truck and car bombings, and barricade-hostage incidents in foreign embassies.

The reaction to such a book would probably have been one of disbelief. Many critics would have dismissed it as being too alarmist or too futuristic. Yet all of those things happened, and what seems today as beyond the capabilities or intentions of terrorists can soon become a reality as technology and politics produces changes in the behavior of individuals, groups, and nations. The next wave of terrorism promises to be even more violent, more technologically advanced, and more innovative than previous periods.

Terrorist Tactics

Terrorists have tended to concentrate on seven basic types of tactics over the years: hijackings, kidnappings, bombings, assassinations, armed assaults (machine gun, rocket, or other violent attacks against people or buildings), barricade-hostage incidents (seizures of embassies or other government or business structures), and product contamination. Some groups have focused on just one or two of these tactics, while others have utilized several of them. The type of tactic a terrorist group chooses will usually depend upon their objectives and their capabilities.

Hijackings, kidnappings, and barricade-hostage incidents are committed when terrorists have specific demands that they believe will be met through violent actions. Hostages are used as bait for the release of comrades in jail, the payment of large ransoms, or the granting of other concessions. Such incidents are also used at times to generate publicity for a cause. These tactics require a certain degree of negotiating skill on the part of the terrorists, since they have to bargain and interact with the authorities. The terrorists also have to be prepared to endure long and tense standoffs with police, government troops, and others as the incident may unfold over days, weeks, or even years.

The risk of capture or death for terrorists is thus higher for these tactics than for most others. The history of terrorism is filled with counterterrorist assaults on hijacked planes or government buildings and embassies where the terrorists—and the hostages—wind up dead. Terrorists who commit hijackings, kidnappings, or embassy/government building seizures also have to be prepared for face-to-face interaction with their victims. This can add to the psychological and stress levels for all involved.

Bombings, assassinations, and armed assaults are more "distant" types of terrorism; the terrorists do not engage in any close personal interaction with their victims. These tactics are chosen when the terrorists want to create a climate of fear in a targeted group or nation through a sustained campaign of violence, retaliate for previous incidents or situations, negatively affect peace processes or other developments they believe are against their interests, or eliminate specific individuals or members of a particular group. Bombings can also be aimed at damaging the infrastructure of a country through blowing up power lines, bridges, government offices, and commercial enterprises.

Bombings have been the most favored terrorist tactic for the past several decades. They have accounted for approximately half of the yearly totals of worldwide terrorist incidents since official statistics were begun in 1968. The reason is that bombs are easy to make or acquire and their use does not often require extensive operational planning. Terrorists with scarce resources can plant dynamite at a facility, set off a remote-controlled explosive device, or use a time-bomb and be safely away from the scene before the authorities arrive. The risk of capture or death by counterterrorist units that is associated with hijackings and kidnappings is thus greatly reduced. Bombings are also attractive to terrorists since they produce immediate effects. The buildings are demolished or damaged, the person or people are killed, the electrical or power systems are blacked out.

Armed assaults and assassinations are also widely used terrorist tactics that usually do not require extensive resources. Armed assaults include both "stand-off" attacks—mortar and rocket fire from a distance in order to overcome existing security at the target—or close-range attacks such as the Abu Nidal massacres at the Rome and Vienna airports. They are also sometimes used to seize weapons from arms depots and police stations or money from banks. Assassination, which is the oldest form of terrorism, going back to the days of the Zealots and Sicariis in the first century and the "Assassins" in the eleventh century, is aimed at the killing of specific individuals. Assassinations can take many different forms, including stabbings, shootings, or bombings of the victims' vehicles while they are in them.

Another tactic used by terrorists is product contamination. Some extremist groups, as discussed earlier, have attempted to damage the export trade of a particular country or simply embarrass a particular government by placing poison or other substances in food or pharmaceutical products. Just the threat of doing so can result in multimillion-dollar losses for businesses as they are forced to remove their products from distribution. This tactic has also been widely used as an extortion device by criminals.

Terrorist tactics can change over time in response to different circumstances. For example, hijackings and embassy seizures were frequent occurrences in the 1970s but subsided in the 1980s as security at airports and at embassies improved. The 1992 annual report on terrorism by the State Department does not even list these tactics in its statistical breakdown of events for that year. According to the State Department, bombings accounted for 57.3 percent of international terrorist incidents for

1992, armed attacks for 14.7 percent, and firebombings (a category that in many other tabulations on terrorism is included with either bombings or armed attacks) for more than 7.5 percent. The State Department also lists sabotage/vandalism as accounting for 8 percent, arson for 5.3 percent, kidnappings for 4.7 percent, and "other" for 2.5 percent.[1]

But statistics on terrorism, as noted earlier, can be extremely misleading. It can mask the tendency for a single, spectacular incident involving any of the terrorist tactics to capture world attention and lead to all types of reactions. Despite the decline in airplane hijackings in the 1980s, one of the most dramatic terrorist episodes of that decade was still the 1985 TWA hijacking in Beirut. Since there can never be perfect security at airports, the potential for terrorists to smuggle weapons on board a plane—or even to use fake weapons as the Croatian separatists did in 1976—will ensure that the world has not seen the last of international hijackings. The same is true for embassy seizures, particularly in a future political environment where many new states have been formed with embassies around the world, making them potential targets for those upset with the revolutionary changes.

Terrorist tactics therefore never really fade away. Some become eclipsed by those that are more frequently committed or widely publicized. But they all remain beneath the surface, only waiting to emerge whenever a group decides to use them. Each of the basic types of terrorist tactics can be expected to continue in the coming years. However, a new generation of terrorists and the proliferation of sophisticated weapons around the world promises to make the future terrorist environment much more ominous.

A New Generation of Terrorists

An important trend affecting the future of terrorism is the coming of age of a new generation of terrorists. There have now been several years, and in some cases several decades, of internal strife in countries around the world. Bosnia, Northern Ireland, Lebanon, Sri Lanka, India, and Peru are just some of the areas where youths have grown up with violence as a natural and normal part of their lives. Having seen numerous car bombings and assassinations and pitched battles between rival forces year-round, many of these youths view violence as the only way to address grievances or retaliate against one's enemies. They are well-schooled in the science of killing and very well may have higher thresholds for the number of casualties or level of violence they are willing to inflict upon their various targets. Despite progress toward peace in some of these conflicts, further radicalization and factionalism is a likely trend as these youths enter into the ranks of the extremist groups. Author-journalist David Lamb captured the essence of the new generation of terrorists in his depiction of Palestinian terrorists:

> If there is a common denominator in the character of the Arab terrorist, it is a sense of hopelessness. He is young, usually poor and has had only a limited education. . . . He feels betrayed—by the West, which created Israel; by the Americans, who support Israel; by the Arabs, who encourage him with words and money but little else. *The world is his enemy. He is less tolerant than his father, just as his children one day will be less tolerant than he. With a gun, he is important. Without one, he is naked.*[2]

Young extremists in other troubled regions also fit the above description. "People don't want words; they want deeds," a twenty-one-year-old Shining Path guerrilla told author-journalist Tina Rosenberg in the late 1980s. "You talk to the masses in simple language, and the simplest and clearest is with bullets and dynamite."[3] The Maoist revolutionary organization, which the U.S. State Department labels one of "the world's most dangerous and ruthless terrorist groups,"[4] has waged a war against the Peruvian government and society since 1980. More than twenty thousand people have died in the conflict, including peasants, government officials, police officers, and guerrillas. The young terrorist spoke about the symbolism of killing people who were much like his father, a policeman who had died in an automobile accident. "To be honest, at first I had a lot of trouble with the idea of killing police," he told Rosenberg. "But now I have been educated, and I understand why it is necessary. They educated me well. I think if my father were alive, he'd approve."[5] The next generation in Peru will probably require even less "education" in the justification of violence against anybody, since they will have lived with it for so long.

For many youths in conflict-ridden areas, there is a desperate need to identify with some type of authority figure who might be able to give their lives some direction and meaning. Unfortunately, the role models often turn out to be the terrorists or guerrillas who are perpetrating much of the violence. "[Abu Nidal] can get all the young people he wants—the young men who have nothing in life and who are willing to sacrifice themselves—because of the strength that they get out of identifying with and working with this powerful figure," observed psychologist Dr. Calvin Frederick about the notorious Palestinian terrorist.[6] Terrorists represent strength to the young people by virtue of the guns and other weapons that they brandish around. They represent authority by means of their commitment to their cause and their rigid beliefs in what they perceive as correct behavior. Identifying with the terrorists or joining their group becomes the logical thing for many of these young people. "In a way you're almost foolish not to become a part of it," said Frederick.[7]

In the villages and cities throughout the world where ethnic-nationalist violence has erupted in the early 1990s, virtually everyone living in the area becomes personally affected—a loved one killed or wounded, a home or business destroyed, a life greatly disrupted. People who may have had little or no prior animosities can become instantaneously radicalized. The high death tolls caused by modern weapons on each side become fuel for those seeking revenge. Long after the fighting ends, the memories still linger. Out of the hundreds of thousands of suffering people will emerge some new terrorists. There might also emerge some new state-sponsors of terrorism from the numerous independent states that are cropping up. "These individual [states] don't have to maintain an army," said former U.S. government official Owen Robinson. "Any mustang state that comes along can gain the eyes of the world through [terrorism] and they can coerce governments into positions that armies did not used to be able to accomplish."[8] The next wave of both state-sponsored and individual terrorism should be intense. "It is going to get worse," said Robinson, "because you got more small states and you have more minority groups within the small states that feel that they have been controlled too strongly in the past by whatever government was in charge. . . . I don't see any way that they can hold down the increase that is coming."[9]

The rank and file of terrorist organizations will continue to be filled with the poor, uneducated, and alienated youths of the Third World and elsewhere. But they will also be joined by other extremists who, reflecting the general trends of a more technologically proficient society, will be sufficiently skilled in the modern technologies of computers, telecommunications equipment, information systems and data bases, and financial networks. This will add a new dimension to terrorist attacks, leading to the inclusion of white-collar or "smart" terrorism to the terrorist repertoire. Terrorists have traditionally avoided sabotaging telecommunications links, computerized financial markets, and international banking networks, since it doesn't have the "big bang" or dramatic effect of more traditional types of terrorist tactics. "Such operations are technically demanding, and they produce no immediate visible effects," terrorism expert Brian Jenkins wrote in the mid-1980s. "There is no drama. No lives hang in the balance. There is no bang, no blood. They do not satisfy the hostility or the publicity hunger of the terrorists."[10]

Jenkins was quite correct in his assessment at that time. For the remainder of the 1980s, terrorists stayed with the proven tactics of bombings, kidnappings, hijackings, and assassinations—increasing the drama each time with more violent or daring attacks. But as the daily life of the public, business community, and government becomes increasingly defined by technological devices and computerized networks in the 1990s, the terrorists will take notice. What once seemed too complicated or not dramatic enough for terrorists to waste time on will become more appealing as they acquire the necessary technical skills.

The global village will provide terrorists with new avenues for disrupting society and governments. There have already been incidents perpetrated by computer hackers where "viruses"—program codes sometimes consisting of just a single line that can sabotage entire data bases and networks—have been introduced by individuals with mischievous aims. Terrorists will likely follow suit as opportunities arise for targeting capitalist and military information systems. A computer virus can also be designed like a time bomb, programmed to lie in wait until a specific date and then begin its destructive work.

Proliferation of High-Tech Weapons

A disturbing trend for the future of terrorism is the proliferation of sophisticated weapons in the Third World—a trend for which both the United States and the former Soviet Union share the blame. This will make the terrorists' task of acquiring and using such weapons much easier. The previous decade witnessed a steady growth in the selling and supplying of deadly weapons, including Stinger shoulder-fired antiaircraft missiles, Semtex plastic explosives, remote-propelled grenades, and other light, small, and portable weapons to various guerrilla armies and government troops. It was not only the superpowers that were involved in transferring these weapons. China, India, and other nations became active players in the Third World arms market of the 1980s, as did a number of private individuals.

While some of the guerrilla wars and regional conflicts that spurred the conventional arms race during the Cold War have ended, the legacy will be there well into the next century as these weapons fall into terrorists' hands. "These 'anti' weapons have now been built by the thousands in the case of antiship missiles, tens of thousands in the case of shoulder-fired antiaircraft missiles, and hundreds of thousands in the case of antitank missiles," write the former director of the Arms Control and Disarmament Agency, Kenneth Adelman, and military analyst Norman Augustine. "All represent major threats under many circumstances—with the latter two classes of weapons being readily carried by a single individual, thereby making them suitable weapons even for terrorists."[11]

The prospect, then, of terrorists firing Stinger missiles at airplanes or antitank missiles at various ground targets in the 1990s cannot be dismissed. High-tech weapons in the hands of terrorists will make many existing security measures at airports, embassies, and other places obsolete. All a terrorist would need to do is hide by the runway of an airport and fire at the plane as it takes off or lands. "Counter measures are possible but would not be perfect," Adelman and Augustine note. "The impact on world commerce would be disconcerting, if not devastating."[12] Adding to the potential for terrorists to obtain these types of weapons is the disbanding of former Soviet-bloc and Soviet military units in the wake of the collapse of communism. This has led to a growing black market in sophisticated military weapons.[13] All an extremist group might need is sufficient cash to buy whatever type of weapon they desire.

The aftermath of the 1991 Gulf War also contributed to a new surge in arms sales and transfers in the Middle East and elsewhere. Part of this was due to the jockeying for position in new regional balances of power following the defeat of Iraq. But another factor spurring the arms sales was that the United States demonstrated the effectiveness of high-tech weaponry in winning the war. Many governments were eager to follow suit by acquiring some of these tools of modern warfare. Immediately after the war, arms salesmen from the United States, Britain, France, Germany, and other nations descended on the Middle East.[14] There was also a report that Iran had committed $7 billion in a secret plan to purchase missiles, tanks, fighter jets, and nuclear technology from China, North Korea, and Russia.[15] While this surging arms trade is geared toward international warfare and not toward terrorism, whenever there is an abundance of weapons floating around in unstable regions the risk of some of the weapons being acquired by terrorists or state-sponsors of terrorists increases.

A potential future trend in terrorism is the evolution of terrorist suicide attacks from the ground to the air. In the 1980s, Islamic extremists introduced the new tactic of crashing trucks and cars filled with explosives into fortified buildings and troop convoys. The same tactic can be used with explosive-laden aircraft. "Aerial terrorism" may well be the new addition to terrorism vocabulary in the 1990s. Terrorists in single-engine, low-flying planes or helicopters to avoid radar, filled with explosives, could easily crash into buildings, populated areas, and other targets. There have already been terrorist attacks—although not suicidal—from the air. A Palestinian terrorist penetrated Israeli border security by using a motorized hang glider to cross over from Lebanon. After landing, he killed several Israeli soldiers before being killed by the Israelis.

One high-tech weapon that could be used by future terrorists in aerial attacks is remotely piloted vehicles (RPVs). These are unmanned, small flying machines that are used for low-level target reconnaissance. Israel used RPVs in its 1982 invasion of Lebanon. RPVs provide assistance to battlefield artillery through live television pictures or film of a particular target. They are also used for electronic warfare purposes since they can cause enemy radar to turn on and therefore reveal itself. While all these are roles advantageous for conventional war, RPVs also possess a capability that would appeal to terrorists who might gain possession of one. RPVs can be used in stand-off attacks as "a cheap flying bomb."[16]

Technological advancements in basic weapons such as the rifle may also prove advantageous to terrorists who gain possession of them. For example, a new service rifle issued to the British army, the SA80 rifle, is easy for new recruits to fire accurately due to its low recoil and optical sights. The rifle can be used as a submachine gun, since it is short and light and can be fired in bursts. The cartridges for the rifle are also small and light, which allows more ammunition to be carried. Users of these weapons also have less need for precise estimation of the range to the target, since the bullet flies on a flatter trajectory than most other rifles. In a terrorist's hands, these types of new rifles could prove quite deadly.[17]

Even if there weren't any advancements in weaponry or the introduction of new terrorist tactics, future terrorist attacks are still likely to result in much higher casualties. Thus far, the highest death toll in a terrorist bombing has been the 329 passengers and crew that perished when Sikh extremists were believed to have blown up the Air India jet over the Atlantic in 1985. The number of deaths in that case was limited only by the size of the plane. The late 1990s is expected to see larger commercial aircraft come into use, including super-jumbo jets capable of carrying more than six hundred people. Since there has never been an innovation in transportation that has not at some time been attacked or utilized by terrorists—car bombings, hijackings, and bombings of jet planes, trains, and ships—the same can be expected of these bigger planes. A successful midair bombing of one of these would thus double the previous death toll for a single terrorist attack.

Terrorists and Weapons of Mass Destruction

Of all the potential future trends in terrorism, though, the one that most worries people is the prospect of terrorists escalating their violence to include weapons of mass destruction. Public and government concern over this matter is only a recent development. For many years, analysts concerned with this threat tended to receive skeptical looks from those who dismissed such thinking as too futuristic. After all, the argument went, why would terrorists want to go into such uncharted waters—with all the uncertainty and risks associated with using nuclear, chemical, or biological weapons—when they had an easier and more readily available arsenal at their disposal, such as conventional bombs, plastic explosives, and automatic guns?

The answer is that terrorists move into new areas of violence when current operations no longer achieve the same effect as previous ones. Terrorists have launched more dramatic and violent attacks in order to attain the same degree of publicity and government responses that their earlier incidents generated. As people become desensitized to "conventional" terrorist attacks, the urge to go higher in casualties and more daring in tactics becomes tempting. The post–Cold War environment is likely to present new opportunities for terrorists to try new methods of killing.

Terrorism has been characterized by cycles of violence where new methods are introduced during different historical periods by groups attempting to gain instant attention to their grievances. As noted earlier, after the Arab defeat by Israel in the June 1967 war, Palestinian extremists introduced a new form of terrorism: international hijackings. They improved upon the methods used by the various individuals who had hijacked planes to Cuba in 1961 by seizing larger planes with more potential hostages, keeping the hostages for longer periods of time, and on one occasion hijacking four planes on the same day. They also blew up planes on the ground and on two occasions in 1970 in midair. The terrorists believed that hijackings and bombings were ways to generate worldwide publicity for their cause and to carry on the war against Israel and its supporters. Similarly, pro-Iranian Shiite terrorists introduced another new method of terrorism in Lebanon in 1983: suicide car and truck bombings. These were seen as an effective tactic to protest the U.S. military presence in that war-torn country. It ultimately proved successful, as the United States withdrew its troops a few months after the bombing of the Marine barracks.

The rapidly changing world of the 1990s should bring with it another cycle of international terrorism. The different causes that give rise to terrorism will find various groups with more powerful weapons. Most terrorist incidents, though, will remain in the familiar category of bombings, hijackings, assassinations, and kidnappings—only more violent. But some groups or individuals are likely to be tempted to gain instant attention through bypassing the old methods of terrorism and trying new ones, just as the Palestinians did in the late 1960s and the pro-Iranian Shiite fundamentalists did in the 1980s.

Weapons of mass destruction are a possible new vehicle of violence for terrorists. Since terrorism is a psychological form of warfare, the introduction of any new weapon or tactic into the terrorists' campaigns of violence will guarantee widespread reaction. The terrorist nuclear threat has increased due to the demise of the Soviet Union. The prospect of unemployed nuclear scientists, rocket engineers, and other technical specialists from the former Soviet Union finding new jobs with Third World or Middle Eastern governments is troubling. Some of these technical experts will be lured by foreign states eager to build their own nuclear arsenals and willing to pay high salaries. Others may find their way into various terrorist groups for either money or adventure. Former German Foreign Minister Hans-Dietrich Genscher expressed the concern of many Western governments when he said that the unemployed Soviet nuclear specialists were "wandering technological mercenaries . . . easy prey for recruiters for irresponsible potentates."[18] Although the director of a nuclear missile production plant responded by pointing out that no single Soviet nuclear specialist would have broad enough knowledge on his or her own to help a government or group build nuclear weapons, the potential spread of nuclear weapons to other nations and possible terrorist groups has nevertheless increased with the disintegration of the Soviet Union.

Who will ultimately control nuclear weapons in the former Soviet Union is another matter that raises concerns in the West. Although the former Soviet republics initially agreed that nuclear weapons would remain under central control by Russia, Ukraine changed its mind and asserted the right to control the nuclear weapons on its soil. Should the Commonwealth of Independent States—the successor to the Soviet Union—disintegrate amid the ethnic-nationalist and religious differences among its many members, it is likely that other states will attempt to control—or sabotage—nuclear facilities and weapons. And once that occurs, the prospects for various extremist groups to gain possession of a nuclear weapon increases.

The second type of weapon of mass destruction is chemical agents. These are more readily available than nuclear weapons, and much easier to handle and use against various targets. They can enter the body through the skin, be inhaled or digested. Nerve agents such as Tabun "GA," Sarin "GB," and VX disrupt the nervous system and can cause paralysis and death. Blister agents such as distilled mustard and nitrogen mustard affect the eyes and skin as well as the lungs and other internal tissues, causing bronchopneumonia. Choking agents such as phosgene affects respiratory organs, resulting in death. Other categories of chemical agents include incapacitating agents such as "CN," "CS," and "BZ," and toxin agents that fall between chemical and biological agents.[19]

As noted above, chemical agents have been used by terrorists and criminals in various product contamination cases. The casualties from these incidents were minimal. But states have used chemical weapons in more dangerous forms in times of war, most notably Iraq and Iran during their conflict in the 1980s. Iraq proved more successful, forcing Iran to agree to a cease-fire after unleashing a barrage of chemical attacks on Iranian troops and cities. Saddam Hussein then turned the weapons on Kurdish rebels in northern Iraq. The lack of a strong international condemnation of Iraq—or Iran—at that time can only serve notice to other states and terrorist groups that they too might unleash chemical weapons and not fear a worldwide backlash from their actions. "It is to me very disturbing that the world community, including the American government, did so little about the Iraqi and Iranian use of chemicals in their war, because in a way they established—and that could be disturbing for terrorists—they established the principal that these things could be used without it provoking as much of an outrage as it should have," said L. Paul Bremer, the chief counterterrorist official in the Reagan administration. "So there will be a temptation by states [to use these weapons] and potentially some of the states could use it for terrorism."[20]

The discovery of a chemical weapons facility in Rabta, Libya, in 1988 greatly worried U.S. officials for obvious reasons. "The prospect of a person like Qaddafi, who has a clear record [of] giving the most dangerous kinds of weapons to any terrorist group who asks, having at his disposal chemical weapons that he could turn over to people like Abu Nidal . . . is something that has to be of some concern," said Bremer.[21] Terrorist groups' interest in chemical weapons dates back several decades. In 1975, German terrorists stole canisters of mustard gas, a blistering agent, from U.S. stockpiles in West Germany and threatened to use it on civilian populations, and that same year German businessmen were arrested in Vienna for attempting to sell the nerve agent Tabun to Palestinian terrorists.[22] In 1987, Colonel Abu al-Tayyib, the commander of Force 17 of the PLO, stated that his group had acquired chemical weapons and would use them against Israel if necessary. He claimed that some Palestinians have been trained in the use of these weapons in other countries.[23]

The most dangerous type of weapon of mass destruction in terms of future terrorist use is biological agents. These include bacteria, viruses, fungi, protozoa, and rickettsiae. Toxins, as noted above, can be considered somewhere between chemical and biological agents since they are chemicals that can be extracted and purified from biological entities.[24] Bacterial agents can cause anthrax, cholera, plague, and typhoid fever, while viral agents can cause smallpox, yellow fever, encephalitis, and influenza. Rocky Mountain spotted fever, A-fever, and African tick-borne fever are among the diseases caused by rickettsiae, while coccidioidomycosis, histoplasmosis, and nocardiosis are diseases within the category of fungi. Among the toxin agents are ricin and botulinal toxin.[25]

Biological agents can be delivered against a target in several ways. One is through aerosol form, which is finely divided particles of liquid or solid distributed through a gas or air. The vehicle for the biological agent could be a missile, a shell, or even a spray can. Another way would be to infect insects or animals and have them spread the disease. Biological agents can enter the human body either through the digestive system, through food or water; through the respiratory system, by inhaling the microorganisms in the air; or through the skin, by means of an insect bite.[26]

Biological agents can be much more devastating in their effect on people than conventional bombs and even chemical weapons, and are more readily attainable and usable for terrorists than nuclear weapons. The fatalities from a successful biological agents attack—release of anthrax spores over populated areas either from a low-flying airplane or a spray can, dissemination of various agents into food supplies, release of botulinal toxin—could be tenfold what we have seen in "conventional" terrorism. The crisis atmosphere it would generate—caring for the sick and dying, coping with national security implications of the attack—would be unlike any we have yet experienced in terrorism.

An experiment conducted by the U.S. Army in the late 1960s demonstrated the potentially devastating effect that a terrorist attack with biological agents could have in a metropolitan area. The target of the mock attack was the New York City subway system. Aerosol clouds of a nonlethal substitute for dry anthrax were sprayed into subway stations through sidewalk vents. Light bulbs containing the harmless agent were also tossed from trains into the subway tunnels. The fake bacteria was then spread to many other stations due to the wind of the speeding trains. The Army took measurements of the harmless bacteria and concluded that had the attack been real, several hundred thousand people would have been killed.[27]

There are several reasons why terrorists might be tempted to utilize biological agents. In addition to the basic terrorist objective of creating fear in the general public and reaching the widest possible audience through their violent incidents, terrorists with biological agents would also be able to perpetrate their attacks more "quietly" in order to avoid detection and aid in their escape after the incident. Biological agents are silent killers, slowly working their way through their victims. Symptoms of a biological agents attack may not appear for hours or even days. Terrorists can thus unleash these agents without raising any suspicions at the scene of the attack. The 1978 assassination of Bulgarian defector

Georgi Markov, as noted earlier, was perpetrated by a man who bumped into Markov with a poison-tipped umbrella containing the deadly agent ricin; the man then simply walked away after "apologizing" for the incident.[28] The silent nature of biological weapons would also give terrorists an advantage in penetrating security at airports and other security-conscious facilities. A terrorist could walk right into a crowded terminal and release an agent or even place it along with a timed-release device in an unsuspected passenger's baggage. The agent could be in a perfume bottle, a shaving can, or any other everyday appliance that would pass right through security.

Terrorists can also use biological agents to inflict large casualties on a nation's military forces. The most deaths caused by a terrorist attack against the U.S. military were the 241 lives lost in the suicide truck bombing at the Marines barracks in Beirut. That would likely pale in comparison with the number of troops killed in a terrorist incident with biological agents. These weapons could incapacitate an entire military base or cause death and illness to all the troops and personnel stationed there.

Biological agents can also be used, along with chemical agents, to extort large sums of money or to undermine a nation's economy and natural resources. There have been several cases in which a country's export trade was targeted by terrorists threatening to poison key products, as well as the Commander Nemo incident in Cyprus. "Any part of the food chain is vulnerable," said Dr. Cornelius G. McWright, the former chief of scientific research for the FBI. "This is from the origin to the store shelf. And this is, for want of a better term, the beauty of this approach. If a product originates in Guatemala, Peru, Chile, anywhere in the world, [a biological agent incident] can occur at the field, it can occur at the loading dock, it can occur aboard ship, it can occur at the unloading dock, or it can occur at the store. So the vulnerability is there. It's just a matter of carrying it out."[29]

Yet despite all the potential payoffs that biological agents may hold for terrorists, with the exception of a few sporadic threats by some groups over the past twenty years and rumors that occasionally circulate about terrorists being trained in the use of biological weapons, there has been little activity by terrorists in this domain. The reasons why can be found in the uncertainty that biological weapons present for terrorists. The risks of personal injury or death are higher when handling these agents rather than chemical, nuclear, or conventional weapons. The reluctance to experiment with unfamiliar weapons is thus a major deterrent. There is also concern among terrorist groups that they might alienate their "constituency" and supporters by killing extraordinarily large numbers of people, as would be the case in most biological agent attacks. These supporters, and the terrorists themselves, could also be killed in the aftermath of an aerial dispersal of a biological agent as winds shift and carry the agent over areas not originally targeted. It is difficult to use biological agents with precision—except for selective assassination operations such as the ricin attack on Markov. The dispersal and delivery problems associated with biological agents are thus an obstacle to their use by terrorist groups. And while terrorists often seek to elicit responses from governments for their attacks, a biological agent incident could easily lead to a widespread crackdown on the group, which could result in its elimination.[30]

There are indications, however, that these self-imposed constraints may be weakening. One of the legacies of the 1991 Gulf War was to bring out into the open the issue of biological agents and warfare. Terrorists have now seen the tremendous fear, anxiety, and reaction that can be generated by threatening to unleash biological—and chemical—agents. Televised pictures of U.S. troops training in the desert in special protective suits that looked more like spaceman outfits than military uniforms, and reporters filing live stories wearing gas masks, all presented vivid pictures of the potential terror of biological weapons. Many news reports and government statements also carried detailed information about biological agents. Terrorists are now likely to be more familiar with these agents and to have developed new ideas for future terrorist violence. Saddam Hussein's ultimate revenge against the West—and the moderate Arab states that aligned against him—could very well be to have lowered the moral barriers against using biological weapons, and to have raised the threshold of violence that some terrorist groups will be willing to accept.

Another development that adds to the potential for terrorists to utilize biological agents is the growth of state-sponsorship of terrorism. State-sponsors could easily train a terrorist group in the proper use of biological agents, thereby eliminating a group's reluctance to experiment with unfamiliar weapons. Governments would also be able to supply terrorist groups with the necessary biological agents. The prospect of new state-sponsors of terrorism emerging from the various ethnic-nationalist conflicts brewing around the world in the 1990s adds to the potential for terrorist incidents with biological agents.

A terrorist group would not even need a state-sponsor to perpetrate an incident with biological agents. "You can look across the world and you could see terrorist groups with professional people within the group," said McWright. "By professional, I'm talking about medically qualified people, engineers, [and] chemists."[31] For groups that do not have such expertise, they would still be able to recruit people with sufficient scientific knowledge to produce the desired biological agents. Furthermore, as is the case with nuclear scientists from the former Soviet Union, there is now an abundance of biological weapons specialists, microbiologists, chemists, and others in need of work following the fall of the Soviet Union. Compared to the "wandering technological mercenaries" that raise fears of nuclear proliferation, it takes even fewer scientists to help governments or terrorist groups develop biological agents.

Technological innovations may also facilitate terrorist use of weapons of mass destruction. Microencapsulation is a technology that could allow for the production of timed-release biological and chemical agents, just as it produces timed-release pharmaceutical drugs and vitamins. This would make the agent the equivalent of a time bomb that terrorists could plan to be released at a particular hour. Microencapsulation also helps reduce the hazards of handling the agent and protects the agent from being neutralized by environmental factors such as light.[32]

Another technology that might assist the production and use of biological agents is "nanotechnology." Some researchers foresee a future world dominated by the science of manipulating matter at the molecular level. Nanomachines—"nano" is a prefix meaning one-billionth and is derived from the Greek word for dwarf, "nanos"—are seen as capable of building anything, molecule by molecule. While there are many positive applications for this new technology, including those in the fields of medicine, industry, and education, its major advocate, research scientist K. Eric Drexler, admits its potential misuse. "In the long run, it seems wise to assume that someone, somewhere, somehow, will escape the bounds of regulation and arms control and apply molecular-manufacturing capabilities to make novel weapons," Drexler writes. He paints a frightening picture of a future arms race with nanotechnology. "The sheer productive capabilities of molecular manufacturing will make it possible to move from a working weapons prototype to mass production in a matter of days. In a more exotic vein, dangerous nanomachines could be developed, including programmable 'germs' (replicating or nonreplicating) for germ warfare."[33]

It is likely that at first the technology to make nanoweapons will be beyond the capabilities of terrorists:

> Terrorism is not an immediate concern. We have lived with nuclear weapons and nerve gas for decades now, and nerve gas, at least, is not difficult to make. As of this writing, no city has been obliterated by terrorists using these means, and no terrorist has even made a credible threat of this sort. The citizens of Hiroshima and Nagasaki, like the Kurds in Iraq, fell victim to nuclear and chemical weapons wielded by governments, not small groups. So long as nanotechnology is technologically more challenging than the simple chemistry of nerve gas, nanoterrorism should not be a primary concern.[34]

But terrorists have demonstrated an ability to adapt to new technologies and weapons either by themselves or with the help of state-sponsors. Drexler hopes there will be warning signs should terrorists attempt to venture into this new field. "In the natural course of events, causes attract protesters before stone-throwers, and produce letter bombs before car bombs. Abuse of nanotechnology is likely to be visible long before it is devastating, and this at least gives some time to try to respond."[35] A terrorist with a "nanoweapon" consisting of biological agents, however, may prove difficult to deal with in terms of existing counterterrorist techniques.

Another technological innovation that may facilitate the use of biological agents by terrorists is recombinant DNA technology, also known as genetic engineering. This may make the development of biological agents both easier and safer for terrorists. "Biological warfare has never been widely used because of the expense and danger involved in processing and stockpiling large volumes of toxic materials and the difficulty in targeting the dissemination of biological agents," writes Jeremy Rifkin. "Advances in genetic engineering technologies over the past decades, however, have made biological warfare a viable possibility for the first time in history."[36] A former deputy secretary of defense testified to Congress in the mid-1980s that genetic engineering makes it "possible to synthesize BW [biological weapon] agents tailored to military specifications. The technology that makes possible so-called 'designer drugs' also makes possible designer BW."[37]

As Rifkin notes, these can have terrorist applications:

> Recombinant DNA "designer" weapons can be created in many ways. The new technologies can be used to program genes into infectious microorganisms to increase their antibiotic resistance, virulence, and environmental stability. It is possible to insert lethal genes into harmless microorganisms, resulting in biological agents that the body recognizes as friendly and does not resist. . . . Genetic engineering can also be used to destroy specific strains or species of agricultural plants or domestic animals, if the intent is to cripple the economy of a country. The new genetic engineering technologies provide a versatile form of weaponry that can be used for a wide variety of military purposes, ranging from terrorism and counterinsurgency operations to large-scale warfare aimed at entire populations. Unlike nuclear technologies, genetic engineering can be cheaply developed and produced, requires far less scientific expertise, and can be effectively employed in many diverse settings.[38]

Since the technology that is used to make biological weapons is also needed by Third World countries to address serious health, agricultural, and other problems, it may become difficult to regulate and monitor the transfer of such technology. The huge profits that are to be made in selling biotech knowledge will lead many companies not to ask questions of potential buyers about their real objectives in attaining such expertise. Technology transfer in the biological field may become one of the great dangers in the future as some governments and groups exploit this new knowledge for destructive purposes.

Biological weapons have been described as the "poor man's atomic bomb."[39] They give terrorists and Third World nations a relatively inexpensive, yet very powerful weapon with which to threaten much stronger states. Biological agents may become to today's terrorists what dynamite was to the nineteenth-century anarchists: a weapon made from science that is perceived as the great equalizer in battles against governments and military forces. The anarchists hailed the invention of dynamite, believing that "in providing such a powerful but easily concealed weapon, science was thought to have given a decisive advantage to revolutionary forces."[40] Since one aspect of terrorism is the "willingness to violate social norms pertaining to restraints on violence," biological agents would provide the mechanism for shattering those restraints. "The history of terrorism reveals a series of innovations, as terrorists deliberately selected targets considered taboo and locales where violence was unexpected," writes terrorist scholar Martha Crenshaw. "These innovations were then rapidly diffused, especially in the modern era of instantaneous and global communications."[41]

Terrorists can produce biological agents even without the use of sophisticated technology. While genetic engineering, microencapsulation, and other high-tech methods would facilitate the development of some biological agents, terrorists can still do a lot of harm with just basic technical and scientific knowledge. "Technologically, we're not [necessarily] talking about moving to a higher realm of technology," said the former FBI science chief, Cornelius McWright. "What we're looking at is an alternate form or alternate weapons system that is available."[42] The term biological weapons tends to evoke images of complicated mechanisms such as bombs and missiles carrying deadly agents. But while the use of biological agents would require a slightly higher degree of scientific expertise on the part of the terrorist group than what is required for shooting a gun or setting off a bomb, it would not be beyond the potential capabilities of most groups.

The first publicized terrorist incident with biological agents, no matter how lethal the agent or how unsophisticated the technique, will likely break down all remaining constraints against the use of such weapons by other groups. The copycat nature of terrorism, in which terrorists tend to copy another group's innovative tactics, will mean that a rash of biological agents threats and incidents will follow the first one. And the first one will not even have to be that "successful" to open up the floodgates. Terrorism is a symbolic form of conflict in which "failed" attacks, such as bombs not exploding or missiles falling short of their target, can still create as much public anxiety as the more successful attacks. The symbolism of terrorism lies in the fact that since terrorists cannot "defeat" their much stronger foes—just as terrorism itself can never be eliminated or defeated—each attack becomes a message from terrorists that they have the ability to make their presence known and that more violence may be in store in the future. Terrorists can also learn from other groups' mistakes and make their weapons and tactics more effective.[43]

Terrorists and Future Media

The mind-boggling advances still to come in global communications will bring terrorist incidents more directly into peoples' homes. The days when terrorism episodes were covered primarily by the newspapers—beginning with the Americans held captive by the Barbary pirates during Jefferson's time and continuing with the hostage/hijacking episodes during the Eisenhower, Kennedy, and Johnson administrations—are long gone. Television news coverage of terrorism, which began to make its impact during the Nixon years but did not truly grow in influence and stature until the Carter, Reagan, and Bush years, now finds itself at a crossroads. "Will technology and direct broadcast satellites make all distributors, from stations to networks to cable companies, obsolete?" asks author and media analyst Ken Auletta.[44] While the answer to that question is still not clear, what is apparent is that the concept of "media" itself will undergo changes as television news, newspapers, radio broadcasts, and magazines are supplemented—and perhaps replaced—by a worldwide electronic hookup of people, events, and information.

The contemporary debates on curbing media coverage or imposing guidelines on terrorism reporting may seem archaic in a future world where the filtering role of the media in bringing information to the public is greatly reduced or eliminated. In the age of instantaneous communications, where everybody with their personal-computer-video-telephone hookup to the world will be both the senders and receivers of information, the individual citizen will become her or his own media. Much like a train that has already left the station, attempts to restrain the media today in its pursuit of any story will be futile as the world marches toward a free-flow, interconnected information society.

One of the trends in communications that is likely to have an impact on the way terrorists and the media interact in the years ahead is the continued globalization of media. This will likely lead to television news broadcasts that originate in one country in the world and are beamed to all other countries, with local foreign reporters doing the coverage and commentary. The Third World is still in the process of developing and discovering the power and impact of mass media, and has not had the luxury or inclination to debate issues such as guidelines for terrorism coverage that have characterized the American media for many years. There are also different cultural perceptions as to what may be "inflammatory," "newsworthy," or "proper," or what may be seen as playing into the terrorists' hands. As noted earlier, the media melee that broke out during a press conference by the TWA 847 hijackers in Beirut was due primarily to the activities of the non-Western local and regional press. However, it is unlikely that those reporters thought that they had done anything wrong. Their job was to cover the story, whatever that took, including pushing and shoving among each other to get photographs and ask questions of the terrorists and hostages.

A glimpse into how foreign television networks present terrorism-related stories was seen during an episode of CNN's "World Report," the innovative program that takes the viewer on a tour of foreign news as reported by those countries' news stations. An Indian television station produced a segment on the deaths of seven Tamil separatist guerrillas—the Tamils are fighting for a separate state in Sri Lanka—who were suspected of involvement in the assassination of Indian Prime Minister Rajiv Gandhi. The video showed an Indian counterterrorist team preparing for an assault on the hide-out. "The commando team, which had already secured the house next to the hide-out, crossed over stealthily, using a ladder, and then ran across the terrace to fix a detonator on the door," the Indian correspondent told viewers as the action unfolded on the television screen. "The door was then burst open and when the commandos stormed down the staircase, they found the seven LTTE men already dead." There were video pictures of the dead terrorists, six of whom were believed to have taken cyanide to avoid being captured alive. The other Tamil guerrilla, suspected of being the mastermind of the Gandhi assassination, shot himself in the head. The CNN anchor had warned viewers before showing the tape that some of the pictures would be "disturbing." Indeed, the Indian television station showed the bloodied body of the Tamil leader in a graphic close-up, with the bullet hole in his temple very clear to viewers.[45] Television newscasts originating from Third World countries may be more likely to focus on the blood and guts aspects of terrorist dramas, since their people have long experienced the bloodshed associated with ethnic-religious and nationalist conflicts. What Americans might perceive as graphic pictures and excess coverage of violence, foreign networks might simply view as routine and normal reporting of everyday life.

The globalization of news will also mean more opportunities for terrorists to get on the airwaves. In the United States, media coverage for any particular terrorist episode depends on several factors. These include the type of news day it is—whether there are more dramatic and significant events happening elsewhere; the geographical location of the terrorist incident, which will determine if a news crew can be put in place quickly and inexpensively; and the nature of the competition—if one network is providing extensive coverage, it will force the other networks to do likewise. But most important of all is whether the victims are Americans. No matter how dramatic another nation's terrorist episodes may be, it is not likely to be perceived by the U.S. networks as having the same potential viewer interest as those involving Americans.

With the eventual introduction of direct foreign news broadcasts, the decision on what to air will be taken out of the hands of the U.S. networks. A television viewer will likely find terrorism reports and episodes from all over the globe with a spin of the dial. What would have been buried in the back pages of a newspaper, or perhaps not even printed, would now be on any one of the hundreds of channels available. There might be the aftermath of a bombing in Belfast on one channel, a live hostage drama from Peru on another, and a hijacking from Japan on a third. While these episodes will not elicit the same emotional reaction among the American public as occurs when the victims are one's fellow citizens, it will nevertheless broaden the global audience that terrorists will have available no matter where they perpetrate their violence. The future of television will be filled with more, not less, terrorism coverage.

It will also be filled with sharper, bigger, and movie-theater type images and sound. This will be the result of high-definition television (HDTV), a second trend in communications that is likely to affect future terrorist-media interaction. The attraction of HDTV lies in its ability to deliver much better images than is currently available on television. Whereas regular television screens contain 525 horizontal lines, HDTV more than doubles that with 1,125 lines. The width of the television screen is approximately twice the size of its height—"the wide-screen HDTV sets sell themselves even when they're turned off"[46]—and there is no distortion in pictures as occurs when the 525-line conventional television image is expanded to a wide screen. "Now, just as FM revolutionized radio, HDTV is about to stage its revolution," writes former CBS News producer Edward Bliss, Jr., "bringing pictures as sharp and almost as large as those in movie houses into viewers' homes."[47]

Certain types of terrorist incidents will be well-suited for this advanced form of television. Imagine a hijacking with pictures of the plane and the hijackers that appear almost life-size, or a firefight between terrorists and counterterrorist units that when shown on HDTV will seem to have all the trappings of a big-budget movie production. Terrorist episodes involving one's fellow citizens will also become even more personalized for a viewer than is the case today, since the drama will be enhanced by the large, detailed, and powerful video portraits of the victims and their families. "HDTV will intensify television," writes Bliss. ". . . News footage, life-size, has to carry more force."[48]

A congressional report on HDTV agreed. " 'Telepresence,' or the sense of 'being there,' is a potentially powerful market inducement for large-screen, high-resolution displays," stated the report by the Office of Technology Assessment. "An example of this sense might be the feeling, when viewing a very high-quality motion picture screen up close, of moving with the airplane or roller coaster when it makes a fast turn, or of unconsciously putting your foot on the brake to prevent an accident. In watching sports, it allows one to have a greater sense of being in the stadium itself. . . ."[49]

The sense of "being there" at a terrorist episode will not only heighten the drama for the viewer, but may also be taken into account by those terrorists that are media conscious. As we noted above, the majority of terrorist groups do not perpetrate their violent acts for the benefit of media attention. But for those that do, HDTV will provide added incentive for being more flamboyant and playing up to the cameras. Blowing up a plane on the ground, waving a gun at the camera, or holding a press conference during a hijacking will all seem more real than before when shown on HDTV.

Among the most futuristic trends in communications that is forecast is the creation of worldwide "integrated systems of digital networks."[50] ISDN usually refers to "integrated *services* digital network," an effort well under way to establish a digital telephone network of diverse electronic services. In this regard, ISDN involves "computer and video equipment [that] would be connected to the phone and used to send and receive words and pictures. It will be possible to search for, and find, information that is in a remote computer miles, or even continents, away and copy it to your own computer."[51] But Leonard Sussman, a communications analyst who served for more than two decades as the executive director of Freedom House, views ISDN as evolving into much more than just an information service. He sees it as a future global *system* of networks that will enable virtually "every man and woman on earth . . . to communicate in a few moments with someone continents away." ISDN will become a "network linkage of tens of thousands of domestic and global communication channels. . . ."[52]

Although ISDN as a fully integrated communication system will not take effect until several decades into the next century, it will be the closest realization yet to McLuhan's "global village." People will be linked together through computer terminals and various other devices, even in the most remote parts of the earth. ISDN will be "carriers of data, voice and pictures over networks linked to other networks."[53] Sussman views this as providing a public forum for anybody:

> There will be far more diversified news, analysis, raw information of the past and present, classical literature, art, music and poetry from all lands and cultures, basic mathematical and physical theories and processes, architectural and technological theories and models, developments in many physical and social sciences, and countless other data flows. There will be room for the avant garde dramatist or artist to test the most innovative ideas and techniques, for the most dissident political or social experimenter to air views that run counter to the mainstream. For in fact, in such a massive network of networks there will no longer be a mainstream. The flow will come from all directions to all directions; from continent to continent; from the periphery to overseas and at home, as well as from the center. This will be made possible by private, corporate entrepreneurs long before some still-oppressive governments permit such diversity.[54]

While this can be an important development for ensuring instant access and interaction among people and ideas, it might also have repercussions for terrorism. Terrorists might be able to use ISDN as a platform for issuing threats and thereby generating new levels of fear. Whereas today, those terrorists that utilize the mass media to reach global audiences can never be certain that their actions or threats will be extensively covered—other things happening in the world that day might be judged more newsworthy by the media—in the age of ISDN the terrorists may not need the media as we know it today. They could send threats *directly* to publics and governments around the world through the interconnected computer network that will be a vital part of ISDN. It is doubtful that any regulatory controls implemented to prevent abuse of ISDN would be effective in deterring an attempt by a terrorist group to penetrate the system. Among the potential terrorist uses of ISDN could be the issuing of threats to contaminate food and pharmeceutical products, threats to kill hostages they may be holding from a kidnapping or hijacking, or threats to unleash weapons of mass destruction unless their various demands are met.

People will also learn of terrorist incidents everywhere from their video computer terminals that will be connected with the entire world. "Third World countries' news will be heard instantly on the new communications networks accessible everywhere, in homes as well as news services worldwide," writes Sussman. The role of the press in providing news to the public will likely be diminished in the age of ISDN. "The journalist will not be needed as intermediary for other users of a terminal anywhere to tap into the Third World news flow," writes Sussman. "That will, indeed, be a new information age, if not 'order.' "[55]

The benefits of ISDN, including universal access to educational, cultural, and economic developments and information, will likely far outweigh the potential negative effects of its use by terrorists. However, as the communications revolution rolls on, it will not discriminate between those who plan to use its technology for positive ends and those who have more devious ideas in mind. The terrorists of tomorrow may therefore have a vast and more powerful array of communication devices at their disposal with which to disseminate their threats and publicize their actions.

Terrorism within U.S. Borders

A major concern for most Americans during the past decade of terrorism was whether it was likely to spread to U.S. shores. This was understandable as news accounts continually told of foreign terrorists blowing up buildings and airplanes and taking hostages throughout the world. Even though there had been several terrorist incidents committed within the United States—by radical leftist revolutionaries; Puerto Rican, Croatian, and Armenian separatists; anti-abortion, ecology, and animal rights extremists; anti-Castro Cubans; and white supremacist groups such as the Aryan Nations, The Order, and Posse Comitatus—it never quite seemed to match the frequency, ferocity, and terror of the international terrorists. For example, during the five-year period between 1987 and 1991, the FBI reported thirty-four terrorist incidents in the United States, with no deaths or injuries occurring and the majority of the attacks taking place in Puerto Rico by Puerto Rican separatist groups.[56] In 1992, the year before the World Trade Center bombing, there were just four minor terrorist incidents in the United States.[57] The few times in the past when foreign terrorists did come to American shores or had their sympathizers do their killing, it was mainly for selective assassinations that did not greatly arouse the American public.

There are several reasons why the United States has been rather fortunate in terms of the level of domestic terrorism and the relative absence of international terrorism within its borders. Unlike many European and Latin American countries where ideological conflicts over capitalism, socialism, and Marxism can spur and sustain domestic terrorist movements, the United States' conflicts tend to be more pragmatic. Many of the major disputes in this country are issue-oriented—abortion, busing, labor and women's rights—with the potential for terrorist groups to exploit deep-seated ideological divisions in society very low. As soon as the issues are resolved or fade away from the public consciousness, the terrorist group loses its raison d'être. Those groups that do attempt to go beyond a single issue and tap revolutionary fervor, such as the Weather Underground, the United Freedom Front, or the Symbionese Liberation Army, do not last very long. They become viewed by most of the public as a fringe element and tend to dissolve as their members are arrested or "retire." The European and Latin American groups, on the other hand, can find new recruits and form new factions, as the philosophical and ideological divisions in their countries never quite die out.

When Judith Clark and other former members of the Weather Underground took part in the Brink's armored truck robbery and murders in Nanuet, New York, in 1981, there was concern expressed in the media and in Congress that the radical group from the late 1960s and early 1970s had reemerged. Senator John East claimed that the incident demonstrated "the continuing threat of terrorism to American citizens," while Congressman John Ashbrook called for "immediate action to halt the growth of terrorism."[58] A staff member on the Subcommittee on Security and Terrorism asserted that the Brink's incident showed that the Weather Underground had escalated its violence from basic bombings to complex robberies and was also aligned with other extremist groups.

But the FBI discovered no evidence of a conspiracy among the Weather Underground and the other groups alleged to have been involved in the Brink's incident, including the Black Liberation Army. Left-wing political groups and civil rights organizations condemned the robbery-murders "as an act of political desperation by politically isolated individuals."[59] The FBI found that the remnants of the Weather Underground and Black Liberation Army "were small in number [and] lacking in public support. . . ."[60] The foundation to support a political revolutionary terrorist campaign in the United States was simply not there.

The United States also does not have the deep ethnic-nationalist, separatist, and religious divisions that are the driving force of much of the terrorism in the Middle East, Europe, and elsewhere. With the exception of Puerto Rican separatists, extremist groups in the United States have not successfully used territorial, ethnic, or religious issues to build a significant following that lasts beyond a few years. The Black Liberation Army and white supremacist and neo-Nazi groups were rejected by the majority of both black and white Americans, and the polarization in society that they sought to create and exploit never materialized. It is therefore unlikely that "home-grown" terrorism will expand in the coming years.

Where domestic terrorism is likely to grow, however, is in the case of foreign ethnic and nationalist groups spreading their violent conflicts into the United States. The pool of potential terrorists is likely to increase with the expected surge in immigration by people escaping the many ethnic-nationalist conflicts of the 1990s. While the majority of the immigrants will be nonviolent, a few will undoubtedly carry not only the scars of their past but also a desire for revenge against their former enemies, some of whom might very well be among the new immigrants themselves. "Along with the poor and hungry," observed terrorism expert Brian Jenkins, "we [do] take in a certain number of bombers. . . ."[61] Miniature versions of the "old" country's violence could very well erupt in the new one.

One form this may take would be for ethnic-nationalist groups to fight among themselves through campaigns of assassinations and bombings, much like previous groups such as the Armenians with respect to Turkish targets and Croatians with respect to Yugoslav targets. With more powerful and sophisticated weapons, the death tolls could become quite high. Furthermore, just as Croatian separatists hijacked a TWA plane in 1976 to protest U.S. policy toward Yugoslavia and gain recognition for their cause, so too may future ethnic-nationalist groups within the United States strike at U.S. government targets to protest various policies.

The potential also exists for international terrorists abroad to forge closer links with some of the new immigrants. Author G. Davidson Smith states that "terrorist pressure upon ethnic communities in America could generate a future increase of foreign-initiated incidents on the US mainland."[62] The FBI, in its annual report on terrorism for 1992, noted that "anti-American terrorist groups and individuals who oppose U.S. policies or U.S. involvement overseas, have a representation throughout the world, including the United States."[63]

As noted earlier, one of the major reasons why terrorists have been reluctant to travel to the United States to attack American targets is the easy availability of U.S. targets overseas. As long as terrorists found an abundance of American symbols to hit, there was no need to try to overcome the logistical problems involved in carrying out an attack in the United States. But modern communications may be reducing that barrier as terrorists in Europe or the Middle East with faxes, cellular phones, and other modern tools could establish efficient command and control systems for terrorist attacks in the United States. This could be done either with the assistance of extremist elements in some ethnic-nationalist communities in the United States, or by establishing their own temporary network of terrorists in this country. If physical security measures improve in Europe and other regions, then initiating attacks within the United States could become a viable option.

Another factor that could motivate international terrorist groups to launch attacks within the United States is the same reason a terrorist group might use biological weapons: the need to rise above the normal "noise" level of terrorism. If their target is U.S. symbols—or global symbols such as the World Trade Center and United Nations headquarters—and they believe the American public and government has become used to anti-U.S. terrorism overseas, then they might be tempted to commit a major bombing, assault, or hijacking within the United States. As good as U.S. security has been against terrorism within its borders, it cannot stop every determined group. The World Trade Center bombing proved that we are as vulnerable to terrorism as any country around the globe. But the quick arrest of most of the participants in that 1993 bombing, and the prevention by police and the FBI of a plot to bomb the U.N. headquarters and other targets in New York, illustrate that terrorists will find it difficult to sustain a campaign of violence in the United States beyond a few spectacular incidents. However, the reaction they will elicit from just one or two major bombings or other violent acts within the United States may be sufficient to meet their objectives.

The future of terrorism will pose challenges to governments and societies throughout the world. The higher levels of violence and more sophisticated techniques that can be expected from tomorrow's terrorists will put governments to the test in designing effective ways to deal with this threat. But the endless nature of terrorism, with its roots embedded in issues ranging from religious fanaticism to political extremism, ensures that no single solution or even mix of policies will prove successful in eliminating terrorism in anybody's lifetime. The view of one observer in the mid-1970s that "there is no doubt that international terrorism . . . could end tomorrow if the nations of the world simply stopped providing safe havens for terrorists"[64] proved to be wishful thinking. Many nations did stop providing safe haven, yet terrorism has persisted.

But if there are no magic formulas for ending terrorism, then there are nevertheless a variety of measures that can be taken to help reduce the threat. How to combat terrorism will remain a central problem for the United States and other governments in the coming years. Our long experience with terrorism holds some lessons as to what works—and does not work—in the battle against this violent form of international behavior.

$$10$$

Lessons Learned

This book has looked into the past and peeked into the future in order to gain insight into the dynamics of a phenomenon that can transfix presidents, inflame and anger the public, and captivate the media at any given moment. The dramatic changes that have taken place around the globe in the past few years call for a new look into how governments and societies can deal with the problem of terrorism. There are now opportunities for addressing some aspects of the terrorist threat in ways that were not possible when the Cold War placed barriers against full and meaningful international cooperation. But there are also many pitfalls that can arise and lead to a repeating of the major mistakes of the past.

Some of these mistakes lie in the way we react to terrorism. Instead of allowing terrorist attacks to throw nations into states of crisis and immediate responses, it will be necessary to learn how to cope with a world where terrorism will increasingly become the unfortunate, but natural, byproduct of the numerous conflicts and grievances that have always plagued civilization. Coping with terrorism, however, does not mean ignoring it. Being "tough" on terrorism requires careful consideration of those practical measures that may help in the struggle against terrorist violence, but not the useless rhetoric or sweeping condemnations of terrorism that sound good but accomplish little. Much can be done to address the terrorist threat in ways that would minimize the benefits to the terrorists and at times raise the cost to them for their actions.

The first step is to take away the psychological advantage that terrorists gain when they threaten or commit violent acts. This can be accomplished by reassessing our reactions to terrorism and determining what are the things that we do that play right into the terrorists' hands. The second step is to identify those measures—both defensive and offensive—that governments around the world need to take that hold the most promise for reducing *some* aspects of international terrorism and preventing its escalation into much more dangerous forms of violence.

Reacting to Terrorism: The Psychological Dimension

Terrorists thrive on the psychological effects their actions have upon others. Whenever a government overreacts to a hostage incident or the public becomes engulfed in fear over potential terrorist attacks, the terrorists achieve an important victory. They are able to demonstrate that small groups using violent tactics can propel themselves onto the world stage and influence the course of events in other countries and regions. They can continually frustrate governments by making their policies seem ineffective with each new bombing or hijacking. But taking away this psychological advantage from terrorists is the one element in combating terrorism that governments and societies have the most control over. It requires a number of changes in the way we typically react to terrorism.

1. Do not declare any official "policy" on terrorism.

A central feature of the terrorist trap has been the tendency to react to terrorism much as one would tackle any other serious issue of the day. Namely, identify the potential source of the problem, announce concrete steps to address and alleviate it, and then wait for the positive results. A mind-set thus evolves in which terrorism is seen as a somehow "manageable" problem that only awaits the right policies and actions. This, however, raises expectations for the public that cannot be fulfilled. Each additional terrorist incident is magnified in importance when compared with the ineffectiveness of official counterterrorist policies.

A policy on terrorism also takes away the flexibility that is often needed to deal with the unique nature of each terrorist incident. It opens up a government to charges of contradictions and inconsistencies when it doesn't follow its own stated programs. The official U.S. policy on terrorism, as set forth in government reports and statements over the past two decades, has been that the United States does not make concessions to terrorists, that it forces state-sponsors of terrorism to pay a price for their actions, and that it pursues all measures to bring terrorists to justice and destroy their operations and networks.[1] The unofficial U.S. policy on terrorism, however, is that concessions are usually made to gain freedom for hostages or to resolve a terrorist crisis, state-sponsors of terrorism are not punished when other policy concerns arise, and only a limited number of terrorists have been brought to justice or groups destroyed.

This is not a weakness in U.S. policy as much as a reflection of the realities in dealing with a threat as diverse as international terrorism with its multitude of actors and its varying causes. It becomes quite difficult to establish clear guidelines for a threat that itself has no clear structure or patterns. The United States has not been alone in its frustrations in dealing with terrorism. All governments have made concessions to terrorists, but simply do not call them concessions. All governments have allowed other issues deemed more important to take precedence over any specific action against terrorists. And all governments have had difficulty in apprehending terrorists outside their borders and bringing them to justice.

Terrorism persists because it takes so little to activate the terrorist machinery—a car bombing in one place, a hijacking in another, a kidnapping somewhere else—and yet there are so many potential payoffs awaiting the terrorists: publicity for their cause, freedom for imprisoned comrades, money or arms for future operations, personal satisfaction in seeking and gaining revenge, and general disruption and sabotage of specific developments or events.

The irony in any government's policy on terrorism is that it doesn't have to be "consistent" in how it approaches the threat, provided that it doesn't profess to be so. There will be times when interactions and requests for assistance will need to be made with state-sponsors of terrorism, just as there will be times when negotiations and concessions may be part of the resolution of a particular incident. The Ford administration's granting of a minor concession to Croatian hijackers in 1976 helped end that incident peacefully. Terrorists don't always announce their intentions and plans, and neither should those governments dedicated to confronting the threat. Flexibility is important in dealing with terrorism, and official policies can often impede that.

The same is true for setting criteria for when military preemptive or retaliatory strikes will be used. We saw how this hampered the Reagan administration in the mid-1980s when it promised that it would initiate military responses to terrorism, but only when it had "irrefutable evidence" linking a group or a state-sponsor to a particular terrorist act. But such evidence is not always present or clear-cut, and the self-constraints can prove embarrassing to the government that establishes them. The United States had to endure the continual taunts from Libyan leader

Muammar Qaddafi about perpetrating terrorism against U.S. targets, and strong suspicions that Libya was involved in several anti-U.S. terrorist attacks, without being able to strike back at Libya until it produced the "incontrovertible evidence." And when the United States finally did produce the evidence—the intercepted messages between the Libyan's people's bureau in East Berlin and Tripoli following the 1986 bombing of a West Berlin discotheque frequented by American servicemen—the result was potential damage to U.S. national security by publicly disclosing secret information concerning U.S. capabilities in electronic eavesdropping on foreign adversaries.

The United States made problems for itself with its official policy on terrorism in regard to Iran and Syria. Throughout the 1980s, there was little likelihood that the United States would ever launch a military strike against states such as Syria or Iran no matter how much evidence was produced linking those states or elements of their governments to anti-U.S. terrorist attacks. The potential damage to U.S. interests in the region, to Mideast peace initiatives, and to a range of other foreign policy concerns all worked against U.S. military operations against such states— but not against Libya, which was isolated in the Arab world. As evidence—but never those elusive "irrefutable" criteria—pointed to Syrian and Iranian involvement in terrorist activity, the United States opened itself up to charges of being inconsistent in fighting terrorism by either not looking hard enough for "irrefutable" evidence or simply ignoring what seemed obvious to most observers. All of this was unnecessary, since the United States did not have to set conditions for military responses to terrorism in the first place.

It is also debatable whether any government really needs an "official" list of state-sponsors of terrorism. The United States has maintained one since 1979, and although it technically imposes trade and other restrictions on those countries on the list, most of these countries—Cuba, Iran, Iraq, Libya, North Korea, Syria, Sudan—have traditionally had little economic relationship with the United States to begin with. The advantage of an official list of state-sponsors is that it publicizes who the state-sponsors of terrorism are and provides an avenue for diplomatic, economic, and other pressure to be applied by both the United States and the world community. But it is not clear that the presence of a particular country on the U.S. list has affected their behavior or that of other countries in their relations with them. Furthermore, since the United States has foreign policy and security interests that require positive interactions at times with some state-sponsors of terrorism, the existence of an official list only adds to the perception of inconsistencies and contradictions in U.S. terrorism policy.

A policy on terrorism does not have to be set in stone or placed on a pedestal for all to see. When public statements by government officials are called for against terrorists, they should be followed by firm action. But whatever can be accomplished through sweeping policy statements or a widely publicized program against terrorism can just as readily and more effectively be pursued through behind-the-scenes pressure against state-sponsors and by persistent efforts to attain international cooperation.

2. Do not create a crisis atmosphere in Washington every time terrorists strike.

Terrorists have been quite successful in generating overreactions by U.S. presidents, the public, and the media during various terrorist attacks. The United States is today in a perpetual pre-crisis mode of thinking and acting about terrorism. The right incident—a hijacking, a major bombing, a hostage-barricade situation—at any time will touch off alarm bells throughout the country. The pattern has been repeated enough times in our recent past to be predictable.

First comes the news of the terrorist incident, followed by reports about who may be involved in the attack and the potential danger to hostages. In the case of bombings, the first reports deal with the number of casualties. This is followed by various statements from government officials condemning the attack, often claiming it is an "act of war." Speculation grows about what the U.S. response will be as numerous "experts" take to the airwaves to give their opinions. Meanwhile, the families and communities of the victims become a focal point for media attention. But throughout all of these developments, the eyes of the nation invariably set upon Washington for signals of how the president will handle this latest act of violence.

The decisions for a president are whether to become caught up in the growing frenzy or to make a determined effort, either through words or behavior, to put the event in a proper context for the public and thereby have a calming effect upon the nation. Presidents Eisenhower, Kennedy, Johnson, Nixon, and Ford all made conscious efforts to prevent terrorist incidents from becoming full-blown crises. Eisenhower, Kennedy, and Johnson used a news conference to send that message, Nixon remained behind the scenes during the 1970 hijacking episodes in Jordan, and Ford encouraged the granting of a minor "concession" to Croatian hijackers to resolve that 1976 incident.

Most of these presidents also responded to the terrorist episodes in ways that made it clear that U.S. foreign policy interests would not be sacrificed by the desire to resolve a terrorist incident or to prevent more from occurring. Eisenhower did not allow the hostage situation in Cuba to force him into a confrontation with Cuban rebels, which he felt would not serve U.S. interests. Kennedy was equally determined to prevent public and congressional anxiety and anger over the wave of hijackings in 1961 from diverting attention away from his foreign policy programs in Latin America. Johnson would not allow hostage situations in the Congo in 1964 or in North Korea in 1968 to change the course of his policies in those regions. And Nixon kept the goal of stability in Jordan and the survival of King Hussein as the measuring stick for any U.S. response during the 1970 hijackings-hostage episode in that country.

All of this changed under Presidents Carter and Reagan. The emotional aspects of responding to terrorism took over as the United States endured crisis after crisis. U.S. foreign policy interests were sacrificed first by Carter, who became preoccupied for more than a year by the hostage episode in Iran, and then by Reagan, who believed that any action, including the selling of arms to Iran, was justified if it meant freedom for a few hostages in Lebanon. And each time a terrorist group hijacked a plane or set off a bomb with Americans as victims, there was an immediate sense of crisis generated in Washington.

George Bush began to break away from this terrorist trap, but left the door open enough for future presidents to fall back into it. He resisted the pro-Iranian Shiite extremists in Lebanon when they tried to dictate to him whom he should send to Syria to receive two American hostages. He did not take the bait from Saddam Hussein when the Iraqi dictator tried to use thousands of foreign hostages, including large numbers of Americans, to prevent the United States from proceeding with plans for Desert Storm and the bombing of Iraq. But the temptation to rally the nation behind him by using the plight of the hostages as the reason why the United States might go to war with Iraq was briefly used during the November 1990 congressional elections. And President Bush did scurry back to the White House in the summer of 1989 when Hizballah threatened to kill American hostages.

Breaking out of a crisis atmosphere over terrorism requires deliberate steps by a president. It is the president who has the most potential to take away the psychological advantage that terrorists gain when a particular incident is escalated into a crisis. Presidents have traditionally been the molders and shapers of public opinion, and their role in terrorism crises is just as crucial. The first step requires achieving a balance between demonstrating compassion and concern for potential victims and hostages on the one hand, yet at the same time making it clear that terrorists cannot be allowed to dictate the course of American foreign policy or to paralyze the nation in an effort to resolve the problem. There may also be times when nothing should be said publicly by a president during a terrorist episode—as Nixon demonstrated during the 1970 Jordan hijackings, but failed to do during the 1973 hostage episode in Sudan— while behind-the-scenes efforts are being pursued to end the situation.

The second step in preventing a terrorist episode from becoming a full-blown crisis is for presidents and high-level government officials to refrain from any rhetoric on terrorism. No matter how strong the temptation may be to equate terrorism with "war" or to issue grandiose statements about "defeating" terrorists, it should be avoided at all costs. Such rhetoric automatically puts the terrorists on an equal footing with the United States and gives them instant recognition and status. It also greatly raises the stakes in the conflict, as well as the expectations for the American public who then expect that if we are indeed in a "war," then we had better win it. But there won't be any General Norman Schwarzkopfs to run blitzkriegs over terrorists as was done over Iraqi troops during the Gulf War. Terrorism will remain an elusive threat on which progress will be made at times, but for which there will not be any decisive victories. The less promised to the public the better.

3. Overdramatization in media coverage of terrorism needs to be reduced, but the media should not be made the scapegoat for the problem of international terrorism.

The media have been placed with an unfair burden in covering terrorism. Terrorism is drama, and the media thrive on drama. Many terrorism experts, politicians, and government officials have blamed the media for playing into the terrorists' hands by providing them with a world stage to promote their violence and threats. Terrorist acts, however, are newsworthy events—the public is interested in them and governments react to them. The long-term risks to freedom of the press that would arise from any imposed restraints on media coverage of terrorism would be a far greater danger to our basic freedoms than any terrorist act could be.

There is no question, though, that some terrorists are quite skilled in manipulating the media to their advantage. The media have also tended at times to overdramatize terrorism with endless reports on hostages and their families, detailed accounts of the violence involved in a particular incident, and speculation on the dangers that may lie ahead during, or in the aftermath of, a terrorist episode. All this greatly adds to the sense of fear that usually accompanies terrorist attacks.

De-escalating the hype over terrorism that is sometimes found in media reporting would be desirable. But this cannot be forced on the media, and the best hope for achieving this is the sense of responsibility that is typical of most reporters, commentators, and news executives. Many newspapers and television networks went through a self-criticism of their role in terrorism reporting following the Hanafi Muslim hostage episode in Washington, D.C., in 1977. This was repeated in the aftermath of the 1979–81 Iran hostage crisis and the 1985 TWA hijacking in Beirut. This should be an ongoing process for the media and not have to wait for the post-mortems of a terrorist incident.

But the sense of crisis and drama over terrorism that has become a staple in recent years is not the fault of the media. As noted earlier, it is still the president and top-level government officials who set the tone for how the public and media will react to terrorism. The media would not have been able to report on the retreat and isolation of Jimmy Carter into the Rose Garden during the Iran hostage crisis if the president had not chosen that course of action. And they would not have covered the ringing of church bells and vigils throughout the nation if the Carter White House had not promoted that activity in an effort to rally the nation behind the hostages and the president. And the media would not have reported the rhetoric on terrorism that was the hallmark of Ronald Reagan throughout the 1980s if the president had not uttered the words or made the threats and promises of swift and effective retribution against terrorists that he did.

If every television camera were taken away from the scene of a terrorist episode and every reporter banned from writing on the subject, there would still be plenty of terrorism to go around. Massacres by Sikh militants in India, assassinations and bombings by IRA or Loyalist extremists in Northern Ireland, kidnappings by Islamic guerrillas in Lebanon or leftist rebels in Colombia would not disappear with the elimination of the media. But since the media *are* a force that will continue to make their presence felt in many terrorist episodes, attention should be focused more on ways to improve their reporting on terrorism for the public rather than on imposing restraints or censorship that runs counter to democratic principles.

The one area where the media have the most potential to improve their record in terrorism reporting lies in their being an educational vehicle for the public. Since terrorism is a volatile and complex issue, the media can play an important, positive role by putting terrorist incidents and threats into a proper context. This would entail providing more background reports on the roots of the various grievances and conflicts that give rise to a particular terrorist incident, as well as reminding viewers or readers of the dangers in overreactions or excessive fears about terrorism. Reporting on terrorism is, in one respect, analogous to reporting on a local fire, earthquake, or some other disaster that can greatly arouse the public. In those cases, news organizations have no problem mixing extensive coverage of the event with continual reassurances to the public about the realities of the situation and the need to avoid panic or overreaction. If this practice were incorporated in some form into media coverage of terrorism, it could provide an important source for reducing the psychological advantages that some terrorists gain when they use the media to evoke fear in large audiences.

4. Be skeptical of statistics on terrorism.

Government officials and politicians like to cite statistics on terrorism to support various positions on the issue. Statistics are used to argue that terrorism is either on the rise or decline, or that progress is being made or impeded against the terrorist threat. But statistics actually tell us very little about the nature and impact of terrorism. And placing too much faith in them can lead to disappointment and frustration for both policy-makers and the general public.

Terrorism's unique characteristic is that just a single major incident can shatter all perceptions of progress in the battle against the terrorist threat. As noted earlier, this tends to make statistics on terrorism and related policy statements appear quite misleading. The major international terrorist incidents for the United States over the past several decades took place during varying periods of worldwide terrorist activity. The 1970 hijackings in Jordan occurred in a year when the volume of terrorism had increased from the previous year. But the 1973 kidnapping and murder of two American diplomats in Sudan was in a "declining" year of activity. Similarly, the taking of American hostages at the U.S. embassy in Iran in 1979 was in a year when the number of terrorist incidents had declined from the previous year, while the 1985 TWA and *Achille Lauro* hijackings were in an "increase" year. The 1983 bombings of the American embassy and Marine barracks in Beirut and the 1988 Pan Am 103 bombing in Scotland occurred in years when the volume of terrorist incidents were almost identical to the previous year. And the 1990 terrorist threats and hostage taking by Saddam Hussein were in a "declining" year in terms of the number of terrorist incidents.[2]

What mattered to the American public and the government was not the volume of terrorist activity, but rather the few spectacular incidents that made it appear that terrorists were everywhere and invulnerable. Since terrorists will always have the ability to strike in some major fashion at any time, it would be better if government officials and politicians refrained from using statistics to bolster any claims about the course and direction of international terrorism.

5. Attempts to define terrorism are futile, and only add to the sense of confusion that people have about what really is terrorism.

No attempt has been made in this book to define terrorism. Most definitions of terrorism are either too narrow and thereby exclude many significant cases of terrorist activity, or are so broad as to be quite useless in understanding the terrorist phenomenon. One scholar found more than one hundred different definitions of terrorism proposed between 1936 and 1981.[3] And this was *before* the onslaught of hundreds more definitions of terrorism with the proliferation of terrorism books and articles in the 1980s.

Definitions of terrorism also lend themselves to contradictions, since they are usually influenced by ideological and political perceptions of the terrorist threat. Some definitions have focused on the victimization of "innocent" people. The President's Commission on Aviation Security and Terrorism defined terrorism as "a deadly weapon of the weak and the cowardly [which] leverages violence against innocent victims."[4] However, under this definition, the killing of military personnel and diplomats would not be considered terrorism. These victims are not "innocent" in the eyes of the terrorists, since they represent the target government that the terrorists view as the enemy. The "innocent victim" definition of terrorism would thus exclude such terrorist incidents as the suicide bombings of the U.S. Marine and French troops barracks in Lebanon, the countless number of assassinations of off-duty military and police officials, and the murders of heads-of-state.

Other definitions have focused on violence committed against "noncombatants." Although the State Department acknowledges that "no one definition of terrorism has gained universal acceptance," its official definition of terrorism is "premeditated, politically motivated violence perpetrated against noncombatant targets by subnational or clandestine agents, usually intended to influence an audience." The term "noncombatant target" includes both civilians and military personnel "who are unarmed and/or not on duty at the time of the attack," as well as military installations or armed military personnel "when a state of hostilities does not exist at the site."[5] But many terrorists do not recognize military personnel—armed or unarmed—as "noncombatants," but rather view them as the enemy with whom they are engaged in a perpetual state of war. For many terrorists, there are no innocents or noncombatants.

The difficulty in defining terrorism has given rise to the famous slogan, "one person's terrorist is another person's freedom fighter." Communities that support various groups in their violent acts do not necessarily see them as "terrorists." Since the essence of terrorism is the effect that violent acts can have on various targets and audiences, it would make more sense to talk about terrorist-type *tactics*—which can be utilized by extremist groups, guerrillas, criminals, or governments—than to attempt to determine who exactly qualifies as a "terrorist." The blowing up of planes, whether done by Canadian or American criminals such as J. Albert Guay and John Gilbert Graham, or by Libyan agents and the

PFLP-GC, is terrorism. The same is true for hijackings, assassinations, bombings, product contaminations, and other violent acts.

Definitional issues are important for academic treatments of terrorism, but are less relevant for policymakers. That is why the international agreements that have been reached on terrorism, including the Hague, Montreal, and New York/United Nations Conventions, all deal with the tactics of terrorists—hijackings, sabotage of aircraft, hostage taking—rather than the controversial issue of what exactly constitutes "terrorism." The more disagreements there are on defining terrorism, the more terrorists can benefit by the added confusion on the issue. Several decades of futile efforts to reach a consensus on defining terrorism should be a clear enough signal to move on to other aspects of the terrorist threat.

Combating Terrorism: Identifying the Payoffs

It used to be said that the two things in life everybody could be sure of were death and taxes. A third, though, could be added to the list. Any speech on terrorism that calls for vigorous action against all terrorists will be guaranteed enthusiastic applause. But combating terrorism requires more than just rhetoric. It requires careful assessment of the costs and benefits of various actions and a concentration on those options that promise the most payoffs.

Intelligence and Law Enforcement

The least publicized, yet most effective, part of the counterterrorist efforts of most countries lies in the areas of intelligence and law enforcement. These are the people who are on the front lines, yet whose quiet work usually gets lost in the hoopla that surrounds the more publicized military, economic, and diplomatic measures.

Many terrorist incidents have been prevented due to the efforts of intelligence agents and analysts, as well as law enforcement personnel in the United States and abroad. Most of these are not publicized in order to prevent compromising intelligence or police methods. Among those that have become known was a plot in the mid-1980s to blow up the American embassy in Rome. This failed after Swiss police arrested a Lebanese man at the Zurich airport and found two pounds of explosives in his possession, as well as a ticket to Rome and an address there. Police found two more pounds of explosives in a locker at the Zurich railroad station. Italian authorities were alerted and they arrested seven Lebanese students who had ties to pro-Iranian Shiite extremists. A search of the students' apartments found a detailed map of the U.S. embassy, notes on vulnerable access points, and arrows pointing to the positions of the guards, television cameras, and concrete blocks. In another case, West German police discovered lists of clubs frequented by U.S. troops, barracks, and the residences and offices of military commanders in a Red Army Faction terrorist safe-house in Frankfurt in 1984.[6]

Among the potential terrorist attacks thwarted by good law enforcement work in the United States was the arrest of a group of Islamic militants in 1993 for plotting to blow up the United Nations headquarters and other targets in New York, and the apprehension of Japanese Red Army terrorist Yu Kikumura in 1987 on the New Jersey Turnpike before he could initiate a series of planned bombings in New York City. Another example was the arrest of members of the El Rukn street gang in Chicago in 1986 after they purchased an inert light antitank weapon from undercover FBI agents. The gang allegedly planned a terrorist attack within the United States in exchange for funding from Libya.[7] In August 1991, the FBI discovered and prevented a plot by the Palestine Liberation Front to commit a terrorist attack against the Kuwaiti mission to the United Nations and/or the ambassador to that mission in New York.[8]

Sometimes the terrorists make foolish mistakes that lead to serious blows to their organization. One of the World Trade Center bombers was caught, leading to other arrests, when he tried to obtain a refund on the rental van that carried the explosives into the trade center. In another case, Spanish police reportedly gained possession of an address book that was mistakenly left in a telephone booth in Barcelona by a member of the Basque separatist group ETA. The Spanish authorities provided information to French police, who, in March 1992, raided a high-level ETA meeting in the Basque region of southwestern France. The leader of the group, Francisco Mugica Garmendia, was arrested, along with two of his top aides, including the ETA's chief bomb maker. Several other ETA members were captured in the raid, while Spanish police arrested five more suspected ETA guerrillas in northern Spain. The police and intelligence breakthrough came on the eve of the World's Fair in Seville and the Summer Olympics in Barcelona.[9]

The International Criminal Police Organization (Interpol) has also provided valuable assistance to countries through its communications network, computerized files, and agents throughout the world. In one case in the late 1970s, the Beirut office of Interpol alerted its counterpart in Nicosia, Cyprus, about a time bomb that was aboard an airliner bound for Rome. Interpol-Nicosia informed the pilot, who then returned the plane to the ground where the bomb was discovered and removed.[10] Interpol's role in counterterrorist matters was improved greatly in 1984, when member nations passed a resolution that changed Interpol's definition of terrorism from a "political" act to a "criminal" act. This allowed members to cooperate fully on terrorist investigations, whereas previously they could not do so under Interpol's constitutional ban on involvement in political, military, religious, or racial matters. Interpol subsequently created a special unit to collect information on terrorists and terrorist acts and provide this information to Interpol members.[11]

The potential for further international cooperation in intelligence on terrorism is higher today than at any previous time. The end of the Cold War has removed many barriers to East-West cooperation on several issues, including political and economic affairs. Cooperation on counterterrorist intelligence matters with the newly formed nations of the former Soviet Union and Eastern Europe should be pursued while the spirit of cooperation is still there on other issues. The United States and other Western nations should also take advantage of the increased awareness level of governments throughout the world concerning the prospects for more terrorism to arise from extremist religious, ethnic, and nationalist groups in the post–Cold War era—as well as from old and new state-sponsors of terrorism—to form new networks of information and knowledge about terrorist group developments.

Establishing an expanded and continually updated network among nations for sharing intelligence on terrorism would yield many benefits. Since no government can monitor, track, and follow up on developments concerning every terrorist group worldwide, a pooling of resources would provide potentially important information. "The issues of intelligence are critical, in terms of trying to determine where people are moving to, what their relationships are," said Robert McGuire, police commissioner of New York City in the late 1970s and early 1980s.[12] For countries such as the United States, whose citizens and symbols are present in virtually every country around the world and who are prone to terrorist attack by a wide variety of groups, there is a definite need to know about the latest developments within terrorist groups in other countries, recent information on the movements of suspected terrorists, discovery of weapons in safe-houses, and so forth. The more that counterterrorist intelligence and police officials from different countries are in continual contact with each other, the more likely it is some incidents may be averted.

A major obstacle, however, to establishing such a network is the understandable concern that sharing secret information with other governments may compromise one's own intelligence-gathering methods or even one's informants and operatives around the world. "It takes a while for people to feel comfortable sharing intelligence," recalled former Secretary of State George Shultz. "And to a certain extent, since valuable intelligence in terrorism involves very delicate techniques of gathering information, there is an uneasiness about it in case it gets out. You can kill somebody by getting it out."[13]

Indeed, the tendency for U.S. politics and government to be beset by numerous leaks, including information relevant to national security matters, greatly troubled other governments. Shultz recalled that foreign governments were hesitant at times to cooperate with the United States in intelligence matters "because we're so leaky. And our Congress and our press insist that everybody has a right to know everything. But if we have a right to know your sources of intelligence, then you're not going to get anybody to tell you something. We had that problem all the time. We wrestled with it."[14]

There is also a reluctance among counterterrorist officials to share information with each other in the general international meetings that are occasionally held to address the problem of international terrorism. "As far as I know, specialized intelligence will never be shared in a large assembly," observed Constantine Melnik, a former French government official who held office during the Algerian civil war and its associated terrorism during the late 1950s and early 1960s. "You will never tell in a large assembly that you have information about one specific German terrorist who is coming to France, and in a given time, in a given little village, and that we have located the village and we are interested to find out when it is the best time to arrest him. This kind of information will never be given on a large scale. . . . And you don't tell about your own techniques."[15]

It is therefore critical that counterterrorist officials and specialists build trust among each other so they can work together to uncover potential terrorist activity and follow up on the movements of suspected terrorists. "I think this has to be done on a very specific level," said Melnik. "If you need the cooperation on the level of criminal polices, then it is very important to let the criminal polices [from different countries] meet together and find out the necessary measures [to take]."[16] The same is true for counterterrorist specialists in aviation and embassy security, terrorist group psychology, and experts on terrorist weapons and tactics.

The area of terrorism in which the role of intelligence will become most critical in the years ahead will be in the potential for terrorists to utilize weapons of mass destruction. Since the repercussions of a terrorist incident with nuclear, chemical, or biological weapons would be much greater than with conventional weapons, in terms of casualties, panic, fear, and other effects, the highest priority will need to be given to preventing even a single incident.

Since all nations could conceivably be affected by terrorists with nuclear, chemical, or biological agents—whereas a hijacking, a conventional bombing, or an assassination could be seen as more isolated—there should be an even higher incentive for governments to cooperate in this area. Among the intelligence indicators that should be conveyed to all other nations and joint efforts undertaken to track them down would be the suspicious theft of certain hazardous or scientific materials that could be used to build nuclear, chemical, or biological weapons; the recruitment of nuclear or biological specialists into the ranks of terrorist groups; or the discovery of documents that would lead one to suspect that a terrorist group was planning or thinking about using these types of weapons. This is an issue in terrorism that needs to be nipped in the bud, so to speak, or at least maintained at a continually heightened level of vigilance to try to prevent such a catastrophe from occurring.

While intelligence-gathering and analysis hold the most promise for making gains in preventing some terrorist incidents, covert operations hold much higher risks. Counterterrorism efforts would be undoubtedly enhanced if terrorist groups could be penetrated by government agents or informers. This would not only yield information about planned attacks, but would also provide opportunities to confuse and trick the terrorists by providing misleading and false information. However, penetrating a terrorist group is difficult since many terrorist groups consist of just a few members, and in some cases, such as in Lebanon, are held together by family ties. Furthermore, some terrorist groups require new members to participate in a violent act to prove their loyalty, thereby negating infiltration by a police or government agent.

The use of surrogates, that is, local indigenous groups, to carry out disruptive operations against terrorists has the advantage of utilizing people who are probably familiar with the villages, towns, and possibly even the movements of various terrorist groups. However, the major pitfall is that it may be difficult to control the activities of any foreign group, as the United States painfully learned in Lebanon in 1985. President Reagan had earlier signed a "finding" that authorized the CIA to train Lebanese units for possible preemptive attacks against terrorists. But the U.S.-trained unit then hired mercenaries, who went on an unauthorized operation that resulted in a car bombing at the Beirut suburb apartment of Hizballah leader Sheikh Mohammed Hussein Fadlallah. Eighty people were killed, and Fadlallah escaped the assassination attempt. Following this fiasco, President Reagan rescinded the finding.[17]

The most widely debated issue concerning covert operations against terrorists is that of assassination. Each time there is a major terrorist incident involving Americans, there are usually calls by various people to repeal the executive order that prohibits the U.S. government from engaging in assassination. This is understandable, since paying back terrorists by the same means that they use would seem to be poetic justice. The Israelis have used assassinations to retaliate against terrorists, including the hunting down of the Black September members responsible for the massacre at the 1972 Olympic Games in Munich; the killing of Abu Jihad, the military commander of the PLO, in 1988; and the killing of Sheikh Abbas Musawi, the head of Hizballah, in an aerial bombing of a convoy he was traveling with in southern Lebanon in 1992.

However, there are several reasons why assassination is not a wise counterterrorist option. First, it does not reduce or eliminate the terrorist threat, since there are others who will take the place of the slain terrorist leader or member. It also creates new martyrs for the terrorist group and provides additional fuel to fan the passions and anger of its supporters. This can lead to further terrorist attacks, as occurred in 1992 when Islamic Jihad claimed responsibility for a car bombing of the Israeli embassy in Buenos Aires following the Israeli attack on Musawi.

Allowing the assassination of terrorists also reduces a government to the level of the terrorists and takes away any potential moral argument that may be used against terrorism. The terrorists thus succeed in bringing the government into its violent playing field. There is also the risk of killing the wrong person. Furthermore, since there is no consensus on what exactly constitutes a "terrorist," there could be room for misuse of the "right" to engage in assassination if it becomes part of a government's counterterrorist strategy. Various foreign individuals or leaders might be targeted under the guise of being "terrorists," when in fact it is for other reasons—political, personal, ideological—that they are marked for death. As national security scholar Loch Johnson writes, "Almost always, [assassination] remains an unworthy, illegal and, for that matter, impractical approach to America's international problems."[18]

Military Responses

The United States record in using military responses to terrorism has been a mixed one. It has been both an exhilarating and bitterly disappointing experience for this country. The interception of the plane carrying the hijackers of the *Achille Lauro* led Ronald Reagan to make his "you can run but you can't hide" boast to terrorists, and the bombing of Libya led him to tell those who participated in the raid that "it's an honor to be your Commander in Chief," while the failure of the Iran hostage rescue mission forced Jimmy Carter to make a painful address to the nation revealing that eight American soldiers lay dead in the Iranian desert. A rescue effort during the *Mayaguez* incident in 1975 resulted in more U.S. troops killed—forty-one—than the number of hostages originally taken off the ship by the Cambodians—thirty-nine. But a joint U.S.-Belgian military operation in the Congo in 1964 led to freedom for thousands of foreign hostages, including many Americans, who were in immediate danger of being massacred by Congolese rebels.

There have been many times when U.S. presidents decided against using military force during hostage incidents. Diplomatic measures were chosen instead of military action when hostages were taken by Cuban rebels in 1958, by the North Korean government in 1968, by Palestinian guerrillas in Jordan in 1970, by pro-Iranian Shiite extremists in Lebanon throughout the 1980s, and by Saddam Hussein in Iraq and Kuwait in 1990. In each of these cases, a military rescue was seen as either too difficult or as placing the lives of the hostages in greater jeopardy. It was also determined that U.S. geopolitical interests could be harmed by involving the United States in a military confrontation in those countries at that time. (The United States did, of course, use military force in Iraq and Kuwait once the Persian Gulf War began in January 1991.) And in all these cases, the hostages were eventually released.

History has shown the greater difficulty involved in hostage rescue missions than in other types of counterterrorist military operations. The U.S. bombing of Libya and the interception of the Egyptian airliner were more successful than the rescue effort in Iran, partly because these were conventional military operations, for which the military is best trained. Intercepting a plane and bombing a target are basically straightforward military operations. Rescuing hostages on foreign enemy soil, however, is an entirely different matter. In addition to the problems involved in having to secretly transport aircraft and troops to within striking distance of the target, there also needs to be perfect timing and coordination in order to catch those holding the hostages by surprise and bring back as many live hostages as possible. All of this raises the risk of failure.[19]

One of the hardest, and most unfair, burdens that the U.S. military—and those of other countries as well—have long had to endure whenever there is a hostage episode is comparisons to the stunning success of the Israelis at Entebbe airport in Uganda in 1976. In a daring rescue mission that has yet to be duplicated, three Israeli C-130 aircraft carried Israeli paratroopers and special forces more than 2,500 miles in the rescue of more than one hundred hostages who had been hijacked on an Air France plane. Three hostages were killed during the raid—a fourth hostage who had been in a hospital was later murdered by the Ugandan government—along with the leader of the rescue mission, seven terrorists, and approximately forty Ugandan troops.

The raid on Entebbe has been considered the model for successful hostage rescue missions. Whenever a government is faced with a large-scale hostage incident, the question is usually raised about whether they can duplicate the Israelis' success. The Israeli raid, however, was unique in several ways and was aided by factors that are unlikely to be present in other incidents. First, the Israelis were familiar with the tactics and capabilities of the Ugandan paramilitary forces, since they had helped train them. Second, the Israelis knew the physical layout of the airport, since an Israeli construction firm had helped build the new terminal building there. And third, the operation caught nearly everyone—the terrorists, the Ugandans, and even the hostages—by complete surprise, as it was among the first long-range rescue operations in the days before terrorists would be prepared for all types of counterterrorist operations.[20]

Yet for every spectacular success in counterterrorist military operations—including the West German commando assault at Mogadishu in 1977—there have been an equal, if not greater, number of spectacular failures. The Germans were not able to rescue the Israeli hostages during the 1972 Olympic Games in Munich, with police sharpshooters engaged in a shoot-out with the terrorists that resulted in the deaths of all nine Israeli hostages. Egyptian commandos attempted to rescue hostages from a hijacked Egyptair plane in Malta in 1985, but more than fifty people—mostly hostages—were killed during the rescue effort. More than one hundred people died in Colombia, including twelve Colombian Supreme Court justices, during a military assault on the Palace of Justice, where rebels were holding hostages in 1985. And twenty-one people were killed when terrorists began shooting passengers and detonating grenades on a hijacked Pan Am plane that was on the ground at the airport in Karachi, Pakistan, in 1986. The hijackers mistakenly believed a rescue attempt was under way after the lights went out in the plane. The presence of Pakistani commandos apparently made the hijackers nervous.

The history of military counterterrorist operations illustrates that no two missions can ever be the same since no two terrorist episodes are ever the same. In hostage incidents, the type of location may be similar—an airplane, an embassy, a house—but the circumstances can vary greatly, including whether the hostages are being held on friendly, neutral, or enemy soil, whether they are being moved around from one location to another, the type of terrorists involved and their weapons, and the impact that a military operation may have on other issues and developments in the region.

The same is true for preemptive or retaliatory strikes against terrorists or their state-sponsors. The political and military repercussions of an operation will vary according to the country that is to be attacked—Libya was always a preferable target for U.S. military responses compared to Syria or Iran. The number of civilian casualties will also vary depending on whether the raid is in an urban or rural area. And there will also be different risks depending on how far the attacking aircraft are required to travel to carry out the mission. The longer the distance, the greater the chance of things going wrong, as when a U.S. plane crashed after having to travel several thousand miles during the raid on Libya.

The unique nature of each terrorist situation thus precludes any over-all military doctrine to counter the terrorist threat. Doctrines reduce flexi-bility, and fighting terrorism demands assessing each incident for the potential repercussions of various responses. However, sometimes just the threat of utilizing military responses to terrorism can be as effective, and less risky, than actually implementing a military attack. During the hostage crisis in Lebanon in 1989, the United States moved the *Coral Sea* off the coast of Lebanon as a warning to the Hizballah extremists of the possible repercussions of killing additional American hostages, as they were threatening to do. No further hostages were killed. And during the Jordan hostage crisis and civil war in 1970, maneuvers by the Sixth Fleet kept the Palestinian terrorists who were holding hundreds of foreign hostages guessing about U.S. intentions. The threat to use military force can also motivate other countries to take stronger measures against ter-rorists as they become fearful that any military operation may cause ter-rorists to respond with a new wave of attacks, or cause dissension and unrest in their own country among those protesting the military action. This occurred after the U.S. raid on Libya as both European and moder-ate Arab states feared additional U.S. strikes and thus increased their cooperation with the Reagan administration in fighting terrorism.

The military option is thus an important one for the United States to keep in its arsenal of counterterrorist strategies. But since it can lead to escalating cycles of violence, as well as result in casualties for hostages, civilians, and one's own armed forces, it needs to be used wisely and selectively.

Economic Sanctions

Economic sanctions against state sponsors of terrorism can serve as a flexible response to terrorism. They are stronger than verbal threats yet weaker than military operations. If the economic sanctions fail to achieve the objective of changing the behavior of a particular state-sponsor, then stronger measures could be adopted. If they succeed, then the sanctions could be lifted without the bitter aftermath that usually follows a mili-tary attack on a country. The economic weapon also serves to demon-strate resolve in the battle against terrorism and can deflect accusations that a government is weak in confronting terrorism.

The major problem with economic sanctions, however, lies in the diffi-culty in gaining universal cooperation. As much as governments may want to cooperate in counterterrorist policies, they do not want to do so at the expense of their own economic interests. When the United States imposed economic sanctions on Libya in the 1980s, it had little effect since European nations such as Italy and West Germany continued to trade with Tripoli, a major trading partner of both nations. U.S. trade with Libya was minimal to begin with, further weakening the effect of sanctions. For example, the Reagan administration imposed an embargo on Libyan oil imports in 1982, yet Libya was supplying only 2 percent of U.S. oil imports. Furthermore, American oil companies were allowed to continue to operate in Libya until 1986 and accounted for the bulk of Libya's oil output until that time. When the United States imposed sanctions against Syria in 1986 for its role in sponsoring terrorism, U.S.-Syrian trade was also minimal.

Even when there are substantial prior economic ties between two nations, the effectiveness of sanctions can be broken by other countries eager to step into the vacuum. "Unilateral economic sanctions can have only limited effect," writes former CIA director Stansfield Turner. ". . . Someone else will usually fill whatever gap we create and take the business away from us besides."[21] The 1986 Vice President's Task Force on Combatting Terrorism headed by George Bush acknowledged the limitations of economic sanctions:

> Multilateral sanctions are difficult to organize and even then may not be effective. Further, they could unify the country against the United States, since sanctions often harm the general populace more than terrorists. In every case the advantages of sanctions must be weighed against other foreign policy objectives.[22]

Economic sanctions can therefore hurt large numbers of innocent people. This includes the civilian population in the target country as well as business interests in the country that is imposing the sanctions. Nevertheless, if compliance by the major trading partners of the state-sponsor can be attained, and other nations prevented from breaking the sanctions, then these are costs that may be necessary to take at times in order to demonstrate resolve against international terrorism. Sanctions may also encourage internal opposition to the state-sponsor's activities as its people grow restless over the economic hardships.

Diplomatic and Legal Measures

Confronting terrorism through diplomatic and legal means has had moderate degrees of success over the years. The closing of Libyan people's bureaus by several European nations in the 1980s eliminated the potential for those missions to be used for terrorist attacks. During the 1991 Gulf War, many governments around the world expelled Iraqi diplomatic and intelligence personnel to reduce the risk of Iraqi-sponsored terrorist incidents. The United States successfully used the 1986 economic summit of industrialized nations in Tokyo to gain a united stand among its allies in applying diplomatic pressure on state-sponsors of terrorism, including measures to limit the size of diplomatic missions of state-sponsors, impose stricter immigration and visa requirements for nationals of countries that sponsor terrorism, and improve extradition procedures to bring to justice international terrorists.

But verbal agreements and promises are not always followed by action. For example, West Germany refused to extradite Mohammed Ali Hamadei to the United States despite his involvement in the murder of U.S. Navy diver Robert Stethem during the hijacking of TWA Flight 847 in Beirut. The West German government, which arrested Hamadei when he tried to enter the country with explosives in his luggage, was fearful of the effect extradition would have on the fate of West German hostages being held in Lebanon. France continued to negotiate with Syria for the release of its hostages in Lebanon even after Britain broke off relations with Damascus over its role in the attempted bombing of an El Al plane at Heathrow Airport.

Another problem with diplomatic countermeasures is the difficulty in rebuilding diplomatic ties once the crisis is over. The United States recalled its ambassador from Syria and scaled down its embassy there after the revelations of Syria's role in the El Al bomb attempt. But Secretary of State George Shultz, who was the major proponent of the "tough" stance against terrorists in the Reagan administration, had second thoughts about the wisdom of that U.S response. "After we had done that, and I saw how difficult it was [subsequently] to get our ambassador back [to Syria], I said we're never going to do that again, as far as I'm concerned, because it works against us," said Shultz in the fall of 1991.[23] When diplomatic ties are broken, a government also loses its ability to monitor events and situations in the foreign country. "I think you just cut off your nose to spite your face when you break diplomatic relations," said Shultz. "When you don't have diplomatic relations you don't have anybody there [and] you deprive yourself of any ability to see for yourself what's going on and to represent your interests. And if you have objections to what a country is doing, to say so. And so it's never appealed to me."[24]

The United States has successfully used a 1973 bilateral agreement with Cuba over extradition or prosecution of hijackers to greatly reduce the incidence of that terrorist threat between the two countries. Multilateral legal conventions have also had a long history as a counterterrorist strategy. One of the earliest was the 1963 Tokyo Convention, which, as noted earlier, required countries to establish jurisdiction over hijackings and other incidents on airplanes that occur outside of their own territory. It did not, however, require the signatories to prosecute or extradite the hijackers. The 1970 Hague Convention and the 1971 Montreal Convention improved on the Tokyo measure by requiring the signatories to prosecute or extradite hijackers (the Hague Convention) or those who commit other acts of violence on a plane, including the placing of bombs (the Montreal Convention). The 1973 Chicago Convention established standards for international airport security while the 1973 New York (U.N.) Convention required governments to extradite or prosecute people who commit violent acts against diplomats and their property. In 1979, the U.N. adopted a convention that required states to prosecute or extradite those who take hostages, while in 1991 the U.N. adopted Resolution 4651 that reaffirmed the international community's commitment to combat terrorism. Another Montreal Convention was signed in 1991 by the United States and forty other nations; this convention required that plastic explosives be marked with chemicals at the time of manufacture in order to improve their preblast detection by various existing technologies.[25]

The major weakness of all international agreements on terrorism is that there are no enforcement mechanisms to ensure compliance. When a nation's self-interest dictates otherwise—fear of retaliation by terrorists in the aftermath of an extradition of a captured terrorist, harmful effects on other policy matters, and so forth—one can be assured that the government will march to its own drum. The conventions also do not cover frequent terrorist acts such as bombings on the ground that are not targeted at diplomatic facilities, assassinations, and other acts. But the legacy of several decades of conventions on some aspects of terrorism demonstrates at least the willingness of the international community to address the terrorist threat. With new independent states coming into existence in the 1990s, it will become important to bring them into the process of counterterrorism cooperation.

Physical Security Measures

An underrated but important tactic in deterring terrorism is establishing good physical security measures at airports, embassies, and other facilities where terrorists might attack. It has also proven to be one of the most frustrating elements in the battle against terrorism. Providing adequate physical security has been a never-ending technological race against terrorists. As soon as new devices are designed and installed to detect weapons or protect against attack, terrorists change tactics or use more sophisticated and lethal weapons to defeat them. It is a contest in which the terrorists hold the ultimate advantage. No matter how many times security measures are effective in preventing terrorist attacks, the terrorists only need to penetrate the system once to demonstrate its weakness. Governments and security personnel are then blamed for allowing the incident to occur. Pan American World Airways was found guilty by a federal jury in 1992 of "willful negligence" for failing to prevent the bombing of Pan Am 103. The Long Commission blamed the Marines commanders in Beirut for not taking strong enough physical security measures to avert the 1983 suicide bombing of the Marines barracks.

Technology has played a crucial role in the evolution of U.S. physical security measures. When hijackings first emerged as an issue of concern in the 1960s, various antiterrorist measures were introduced to thwart this new form of piracy. These included the use of psychological and personality profiles at airports to identify potential hijackers and the placement of sky marshals aboard some flights. While these measures gave notice to hijackers that governments were taking the terrorist threat seriously, they were basically selective programs that did not greatly reduce the threat of plane hijackings. Planes continued to be hijacked as the terrorists used various methods to smuggle weapons past airport check-in gates.

The introduction of metal detectors and x-ray machines in the early 1970s helped reduce the incidence of hijackings, but it also served to move terrorists into higher forms of violence. Midair bombings and the use of plastic explosives, which the security devices could not detect, became new weapons in the terrorists' arsenal. Plastic explosives, which are putty-like substances that can be molded into any shape or form, are suspected of having been used in the February 1970 midair bombings of a Swissair transport plane over Switzerland that killed forty-seven people on board and of an Austrian Airlines plane near Frankfurt that same day. The pilot of the Austrian plane was able to land the plane safely. Plastic explosives were used in several midair bombings of the 1980s, including the blowing up of the Air India plane in 1985 and the Pan Am plane over Lockerbie in 1988.

It was in the aftermath of the Lockerbie tragedy that efforts to detect plastic explosives aboard planes were accelerated. Thermal neutron analysis (TNA) machines were installed at selected airports in the United States, with plans to introduce them abroad. These state-of-the-art detection systems bombard luggage with neutrons, which in turn emit gamma radiation when they interact with nitrogen atoms. Since most explosives contain nitrogen, the gamma radiation can alert security officials to their presence.[26] However, initial testing of these systems has shown that they cannot detect small amounts of plastic explosives that would still be capable of destroying aircraft. The President's Commission on Aviation Security and Terrorism found that the bomb that was used to blow up Pan Am 103 weighed half or less than the amount that the TNA machines would be able to reliably detect. The commission thus recommended deferring implementation of the TNA system until there is the "development of more effective TNA machines or an alternative technology."[27]

The TNA case illustrates some of the obstacles that those committed to fighting terrorism by enhancing physical security face. State-of-the-art technological devices are usually expensive; one TNA machine costs close to $1 million. And it can quickly become obsolete if terrorists move away from using plastic explosives. "What we're talking about [is] spending hundreds of millions of dollars on pieces of equipment that could only do one thing," said Dr. Geoff Goesling, a research engineer at the University of California at Berkeley, who examined the feasibility of installing TNA machines at airports for the FAA. "And if it became clear that there wasn't the threat anymore [of plastic explosives], we spend all this money and these white elephants [TNA machines] are sitting in airports around the world, unusable, and now we have to start all over again."[28]

The TNA debate also raises the broader question of the monetary costs for security against a low probability threat, such as bombings, as opposed to other problems in air safety, such as icing on wings of planes that can cause crashes after takeoff. "We have finite resources to deal with any class of problems and terrorism is just one class of problem," said Goesling. "It would be a shame if we spent so much effort on terrorism . . . that we reduce our efforts on other aviation safety questions."[29] Nevertheless, if a terrorist bombing or hijacking of a plane can be averted through a particular security device or procedure, it would seem likely that the public would support it no matter how much the cost or its effect on other aviation safety issues.

One obstacle to adequate physical security is the suicide terrorist. When terrorists are prepared to die for their cause, the task of antiterrorist planners becomes much more difficult. No degree of physical security may be adequate to prevent the suicide terrorist who is not concerned with escaping after the attack. Trying to keep one step ahead of this type of terrorist was a problem for the United States in Lebanon in the 1980s. At the time of the suicide bombing of the American embassy annex in Christian East Beirut in 1984, work was under way to improve security of the facility in the wake of the previous year's bombings of the Marine barracks and U.S. embassy in Beirut. Concrete barriers had been erected, but a steel gate that was to block the entry road to the annex was not yet installed. The terrorist was thus able to maneuver around the concrete barriers and detonate the bomb.

Physical security planners also face the problem of the stand-off attacks. Terrorists can simply extend the distance from which they initiate an attack in order to penetrate existing security around the perimeter of the target. During the 1986 economic summit in Tokyo, the Japanese terrorist group Middle Core Faction fired several homemade rockets from an apartment house nearly two miles away from the location where the foreign leaders were meeting under very tight security. Modern weapons allow for even further stand-off assaults by terrorists. Terrorists can also use sophisticated timing devices on explosives to penetrate security. The Irish Republican Army planted a bomb with a long delay fuse—estimates ranged from several days to several weeks—at a hotel where the Conservative party was holding its 1984 convention. This enabled the IRA to place the bomb at the hotel before tight security was put into effect. The bomb went off and narrowly missed killing Prime Minister Margaret Thatcher. "You can build timers now up to four years," observed Owen Robinson, a former U.S. government official. "Now if the terrorists are sophisticated enough to build it into the building itself, you haven't got a prayer of finding it."[30]

Despite these problems, physical security remains one of the more successful aspects of U.S. counterterrorism strategy. The number of terrorist incidents would have been much higher had current measures at airports, embassies, and other facilities not been in place. Security measures against terrorists will require continual updating and improving of technology, since the terrorists cannot be expected to stand still and watch their operations stymied by existing measures. They will improve their weapons and tactics to overcome any barriers. "Terrorists can attack anything, anywhere, anytime, limited only by operational considerations," writes terrorism expert Brian Jenkins.[31] The United States and other nations will need to keep their guard up even during "quiet" periods on the terrorist front. Physical security is a critical first line of defense.

America's experience with terrorism has been unique. The ideological and ethnic and religious divisions in society that are the roots of terrorism for most of the countries of the world have not exploded into sustained terrorist activity within the United States. But what has been absent from American soil has been more than made up overseas. Whereas the major terrorist threat for most governments lies within their borders, for the United States it is worldwide. No other country has had to face the diversity in the types of terrorist groups that can attack its citizens and facilities as has the United States: Palestinian and Islamic extremists in the Middle East, Europe, and Africa; Marxist-Leninist revolutionaries and other radical leftists in Latin America, Asia, and Europe; ethnic-nationalist separatists in virtually all regions of the world.

The United States will remain the favorite target of terrorists worldwide by virtue of its power, prestige, and influential role in many regions; U.S. symbols have accounted for approximately one-third of the yearly total of international terrorist incidents for decades. This will make the task of dealing with terrorism a perpetually frustrating one for the United States. There are simply things that are beyond the control of U.S. security planners, intelligence analysts, policymakers, and others when the threat comes from foreign soil. The major successes against terrorism by governments have come when the terrorist threat was domestic, allowing the government to bring the full brunt of their police, military, legal, and public pressure to bear against the terrorists. The Turkish military crushed the rightist and leftist terrorism that was destroying the country in the late 1970s; the Uruguayan military put down the terrorist threat of the Tupamaros in 1972; the Italian government used a combination of internal security and police measures along with promises of reduced sentences for those who gave information to reduce the Red Brigades terrorist threat.

Given the enormity of the counterterrorist task facing the United States, it makes more sense to shift away from the unattainable goals of the past—the sweeping policy statements on defeating terrorism, the casting of the problem in black-and-white terms, the unrealistic promises of never negotiating with or making concessions to terrorists—and focus instead on more achievable goals in the struggle against terrorism. The most important of these lies in the much-maligned "defensive" measures. Physical security, intelligence, and law enforcement have saved many lives and prevented the destruction of many facilities. Yet in the macho view that the best way to confront terrorism is to fight fire with fire, defensive measures are usually scoffed at as having only a minimum effect. Some even see negative effects in emphasizing defensive measures since it "has, in essence, made us sitting ducks [and] [i]t has not deterred terrorists from trying again and again. . . ."[32] But it is unrealistic to expect that terrorists can be completely deterred from embarking upon violent attacks. What good physical security and intelligence can do is reduce the risk at times to people and facilities of being targeted by terrorists. In battles against as wide and pervasive a threat as terrorism is, that is no small accomplishment.

Achievable goals also lie in bolstering the international community's legal framework. The United Nations has assumed a more influential role in the post–Cold War era, responding to ethnic-nationalist conflicts around the world by sending peacekeeping forces and by imposing sanctions on aggressive states. This assertive role can be expanded into the world of terrorism to help provide enforcement mechanisms for states to abide by the existing multilateral conventions on hijacking, bombings of aircraft, and kidnapping, as well as to help design even more encompassing agreements on other potential terrorist activities. The U.N. sanctions against Libya for its refusal to hand over two suspects wanted by the United States and Britain for their role in the bombing of Pan Am 103, and four other Libyans wanted by France for its investigation of the bombing of a French airliner over Niger in 1989, is an example of how the U.N. can be brought into the fight against terrorism.

A third achievable goal lies in the use of the military for selective operations against terrorists and their state-sponsors. What was unattainable in the past was to expect that the military could apply quick-fix solutions to the problem of terrorism, or that its special units, such as Delta Force and the Navy SEALS, could successfully do battle against terrorists worldwide, no matter what the terrain or the circumstances. It was also unrealistic, based upon other governments' experiences, to expect that hostage rescue efforts could be carried out without casualties, including the hostages. But military successes against terrorists are possible and advisable when the terrain, environment, and distance the military has to travel are all working in favor of the attacking forces, and the costs of inaction are deemed greater than any potential repercussions.

The most achievable goal of all, however, in combating terrorism lies in changing our reaction to the threats and violence of terrorists. From the days of the Barbary pirates to those of Saddam Hussein, the one continuing strain has been the ability of terrorists to evoke widespread fear in society. As we draw close to a new century, there needs to be a recognition that we have possessed within ourselves all along the most powerful weapon against international terrorism. While we cannot prevent every single incident from occurring or take away every potential bomb from the terrorists, we can take away the reaction that they seek, which is panic, fear, and disruption in our lives.

Epilogue

"The terrorism happened when I was young," reflected Miriam Beeber in the spring of 1992. "That was really my first experience in life." She could look back upon her odyssey of terror at the hands of the PFLP in the Jordanian desert in 1970, knowing that although it cannot be erased from her memory—"I've never talked about it that much because it does have emotional tension"—it can nevertheless be put into perspective: "I've had so many [other] experiences in my life [since] . . . that the terrorism to me [was] just one very intense episode."[1] She survived her terrorism ordeal to become an anthropologist, traveling around the world and eventually marrying and becoming the mother of two children. She settled in a university town in Arizona.

Although there was no twenty-five-year reunion in 1992 for Midwood High School's 1967 graduating class, for a brief time in the late 1980s, Beeber and fellow honor student Judith Clark lived very close to each other. Clark continued to have problems while serving her life sentence in a state prison for women in New York. In 1985 she was placed in an isolated cell for two years, following an administrative hearing that found she had attempted to smuggle out information about the prison's security system. When the state prison underwent construction work in 1987, the authorities believed that the facility would be vulnerable to escapes during that period and that Clark would be a high risk based upon her previous behavior. They transferred her temporarily to a federal prison in Arizona—in the same university town where Miriam Beeber was living.

The transfer across the country led the *New York Times* to publish an editorial protesting the action. The editorial, titled "Punish the Mother, Not the Daughter," presented the case for keeping Clark in New York for the benefit of her seven-year-old daughter, who had been born a few months before the Brink's incident. "Every week for six years, Harriet Clark . . . has spent the better part of a day visiting her mother at the Bedford Hills Correctional Center, a maximum-security women's prison. The family makes a plausible case that the sudden termination of the visits inflicts serious damage on the child. . . . The prison's concern for security surely comes first. But if there are other ways to meet it, why visit the sins of the mother upon the child?"[2] When a reporter asked Clark a few months after her 1981 arrest if she did not feel that she had endangered the welfare of her daughter by her involvement in the Brink's incident, she replied that her baby was being cared for by "comrades." "I don't want my child to grow up in a corrupt society," Clark told the reporter.[3]

Images of what society should be or who should be held responsible for various grievances have long characterized political and social movements. But those who have resorted to terrorism cross a line that most politically active groups never contemplate. What is beyond comprehension to most people—the killing and emotional scarring of victims with no apparent connection to a terrorist's agenda—is all too clear to those who engage in the violence. The retort of the French anarchist Emile Henry a century ago—that "there are no innocent"—still holds true today. The most formidable aspect of terrorism will remain the endless supply of extremists willing to kill, kidnap, or hijack in the name of some cause.

Yet by the autumn of 1992, America could be described as in a state of limbo with respect to international terrorism. The tough talk on terrorism that had been so prevalent in the 1980s was no longer heard as frequently but would still arise on occasion, particularly whenever a Muammar Qaddafi or a Saddam Hussein was in the news. The hostages from Lebanon had been home for almost a year, yet there were still occasional kidnappings of Americans overseas; during the winter an American businessman was seized by communist rebels in the Philippines and held for two months before being rescued by Filipino police. The Cold War was quickly becoming a distant memory, but daily reports of bloodshed in the former Yugoslav republic of Bosnia-Herzegovina reminded people that violence and terrorism did not end with the termination of superpower conflicts. And while there had not been a spectacular anti-

U.S. terrorist attack since the bombing of Pan Am 103, there were still plenty of major terrorist attacks occurring elsewhere in 1992—including the blowing up of the Israeli embassy in Buenos Aires and the bombing of an Air France ticket counter in Algiers—to suggest that it might only be a matter of time before U.S. targets were once again involved in major terrorist assaults.

The World Trade Center bombing was just such an assault. The 1993 blast brought America back to reality about the terrorist threat, and if history is to be any guide, then America certainly has not seen the last of such attacks. What began with hostage taking in the faraway shores of the Mediterranean at the beginning of the republic continued at home with bombings during the turbulent years of labor-management conflicts, and what struck again with a fury during the decades of midair plane bombings, hijackings, and suicide truck bombings overseas had clearly proven itself to be a phenomenon with lasting power. Anguish and frustration over combating terrorism was a common trait during Washington's and Jefferson's time, as well as during Carter's, Reagan's, and Bush's time. Victims suffered at the hands of the Barbary pirate states centuries ago and at the hands of Hizballah, Palestinian extremists, and numerous other state-sponsored and independent terrorist groups just a few years ago. Like a menacing cloud before a storm, terrorism has always been lurking in the background, awaiting only the right moment to pour down its violence.

The legacy of the past and the realities of the current world situation should have suggested the folly of believing that terrorism can somehow be eliminated. Yet old habits die hard, and the desire to view terrorism as a solvable problem could still be found in some quarters during the 1990s. One article on terrorism, published in the spring of 1992, concluded on the following optimistic note: "A willingness to take direct action against terrorists and the states that underwrite their violence could break the back of terrorism for a long time to come."[4] But as American presidents and the American public painfully learned over the years, there never was a "back of terrorism" to break, and no matter how much "direct action" was taken, terrorists always seemed to rebound and strike again. The world of terrorism was a chameleon-like world of shifting groups and state-sponsors, changing tactics and causes, new weapons and higher levels of violence.

There was, nevertheless, much that America could be proud of after many years of grappling with the terrorist threat. The United States had established itself in the early 1970s as the leader of the democratic world's response to international terrorism. Pressure was put upon states to deny safe passage to terrorists and to punish or extradite those responsible for terrorist attacks. Although many of these efforts were initially frustrated by some governments' desires to pursue their self-interests, gradually an increasing number of countries began cooperating in combating a form of violence that could affect them all.

The United States had also taken the lead in helping other governments improve their physical security and intelligence measures in combating terrorism. Through the State Department's antiterrorism assistance program, thousands of law enforcement and security personnel from foreign nations were trained in the United States. The United States also provided airport security and communications equipment to many governments. A multimillion-dollar effort was begun in the 1980s to improve physical security at our own embassies overseas, and there has been continual monitoring of security measures at international airports throughout the world to decrease the risk of terrorist incidents.

The United States demonstrated that it could go on the offensive against some terrorists and some state-sponsors when all other measures failed. The years of frustration in dealing with the taunts and activities of Qaddafi finally led to the raid on Libya. That no action was taken against more powerful and influential Middle East actors and state-sponsors of terrorism such as Iran and Syria underscored the limitations in using military force as a counterterrorist weapon. The raid nevertheless served as a warning that, with the exception of assassination, there were no options that the United States would preclude in its battle against terrorism. President Bill Clinton emphasized this strategy early in his presidency, launching a military strike against Iraq's intelligence command center in retaliation for an Iraqi plot to assassinate George Bush during a 1993 visit to Kuwait.

Arrests of terrorists in the United States and abroad were also made, some by luck, as in the case of the New Jersey state trooper who spotted a nervous Yu Kikumura at a rest stop on the New Jersey Turnpike, and some by cunning, as in the FBI sting operation that lured Fawaz Younis onto a boat off the coast of Cyprus. Other governments arrested an increasing number of terrorists in the 1990s, including the French capture of top leaders of the Basque separatist ETA movement and the Peruvian government's arrest of Shining Path leader Abimael Guzman Reynoso. While most terrorists remained beyond the reach of the law, the imprisonment of even a small percentage of them was still a boost to America and other countries' counterterrorist efforts.

Much had been accomplished indeed in the struggle against terrorism. But much more remained uncertain as the 1990s evolved. Among the growing list of questions was how the new states that were coming into existence in the post–Cold War era—the numerous independent and semi-independent entities born from the collapse of communism—were going to evolve as players in the world of international terrorism. Would they become active participants in the international community's efforts to bring terrorists to justice, to impose sanctions on state-sponsors of terrorism, to enhance physical security at facilities, to share intelligence on terrorist groups and developments? Or would some turn a blind eye to terrorists, as many states did in the 1970s and 1980s, hoping that by providing safe passage and sanctuary they would be spared terrorist attacks on their own territory? There was also the potential for some of these states to sponsor terrorist activity if they believed such action might serve their interests.

The early 1990s raised concerns about the terrorist repercussions of the ethnic-nationalist and religious conflicts that were brewing around the world. Long after the fighting dies out, lingering hatreds and bitterness among the various groups were likely to find an outlet in international terrorist attacks. There was also uncertainty about the aftermath of any potential peace settlement in the Middle East. The history of terrorism has been filled with cases in which extremists have sabotaged peace accords with violent attacks or continued their terrorism even after peace was reached.

Another question mark in the world of terrorism was how future American presidents would handle the terrorist threat. Each president has had his own style for dealing with terrorism. Jefferson's compassion for the hostages held in the Barbary prisons led him to cut deals with the terrorists in order to gain the captives' freedom, but also to use military force against the Barbary states to free them. Teddy Roosevelt threatened military action in Tangier, but this was to pressure the Moroccan government to negotiate with the leader of a rebel group holding what was believed to be an American hostage. Truman, Eisenhower, Kennedy, and Johnson all favored a low-key approach to their terrorist incidents, while Nixon utilized intense behind-the-scenes efforts to help resolve the PFLP hijacking-hostage episode. Ford's brief time in office found him yielding to the demands of Croatian separatists during a hijacking, but using military force against the Cambodian government during the *Mayaguez* incident. Carter chose the patient approach to try to end the hostage crisis in the American embassy in Iran, while Reagan opted for the tough stance on terrorism during his years in office. Yet both wound up becoming victims of the emotional desire to free hostages no matter what the costs to American prestige or interests. Bush was able to avoid the trap of his predecessors on the issue of hostages, but nevertheless found himself in an embarrassing position on the issue of state-sponsorship of terrorism. After repeatedly denouncing governments that support terrorism, Bush still courted the assistance of a well-known state-sponsor, Syria, when that government's help was needed during the war with Iraq. Clinton's record in the battle against terrorism during his first year in office revealed a low-key style, as he avoided any rhetoric about terrorism in the aftermath of the World Trade Center bombing, but also showed a willingness to bomb Iraq as a state-sponsor of terrorism.

The central role that presidents have played in the history of America's response to terrorism will continue in the coming years. Future presidents will not only decide whether the United States should use its military might to try to punish terrorists and retaliate against state-sponsors of terrorism or instead focus on economic and diplomatic sanctions, they will also influence the way the American public perceives and reacts to terrorism. Through their statements and actions, presidents will help determine whether a particular terrorist episode becomes a full-fledged crisis for the country. The burden for presidents will be to achieve a balance between responding firmly to terrorism and demonstrating compassion for hostages and other victims of terrorism on the one hand, while not jeopardizing the long-term interests of the nation on the other hand. It will be a task that will require all the skills of presidential leadership.

One of the biggest concerns in terrorism in the 1990s is the continued proliferation of sophisticated weapons worldwide. There is no indication that governments will be able to prevent some of these arms, particularly the small, mobile, and light weapons, from falling into the hands of terrorists and extremist groups. There are not only more modern weapons being traded, sold, bartered, and moved across borders, but there are more players entering the game as well. Joining the United States in peddling arms to such volatile regions as the Middle East are China, France, Germany, and Russia.

Illustrating the problems that previous weapon transfers can cause, the United States was trying to figure out in the 1990s how to get back, if at all possible, the numerous Stinger antiaircraft missiles that it had given to Afghan Muslim rebels in the 1980s. The rebels' victory over the former Soviet-backed government in Kabul in 1992 led to concerns that a surplus of the high-tech weapons ultimately could be transferred to international terrorist groups or to state-sponsors of terrorism, such as Iran. These shoulder-fired weapons, which can bring down airplanes flying up to 18,000 feet, were already floating around the world's arms markets by the 1990s. The Persian Gulf nation of Qatar purchased Stingers on the black market in 1988, while in 1991, three Croatians and an American gun shop owner were arrested by U.S. customs agents as they attempted to buy twenty Stinger missiles for use in the Yugoslav civil war.[5]

Technology and violence have marched together since the beginning of time. From stone-age weapons such as axes, daggers, and swords, to the invention of gunpowder in the fourteenth century and dynamite in the nineteenth century, technology has provided a continual source of creativity for the making of lethal weapons. Nobody at the end of the twentieth century can be quite sure where all this ultimately will lead. One thing that is certain is that modern-day innovations in weaponry have made violence by anybody—a nation, a group, an individual—more proficient and deadlier than previous times. It is one of the great ironies of history that with the end of the Cold War the world can breathe a sigh of relief over the prospects of nuclear annihilation by the superpowers, but will have to hold its breath with respect to terrorists, guerrilla groups, and various governments unleashing high-tech weapons or nuclear, chemical, and biological weapons.

While the United States and the international community were taking steps in order to address the potential threat of *states* utilizing weapons of mass destruction, little was being done to deal with the terrorist threat in this domain. The heightened worldwide concern about terrorists and biological weapons that was generated during the Gulf War had all but faded a few years afterward. "Where are the dead bodies from terrorist attacks with biological agents?" was the typical response U.S. intelligence analysts were receiving from others in the government when they raised the prospects of terrorists venturing into this domain. Policymakers tend to work with what is familiar, and in the world of terrorism, that means the blowing up of things or the seizing of people and objects. Yet the continued neglect of the terrorist threat of using weapons of mass destruction would greatly diminish the significance of any treaties dealing with state use of such weapons. What foreign governments can do on a grand scale with chemical and biological weapons, terrorist groups can do on a smaller scale with equally dangerous results. The terrorists do not need elaborate weapons programs, but rather with simple procedures and planning can cause great harm with chemical, and particularly biological, agents.

The establishment of a worldwide monitoring and intelligence network aimed at uncovering terrorist plans and activity in this area would be a crucial first step in addressing the threat. Through the informal intelligence contacts between different governments and joint international efforts to identify all possible indicators of a terrorist group or individual's ability and willingness to use biological and chemical agents, the risk of such a terrorist event occurring might be greatly reduced. A second important step would be to design counterterrorist response options to scenarios in which terrorists either are threatening to unleash chemical or biological agents or have already done so. It would be quite ironic if after all the years when U.S. government officials had talked about terrorism as a war and as a threat to national security—always having in mind the bombings, hijackings, and kidnappings that terrorists were skilled at doing, but that never really posed a serious threat to U.S. security interests—they would now ignore the one area in which terrorists can indeed threaten the security of a nation and cause an unprecedented number of casualties in the process.

For those Americans that have been touched by terrorism, however, just one casualty has been one too many. Issues of national security and foreign policy—the things that governments have to be concerned with in responding to terrorism—are just abstract principles to most victims and their families. There is no replacing a loved one killed by a terrorist bomb or bullet, and there can never be a clean wiping of the slate for former hostages. Whether a victim's ordeal was a few hours being held captive in an airplane or a few years being chained to a wall in a Beirut apartment, the memories linger and lives are affected forever. As with any diverse group of people that have been victimized by a traumatic event, some adjust well and some do not. But most never forget their terror, even if they eventually may come to forgive or understand their tormentors' motives.

Most of America's victims of terrorism have had to bear their burden alone. Long after public interest in their episodes fades, they still have to find ways to cope with the anguish that remains. One of the few times when people directly affected by terrorism banded together for both emotional and political support was in the aftermath of the bombing of Pan Am 103. The families of the victims had a political agenda they wanted addressed, namely, the punishment of those responsible for the murder of their loved ones and the implementation of better aviation security measures. But they also needed to find ways to deal with their grief. "I don't think friends and family can really understand what it's like," said Rosemary Wolfe, stepmother of Miriam Wolfe, one of the Syracuse University students killed in the Pan Am bombing. "Only somebody who has gone through it really understands what it's like, and so that's why I think it's been very important for us [to have each other]."[6]

Even the compassion of others can sometimes rub the victims of terrorism the wrong way. When Syracuse University unveiled a plaque in memory of the thirty-five students who were aboard Pan Am 103, the university thought they would offend family members if they used words such as "bombing" or "terrorism" on the brief inscription on the plaque. They therefore chose the phrase "plane crash" to describe the incident. When Rosemary Wolfe and her husband, Jim, arrived at the hotel the night before the unveiling, they found several families gathered in the lobby and visibly upset. One of the relatives of a Pan Am victim had taken a peek at the plaque and informed the others about its wording. "We immediately got in touch with the Syracuse people, and one of them came over and met with us at 9:30 that night in the hotel," recalled Rosemary Wolfe. The families explained to the university representative that their loved ones died due to terrorism and that the words "plane crash" did not convey the true meaning of the tragedy. "It was a bombing, we want it called a bombing, and we want the world to remember that it was a bombing," the families told the university official. While it was too late to change the wording for the next day, it was eventually changed. The plaque, which is located at the main entrance to the university, has the names of the students inscribed on it and reads as follows: "This place of remembrance is dedicated to the memory of the 35 students enrolled in Syracuse University's Division of International Programs Abroad who died with 235 others as the result of a plane crash, December 21, 1988 over Lockerbie, Scotland *caused by a terrorist bomb*."[7]

Keeping alive the memories of those killed by terrorists can take many forms. In the fall of 1992, Jack Plaxe, a high school friend of John Flynn, who died in the Pan Am 103 bombing, returned to the small school in New Jersey along with several of Flynn's other friends and former teachers. Their plan was to have a memorial ceremony for Flynn, but not one devoted solely to personal remembrances of their friend. Rather, their purpose was also to educate a new generation of students about the threat of terrorism. "We're going to talk to the student body to basically sensitize them to the [terrorism] issue," Plaxe said on the eve of the visit, "to make sure that they remember Pan Am 103, because a lot of them are young."[8]

Remembering terrorism and remembering its victims will be part of the legacy that we leave to future generations. Their burden will be to deal with an increasingly violent world where terrorists continue to strike for age-old reasons, and where governments try to find ways to combat the threat, while individuals are left to cope with terrorism's inevitable tragedies.

Interviews

HOWARD BANE, former Central Intelligence Agency official, May 3, 1990, Fairfax, Virginia.

COLONEL (RET.) CHARLES BECKWITH, former commander of Delta Force, May 16, 1990, Austin, Texas.

MIRIAM BEEBER, hostage on 1970 TWA plane hijacked to Jordan by the Popular Front for the Liberation of Palestine (PFLP), June 11, 1992, Tucson, Arizona.

RANDY BEERS, director of counterterrorism, National Security Council, 1988–1992, September 22, 1992, Washington, D.C.

WARREN BENSON, hostage on 1976 TWA plane hijacked to France by Croatian separatists, June 11, 1992, Tucson, Arizona.

L. PAUL BREMER, ambassador at large for counterterrorism, 1986–1989, May 23, 1990, New York, New York.

EMILY BRETZ, wife of hostage Rudy Bretz, March 27, 1992, Malibu, California.

RUDY BRETZ, hostage on 1976 TWA plane hijacked to France by Croatian separatists, March 27, 1992, Malibu, California.

TOM BROKAW, anchor, NBC News, June 26, 1990, New York, New York.

MCGEORGE BUNDY, special assistant for national security affairs, 1961–1965, March 5, 1990, Irvine, California.

JULIENE BUSIC, hijacker of 1976 TWA plane to France, April 9, 1992, South San Francisco, California.

ZVONKO BUSIC, hijacker of 1976 TWA plane to France, December 1, 1992, and January 12, 1993 (telephone interviews, U.S. penitentiary, Lewisburg, Pennsylvania).

WARREN CANRIGHT, publisher, *Chesterton (Indiana) Tribune,* November 4, 1993 (telephone interview).

MAJOR RHONDA CORNUM, U.S. Army flight surgeon during Persian Gulf War and prisoner-of-war in Iraq, May 25, 1992, Los Angeles, California.

ROBERT CUMMINGS, court reporter during 1982–1983 trial of former Weather Underground members, September 2, 1992 (telephone interview).

SAM DONALDSON, correspondent, ABC News, June 19, 1990, Washington, D.C.

DR. CALVIN J. FREDERICK, psychologist, University of California at Los Angeles and Veterans Administration Medical Center, August 4, 1992, Los Angeles, California.

LESLIE GELB, columnist, *New York Times,* June 26, 1990, New York, New York.

PTOR GJESTLAND, financial trader in the World Trade Center on the day of the bombing in 1993, August 20, 1993 (telephone interview).

GEOFF GOESLING, researcher, University of California, Berkeley, April 10, 1992, Berkeley, California.

GENERAL (RET.) ANDREW GOODPASTER, staff secretary to President Dwight D. Eisenhower and former supreme allied commander, Europe, May 2, 1990, Washington, D.C.

LARRY GROSSMAN, President of NBC News, 1984–1988, May 21, 1990, New York, New York.

CATHERINE HODES, hostage on 1970 TWA plane hijacked to Jordan by the PFLP, March 21, 1992 (telephone interview).

MARTHA HODES, hostage on 1970 TWA plane hijacked to Jordan by the PFLP, April 15, 1992 (telephone interview).

YOUSSEF IBRAHIM, reporter, *New York Times*, July 18, 1990, Paris.

DAVID JACOBSEN, hostage in Beirut from May 1985 to November 1986, June 30, 1992, Huntington Beach, California.

FATHER LAWRENCE MARTIN JENCO, hostage in Beirut from January 1985 to July 1986, May 11, 1992, Los Angeles, California.

BRIAN JENKINS, international terrorism expert, June 22, 1992, Santa Monica, California.

HOWARD JOHNSON, resident of Chesterton, Indiana, November 8, 1993 (telephone interview).

GALE MCGEE, former senator (D-Wyoming), June 19, 1990, Washington, D.C.

ROBERT MCGUIRE, police commissioner, New York City, 1978–1983, May 23, 1990, New York, New York.

DR. CORNELIUS G. MCWRIGHT, former supervisory special agent and chief of scientific research, Federal Bureau of Investigation, July 29, 1992, Santa Monica, California.

DR. J. WILLIAM MAGEE, former supervisory special agent and chief chemist, Federal Bureau of Investigation, April 30, 1990, Arlington, Virginia.

CONSTANTINE MELNIK, former French government official, July 17, 1990, Paris.

ALLEN MORRISON, spokesperson for the Port Authority of New York and New Jersey, in the World Trade Center on the day of the bombing in 1993, August 27, 1993 (telephone interview).

JEANNE MURRY, wife of hostage Thomas Murry, March 27, 1992, Newbury Park, California.

THOMAS MURRY, hostage on 1985 TWA plane hijacked to Beirut, Lebanon, by Shiite extremists, March 27, 1992, Newbury Park, California.

RITA ODE, wife of hostage Robert Ode, June 12, 1992, Sun City West, Arizona.

ROBERT ODE, hostage in American embassy in Iran, 1979–1981, June 12, 1992, Sun City West, Arizona.

JACK PLAXE, high-school friend of John Flynn, killed in bombing of Pan Am 103, September 24, 1992 (telephone interview).

OWEN ROBINSON, former U.S. government official, May 1, 1990, Arlington, Virginia.

JAMES ROSCOE, hostage on 1976 TWA plane hijacked to France by Croatian separatists, March 25, 1992 (telephone interview).

ANDY ROSS, owner of bookstore firebombed in 1988 for carrying Salman Rushdie's *The Satanic Verses*, April 10, 1992, Berkeley, California.

WALT ROSTOW, special assistant for national security affairs, 1964–1969, May 16, 1990, Austin, Texas.

DEAN RUSK, secretary of state, 1961–1969, April 23, 1990, Athens, Georgia.

PIERRE SALINGER, former chief foreign correspondent, ABC News, and White House press secretary, 1961–1964, July 12, 1990, London.

DANIEL SCHORR, senior news analyst, National Public Radio, June 18, 1990, Washington, D.C.

GERALD SEIB, reporter, *Wall Street Journal*, abducted by Iranian government agents in 1987, September 23, 1992, Washington, D.C.

GEORGE SHULTZ, secretary of state, 1982–1989, November 25, 1991, Palo Alto, California.

RICHARD TUFARO, former staff member of the White House Working Group on Terrorism, 1972–1974, May 23, 1990, New York, New York.

ED TURNER, executive vice president, Cable News Network, June 24, 1990, Atlanta, Georgia.

JACK VALENTI, special assistant to President Lyndon B. Johnson, 1964–1968, April 30, 1990, Washington, D.C.

CYRUS VANCE, secretary of state, 1977–1980, May 22, 1990, New York, New York.

MICHAEL WINES, reporter, *New York Times*, June 22, 1990, Washington, D.C.

ROSEMARY WOLFE, stepmother of Miriam Wolfe, killed in bombing of Pan Am 103, September 23, 1992, Washington, D.C.

JOHN YAO, engineer with the Port Authority of New York and New Jersey and in the World Trade Center on the day of the bombing in 1993, August 29, 1993 (telephone interview).

Z (pseudonym for Armenian terrorist convicted of plotting to bomb Turkish consulate general office in Philadelphia in 1982), April 1, 1992, Los Angeles, California.

Notes

Prologue

1. *Department of State Telegram, September, 1970, White House Central Files,* Richard Nixon Presidential Materials Staff, National Archives and Records Administration, Alexandria, Virginia.
2. *New York Times,* September 29, 1970, p. 18.
3. *New York Times,* October 22, 1981, p. 1; December 24, 1982, Section II, p. 6.
4. *New York Times,* February 16, 1982, p. B4.
5. *New York Times,* September 15, 1983, p. B7.
6. *New York Times,* October 7, 1983, p. B2.
7. Ibid.
8. Interview (telephone), Robert Cummings, September 2, 1992.
9. Albert Parry, *Terrorism: From Robespierre to Arafat* (New York: Vanguard Press, 1976), pp. 87–88.
10. *New York Times,* September 11, 1976, p. 7.
11. *Report of the President's Commission on Aviation Security and Terrorism,* Washington, D.C., May 15, 1990, p. i.

1. Welcome to Reality

1. ABC News "Nightline," August 2, 1993, show #3181, Journal Graphics.
2. Interview (telephone), Ptor Gjestland, August 20, 1993.
3. David Wise, "The Terrorists among Us," *Los Angeles Times,* March 7, 1993, Section M, p. 1.
4. *New York Times,* June 25, 1993, p. 1.
5. ABC News "Nightline," August 2, 1993, show #3181, Journal Graphics.
6. *New York Times,* March 28, 1993, pp. 1, 18.
7. *Wall Street Journal,* January 6, 1993, p. 5.
8. *New York Times,* July 15, 1993, p. 16.
9. ABC News "Nightline," August 2, 1993, show #3181, Journal Graphics.
10. Statement of Stanley Brezenoff, executive director, the Port Authority of New York and New Jersey, "Regarding the Bombing of the World Trade Center," before the House Subcommittee on Crime and Criminal Justice, Washington, D.C., March 9, 1993.
11. Interview (telephone), Allen Morrison, August 27, 1993.
12. Interview (telephone), John Yao, August 29, 1993.
13. Interview (telephone), Ptor Gjestland, August 20, 1993.

2. The Endless Nature of Terrorism

1. J. M. Roberts, *The Pelican History of the World* (London: Penguin, 1987), p. 925. For two excellent historical narratives of the conflict in Northern Ireland, see J. Bowyer Bell, *The Irish Troubles: A Generation of Violence, 1967–1992* (New York: St. Martin's, 1993), and Tim Pat Coogan, *The IRA: A History* (Niwot, Colorado: Roberts Rinehart, 1993).

2. Martha Crenshaw, "The Causes of Terrorism," in Charles W. Kegley, Jr., ed., *International Terrorism* (New York: St. Martin's Press, 1990), p. 123.

3. *Patterns of Global Terrorism: 1990,* Department of State Publication 9862, Office of the Secretary of State, Office of the Coordinator for Counterterrorism, U.S. Department of State, Washington, D.C., April 1991, p. iii.

4. Colin Legum, "What Is Terrorism," *London Observer,* November 26, 1972, reprinted in *Current,* January 1973, pp. 3–9.

5. David C. Rapoport, "Religion and Terror: Thugs, Assassins, and Zealots," in Kegley, *International Terrorism,* p. 155.

6. Amir Taheri, *Holy Terror: Inside the World of Islamic Terrorism* (Bethesda, Maryland: Adler & Adler, 1987), pp. 36–43.

7. Quoted in Bernard Lewis, *The Assassins: A Radical Sect in Islam* (New York: Octagon, 1980), p. 5.

8. Ibid., pp. 12, 130, 134.

9. Rapoport, "Religion and Terror," pp. 147–49.

10. R. R. Palmer, *Twelve Who Ruled: The Committee of Public Safety during the Terror* (Princeton: Princeton University Press, 1941), p. 266.

11. Daniel Gerould, *Guillotine: Its Legend and Lore* (New York: Blast Books, 1992), p. 13.

12. George Rude, ed., *Robespierre* (Englewood Cliffs, New Jersey: Prentice-Hall, 1967), p. 8; Parry, *Terrorism,* pp. 53–54.

13. Palmer, *Twelve Who Ruled,* pp. 260, 276.

14. Parry, *Terrorism,* pp. 21, 56–60.

15. Stanley Loomis, *Paris in the Terror* (Philadelphia: Lippincott, 1964), pp. 339–40.

16. Rude, *Robespierre,* p. 76.

17. Dumas Malone, *Jefferson and the Rights of Man* (Boston: Little Brown, 1951), pp. 27–28. For a discussion of U.S. policy toward the Barbary states, see Ray W. Irwin, *The Diplomatic Relations of the United States with the Barbary Powers, 1776–1816* (Chapel Hill: University of North Carolina Press, 1931); Samuel Flagg Bemis, ed., *The American Secretaries of State and Their Diplomacy,* vol. 2 (New York: Knopf, 1928); Richard Hofstadter, William Miller, Daniel Aaron, *The American Republic,* vol. 1: *To 1865* (Englewood Cliffs, New Jersey: Prentice-Hall, 1959).

18. Irwin, *Diplomatic Relations,* pp. 9–10.

19. A. B. C. Whipple, *To the Shores of Tripoli: The Birth of the U.S. Navy and Marines* (New York: Morrow, 1991), p. 41.

20. Irwin, *Diplomatic Relations,* p. 204.

21. Malone, *Jefferson and the Rights of Man,* p. 32; Irwin, *Diplomatic Relations,* p. 45.

22. Irwin, *Diplomatic Relations,* pp. 11, 44–46, 70; Malone, *Jefferson and the*

Rights of Man, pp. 28, 31–32; Gardner W. Allen, *Our Navy and the Barbary Corsairs* (Hamden, Connecticut: Archon Books, 1965 [first published in 1905]), pp. 2, 41–42.

23. Irwin, *Diplomatic Relations*, p. 17; Malone, *Jefferson and the Rights of Man*, p. 31.

24. Irwin, *Diplomatic Relations*, p. 55.

25. Thomas Jefferson, *Public and Private Papers* (New York: Vintage Books/Library of America, 1990), p. 176.

26. Barbara W. Tuchman, "Perdicaris Alive or Raisuli Dead," *American Heritage*, August 1959, p. 18.

27. Ibid., p. 19.

28. *New York Times*, May 21, 1904, p. 1.

29. Lewis L. Gould, *The Presidency of Theodore Roosevelt* (Lawrence: University of Kansas Press, 1991), p. 136.

30. Tuchman, "Perdicaris," p. 21.

31. Ibid., p. 98.

32. *New York Times*, June 18, 1904, p. 8.

33. Ibid., June 20, 1904, p. 9.

34. Tuchman, "Perdicaris," p. 99.

35. *New York Times*, June 23, 1904, p. 1.

36. Ibid., p. 1.

37. Tuchman, "Perdicaris," p. 100.

38. Ibid., p. 100.

39. Tyler Dennett, *John Hay: From Poetry to Politics* (New York: Dodd, Mead, 1934), p. 401.

40. Dennett, *John Hay*, p. 402; Tuchman, "Perdicaris," pp. 21, 98, 100–101. When the incident was over, Gummere had Perdicaris sign a confession that he had never tried to resume American citizenship since the 1860s. No action was taken against Perdicaris who continually referred to his American citizenship both during and after the crisis. In a speech in April 1905, he praised the "big stick" policy of President Roosevelt, saying "such action should always be taken when an American citizen is imprisoned without cause as I was" (*New York Times*, April 28, 1905, p. 3). It would have been too embarrassing for the Roosevelt administration to reveal its knowledge of his background. See Tuchman, "Perdicaris," p. 101, for a further discussion of this matter.

41. *New York Times*, June 27, 1904, p. 1; Tuchman, "Perdicaris," p. 101.

42. *New York Times*, June 27, 1904, p. 1.

43. Ibid., July 17, 1904, p. 4.

44. Ibid., April 28, 1905, p. 3.

45. Ibid., April 29, 1905, p. 10.

46. Parry, *Terrorism: From Robespierre to Arafat*, pp. 95–96.

47. Wayne G. Broehl, Jr., *The Molly Maguires* (Cambridge, Massachusetts: Harvard University Press, 1964), pp. 247–48.

48. Philip S. Foner, *History of the Labor Movement in the United States*, vol. 1: *From Colonial Times to the Founding of the American Federation of Labor* (New York: International Publishers, 1947), p. 461.

49. Sidney Lens, *The Labor Wars: From the Molly Maguires to the Sitdowns* (New York: Doubleday, 1973), p. 27.

50. William Burns, *The Masked War* (New York: Doran, 1913), p. 44. Reprinted as part of Mass Violence in America series, Robert M. Fogelson and Richard E. Rubenstein, advisory eds. (New York: Arno Press and The New York Times, 1969).

51. Foner, *History of the Labor Movement in the United States,* vol. 5: *The AFL in the Progressive Era, 1910–1915* (New York: International Publishers, 1980), p. 13.

52. Page Smith, *America Enters the World,* vol. 7: *A People's History of the Progressive Era and World War I* (New York: McGraw-Hill, 1985), pp. 252–60. Darrow was later indicted for bribing two jurors in the McNamara trial. He was acquitted in one case, but there was a hung jury in the other case. The prosecutor did not file charges again against Darrow. For an excellent account of Darrow's bribery trial and the trial of the McNamara brothers, see Geoffrey Cowan, *The People v. Clarence Darrow: The Bribery Trial of America's Greatest Lawyer* (New York: Times Books/Random House, 1993).

53. Ibid., pp. 258–60.

54. Foner, *History of the Labor Movement,* vol. 5, p. 31.

55. Crenshaw, "The Logic of Terrorism: Terrorist Behavior as a Product of Strategic Choice," in Walter Reich, ed., *Origins of Terrorism: Psychologies, Ideologies, Theologies, States of Mind* (New York: Cambridge University Press and Woodrow Wilson International Center for Scholars, 1990), p. 15.

56. Foner, *History of the Labor Movement,* vol. 5, p. 8.

57. Donald Robinson, ed., *Under Fire: Israel's Twenty-Year Struggle for Survival* (New York: Norton, 1968), p. 23.

58. Thurston Clarke, *By Blood and Fire: The Attack on the King David Hotel* (New York: Putnam's, 1981), p. 76.

59. Ibid., p. 247.

60. Amos Perlmutter, *Israel: The Partitioned State* (New York: Scribner's, 1985), p. 104.

61. Clarke, *By Blood and Fire,* p. 257.

62. Paul Johnson, *Modern Times: The World from the Twenties to the Eighties* (New York: Harper and Row, 1983), p. 483.

63. Clarke, *By Blood and Fire,* p. 260.

64. Perlmutter, *Israel: The Partitioned State,* p. 105.

65. *The Toronto Globe and Mail,* September 30, 1949, p. 1; March 6, 1950, p. 9.

66. *The Toronto Globe and Mail,* September 29, 1949, p. 2.

67. *The Toronto Globe and Mail,* September 24, 1949, p. 2; September 26, 1949, p. 1.

68. *The Toronto Globe and Mail,* March 15, 1950, p. 1.

69. E. J. Kahn, Jr., "Annals of Crime: It Has No Name," *New Yorker,* November 14, 1953, p. 133.

70. Interview, J. William Magee, Arlington, Virginia, April 30, 1990.

71. *The Denver Post,* November 14, 1955, pp. 2, 3; November 15, 1955, p. 3.

72. *The Denver Post,* November 15, 1955, p. 3.

73. *New York Times,* November 15, 1955, p. 28.

74. *New York Times*, March 13, 1957, p. 33.

75. Earl Parker Hanson, *Puerto Rico: Ally for Progress* (New York: Van Nostrand, 1962).

76. Robert H. Ferrell, ed., *Off the Record: The Private Papers of Harry S Truman* (New York: Harper and Row, 1980), p. 199.

77. Ibid., p. 199.

78. Interview, Dean Rusk, April 23, 1990, Athens, Georgia.

79. *New York Times*, March 2, 1954, p. 16; March 4, 1954, p. 1; Hanson, *Puerto Rico*, p. 66.

80. *New York Times*, March 5, 1954, p. 2.

81. Alan Weisman, "An Island in Limbo," *New York Times Magazine*, February 18, 1990, p. 31. In 1990, the committee organizing African National Congress leader Nelson Mandela's visit to New York City invited three members of the Puerto Rican group that shot the congressmen to be speakers at a Harlem rally. Mayor David Dinkins objected, calling the three "assassins." This led to protests by the Hispanic community in New York, as well as by the mayor's own adviser on Hispanic affairs. The latter called for Dinkins to apologize for his characterization of the Puerto Rican nationalists. The mayor obliged, stating that he may have spoken too quickly when he used the term "assassins." The three were allowed to address the Harlem rally. See Andy Logan, "Around City Hall: Grand Tour," *The New Yorker*, July 9, 1990, p. 81.

82. Interview, Gen. (Ret.) Andrew J. Goodpaster, Washington, D.C., May 2, 1990.

83. The arms flow had stopped, except for a May transfer of 300 small rocket heads. The administration stated that the shipment was necessary to "correct" an error that was made at the time of delivery several months before the embargo went into effect.

84. Georgie Anne Geyer, *Guerrilla Prince: The Untold Story of Fidel Castro* (Boston: Little, Brown, 1991), p. 185.

85. Carlos Franqui, *Diary of the Cuban Revolution* (New York: Viking Press, 1980), p. 358.

86. Ibid., pp. 364–65.

87. Ibid., p. vi.

88. *Congressional Record*, July 1, 1958, p. 12867.

89. Ibid., p. 12875.

90. *Papers of John Foster Dulles, Box 12, Telephone Call to President, July 2, 1958*, The Dwight D. Eisenhower Library, Abilene, Kansas.

91. Interview, Gen. (Ret.) Andrew J. Goodpaster, May 2, 1990, Washington, D.C.

92. Interview, Gen. (Ret.) Andrew J. Goodpaster, May 2, 1990, Washington, D.C.

93. *White House Central Files, 6F, 122-Cuba, July 2, July 15, 1958*, The Dwight D. Eisenhower Library, Abilene, Kansas.

94. *White House Central Files, 6F, 122-Cuba, July 1, 1958*, The Dwight D. Eisenhower Library, Abilene, Kansas.

95. *New York Times*, July 2, 1958, p. 1. However, when the East Germans de-

tained the American servicemen, Dulles responded to a question about what the United States planned to do by stating that "when you have people kidnapped, you deal with the kidnappers" (*New York Times,* July 3, 1958).

96. *Papers of James Hagerty, Presidential Press Conference Material, Box 64, Memorandum for the President, July 2, 1958,* The Dwight D. Eisenhower Library, Abilene, Kansas.

97. *New York Times,* July 2, 1958.

98. *New York Times,* July 19, 1958.

99. Fred I. Greenstein, *The Hidden-Hand Presidency: Eisenhower as Leader* (New York: Basic, 1982), pp. 235, 233.

100. Interview, Gen. (Ret.) Andrew J. Goodpaster, May 2, 1990, Washington, D.C.

101. *New York Times,* November 12, 1958, p. 3.

3. The Threat Emerges

1. *Oral History Statement by Pedro Theotonio Pereira, December 18, 1966,* John F. Kennedy Library Oral History Program, John F. Kennedy Library, Boston, Massachusetts.

2. Ibid.

3. Interview, Dean Rusk, April 23, 1990, Athens, Georgia.

4. Ibid.

5. *Memorandum on Hijacking* (folder 1-2c), John F. Kennedy Presidential Library, Boston, Massachusetts.

6. Ibid.

7. *Public Papers of the Presidents of the United States, John F. Kennedy, Containing the Public Messages, Speeches, and Statements of the President, January 20 to December 31, 1961,* "Telegrams of Commendation Following the Capture of Highjackers of a Jet Airliner in El Paso, Texas, August 4, 1961," U.S. Government Printing Office, Washington, D.C., 1962.

8. *New York Times,* August 4, 1961.

9. *New York Times,* July 30, 1961, Section IV, p. 4. The cartoon originally appeared in the *Buffalo Courier-Express.*

10. *Memorandum on Hijacking, FAA Action* (folder 1-2c), John F. Kennedy Presidential Library, Boston, Massachusetts.

11. *Memorandum on Hijacking, Possible Future Actions under Investigation* (folder 1-2c), John F. Kennedy Presidential Library, Boston, Massachusetts.

12. *Washington Post,* August 10, 1961, p. 1.

13. *Washington Post,* August 10, 1961, p. A9.

14. *Memo to McGeorge Bundy: Hijacking of Pan American DC8 on 9 August* (folder 1-2c), John F. Kennedy Presidential Library, Boston, Massachusetts.

15. *Telegram to the President, dated August 10, from Enrique Ariza; Memo to McGeorge Bundy: Hijacking of Pan American DC8 on 9 August,* John F. Kennedy Presidential Library, Boston, Massachusetts.

16. *Memo to McGeorge Bundy: Hijacking of Pan American DC8 on 9 August* (folder 1-2c), John F. Kennedy Presidential Library, Boston, Massachusetts. Turbay would eventually become president of Colombia, but would also suffer a

personal tragedy at the hands of narcoterrorists. In 1990 his daughter was taken hostage by drug traffickers and killed during a police effort to free her in January 1991.

17. *Congressional Record,* August 9, 1961, p. 15242; *New York Times,* August 10, 1961.

18. *Washington Post,* August 10, 1961; *Congressional Record,* August 9, 1961, p. 15224.

19. *Congressional Record,* August 9, 1961, p. 15234.

20. Chalmers M. Roberts, "Impatient Nation Taking on Belligerent Mood," *Washington Post,* August 11, 1961, p. A6.

21. Arthur Krock, "The Approaching Limits of Reiteration," *New York Times,* August 10, 1961, p. 26.

22. *Los Angeles Times,* August 10, 1961, p. 1.

23. Interview, Pierre Salinger, London, July 12, 1990.

24. Ibid.

25. *Public Papers of the Presidents of the United States, John F. Kennedy, Containing the Public Messages, Speeches, and Statements of the President, January 20 to December 31, 1961,* "The President's News Conference of August 10, 1961," U.S. Government Printing Office, Washington, D.C., 1962.

26. Interview, Gale McGee, June 19, 1990, Washington, D.C.

27. Interview, Dean Rusk, April 23, 1990, Athens, Georgia.

28. Interview, McGeorge Bundy, Irvine, California, April 5, 1990.

29. *Chronology of Significant Events,* Lyndon Baines Johnson Presidential Library, Austin, Texas.

30. *CIA Cable,* October 16, 1964, Lyndon Baines Johnson Presidential Library, Austin, Texas.

31. *USIA Report on the Congo Rebellion,* Lyndon Baines Johnson Presidential Library, Austin, Texas.

32. *The Situation in the Congo, CIA Report,* October 20, 1964, Lyndon Baines Johnson Presidential Library, Austin, Texas.

33. *Memorandum for the President,* Bundy to Johnson, August 11, 1964, Lyndon Baines Johnson Library, Austin, Texas.

34. Interview, Dean Rusk, April 23, 1990, Athens, Georgia.

35. *Memorandum to the President,* Bundy to Johnson, November 16, 1964, Lyndon Baines Johnson Library, Austin, Texas.

36. *Research Memorandum, U.S. Department of State, Director of Intelligence and Research,* November 18, 1964, Lyndon Baines Johnson Library, Austin, Texas.

37. Ibid.

38. *U.S. Mission in Geneva Cable,* November 3, 1964, Lyndon Baines Johnson Library, Austin, Texas.

39. *Department of State Telegram,* November 17, 1964, to Leopoldville and Bujumbura, Lyndon Baines Johnson Library, Austin, Texas.

40. *Research Memorandum, U.S. Department of State, Director of Intelligence and Research,* November 18, 1964, Lyndon Baines Johnson Library, Austin, Texas.

41. *U.S. Embassy Leopoldville Cable,* November 20, 1964, Lyndon Baines Johnson Library, Austin, Texas.

42. *New York Times*, November 25, 1964.

43. Interview, Dean Rusk, April 23, 1990, Athens, Georgia.

44. Interview, Cyrus Vance, May 22, 1990, New York, New York.

45. Interview, Jack Valenti, April 30, 1990, Washington, D.C.

46. Interview, Jack Valenti, April 30, 1990, Washington, D.C.

47. *Press Conference No. 34 of the President of the United States*, November 28, 1964, Lyndon Baines Johnson Presidential Library, Austin, Texas.

48. Interview, Walt Rostow, May 16, 1990, Austin, Texas.

49. Interview, Cyrus Vance, May 22, 1990, New York, New York.

50. Interview, Walt Rostow, May 16, 1990, Austin, Texas.

51. Dean Rusk, *As I Saw It, As Told to Richard Rusk* (New York: Norton, 1990), pp. 394–95.

52. Parry, *Terrorism*, p. 325.

53. Quoted in Walter Laqueur and Yonah Alexander, eds., *The Terrorism Reader*, revised edition (New York: Meridian, 1987), p. 173.

54. Christopher Dobson and Ronald Payne, *The Terrorists: Their Weapons, Leaders and Tactics* (New York: Facts on File, 1982), pp. 204–206.

55. Ibid.

56. Ibid.; *Report of the President's Commission on Aviation Security and Terrorism*, May 15, 1990, Washington, D.C., p. 162.

57. Interview, Miriam Beeber, June 11, 1992, Tucson, Arizona. See also Jorg Andrees Elten, "'This Is a Hijacking,' " *Reader's Digest*, July 1971, pp. 213-56 (the article originally appeared in the German magazine *Stern*, December 20, 27, 1970; January 3, 10, 17, 24, 31, 1971; February 7, 14, 21, 1971).

58. Interview (telephone), Catherine Hodes, March 21, 1992.

59. Interview (telephone), Catherine Hodes, March 21, 1992.

60. Elten, "'This Is a Hijacking,' " p. 247.

61. Interview, Miriam Beeber, June 11, 1992, Tucson, Arizona.

62. Interview, Miriam Beeber, June 11, 1992, Tucson, Arizona.

63. *Memorandum for H. R. Haldeman*, September 23, 1970, Richard Nixon Presidential Materials Staff, National Archives and Record Administration, Alexandria, Virginia.

64. Henry Kissinger, *White House Years* (Boston: Little Brown, 1979), p. 602.

65. Ibid., p. 602.

66. Interview, Miriam Beeber, June 11, 1992, Tucson, Arizona.

67. Interview, Miriam Beeber, June 11, 1992, Tucson, Arizona.

68. Kissinger, *White House Years*, p. 602.

69. *White House Central Files*, November 7, 1970, Richard Nixon Presidential Materials Staff, National Archives and Records Administration, Alexandria, Virginia.

70. *New York Times*, September 11, 1970, p. 14.

71. *Congressional Record*, September 10, 1970, p. 31180.

72. Kissinger, *White House Years*, p. 603.

73. Interview, Richard Tufaro, May 23, 1990, New York, New York.

74. James Reston, "The Impotence of Power," *New York Times*, September 11, 1970, p. 40.

75. C. L. Sulzberger, "Foreign Affairs: Skyjack—Gnats and Sledges," *New York Times*, September 11, 1970, p. 40.

76. Interview, Ed Turner, April 24, 1990, Atlanta, Georgia.

77. Interview, Miriam Beeber, June 11, 1992, Tucson, Arizona.

78. Interview (telephone), Catherine Hodes, March 21, 1992.

79. Interview (telephone), Martha Hodes, April 15, 1992.

80. *New York Times*, September 8, 1972, p. 12. For an account of the Munich massacre, see Edgar O'Ballance, *Language of Violence: The Blood Politics of Terrorism* (San Rafael, California: Presidio, 1979), pp. 115–27; Norman Antokol and Mayer Nudell, *No One a Neutral: Political Hostage-Taking in the Modern World* (Medina, Ohio: Alpha Publications of Ohio, 1990), pp. 65–69.

81. *New York Times*, September 7, 1972, p. 19.

82. *New York Times*, September 6, 1972, p. 18.

83. Ibid., p. 44.

84. *Department of State Bulletin*, October 23, 1972, "President Nixon Establishes Cabinet Committee to Combat Terrorism."

85. Marc Celmer, *Terrorism, U.S. Strategy, and Reagan Policies* (New York: Greenwood, 1987), pp. 17–19.

86. Interview, Richard Tufaro, May 23, 1990, New York, New York.

87. *New York Times*, March 3, 1973, pp. 1–2. For an excellent account of this hostage crisis, see David A. Korn, *Assassination in Khartoum* (Bloomington: Indiana University Press, 1993).

88. Judith Miller, "Bargain with Terrorists?" *New York Times Magazine*, July 18, 1976, p. 38.

89. Ibid., p. 37.

90. Ibid.

91. Interview, Brian Jenkins, June 21, 1992, Santa Monica, California.

92. Interview (telephone), James Roscoe, March 25, 1992.

93. Interview, Warren Benson, June 11, 1992, Tucson, Arizona.

94. Interview, Juliene Busic, April 9, 1992, South San Francisco, California.

95. Interview, Juliene Busic, April 9, 1992, South San Francisco, California.

96. Interview (telephone), Zvonko Busic, January 12, 1993.

97. Interview, Juliene Busic, April 9, 1992, South San Francisco, California.

98. *New York Times*, September 11, 1976, p. 1; September 12, 1976, p. 1.

99. Interview, Rudy Bretz, March 27, 1992, Malibu, California.

100. Interview, Juliene Busic, April 9, 1992, South San Francisco, California.

101. *New York Times*, September 12, 1976, p. 22.

102. *Los Angeles Times*, September 12, 1976, p. 1.

103. Interview, Rudy Bretz, March 27, 1992, Malibu, California.

104. *New York Times*, September 11, 1976, p. 7; September 12, 1976, p. 22.

105. *New York Times*, September 12, 1976, p. 23.

106. Interview, Rudy Bretz, March 27, 1992, Malibu, California.

107. Interview, Juliene Busic, April 9, 1992, South San Francisco, California.

108. Interview (telephone), James Roscoe, March 25, 1992.

109. *New York Times*, September 14, 1976, p. 32.

110. Interview (telephone), James Roscoe, March 25, 1992.

111. *New York Times,* September 13, 1976, p. 18.

112. J. Bowyer Bell, *A Time of Terror* (New York: Basic, 1978), pp. 31, 34–35.

113. Interview, Rudy Bretz, March 27, 1992, Malibu, California.

114. Interview, Emily Bretz, March 27, 1992, Malibu, California.

115. Interview, Warren Benson, June 11, 1992, Tucson, Arizona; Letters to Benson (private collection).

116. Interview, Juliene Busic, April 9, 1992, South San Francisco, California.

117. Interview, Juliene Busic, April 9, 1992, South San Francisco, California.

118. Interview, Juliene Busic, April 9, 1992, South San Francisco, California.

119. Interview, Juliene Busic, April 9, 1992, South San Francisco, California.

120. Interview (telephone), Zvonko Busic, December 1, 1992.

121. Interview (telephone), Zvonko Busic, January 12, 1993.

122. Interview (telephone), Zvonko Busic, January 12, 1993.

123. *New York Times,* September 14, 1976, p. 32.

124. *New York Times,* September 13, 1976, p. 18.

125. Robert L. Pfaltzgraff, Jr., and Jacquelyn K. Davis, *National Security Decisions: The Participants Speak* (Lexington, Massachusetts: Lexington, 1990), p. 276.

4. The Setting of the Terrorist Trap

1. The timing of the hostages' release has been a controversial issue for more than a decade. A 1991 book by Gary Sick, Carter's principal aide on Iran on the National Security Council, argued that a secret deal was made by the Reagan campaign team, headed by William Casey, with the Iranian government to not free the hostages until after the November 1980 presidential election. This was to ensure that there would not be an "October surprise" by the Carter administration in which the president could ride a wave of enthusiasm over the hostages' freedom to victory at the polls. The center of the argument is that Casey, who would become CIA director under Reagan, met with the Iranians during the summer of 1980 in Madrid and during the fall in Paris, and promised that Reagan would cut a better deal with them than Carter, including sending military equipment and arms to Tehran. "If the evidence . . . means what it seems to mean," wrote Sick, "we must conclude that in 1980 a deception was inflicted on the hostages, the government, and the American people that has few if any parallels in our history" (Gary Sick, *October Surprise: America's Hostages in Iran and the Election of Ronald Reagan* [New York: Random House, 1991], p. 7).

But the evidence is circumstantial. Casey's schedule during the campaign left open the possibility that he could have been in Europe for the alleged secret meetings, but no "smoking gun" has yet turned up to verify that he met with the Iranians. Some of the people who claimed to have knowledge of the meetings or even to have taken part in them have been discredited by media investigations of their stories (see, for example, "Frontline," "Investigating the October Surprise," show #1016, April 7, 1992, Journal Graphics). While it would be quite natural in the high-stakes game of presidential politics to expect that the Reagan team was hoping that the hostages would not be released right before the election, it is quite another to expect that they would actually plot to keep Americans in captivity. The risk that disclosure of such dealings would have had on Reagan's presidential chances would seem to argue otherwise. But like many conspiracy theories, this one will continue to be debated until there is conclusive evidence presented, if ever, one way or the other.

2. Allen Otten, quoted in Erwin C. Hargrove, "Jimmy Carter: The Politics of Public Goods," in Fred I. Greenstein, ed., *Leadership in the Modern Presidency* (Cambridge, Massachusetts: Harvard University Press, 1988), p. 253; the second quote is by Hargrove, p. 254.

3. Zbigniew Brzezinski, *Power and Principle: Memoirs of the National Security Adviser, 1977–1981* (New York: Farrar, Straus, Giroux, 1983), p. 525.

4. *New York Times*, March 10, 1977.

5. *New York Times*, March 11, 1977, p. D9.

6. Ibid., p. 12.

7. Ibid.

8. Ibid.

9. William Regis Farrell, *The U.S. Government Response to Terrorism: In Search of an Effective Strategy* (Boulder, Colorado: Westview, 1982), p. 91.

10. *New York Times*, March 19, 1977, p. 33.

11. Ibid., March 12, 1977, p. 22.

12. Bernard Gwertzman, "Cyrus Vance Plays It Cool," *New York Times Magazine*, March 18, 1979; Cyrus Vance, *Hard Choices: Critical Years in America's Foreign Policy* (New York: Simon and Schuster, 1983), pp. 342–43.

13. Harold Saunders, "Talking Points: Security Precautions in Tehran," *Memo to Jody Powell*, November 15, 1979, Jimmy Carter Presidential Library, Atlanta, Georgia; "The Iran Hostage Crisis in Perspective," prepared statement of Hon. Harold H. Saunders, former assistant secretary of state for Near Eastern and South Asian affairs, *Hearings before the Committee on Foreign Affairs, House of Representatives, Ninety-Seventh Congress, First Session*, February 17, 19, 25, and March 11, 1981, U.S. Government Printing Office, Washington, D.C., 1981 ("Iran's Seizure of the United States Embassy"), pp. 10–11.

14. Vance, *Hard Choices*, pp. 372–73; Saunders, "Talking Points."

15. Vance, *Hard Choices*, p. 376.

16. Interview, Cyrus Vance, May 22, 1990, New York, New York.

17. Interview, Robert Ode, June 11, 1992, Sun City West, Arizona.

18. Interview, Robert Ode, June 11, 1992, Sun City West, Arizona.

19. Interview, Cyrus Vance, May 22, 1990, New York, New York.

20. Hamilton Jordan, *Crisis: The Last Year of the Carter Presidency* (New York: Berkley, 1982), p. 33.

21. Ibid., p. 35.

22. Interview, Cyrus Vance, May 22, 1990, New York, New York.

23. Interview, Sam Donaldson, June 19, 1990, Washington, D.C.

24. Jordan, *Crisis*, p. 35.

25. "Timely Public Responses to the Iranian Situation," *Memo from Al McDonald to Hamilton Jordan*, November 8, 1979, Jimmy Carter Presidential Library, Atlanta, Georgia.

26. *Memorandum for Press Office Staff from Charles Goodwin, Attached Letter from Jody*, November 27, 1979, Jimmy Carter Presidential Library, Atlanta, Georgia.

27. *Letter from Philip T. Kelly to Jimmy Carter,* White House Central Files, Box CO-33, Folder CO-71, December 6, 1979, Jimmy Carter Presidential Library, Atlanta, Georgia.

28. *Letter from Jody Powell to Gladys Reckley,* December 21, 1979; *News Release, Governor Calls on Alaskans to Unite in Daily Prayers for the Release of American Hostages,* December 6, 1979, White House Central Files, Box CO-33, Folder CO-71, Jimmy Carter Presidential Library, Atlanta, Georgia.

29. *Memorandum from Anne Wexler and Bob Maddox to the President,* November 14, 1979, Collection: Press/Granum, Box 75, Folder "American Hostages in Iran," 11/7/79-11/30/79, Jimmy Carter Presidential Library.

30. *New York Times,* November 10, 1979, p. 1.

31. *Remarks of the President at the 13th Constitutional Convention of the AFL-CIO,* Sheraton Washington Hotel, November 15, 1979, Office of the White House Press Secretary, Jimmy Carter Presidential Library, Atlanta, Georgia (italics added).

32. Ibid.

33. *New York Times,* November 19, 1979, p. 13.

34. *(Interviews) in Driveway after Leadership Breakfast,* November 27, 1979, Jimmy Carter Presidential Library, Atlanta, Georgia.

35. *Memorandum from Hugh Carter to Ray Jenkins,* November 21, 1979, Jimmy Carter Presidential Library, Atlanta, Georgia.

36. *Letter from Robert Henley to Jody Powell, November 14, 1979; Letter from Jody Powell to Robert Henley,* November 30, 1979 (italics added), Jimmy Carter Presidential Library, Atlanta, Georgia. .

37. "Tehran Radio Notes Kennedy's Statement on Iran, Deposed Shah, December 4, 1979," *Foreign Broadcast Information Service 82; Carter Note to Powell,* December 5, 1979, Jimmy Carter Presidential Library, Atlanta, Georgia.

38. *Statement by the President,* November 17, 1979 (handwritten note to Jody Powell from "David"), Jimmy Carter Presidential Library, Atlanta, Georgia.

39. *Public Opinion,* February/March 1980, p. 29; December/January 1981, p. 27.

40. Jimmy Carter, *Keeping Faith: Memoirs of a President* (New York: Bantam, 1982), p. 460.

41. *Memorandum from Attorney General Benjamin Civiletti to the President,* November 15, 1979, Staff Offices/Counsel Cutler, Box 87, Folder "Iran Demonstrations, November 1979," Jimmy Carter Presidential Library, Atlanta, Georgia.

42. *Memorandum from Attorney General Benjamin Civiletti to the President,* August 27, 1980, Staff Offices/Counsel Cutler, Box 87, Folder "Iran Demonstrations, August 1980," Jimmy Carter Presidential Library, Atlanta, Georgia.

43. Jordan, *Crisis,* p. 32.

44. *Letter from Vivian Homeyer to President Carter,* March 13, 1980; *Letter from President Carter to Vivian Homeyer,* March 25, 1980 (Graham collection), Jimmy Carter Presidential Library, Atlanta, Georgia.

45. Carter, *Keeping Faith,* p. 460.

46. Gary Sick, *All Fall Down: America's Tragic Encounter with Iran* (New York: Penguin, 1985), p. 260.

47. Interview, Cyrus Vance, May 22, 1990, New York, New York.

48. *(Interviews) in Driveway after Leadership Breakfast*, November 27, 1979, Jimmy Carter Presidential Library, Atlanta, Georgia.

49. Interview, Jack Valenti, April 30, 1990, Washington, D.C.

50. Interview, Cyrus Vance, May 22, 1990, New York, New York.

51. Carter, *Keeping Faith*, p. 480.

52. Interview, Cyrus Vance, May 22, 1990, New York, New York.

53. *Memorandum from Gary Sick to Jody Powell*, January 8, 1980, Collection: Press/Powell, Box 63, Folder "Hostages in U.S. Embassy in Iran, 1979–81," Jimmy Carter Presidential Library, Atlanta, Georgia.

54. *Letter from Philip Kennedy to President Carter*, December 5, 1979, White House Central Files, Jimmy Carter Presidential Library, Atlanta, Georgia.

55. Interview, Cyrus Vance, May 22, 1990, New York, New York.

56. Interview, Cyrus Vance, May 22, 1990, New York, New York.

57. Interview, Pierre Salinger, July 12, 1990, London. See also Salinger, *America Held Hostage: The Secret Negotiations* (New York: Doubleday, 1981), pp. 57–59.

58. Salinger, *America Held Hostage*, pp. 95, 158; Jordan, *Crisis*, pp. 118–19.

59. Salinger, *America Held Hostage*, pp. 168-86; Sick, *All Fall Down*, pp. 311–17, 168–86; Jordan, *Crisis*, pp. 164, 178. Salinger provides an excellent account of all the secret negotiations that occurred throughout the hostage crisis, and also includes in the appendix the text of all the different drafts in the scenarios that were agreed to by Jordan and the two intermediaries, Bourguet and Villalon. Jordan provides a firsthand account of the intricacies involved in his secret meetings aimed to resolve the hostage crisis.

60. Carter, *Keeping Faith*, p. 505.

61. *Announcement by the President*, Office of the White House Press Secretary, April 7, 1980, Jimmy Carter Presidential Library, Atlanta, Georgia.

62. "Days of Captivity: The Hostages' Story," *New York Times*, February 14, 1981, p. A12.

63. Interview, Robert Ode, June 11, 1992, Sun City West, Arizona.

64. "Days of Captivity: The Hostages' Story," *New York Times*, February 14, 1981, p. A12.

65. Jordan, *Crisis*, p. 388.

66. Interview, Robert and Rita Ode, June 11, 1992, Sun City West, Arizona.

67. Interview, Robert Ode, June 11, 1992, Sun City West, Arizona.

68. Quoted in Tim Wells, *444 Days: The Hostages Remember* (New York: Harcourt Brace Jovanovich, 1985), pp. 375–77.

69. Interview, Colonel (Ret.) Charles Beckwith, May 16, 1990, Austin, Texas.

70. *Office of the White House Press Secretary, The White House*, April 25, 1980.

71. *Office of the White House Press Secretary, The White House, Statement by the President on Hostage Rescue Attempt, The Oval Office*, April 25, 1980.

72. Salinger, *America Held Hostage*, p. 238.

73. Interview, Cyrus Vance, May 22, 1990, New York City.

74. Sick, *All Fall Down*, p. 347.

75. *Cyrus Vance Letter to President Carter*, April 21, 1980, Jimmy Carter Presidential Library, Atlanta, Georgia.

76. Interview, Sam Donaldson, June 19, 1990, Washington, D.C.

77. Jordan, *Crisis*, p. 247.

78. Interview, Cyrus Vance, May 22, 1990, New York, New York.

79. Christopher Dobson and Ronald Payne, *The Terrorists: Their Weapons, Leaders, and Tactics* (New York: Facts on File, 1979), pp. 138–39, 222; David C. Martin and John Walcott, *Best Laid Plans: The Inside Story of America's War against Terrorism* (New York: Harper and Row, 1988), p. 40.

80. Colonel Charlie A. Beckwith and Donald Knox, *Delta Force* (New York: Harcourt Brace Jovanovich, 1983), p. 215.

81. Interview, Colonel (Ret.) Charles Beckwith, May 16, 1990, Austin, Texas.

82. Interview, Colonel (Ret.) Charles Beckwith, May 16, 1990, Austin, Texas.

83. Interview, Colonel (Ret.) Charles Beckwith, May 16, 1990, Austin, Texas.

84. Beckwith and Knox, *Delta Force*, pp. 155–63, 181–86.

85. Interview, Colonel (Ret.) Charles Beckwith, May 16, 1990, Austin, Texas.

86. Interview, Colonel (Ret.) Charles Beckwith, May 16, 1990, Austin, Texas.

87. Interview, Howard Bane, May 3, 1990, Fairfax, Virginia.

88. *New York Times*, August 24, 1980, p. 1.

89. Interview, Colonel (Ret.) Charles Beckwith, May 16, 1990, Austin, Texas. The following account of the planning and implementation of the rescue effort is based on interviews with Beckwith and Howard Bane, the CIA officer responsible for the rescue mission, as well as the following sources: Carter, *Keeping Faith*, pp. 506–22; Sick, *All Fall Down*, pp. 348–56; Beckwith and Knox, *Delta Force*, pp. 253–80; Jordan, *Crisis*, pp. 252–57; Vance, *Hard Choices*, pp. 408–13; Brzezinski, *Power and Principle*, pp. 487–500; Salinger, *America Held Hostage*, pp. 234–44; David C. Martin and John Walcott, *Best Laid Plans*, pp. 6–42; *Report on Iranian Rescue Mission*, Joint Chiefs of Staff, May 7, 1980, Jimmy Carter Presidential Library, Atlanta, Georgia.

90. Carter, *Keeping Faith*, p. 515; Beckwith and Knox, *Delta Force*, pp. 269–70.

91. Interview, Colonel (Ret.) Charles Beckwith, May 16, 1990, Austin, Texas.

92. Stansfield Turner, *Terrorism and Democracy* (Boston: Houghton Mifflin, 1991), pp. 129–30.

93. Interview, Colonel (Ret.) Charles Beckwith, May 16, 1990, Austin, Texas.

94. Tom Wicker, "A Puzzle of Timing," *New York Times*, April 27, 1980, p. E23; James Reston, "A Second Rescue Mission," *New York Times*, April 27, 1980, p. E23.

95. William Pfaff, "To Our Allies, It Is Another American Default," *Los Angeles Times*, April 27, 1980, Part V, pp. 1, 5.

96. *New York Times*, August 24, 1980, pp. 1, 19.

97. Turner, *Terrorism and Democracy*, p. 141.

98. Brzezinski, *Power and Principle*, pp. 488, 494–95.

99. Interview, Colonel (Ret.) Charles Beckwith, May 16, 1990, Austin, Texas.

100. Interview, Howard Bane, May 3, 1990, Fairfax, Virginia; Beckwith and Knox, *Delta Force*, p. 264; Martin and Walcott, *Best Laid Plans*, p. 11.

101. Interview, Colonel (Ret.) Charles Beckwith, May 16, 1990, Austin, Texas.

102. Interview, Howard Bane, May 3, 1990, Fairfax, Virginia.

103. *Letter/memo from Hamilton Jordan to President Carter*, April 28, 1980, Jimmy Carter Presidential Library, Atlanta, Georgia.

104. Carter, *Keeping Faith*, p. 518.

105. Sick, *All Fall Down*, pp. 360, 421.

106. Salinger, *America Held Hostage*, pp. 239–40.

107. For a detailed treatment of the period between the formation of the Majlis in May and the final agreement freeing the hostages seven months later, see Sick, *All Fall Down*, pp. 361–98; Salinger, *America Held Hostage*, pp. 248–305.

108. Carter, *Keeping Faith*, p. 559.

109. Jordan, *Crisis*, pp. 325–26.

110. Carter, *Keeping Faith*, p. 594.

111. *Memorandum, Untitled and Unsigned, The White House*, Jimmy Carter Presidential Library, Atlanta, Georgia.

112. *New York Times*, December 25, 1980, pp. 1, 4.

113. "Iran Hostage Crisis Tenth Anniversary," "Nightline," November 3, 1989, show #2205, Journal Graphics, New York, p. 6.

114. Bernard Lewis, "The Roots of Muslim Rage," *Atlantic Monthly*, September 1990, pp. 59–60, 56.

115. Interview, Cyrus Vance, May 22, 1990, New York, New York.

116. Wells, *444 Days*, p. 438.

5. Tough Talk on Terrorism

1. *New York Times*, January 28, 1981, p. 14; January 29, 1981, p. 10.

2. Ronald Reagan, *An American Life* (New York: Simon and Schuster, 1990), p. 267.

3. Ibid., p. 361.

4. *New York Times*, January 29, 1981, p. 10.

5. *New York Times*, June 30, 1979, p. 3.

6. Claire Sterling, *The Terror Network* (New York: Berkley, 1982), p. 10.

7. Ibid., pp. 14–15.

8. Ibid., pp. 15, 12–13.

9. Joseph E. Persico, *Casey: From the OSS to the CIA* (New York: Viking Penguin, 1990), pp. 220–21; "CIA on International Terrorism, June 15, 1981," *Historic Documents of 1981*, Cumulative Index 1977–1981, Congressional Quarterly, Inc., 1982, pp. 461–75; David C. Martin and John Walcott, *Best Laid Plans: The Inside Story of America's War against Terrorism* (New York: Harper and Row, 1988), pp. 51–56.

10. Leroy Thompson, *The Rescuers: The World's Top Anti-Terrorist Units* (Boulder, Colorado: Paladin, 1986), pp. 81–83; Martin and Walcott, *Best Laid Plans*, pp. 57–66.

11. Thomas L. Friedman, *From Beirut to Jerusalem* (New York: Anchor Doubleday, 1990 [first published by Farrar Straus Giroux in 1989]), pp. 50–51.

12. Wadi D. Haddad, *Lebanon: The Politics of Revolving Doors* (Washington, D.C.: Center for Strategic and International Studies, Georgetown University, Washington Papers/114), pp. 47–55.

13. Ibid., p. 76.

14. Ibid., pp. 77–79.

15. Friedman, *From Beirut to Jerusalem*, p. 505.

16. Friedman, *From Beirut to Jerusalem*, p. 161.

17. Caspar Weinberger, *Fighting for Peace: Seven Critical Years in the Pentagon* (New York: Warner, 1990), p. 151.

18. Ibid., p. 152.

19. Ibid., p. 154.

20. For a discussion of the terrorist attacks against the United States in Lebanon in 1983, see Martin and Walcott, *Best Laid Plans*, pp. 103–60; Neil Livingstone and David Halevy, *Inside the PLO: Covert Units, Secret Funds, and the War against Israel and the United States* (New York: Morrow, 1990), pp. 265–67; Friedman, *From Beirut to Jerusalem*, pp. 197–211.

21. Livingstone and Halevy, *Inside the PLO*, pp. 264–67; Martin and Walcott, *Best Laid Plans*, pp. 154–55.

22. Friedman, *From Beirut to Jerusalem*, pp. 200–201.

23. *Historic Documents of 1983*, Reports on Terrorist Bombing of U.S. Marines in Beirut, December 19 and 28, 1983 (DOD Commission on Beirut International Airport [BIA] Terrorist Act of 23 October 1983) Congressional Quarterly Inc., Washington, D.C., 1984, p. 948.

24. Martin and Walcott, *Best Laid Plans*, p. 133.

25. Reagan, *An American Life*, pp. 463-64.

26. Ibid., p. 466.

27. Weinberger, *Fighting for Peace*, p. 173.

28. *Historic Documents of 1983*, p. 940.

29. Ibid., p. 964 (italics added).

30. Martin and Walcott, *Best Laid Plans*, p. 157; Celmer, *Terrorism, U.S. Strategy, and Reagan Policies*, p. 63; *New York Times*, April 17, 1984, p. 3.

31. *New York Times*, April 18, 1984, p. 13; April 17, 1984, p. 3.

32. Interview, George Shultz, November 25, 1991, Palo Alto, California.

33. *Department of State Bulletin*, vol. 84, no. 2089, August 1984, pp. 29–30, 33.

34. *Department of State Bulletin*, vol. 84, no. 2093, December 1984, pp. 12–17.

35. *New York Times*, October 26, 1984, p. 1, p. 12; October 27, 1984, pp. 1, 6; October 28, 1984, pp. 1, 7.

36. *New York Times*, October 28, 1984, p. 7.

37. Interview, George Shultz, November 25, 1991, Palo Alto, California.

38. Reagan, *An American Life*, pp. 477, 661.

39. *Department of State Bulletin*, vol. 84, no. 2091, October 1984, p. 19.

40. Interview, George Shultz, November 25, 1991, Palo Alto, California.

41. Reagan, *An American Life*, p. 511.

42. Weinberger, *Fighting for Peace*, p. 188.

43. Ibid., p. 164.

44. *Department of State Bulletin*, vol. 84, no. 2088, July 1984, p. 40.

45. Weinberger, *Fighting for Peace*, pp. 441–42.

46. Interview, George Shultz, November 25, 1991, Palo Alto, California.

47. George P. Shultz, *Turmoil and Triumph: My Years as Secretary of State* (New York: Scribner's, 1993), p. 231.

48. *New York Times*, October 28, 1984, p. 1.

49. Interview, L. Paul Bremer, May 24, 1990, New York, New York.

50. Capt. John Testrake (with David J. Wimbish), *Triumph over Terror on Flight 847* (Old Tappan, New Jersey: Fleming H. Revell, 1987), pp. 79–81.

51. Reagan, *An American Life*, p. 494.

52. Interview, Thomas Murry, March 27, 1992, Newbury Park, California.

53. Interview, Thomas Murry, March 27, 1992, Newbury Park, California.

54. Reagan, *An American Life*, pp. 494-95.

55. Ibid., p. 495.

56. Testrake, *Triumph over Terror*, pp. 131–32.

57. Martin and Walcott, *Best Laid Plans*, pp. 178–79.

58. Interview, Thomas Murry, March 27, 1992, Newbury Park, California.

59. Interview, Larry Grossman, May 21, 1990, New York, New York.

60. Interview, Ed Turner, April 24, 1990, Atlanta, Georgia.

61. Martin and Walcott, *Best Laid Plans*, p. 198.

62. Ibid., pp. 200–202.

63. Interview, Thomas Murry, March 27, 1992, Newbury Park, California.

64. Interview, Thomas Murry, March 27, 1992, Newbury Park, California.

65. Tony Atwater, "Network Evening News Coverage of the TWA Hostage Crisis," in Yonah Alexander and Richard Latter, eds., *Terrorism and the Media: Dilemmas for Government, Journalists, and the Public* (New York: Brassey's [U.S.], 1990), p. 90.

66. *New York Times*, June 25, 1985, p. 1.

67. Martin and Walcott, *Best Laid Plans*, p. 184.

68. "Remarks Announcing the Release of the Hostages from the Trans World Airlines Hijacking Incident, June 30, 1985," *Public Papers of the Presidents of the United States, Ronald Reagan, 1985 (In Two Books), Book II—June 29 to December 31, 1985* (Washington, D.C., United States Government Printing Office, 1988), p. 886.

69. Interview, Thomas Murry, March 27, 1992, Newbury Park, California.

70. Jeffrey D. Simon, "The Implications of the *Achille Lauro* Hijacking for the Maritime Community," in Brigadier (Ret.) Brian A. H. Parritt, CBE, ed., *Violence at Sea: A Review of Terrorism, Acts of War and Piracy, and Countermeasures to Prevent Terrorism* (Paris: International Chamber of Commerce [ICC], 1986), pp. 19–20.

71. Ibid., p. 18.

72. Martin and Walcott, *Best Laid Plans*, pp. 252–56.

73. Livingstone and Halevy, *Inside the PLO*, p. 258. Italy freed the two Palestinian accomplices in January 1991 as part of an amnesty program. Each was freed with about two years left on his sentence. Prime Minister Giulio Andreotti denied that the release was part of a deal Italy struck with the PLO to protect Italy from terrorism (*New York Times*, February 10, 1991, p. 13).

74. Interview, George Shultz, November 25, 1991, Palo Alto, California.

75. "Remarks and a Question-and-Answer Session with Reporters, October 11, 1985," *Public Papers of the Presidents of the United States, Ronald Reagan, 1985 (In Two Books), Book II—June 29 to December 31, 1985*, p. 1232 (italics added).

76. Interview, Sam Donaldson, June 19, 1990, Washington, D.C.

77. Ibid.

78. *New York Times*, November 25, 1985, p. 1; November 29, 1985, p. 13. Two hostages were killed prior to the rescue operation.

79. *New York Times,* December 29, 1985, p. 1.

80. Weinberger, *Fighting for Peace,* p. 175; Reagan, *An American Life,* pp. 280, 518.

81. *New York Times,* January 13, 1986, p. 8.

82. Weinberger, *Fighting for Peace,* pp. 182–86.

83. Ibid., p. 188; Livingstone and Halevy, *Inside the PLO,* p. 144; Reagan, *An American Life,* pp. 517–18.

84. *New York Times,* April 17, 1986, p. 24.

85. Jeffrey D. Simon, *U.S. Countermeasures Against International Terrorism,* R-3840-C³I, The RAND Corporation, Santa Monica, California, March 1990, pp. 27–28.

86. *New York Times,* April 19, 1986, pp. 1, 4; David Jacobsen with Gerald Astor, *Hostage: My Nightmare in Beirut* (New York: Donald I. Fine, 1991), p. 168.

87. Weinberger, *Fighting for Peace,* p. 199.

88. *New York Times,* April 24, 1986, p. 8.

89. Ibid., p. 23.

90. Ibid., p. 23.

91. Interview, George Shultz, November 25, 1991, Palo Alto, California.

92. Interview, George Shultz, November 25, 1991, Palo Alto, California.

93. Interview, L. Paul Bremer, May 24, 1990, New York, New York.

94. Interview, L. Paul Bremer, May 24, 1990, New York, New York.

95. Reagan, *An American Life,* p. 513.

96. "Address to the Nation on the Iran Arms and Contra Aid Controversy, March 4, 1987," *Public Papers of the Presidents of the United States, Ronald Reagan, 1987 (In Two Books), Book I—January 1 to July 3, 1987,* p. 209; *The Tower Commission Report: The Full Text of the President's Special Review Board* (New York: Bantam, 1987), pp. 36, 79.

97. Interview, George Shultz, November 25, 1991, Palo Alto, California.

98. *New York Times,* February 3, 1987, p. 3; February 7, 1987, p. 3.

99. Interview, George Shultz, November 25, 1991, Palo Alto, California.

100. Interview, Gerald Seib, September 23, 1992, Washington, D.C.

101. Interview, Gerald Seib, September 23, 1992, Washington, D.C.

102. *The Tower Commission Report,* p. 18.

103. Persico, *Casey,* pp. 472–73. This same pattern of not revealing the death of a hostage until an opportune time occurred in August 1989. Hizballah threatened to kill Lt. Col. William Higgins, the U.N. peacekeeping commander who had been kidnapped in January 1989 in southern Lebanon, unless the Israelis released Sheik Abdul Karim Obeid, a Hizballah leader whom they had abducted from Lebanon. Hizballah then produced a video of Higgins hanging from a post, and threatened more violence against American hostages. But U.S. analysts believed that Higgins had been killed months and perhaps as long as a year before the August 1989 incident.

104. David Jacobsen with Gerald Astor, *Hostage: My Nightmare in Beirut* (New York: Donald I. Fine, 1991), p. 236.

105. Interview, David Jacobsen, June 30, 1992, Huntington Beach, California.

106. Interview, Father Lawrence Martin Jenco, May 11, 1992, Los Angeles, California.

107. Interview, David Jacobsen, June 30, 1992, Huntington Beach, California.

108. Jacobsen, *Hostage,* pp. 370–71, 316–17, 472–73; *New York Times,* February 27, 1987, p. 7.

109. *The Tower Commission Report,* pp. 29–30.

110. Jacobsen, *Hostage,* pp. 3–10.

111. Interview, Father Lawrence Martin Jenco, May 11, 1992, Los Angeles, California.

112. Jacobsen, *Hostage,* pp. 183–85, 194–96.

113. Ibid., pp. 48, 57, 210, 246–47.

114. Interview, Father Lawrence Martin Jenco, May 11, 1992, Los Angeles, California.

115. Interview, David Jacobsen, June 30, 1992, Huntington Beach, California.

116. Interview, David Jacobsen, June 30, 1992, Huntington Beach, California.

117. Interview, David Jacobsen, June 30, 1992, Huntington Beach, California.

118. ABC News, "20/20," transcript #1216, April 17, 1992, p. 4. In his memoirs, *Taken on Trust* (New York: Harcourt Brace, 1993), Terry Waite describes some of his interactions with Tom Sutherland while they were hostages: "Tom has latched on to me and pours out his life story. Once he begins, he continues to speak for hour after hour. . . . My feelings towards him are mixed. I have an enormous sympathy for this clever, humiliated individual but a growing weariness with his story" (p. 352).

119. Interview, David Jacobsen, June 30, 1992, Huntington Beach, California. Terry Anderson agrees with Jacobsen's assessment in his own memoirs, *Den of Lions: Memoirs of Seven Years* (New York: Crown, 1993). Anderson writes, "David is as arrogant and bullheaded as I am . . . " (p. 119).

120. Interview, Father Lawrence Martin Jenco, May 11, 1992, Los Angeles, California.

121. Interview, David Jacobsen, June 30, 1992, Huntington Beach, California.

122. Interview, Father Lawrence Martin Jenco, May 11, 1992, Los Angeles, California.

123. Interview, David Jacobsen, June 30, 1992, Huntington Beach, California.

124. Interview, Father Lawrence Martin Jenco, May 11, 1992, Los Angeles, California.

125. Interview, Father Lawrence Martin Jenco, May 11, 1992, Los Angeles, California.

126. Interview, Father Lawrence Martin Jenco, May 11, 1992, Los Angeles, California.

127. Reagan, *An American Life,* p. 524.

128. Ibid., p. 525

129. Interview, Father Lawrence Martin Jenco, May 11, 1992, Los Angeles, California.

130. Interview, David Jacobsen, June 30, 1992, Huntington Beach, California; *New York Times,* November 8, 1986, p. 3.

131. Interview, David Jacobsen, June 30, 1992, Huntington Beach, California.

132. Interview, Father Lawrence Martin Jenco, May 11, 1992, Los Angeles, California; interview, David Jacobsen, June 30, 1992, Huntington Beach, California.

133. *New York Times,* June 17, 1992, p. 14; December 9, 1992, p. 1. North would reemerge in the public eye as he ran for the Republican nomination for senator in Virginia in 1994.

134. *New York Times,* June 17, 1992, p. 1.

135. *Los Angeles Times,* June 26, 1992, p. 1.

136. Interview, George Shultz, November 25, 1991, Palo Alto, California.

137. Interview, George Shultz, November 25, 1991, Palo Alto, California.

138. Lou Cannon, *President Reagan: The Role of a Lifetime* (New York: Simon and Schuster, 1991), p. 642.

139. Ibid., p. 643.

140. Reagan, *An American Life,* p. 532.

141. Donald T. Regan, *For the Record: From Wall Street to Washington* (New York: St. Martin's, 1989), p. 35.

142. Interview, Sam Donaldson, June 19, 1990, Washington, D.C.

143. One that did—the bombing of a USO club in Naples—led Reagan to once again focus his efforts on toppling Qaddafi. The United States suspected the Libyan dictator of involvement in the attack. A covert plan was approved in the final months of the Reagan presidency to use Libyan commandos—who had been captured in a border war between Libya and Chad by the Chadian army—to wage a new war against Qaddafi. The prisoners-of-war were trained by the United States to become a paramilitary force with the objective of destabilizing the Qaddafi regime. But before they could even launch any serious operations, Chad fell to Libyan-backed rebels. See *New York Times,* March 12, 1991, p. 7.

144. Patrick Clawson, "Terrorism in Decline?" *Orbis,* Spring 1988.

6. The Mother of All Hostage Takers

1. Reagan, *An American Life,* p. 255.

2. Celmer, *Terrorism, U.S. Strategy, and Reagan Policies,* p. 25.

3. *Public Report of the Vice-President's Task Force on Combatting Terrorism* (Washington, D.C.: U.S. Government Printing Office, February 1986).

4. *The Tower Commission Report,* pp. 228, 384–89.

5. Theodore Draper, *A Very Thin Line: The Iran-Contra Affairs* (New York: Hill and Wang, 1991), pp. 573–74.

6. *Public Report of the Vice-President's Task Force on Combatting Terrorism,* p. 10.

7. Ibid., pp. 15, 17, 19, 21.

8. Ibid., pp. 12, 23.

9. *The Tower Commission Report,* p. 462.

10. Ibid., p. 4.

11. *Public Report of the Vice-President's Task Force on Combatting Terrorism,* p. 21.

12. Ibid., pp. 22–23.

13. Ibid., p. 7.

14. *The National Journal,* June 13, 1987; *New York Times,* May 20, 1988, p. 1.

15. Interview, L. Paul Bremer, May 24, 1990, New York, New York.

16. Peggy Say and Peter Knobler, *Forgotten: A Sister's Struggle to Save Terry*

Anderson, America's Longest-Held Hostage (New York: Simon and Schuster, 1991), pp. 59–60.

17. Steven Emerson and Brian Duffy, *The Fall of Pan Am 103: Inside the Locker-bie Investigation* (New York: Putnam's, 1990), pp. 27–28, 43; *New York Times*, December 24, 1988, p. 5.

18. Interview, Randy Beers, September 22, 1992, Washington, D.C.

19. Interview, Rosemary Wolfe, September 23, 1992, Washington, D.C.

20. Emerson and Duffy, *The Fall of Pan Am 103*, p. 83.

21. *Report of the President's Commission on Aviation Security and Terrorism*, Washington, D.C.: May 15, 1990, Appendix E, "Acts of Aviation Sabotage," pp. 160–66.

22. *New York Times*, December 29, 1988, pp. 1, 10; Emerson and Duffy, *The Fall of Pan Am 103*, pp. 98–99.

23. Emerson and Duffy, *The Fall of Pan Am 103*, pp. 131–40; *Report of the President's Commission on Aviation Security and Terrorism*, p. 7.

24. *New York Times*, November 15, 1991, p. 6.

25. ABC News, "PrimeTime Live," December 20, 1990, transcript, Journal Graphics, New York, 1990, p. 15.

26. *New York Times*, December 30, 1988, p. 10.

27. Ibid., January 2, 1989, p. 3.

28. Ibid., December 30, 1988, p. 10 (italics added).

29. Ibid., p. 10.

30. Ibid., January 2, 1989, p. 3.

31. ABC News, "PrimeTime Live," December 20, 1990, p. 6.

32. Interview, Pierre Salinger, July 12, 1990, London.

33. *Report of the President's Commission on Aviation Security and Terrorism*, pp. 1–2, 3, 142–43.

34. Ibid., p. i.

35. *New York Times*, May 16, 1990, p. 11.

36. *Wall Street Journal*, May 4, 1989, p. A3.

37. *Report of the President's Commission on Aviation Security and Terrorism*, p. 115.

38. Ibid., p. i.

39. *New York Times*, May 16, 1990, p. 8.

40. Emerson and Duffy, *The Fall of Pan Am 103*, pp. 221–25. Internal divisions over strategy and personality conflicts among some of the group's leaders eventually led to the formation of a splinter organization, The Families of Pan Am 103/Lockerbie. For an excellent account of this, as well as an in-depth look at the personal experiences of many of the relatives of those killed in the bombing, see Matthew Cox and Tom Foster, *Their Darkest Day: The Tragedy of Pan Am 103 and Its Legacy of Hope* (New York: Grove Weidenfeld, 1992).

41. Interview, Tom Brokaw, June 26, 1990, New York, New York.

42. The PFLP-GC timers had been rigged with an altimeter, which is a barometric device that measures changes in a plane's altitude. The purpose of an altimeter is to ensure that the bomb does not explode while the plane is on the ground, which would leave more evidence and recoverable wreckage than one in

midair. Thus far, investigators have not recovered an altimeter from the Pan Am bombing. But some investigators still believe an altimeter may have been used. According to British journalist David Leppard, who wrote a book about Pan Am 103, *On the Trail of Terror,* and who interviewed Thomas Hayes, a forensics expert who conducted the main analysis of the timing device from Pan Am 103, there is still plenty of doubt about the type of timer that was used in the bombing. "His authoritative view is that not enough of the bomb's timing device has been recovered to make a definite judgment about whether it was a dual device containing a barometric switch and a timer, or a single trigger device, which was activated by just a timer." Quoted in Roy Rowan, "Pan Am 103: Why Did They Die?" *Time,* April 27, 1992, p. 30.

43. *New York Times,* November 15, 1991, p. 6.

44. A. M. Rosenthal, "White House Rap," *New York Times,* November 22, 1991, p. 31.

45. L. Paul Bremer, "Iran and Syria: Keep the Bums Out," *New York Times,* December 17, 1991, p. 21.

46. Robin Wright, *Sacred Rage: The Wrath of Militant Islam* (New York: Simon and Schuster, 1985), pp. 80–83.

47. Livingstone and Halevy, *Inside the PLO,* pp. 40–41.

48. Ibid., p. 41.

49. *Los Angeles Times,* August 6, 1989, p. 9.

50. Emerson and Duffy, *The Fall of Pan Am 103,* pp. 117–19.

51. *Los Angeles Times,* August 6, 1989, p. 9.

52. ABC News, "Nightline," July 31, 1989, show #2136, Journal Graphics, New York, p. 3.

53. *New York Times,* July 29, 1989, p. 5.

54. Ibid., p. 5.

55. ABC News, "Nightline," July 31, 1989, pp. 2–3.

56. "Remarks to the National Governors' Association in Chicago, Illinois, July 31, 1989," *Public Papers of the Presidents of the United States, George Bush, 1989 (In Two Books), Book II-July 1 To December 31, 1989* (Washington, D.C.: U.S. Government Printing Office, 1990), pp. 1035–36.

57. ABC News, "Nightline," August 1, 1989, show #2137, Journal Graphics, New York, p. 7.

58. Say and Knobler, *Forgotten,* pp. 260–61.

59. Robert Pear, "Has America Learned to Deal with Iran?" *New York Times,* April 29, 1990, section IV, p. 3.

60. *New York Times,* April 20, 1990, p. 1.

61. *New York Times,* April 21, 1990, p. 3.

62. William Raspberry, "Hostages: Bush Has Played It Right," *Washington Post,* May 2, 1990, p. 23.

63. Robert Pear, "Has America Learned to Deal with Iran? *New York Times,* April 29, 1990, p. E3.

64. Interview, Dean Rusk, April 23, 1990, Athens, Georgia.

65. Daniel Yergin, *The Prize: The Epic Quest for Oil, Money, and Power* (New York: Simon and Schuster, 1991).

66. Judith Miller and Laurie Mylroie, *Saddam Hussein and the Crisis in the Gulf* (New York: Times Books/Random House, 1990), p. 219.

67. Pierre Salinger and Eric Laurent, *Secret Dossier: The Hidden Agenda behind the Gulf War* (New York: Penguin Books, 1991), pp. 45–63, 68–69; Adel Darwish and Gregory Alexander, *Unholy Babylon: The Secret History of Saddam's War* (New York: St. Martin's, 1991), pp. 267–71.

68. Ibid., p. 155.

69. *New York Times,* November 24, 1991, p. 1.

70. Quoted in A. M. Rosenthal, "Pan Am 103 and Mr. Bush," *New York Times,* December 21, 1990, p. 19.

71. Ibid.

72. *Patterns of Global Terrorism: 1990,* Department of State Publication 9862, Office of the Secretary of State, Office of the Coordinator for Counterterrorism, U.S. Department of State, Washington, D.C., April 1991, p. 34.

73. Salinger and Laurent, *Secret Dossier,* p. 51.

74. Quoted in "MacNeil/Lehrer Newshour," August 20, 1990, transcript, "Strictly Business," 1990, p. 7.

75. Ibid., p. 1.

76. *Washington Post,* September 12, 1990, p. A34.

77. Bob Woodward, *The Commanders* (New York: Simon and Schuster, 1991), p. 316.

78. Ibid., pp. 317–18.

79. *New York Times,* November 1, 1990, p. 1.

80. *New York Times,* November 2, 1990, p. 7.

81. *New York Times,* August 24, 1990, p. 8; Efraim Karsh and Inari Rautsi, *Saddam Hussein: A Political Biography* (New York: The Free Press, 1991), p. 234.

82. Karsh and Rautsi, *Saddam Hussein: A Political Biography,* p. 236.

83. Ibid., pp. 237–43.

84. *Los Angeles Times,* January 24, 1991, p. 18.

85. *New York Times,* February 8, 1991, p. 1, *Los Angeles Times,* February 8, 1991, pp. 1, 30.

86. *Los Angeles Times,* January 18, 1991, p. 16.

87. Interview, Major Rhonda Cornum, May 25, 1992, Los Angeles, California.

88. Major Rhonda Cornum as told to Peter Copeland, *She Went to War: The Rhonda Cornum Story* (Novato, California: Presidio, 1992), pp. 49–50; Elaine Sciolino, "Women in War: Ex-Captive Tells of Ordeal," *New York Times,* June 24, 1992, p. 1.

89. Interview, Major Rhonda Cornum, May 25, 1992, Los Angeles, California.

90. Interview, Major Rhonda Cornum, May 25, 1992, Los Angeles, California.

91. Interview, Randy Beers, September 22, 1992, Washington, D.C.

92. Less than a year later, Bush's approval rating had dropped to 45 percent. See *New York Times,* January 28, 1992, p. 1.

93. Interview, George Shultz, November 25, 1991, Palo Alto, California.

94. ABC News, "Nightline," December 4, 1991, show #2748, Journal Graphics.

95. Interview, David Jacobsen, June 30, 1992, Huntington Beach, California.

96. Interview, David Jacobsen, June 30, 1992, Huntington Beach, California.

97. Interview, David Jacobsen, June 30, 1992, Huntington Beach, California.

98. Interview, David Jacobsen, June 30, 1992, Huntington Beach, California.

99. Interview, Father Lawrence Martin Jenco, May 11, 1992, Los Angeles, California.

7. Media Players

1. Jack Gould, "On Television: No Comment," *New York Times*, November 13, 1955, section 2, p. 9 (italics added).

2. For a lively discussion of the talk show phenomenon, see Alan Hirsh, *Talking Heads: Political Talk Shows and Their Star Pundits* (New York: St. Martin's, 1991).

3. Marshall McLuhan, *Understanding Media: The Extensions of Man* (New York: Mentor/Penguin, 1964), pp. 292–93.

4. Edward Bliss, Jr., *Now the News: The Story of Broadcast Journalism* (New York: Columbia University Press, 1991), pp. 69–70.

5. McLuhan, *Understanding Media*, pp. 293–94.

6. Ibid., p. 261.

7. McLuhan and Bruce R. Powers, *The Global Village: Transformations in World Life and Media in the Twenty-first Century* (New York: Oxford University Press, 1989), p. 115. The book was put together between 1976 and 1984.

8. Interview, Pierre Salinger, July 12, 1990, London.

9. Dan Nimmo and James E. Combs, *Nightly Horrors: Crisis Coverage in Television Network News* (Knoxville, Tennessee: University of Tennessee Press, 1985), p. 142.

10. ABC News, "Nightline," November 3, 1989, show #2205, Journal Graphics, p. 8.

11. "News Directors on the Defensive in Nashville," *Broadcasting*, September 16, 1985, pp. 76–78.

12. Interview, Daniel Schorr, June 18, 1990, Washington, D.C.

13. Patrick Clawson, "Why We Need More but Better Coverage of Terrorism," in Charles W. Kegley, Jr., ed., *International Terrorism: Characteristics, Causes, Controls* (New York: St. Martin's, 1990), p. 242.

14. Christopher Andrew and Oleg Gordievsky, *KGB: The Inside Story* (New York: Harper Collins, 1990), pp. 64–65.

15. Quoted in Seven Anzovin, ed., *Terrorism* (New York: Wilson, 1986), p. 98.

16. Interview, Juliene Busic, April 9, 1992, South San Francisco, California.

17. Interview, Z, April 1, 1992, Los Angeles, California.

18. Interview, Michael Wines, June 22, 1990, Washington, D.C.

19. Interview, Cyrus Vance, May 22, 1990, New York, New York.

20. Interview, George Shultz, November 25, 1991, Palo Alto, California.

21. Interview, L. Paul Bremer, May 24, 1990, New York, New York.

22. Interview, Michael Wines, June 22, 1990, Washington, D.C.

23. Interview, Leslie Gelb, June 26, 1990, New York, New York.

24. A notable exception was the *New York Times'* publication of the Pentagon Papers in 1971, despite the Nixon administration's attempt to prevent it.

25. Interview, Larry Grossman, May 21, 1990, New York, New York.

26. Interview, Ed Turner, April 24, 1990, Atlanta, Georgia.

27. Interview, Cyrus Vance, May 22, 1990, New York, New York.

28. Interview, Ed Turner, April 24, 1990, Atlanta, Georgia.

29. *Communications Daily, Television Digest, Inc.*, May 8, 1986, Services of Mead Data Central.

30. Interview, Tom Brokaw, June 26, 1990, New York, New York.

31. Interview, Tom Brokaw, June 26, 1990, New York, New York.

32. Interview, Michael Wines, June 22, 1990, Washington, D.C.

33. Nimmo and Combs, *Nightly Horrors*, p. 18 (italics added).

34. Interview, Jeanne Murry, March 27, 1992, Newbury Park, California.

35. Interview, Jeanne Murry, March 27, 1992, Newbury Park, California.

36. Interview, Andy Ross, April 10, 1992, Berkeley, California.

37. Interview, Andy Ross, April 10, 1992, Berkeley, California.

38. Interview, Andy Ross, April 10, 1992, Berkeley, California.

39. *New York Times*, March 11, 1977, p. 12.

40. *New York Times*, March 19, 1977, p. 33; Rudolf Levy, "Terrorism and the Mass Media," *Military Intelligence*, October-December 1985, p. 36.

41. *New York Times*, March 19, 1977, p. 33.

42. "CBS News Standards," in Yonah Alexander and Richard Latter, *Terrorism and the Media: Dilemmas for Government, Journalists and the Public* (New York: Brassey's [U.S.], 1990), pp. 139–40; *New York Times*, April 15, 1977, p. C28.

43. *Broadcasting*, August 5, 1985, p. 60.

44. *NBC Memorandum*, July 24, 1985.

45. Interview, Sam Donaldson, June 19, 1990, Washington, D.C.

46. Interview, Sam Donaldson, June 19, 1990, Washington, D.C.

47. Interview, L. Paul Bremer, May 24, 1990, New York, New York.

48. Interview, Robert McGuire, May 23, 1990, New York, New York.

49. *New York Times*, August 13, 1991, p. 6.

50. *New York Times*, April 9, 1988, p. 8.

51. Ibid.

52. *Cyprus Mail*, April 17, 1988, p. 1.

53. Interview, Youssef Ibrahim, July 18, 1990, Paris.

54. Interview, Youssef Ibrahim, July 18, 1990, Paris.

55. *New York Times*, April 17, 1988, p. 17 (also p. 1).

56. Interview, Youssef Ibrahim, July 18, 1990, Paris.

57. Interview, Youssef Ibrahim, July 18, 1990, Paris.

58. *New York Times*, April 17, 1988, pp. 1, 17.

59. Interview, Youssef Ibrahim, July 18, 1990, Paris.

60. Timothy Gallimore, "Media Compliance with Voluntary Press Guidelines for Covering Terrorism," in Yonah Alexander and Robert Picard, eds., *In the Camera's Eye: News Coverage of Terrorist Events* (New York: Brassey's [U.S.], 1991), pp. 103–18.

61. Ibid. Gallimore quote on p. 114. On some items, including not relying on authorities or terrorists as sole news sources, Gallimore found that the media did not violate its own guidelines.

62. For an excellent treatment of the rise of CNN, see Hank Whittemore, *CNN: The Inside Story* (Boston: Little, Brown, 1990). The quote on Sherman is on p. 102, by Flip Spiceland. The quote on Bush is from the *New York Times*, August 11, 1989, p. 12, reprinted in Whittemore, p. 301.

63. Ibid., pp. 129–30.

64. Ibid., pp. 270–71.

65. Martin and Walcott, *Best Laid Plans*, p. 191 (North quote cited); "The Presidency, the Press and the People," KPBS Television and the University of California, San Diego, January 5, 1990 (Moyers quote, p. 32, transcript PBS Distribution, April 2, 1990); *New York Times*, August 11, 1989, p. 12, cited in Whittemore, *CNN: The Inside Story*, pp. 301-302 (Fitzwater and presidential aide quote); Ken Auletta, "Raiding the Global Village," *The New Yorker*, August 2, 1993, p. 25 (CNN seen in 200 countries noted).

66. Interview, George Shultz, November 25, 1991, Palo Alto, California.

67. Interview, Ed Turner, April 24, 1990, Atlanta, Georgia.

68. The broadcasts reported here and in the following paragraphs are from two videotapes that CNN produced recounting the Gulf War. These are *Desert Storm: The War Begins*, narrated by Bernard Shaw, CNN Special Reports, Cable News Network, Inc., 1991, Turner Home Entertainment; and *Desert Storm: The Victory*, narrated by Bernard Shaw, CNN Special Reports, Cable News Network, Inc., 1991, Turner Home Entertainment. The broadcasts are also described in the excellent account of CNN's war coverage by Robert Wiener, *Live from Baghdad: Gathering News at Ground Zero* (New York: Doubleday, 1992).

69. *Los Angeles Times*, January 23, 1991, p. 12 (p. 1).

70. There were also accusations by other networks that CNN may have traded special concessions, such as use of CNN's communications apparatus, with the Iraqis in order to be allowed to remain in Baghdad. CNN denied the accusations, claiming they allowed the Iraqis to use CNN's satellite telephones only to relay requests for visas for other journalists. See *New York Times*, February 12, 1991, p. B1.

71. The senator was Alan Simpson, a Republican from Wyoming (see *Los Angeles Times*, February 20, 1991, p. 1) and the media critic was Reed Irvine, chairman of Accuracy in Media, who made his comments on the "MacNeil/Lehrer Newshour," February 14, 1991 (see the transcript by Strictly Business, Overland Park, Kansas, show #3969, p. 7).

72. Reuven Frank, *Out of Thin Air: The Brief Wonderful Life of Network News* (New York: Simon and Schuster, 1991), p. 41.

73. Interview, Ed Turner, April 24, 1990, Atlanta, Georgia.

74. *Los Angeles Times*, January 23, 1991, p. E1; February 5, 1991, p. A5.

75. *Los Angeles Times*, January 23, 1991, p. E3.

76. Ken Auletta, *Three Blind Mice: How the TV Networks Lost Their Way* (New York: Random House, 1991), p. 563.

77. Interview, George Shultz, November 25, 1991, Palo Alto, California.

8. Roots

1. *Wall Street Journal*, July 15, 1992, p. 1.

2. The discussion that follows does not attempt to assess every possible "motivation" of terrorists and the associated underlying "causes." The distinction between a "cause," and a "motivation," is often a gray one. Something may drive a person to commit a terrorist act—desire to sabotage peace talks, gain revenge, eliminate an enemy, etc. The underlying causes of those "motivations" could be religious extremism, poverty, political alienation, and so forth. But the motivation can also be considered a "cause," as gaining revenge or sabotaging a peace conference could be the root of the terrorist act itself. And various causes can overlap with motivations, so that poverty and alienation may lead to religious extremism, which in turn leads to terrorism, or religious extremism by itself may be both the motivation and cause of the terrorist act. This discussion treats the "roots" of terrorism as both causes and motivations in order to present the diversity of reasons why people are driven to commit terrorist acts.

3. David C. Rapoport, "Sacred Terror: A Contemporary Example from Islam," in Walter Reich, ed., *Origins of Terrorism: Psychologies, Ideologies, Theologies, States of Mind* (New York: Woodrow Wilson International Center for Scholars Cambridge University Press, 1990), p. 118.

4. Amir Taheri, *Holy Terror: Inside the World of Islamic Terrorism* (Bethesda, Maryland: Adler and Adler, 1987), p. 10.

5. Ibid., p. 128.

6. Wright, *Sacred Rage,* p. 37.

7. Rapoport, "Sacred Terror," pp. 116–17. The quotes are from Adel Hamouda, *Ightiyahl Ra'is* (The Assassination of a President), 4th ed., trans. Ibrahim Karawan (Cairo: Sina [Sinai]), p. 84, cited in Rapoport.

8. Merari, "The Readiness to Kill and Die," p. 196. The IRA also utilized involuntary suicide attacks in its campaign of violence in Northern Ireland. In one case, the IRA kidnapped a man from his home, tied up his parents (or held them hostage) and forced him to drive a truck with explosives to a British army checkpoint. The man, however, jumped from the truck at the last moment, shouting a warning to the troops. The bomb detonated, but nobody was injured. In an earlier, similar incident, seven people were killed. See *New York Times,* November 24, 1990, p. 5.

9. William Langewiesche, "The World in Its Extreme," *Atlantic Monthly,* November 1991, p. 110.

10. Bernard Lewis, "The Roots of Muslim Rage," *Atlantic Monthly,* September 1990, p. 48.

11. Ibid., p. 48.

12. Ayla Hammond Schbley, "Resurgent Religious Terrorism: A Study of Some of the Lebanese Shi'a Contemporary Terrorism," *Terrorism,* vol. 12, 1989, p. 224.

13. *Financial Times,* January 4–January 5, 1992, p. 3.

14. *The Economist,* June 13, 1992, p. 40.

15. Lewis, "The Roots of Muslim Rage," p. 60.

16. *The Economist World Atlas and Almanac* (London: Economist Books, 1991), pp. 161, 220.

17. Seton-Watson, *The East European Revolution,* p. 6.

18. *Financial Times*, September 21–22, 1991, p. 7.

19. *Los Angeles Times*, October 9, 1991, p. 7. During World War II, the Nazis created a puppet state in Croatia that committed atrocities against the Serbs.

20. *Los Angeles Times*, February 15, 1993, p. 1.

21. "Larry King Live," transcript #620, August 4, 1992, CNN, Journal Graphics.

22. Interview, Z, April 1, 1992, Los Angeles, California.

23. Interview, Z, April 1, 1992, Los Angeles, California.

24. Interview, Z, April 1, 1992, Los Angeles, California.

25. Interview, Z, April 1, 1992, Los Angeles, California.

26. *Los Angeles Times*, October 27, 1982, part II, pp. 1, 3.

27. Interview, Z, April 1, 1992, Los Angeles, California.

28. Interview, Z, April 1, 1992, Los Angeles, California.

29. Interview, Juliene Busic, April 9, 1992, South San Francisco, California.

30. Interview, Juliene Busic, April 9, 1992, South San Francisco, California.

31. Interview, Z, April 1, 1992, Los Angeles, California.

32. *New York Times*, November 10, 1991, p. 3. Illustrating the continuing definitional problems associated with terrorism, Turkish authorities announced they would allow the plane and the hijackers to return to the Chechen-Ingish republic since the hijacking was more an act of protest rather than an act of terrorism.

33. "CBS Radio News," November 11, 1991.

34. Parry, *Terrorism: From Robespierre to Arafat*, p. 395.

35. Christopher Dobson and Ronald Payne, *The Terrorists: Their Weapons, Leaders, and Tactics* (New York: Facts on File, 1979), p. 161.

36. *Wall Street Journal*, December 27, 1991, p. 8.

37. Dobson and Payne, *The Terrorists*, pp. 80, 151–52, 225; Cesare Medail, Gastone Alecci, Lietta Tornabuoni, "Covering Terrorism," *Corriere Della Sera*, March 21, 22, 23, 1978.

38. Dobson and Payne, *The Terrorists*, p. 225.

39. *Patterns of Global Terrorism: 1990*, pp. 72–73.

40. Ibid., p. 63.

41. Christopher Hewitt, "Terrorism and Public Opinion: A Five-Country Comparison," *Terrorism and Political Violence*, Summer 1990, pp. 145–70.

42. Dobson and Payne, *The Terrorists*, p. 55.

43. Patricia Steinhoff, "Portrait of a Terrorist: An Interview with Kozo Okamoto," *Asian Survey*, September 1976, pp. 844–45.

44. *Los Angeles Japanese Daily News*, February 10, 1989.

45. Sabri Sayari, "Patterns of Political Terrorism in Turkey," *TVI: Terrorism, Violence, Insurgency Journal*, vol. 6, no. 1, Summer 1985, p. 43.

46. *Financial Times*, November 14, 1991, p. 7.

47. Paul Wilkinson, *Terrorism and the Liberal State* (second edition) (London: Macmillan Education, 1986), pp. 277–78.

48. *Patterns of Global Terrorism: 1990*, p. 37.

49. Ibid., p. 32.

50. Ibid., pp. 32, 34.

51. Interview, L. Paul Bremer, May 24, 1990, New York, New York.

52. Interview, George Shultz, November 25, 1991, Palo Alto, California.

53. *Patterns of Global Terrorism: 1990*, pp. 33–36; *Libya's Continuing Responsibility for Terrorism*, U.S. Department of State, November 1991, p. 5.

54. *Patterns of Global Terrorism: 1990*, p. 50; *Libya's Continuing Responsibility for Terrorism*, p. 8.

55. *Libya's Continuing Responsibility for Terrorism*, pp. 9–12.

56. Brian Jenkins, *International Terrorism: The Other World War*, R-3302-AF, The Rand Corporation, Santa Monica, California, November 1985, p. 19.

57. *Financial Times*, January 2, 1992, p. 3.

58. Interview, George Shultz, November 25, 1991, Palo Alto, California.

59. Rachel Ehrenfeld, *Narco-Terrorism* (New York: Basic Books, 1990), pp. 86–87.

60. Robert Kupperman and Jeff Kamen, *Final Warning: Averting Disaster in the New Age of Terrorism* (New York: Doubleday, 1989), pp. 190–91.

61. Peter R. Andreas, Eva C. Bertram, Morris J. Blachman, and Kenneth E. Sharpe, "Dead-End Drug Wars," *Foreign Policy*, Winter 1991–92, p. 111.

62. Ibid., p. 113.

63. Ibid., p. 111.

64. Livingstone and Halevy, *Inside the PLO*, p. 55.

65. Interview, George Shultz, November 25, 1991, Palo Alto, California.

66. Ehrenfeld, *Narco-Terrorism*, p. 141; Claire Sterling, *Octopus: The Long Reach of the International Sicilian Mafia* (New York: Touchstone Books/Simon and Schuster, 1990), pp. 36–37.

67. Andreas et al., "Dead-End Drug Wars," p. 108.

68. *New York Times*, January 13, 1992, p. 6; January 14, 1992, p. 10.

69. Narcoterrorism was an exception due to the wide scope of the violence and the large organizational base that was behind it. But even narcoterrorism had a political objective in that it was aimed at intimidating judicial and government officials against extraditing and arresting the drug barons.

70. Brian Jenkins, "The Threat of Product Contamination," *TVI Report*, vol. 8, no. 3, pp. 1–3.

71. Ibid., pp. 1–3.

72. Wilkinson, *Terrorism and the Liberal State*, p. 51.

73. *Cyprus Mail*, May 16, 1987, p. 1.

74. Melvin Berger, *Hazardous Substances: A Reference* (Hillside, New Jersey: Enslow, 1986), p. 55.

75. *Cyprus Mail*, May 16, 1987, p. 1.

76. *Cyprus Mail*, May 16, 1987, p. 1; May 17, 1987, pp. 1, 3; May 19, 1987, p. 1; *Foreign Broadcast Information Service* (FBIS/JPRS), June 9, 1987, pp. 60–61.

77. *Cyprus Mail*, May 16, 1987, p. 1; *Foreign Broadcast Information Service* (FBIS/JPRS), June 9, 1987, p. 59.

78. *Cyprus Mail*, May 17, 1987, p. 3; May 19, 1987, p. 1.

79. *Cyprus Mail*, May 17, 1987, p. 3.

80. Cited in Crenshaw, "The Causes of Terrorism," p. 126.

81. Jerrold M. Post, "Rewarding Fire with Fire: Effects of Retaliation on Terrorist Group Dynamics," *Terrorism*, vol. 10, 1987, p. 24.

82. Jerrold M. Post, "Terrorist Psycho-logic: Terrorist Behavior as a Product of Psychological Forces," in Reich, *Origins of Terrorism*, p. 27.

83. Crenshaw, "The Causes of Terrorism," p. 120.

84. Ibid., p. 120.

85. Cited in Konrad Kellen, *On Terrorists and Terrorism*, N-1942-RC, The Rand Corporation, Santa Monica, California, December 1982, p. 15. However, Ferracuti argues that right-wing terrorists "are frequently psychopathological and the ideology is empty; in left-wing terrorism, ideology is unrealistic and terrorists are more normal and fanatical." But as Kellen points out, there may be more than psychological explanations in separating the right-wing and left-wing terrorist personality. "Right-wing terrorists tend to be racists and nationalists, whereas left-wing terrorists tend to be anarchical millennialists" (p. 16).

86. Crenshaw, "The Causes of Terrorism," p. 121.

87. Walter Reich, "Understanding Terrorist Behavior: The Limits and Opportunities of Psychological Inquiry," in Reich, *Origins of Terrorism*, p. 270.

88. Post, "Terrorist Psycho-logic," p. 33.

89. Michael Baumann, *Terror or Love: Bommi Baumann's Own Story of His Life as a West German Urban Guerrilla*, with statements by Heinrich Boll and Daniel Cohn-Bendit, trans. Helene Ellenbogen and Wayne Parker (New York: Grove, 1977), p. 108.

90. Alison Jamieson, "Entry, Discipline, and Exit in the Italian Red Brigades," *Terrorism and Political Violence*, Spring 1990, pp. 18–19.

91. *Der Spiegel*, #25, June 18, 1990, Department of State, Division of Language Services, pp. 28–29.

92. Ibid., pp. 29–30.

93. Ibid., p. 7; p. 15; *Chicago Tribune*, June 8, 1990, p. 16.

94. Daniel Lang, "A Reporter at Large: The Bank Drama," *The New Yorker*, November 25, 1974, pp. 56–126.

95. Albert Bandura, "Mechanisms of Moral Disengagement," in Reich, *Origins of Terrorism*, pp. 183–84.

96. Lang, "A Reporter at Large," p. 92.

97. Ibid., p. 92.

98. Norman Antokol and Mayer Nudell, *No One a Neutral: Political Hostage-Taking in the Modern World* (Medina, Ohio: Alpha, 1990), p. 148.

99. Lang, "A Reporter at Large," p. 118.

100. Reagan, *An American Life*, p. 524.

101. Georgie Anne Geyer, "Terrorists Are 'Nice Guys,' Their Victims Say—Why?" *Los Angeles Times*, October 5, 1976, part II, p. 5.

102. Interview, Father Lawrence Martin Jenco, Los Angeles, California, May 11, 1992.

103. Interview, Father Lawrence Martin Jenco, Los Angeles, California, May 11, 1992.

104. Interview, David Jacobsen, June 30, 1992, Huntington Beach, California.

105. Jacobsen, *Hostage*, p. 289.

106. Interview, Juliene Busic, April 9, 1992, South San Francisco, California.

107. Interview, Juliene Busic, April 9, 1992, South San Francisco, California.

108. "Mile Hijack Club Newsletter," vol. 1, no. 1, September 14, 1976, p. 1 (private collection of Warren Benson). Benson received the letter but was not the organizer of the reunion.

9. Future Trends

1. *Patterns of Global Terrorism: 1992*, Department of State Publication 10054, Office of the Secretary of State, Office of the Coordinator for Counterterrorism, U.S. Department of State, Washington, D.C., April 1993, p. 56.

2. David Lamb, *The Arabs: Journeys beyond the Mirage* (New York: Vintage, 1987, 1988), p. 89 (italics added).

3. Tina Rosenberg, *Children of Cain: Violence and the Violent in Latin America* (New York: Morrow, 1991), p. 152.

4. *Patterns of Global Terrorism: 1991* (Washington, D.C.: Department of State Publication 9963, Office of the Secretary of State, Office of the Coordinator for Counterterrorism, April 1992), p. 64.

5. Rosenberg, *Children of Cain*, p. 154.

6. Interview, Dr. Calvin J. Frederick, August 4, 1992, Los Angeles, California.

7. Interview, Dr. Calvin J. Frederick, August 4, 1992, Los Angeles, California.

8. Interview, Owen Robinson, May 1, 1990, Arlington, Virginia.

9. Interview, Owen Robinson, May 1, 1990, Arlington, Virginia.

10. Brian Michael Jenkins, *Future Trends in International Terrorism*, P-7176, The Rand Corporation, Santa Monica, California, December 1985, p. 20.

11. Kenneth L. Adelman and Norman R. Augustine, *The Defense Revolution: Intelligent Downsizing of America's Military* (San Francisco: Institute for Contemporary Studies, 1990), p. 56.

12. Ibid.

13. *Patterns of Global Terrorism: 1991*, p. 12.

14. James Adams, "The Arms Trade: The Real Lesson of the Gulf War," *Atlantic Monthly*, November 1991, p. 36.

15. Youssef Ibrahim, "Iran Said to Commit $7 Billion to Secret Arms Plan," *New York Times*, August 8, 1992, p. 3.

16. *Weapons: An International Encyclopedia from 5000 BC to 2000 AD* (New York: St. Martin's, 1990), p. 291.

17. Ibid., p. 280.

18. *Financial Times*, January 24, 1992, p. 1. A CIA report also warned of ex-Soviet nuclear experts potentially selling their services abroad. See *New York Times*, January 1, 1992, p. 1.

19. *Weapons: An International Encyclopedia*, p. 268.

20. Interview, L. Paul Bremer, May 24, 1990, New York, New York.

21. Interview, L. Paul Bremer, May 24, 1990, New York, New York.

22. Kupperman and Kamen, *Final Warning*, pp. 101–102; Eric Morris and Alan Hoe, with John Potter, *Terrorism: Threat and Response* (New York: St. Martin's, 1988), pp. 95–96.

23. *Cyprus Mail*, January 13, 1987, p. 1 (reprinted in Foreign Broadcast Information Service [FBIS], January 13, 1988, p. 16).

24. Joseph D. Douglas, Jr., and Neil C. Livingstone, *America the Vulnerable: The*

Threat of Chemical and Biological Warfare (Lexington, Massachusetts: Heath, 1987), p. 13; Brian Beckett, *Weapons of Tomorrow* (London: Orbis, 1982), p. 108; Jeffrey D. Simon, *Terrorists and the Potential Use of Biological Weapons: A Discussion of Possibilities*, R-3771-AFMIC, The Rand Corporation, Santa Monica, California, December 1989, p. 3.

25. *Weapons: An International Encyclopedia*, p. 277.

26. Ibid.

27. Kupperman and Kamen, *Final Warning*, pp. 106–107; *New York Times*, September 19, 1975; *International Herald Tribune*, April 23, 1980.

28. Beckett, *Weapons of Tomorrow*, p. 107; Simon, *Terrorists and the Potential Use of Biological Weapons*, p. 10.

29. Interview, Dr. Cornelius G. McWright, July 29, 1992, Santa Monica, California.

30. Simon, *Terrorists and the Potential Use of Biological Weapons*, pp. v–vi.

31. Interview, Dr. Cornelius G. McWright, July 29, 1992, Santa Monica, California.

32. Douglas and Livingstone, *America the Vulnerable*, pp. 72–73.

33. K. Eric Drexler and Chris Peterson, with Gayle Pergamit, *Unbounding the Future: The Nanotechnology Revolution* (New York: Morrow, 1991), pp. 34, 256, 259.

34. Ibid., p. 256.

35. Ibid.

36. Jeremy Rifkin, *Biosphere Politics: A Cultural Odyssey from the Middle Ages to the New Age* (New York: Harper Collins, 1992), pp. 145–46.

37. Ibid., p. 147 (quote is by former Deputy Secretary of Defense Douglas Feith).

38. Ibid., pp. 147–48.

39. Neil C. Livingstone and Joseph D. Douglass, Jr., *CBW: The Poor Man's Atomic Bomb*, Institute for Foreign Policy Analysis, National Security Paper, no. 1, Cambridge, Massachusetts, January 1984. See also Douglass and Livingstone, *America the Vulnerable*.

40. Crenshaw, "The Logic of Terrorism: Terrorist Behavior as a Product of Strategic Choice," in Reich, *Origins of Terrorism*, p. 15.

41. Ibid.

42. Interview, Dr. Cornelius G. McWright, July 29, 1992, Santa Monica, California.

43. Simon, *Terrorists and the Potential Use of Biological Weapons*, p. vi.

44. Auletta, *Three Blind Mice*, pp. 576–77.

45. CNN "World Report," August 25, 1991.

46. Stewart Brand, *The Media Lab: Inventing the Future at M.I.T.* (New York: Penguin, 1987), p. 72.

47. Bliss, *Now the News*, p. 462.

48. Bliss, *Now the News*, p. 463.

49. U.S. Congress, Office of Technology Assessment, *The Big Picture: HDTV and High-Resolution Systems*, OTA-BP-CIT-64, Washington, D.C.: U.S. Government Printing Office, June 1990, p. 55.

50. Sussman, *Power, the Press, and the Technology of Freedom*, p. 5.

51. David Meek, "Connecting the Global Village—ISDN," *The Macintosh AnswerSource*, Fall 1991, p. 18.

52. Sussman, *Power, the Press, and the Technology of Freedom*, pp. 5, 24.

53. Ibid., p. 6.

54. Ibid., p. 61.

55. Ibid., p. 25; p. 126.

56. *Terrorism in the United States: 1991*, U.S. Department of Justice, Federal Bureau of Investigation, Terrorist Research and Analytical Center, Counterterrorism Section, Intelligence Division, pp. 7–8.

57. *Terrorism in the United States: 1982-1992*, U.S. Department of Justice, Federal Bureau of Investigation, Terrorist Research and Analytical Center, Counterterrorism Section, Intelligence Division, pp. 2–3.

58. Beau Grosscup, *The New Explosion of Terrorism* (Far Hills, New Jersey: New Horizon, 1991), p. 94.

59. Ibid., pp. 98–99.

60. Ibid., p. 98.

61. Interview, Brian Jenkins, June 21, 1992, Santa Monica, California.

62. G. Davidson Smith, *Combating Terrorism* (London: Routledge, 1990), p. 37.

63. *Terrorism in the United States: 1982-1992*, p. 16.

64. Robert A. Liston, *Terrorism* (Nashville: Thomas Nelson, 1977), p. 136.

10. Lessons Learned

1. *Patterns of Global Terrorism: 1989*, Washington, D.C., Department of State Publication 9743, Office of the Secretary of State, Office of the Coordinator for Counter-Terrorism, April 1990, pp. iii–iv.

2. *Patterns of Global Terrorism: 1990*, p. 39.

3. Alex Schmid, *Political Terrorism: A Research Guide* (New Brunswick: Transaction, 1984), cited in Walter Laqueur, "Reflections on Terrorism," *Foreign Affairs*, October 1986.

4. *Report of the President's Commission on Aviation Security and Terrorism*, p. 113.

5. *Patterns of Global Terrorism: 1990*, p. iv.

6. Jeffrey D. Simon, *U.S. Countermeasures against International Terrorism*, R-3840-C³I, The Rand Corporation, Santa Monica, California, March 1990, p. 9; *New York Times*, November 28, 1984; *Christian Science Monitor*, November 29, 1984; *Los Angeles Times*, July 12, 1984.

7. *Terrorism in the United States: 1991*, p. 17.

8. Ibid., p. 3.

9. *Los Angeles Times*, March 31, 1992, p. 1; *Financial Times*, March 31, 1992, p. 2; *New York Times*, March 31, 1992, p. 7.

10. Simon, *U.S. Countermeasures*, p. 9; *International Herald Tribune*, October 21–22, 1978.

11. Simon R. A. Crawshaw, "Anti-Terrorism Networks: Information and Intelligence for Fighting International Terrorism," *The Futurist*, March–April 1989, p. 13.

12. Interview, Robert McGuire, May 23, 1990, New York, New York.

13. Interview, George Shultz, November 25, 1991, Palo Alto, California.

14. Interview, George Shultz, November 25, 1991, Palo Alto, California.

15. Interview, Constantine Melnik, July 17, 1990, Paris.

16. Interview, Constantine Melnik, July 17, 1990, Paris.

17. Joseph E. Persico, *Casey: From the OSS to the CIA* (New York: Viking Penguin, 1990), p. 435.

18. Loch K. Johnson, "On Drawing a Bright Line for Covert Operations," *American Journal of International Law*, April 1992, p. 307.

19. Jeffrey D. Simon, *U.S. Countermeasures against International Terrorism*, p. vii.

20. Ibid., p. 35; Ernest Evans, *Wars without Splendor: The U.S. Military and Low-Level Conflict* (New York: Greenwood, 1987), p. 38; *New York Times*, July 5, 1976.

21. Turner, *Terrorism and Democracy*, p. 232.

22. *Public Report of the Vice-President's Task Force on Combatting Terrorism*, p. 14; also cited in Simon, *U.S. Countermeasures*, p. 15.

23. Interview, George Shultz, November 25, 1991, Palo Alto, California.

24. Interview, George Shultz, November 25, 1991, Palo Alto, California.

25. *Patterns of Global Terrorism: 1991*, p. 26; Simon, *U.S. Countermeasures*, pp. 17–18.

26. *Washington Post*, December 24, 1988, p. 11.

27. *Report of the President's Commission on Aviation Security and Terrorism*, p. iv.

28. Interview, Geoff Goesling, April 10, 1992, Berkeley, California.

29. Interview, Geoff Goesling, April 10, 1992, Berkeley, California.

30. Interview, Owen Robinson, May 1, 1990, Arlington, Virginia.

31. Jenkins, *Future Trends*, p. 20.

32. Mark Edington, "Taking the Offensive: The Case for Major Changes in the Way the United States Confronts Terrorism," *Atlantic Monthly*, June 1992, p. 42.

Epilogue

1. Interview, Miriam Beeber, June 11, 1992, Tucson, Arizona.

2. *New York Times*, January 11, 1988, p. 18.

3. M. A. Farber, "Behind the Brink's Case: Return of the Radical Left," *New York Times*, February 16, 1982, p. B4.

4. Edington, "Taking the Offensive," p. 50.

5. *New York Times*, April 26, 1992, p. 4.

6. Interview, Rosemary Wolfe, September 23, 1992, Washington, D.C.

7. Italics added.

8. Interview (telephone), Jack Plaxe, September 24, 1992.

Acknowledgments

During the years that I worked on this book, I always looked forward to the time that I would be writing the acknowledgments. Not only would that mean that the book was finished—something every writer looks forward to—but also that there would be an opportunity to formally thank the people who played such an important part in this project. Now that the time has come, I am sure that I will inadvertently leave out many names. I apologize in advance for any omissions.

First and foremost, I want to thank the more than fifty people—listed in a separate section—who agreed to be interviewed. All of them gave willingly of their time and spoke openly about what was, for several of them, a very difficult and emotional period in their lives. Their stories were indispensable for providing an oral history of America's experience with terrorism and for hopefully bringing the book alive for the reader.

The staffs at the presidential libraries were very helpful. I wish to thank Anita Smith and Pauline Testerman at the Harry S Truman Library; Kathleen Struss at the Dwight D. Eisenhower Library; Donna Cotterell and Ron Whealan at the John F. Kennedy Library; E. Philip Scott and Regina Greenwell at the Lyndon B. Johnson Library; Mary Young at the Richard Nixon Presidential Materials Project; David Stanhope at the Jimmy Carter Library; Steve Branch and Lisa Osburn at the Ronald Reagan Library; and Mary Finch at the George Bush Presidential Materials Project.

Among those who diligently answered all my research requests and whom I gladly acknowledge are the following: Athena Angelos; Laura Allen at *American Heritage Magazine*; Jennifer Brathovde and Pamela Poze at the Library of Congress; Damien Brouillard at the *Washington Post*; Cathy Cherbose and Jennifer Watts at the Henry E. Huntington Library and Art Gallery; Thomas Coughlin at the New York State Correctional Services; Matthew Cox at the *Syracuse Post-Standard*; Stephanie Cross at the White House; Wallace Dailey at the Theodore Roosevelt Collection at Houghton Library at Harvard University; Francine Della Catena at the *Los Angeles Times*; Carolyn George at the Westchester Public Library in Chesterton, Indiana; Fred Greenstein at Princeton University; Steve Hayworth at Turner Broadcasting System; Sister Martin Joseph at the E. H. Butler Library of the State University College at Buffalo; Holly Jones at Wide World Photos; Jim Lake; Linda Kloss, Bobby Cotter and I. Ray McElhaney, Jr., at the FBI; Barbara Mancuso at the *New York Times*; Nancy Nassereddine and Jocelyn Clapp at Bettmann Archive/Newsphotos; Steve Neff at the *Denver Post*; Fred Pernell at the National Archives; Debra Seals at the U.S. Department of State; Diane Sloan at Syracuse University's Public Affairs Office; Mary Ternes at the D.C. Public Library; Doug Turner at the *Buffalo Evening News*; Bob Waller at the U.S. Department of Defense; Susan Williams at Agence France-Presse.

I am also grateful to a number of people, both in the United States and abroad, who contributed to the book but wished to remain anonymous. The Rand Corporation provided support during an early stage in the research and writing, and I wish to thank Connie Greaser for her enthusiasm. I also want to acknowledge with much appreciation the interest shown in this book by several friends, associates, and people with whom I have worked over the years. They are: Pat Allen, Jerry Aroesty, Clyde Asakura, Debbie Asakura, Koki Asakura, Pearl Asakura, Robin Asakura, Valerie Bernstein, David Boren, Molly Boren, Carl Builder, Bob Byman, Kenneth Chin, Sandra Chin, David Cohen, Alberto Coll, Tad Daily, Jim Dyson, Brooke England, Barry Erlick, Linda Flock, Cindy Forrestal-Snell, Karen Gardela, Marilyn Grace, Gil Guzman, Harlan Hahn, Patty Hitsous, Robert Hitsous, Mari Hope, Ken Horn, Terry Jenkins, Steven Kafka, Zalmay Khalizad, Eddie Kamiya, Janet Kamiya, Larry Karp, Konrad Kellen, Sherman Lamb, Jim Lebovic, Paul Levine, Gordon McCormick, Alice McGillion, Stephan Meyers, Janine Meyers, Peter Miller, Maureen Murphy, David Ochmanek, Geri Petty, Niko Pfund, Hellen Purkitt, Stephanie Rice, David Ronfeldt, James Rosenau, Bill Sater, Hatsue Schmitt, Ben Schwarz, Larry Snell, Emiko Shimazu, Tom Sizemore, Shoshana Snyder, Warren Spenser, Gail Suber, Joni Terpstra, Tom Tompkins, David Veness, Sue Walther, Ted Warner, David Weaver, Michael White, Mary Yanokawa, Connie Young.

A special word of thanks goes to Brian Jenkins, who pioneered the study of international terrorism and remains one of the most astute and respected observers in the field today. I learned a great deal about terrorism from Brian while we were colleagues, and he provided valuable feedback to my own ideas during our many long-distance runs in southern California. He was extremely helpful for many aspects of this book.

Arthur Alexander, Martin Balaban, Lisa Bankoff, Ed Kobak, Ron Lear, Cornelius McWright, John Mueller, Pierre Salinger, Sabri Sayari, Bernadine Siuda, Lorron Snell, Douglas Snyder, Kevin Terpstra, Ed Turner, and Carole Wood expressed continual interest in this book and their support is greatly appreciated. I also want to thank Steven Emerson and Loch Johnson for reading the entire manuscript and providing important insight.

I was fortunate to work with an exceptional editorial staff at Indiana University Press. I would like to thank Bob Sloan for taking special interest in this project and providing excellent advice. I am also very grateful to Terry Cagle, Sue Havlish, Pam Albert, Dick Granich, Darrin Pratt, Marvin Keenan, Kathleen Ketterman, Cindy Ballard, Jan Wood, and Lisel Virkler for their tireless efforts on my behalf.

Words cannot express the gratitude I have for my sister, Ellen Sandor, who believed in this book and was instrumental in bringing it to completion. Nobody could ask for a better sister. Richard Sandor, Julie Sandor, and Penny Sandor were also enthusiastic believers and I express heartfelt appreciation to all of them.

Finally, I would like to thank whoever may be reading these pages for giving me the opportunity to communicate through the wonderful world of books.

Index

JEFFREY D. SIMON is an author, consultant, and lecturer on terrorism and security issues, based in Santa Monica, California. He received a B.A. degree in history from the University of California at Berkeley, an M.A. degree in political science from Indiana University, and a Ph.D. in political science from the University of Southern California. He worked for several years at the Rand Corporation, where he specialized in terrorism and political violence. He has published Op-Ed pieces and articles for several journals and newspapers, including the *Journal of the American Medical Association, Foreign Policy,* the *New York Times,* the *Los Angeles Times,* the *Boston Globe,* and *USA Today.*